ADVANCED NEURAL COMPUTERS

ADVANCED NEURAL COMPUTERS

Edited by

Rolf ECKMILLER
Division of Biocybernetics
Department of Biophysics
Heinrich Heine University Düsseldorf
F.R.G.

1990

NORTH-HOLLAND
AMSTERDAM • NEW YORK • OXFORD • TOKYO

ELSEVIER SCIENCE PUBLISHERS B.V.
Sara Burgerhartstraat 25
P.O. Box 211, 1000 AE Amsterdam, The Netherlands

Distributors for the United States and Canada:

ELSEVIER SCIENCE PUBLISHING COMPANY INC.
655 Avenue of the Americas
New York, N.Y. 10010, U.S.A.

Library of Congress Cataloging-in-Publication Data

Advanced neural computers / edited by Rolf Eckmiller.
p. cm.
Includes bibliographical references and index.
ISBN 0-444-88400-9 (U.S.)
1. Neural computers--Congresses. 2. Neural networks (Computer science)--Congresses. I. Eckmiller, Rolf, 1942- .
QA76.87.A37 1990
006.3--dc20 90-39685
CIP

ISBN: 0 444 88400 9

Printed in The Netherlands

PREFACE

This book is the outcome of the International Symposium on Neural Networks for Sensory and Motor Systems (NSMS) held in Neuss (near Düsseldorf (FRG)) from 22 to 24 March, 1990.

The NSMS symposium assembled 45 invited experts from Europe, America, and Japan representing the fields of Neuroinformatics, Computer Science, Computational Neuroscience, and Neuroscience.
More than 150 additional scientists from various countries representing a number of research institutes and companies with interest in neural computing participated in the discussions and made poster presentations.

The 45 invited contributions in this book are arranged in six sections ranging from Biological Sensory and Motor Systems via Theory of Artificial Neural Networks and Neural Network Simulators to Pattern Recognition and Motor Control with Artificial Neural Networks.

The readibility of this book was enhanced by a number of measures:
* The invited papers are arranged in six sections.
* The collection of References from all Contributions provides an alphabetical list of all references quoted in the individual contributions.
* A separate List of General References serves newcomers in this field to find other recent books.
* Separate Author and Subject Indices facilitate access to various details.

It is hoped that this book as a rapidly published report on the 'State of the Art in Neural Computing' and as a reference book for future research in the highly inter-disciplinary field of 'Theory and Applications of Neural Computers' will provide useful in the endeavour to: *Transfer Concepts of Brain Function and Structure to Novel Neural Computers with Adaptive, Dynamical Neural Net Topologies.*

The editor wishes to thank Claudia Berge, Miriam Buck, and Sandra Winter for their efficient and thorough technical and managerial assistance, which was essential to meet the tight deadline for preparation of the final book manuscript.
The subsequent expert work of the publisher made it possible to make this book available in high quality within less than four months after the NSMS symposium.

Düsseldorf, June 1990 — The Editor

ACKNOWLEDGEMENT OF SPONSORSHIP

The generous sponsorship of several American and German Governmental Ministries and Agencies, which made the International Symposium on Neural Networks for Sensory and Motor Systems (NSMS) and thereby this book possible, is gratefully acknowledged:

Air Force Office of Scientific Research (AFSC) / Washington (USA)

Defence Advanced Research Project Agency (DARPA) / Arlington (USA)

Minister für Wissenschaft und Forschung des Landes Nordrhein-Westfalen / Düsseldorf (FRG)

Office of Naval Research (ONR) / Arlington (USA)

Office of Naval Research (ONR), European Office / London (UK)

TABLE OF CONTENTS

Section 1: General Introduction

Section 2: Biological Sensory and Motor Systems

Section 3: Theory of Artificial Neural Networks

Section 4: Neural Network Simulators

Section 5: Pattern Recognition with Neural Networks

Section 6: Motor Control with Neural Networks

Section 1
General Introduction

Advanced Neural Computers / R. Eckmiller (Editor)

Proiegomena to an Analysis of Form and Structure

Eduardo R. Caianiello

Dipartimento Fisica Teorica
University of Salerno
Salerno, Italy

I. INTRODUCTION

1. - This title is meant as an expression of realistic humility, in front of problems whose extension and depth I deem to be much beyond our present grasp. As an example, the task of understanding in full the structure of English or Japanese, and of making an acceptable translation from one into the other, appears of a magnitude comparable to that of the study of cerebral activity. This was in fact the reason that prompted our first researches on the subject in the early 60's [1,2]: our purpose was to learn something about the latter by studying the "produce" of the brain, conceived as a biological machine (almost a heresy at that time) whose inner workings we had just started modeling with mathematical equations describing Neural Nets and their learning mechanisms.

Our methodological approach provided several insights, which were, when possible, subjected to computer analyses (of texts in several languages) that well corresponded to our expectations, thus stimulating further researches, still under way. Implementation with Neural Nets is being also considered, but will not be discussed here. I present it, in sketchy outline but with several improvements with respect to earlier studies, because I think it paradigmatic for many problems of interest to us. E.g., a robot may be described by specifying the "translation" it performs from a "sensory" to a "motor" language: a problem for which the appellative "prolegomena" given to these considerations seems not inappropriate. They may be taken, in a generalized sense, to belong to "mathematical linguistics". The major difference between most approaches in this area and ours is that we consider the language which we happen to study as our "universe", which we treat as a physicist does with his: he cannot change it at will and is forbidden from making a priori assumptions on its laws. Likewise, we demand that what structures, grammars, etc. may exist in a "language" must be found by applying a systematic methodology, not postulated as already known.

The major conceptual difference from earlier works is given by our refounding the whole approach on properties of the Kullback-Leibler entropy. Basic notions become more perspicuous and rigorous, some statements proposed before as heuristic become mathematical corrolaries.
We name this improved version "Procrustes II", since our previous work was called

"Procrustes" (after the name of the first theorist in our history)

2.- The "form of an object is understood as a quality bestowed upon it by the "observer" (a typical Kantian phenomenon). It includes "pattern", "image", etc. . "Form" is thus a "set property"; the "observer" is defined in turn through the set of elements stipulated by him to have the same form (e.g. according to weight, colour, shape, nutritional value...) . It is well known that a "set consisting of a single element" is a quite different object from that single element alone: the difference is the observer! This raises profound system-theoretical questions (think also of Quantum Mechanics), which will not concern us here. The operation performed by the observer when defining a form coincides with "abstraction", typical, in our approach, of learning neural nets [3]. Iteration of this operation creates hierarchies and heterarchies of sets, or forms, or "features" (as such partial sets are often called when seen from a higher level). The study of this global process we call "Structural Analysis". Considerations which we do not report here [4] show that it involves usually a "Quantification" into the discrete (and finite) domain (think of our "seven" notes or colours as contrasted with the underlying physical continuum). We shall assume, as starting point, that the objects we deal with are quantified, either naturally or because of some preliminary pre-processing.

We propose to analyze structures as "nested sequences of substructures". The analogy with a typed linguistic text is cogent; we shall use, proceeding "bottom-up", the words "letter", "syllable", word",...
This may be misleading, because it implies an underlying "linear dimension" as for a typwritten text, i.e. the existence of "complete ordering" relations, which may well not be"natural" in the analysis, say, of pictures. In such cases we assume, for the purpose of the present discussion, such relations to be the result of some prescription, as always possible in the discrete: think of TV scanning, or of the saccadic eye movements of Yarbus. By so doing, we deal in fact with the most complex situation, that of "strings" of elements in which "order" is essential; suppression of order would simplify our treatment into that of "clusters", an easier task not treated here (it would imply a reconsideration of the "codes" discussed next).

3.- We shall call henceforth "language" a given (extensively or potentially, finite or infinite) set of "texts" written in terms of "letters" of an "alphabet" A (e.g. English letters, or Kanji and Kana). Our attention will be concentrated on a single text T (the addition of more texts will enrich later our knowledge). A "code" is a collection of strings (code words) of letters of A. We defined [5] a code "closed" if "left cancellation" of a code word gives again a code word: thus, if $a_1a_2a_3$ is a code word, a_2a_3 and a_3 are also code words .

"Natural codes" are defined as those which contain "terminal letters": in our analysis a subset of them, "closed natural codes" (CNC), will play a relevant role.

"Instantaneous codes" are the subclass of "uniquely decipherable codes" for which the end of a code word is recognizable without exploration of the next letter. We defined "closed instantaneous codes" (CIC) the subclass of instantaneous codes which is closed under left cancellation, except that it does not contain as words suffixes which have code words as prefixes: thus $a_1a_2a_3a_4$; a_3a_4; a_3a_2; a_2; a_4 is a CIC (the suffix $a_2a_3a_4$ is forbidden). CIC's contain terminal symbols also within their code words, and are thus wider than CNC's, in terms of which they can be further analyzed.

The interest of CIC and CNC lies for us in the fact that our algorithm was proved to converge always to one of these two codes (applications to texts written with other types of codes prove this assertion; for a discussion, see ref. [5])

II - Preliminary Remarks

1.- Two main topics are relevant for our structural analysis:

- frequency count;

- search for individual structures, no matter how rare.

We have restricted our attention only to the second, which presented the greater challenge and is a necessary pre-requisite for the first; a study of texts in various languages, especially Italian, substantiated our conclusions. There is of course no doubt that both topics are important in a complete analysis of the type we propose.

2.- Our search for structural levels has to meet two basic demands:

- finding, proceeding bottom-up, a hierarchy of nested substructures, none excluded, in terms of which our texts may be fully described;

- destroying the evident influence of higher structures on the distribution of lower ones. (One may read thus most of Italian literature without ever meeting the word "soqquadro", which denotes a situation of "total upsetting wantonly created", and is the only Italian word to have the sequence "qqua"; yet this string cannot be ignored by our search!)

The second is easily answered at the first two steps:

- transition from the study of "language" to that of a single "text" T .

- transition from the text T to the corresponding "reduced text", or vocabolary, W , which contains each word of T only once.

The latter is paradigmatic for our procedure; the reader may compare our approach, for analogies and differences, with C. Shannon's celebrated analysis of English. Assume level "1" to be given by the alphabet letters (because given, or as a higher level from some binary, or Morse, code); call level "K" that given by all the words of the reduced text W . Think now of two sets of B. Russell's monkeys, one with letter-keyboards, the other with word-keyboards: the first will reproduce all that we want and can of structure at level "1", the second at level "K". How the destruction of the damaging influence of higher levels comes about is quite clear in both cases.

3.- Our aim is to obtain, at whatever levels may exist between "letters" and "words", this same result. It suffices to consider only one intermediate level between the two just named, that of "syllables". It is the old problem of "parsing", when no indications are elicitable from the text on how to divide words into syllables. We can replace monkeys with semigroup theory: we demand that our "syllables", if written as strings of alphabet letters, generate a "submonoid" (that covers W) which is a "free submonoid" of the monoid generated by the letters. Our algorithms must therefore automatically, on reading the text, retrieve the generators of the free submonoid that is smaller than the monoid generated by letters and larger than that generated by words. (We have assumed just one intermediate level, but the extension to whole hierarchies should be evident).

III - Information as Kullback-Leibler Entropy

1.- Our purpose is not to repeat statements and proofs already available in the references, but rather to "distill" out of them, with greater mathematical clarity than was then possible, the crucial points that we deem of value for further investigation; the result ought to be a vast improvement, because the use of "conjectures" then made, turned now into legitimate mathematical statements, will allow great gains in computational speed.

We only discuss here, as an illustration, the paradigm "letter - syllable - word" just quoted. If we denote A* the monoid generated by the alphabet A, we propose to find a set of syllables S such that:

$A^* \sqsupset \quad S^* \sqsupset \quad W^*$ (in the strong sense, or else there is no intermediate level between A and W).

2.- We are interested in structures, not in frequencies. We build therefore at each stage probability schemes of "microcanonical" type, as follows. Our search for S must start and stop automatically (words are assumed to have a finite maximal length); it proceeds, by iteration, through the construction of "intermediate provisional alphabets" containing letters, digrams, trigrams..., until the previous alphabet is identically reproduced. It constitutes the wanted S : our procedure, explained next, guaranties that S is a CNC or a CIC.

Call X_α a string of (one or more) letters, y_h the letter next to it at right in the word. Call $p(X_\alpha\, y_h)$ the probability (to be specified later) that the string $X_\alpha\, y_h$ exists in W. Consider then the marginal probabilities

$$p(X_\alpha) = \Sigma_h \; p(X_\alpha\, y_h), \qquad\qquad p(y_h) = \Sigma_\alpha \; p(X_\alpha\, y_h)$$

and the conditional probabilities

$$p(y_h / X_\alpha) = p(X_\alpha\, y_h) / p(X_\alpha);$$

$$p(X_\alpha / y_h) = p(X_\alpha\, y_h) / p(y_h);$$

form the entropies

$$H(Y) = -\Sigma_h \; p(y_h) \log p(y_h)$$

$$H(Y / X\;) = -\Sigma_h \; p(y_h / X_\alpha) \log p(y_h / X_\alpha)$$

$$H_X(Y) = \Sigma_\alpha \; p(X_\alpha)\, H(Y / X_\alpha) \qquad \text{(equivocation)}$$

and from them the "mutual information", or "divergence", or "Kullback-Leibler entropy" (all synonims; the last concept is the most interesting for us, as it implies a "measure" of how near we are to our aim):

$$H(X;Y) = H(Y) - H_X(Y) = H(X) + H(Y) - H(X,Y) =$$

$$= \Sigma_{\alpha,h}\ p(x_\alpha y_h) \log\{p(x_\alpha y_h) / p(x_\alpha)\, p(y_h)\}.$$

The gain in information with respect to the average information on y when X_α is known is:

$$\xi(X_\alpha) = H(Y) - H(Y / X_\alpha)$$

3. - Proceed now as follows.

<u>Step</u> 1):

a) Construct a histogram having as abscissae and ordinates the letters of A; set in it a "1" whenever the digram $X_\alpha\, y_h$ <u>exists</u> in W, no matter how many times, a "0" otherwise (here, X_α is a single letter of A);

b) Call D the total number of 1's in histogram (we treat only the case $D < A^2$ here, denoting with A also the number of letters of A); set

$$p(X_\alpha\, y_h) = \begin{cases} 1/D & \text{if } X_\alpha\, y_h \in D \sqsubset A^2 \\ 0 & \text{if } X_\alpha\, y_h \notin D \end{cases}$$

c) Compute $\xi(X_\alpha)$ for all values on abscissa; if

$\xi(X_\alpha) \leq H(X;Y)$ take all monograms X_α as letters of first provisional alphabet;

if

$\xi(X_\alpha) > H(X;Y)$ remove X_α from letteral alphabet A, complete first provisional alphabet with <u>all</u> such digrams.

<u>Step</u> 2):

Set as abscissae X_α all elements of first provisional alphabet, as ordinates all letters of A. Iterate step 1).

<u>Step</u> 3) etc.: Iterate.

<u>End</u>: When iteration reproduces previous alphabet. This is taken as that of wanted syllables. Wanted structure is found.

The main point is now easily understood. Looking at the Kullback-Leibler entropy, we see that it <u>vanishes</u> when $p(X_\alpha y_h) = p(X_\alpha)p(y_h)$: the wanted "syllabic" alphabet is reached when none of the symbols that have been constructed with our procedure yields information on the next letter, as expressed by the factorization of the probability. This situation is "ideal", because any text we examine can only be finite; one can however (thus destroying the constraints posed by word-structure on syllable-finding) easily replace the "word level" with one in which "all" syllables are assumed freely adjoinable. This, again, acts like a thermodynamic limit, and simplifies computation greatly. It also implies that $p(y_h)$ is taken not as the marginal probability of y_h ("last" letter of a string), but of y_h as any letter of the alphabet (assumed equiprobable). In earlier works we found, empirically, this to be indeed the best choice.

3.- Discussion.

We have thus built a sequence of "vocabularies", each listing the structures of a level.. This is only a first start, which however indicates several problems that can be studied next with in ways not only heuristic. They are mentioned in ref.[5-8]. Our specific aim demanded the exclusion of direct "frequency counts" (but information on the frequency of a symbol among those of higher levels might be usefully obtained). Such counts will be of course of major importance for other parts of the structural analysis we propose, of which only the mere beginnings are here reported.

References

[1] Caianiello, E.R. and Crocchiolo, Programma Procuste per l'Analisi di Linguaggi Naturali, Calcolo, 2, 83, (1965).

[2] Caianiello, E.R., On the analysis of natural languages, Odessa, Proceedings of the 3rd All Union SSR Congress on Cybernetics (1965).

[3] Caianiello, E.R., Outline of a theory of thought processes and thinking machine, J. Theor. Biol., 1, p. 209 (1961).

[4] Caianiello, E.R., Some remarks on organization and structure, Biological Cybernetics,26,p. 151, (1977).

[5] Caianiello, E. R. and Capocelli, R.M., On form and language: the Procuste's algorithms for feature extraction, Kybernetik, 8,p. 223, (1971).

[6] Caianiello, E.R. and Capocelli, R.M., Structural analysis of hierarchical systems, Proc. of 3rd joint conference Pattern Recognition, (1976).

[7] Caianiello , P., Neural models, structure and learning, Proc. of 1st Italian workshop on parallel architecture and neural networks, (Word Scientific, Singapore, 1988).

[8] Caianiello , P., Learning by data compression in neural nets, Proc. of2nd Italian workshop on parallel architecture and neural networks, (Word Scientific, Singapore, 1988).

Advanced Neural Computers / R. Eckmiller (Editor)

The Truck Backer-Upper: An Example of Self-Learning in Neural Networks

Derrick Nguyen and Bernard Widrow

Information Systems Laboratory
Department of Electrical Engineering
Stanford University
Stanford, CA 94305

Neural networks can be used to solve highly nonlinear control problems. A two-layer neural network containing 26 adaptive neural elements has learned to back up a computer simulated trailer truck to a loading dock, even when initially "jackknifed." It is not yet known how to design a controller to perform this steering task. Nevertheless, the neural net was able to learn of its own accord to do this, regardless of initial conditions. Experience gained with the truck backer upper should be applicable to a wide variety of nonlinear control problems that appear in power systems.

1 Introduction

The control of severely nonlinear systems has for the most part escaped the attention of control theorists and practitioners. This paper addresses the issue from the point of view of utilizing self-learning techniques to achieve nonlinear controller design. The methodology shows promise for applications to control problems that are so complex that analytical design techniques either do not exist or will not exist for some time to come. Neural networks can be used to implement highly nonlinear controllers whose weights or internal parameters can be chosen or determined by a self-learning process.

Backing a trailer truck to a loading dock is a difficult exercise for all but the most skilled truck drivers. Anyone who has tried to back up a house trailer or a boat trailer will realize this. Normal driving instincts lead to erroneous movements. A great deal of practice is required to develop the requisite skills.

When watching a truck driver backing toward a loading dock, one often observes the driver backing, going forward, backing again, going forward, etc., and finally backing to the desired position along the dock. The forward and backward movements help to position the trailer for successful backing up to the dock. A more difficult backing up sequence would only allow backing, with no forward movements permitted. The specific problem treated in this paper is that of the design by self-learning of a nonlinear controller to control the steering of a trailer truck while backing up to a loading dock from an arbitrary initial position. Only backing up is allowed. Computer simulation of the truck and its controller has demonstrated workability, although no mathematical proof yet exists. The experimental controller contains 26 adaptive ADALINE units [1] and exhibits exquisite backing up control. The trailer truck can be initially "jackknifed" and aimed in many different directions, toward and away from the dock, but as long as there is sufficient clearance, the controller appears to be capable of finding a solution.

Figure 1 shows a computer-screen image of the truck, the trailer, and the loading dock. The critical state variables representing the position of the truck and that of the loading dock are θ_{cab}, the angle

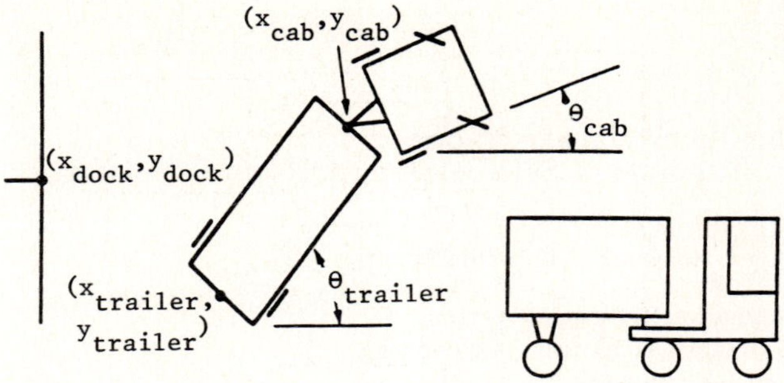

Figure 1: The truck, the trailer, and the loading dock

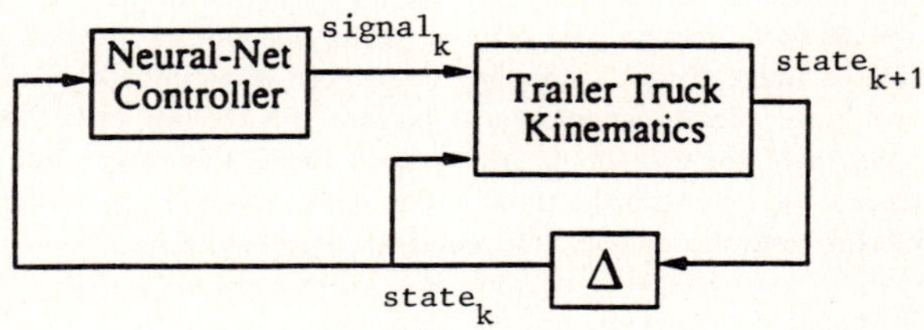

Figure 2: Overview Diagram

of the truck, x_{cab} and y_{cab}, the cartesian position of the yoke, $x_{trailer}$ and $y_{trailer}$, the cartesian position of the rear of the center of the trailer, and x_{dock} and y_{dock}, the cartesian position of the center of the loading dock. Definition of the state variables is illustrated in Figure 1.

The truck backs up until it hits the dock, then stops. The goal is to cause the back of the trailer to be parallel to the loading dock, and to have the point $(x_{trailer}, y_{trailer})$ be aligned as closely as possible with point (x_{dock}, y_{dock}). The controller will learn to achieve this objective.

2 Training

The approach to self-learning control that has been successfully used with the truck backer-upper involves a two-stage learning process. The first stage involves the training of a neural network to be an emulator of the truck and trailer kinematics. The second stage involves the training of a neural-network controller to control the emulator. A similar approach has been used by Widrow [2, 3] and by Jordan [4]. Once the controller knows how to control the emulator, it is then able to control the actual trailer truck. Figure 2 gives an overview, showing how the present state vector $state_k$ is fed to the controller which in turn provides a *steering* $signal_k$ between -1 (hard right) and $+1$ (hard left) to the truck. The time index is k. Each time cycle, the truck backs up by a fixed small distance. The next state is determined by the present state and the steering signal, which is fixed during the cycle.

Figure 3 shows a block diagram of the process used to train the emulator. The truck backs up randomly, going through many cycles with randomly selected steering signals. By this process, the emulator "gets the feel" of how the trailer and truck behave. The emulator, chosen as a two layer

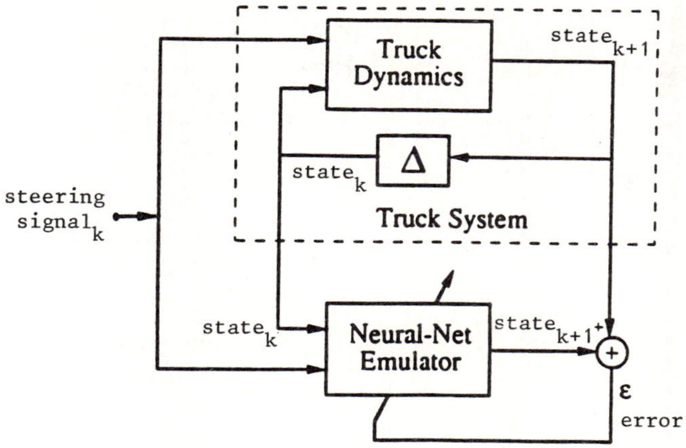

Figure 3: Training the neural-net truck emulator

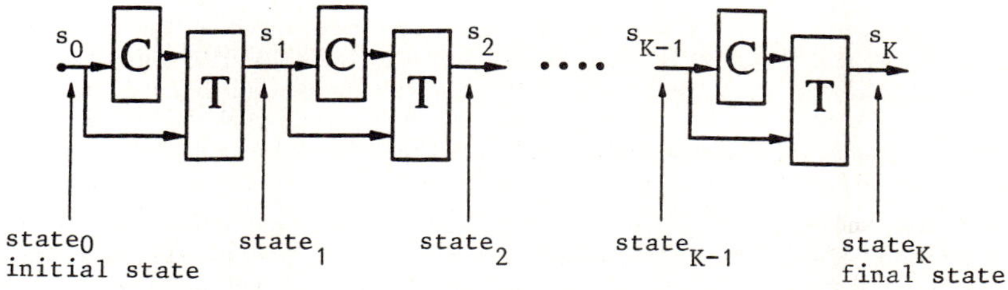

Figure 4: State transition flow diagram

neural network, learns to generate the next positional state vector when given the present state vector and the steering signal. This is done for a wide variety of positional states and steering angles. The two-layer emulator is adapted by means of the back-propagation algorithm [5, 6, 7]. The first layer had six present state inputs plus the present steering signal input. This layer contained forty five hidden adaptive ADALINE units producing six next-state predictions. Once the emulator is trained, it can then be used to train the controller.

Refer to Figure 4. The identical blocks labeled C represent the controller. The identical blocks labeled T represent the truck and trailer emulator. Suppose that the truck is engaged in backing up. Let C be chosen randomly and be initially fixed. The initial state vector s_0 is fed to C, which produces the steering signal output which sets the steering angle of the truck. The backing up cycle proceeds with the truck and trailer soon arriving at the next state s_1. With C remaining fixed, the backing up process continues from cycle to cycle until the truck hits something and stops. The final state s_K is compared with the desired final state (the rear of the trailer parallel to the dock with proper positional alignment) to obtain the final state error vector ϵ_K. This error vector contains three elements (which are the errors of interest), $x_{trailer}$, $y_{trailer}$ and $\theta_{trailer}$, and is used to adapt the controller C.

The method of adapting the controller C is illustrated in Figure 5. The final state error vector ϵ_K is used to adapt the blocks labeled C, which are maintained identical to each other throughout the

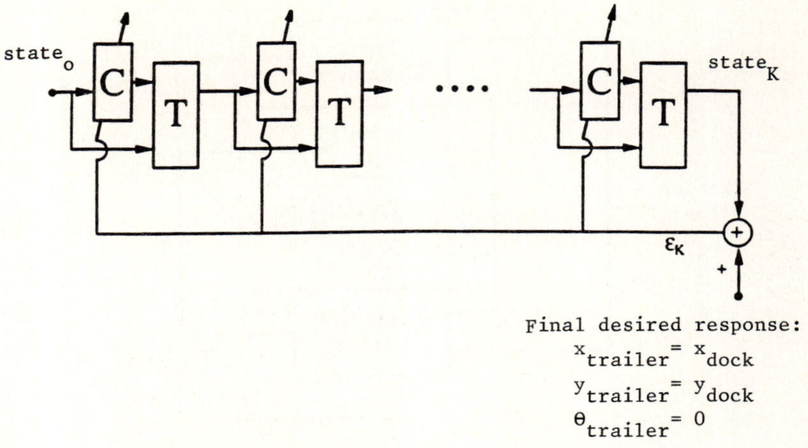

Figure 5: Training the controller with back-propagation

adaptive process. The controller C is a two-layer neural network. The first layer has the six state variables as inputs, and this layer contains twenty five adaptive ADALINE units. The second or output layer has one adaptive ADALINE unit and produces the steering signal as its output.

The procedure for adapting C goes as follows. The weights of C are chosen initially at random. The initial position of the truck is chosen at random. The truck backs up, undergoing many individual back up cycles, until it stops. The final error is used by back-propagation to adapt the controller. Each of the C blocks could be tentatively adapted by back-propagation if they were independent of each other, but the actual weight changes in C are taken as the sum of the tentative changes. In this way, the C blocks are maintained identical to each other. The weights are changed by this constrained back-propagation algorithm to reduce the sum of the squares of the components of the final state error ϵ_K by following the negative of the gradient, using the method of steepest descent. The entire process is repeated by placing the truck and trailer in another initial position, and allowing it to back up until it stops. Once again, the controller weights are adapted. And so on.

Figure 6 shows details of one of the state transition stages of Figure 5. One can see the structure of controller C and of emulator T, and how they are interconnected. Each stage of Figure 5 amounts to a four-layer neural network. The entire process of going from an initial state to the final state can be seen from Figures 4 and 5 to be analogous to a neural network having a number of layers equal to four times the number of backing up steps when going from the initial state to the final state. The number of steps varies of course with initial position of the truck and trailer.

The diagram of Figure 5 was simplified for clarity of presentation. The output error does not go directly to the C-blocks as shown, but back-propagates through the T-blocks and C-blocks. Thus, the error used to adapt each of the C-blocks does originate from the output error ϵ_K, but travels through the proper back-propagation paths. For purposes of back-propagation of the error, the T-blocks are the truck emulator. But the actual truck kinematics are used when sensing the error ϵ_K itself.

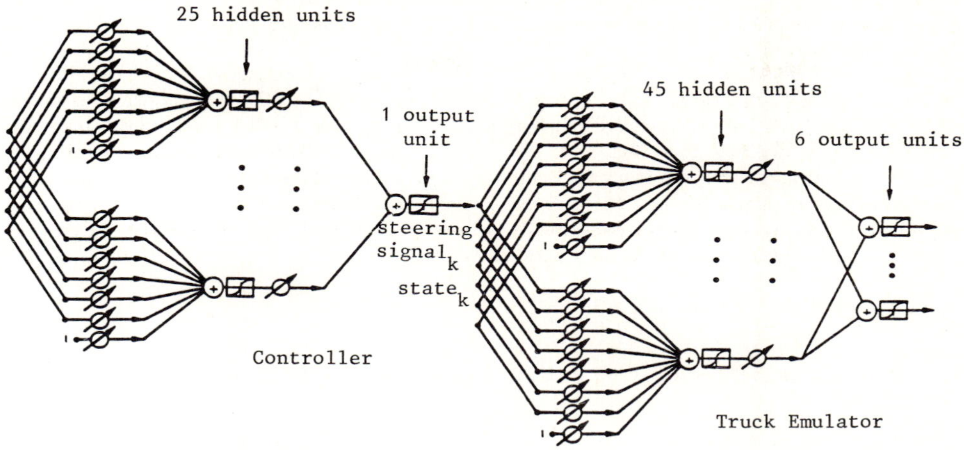

Figure 6: Details of emulator and controller

3 Summary and Results

The truck emulator was able to represent the trailer and truck when jackknifed, in line, or in any condition in between. Nonlinearity in the emulator was essential to represent the truck and trailer. The angle between truck and trailer were not small. *Sin* θ could not be represented approximately as θ. Nonlinearity in the controller was also essential. Self-learning processes were used to determine the parameters of both the emulator and the controller. Thousands of back ups were required to train these networks. Without the learning process however, substantial amounts of human effort and design time would have been required to devise the controller.

The training of the controller was divided into several "lessons". In the beginning, the controller was trained with the truck initially set to points very near the dock and the trailer pointing at the dock. Once the controller was proficient at working with these initial positions, the problem was made harder by starting the truck farther away from the dock and at increasingly difficult angles. This way, the controller learned to do easy problems first and more difficult problems after it mastered the easy ones. There were 16 lessons in all. In the easiest lesson the trailer was set about half a truck length from the dock in the x direction pointing at the dock, and the cab at a random angle between ±30 degrees. In the last and most difficult lesson the rear of the trailer was set randomly between 1 and 2 truck lengths from the dock in the x direction and ±1 truck length from the dock in the y direction. The cab and trailer angle was set to be the same, at a random angle between ±90 degrees. The controller was trained for about 1000 truck backups per lesson during the early lessons, and 2000 truck backups per lesson during the last few. It took altogether about 20000 backups to train the controller.

The controller learned to control the truck very well with the the above training process. Near the end of the last lesson, the root mean square error of $y_{trailer}$ was about 3 percent of a truck length. The root mean square error of $\theta_{trailer}$ was about 7 degrees. There is no error in $x_{trailer}$ since a truck backup is stopped when $x_{trailer} = x_{dock}$. One may, of course, trade off the error in $y_{trailer}$ with the error in $\theta_{trailer}$ by giving them different weightings during training.

Results with the adaptive controller are illustrated in Figures 7, 8, 9, and 10. The controller has already been trained and its weights remained fixed for all the experiments. The truck and trailer were placed in a variety of initial conditions, and backing up was effected in each case. Initial and final states are shown in the computer screen displays, and the dynamics of backing up is illustrated by the time-lapse plots.

The truck backer-upper learns to solve sequential decision problems. The control decisions made early in the backing up process have substantial effects upon final results. Early moves may not always be in a direction to reduce error, but they position the truck and trailer for ultimate success. In many respects, the truck backer-upper learns a control strategy that is like a dynamic programming problem solution. The learning is done in a layered neural network. Connecting signals from one layer to another corresponds to idea that the final state of a backing up cycle is the same as the initial state of the next backing up cycle.

Future research will be concerned with:

- Determination of complexity of emulator as related to complexity of the system being controlled.
- Determination of complexity of controller as related to complexity of emulator.
- Determination of convergence and rate of learning for emulator and controller.
- Proof of robustness of control scheme.
- Analytic derivation of non-linear controller for truck backer-upper, and comparison with self learned controller.
- Re-learning in the presence of movable obstacles.
- Application of self-learning neural networks to control of power generators, power system apparatus, and to power distribution systems.

This research was sponsored by SDIO Innovative Science and Technology Office and managed by ONR under contract #N00014-86-K-0718, by the Department of the Army Belvoir R D & E Center under Contract #DAAK70-89-K-0001, and by grants from the Thomson CSF Company and the Lockheed Missiles and Space Company.

This material is based on work supported under a National Science Foundation Graduate Fellowship. Any opinions, findings, conclusions, or recommendations expressed in this publication are those of the authors and do not necessarily reflect the views of the National Science Foundation.

References

[1] B. Widrow and M. E. Hoff, Jr. Adaptive switching circuits. In *1960 IRE WESTCON Conv. Record, Part 4*, pages 96–104, 1960.

[2] Bernard Widrow and Samuel D. Stearns. *Adaptive Signal Processing.* Prentice-Hall, Inc., Englewood Cliffs, N.J., 1985.

[3] B. Widrow. Adaptive inverse control. In *Adaptive Systems in Control and Signal Processing 1986.* International Federation of Automatic Control, July 1986.

[4] M. I. Jordan. Supervised learning and systems with excess degrees of freedom. COINS 88-27, Massachusetts Institute of Technology, 1988.

[5] P. Werbos. *Beyond Regression: New Tools for Prediction and Analysis in the Behavioral Sciences.* PhD thesis, Harvard University, Cambridge, MA, August 1974.

[6] D.B. Parker. Learning logic. Technical Report TR-47, Center for Comput. Res. Econ. and Manage., Mass. Inst. Technol., 1985.

[7] David E. Rumelhart and James L. McClelland, editors. *Parallel Distributed Processing*, volume 1, chapter 8. The MIT Press, Cambridge, Mass., 1986.

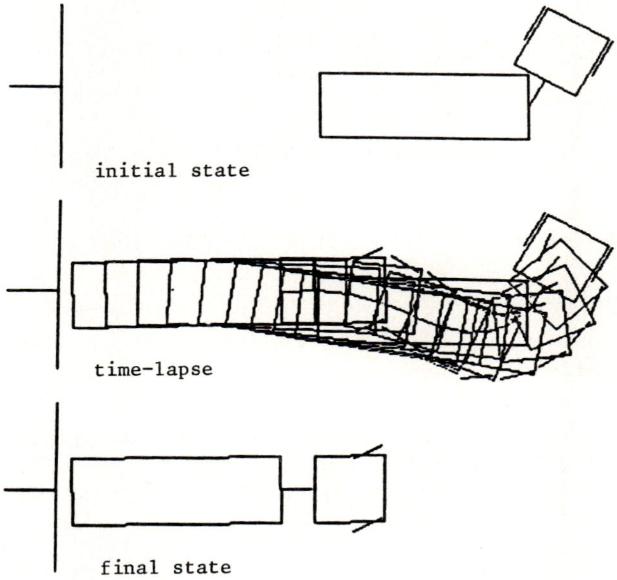

Figure 7

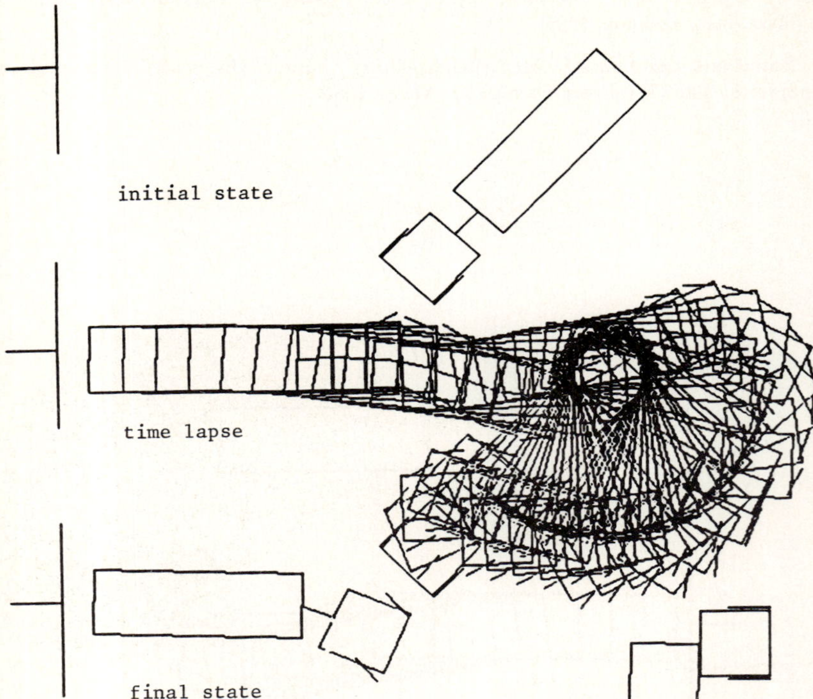

Figure 8

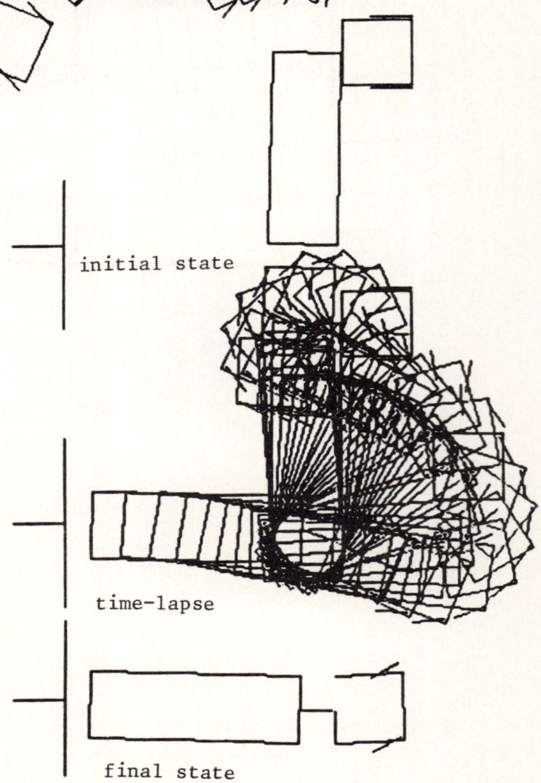

Figure 9

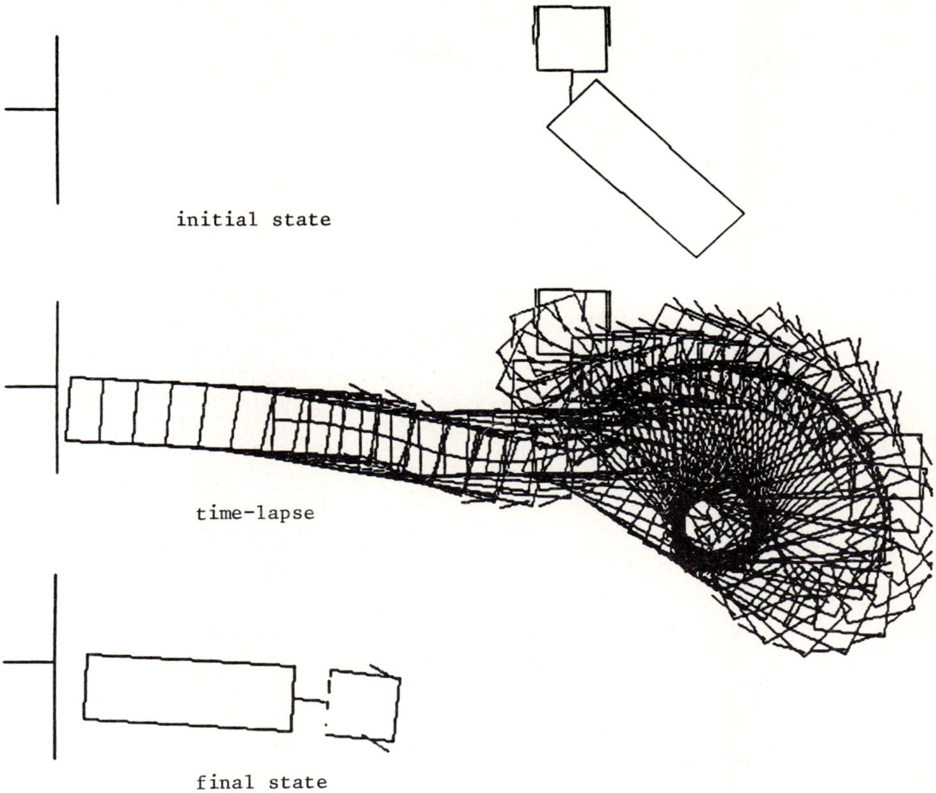

Figure 10

Advanced Neural Computers / R. Eckmiller (Editor)

DIE LERNMATRIX - THE BEGINNING OF ASSOCIATIVE MEMORIES

Karl STEINBUCH

Formerly University of Karlsruhe, Germany (Now retired)

1. INTRODUCTION

Comparison of information processing by man and by computers (of John von Neumann's structure) shows:

+ Computers can simulate all - or most - information processing modes of man.
+ But for very simple modes of man's information processing, computers are less appropriate (for example for pattern recognition).

This was the starting point of considerations about 30 years ago - and I rapidly came to the "conditioned reflexes", which the famous russian physiologist I.P. Pavlov had discovered at the beginning of our century.

In Pavlov's well known experiment, a dog was conditioned to salivate upon the signal of a bell - a signal, which has been without any effect before.

Conditioned reflexes suppose circuits, whose rules of operation are being changed as a function of input information. Apparently they provide for storage of variable logical operation.

I proposed several simple technical realizations of conditioned reflexes, for example formation of threads of metallic silver in an environment of silver bromide or ferro-magnetic realizations which are useful for reversible connections.

Basic idea hereby was not to simulate organisms, but rather to find simple technical prinziples for learning processes.

In order not to confuse terminology, the expression "conditioned reflex" will not be used, but "conditioned connection".

Basically, two kinds of circuitry could be conceived, dependend on whether binary or non-binary patterns are to be processed.

2. BINARY LEARNING MATRIX

The structure of a learning matrix is indicated in Figure 1.

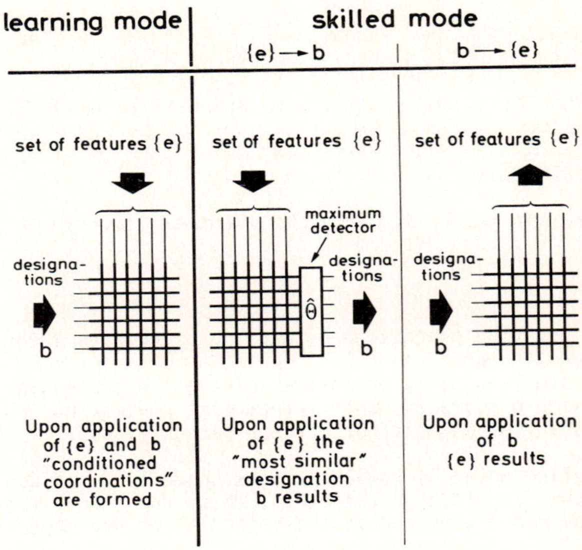

FIGURE 1

The Learning matrix, principle

Two sets of conductors intersect forming a matrix like structure. The cross-points of the matrix behave as" conditioned connections". The vertical conductors carry a set of features or a pattern $\{e\}$ consisting of binary signals, e.g. black and white.

The horizontal set of conductors carries statements of designations b . In this set only one at a time will be marked by a signal, the statements of designation are offered in a "1-out-of-m-code".

Two modes of operation can be distinguished:

1) a learning state, during which both a pattern $\{e\}$ and an associated designation b are applied to the learning matrix and therefore the conditioned connections may be built up, and
2) a skilled state or knowing phase during which alternatively
   + upon application of an arbitrary set of features $\{e\}$ the most similar designation b or
   + upon application of designation b the associated pattern $\{e\}$ will be signalized.

In some cases it is useful and by special arrangements of realization as well possible to gradually change the learned coordination between patterns e and particular designation b simply by continuous operation (feature of read-justment). The conditioned connections mentioned above are in this sense functional elements whose logical operation changes with experience or former performance.

How learning may be achieved, depends on the special technical realization of the matrix.

In the case of an electro-chemical realization, no conductivity exists at all at the beginning of the learning state.

In the case of a ferro-magnetic realization, the magnetic elements representing intersecting points are at the beginning in the zero point of the hysteresis loop.

Learning is performed by applying the set of features mentioned before to the column inputs and at the same time a certain signal to the special row into which the pattern is to be stored.

In fig. 2 it is assumed, that four different patterns have been learned by the matrix in the sense discussed.

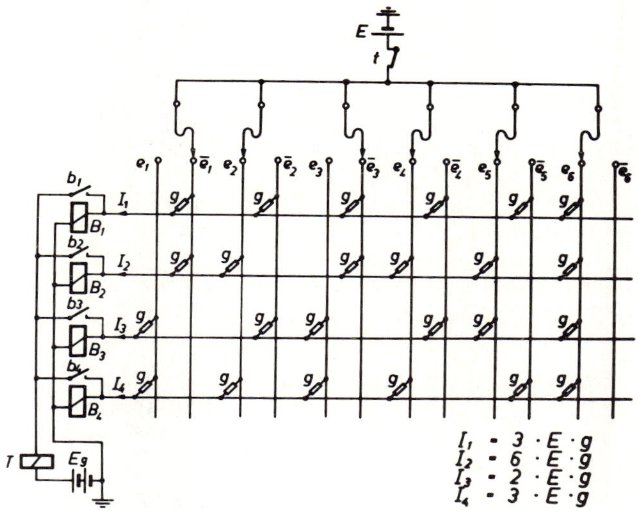

FIGURE 2

Learning matrix, knowing state

As fig. 2 shows, for each input element one double column has been provided. This is necessary in order to make use of the information e = 0 , otherwise the pattern $\{e\}$ = 11111 would suppress all the other ones.

When learning is completed, skilled or knowing mode operation may start. The principle of it, too, is indicated in fig. 2. Again a pattern is presented to the column heads, let us say in form of a set of voltages, which are now coupled to the left hand column input if the particular feature **e** is 1 or to the right hand one if it is 0 . In fig. 2 $\{e\}$ = 010111 is applied as an input. On the rows leads the coincidences with the stored patterns are summed up.

Apparently the one having the greatest similarity to the pattern applied will carry the largest current.

A coincidence in all positions causes a current contribution by all double columns. Hence the current on the row corresponding to the pattern applied (provided it has been learned before by the matrix) will have a maximum value. Lack of coincidence in one or more positions will result in smaller currents. Actually one can state that the row current will be smaller the larger the Hamming distance is between the pattern applied and the one stored in the particular row. The largest current will operate the correspondent relay which upon operation switches the fast relay T disconnecting the inputs. This is to demonstrate the behaviour of the maximum detection circuit, which in reality consists of transistors, diodes a.s.o.

In summary, a learning matrix determines the most similar pattern to a given input set of events, this is a maximum likelihood detection.

So far only conductivities at the intersection points have been discussed. Probably of greater importance are ferro-magnetic storage elements providing for the additional features of reversibility of the matrix and its learning processes and for relearning. By making use of half-current pulses of short duration (as compared with the switching time of the magnetic material) a core representing a storage element can be changed stepwise like a multiple state magnetic counter.

Hereby the stored value corresponds to a whole series of applied patterns each changing the row elements by just a small amount. Reading has to be nondestructive, the signals of all rows are fed into a maximum detection circuit selecting again the row containing the most similar pattern to the one applied.

3. NON-BINARY LEARNING MATRIX

Besides binary learning matrices discussed so far another type can be conceived dealing with analogue signals.

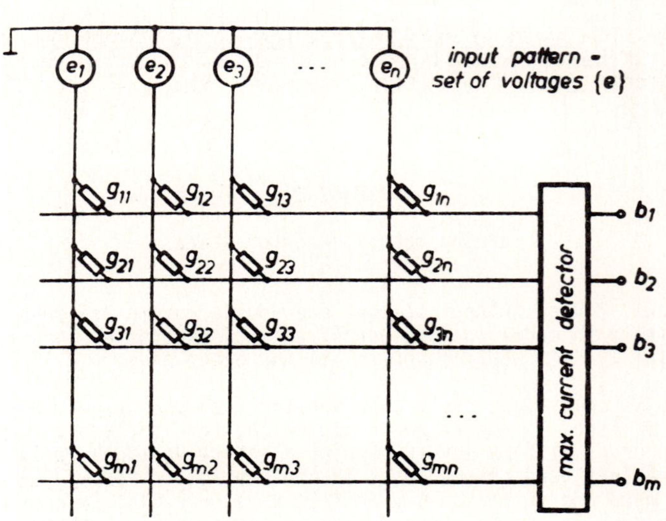

FIGURE 3

Non - binary Learning matrix

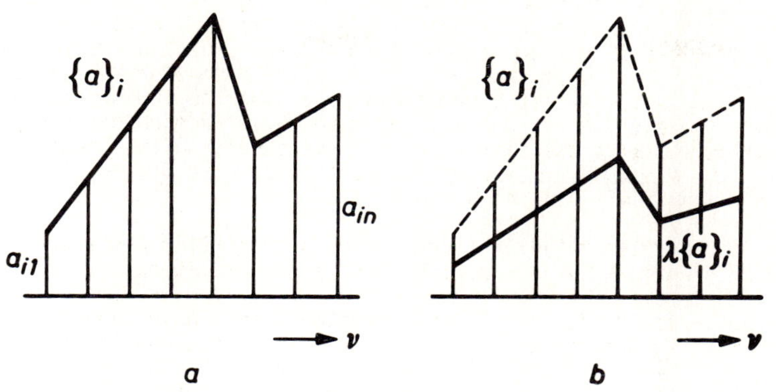

FIGURE 4

Sampled Patterns

Fig. 4 a shows a typical pattern or set of features which can be processed by the matrix. Into the columns a signal is fed, e.g. a voltage e corresponding in magnitude to the particular sample value of the analogue pattern. By an appropriate learning process the elements along a certain row likewise have been brought to a proportional value $a_{i\nu}$.

A simple calculations shows:

+ the learned patterns must be normalized with respect to their energy. The learned (stored) patterns are called "unity patterns" or "perceptual forms".
+ the recognition by the learning matrix is invariant to affine transformed patterns. Affine transformation fo a pattern means multiplying each one of its attributes by the same positive constant (Fig. 5).

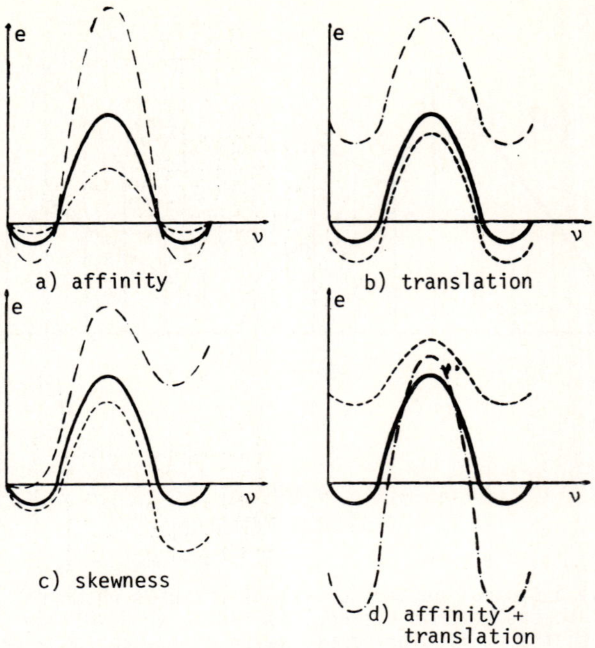

FIGURE 5

Some invariants

Still one problem remains: Such a matrix using resistors is not able to deal with patterns containing negative attributes. But an arrangement using "contradictory" columns for each input solves this problem.

Arrangements similar to the non-binary matrix are known (Chow 1957). But it has been assumed, so far, that the magnitudes of the connecting elements are set "a priori" proportional to the attributes of the learned patterns, for instance by soldering in ordinary resistors.

A learning non-binary matrix could be realized with almost all physical means which have already been used in binary learning matrices, such as chemical cells, the resistance of which can be altered by currents fed into the cell. However, the most versatile elements are magnetic devices. With irreversible connecting elements some difficulties could arise, for instance the impossibility of relearning.

4. CIRCUITS WITH SEVERAL LEARNING MATRICES

Interesting aspects arise from combined circuits of learning matrices. They easily could be arranged by means of intermediate storage to use a set of meanings coming out in sequence of a first learning matrix as an input set to a second matrix (see Fig. 6).

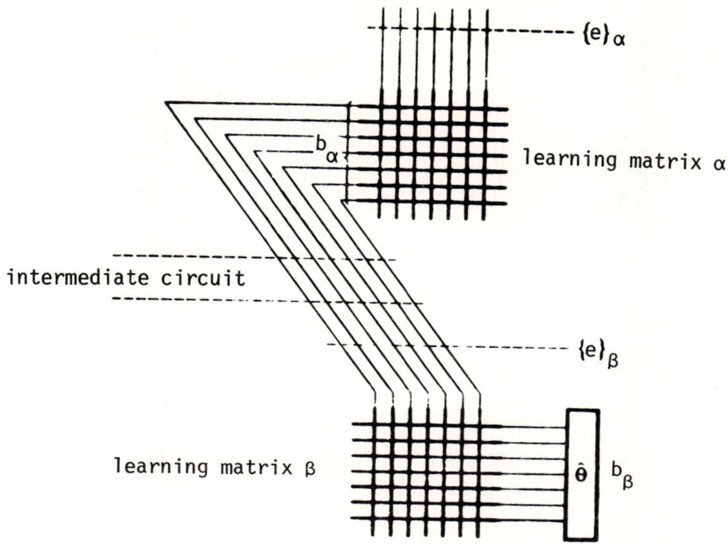

FIGURE 6

Layers of Learning matrices

By that combination e.g. words could be recognized of the single letters being the meanings of the first matrix. This could be extended to recognition of sentences using another intermediate circuit. This method resembles to the ability of organic systems to restore disturbed code words, e.g. wrongly spelled words.

Another way of making use of several learning matrices is the parallel circuit of two of them: Coupled learning matrices, "learning matrix - dipoles".

Two kinds of coupling are possible.

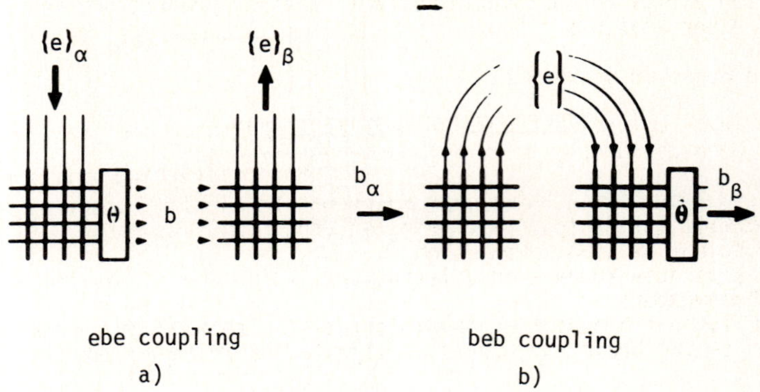

FIGURE 7

LM - Dipoles

+ ebe - coupling: transforming a set of characteristics into another one having meaning b as an invariant. This may be a model for translation of the meaning of one language into another.
+ beb - coupling: transforming the meaning, keeping a set of features $\{e\}$ invariant.

5. APPLICATIONS

When I had found and realized the learning matrix some 30 years ago, I was very optimistic about practical applications.
For example:

a) Automatic Pattern Recognition
So far the types of characters to be recognized had to be known a priori in order to construct and wire the logical network. A learning matrix could shift from one learned alphabet (e.g. latin typewriter) to another (certain types of printing, Greek letters, Kyrillic letters a.s.o.). Naturally one must not use black/white information as considered above but rather symptoms of shape, topological symptoms a.s.o.

b) Automatic Speech Recognition
Learning here can bridge the gap between individual differences in speaking.

c) Machine Translation could probably make good use of learning matrices adjusting the semantics to a certain text.

d) Information retrieval: Here new aspects are given by the fact, that the maximum likelihood decision is merely based on the information itself - no adress is needed. Thus a publication easily may be located by simply calling up the key-words.

e) For chemical analysis by means of spectrogramms a circuit consisting of a non-binary learning matrix may be conceived, where rather than a maximum detector the output row signals indicate the percentage of different compounds.

It may be too useful for automatic control, weather prediction, medical diagnosis, expert-systems a.s.o.

These where hopes 30 years ago.

But meanwhile my optimism concerning practical application of the learning matrix has been reduced.

Nevertheless, I estimate that the learning matrix has some exciting possibilities: It permits the design of information processing networks
+ which must not be programmed - and
+ which may perhaps surpass the limitations, which Goedel has stated for "normal" computers.

I am grateful, that a hungarian physiologist (J. Szentagothai) remarked, that he observed in the brain structures similar to the learning matrix.

References:

Steinbuch, K.	"Die Lernmatrix" Kybernetik 1 (1961) H. 1, S 36-45
Hönerloh, H.J. Kraft, H.	"Technische Verwirklichung der Lernmatrix" In Billing, H. (Ed.) "Lernende Automaten" R. Oldenbourg, München 1961
Görke, W. Kazmierczak, H. Wagner, S.W.	"Anwendungen der Lernmatrix" in Billing, H. (Ed.) "Lernende Automaten" R. Oldenbourg, München 1961
Steinbuch, K. Frank, H.	"Nichtdigitale Lernmatrizen als Perzeptoren" Kybernetik 1 (1961) S. 117-124
Chow, C.L.	"An Optimum Character Recognition System Using Decision Function" Trans. IRE EC - 6 H. 4

Section 2
Biological Sensory and Motor Systems

Advanced Neural Computers / R. Eckmiller (Editor)

MODEL OF VISUO-MOTOR TRANSFORMATIONS PERFORMED BY THE CEREBRAL CORTEX TO COMMAND ARM MOVEMENTS AT VISUAL TARGETS IN THE 3-D SPACE

Y.Burnod[1], R.Caminiti[2], P.Johnson[2], Ph.Granguillaume[1], I.Otto[1]
[1] Institut des Neurosciences, Univ. Paris VI
[2] Istituto di Fisiologia, Univ. La Sapienza.

We propose a biologically realistic neural network to perform arm reaching movements in the 3-D space, and which is consistent with anatomical and physiological data on the cortical areas involved in the command of these movements. Studies of the neuronal activities in the motor and premotor cortices of behaving monkeys have shown that individual neurons, related to motor synergies, are broadly tuned to preferred directions in the 3-D space [1]. Recent data demonstrate that these cell preferred directions rotate with the initial position of the arm [2]. Furthermore, the rotation of the arm in space predicts the rotation of the whole population of preferred directions. These results support the hypothesis that cortical neural circuits compute the appropriate motor command by projecting visual information on a reference frame rotating with the arm.
This computation can be performed by two processing layers made of units which model the properties of the cortical column, as the basic neuronal circuits common to all cortical areas. During spontaneous movements of the arm, the learning rules can memorize a relation, between somatic and visual information, which can be approximated by a bilinear form. Such bilinear combination explains the projection of visual information on a coordinate system rotating with the arm, and the invariant properties of cellular activities in the motor area. Neural circuits converging toward a single neuron in the motor cortex can easily learn and generalize such invariant properties in a 2-D subspace, but not in the whole 3-D space. However, the uniform distribution of cell preferred directions can explain the computation of the correct solution by a population of motor cortical neurons. These two predictions of the model are consistent with the experimental results.

I. BIOLOGICAL CONSTRAINTS

In order to propose a biologically realistic neural network that can learn visually guided movements of the arm in the 3-D space, it is necessary to meet at least three essential requirements, at three levels of the biological organization :

1. The global processing of the whole population of units performs a continuous transformation from visual into motor coordinates and results in a reaching movement. Parallel processing by all these units produce the correct command which orients the movement toward the target whatever the initial position of the hand as given in retinal and body coordinates. Several models have been proposed for the learning of arm kinematics and dynamics (review in [3]), and for the computation of invariant properties of sensorimotor transformations [4].

2. In the cortical areas involved in visuomotor tasks (parietal, motor, premotor), the activities of neurons recorded during a 3-D reaching movement should be explained by the model. These activities can be interpreted in relation with sensory inputs, motor outputs and learning conditions [5].

3. At the local level, the processing units should model the operations and learning properties of the cortical column which is the basic neuronal circuit of the cerebral cortex [6]. The operations performed by this unit have been modelled in relation with the behavioral adaptations performed by different cortical areas [7].

II. INVARIANT PROPERTIES OF MOTOR CORTICAL NEURONS.

Experiments are designed in order to quantify the cortical processes which result in the appropriate command of a 3-D arm reaching movement. Neuronal activity is recorded in the shoulder zone of the motor cortex of monkeys performing a 3-D movement of the hand between two points determined at each trial by a conditioning program. These trajectories follow eight possible directions which can be performed in three different parts of the work space, due to three initial positions of the arm.

1. Directional properties of neuronal activities.

Within each part of the workspace, it has been shown in previous studies that there is a particular movement direction for which the cell discharge frequency is maximal [1]. For a constant initial position of the arm, it is thus possible to define, for each recorded neuron, a preferential direction.

2. Population code.

Although single cells were broadly tuned to a particular direction in the 3-D space, the direction of the effective movement of the arm can be predicted with a population of cortical neurons by summing their preferred direction vectors weighted by their activities [1]. The set of preferred directions of the recorded cells covers the entire 3D-continuum, and their distribution is uniform in all the 3 parts of the work space.

3. Shift of preferred directions with the initial position of the arm

When the initial position is changed, the orientation of the preferred direction for each cell rotates in space [2]. In order to quantify the rotation of the whole set of preferred direction in the shoulder zone of the motor cortex, a spherical regression analysis has been performed between the different initial conditions. This statistical analysis shows that the rotation of the whole set of preferred directions exactly follows the rotation of the shoulder joint between the different initial positions of the arm.

All the results obtained in recording cells of the motor cortex are consistent with the following assessments : (1) the motor cortical cells command muscle synergies, which can be represented by a vector corresponding to the sum of the individual muscles actions ; (2) the orientation of such a synergy vector does not remain constant with respect to an extrapersonal coordinate system, but rotates with the position of the arm in space and has invariant property in an arm centered reference system ; (3) for both shoulder and elbow joints, a cortical command sent to the muscles will change the arm position in a constant way within this intrinsic coordinate system (Ref in [2]).

In the task which is experimentally analyzed, information about the desired trajectory of the hand (visual, oculomotor and proprioceptive) is projected on a body coordinate system, since the body does not move, and the eyes fixate the target before the movement. Consequently, the cortical neural network has to compute the projection of this information in a reference system rotating with the arm in order to produce the appropriate motor command.

The shift of cells preferred directions was evident even in the early phase of the reaction time, suggesting that the computation is performed before the initiation of the movement, and then without the sensory feedback loop due to the movement.

III. SENSORIMOTOR COMBINATIONS IN CORTICAL AREAS.

The shift of cell preferred directions with the initial position of the arm reflects the computation of the appropriate motor output by the combination between two different sources of inputs : (1) an information about the position of the arm with respect to the body (for example angles of the shoulder and elbow joints) ; (2) an information about the trajectory to be performed as defined by the visual system (image of the hand when the target is centered on the fovea), and the oculomotor system (angle of gaze).

Computations from experimental data give a vectorial interpretation to cell properties (cell preferred directions), and allow to delimit the "combinatory domain" of cortical circuits converging on a cell , with at least two parameters :

- The dimension (Dc) of the combinatory domain: vectorial inputs from the two sensory sources may be matched in the whole space (3D), or within a plane (2D) or in only one specific direction.
- The combinatory order (Oc): only pairs of vectors leading to a common output are matched (Oc=1), or all the possible combinations are effected (Oc=2).

The cell's preferred direction does not rotate if Dc=1, and rotates in a plane if Dc=2. The rotation of the cell's preferred direction can follow the rotation of the arm if Oc=1. Experimental results are consistent with a computation of the motor command by two processing layers, as shown in Figure 1 :

- a **matching layer** models bimodal associative cortical maps (somatic+visual) in the parietal lobe (Dc=1 and Oc=1).
- an **output layer** model motor and premotor cortex which receives information from parietal neurons; it combines them in a subspace (Dc=2) and in an ordered way (Oc=1)

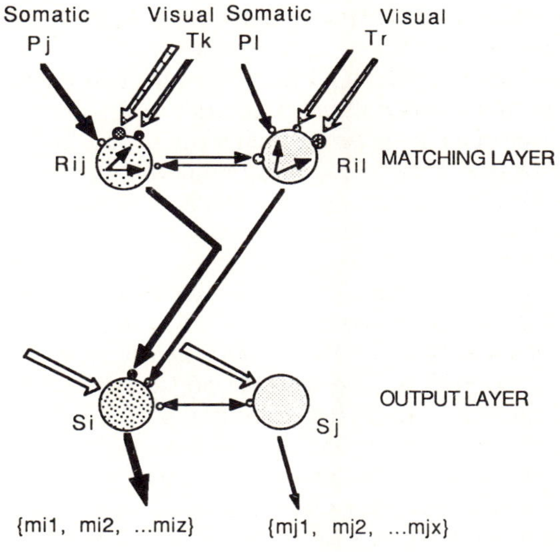

figure 1 :

Furthermore, it is important to take into account the direct internal relation from the output layer to the matching layer ("efferent copy" of the motor command) This architecture is consistent with anatomical data on the relations between premotor and parietal regions.

The properties of the cortical combinations are due both to anatomical connections, and reinforcement of specific pathways by learning.

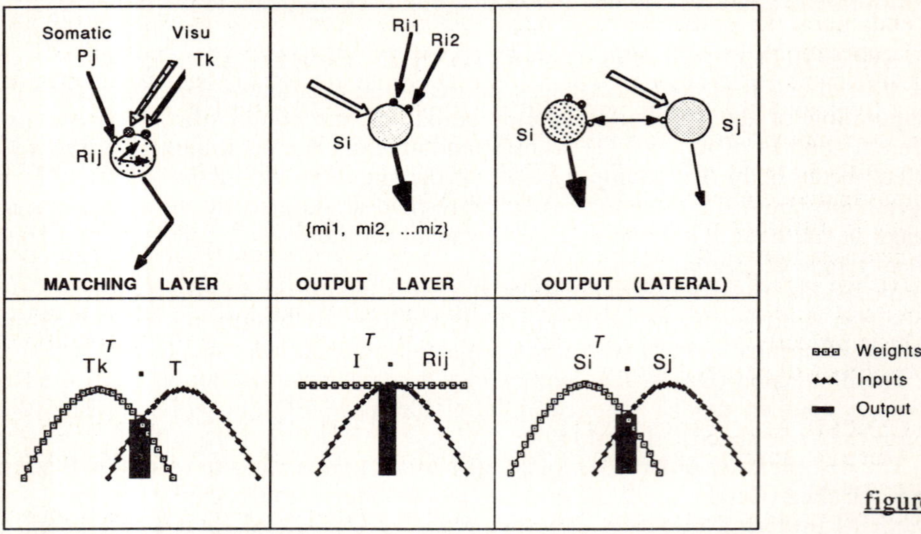

figure 2

In the model, three types of relations between units are learned (in Figure 2) A representation of the 3-D external space is learned by the adjustment of lateral connections between output units (right column). A global transformation of visual inputs by somatic signals is learned in two steps (left and middle columns), thanks to the visual feedback signals produced by spontaneous movements of the arm.

IV. PROCESSING UNITS: MODEL OF THE CORTICAL COLUMN.

Activation and learning properties of the processing units in these two layers should not be chosen arbitrary, but should be designed as close as possible to the main known features of the real intracortical network [7]. Such units do not correspond to single neurons but to cortical columns, which are repetitive multicellular neuronal circuits, with common properties whatever the adaptation they produce within each specific cortical region.

Two properties of cortical columns are important for the command of visually-guided hand movements :

1. **Activation rules** : the coactivation of two inputs from independent sources (for example proprioceptive and visual) can generate a strong non-linear increase of activity (gating and amplification). An increasing activity can result first in an activation, and after in an inhibition of related units with lower activities (conditional inhibition).

2. **Learning rules** correspond to operant conditioning. If a column, strongly active, participates to an action outside the cortex, and if this action results in a reactivation of a cortical input of the column, this input will gain by learning a new influence : after learning, columns selectively activate other columns whose actions were previously efficient to result in their reactivation. These rules allow to build multilayered networks with feedback, feedforward, and local connections, which

are efficient not only to learn movements, but also pattern recognition with a very fast learning process.

After learning, the operation which is performed by columns on their inputs depends upon the probabilities of coactivation between strong inputs and outputs. Such operations can be approximated either as logical operators AND/OR on activity levels, or more continuously by sums or products, considering that the firing frequency signals the probability that the preferred feature is present :

a) If two inputs come from independent sources, and each one alone has a low probability to be related to the appropriate output, the input-output operation can be approximated either by an AND gate or a product.

b) But if different inputs lead to the same output and each one is sufficient to produce this output, the operation can be approximated either by an OR gate, or a sum (if the inputs are mutually exclusive).

Subsets of columns can thus function as SigmaPi units, but this operation is not an intrinsic property of the column, but a learned operation adjusted to the conditional probabilities of external events.

V. CORTICAL REPRESENTATIONS OF MUSCLES AND 3-D SPACE.

1. Output interactions of motor cortical neurons represent muscle synergies.

A cortical column "i" in the motor area, with an activity si(t) commands a muscle synergy represented as a family of vectors (motor units Mi1,...,Miz) with orientations corresponding to muscle axes relative to the joint and magnitudes (mi1,..., miz) proportional to the number of similar units activable by this column. Consequently, the maximal activity of a cell "i" represents a "synergy vector" S_i due to the effects of target motor units $(m_{i1}.M_{i1},...,m_{iz}.M_{iz})$.

The activity si(t) at any time represents the component of the movement direction on the synergy vector Si. The projections of a synergy vector Si on an arm-centered coordinate system are fixed, given that the relation between Si and muscle contractions only depends on skeletal geometry and muscle dynamics. Each synergy vector Si is thus linked to a coordinate system rotating with the shoulder joint, and for each arm position P, corresponds to a vector Si(P) in the 3D external space.

An optimal ballistic command si(t) for moving the arm in a given direction T(t) can be computed from the inputs by :

$$s_i(t) = \lambda S_i^T(P).T(t) \text{ depends on } P_j \text{ and then } T(t) = 1/n \sum_{i=1}^{N} s_i(t).S_i$$

The contribution si(t) of a cell to the required arm movement will be highest, when the orientation of its synergy vector Si(P) is parallel to the desired direction T(t).

2.Lateral interactions in the motor cortex represents the 3-D external space.

Experimental results show that both in motor and premotor areas, the distribution of synergy vectors Si is **uniform** in the 3D space, for any initial position of the arm. Thanks to this property, internal cortical and external 3-D representations are equivalent :

- The whole set of synergy vectors (Si, i=1,N) can be generated by a set of rotations Qr of a 3-D orthonormal basis (C_1, C_2, C_3) :

$$S_{ri} = \mathbf{Q_r}\, C_i \qquad \text{with } r=1,n \text{ and } i=1,3$$

- Any vector T with coordinates C(T,0) in the 3-D external cartesian space, is redundantly described within the cortex by its coordinates C(T,r) on a set of 3-D orthonormal bases (S_{r1},S_{r2},S_{r3}) :

$$C(T,r)= \mathbf{Q}.C(T,0)$$

$$T = \sum_{i=1}^{3} [S_{ri}^{T}(P).T(t)]S_{ri} \quad \text{in each base "r"}$$

$$T = 1/n \sum_{i=1}^{n} [S_{i}^{T}(P).T(t)]S_{i} \quad \text{in the whole population } i = 1, N$$

The population vector which sums all the representations (right part of equation), is equivalent to the vector in the 3-D space (left part). The variability within each basis can be high, since the variability of the population vector decreases with the number of parallel representations.

The important point is the global coherence of the internal cellular representation of the 3-D external space. Any transformation (for example a rotation) in the outside world can be represented by an equivalent transformation within each cortical basis of 3 orthogonal vectors, and thus within the whole set of neurons. A motor operation which is learned in a few directions can be generalized to the other directions.

Learning-dependent changes of lateral interactions I(Si,Sj) between any pairs of columns with synergy vectors Si and Sj stabilize this cortical representation of the the 3-D external space. After learning (Figure 2, right column) :

$$I(S_i,S_j) = \mathrm{Prob}(S_i / S_j) \qquad \text{learning rule of the model}$$

$$= S_i^{T}.S_j \qquad \text{property of the 3-D external space}$$

Consequently, lateral interactions between two sets of units forming two different basis (Sri), (Spi) will converge towards the rotation matrix which relates them :

$$(S_{ri}^{T}.S_{pi}) = \mathbf{Q_{p-r}}$$

and the influence I[C(T,p), (Sr)] on columns "r" due to the representation of vector T in the basis "p" will be :

$$I[C(T,p),(S_r)] = k\, \mathbf{Q_{p-r}}.C(T,p) \qquad \text{after learning}$$

$$= k.C(T,r) \qquad \text{(coordinate transformation)}$$

$$\sum_{p=1}^{n-1} I[C(T,p),(S_r)] = K.C(T,r) \qquad \text{total lateral influence}$$

The result of all lateral interactions due to the redundant representation of the same vector T produces an effect which is proportional to the direct representation, and thus stabilizes it.

VI. MOVEMENT DEPENDENT MATCHING OF SENSORY INPUTS.

In this model, learning in the matching layer occurs with the sensory feedbacks produced by spontaneous movements of the hand.

In this layer, before learning, units Rij are biased both for specific arm positions (Pj) and efferent copies of motor synergies (Si). They receive through adjustable weights a subset of inputs (T1,.. Tn) which signal for the target position This target information can come either from visual fixation units tuned with the position of the eye in a body coordinate system, or from units which signal the displacement of the hand in retinal coordinates.

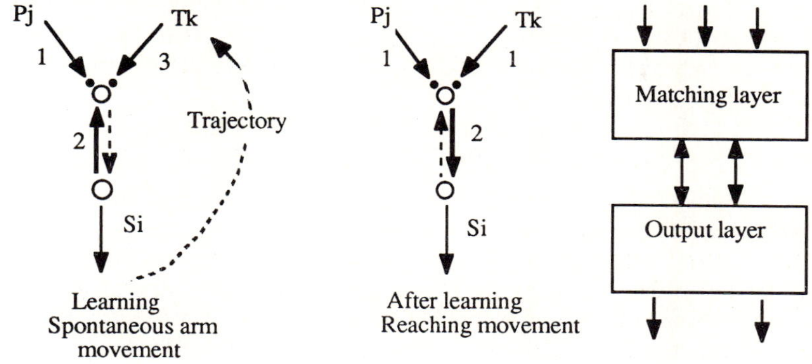

Figure 3

As shown in Figure 3 (left part), spontaneous movements produce a strong output and an efferent copy Si (2), which activates the unit Rij gated by the arm-positional signal Pj (1). Unit Rij is then reactivated by visual (or eye-position) inputs Tk (3) which are directly related to the trajectory of the hand in the visual field (or its final position). The influence of the input Tk on unit Rij will be :

$$I(T_k,R_{ij}) = Prob(T_k / R_{ij}) \quad k = 1,n \qquad \text{learning rule}$$
$$= Prob(T_k / (S_i,P_j)) \qquad \text{connectivity}$$

If the optimal visual input is Tk, the influence, after learning, of any vector T(t) on the matching unit Rij can be approximated by :

$$I(T(t),R_{ij}) = T_k^T.T(t)$$

When the eyes fixate a target, the information about the desired trajectory (or target position) will optimally activate certain matching units Rij which are gated by the arm position Pj, and then motor units Si (for initial position Pj) producing a movement in the direction of the target.

Several matching units Rij converge to the same command output Si. Learning establishes a one to one relation Mi, from a finite dimensional vector space E (generated by the 2n basic directions Pj,Tk) onto itself, such as

$$T_k = M_i(P_j) \quad \text{if for } (T_k,P_j)\ ,\ s_i(t) \text{ is maximal.}$$

In a general way, for a given muscular command Si, and an initial position Pj, the arm moves within a plane. The angle between the trajectory Tk, and the initial position of the arm Pj remains constant. Consequently, the restriction of the application Mi on this plane is a rotation.

VII. GENERALIZATION OF LEARNING.

After learning, the ballistic motor command si(t) (i=1,N) is computed in two processing steps (f1 by the matching layer, and f2 by the output layer), which combine two sources of information, P (initial arm position) and T (target position or desired trajectory) : $si(t) = f2.f1(P,T)$

The global operation f1.f2 can be approximated by a bilinear form :

1. In the matching layer (left column of Fig.2), the two inputs come from independent sources, and each one alone has a low probability to be related to the appropriate motor command. Consequently, after learning, the operation performed by the unit can be approximated by an AND gate or more continuously by a product (see section IV) :

Output activity $r_{ij}(t)$ is maximal if ($P=P_j$ AND $T=T_k$)

$r_{ij}(t) = prob(P=P_j \text{ AND } T=T_k) = prob(P=P_j).prob(T=T_k) = p_j.t_k$

Such combination has been described in the posterior parietal cortex between retinal inputs and eye position [5].

2. In the output layer (middle column of Fig.2), different combinations of inputs (Ri1, Ri2) lead to the same output Si and are mutually exclusive (different positions Pj); after learning, the input output operation (on vector R= rij(t) j=1,n) can be approximated by an OR gate or more continuously by a sum :

Output activity $s_i(t)$ is maximal if ($R=R_{i1}$ max OR R_{i2} max)

$s_i(t)= prob(R=R_{i1} \text{ OR } R=R_{i2}) = r_{i1}(t) + r_{i2}(t)$

Consequently, after learning, the operation f1.f2 performed by the two layers of the network can be approximated by a bilinear form :

$s_i(t) = f2.f1[P(t),T(t)]$

$s_i(t)$ is maximal IF ($P=P_j$ AND $T=T_k$) OR ($P=P_l$ AND $T=T_r$)

$$s_i(t) = P^T(t).\mathbf{M}_i.T(t)$$

where Mi is the matrix which is learned with the spontaneous movements, and whose lines are formed by the subsets of synaptic weights (due to Tki) on Rij.

The bilinear form shows how the correspondence learned on a small number of directions (Pj,Tk) can be generalized to any type of combinations (P(t),T(t)).

VIII. PREDICTIONS OF THE MODEL : INVARIANT PROPERTIES.

Furthermore, the bilinear combination predicts the main experimental results on cell activities recorded in the motor area in relation with visually guided 3D arm movements :

1. Cell preferred directions for a given initial position.

For a constant initial position, the form is linear and the command can be represented by its effect on the trajectory in the 3-D space, in agreement with the experimental results. The cells are broadly tuned for a preferred direction Ti which corresponds to : $T_i(t) = S_i[P(t)] = \mathbf{M}_i^T.P(t)$

and the activity in the motor cortex can then be described, for a trajectory T, by :

$$s_i(t) = T_i^T.T(t) = S_i[P]^T.T(t)$$

2. Invariant properties of cell activities in the motor cortex.

When the arm rotates (rotation Hr) from P0 to Pr, the cell preferred direction T0, for P0, will change to Tr :

$$P_r = \mathbf{H_r}.P_0 \qquad \text{and} \qquad T_r = \mathbf{M_i^T}.\mathbf{H_r}.\mathbf{M_i}.T_0$$

Consequently, the preferred direction of each cell changes in an ordered way with the initial position of the arm, but this individual change does not necessarily match the arm rotation in the 3-D space.

But Mi for a given muscular command Si stands for a rotation within a subspace which represents a plane in the 3-D external space. The applications Mi and Hr restricted to the 2-D subspace generated by (P0,T0) are rotations and are commutative. Consequently, the cell preferred direction rotates exactly as the arm :

$$T_r = \mathbf{H_r}.T_0 \quad \text{and} \quad s_i(t) = P^T.\mathbf{M_i}.T = (\mathbf{H}.P)^T.\mathbf{M_i}.(\mathbf{H}.T)$$

when the initial position of the arm and the trajectory are rotating in the same way, the command is unchanged.

The model predicts that the preferred direction of a single neuron in the motor cortex will rotate like the arm within a specific subspace but not in the whole 3D space.

3. Population code for computation in the 3D space.

When the arm rotates between two position in a plane, it is possible to divide the whole 3D space by this plane (P0Pr). Since the distribution of preferred direction is uniform, each vector Ti in one hemisphere has a correspondent Ti' which is symmetrical with respect to the plane (P0Pr). The vectorial sum Ti+Ti' belongs to the plane of rotation of the arm and rotates like the arm. The whole population can thus be divided in N doublets (Ti,Ti') and the whole set of vectors will rotate in the same way as the arm in the 3-D space.

These theoretical results predict the results of the spherical regression analysis on the experimental data [2].

[1] Georgopoulos, A.P., Schwartz, A.B., Kettner, R.E. 1986. Neuronal Population Coding of a movement Direction. Science 233: 1416-19.

[2] Caminiti, R., Johnson ,P.B., Urbano, A. 1990. Making arm movements within different parts of space, dynamic aspects in the primate motor cortex. Journal of Neuroscience, in Press.

[3] Atkeson, C.G. 1989. Learning arm kinematics and dynamics. Ann. Rev. Neurosci. 12: 157-83

[4] Kuperstein, M. 1988 . An Adaptative Neural Model for Mapping Invariant Target Position Behav. Neurosci. 102.1: 148-162

[5] Zipser, D. , Andersen, R.A., 1988. A back propagation programmed network that simulates response properties of a subset of posterior parietal neurons. Nature, 331. 6158: 679-684

[6] Mountcasle, V.B. 1978. An organizing principle for cerebral function : the unit module and the distributed system. In The mindful brain, F.O. Schmitt ed., MIT Press, Cambridge Mass. pp. 7-50

[7] Burnod, Y. 1988. An adaptative neural network : The cerebral cortex. Masson, Paris.

This research is supported by the program BRAIN of the EEC.
We thank Emmanuel Guigon and Bernadette Dorizzi for helpful comments.

Advanced Neural Computers / R. Eckmiller (Editor)

NEURAL NETWORK MODELS OF THE PRIMATE MOTOR SYSTEM

Eberhard E. FETZ and Larry E. SHUPE

Department of Physiology & Biophysics and
Regional Primate Research Center
University of Washington
Seattle, WA 98195

Dynamic neural network models that incorporate time-varying activity and allow unrestricted connectivity were trained by back-propagation to generate discharge patterns of cells previously observed in behaving monkeys. Neuronal recordings in monkeys performing a simple alternating step-tracking task have shown that forearm motor units and connected premotoneuronal cells fire with characteristic patterns: phasic-tonic, tonic, decrementing, etc.. To investigate the properties of networks that could transform a step input of target position to the four observed discharge patterns of flexor and extensor motor units we trained dynamic network models to generate these firing patterns as outputs. These networks have hidden units with either excitatory or inhibitory connections to each other and to the output "motor units". Network solutions have been found for a variety of connection matrices corresponding to different network topologies. The activity of many hidden units resembles the discharge patterns that have been observed in physiological recordings of neurons in motor cortex and red nucleus. In networks receiving both sustained (step) input and transient input signals, preferential connections can develop within subsets of phasic and tonic units.

The function of specific hidden units in the network can be tested by making selective lesions of particular units and determining the behavior of the remaining network. When relatively few hidden units with similar activations are strongly interconnected, removing a particular unit can have appreciable consequences in eliminating corresponding components of activity in other units. The output effects of a given unit can also be tested by delivering a simulated stimulus and analyzing the propagated network response. Delivering the stimulus pulse during various phases of the ongoing task shows how the impulse response is modulated by the changing activation patterns.

1. INTRODUCTION: PHYSIOLOGICAL NETWORKS

The neural circuitry controlling forelimb muscles of the primate has been elucidated by experiments on the anatomical connections and physiological discharge patterns of the neurons during movements. Particularly revealing are experiments in which both the activity and output connections of the same cells can be determined. The premotoneuronal cells which affect muscle activity can be identified in behaving monkeys by spike-triggered averaging of EMG recordings, which can reveal post-spike facilitation or suppression of target muscles [2,3]. The response patterns of corticomotoneuronal (CM) cells and rubromotoneuronal (RM) cells have been documented during simple alternating flexion/extension task designed to relate activity to changes in force and to sustained static force [1,2]. The types of discharge patterns observed in CM and RM cells, as well as in single motor units (MU) of agonist muscles, fall into specific classes [1-3,5]. During a ramp-and-hold movement, all three groups include cells that show phasic-tonic discharge. The phasic component is related to the changing force and the tonic component is proportional to the amount of static force exerted. All groups also include tonic cells which show steady discharge throughout the hold period in proportion to the active force. Each region also has cells with unique firing properties. A large proportion of motor units show decrementing discharge, which decreases gradually through the hold period. The RM population is unique in having cells that fire during both flexion and extension. In particular, an unmodulated group of RM cells shows steady discharge during active movement that is unmodulated with the task [2]. Other response patterns have been observed in additional cells that do not facilitate motoneurons. In cerebral cortex many non-CM cells fire phasically at onset of movement and many of these fire bidirectionally with flexion and extension.

2. DYNAMIC NETWORK MODELS

To investigate the possible functional role of these cells and to determine whether other types of discharge patterns might be required to transform a step signal to the observed output of motoneurons, we developed a model that can incorporate these firing patterns. The network utilizes the back-propagation algorithm of the temporal flow model developed by Watrous [7], and is similar to the dynamic network algorithms recently described by Williams and Zipser [8]. These networks allow arbitrary interconnections between all elements; thus, in addition to feed-forward connections, they also permit cross-connections within layers as well as feedback connections. Secondly, the networks incorporate dynamic time-varying activity of units, representing the firing rates of neurons. In our simulations we have used as outputs the averaged firing rates of motor units recorded in monkeys performing a step-tracking task [5].

The input-output function of each unit is the standard sigmoidal function, with an offset to assure that units generate negligible output in the absence of input to the unit. The input consists of the summed activation of all other cells connected to the unit times their synaptic weight; a source of steady input may also be derived from a bias element. The synaptic weights are initially assigned randomly, and then modified by the back-propagation algorithm to reduce the error for the specified target output activations.

Figure 1 shows a neural network which simulates the input-output transformation performed by a monkey during the step-tracking task. The monkey sees a step change in target position, alternating between flexion and extension target zones. This is represented by sustained step input to the network for both flexion (fs) and extension (es). Since many visual cells discharge transiently, we also provided brief transient input at the onset of each target change (fb & eb). The network transforms these input signals to the observed response patterns of motor units at the output. The four types of motor unit patterns observed experimentally -- tonic, phasic-tonic, decrementing and phasic -- are generated for both flexor and extensor movements (ft to ep). The intervening hidden units consist of twelve excitatory and twelve inhibitory neurons (a and b units, respectively). The squares in the matrix symbolize the strength of the

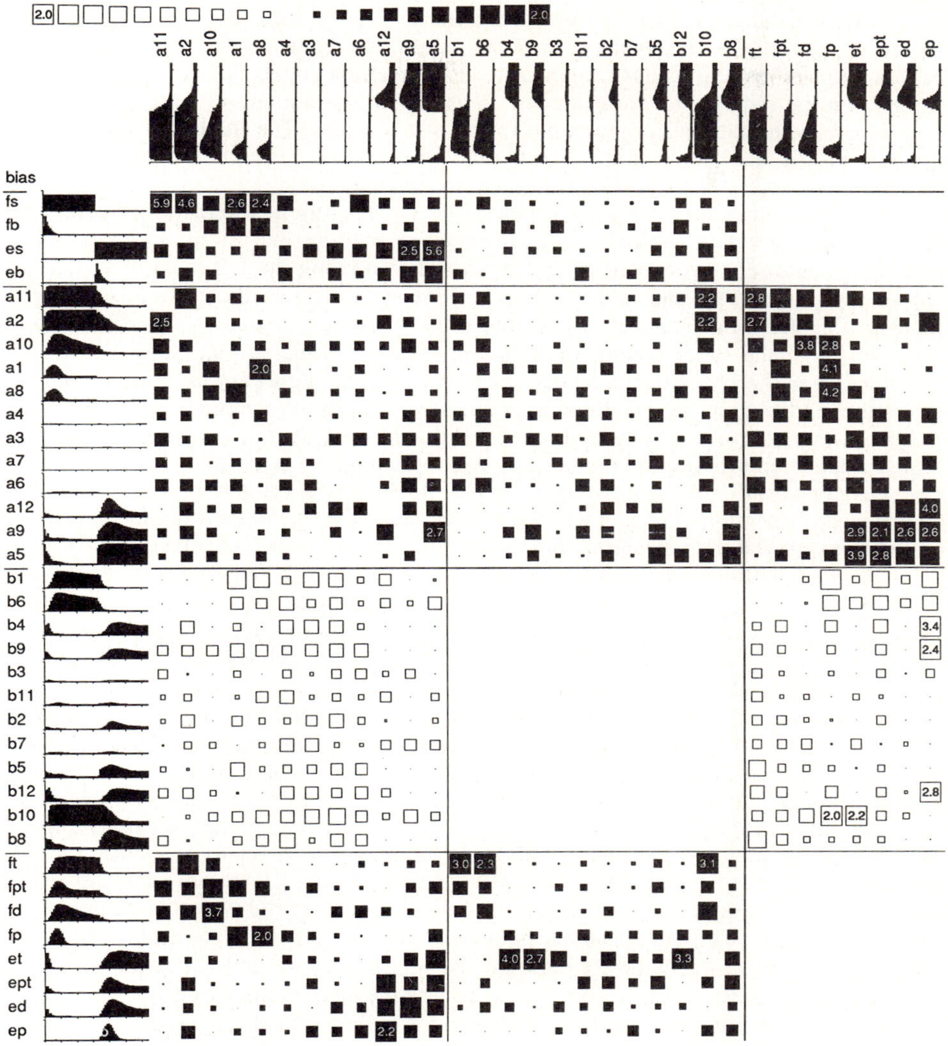

Fig. 1. Network transforming step and transient inputs to firing patterns of motor units at output. Unit activations during a flexion-extension cycle are shown at left and along the top. The weight matrix gives the strength of connections from the row to column units (scale at top). The rows represent, from top to bottom, the bias (which was eliminated for this simulation), the inputs (fs to eb), the excitatory hidden units (a's), inhibitory hidden units (b's) and the output flexor and extensor motor units (ft to ep). The target output patterns are tonic (ft & et), phasic-tonic (fpt & ept), decrementing (fd & ed) and phasic (fp & ep).

synaptic connection from the row unit to the column unit. Black squares designate excitatory weights and open squares represent inhibitory weights. The size of each square is proportional to the strength of the connection, except those which exceed the calibrated scale are designated numerically. Self-recurrent connections (corresponding to weights on the diagonal) were excluded. The excitatory hidden units are connected to each other, to the inhibitory group and to the output cells. The inhibitory hidden units connect to the excitatory units and to the output cells. There are also feedback connections from the output units back to the hidden units.

Figure 1 illustrates the weight matrix and the activation patterns of all units after 2000 training iterations, which was sufficient to produce the eight different output patterns. The discharge pattern of each unit is shown along the left, next to the row of output weights of that unit, and is shown again at the top of the column of weights representing the input connections to that unit. To better visualize the relationships between units, the hidden units were further sorted in order of the strength of their contribution to the phasic-tonic output units. The sorting algorithm used the product of activation and weight to the flexion phasic-tonic motor unit minus activation times weight to the extension phasic-tonic unit. Thus, the first hidden unit (a11) makes the largest relative contribution to the flexion phasic-tonic output unit (fpt). This hidden unit also developed the strongest weights to the flexion tonic output unit (ft), and also contributed connections to the other flexor units. Such divergent connections to different motor units, as well as to synergist muscles are representative of CM cells [1].

The activation patterns of the hidden units show several interesting features. The discharge patterns in the hidden units involve some recognizable variants of the output patterns, i.e., tonic, phasic, phasic-tonic, and decrementing patterns. Secondly, although the activation profiles of the target motor units are identical for the flexion and the extension groups, the network solution involves a different assignment of hidden units devoted to each. There are more excitatory and fewer inhibitory hidden unit activations related to flexion than to extension, yet they produce essentially identical output effects. Physiological experiments have revealed similar asymmetries between flexor and extensor related premotoneuronal cells [2].

Another striking feature of the connections are the preferentially strong connections within the sets of units with sustained and transient activity. Thus, the first two flexor hidden units exhibiting tonic activity (a11 & a2) are strongly interconnected with each other and receive potent input from the flexion step and connect strongly to the tonic output unit. Similarly, the transient input (fb) is most strongly connected to the phasic hidden units (a1 & a8), which are strongly interconnected with each other and which also have strong reciprocal connections with the phasic output unit (fp).

Despite this tendency for sustained and transient signals to propagate through segregated pathways, most cells receive a mixture of phasic and tonic input signals. For example, the phasic flexor motor unit (fp) receives input not only from the phasic hidden units (a1 & a8), but also from cells with sustained activity (a11 & a10); indeed, some of its phasic activity is derived from the difference between excitatory and inhibitory tonic cells with different onset times (e.g., a11 and b1). Such a subtraction of a delayed tonic pattern is used to produce phasic output in network simulations which receive only step inputs [4].

We expected the network to develop reciprocal inhibition between the flexion and extension groups. Although a few inhibitory units activated during one phase of movement (e.g. extension) do affect primarily reciprocally activated motor units (e.g., b8 & b5), just as many inhibit coactivated motor units (e.g., b12). Interestingly, the major drive on the tonic inhibitory units with connections on synergistic motor units is derived from recurrent feedback from the motor units (e.g., et to b4 & b9, which in turn inhibit ep). This recurrent feedback makes these inhibitory hidden units more analogous to the Renshaw cells of the spinal cord than to the Ia inhibitory neurons. Another group of inhibitory hidden units develop connections to both flexor and extensor motor units (b1 & b10), a patterns that has no known correlate in physiological studies.

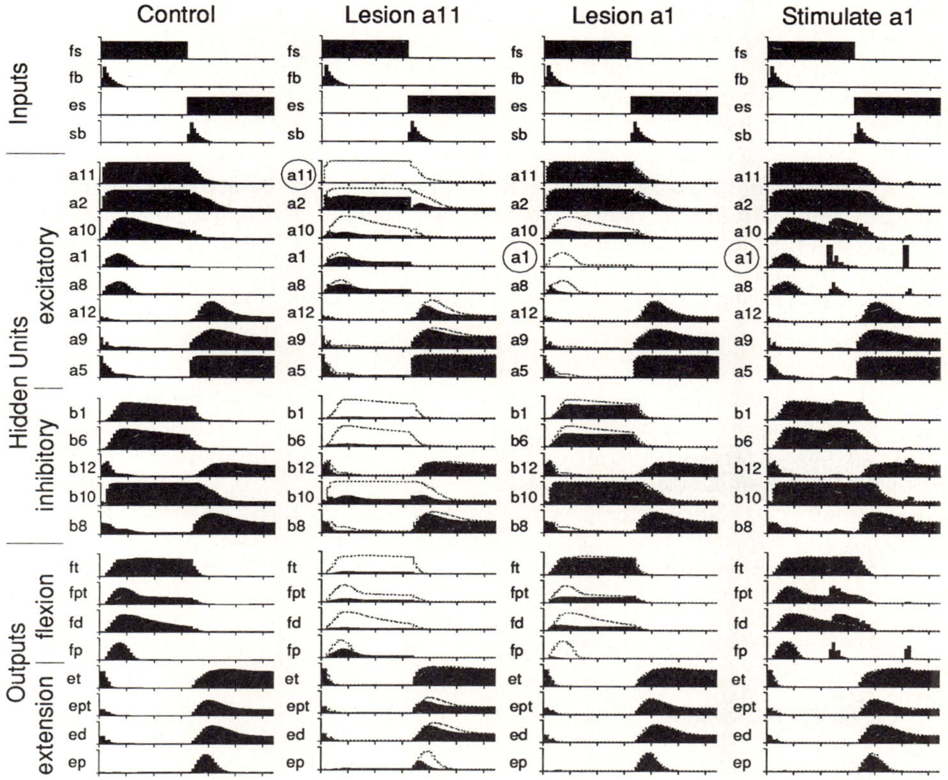

Fig. 2. Effect of lesioning and stimulating specific hidden units in the network in Fig. 1. The activations of representative units are shown for the unmanipulated, intact network (control, first column); after lesioning the tonic excitatory hidden unit a11 (second column); after lesioning the phasic excitatory hidden unit a1 (third column); and after stimulating the phasic excitatory hidden unit a1 (fourth column). The modified activations are shown superimposed on a stippled profile of the control activations.

3. MANIPULATION OF HIDDEN UNITS

3.1 LESIONS

The function of hidden units in the network can be tested by making selective lesions -- i.e., by eliminating the activation of particular units and analyzing the behavior of the remaining network. Fig 2 illustrates the effects of removing one of the tonic hidden units (a11) and one of the phasic hidden units (a1). The control activations of the units in the intact network are shown in the first column. A lesion of the tonic hidden unit a11 (second column) eliminates much of the tonic activity of the output and of the other hidden units. In contrast, lesioning the phasic unit (third column) eliminates the phasic activity of the output flexor units (fpt, fd and fp), as well as eliminating activity of the other phasic hidden unit (e8). The effects of these lesions are quite substantial because the network has relatively few units carrying a particular pattern, and these are strongly interconnected.

3.2 STIMULATION

The output effects of a given unit can also be tested by delivering a simulated stimulus and analyzing the propagated network response. The fourth column in Fig. 2 shows the effect of brief activation pulses delivered to a1 during the flexion and extension phase of the activity. The second pulse, during extension, evokes a response in the phasic output unit as well as in some of the active inhibitory hidden units.

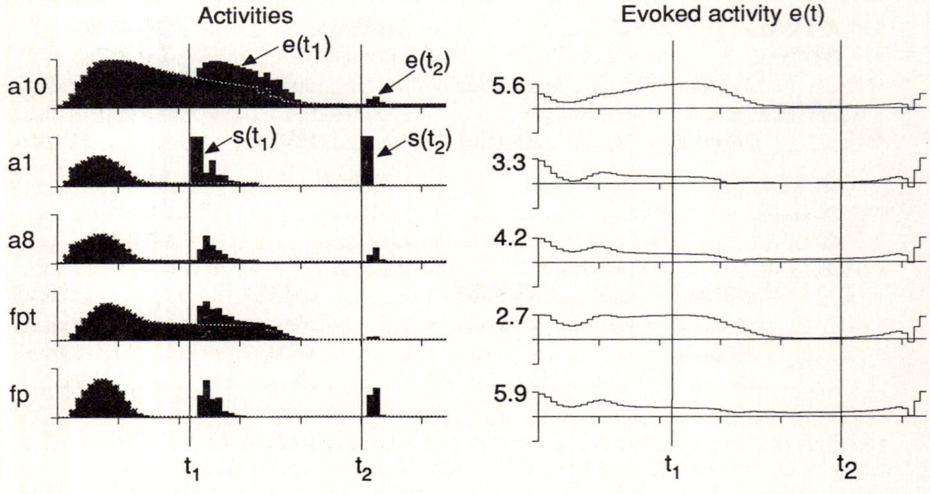

Fig. 3 Modulation of stimulus-evoked activity during the movement cycle. Left: unit a1 stimulated with a pulse during flexion (at time t_1) and extension (t_2). Response in three representative hidden units (a10, a1 & a8) and two flexion motor units (fpt & fp). The evoked response e(t) was calculated as the difference between stimulated and control activation. Right: Magnitude of evoked response plotted as a function of stimulus delay in the cycle.

In contrast, the first pulse, delivered during the flexion phase, evokes a stronger response in the phasic output unit, as well as more prolonged responses in the phasic-tonic and decrementing units; it also evokes activity in some of the excitatory hidden units.

The appearance of larger evoked responses in certain phases of the movement than in others is clearly related to the gating function of the activation of the intervening units. Such modulation of evoked responses is well-known in motor systems physiology [6]. To investigate this phenomenon more systematically, we delivered stimulus pulses at successive times during the movement cycle and measured the evoked response, defined as the difference between the stimulated and control activation (Fig. 3). Plotting the evoked response as a function of time in the flexion-extension cycle revealed modulations that were not simply proportional to the activation of the stimulated or target cell, but were more complex functions of the activations of the intervening units. The units with sustained activation patterns, such as a10, tended to exhibit more prolonged responses to the pulse than units with transient activity. In all cases the magnitude of the response evoked from this flexion unit was enhanced during the flexion period.

4. CONCLUDING COMMENTS

These preliminary observations suggest that dynamic network models may provide a useful tool for simulating neural mechanisms that generate patterns of activity in motor systems. Although these networks are still quite artificial in their connectivity, they develop many of the properties of biological networks [4]. Among the less realistic features of the present simulation are the ubiquitous recurrent interconnections of the hidden units. Such connectivity can lead to solutions in which relatively few interconnected units carry representative signals. It should be noted that such units could be interpreted as representing a larger population of neurons, and their connection weights interpreted as being proportional to the size of the population. Although these networks are highly abstracted, by incorporating profiles of physiological activity and by observing more realistic anatomical connectivity, we believe these models can be constrained to produce plausible simulations of sensorimotor integration.

ACKNOWLEDGEMENTS

This work was supported by the Office of Naval Research (contract number N00018-89-J-1240), and NIH grants RR00166 and NS12542.

REFERENCES

[1] Cheney, P.D. and Fetz, E.E. Functional classes of primate corticomotoneuronal cells and their relation to active force. *Journal of Neurophysiology 44*: 773-791 (1980).

[2] Cheney, P.D., Mewes, K. and Fetz, E.E. Encoding of motor parameters by corticomotoneuronal (CM) and rubromotoneuronal (RM) cells identified by spike-triggered averaging in the awake monkey. *Behavioral Brain Research 28*:181-191 (1988).

[3] Fetz, E.E., Cheney, P.D., Mewes, K. and Palmer, S. Control of forelimb muscle activity by populations of corticomotoneuronal and rubromotoneuronal cells, in Peripheral Control of Posture and Locomotion, J.A.H. Allum and M. Hulliger, eds., *Progress in Brain Research 80*: 437 - 449 (1990).

[4] Fetz, E.E., Shupe, L.E. and Murthy, V.N. Neural networks controlling wrist movements, *Proceedings, IJCNN 90*, in press.
[5] Palmer, S.S. and Fetz, E.E. Discharge properties of primate forearm motor units during isometric muscle activity. *Journal of Neurophysiology 54*:1178-1193, (1985).
[6] Rossignol, S., Lund, J.P. and Drew, T. The role of sensory inputs in regulating patterns of rhythmical movements in higher vertebrates. In: Cohen, A., Rossignol, S. and Grillner, S. (eds), Neural Control of Rhythmic Movements in Vertebrates, (John Wiley & Sons, 1988) pp. 201 - 283.
[7] Watrous, R. L. and Shastri, L. Learning phonetic features using connectionist networks: an experiment in speech recognition. *Technical Report MS-CIS-86-78*, (Linc Lab 44, University of Pennsylvania, 1986).
[8] Williams, R. J. and Zipser, D. A learning algorithm for continually running fully recurrent neural networks. *Neural Computation 1*: 270 - 280 (1989).

Advanced Neural Computers / R. Eckmiller (Editor)

Neural Representation of Motor Synergies

Pietro Morasso

Department of Computer Science, University of Genoa
Via Opera Pia 11A, I-16145 Genoa, Italy

1. Introduction

The generation of synergies of motor commands and of the predicted patterns of their motor consequences are two complementary aspects at the core of motor control. The connectionist framework that is proposed here is based on the concept that the elastic properties of the human musculature not only represent a significant low-level feature of the motor system, but can also provide an organising principle for the global computational architecture. Muscle elasticity allows indeed to define a global elastic potential function whose equilibrium configurations, tuned by the patterns of neuromuscular activity, determine postures. At the same time, muscle elasticity provides a unified treatment of posture and movement because "postural attractors" can be turned into mechanisms of trajectory formation by modifying the shape of the potential field in the direction of the intended movement.

In order to obtain this goal, a principle has been formulated (Mussa Ivaldi, Morasso and Zaccaria, 1988) according to which synergies of motor commands can be generated via the *internal simulation of passive movements*, i.e. movements driven by external disturbances and constrained by the optimal distribution of elastic energy to the different muscles. A parallel and distributed computational architecture was preliminarily proposed (Morasso et al, 1989) which operates via relaxation in a similar way to a Hopfield net. The model is called M-Net (Motor relaxation Network) and is driven by a computational energy which mirrors the elastic potential energy of the muscles. The model has a somatotopic structure and is constructed as a network of units which correspond to the different constituent parts of the musculo-skeletal system: S-units (skeletal segments), M-units (muscles, either single-joint or multiple-joint), and L-units (ligaments of the joints). The units exchange force and displacement signals and the dynamics of the network is automatically seeking an equilibrium configuration.

The state of the network can be "perturbed" by a parallel set of external forces which express the concurrent goals of an action. The dynamics of the network implies two operations: (i) an isotonic relaxation driven by the external forces and (ii) an isometric update where muscle activities are modified in order to substitute the effect of the same forces. It is important to remark that a performing M-net provides two streams of output data at the same time:

- A stream of *muscle activations*, i.e a motor synergy;
- A stream of *kinematic expectations* (the expected time course of muscle lengths, joints rotations, trajectories of the skeletal segments) that represent what von Holst called "efferent copy".

2. Motor Relaxation and Hopfield Networks

The idea that relaxation can be one of the fundamental mechanisms of motor planning&control comes from the study of the spring-like properties of muscles. Their role in controlling posture and movement was clearly demonstrated for the first time by Feldman (1966), who observed that in a simple joint the angular position is identified by the intersection of the length-tension curves of agonist and antagonist muscles, i.e. it is a result of *passive* mechanical properties and not of *active* feedback control. Subsequently, experiments with single-joint and multiple-joint movements were performed which confirmed the original idea (Bizzi et al. 1976, Polit et al. 1979, among others). From this came the *equilibrium trajectory hypothesis* (Hogan 1984, Bizzi et al. 1984), according to which arm movements are achieved by gradually shifting the hand equilibrium position encoded by neuro-muscular activities, and later the already mentioned *passive motion paradigm* (PMP) (Mussa Ivaldi, Morasso, and Zaccaria 1988), i.e. the concept that plans of movement can be obtained by the simulation of an internal model of the muskulo-skeletal system, subjected to virtual disturbances that correspond to the intended movements.

The PMP can be naturally implemented by a relaxation network (m-net) which seeks equilibrium states of some computational energy function analogous to the mechanical potential energy of the musculo-skeletal system. This is obtained by a *somatotopic network* of neural assemblies in which we allocate units for representing the skeletal segments, the muscles, and the ligaments. Such units are not fine-grained as neurons but are mid-grained as cortical columns or similar cell assemblies in other parts of the brain; they must deal with vectorial quantities (as regards both input and output) and perform simple but not trivial mechanic calculations. However, these calculations need not be very precise because the same redundancy, which challenges the architect of the motor controller, guarantees at the same time a certain robustness to "noise" in the computational process distributed to a large number of units.

Let us now briefly discuss the analogy with Hopfield networks which are prototypical relaxation systems. Hopfield networks, either discrete (Hopfield 1982) or continuous (Hopfield 1984), are arrays of units interconnected through a matrix of weights T. In the continuous case, in particular, each unit (which is represented by a pair of amplifiers with a local memory, i.e. an RC circuit) is characterised by an output voltage V, an external input current I, and an array of cross-connecting resistors of admittance T_{ji} that convey to each unit a net input current. The global network is a dynamical system whose state variables can be identified with the energy storage elements, i.e. the capacitors. It consists essentially of two parts: An additive part (a linear summation) and a non linear part (a sigmoidal function). Hopfield demonstrated that for such a network it is possible to define a potential energy function if the additive part is symmetric, i.e. if the connection matrix T is symmetric and its principal diagonal is null (i.e. there are no self-connections). In these conditions, the network admits equilibrium configurations and its dynamics can be characterised as a convergent flow from the initial configuration toward the nearest equilibrium configuration. Moreover, the sigmoidal non-linearity guarantees that the equilibrium states are bounded in an hypercube.

Motor relaxation networks implement a distributed computational model that represents a muskulo-skeletal structure, i.e. a *mechanical circuit* of skeletal bodies and viscous-elastic elements. Considered as a dynamical system, its state vector can be identified with the set $\underline{l}$ of lengths of all the elastic elements, because they can store energy.
Here we need a few words of comments as regards the elastic elements: in our model we explicitly represent not only muscles but also ligaments. The reason for including them does not come just from a requirement of representational fidelity but from a computational necessity. A generic requirement of a distributed somatotopic network is that it performs *local* computations. In a complex articulated structure like the skeleton, the joints are kinematic constraints that are difficult to express in general because the number of degrees of freedom changes during actions and exact calculations would need the "global" analysis of entire kinematic chains. By using ligaments in the computational model, it is possible to transform exact kinematic constraints into soft elastic constraints, i.e. *local* computations, whatever is the interaction between the skeleton and the environment.

The output variables of the network are the actual lengths of all the elastic elements and are derived from a non-linear transformation of the output of the s-units; this is a geometric transformation that expresses how muscles and ligaments are connected with skeletal structures. The input variables (to the s-unts) are force vectors (not simply scalars like in the Hopfield networks) and are computed (similarly to the Hopfield model) by means of a summation of external inputs (virtual disturbance forces) and cross-connections coming from feedback of the output variables. Although the summation is linear, the connection functions are not constant weights but non-linear functions that correspond the length-tension curves of muscles and ligaments. Nevertheless, the interconnection pattern retains the essential requirement of symmetry, intrinsic in the underlying physical system that guarantees stability of the relaxation process.

3. Behaviour of the Network

Let us now consider in more detail the behaviour of the network whose units, as outlined in the previous section, are divided into three classes:

Skeletal segment units (S-units);
Muscle units (M-units);
Ligament units (L-units).

M-units and S-units behave as impedances, i.e. they receive positional information and react feeding back force information. S-units, on the contrary, behave as admittances, i.e. they receive force information and react modifying positional parameters.

3.1 S-units

S-units model the different skeletal body segments, represented as rigid bodies to which complex sets of forces are applied. Let us define the input variables, output variables, state variables, parameters, and activation function.

- Input variables: These are the various types of force vectors $(\vec{f})$ applied to the s-unit that either represent *internal forces* (applied by m-units, l-units, and gravity) and *external forces* (used to express motor goals or environmental constraints).
- State variable: It is a homogeneous matrix H that identifies the position/orientation of a Cartesian frame fixed in the skeletal segment with respect to a reference frame in the environment.
- Parameters: There are positional parameters $(\vec{p}_0)$ that represent the application points of the various force vectors, referred to the local frame, and the mass M of the skeletal segment.
- Output variables: These are the current position vectors $(\vec{p})$ of the various application points expressed in a reference frame common to all the s-units.
- Activation function: It updates the output variables by simulating a viscous behaviour, i.e. it first computes the resultant force and torque vectors and then selects the vectors of rotation and translation velocity proportionally to the two resultants. This allows to update H and then to transform the positional parameters into their updated output values. At equilibrium, the resultant vectors will be null.

3.2 M-units

M-units model single and multi-joint muscles as elastic lines passing through pulleys and fixed at their extremities onto two different bones. Ignoring friction, the tension is constant in all the tracts of the same muscle: only some of them change their length during movement and are dubbed *active tracts* but also the other tracts are relevant because the muscle force is a function of the total length of the muscle, described by its length-tension curves. In particular, an m-unit is defined as follows:

- Input variable: It is a list of the insertion points $(\vec{p})$ of the muscle, with an indication of the active tracts.
- Parameters: These are the parameters of the length-tension curves. The curves were derived from a detailed model of the mechano-electro-chemical characteristics of muscles proposed by Hatze (1981) by considering the steady-state relations of a typical motor unit, representative of the whole muscle. We obtain families of curves indexed by the firing-rate V which are characterised by three parameters: the maximum isometric force $\hat{f}$, the length $\hat{l}$ at which this is achieved (the *optimal length*) and a normalised coefficient (σ) which measures the *spread* of the length-tension curves, in a similar way to the standard deviation for a gaussian function.
- Output variables: These are the pairs of force vectors $(\vec{f},-\vec{f})$ in each active tract. Mono-articular muscles only have one pair. The two vectors of each pair add up to zero and are applied to the two s-units that are connected by that muscle tract.
- Activation function: It has two modes of operation, passive and active. In the passive mode, it uses the length-tension curves, for the current length and level of neural command V. From this it forms the pairs of force vectors.

In the active mode it updates the neural command V.

3.3 L-units

L-units are used primarily in order to model joints. Joints are kinematic constraints among adjacent linkages that allow restricted motions within joint limits. L-units model both types of constraints in a soft way, as appropriate ensembles of (high stiffness) springs. For example, a spherical joint is modeled with a single spring, a hinge with two springs, and also joint limits can be represented by means of additional springs. L-units can be used to represent multi-joint ligaments, such as the retinacular ligament in the fingers, which is essential for the ordered succession of inter-phalangeal joint rotations. L-units are basically equivalent to m-units operating in the passive phase. In summary, an l-unit is defined as follows:

- Input variable: It is a list of insertion points.
- Parameters: Using a linear model for simplicity, we just need two parameters, the rest-length (l_0) and the stiffness k.
- Output variables: These are the pairs of force vectors in each active tract.
- Activation function: It uses the length-tension curve characteristic of the ideal spring. From this it forms the pairs of force vectors.

3.4 External Inputs

External inputs are additional force vectors applied to s-units in order to take into account motor goals or environmental constraints. Together, these forces are the inputs to an m-net, as a global dynamic system. In a larger computational architecture these forces come from the interaction between an m-net, considered as a synergy generation mechanism, and other nets, that take into account planning and peripheral feedback. The analysis of the computational requirements of this network are outside the scope of the paper. The basic feature is that the PMP can be implemented by means of *attracting* forces that pull selected *end-effectors* toward desired targets.

3.5 Alternation of Passive and Active Phases

The PMP implies an alternation of *passive* and *active phases* during the generation of a motor plan. The internal model that is advocated by the PMP is an analogic device for transforming an intention of movement, expressed as a virtual disturbance applied to the internal model, into a pattern of motions of all the joints and muscles; to this, however, we must add one more logical step, i.e. the derivation of the activation patterns that would have produced the same result of the virtual disturbance. This is the active part of the motor plan and we have two alternatives: one is to perform it concurrently with the passive simulation, the other is to alternate the two phases, by allowing a sequence of equilibrium states along a trajectory and by updating the motor commands intermittently, near equilibrium configurations. We opted for the second alternative, as regards the implemented model, because a concurrent passive/active network is very complex and highly prone to instability.

Therefore, during the passive phase an m-net evolves toward an equilibrium state compatible with a given set of external forces and motor command variables. Only when equilibrium is reached, the motor commands can be safely updated without risking instability of the network. These changes displace the equilibrium of the network which is re-gained in another relaxation phase.

It is possible to outline a variety of strategies for updating the activity levels of the m-units during the active phase. In particular, a *compliance strategy* is appropriate for implementing the PMP because, if the motion was caused by an attractor, it generates muscle activations that tend to cancel out its effect, i.e. to "substitute" or "unload" it. A *resistance strategy*, however, is necessary when dealing with contact forces and complex strategies might be necessary in arbitrary motor tasks.

We barely started to investigate this topic that we deem fundamental for distributed models of motor control. The problem is that the choice among the different strategies cannot be done locally, i.e. inside each m-unit on the basis of purely local information. We need some element of globality which then primes a local mechanism. Moreover, we need to take into account whether an m-unit is operating in the area of positive or negative stiffness.
As regards the compliance strategy, that was used in the simulation experiments reported in the next section, it can be implemented by means of the following rule:

$$\Delta f_a = \gamma \cdot \Delta f_p$$

where Δf_p denotes, for a given m-unit, the variation of muscle force due to the last passive phase of relaxation and Δf_a is the selected variation of active force from which the variation of the neural command can be derived; γ is a gain factor which must be negative if the muscle operates in the area of positive stiffness and negative in the opposite case.

4. Simulation Results

A few simulation experiments have been performed with an m-net simulator which runs on an HP-9000 workstation under Unix. In particular, let us consider a simulation involving movements of the finger. A network was developed which contains four s-units, ten l-units, and three m-units (the network is reported in appendix, according to the formalism of the simulation package).

The s-units identify the three phalanxes and the metacarpal joint. For each of them we defined a reference frame, centered in the proximal joint and oriented in such a way that x points to the subsequent joint and y is directed as the rotation axis.

Each one of the three joints was modelled by means of three l-units: a pair of collateral ligaments, with high stiffness and zero rest-length that define the rotation axis, and a palmar ligament, with smaller stiffness and non-zero rest length, which simulates the effect of the volar element and avoids the occurrence of hyper-extension. The tenth ligament models with a soft spring the retinacular oblique ligament which cross-connects the two inter-phalangeal joints.

The three m-units represent a flexor profundus, an extensor digitorum, and an interosseus. The first two muscles span all the three joints, following a palmar or dorsal pathway, respectively. The interosseus is a double-joint muscle and has an opposite effect on the two articulations (flexion of the metacarpo-phalangeal joint and extension of the proximal inter-phalangeal joint).

The parameters of the different units were partly derived from the experimental data reported by Tubiana (Tubiana, 1981) and partly from internal constraints of consistency. With this network we performed a number of simulation experiments like the flexion shown in figures 1 and 2, which is driven by a single attractor connected to the fingertip. Figure 2, in particular, shows, for each of the three muscles, the time-course of its length, force and α-activity, i.e. both the motor synergy and the kinematic expectations. In another experiment we collected flexion/extension movements of the finger by means of an optoelectronic device and we tried to reproduce similar patterns by means of a the same m-net driven by an attractor mimicking the fingertip of the original movement. The results are encouraging, although not perfect. Additional support to the model comes from the emulation of known deformities, such as the "swan-neck" deformity, which comes from a weak retinacular ligament, and the deformity known as "boutonniere" which is determined by a broken insertion of the extensor.

References

- Bizzi, E., Polit, A., and P. Morasso (1976) Mechanisms underlying achievement of final head position. J. Neurophysiology, 39, 435-444.
- Bizzi, E., Accornero, N., Chapple, W., and N. Hogan (1984) Posture control and trajectory formation during arm movements. J. Neuroscience, 4, 2738-2744.
- Feldman, A.G. (1966) Functional tuning of the nervous system with control of movement or maintenance of a steady posture. Biophysics, 11, 565-578.
- Hatze, H. (1981) Myocybernetic control models of skeletal muscle, characteristics and applications. University of South Africa, Pretoria.
- Hogan, N. (1984) An organizing principle for a class of voluntary movements. J. Neuroscience, 4, 2745-2754.
- Hopfield, J.J. (1982) Neural networks and physical systems with emergent collective computational abilities. Proc. Nat. Acad. Sci. USA, 79,2554-2558.
- Hopfield, J.J. (1984) Neurons with graded response have collective computational properties like those of two state neurons. Proc. Nat. Acad. Sci. USA, 81, 3088-3092.
- Mussa Ivaldi, F.A., Morasso, P., and R. Zaccaria (1988) Kinematic networks - A distributed model for representing and regularizing motor redundancy. Biological Cybernetics, 60, 1-16.
- Morasso, P., Mussa Ivaldi, F.A., Vercelli, G., and R. Zaccaria (1989) Connectionism in Perspective (Pfeifer, Schreter, Fogelman-Soulie, and Steels Eds), Elsevier Science Publishers, 413-420.
- Polit, A. and E. Bizzi (1979) Characteristics of motor programs underlying arm movements in monkeys. J. Neurophysiology, 42, 183-190.
- Tubiana, R. (1981) The Hand, volume I. W.B. Saunders Co., Philadephia.

Acknowledgments

This work was partly supported by the Esprit Projects FIRST and ROBIS, and by a National Program on Robotics of the Italian Research Council.

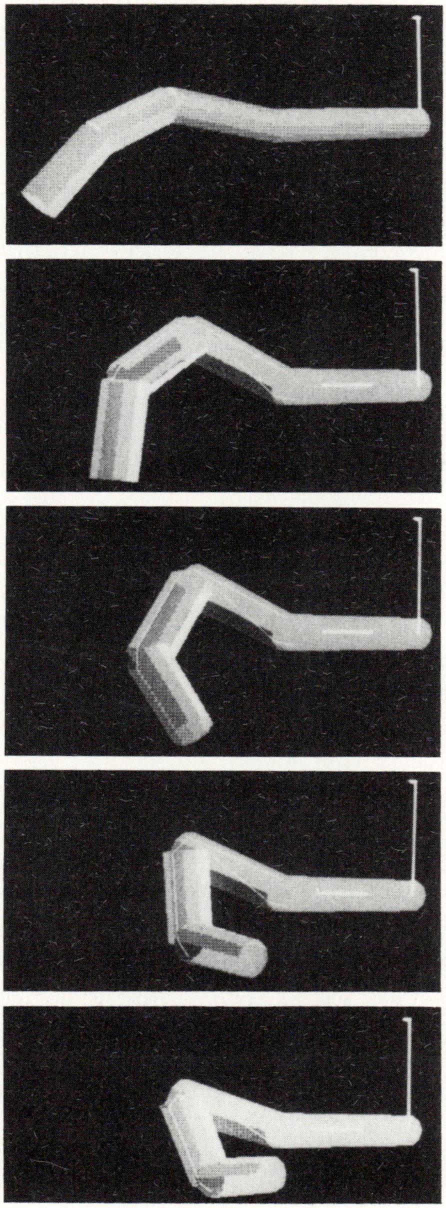

Figure 1. Simulation of a finger flexion.

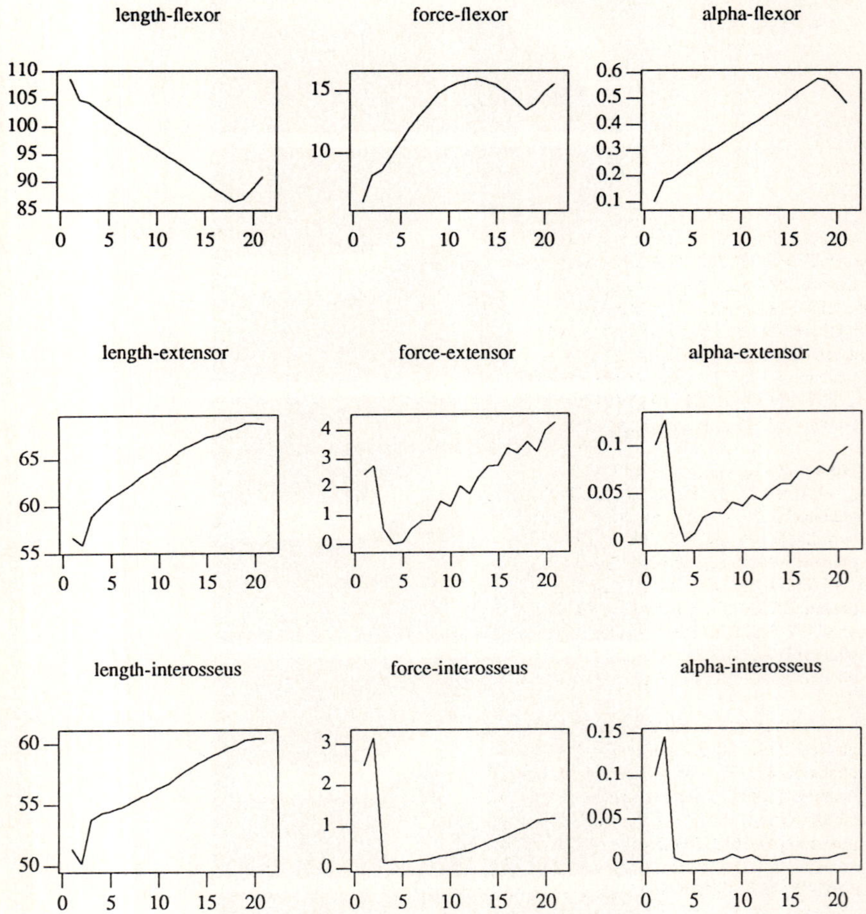

Figure 2. Patterns of muscle contraction for a finger flexion.

Appendix: M-net of the finger

The following is the m-net representation of a finger. Lengths are expressed in millimeters and forces in kilograms.

```
BONES

   metacarp:X(1.,0.,0.),Y(0.,1.,0.),Z(0.,0.,1.),R(0.,0.,0.)
          MASS(50),CG(42.,0.,0.)
   phalanx1:X(1.,0.,0.),Y(0.,1.,0.),Z(0.,0.,1.),R(84.,0.,0.)
          MASS(20),CG(24.,0.,0.)
   phalanx2:X(1.,0.,0.),Y(0.,1.,0.),Z(0.,0.,1.),R(132.,0.,0.)
          MASS(20),CG(15.,0.,0.)
   phalanx3:X(1.,0.,0.),Y(0.,1.,0.),Z(0.,0.,1.),R(162,0.,0.)
          MASS(15),CG(15.,0.,0.)
LIGAMENTS
  mpjoint_l:STIFF(30.),RESTL(0.),LEN(0.)
          metacarp(84.,5.,0.)>phalanx1(0.,5.,0.)
  mpjoint_r:STIFF(30.),RESTL(0.),LEN(0.)
          metacarp(84.,-5.,0.)>phalanx1(0.,-5.,0.)
 pipjoint_l:STIFF(30.),RESTL(0.),LEN(0.)
          phalanx1(48.,5.,0.)>phalanx2(0.,5.,0.)
 pipjoint_r:STIFF(30.),RESTL(0.),LEN(0.)
          phalanx1(48.,-5.,0.)>phalanx2(0.,-5.,0.)
 dipjoint_l:STIFF(30.),RESTL(0.),LEN(0.)
          phalanx2(30.,5.,0.)>phalanx3(0.,5.,0.)
 dipjoint_r:STIFF(30.),RESTL(0.),LEN(0.)
          phalanx2(30.,-5.,0.)>phalanx3(0.,-5.,0.)
 mpjoint_vol:STIFF(5.),RESTL(12.02),LEN(9.16)
          phalanx1(4.58,0.,-5.)>metacarp(79.42,0.,-5.)
pipjoint_vol:STIFF(20.),RESTL(16.51),LEN(15.7)
          phalanx1(40.15,0.,-5.)>phalanx2(7.85,0.,-5.)
dipjoint_vol:STIFF(12),RESTL(9.62),LEN(8.39)
          phalanx2(25.80,0.,-5.)>phalanx3(4.20,0.,-5.)
   retinac:STIFF(1.5),RESTL(35.),LEN(35.)
          phalanx1(40.15,0.,-5.)>phalanx2(7.85,0.,-5.)
          phalanx2(29.24,0.,5.)>phalanx3(.76,0.,5.)
MUSCLES
      ext:FMAX(9.45),LMAX(62.88),SPD(.433),LEN(56.76)
          phalanx2(29.24,0.,5.)>phalanx3(.76,0.,5.)
          phalanx1(47.565,0,5)>phalanx2(.435,0.,5.)
          phalanx1(1.82,0.,5.)>metacarp(83.18,0.,5.)
    inter:FMAX(5.),LMAX(51.05),SPD(.433),LEN(51.38)
          phalanx1(47.565,0,5)>phalanx2(.435,0.,5.)
          phalanx1(4.58,0.,-5.)>metacarp(79.42,0.,-5.)
     flex:FMAX(16.8),LMAX(93.05),SPD(.433),LEN(108.62)
          phalanx1(40.15,0.,-5.)>phalanx2(7.85,0.,-5.)
          phalanx2(25.80,0.,-5.)>phalanx3(4.20,0.,-5.)
          phalanx1(4.58,0.,-5.)>metacarp(79.42,0.,-5.)
```

Advanced Neural Computers / R. Eckmiller (Editor)

Vestibular Head- Eye Coordination: a Geometrical Sensorimotor Neurocomputer Paradigm[#]

Andras J. PELLIONISZ[*$], Barry W. PETERSON[+] and David L. TOMKO[$]

[*]New York University Medical Center
550 First Ave, New York, NY, 10016 USA

[+]Northwestern University
303 E Chicago Ave, Chicago, IL, 60611 USA

[$]NASA Ames Research Center
Vestibular Research Facility, Moffett Field, CA 94035 USA

1. Introduction

Brain-Like Computers and Brain Research

Neurocomputer research is coping with a dilemma. There are reasons for disassociating the strategy of creating brain-like computers from "wet brain" research. There are more than equally strong reasons, however, for the opposite; strengthening this precious but hitherto weak linkage. The first choice would permit rapid progress in technology; cut loose from constraints of the much slower process of theoretical understanding of biological brains. The disadvantage is that "Neural Networks" may thus repeat earlier cycles experienced in Cybernetics and Artificial Intelligence that could not or would not rely on wet brain research. As a result, efforts dried up and waned after initial surges of success. The remaining choice is to closely tie experimental-theoretical neurobiological research to technological development of brain-like machines [34],[38],[2],[50],[16],[30]. This latter strategy also has disadvantages. Establishing such a bond is extremely difficult given major differences between neuroscience and neural net implementation for instance in the extent of mathematical formalism, culture, funding structure and even philosophy. Nonetheless, a synthesis of experimental and theoretical-technological aspects may be the only way to create a discipline from interdisciplinary explorations. While difficult, it should be possible – just as it was in case of the process of creating a flourishing nuclear technology. Interdisciplinary studies, between and beyond classical physics and chemistry, led to forging a new discipline of nuclear physics, with its own mathematical understructure (quantum mechanics). Establishment of the basic science could later safely serve as a foundation on which to build a new technology. A similar scientific-technological integration, necessary today for putting neural net technology on solid grounds of a basic science, is therefore not unprecedented – only difficult.

The potential benefits from such a link are that it anchors the field of Neural Net research and that the biological brain proves the functionality of neural net solutions that follow nature's model. Opting for the assured solution based on natural evolution entails two key requirements, however. The first is to settle down to a much longer haul than most workers or agencies would like to commit themselves. The second is to carefully select those systems in the biological brain that provide us with the best paradigms of neurocomputing. Is it possible to identify a clearly defined "neurocomputer" actually existing in the biological brain?

Supported by NS22999-DC00332 by NIH to AJP and BWP and by NCA2-426 and 471 by NASA to AJP and DLT

2. Vestibulo-Cerebellar Coordination as a Sensorimotor Neurocomputing Paradigm

The authors contend that vestibulo-cerebellar neuronal nets offer among the best and clearest examples of an actual well-performing neurocomputer. It is known that during evolution nature developed this system for maintaining stable position, posture and movement of bodies, such that they can perform coordinated fast action in a turbulent environment [29]. Vestibulo-cerebellum first appeared in the course of evolution with sharks, providing a performance-margin ensuring a remarkable evolutionary survival of this epitome of navigation. Vestibulo-cerebellum attains an outstandingly high proportion of the brain in birds. Accordingly, they are masters of flying; rapidly changing their body-shape to adapt to turbulent conditions. Flight is controlled by an "on-board, real-time" neurocomputer that relies on an error-tolerant, gracefully degrading, massively parallel (and therefore fast) neural network. In addition, it need not rely on supercomplex software (that characterizes, and causes most of the breakdowns, of present-day serial computer systems). Technological implementation of the nature-perfected vestibulo-cerebellar neurocomputer should be obvious.

Because of complexities of biology, presently only partial knowledge is available concerning the mathematical principles upon which vestibulo-cerebellar neural networks operate. A specific subsystem, however, is relatively well known. The vestibulo-cerebellum is an integral part of gaze-stabilization systems, such as those which generate eye- and head-movements that compensate for displacements of the body and thus ensure a steady gaze [10]. Also, the pursuit and saccadic eye movement system provides perhaps the fastest and most precise biological example of target-tracking and interception [13]. Because the overall function is so important and well-defined, and because the underlying biological mechanism is confined and relatively simple, the gaze system has been the target of intense research. In a pioneering stage (1968-1981, see review in [53]) concepts and experimental methods were borrowed from system theory of linear electronic circuits; since sinusoidal input-output function of gaze stabilization is somewhat akin to that of amplifiers. Fig.1. illustrates reasons why researchers should move beyond traditional sinewave (suitable for harmonic analysis of linear systems) recognizing that the CNS is laden with nonlinear characteristics such as inhibition, delay and differentiation.

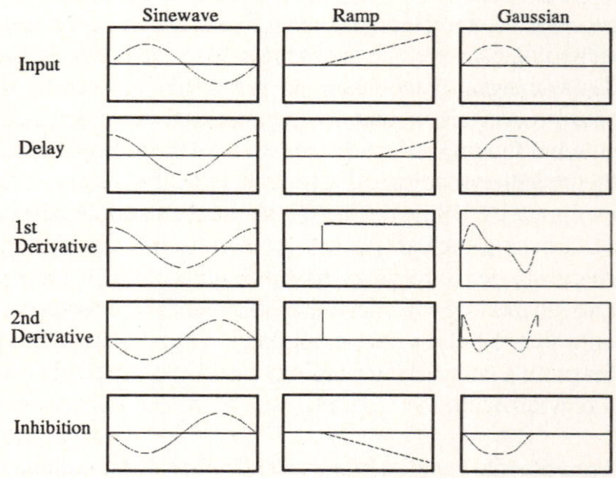

Fig.1. Demonstration of value of non-sinusoidal (Gaussian) test function for sensorimotor gaze research. Ramp and Gaussian functions can reveal temporal tuning of neck muscles that is based on derivative function.

Comparison of columns 1-2-3 reveals that sinusoidal test-functions are mathematically unsuited to detect derivative function; as "phase" confuses delays, derivatives and inhibition. In contrast, ramp-function and Gaussian function clearly distinguish such profiles. Gaussian function has the additional advantage over the ramp-function of being a derivable "smooth" curve.

A second, even stronger mathematical rationale for moving beyond the traditional analyses of natural neurocomputing systems is depicted in Fig.2. Neurocomputing will succeed, or fail, depending on whether it can meet two crucial challenges. The easier task is the development of the suitable technology. The more difficult is to discern (and/or develop) the mathematics *intrinsic* to neural net function.It was argued elsewhere [38] that a departure from the *algebraic* mathematical language of traditional serial computers [31] is long overdue. An emerging geometrical school of brain theory would also have to improve upon its classical mathematical formalism of Cartesian vectors [60], as evidence accumulates that neural geometry is non-Euclidean [40],[41],[43],[18].

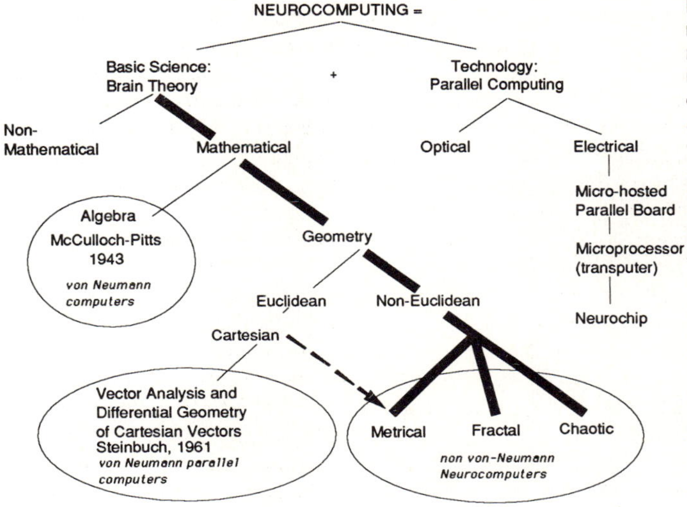

Fig. 2. A major challenge to neurocompuing: to establish the mathematics intrinsic to neural networks. To mathematically characterize the massively parallel neural processor of the CNS, the use of arrays (vectors and matrices) is necessary. The realization that such n-tuplets are points in a mathematical space which may be endowed with a non-Euclidean geometry, opens up research on functional spaces with slight deviation from (Euclidean) metrical spaces, as well as drastically non-Euclidean fractal and chaotic geometries. The mathematics of biological "neurocomputers" has to be discerned from actual neuronal networks of e.g. vestibulo-cerebellar system.

A new trend is necessitated not only for methodological reasons of mathematics. There is also a need to explore the actual neurocomputer mechanisms beneath the rotational input-output function of body movements. The conceptual turnaround, completed recently by a pioneer of such system-theoretical studies of gaze [2], is very telling; the authors argue strongly in favor of a drastic change from the earlier approaches to *"Distributed Parallel Processing in the Vestibulo-Oculomotor System"* since earlier models*" have generally taken the form of black-box diagrams (for example,* [53]*) representing the flow of hypothetical signals between idealized signal-processing blocks. They approximate overall oculomotor behavior but indicate little about how real eye-movement signals would be carried and processed by real neural networks" [2].* An alternative concept, inherently based on distributed parallel processing, was proposed a decade before. Tensor network theory was developed to explain the function of massively parallel neuronal networks in terms of transformation of multidimensional generalized vectors [44]. Implications of this principle on theory and modeling of gaze reflexes, such as the vestibulo-ocular reflex, were immediately pursued; as evidenced by the Chapter *"The vestibulo-ocular 'reflex' as a tensorial response"* in [45]. Similar to other new shifts of scientific axioms, the approach to vestibular system as a distributed parallel processor encountered a delayed response. Nevertheless, through a decade, there was much progress in modeling gaze, with a clear trend towards multidimensional approaches; both using extrinsic vectors [55],[54],[24],[2] or intrinsic generalized vectors (tensors); [45],[46],[35],[58],[23],[47],[36],[49],[15],[28],[11],[9],[25],[26],[50]. As for tensor network theory, the fundamental principle of the CNS as a distributed parallel processor that uses a *vectorial language* was experimentally substantiated in general [20]. The theory has evolved into a cohesive approach [37],[12]. Different generalizations of tensor network theory have also been attempted [19],[14]. Most importantly, the approach concluded in experimentally verifiable quantitative theoretical hypotheses that were tested and confirmed both by independent workers [21] as well as in collaborative experimental research [52],[48].

Our work on the vestibulocollic reflex (VCR) illustrates the success of the tensorial approach in predicting CNS programming of motor patterns. This reflex converts signals coding head velocity from 6 semicircular canals (SCCs) into patterns of activity of 30 muscles that move the head. Since normal head movements involve perhaps 6-10 degrees of freedom [62], there are potentially an infinite number of motor patterns that could execute a given head movement. Yet the VCR employs a single unique pattern ([4];[8]), suggesting that CNS processing is organized around some optimizing strategy. Modeling efforts described below show that this strategy corresponds quite closely to that proposed by [35].

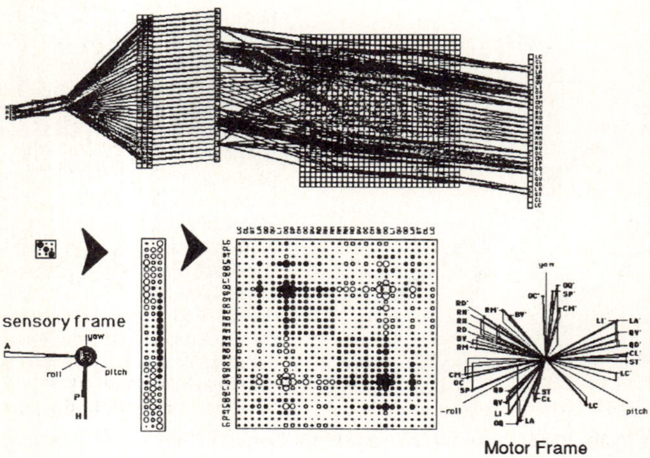

Fig. 3. Tensor network model of VCR in the cat. The sensorimotor transformation in the model occurs in 3 stages (patch diagrams from left to right): $\mathbf{g}^{pr}$, sensory metric tensor, $\mathbf{c}_{ip}$, sensorimotor embedding tensor and $\mathbf{g}^{ie}$ neck motor metric tensor. These tensorial operations are expressed in the reference frames of the VCR by matrices, which are here represented by patch diagrams in which positive and negative components are shown by filled and open circles whose areas are proportional to the size of the component. The CNS can implement these matrices by neuronal networks as indicated in the upper part of the diagram where size and strength of connections are indicated by line thickness and shading (black for excitation, grey for inhibition). From [48].

The model, which is shown in Fig 3, is *based entirely* upon measured geometry of the SCCs and neck muscles [5]. It implements the transformation between SCC signals and neck muscle activation in 3 stages. These are(see patch-diagrams from left to right in Fig.3):

1. Sensory metric tensor. This transforms the incoming covariant signal in the SCC coordinate frame into a contravariant representation in that frame. Since the 6 canals act as 3 pairs coding movement in 3-dimensional space, the 3X3 matrix required for this transformation may be found by simply inverting the matrix consisting of cosines of angles between the 3 SCCs.

2. Sensorimotor embedding tensor. This projects the 3 independent components of the contravariant SCC signal upon the axes of the 30 neck muscles. It is just a 3X30 matrix of cosines of angles between canal sensitivity axes and muscle pulling directions.

3. Neck motor metric tensor. The covariant neck motor signal resulting from 2 must be transformed into the contravariant representation required at the output of the VCR. As at stage 1, what we require is the inverse of the matrix {M} of cosines of angles between axes of the coordinate frame. Here, however, this is a 30X30 matrix which has no unique inverse. Therefore the model utilizes the Moore-Penrose Generalized Inverse (MPGI) as proposed by [35]. Mathematically (cf:[1]) the components of the MPGI are obtained from the outer (dyadic matrix) product of the eigenvectors of {M}. Biologically, it could be generated in a plastic neural network by the meta-organization process described by [47]. From the point of view of mechanics, the MPGI is an efficient choice since it tends to minimize co-contraction of muscles with opposing actions thus preventing wasteful expenditure of energy.

As shown in Fig. 4, the model predicts the VCR motor pattern within experimental error. This indicates that the choice of the MPGI as an optimizing principle approximates the kinematic selection process embodied in VCR circuitry and also confirms the utility of the tensorial approach in general. The model is also a true neural network model in that it suggests what some of the intermediate signals present in that circuitry could be. For instance, even though the patterns of activity of neck muscles are contravariant and therefore do not exhibit signals that are maximal along the pulling directions of

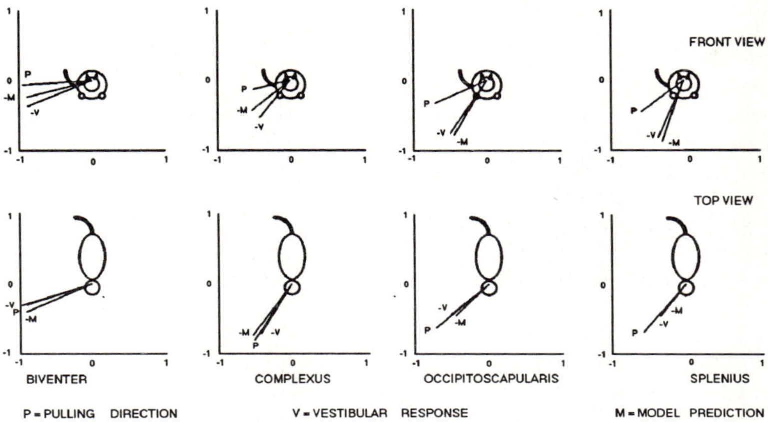

Fig.4. Experimental confirmation of theoretical predictions of tensorial VCR model. Comparison of pulling directions (P), directions of head rotation generating maximal VCR activation (V) and model predictions of V(M) for 4 neck muscles. Note close alignment of V and model predictions M (from [48]

neck muscles, the model suggests that covariant signals, which *would* be maximal along those directions should be found in the CNS. Experiments are now under way to see if activity of brainstem neurons corresponds to those suggested by this model or the elaboration of it shown in Fig 5.

Fig.5 Skeletomuscular Model of the Eye-Head System (inset at left; see in detail in [27,39]), matched by a Network Model of Vestibular Coordinate Transformation.(inset at right; see in detail in 42]).

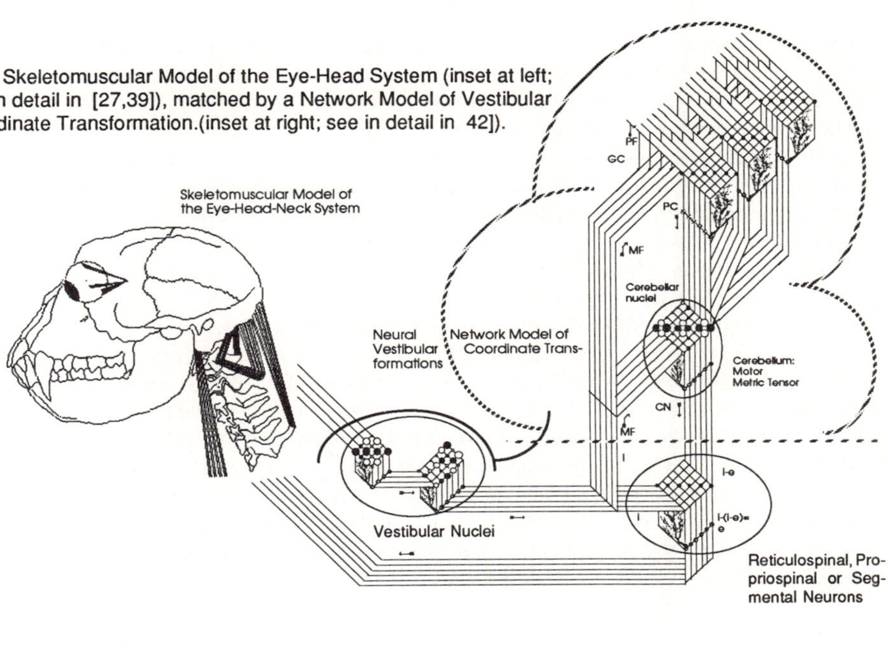

3. Skeletomuscular Systems' Modeling: Biomechanics of Intrinsic Coordinates

The approach of generalized coordinates intrinsic to CNS function requires an anatomical data-base. While coordinate-components of head acceleration are established by the vestibular semicircular canal system whose spatial (bone-embedded) orientation-directions can be well established [15],[23], some functional coordinate systems are changeable during movements; e.g. oculomotor and neck-motor muscle-coordinates [58],[45],[47],[59],[52],[9] and especially limb muscle coordinates [21],[11],[25]. Quantitative application of the tensorial neurocomputer-paradigm to actual neurobiological systems requires, therefore, both the anatomical measurement of such data, as well as the construction (in the temporary absence of suitable biomechanical models) of computer models of skeletomuscular apparatus [39],[28]. In a joint study (by A.J.P. and D.L.T.) of the vestibular eye-head coordination in the monkey, a skeletomuscular model is to be used to quantitatively account for eye- and neck-muscle pulling directions changing with gaze movements. Such a model of the monkey eye-head system is shown as part of Fig.5., following similar earlier modeling studies in the cat [39] and the monkey [27].

4. Development of Neural Network Theory & Experimentation

Fig. 5. also shows a neural network model [39] that is capable of implementing the three tensor transformations of vestibular sensory metric, sensorimotor embedding and motor metric tensors shown in a comprised manner in [51],[48],[50]. On one hand, this network is much further elaborated as it involves the vestibulo-*cerebellar* neuronal circuitry that is capable of transforming k-dimensional vestibular input into an n-dimensional eye- and neck-muscle output. For clarity, k-4 and n=6 was shown to both demonstrate and increase of dimensionality as well as keeping the complexity of the diagram reasonable (see an elaboration of such vestibulo-cerebellar sensorimotor transfer in [42]) The actual dimensions are much higher; as the vestibular input involves not only the 6 semicircular canals but also the otolith system, and the eye-head system involves at least 30+6 muscles each of which representing a space-*time* coordinate of gaze. Thus, future challenges ahead of us include: a) developing the vestibular model to involve the otolith-system based on physiological- [17],[57] and anatomical data [56], b) developing the vestibulo-cerebellar gaze coordination model to full space-*time* representation (to integrate theoretical considerations [46] with experimental findings on spatio-temporal sensory fusion [3],[4], c) Developing the neural network model, such as shown in Fig.3., to account for adaptive properties of gaze reflexes. A modifiability is evident both in terms of changing the neural network transformation according to the change of muscle pulling directions during movement (this can be accomplished by the modification of vestibulo-cerebellar function by the climbing fibers; c.f. [42]) as well as adaptation of performance to changes in the external geometry (see experimental observations [7],[6] and theoretical studies [47]).

5. Advanced Experimental Paradigms: Linear Vestibulo-Ocular Reflex; Gaussian Testing

The above challenges necessitate an increased reliance on novel experimental paradigms. The linear vestibulo-ocular reflex (LVOR; see [22],[32],[61],[33]) provides an ideal complement to angular VOR studies, since based on data derived from this experimental paradigm the vestibular-eye-neck model could be developed to both include the otolith-driven compensatory gaze reflexes (whose investigation is necessary for vestibular canal- and otolith convergence for space-*time* representation; [4]), as well as the fusion of vestibular and visual inputs (whose modeling is essential to gain an understanding of the internalization of external geometry by vestibular and visual mapping). Secondly, in order to reveal temporal derivatives necessary for predictive spacetime performance, the use of the proposed Gaussian analysis will be required (c.f. Fig. 1).

6. References

1. Albert, A. "Regression and the Moore-Penrose pseudo-inverse." 1972 Academic Press. New York.
2. Anastasio, T. J. and D. A. Robinson. Distributed parallel processing in the vestibulo-oculomotor system. Neural Comp. 1(2): 230-241, 1989.
3. Baker, J., G. Goldberg, G. Hermann and B. Peterson. Optimal response planes and canal convergence in secondary neurons in vestibular nuclei of alert cats. Brain Research. 294: 133-137, 1984.
4. Baker, J., J. Goldberg and B. Peterson. Spatial and temporal response properties of the vestibulocollic reflex in decerebrate cats. J. Neurophysiol. 54: 735-756, 1985.
5. Baker, J. and C. Wickland. "Kinematic properties of the vestibulocollic reflex." Control of Head Movement. Peterson and Richmond ed. 1988 Oxford Univ.Press. New York.
6. Baker, J., C. Wickland and B. Peterson. Dependence of cat vestibulo-ocular reflex direction adaptation on animal orientation during adaptation and rotation in darkness. Brain Res. 408: 339-343, 1987.
7. Baker, J. F., S. I. Perlmutter, B. W. Peterson, S. A. Rude and F. R. Robinson. Simultaneous opposing adaptive changes in cat vestibulo-ocular reflex direction for two body orientations. Exp. Brain Res. 69: 220-224., 1988.
8. Banovetz J.M., Rude S.A., Perlmutter S.I., Peterson B.W., Baker J.F. A Comparison of neck reflexes in the alert and decerebrate cats. Soc Neurosci. Abstr. 13: 1312, 1987.
9. Berthoz, A., M. Benhamou and A. J. Pellionisz. Postural positions yielding aligned Eigenvectors of coordinate frames intrinsic to vestibular and head-neck muscle systems in human. Soc. Neurosci. Absts. 14/2: 1235, 1988.
10. Berthoz, A. and G. Melvill-Jones. "Adaptive Mechanisms in Gaze Control." Reviews in Oculomotor Research. 1985 Elsevier. Amsterdam.
11. Bloedel, J. R., S. Tillery and A. J. Pellionisz. Experimental-theoretical analysis of the intrinsic geometry of limb movements. Soc. Neurosci. Absts. 14/2: 953, 1988.
12. Churchland, P. "Neurophilosophy: Towards a unified understanding of the mind-brain." 1985 Bradford Books/ MIT Press. Boston.
13. Cohen, B. Vestibular and oculomotor physiology. Int. Mtg. Barany Soc. Ann. N.Y.Acad. Sci. 347: 892, 1981.
14. Collins, T. J. Cerebral cortical parallel processing using a metric tensor. Proc. Internatl. Neur. Network Society 2nd Annual Meeting. 85, 1988.
15. Daunicht, W. and A. Pellionisz. Spatial arrangement of the vestibular and the oculomotor system in the rat. Brain Res. 435: 48-56, 1987.
16. Eckmiller, R. and C. Malsburg von. Neural Computers. Proc of the NATO Adv. Research Workshop, Springer. 1988.
17. Fernandez, C. and J. M. Goldberg. Physiology of peripheral neurons innervating otolith organs of the squirrel monkey. I. Response to static tilts and to long duration centrifugal force. J. Neurophysiol. 39: 970-984, 1976.
18. Freeman, W. Simulation of chaotic EEG patterns with a dynamic model of the olfactory system. Biol. Cybern. 55: 1987.
19. Gaál, G. Non-orthogonal hormonal coordinate axes calculated from correlation matrices according to tensor network theory. Neurosci. Suppl. 22 S146: 1987.
20. Georgopoulos, A. Coding of the Direction of Reaching by Neural Populations. International Joint Conference for Neural Networks. 1: 169, 1990.
21. Gielen, C. C. A. M. and E. J. van Zuylen. Coordination of arm muscles during flexion and supination: Application of the tensor analysis approach. Neuroscience. 17: 527-539, 1986.
22. Goldberg, J. M. and C. Fernandez. Responses of peripheral neurons to angular and linear accelerations in the squirrel monkey. Acta Otolaryngol. 80: 101-110, 1975.
23. Graf, W. and A. Pellionisz. Morphology and a tensor network model of the three-neuron vestibulo-ocular reflex arc in cat. Soc. Neurosci. Abst. 11: 1041, 1985.
24. Henn, W. and B. Cohen. Proc. of the Symp: Representation of 3-Dimensional Space in the Vestibular, Oculomotor and Visual Systems. Org.by the Bárány Society, Bologna, Italy. 1988.
25. Laczkó, J., A. Pellionisz, H. Jongen and C. C. A. M. Gielen. Computer modeling of human forelimb muscle activation in multidimensional intrinsic coordinate frames. Soc. Neurosci. Absts. 14/2: 955, 1988.
26. Laczkó, J., A. J. Pellionisz, B. W. Peterson and T. S. Buchanan. Multidimensional sensorimotor "patterns" arising from a graphics-based tensorial model of the neck-motor system. Soc. Neurosci. Absts. 13: 372, 1987.
27. Lestienne, F., P. Liverneaux and A. Pellionisz. Morpho-anatomy of sub-occipital muscles in monkey: a tensor model of the musculo-skeletal head-neck system. Reunion Commune de la Physiological Society et de l'Association des Physiologistes. J. Physiol. (Lond). : 2P, 1988.
28. Liverneaux, P., A. J. Pellionisz and F. G. Lestienne. Morpho-anatomy and muscular synergy of sub-occipital muscles in Macaca Mulatta: Study of head-trunk coordination. Neurosci. Suppl. to Vol. 22: S847, 1987.
29. Llinás, R. . "Neurobiology of cerebellar evolution and development." 1969 Am. Med. Assoc. Chicago.
30. Massone, L. and E. Bizzi. On the Role of Input Representations in Sensorimotor Mapping. International Joint Conference for Neural Networks. 1: 173-176, 1990.
31. McCulloch, W. S. and W. Pitts. A logical calculus of the ideas immanent in nervous activity. Bull. Math. Biophys. : 5, 115-133., 1943.
32. Paige, G. D. and D. L. Tomko. Linear vestbular-ocular reflex (LVOR) of squirrel monkey: II. Visual-vestibu-

lar interactions. Soc. Neurosci. Abstr. 14(1): 332, 1988.

33. Paige, G. D. and D. L. Tomko. Eye movements and visual-vestibular interactions during linear head motion. Symposium on head movement control. (in press), 1989.

34. Pellionisz, A. Brain Theory: Connecting Neurobiology to Robotics. Tensor Analysis: Utilizing Intrinsic Coordinates to Describe, Understand and Engineer Functional Geometries to Intelligent Organisms. J. Theoret. Neurobiol. : 185-211, 1983.

35. Pellionisz, A. Coordination: A vector-matrix description of transformations of overcomplete CNS coordinates and a tensorial solution using the Moore-Penrose generalized inverse. J. Theoret. Biol. 110: 353-375, 1984.

36. Pellionisz, A. "Tensorial aspects of the multidimensional approach to the vestibulo-oculomotor reflex and gaze." Adaptive Mechanisms in Gaze Control. Berthoz and Melvill-Jones ed. 1985 Elsevier. Amsterdam.

37. Pellionisz, A. "Tensor network theory of the central nervous system." Encyclopaedia of Neuroscience. Adelman ed. 1987 Birkhäuser. Boston.

38. Pellionisz, A. Tensor geometry: A language of brains and neurocomputers. Generalized coordinates in neuroscience and robotics. Neural Computers. Computers and Systems Sciences: 381-391, 1988.

39. Pellionisz, A. Tensorial aspects of the multidimensional massively parallel sensorimotor function of neuronal networks. Progress in Brain Research. Vestibulospinal Control of Posture and Movement: 341-354, 1988.

40. Pellionisz, A. Brain geometry: The need of researching association of covariant and contravariant coordinates that organizes a cognitive space by relating multisensory-multimotor representations. 3rd IEEE Internatl. Conf. on Neuronal Networks. 711-715, 1989.

41. Pellionisz, A. Fractal geometry of Purkinje neurons: Relationships among Metrical and non-metrical neural geometries. Soc. Neurosci. Absts. 15(I.): 180, 1989.

42. Pellionisz, A. Tensor network model of the cerebellum and its olivary system. The Olivo-Cerebellar System in Motor Control. 400-424, 1989.

43. Pellionisz, A. "Neural geometry: Towards a fractal model of neurons." Models in Brain Function. Cotterill ed. 1990 Cambridge Univ. Press. Cambridge.

44. Pellionisz, A. and R. Llinás. Brain modeling by tensor network theory and computer simulation. The cerebellum: Distributed processor for predictive coordination. Neurosci. 4: 323-348, 1979.

45. Pellionisz, A. and R. Llinás. Tensorial approach to the geometry of brain function: Cerebellar coordination via metric tensor. Neurosci. 5: 1125-1136, 1980.

46. Pellionisz, A. and R. Llinás. Space-time representation in the brain. The cerebellum as a predictive space-time metric tensor. Neurosci. : 2949-2970, 1982.

47. Pellionisz, A. and R. Llinás. Tensor Network Theory of the metaorganization of functional geometries in the CNS. Neurosci. 16: 245-274, 1985.

48. Pellionisz, A. and B. W. Peterson. "A tensorial model of neck motor activation." Control of Head Movement. Peterson and Richmond ed. 1988 Oxford University Press. Oxford.

49. Pellionisz, A., J. Soechting, C. Gielen, J. Simpson, B. Peterson and A. Georgopoulos. Workshop: Multidimensional analyses of sensorimotor systems. Soc. Neurosci. Absts. 12: 1, 1986.

50. Peterson, B. W. Modeling of Spatial Transformations in Vestibular Reflex Systems. International Joint Conference for Neural Networks. 1: 152-156, 1990.

51. Peterson, B. W., A. J. Pellionisz, J. A. Baker and E. A. Keshner. Functional morphology and neural control of neck muscles in mammals. Proc. Symp. on Axial Movement Systems: Biomechanics and Neural Control. 1987.

52. Peterson, B. W., A. J. Pellionisz, J. A. Baker and E. A. Keshner. Functional morphology and neural control of neck muscles in mammals. Am. Zoology. 29: 139-149, 1989.

53. Robinson, D. The use of control systems analysis in the neurophysiology of eye movements. Ann Rev Neurosci. 4: 463-503, 1981.

54. Robinson, D. The coordinates of neurons in the vestibulo-ocular reflex. Adaptive Mechanisms in Gaze Control Facts and Theories. 297-311, 1985.

55. Robinson, D. A. The use of matrices in analyzing the three-dimensional behavior of the vestibulo-ocular reflex. Biol. Cybern. 46: 53-66, 1982.

56. Ross, M. D. Morphological evidence for parallel processing of information in rat macula. Acta Otolaryngol. 106: 213-218, 1988.

57. Schor, R. H., A. D. Miller, S. J. B. Timerick and D. L. Tomko. Responses to head tilt in cat central vestibular neurons. II. Frequency dependence of neural response vectors. J. Neurophysiol. 53: 1444-1452, 1985.

58. Simpson, J. and A. Pellionisz. The vestibulo-ocular reflex in rabbit as interpreted using the Moore-Penrose generalized inverse transformation of intrinsic coordinates. Soc. Neurosci. Absts. 10: 909, 1984.

59. Simpson, J., D. Rudinger, H. Reisine and V. Henn. Geometry of extraocular muscles of the rhesus monkey. Soc. Neurosci. Absts. 12: 1186, 1986.

60. Steinbuch, K. Die Lernmatrix. Kybernetik. : 1, 36-45., 1961.

61. Tomko, D. L. and G. D. Paige. Linear vestibular-ocular reflex (LVOR) in squirrel monkey: I. Basic characteristics. Soc. Neurosci. Abstr. 14(1): 332, 1988.

62. Vidal , P. P., W. Graf and A. Berthoz. The orientation of the cervical vertebral column in unrestrained awake animals. I. Resting position. Exp. Brain Res. 61: 549-559, 1986.

Advanced Neural Computers / R. Eckmiller (Editor)

THE REPRESENTATION OF INFORMATION IN THE TEMPORAL LOBE VISUAL CORTICAL AREAS OF MACAQUES.

Edmund T. Rolls

University of Oxford
Department of Experimental Psychology
South Parks Road
Oxford OX1 3UD, England

Visual pathways project by a number of cortico-cortical stages from the primary visual cortex, the striate cortex, until they reach the inferior temporal visual cortex, area TE (Cowey, 1979; Gross, 1973; Desimone and Gross, 1979; Seltzer and Pandya, 1978; Rolls, 1990a,d; see Fig. 1). The inferior temporal cortex is among the highest unimodal visual cortical areas known. In addition, there are a set of cortical areas in the anterior part of the superior temporal sulcus which also receive visual inputs (Seltzer and Pandya, 1978; Baylis, Rolls and Leonard, 1987) (see Fig. 1). Of these areas, TPO receives inputs from temporal, parietal and occipital cortex; PGa and IPa from parietal and temporal cortex; and TS and TAa primarily from auditory areas (Seltzer and Pandya, 1978).

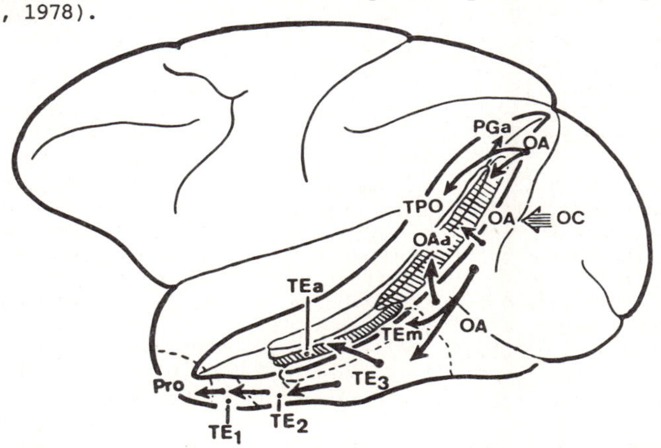

Fig. 1. Forward projections in the temporal lobe from visual areas of the macaque monkey. OC is the primary (striate) cortex, the TE areas are the inferior temporal visual cortex, and the superior temporal sulcus has been opened. (From Seltzer and Pandya, 1978).

In order to investigate the information processing being performed by these parts of the temporal lobe, the activity of single neurons has been analysed in each of these areas in the rhesus monkey (Baylis, Rolls and Leonard, 1987). There is considerable specialization of function in these different temporal cortical areas concerned with vision. For example, areas TPO, PGa and IPa are multimodal, with neurons which respond to visual, auditory and/or somatosensory inputs; the inferior temporal gyrus and adjacent areas (TE3,TE2,TE1,TEa and TEm) are primarily unimodal visual areas; areas in the cortex in the anterior and dorsal part of the superior temporal sulcus (e.g. TPO, IPa and IPg) have neurons specialized for the analysis of moving visual stimuli; and neurons responsive primarily to faces are found predominantly in areas TPO, TEa and TEm (Baylis, Rolls and Leonard, 1987).

The analysis of visual information taking place in some of these areas will be considered in this paper, to highlight the ways in which information is represented in these areas, and to consider ways in which some of the computations may be being performed. The particular population of neurons considered to illustrate these points is that with responses selective for faces (see Rolls, 1984,1990a,b,1991). The responses of these neurons to faces are selective in that they are 2-10 times as large to faces as to gratings, simple geometrical stimuli, or complex 3-D objects (Perrett, Rolls and Caan, 1982; Rolls, 1984; Baylis, Rolls and Leonard, 1985, 1987).

Ensemble encoding of object identity.

In experiments to investigate how a particular object in the environment might be represented by the activity of neurons in temporal lobe visual cortical areas, the responses of the face selective neurons to the faces of different individuals have been examined. It has been shown that in many cases (77% of one sample), these neurons are sensitive to differences between faces (as shown by an analysis of variance (Baylis, Rolls and Leonard, 1985)). However, each neuron does not respond only to one face. Instead, each neuron has a different relative response to each of the members of a set of faces. To quantify how finely these neurons were tuned to the faces of particular individuals, a measure derived from information theory, the breadth of tuning metric developed by Smith and Travers (1979), was calculated. This is a coefficient of entropy (H) for each cell which ranges from 0.0, representing total specificity to one stimulus, to 1.0 which indicates an equal response to the different stimuli. The breadth of tuning of the majority of the neurons analyzed was in the range 0.8 - 1.0. It was thus clear from this and other quantitative measures of the tuning of these face-responsive neurons that they did not respond only to the face of one individual, but that instead typically each neuron responded to a number of faces in the stimulus set (which included 5 different faces) (Baylis, Rolls and Leonard, 1985). Such evidence shows that only across a population or ensemble of such cells is information conveyed which would be useful in making different behavioral responses to different faces.

It may also be noted that it is unlikely that there are further processing areas beyond those described where ensemble coding changes into grandmother cell encoding, in that anatomically there do not appear to be a whole further set of visual processing areas present in the brain; and from the temporal lobe visual areas such as those described, outputs are taken to limbic and related regions such as the amygdala and via the entorhinal cortex the hippocampus. Indeed, tracing this pathway onwards, Leonard, Rolls, Baylis and Wilson (1985) have found a population of neurons with face-selective responses in the amygdala, and in the majority of these neurons, different responses occur to different faces, with ensemble not unique coding still being present.

Given this empirical evidence for ensemble encoding, that is for distributed representation, in these parts of the visual system, we can ask what the advantages are of this type of coding. It has been suggested (Rolls, 1987, 1989, 1990a,c,d) that the advantages arise from the fact that the outputs of these cortical areas reach structures such as the amygdala which are involved with making associations between visual representations of objects and with primary reinforcing stimuli such as the taste of food using pattern association neuronal networks; and such as the hippocampus which are involved in recognition and episodic memory using auto-association neuronal networks. The advantages of distributed representations for the inputs to such association neuronal networks include pattern completion, generalization, and graceful degradation (or graceful performance with an imperfect specification of the connectivity during development) (see Rolls, 1987, 1989). The type of tuning found in at least some temporal lobe cortical visual areas is thus seen as a delicate compromise between very fine tuning, which has the advantage of low interference in neuronal network operations but the disadvantage of losing the emergent properties of storage in neuronal networks, and broad tuning, which has the advantage of allowing the emergent properties of neuronal networks to be realised but of leading to interference between the different memories stored in the network (see Rolls, 1987, 1989).

The development of specificity of the neuronal responses.

Given the fundamental importance of a computation which results in relatively finely tuned neurons which across ensembles but not individually specify objects in the environment, we have investigated whether experience plays a role in determining the selectivity of single neurons which respond to faces. The hypothesis being tested was that visual experience might guide the formation of the responsiveness of neurons so that they provide an economical and ensemble-encoded representation of items actually present in the environment. To test this, we investigated whether the responses of the face-selective neurons were at all altered by the presentation of new faces which the monkey had never seen before. It might be for example that the population would make small adjustments in the responsiveness of its individual neurons, so that neurons would be provided with filter properties which would enable the population as a whole to discriminate between the faces actually seen. We thus asked whether when a set of totally novel faces was introduced, the responses of these neurons were fixed and stable from the first presentation, or instead whether there was some adjustment of responsiveness over repeated presentations of the new faces. First, it was shown for each neuron tested that its responses were stable over 5–15 iterations of a set of familiar faces. Then a set of new faces was shown in random order, and the set was repeated with a new random order over many iterations. It was found that some of the neurons studied in this way altered the relative degree to which they responded to the different members of the set of novel faces over the first few (1–2) presentations of the set (Rolls, Baylis, Hasselmo and Nalwa, 1989). Thus there is now some evidence from these experiments that the response properties of neurons in the temporal lobe visual cortex are modified by experience, and that the modification is such that when novel faces are shown, the relative responses of individual neurons to the new faces alter. It is hypothesized that alteration of the tuning of individual neurons in this way results in a good discrimination over the population as a whole of the faces known to the monkey.

In searching for models to help understand better the representation of information across ensembles of neurons, and how optimal categorisation of the inputs actually presented is developed by the population, we have found neuronal net models with competition to be helpful. These, and the way in which their operation may be guided by backprojections in the cerebral cortex, are considered below and elsewhere (Rolls, 1989).

A Neuronal Representation Showing Invariance.

One of the major problems which must be solved by a visual system is the building of a representation of visual information which allows recognition to occur relatively independently of size, contrast, spatial frequency, angle of view, etc. To investigate whether these neurons in the temporal lobe visual cortex are at a stage of processing where such invariance is being represented in the responses of neurons, the effect of such transforms of the visual image on the responses of the neurons has been investigated.

To investigate whether the responses of these neurons show some of the perceptual properties of recognition including tolerance to isomorphic transforms (i.e. in which the shape is constant), the effects of alteration of the size and contrast of an effective face stimulus on the responses of these neurons were analysed quantitatively in macaque monkeys (Rolls and Baylis, 1986). It was shown that the majority of these neurons had responses which were relatively invariant with respect to the size of the stimulus. The median size change tolerated with a response of greater than half the maximal response was 12 times. Also, the neurons typically responded to a face when the information in it had been reduced from 3D to a 2D representation in gray on a monitor, with a response which was on average 0.5 that to a real face. Another transform over which recognition is relatively invariant is spatial frequency. For example, a face can be identified as a line drawing (in which only high spatial frequencies are present), and when it is blurred (when it contains only low spatial frequencies). It has been shown that if the face images to which these neurons respond are low-pass filtered in the spatial frequency domain (so that they are blurred), then many of the neurons still respond when the images contain frequencies only up to 8 cycles per face.

Similarly, the neurons still respond to high-pass filtered images (with only high spatial frequency edge information) when frequencies down to only 8 cycles per face are included (Rolls, Baylis and Leonard, 1985; Rolls, Baylis and Hasselmo, 1987). Face recognition shows similar invariance with respect to spatial frequency. These neurons also show considerable invariance with respect to retinal translation (Azzopardi and Rolls, 1989).

An Object-Centered Representation of Visual Information.

The findings that the responses of these neurons show considerable invariance over changes in the size, contrast and retinal translation of face stimuli is evidence that the encoding is not in retinal coordinates. Alternatives are that it is in viewer-centered or object-centered coordinates.

Some neurons with responses selective for faces only respond if the face is moving (Perrett et. al., 1985). It is noted that encoding of gestures is likely to be important in the social behavior of primates. We took advantage of the fact that these neurons respond to moving faces to investigate whether the encoding of faces by these neurons is in viewer-centered or object-centered coordinates (Hasselmo, Rolls, Baylis and Nalwa, 1989). For 10 neurons it has been shown that the neuron responds to particular movements which can only be described in object-centered coordinates. For example, four neurons responded vigorously to a head undergoing ventral flexion, irrespective of whether the view of the head was full face, of either profile, or even of the back of the head. These different views could only be specified as equivalent in object-centered coordinates. Further, for all of the neurons that were tested in this way, the movement specificity was maintained across inversion, responding for example to ventral flexion of the head irrespective of whether the head was upright or inverted. In this procedure, retinally encoded or viewer-centered movement vectors are reversed, but the object-centered description remains the same. It was of interest that the neurons tested generalized across different heads performing the same movements.

Further evidence supporting the hypothesis that some of the neurons in this region use object-centered descriptions is that their selectivity between the faces of different individuals is maintained across anisomorphic transforms of the stimulus. For example, some neurons reliably responded differently to the faces of two different individuals independently of viewing angle. However, in most cases (16/18 neurons) although the identity of the face was reflected in the neuronal response, the response was not perfectly view-independent, and viewing angle also influenced the response. It is possible that these latter neurons represent an intermediate stage in the computation of object-centered descriptions (Hasselmo, Rolls, Baylis and Nalwa, 1989).

The functions of backprojections in neuronal networks in the neocortex in the storage and recall of visual memories.

In order to form new (declarative) memories, including memories of visual objects such as faces, limbic structures such as the hippocampal system and perhaps the amygdala are necessary (Mishkin, 1982; Squire, 1986; Squire and Zola-Morgan, 1988; Rolls, 1990a-c). (Declarative memories can be described by humans, in contrast to procedural memories for motor and related skills which are not dependent on limbic strucures.) Although these limbic structures are necessary for the formation of these memories, the memories are not stored in the limbic strucures in the long term but instead are stored in the neocortical areas which perform for example visual processing, in that old memories are at least partially spared in patients with damage to limbic structures. High order neocortical areas such as the inferior temporal visual cortex send projections to these limbic strucures, and in turn receive backprojections from these limbic structures (see Rolls, 1989, 1990c). Because of the importance of these backprojections in the storage of visual information in the neocortex, their connections to the visual association cortex, and their functions in the operation of the visual association cortex, are considered next.

The forward and backward projections which will be considered are shown in Fig. 2 (for further anatomical information see Peters and Jones, 1984).

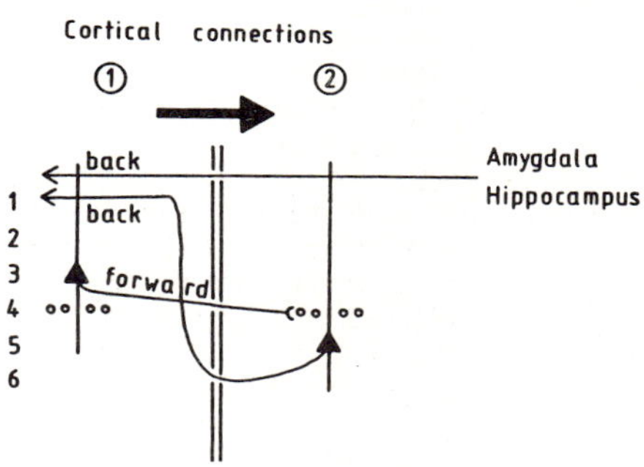

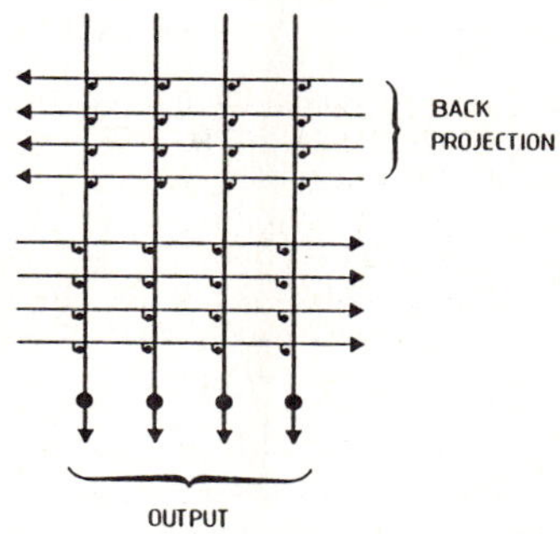

Fig. 2 (left). Schematic diagram of forward and backward projections in the neocortex. The arrow from left to right connecting the cortical area 1 to 2 shows the forward direction. The superficial pyramidal cells (triangles) in layers 2 and 3 project forward to terminate in layer 4 of the next cortical area. The deep pyramidal cells in the next area project back to layer 1 of the preceding cortical area, in which there are apical dendrites of pyramidal cells. The hippocampus and amygdala also are the source of backprojections which end in layer 1. Spiny stellate cells are represented by small circles in layer 4. See text for further details.

Fig. 3 (right). The architecture used to simulate the properties of backprojections. The forward ('input stimulus') and backprojected axons make Hebb modifiable synapses onto the same set of vertical dendrites, which represent cortical pyramidal cells.

In primary sensory cortical areas, the main extrinsic 'forward' input is from the thalamus, and ends in layer 4, where synapses are formed onto spiny stellate cells. These in turn project heavily onto pyramidal cells in layers 3 and 2, which in turn send projections forward to terminate strongly in layer 4 of the next cortical layer (on small pyramidal cells in layer 4 or on the basal dendrites of the layer 2 and 3 (superficial) pyramidal cells). (Although the forward afferents end strongly in layer 4, the forward afferents have some synapses also onto the basal dendrites of the layer 2 pyramidal cells, as well as onto layer 6 pyramidal cells and inhibitory interneurons). Inputs reach the layer 5 (deep) pyramidal cells from the pyramidal cells in layers 2 and 3 (Martin, 1984), and it is the deep pyramidal cells which send backprojections to end in layer 1 (predominantly) of the preceding cortical area (see Fig. 2), where there are apical dendrites of pyramidal cells. In addition to these cortoco-cortical backprojections, there are also axons and terminals in layer 1 in later areas in the cortical hierarchy including the inferior temporal visual cortex from the amygdala and (via the subiculum, entorhinal cortex and parahippocampal cortex) from the hippocampal formation (see Fig. 2) (Van Hoesen, 1981; Turner, 1981; Amaral and Price, 1984; Amaral, 1986, 1987). Now the amygdala and hippocampus are stages of information processing at which the different sensory modalities (such as vision, hearing, touch, and taste for the amygdala) are brought together, so that correlations between inputs in different modalities can be detected in these regions, but not at prior cortical processing stages in each modality, as these cortical processing stages are unimodal. Now, as a result of bringing together the two modalities, significant correspondences between the two modalities can be detected. One example might be that a particular visual stimulus is associated with the taste of food. Another example might be that another visual stimulus is associated with painful touch. Thus at these limbic stages of processing, but not before, the significance of for example visual and auditory stimuli can be detected and signalled, and sending this information back to the neocortex thus can provide a signal which indicates to the cortex that information should be stored, but even more than this, provides a signal which could help the neocortex to store the information efficiently. It is proposed below that one function of backprojections from these limbic strucures is to guide the formation of long-term memories in structures such as the inferior temporal visual cortex so that neuronal networks in these cortical areas need not operate in an unsupervised way, but can benefit from feedback from further on in processing.

The way in which backprojections could assist learning in the cortex can be considered using the architecture shown in Fig. 3. The (forward) input stimulus occurs as a vector applied to (layer 3) cortical pyramidal cells through modifiable synapses in the standard way for a competitive net (see Rolls, 1989). The lower set of synapses on the pyramidal cells would then start by competitive learning to set up representations on the lower parts of these neurons which would represent correlations in the input information space, and could be said to correspond to features in the input information space, where a feature is defined simply as the representation of a correlation in the input information space.

Consider now the application of one of the (forward) input stimulus vectors with the conjunctive application of a pattern vector via the backprojection axons with terminals in layer 1. Given that all the synapses in the matrix start with random weights, some of the pyramidal cells will by chance be strongly influenced both by the (forward) input stimulus and by the backprojecting vector. These strongly activated neurons will then compete with each other as in a standard competitive net, to produce contrast enhancement of their firing patterns. Next, Hebbian learning takes place as in a competitive net, with the addition that not only the synapses between forward projecting axons and active postsynaptic neurons are modified, but also the synapses in layer 1 between the backward projecting axons and the (same) active postsynaptic neurons are modified.

This functional architecture has the following properties. First, the backprojections, which are assumed to carry signals which reflect information derived by convergence of different cortical areas in the next cortical processing stage or in the hippocampus and amygdala, help the neurons to learn to respond differently to (and thus separate) input stimuli (on the forward projection lines) even when the forward input stimuli are very similar. (For neuronal network simulations of this see Rolls, 1989). Another way in which the learning of pyramidal cells can be influenced is that if two relatively different input stimuli are being received, but the same backprojecting signal occurs with these two somewhat different forward inputs, then the pyramidal cells will be guided by the tutor to build the representation of the forward input stimuli on the same pyramidal cells. If the representations of the forward inputs built by modification of the synapses on the pyramidal cells are considered as vectors in a multidimensional space, then the representations in this case will be forced towards each other as a result of the operation of the common backprojecting tutor.

In the cerebral cortex, the backprojecting tutors can be of two types. One originates from the amygdala and hippocampus, and by benefiting from cross-modal comparison, can provide a useful backprojected vector. This backprojection moreover may only be activated if the multimodal areas detect that the visual stimulus is significant, because for example it is associated with a pleasant taste. This provides one way in which guidance can be provided for a competitive learning system as to what it should learn, so that it does not attempt to lay down representations of all incoming sensory information, but only those shown to be significant as a result of a comparison made with inputs originating in a different modality. Another way for this important function to be achieved is by activation of neurons which 'strobe' the cortex when new or significant stimuli are shown. The cholinergic system originating in the basal forebrain (which itself receives information from the amygdala), and the noradrenergic input to layer 1 of the cortex from the locus coereleus may also contribute to this function (see Rolls, 1987; Bear and Singer, 1986). However, in that there are relatively few neurons in these basal forebrain and noradrenergic systems, it is suggested that these projections only provide a simple 'strobe' (see Rolls, 1987). In contrast there are sufficient axons in the backprojecting systems from the hippocampus and amygdala to carry pattern-specific information, so that the hypothesis presented here is therefore that these backprojections guide how information is consolidated, by influencing how information is stored on pyramidal cells in the way described above. The situations in which the amygdala and hippocampal backprojections guide learning (and also recall and attention as discussed below) are probably different in the following way. It is suggested that the amygdala is particularly involved when associations are made between a neutral stimulus (such as a visual stimulus) and a reinforcing stimulus (arising from for example the taste or touch inputs it receives) (see Rolls, 1985, 1990b). In contrast, it is suggested that the hippocampus is particularly involved when conjunctions must be detected between spatial inputs (received by the major inputs of the hippocampus which originate from the parietal cortex) and its other inputs (from for example the inferior temporal visual cortex), in for example conditional spatial and object-place learning tasks (see above and Rolls, 1989, 1990c).

The second type of backprojection is that from the next cortical area in the hierarchy. This next cortical area operates in the same manner, but because it receives convergent inputs from different cortical regions in the preceding cortical processing stage, is able to build representations which reflect categories which can only be formed as a result of the convergence. This next cortical stage then projects back these representations as tutors to the preceding stage, to effectively build at the preceding stage better filters for the diagnosis of the categories being found at the next stage.

A second property of this architecture is that it provides for recall. Recall of a previously stored representation by another stimulus or event occurs in the following way. If only the tutor is presented, then the neurons originally activated by the forward projecting input stimuli are activated. This occurs because the synapses from the backprojecting axons onto the pyramidal cells have been modified only where there was conjunctive forward and backprojected activity during learning. Recall could operate as a result of signals backprojected directly from the amygdala or parahippocampal gyrus, or indirectly through series of back-connected cortical stages.

A third property of this architecture is that attention could operate from higher to lower levels to selectively facilitate only certain pyramidal cells by using the backprojections. Indeed, the backprojections described could produce many of the "top-down" influences which are common in perception. A fourth property is that semantic priming could operate by using the backprojecting neurons to provide a small activation of just those neurons in earlier stages which are appropriate for responding to that semantic category of input stimulus.

A fifth property of such a return mechanism would be a positive feedback effect which would result in better storage in the cerebral cortex in the long term. This would operate so that when a useful tutor had been built at a higher level this would influence the earlier stage(s) so that a better filter would be built at the earlier level. This in turn would lead to formation of an even better tutor at the higher stage, and so on repeatedly. This might provide a neurophysiological and computational basis for any gradient of retrograde amnesia which may occur for the period just before disruption of temporal lobe function (Squire, 1986; Squire and Zola-Morgan, 1988). A sixth property of the backprojections is that they might assist the stability of the preceding competitive networks by providing a relatively constant guiding signal as a result of associations made at a higher stage, to for example an unconditioned taste or somatosensory input. A seventh property of such a return mechanism would be a dynamic (short term) positive feedback effect by which higher levels might affect the tuning of lower levels to help the system settle into the best fit to multiple constraints. This process might also, perhaps by temporal correlations, help to bind together representations at an earlier stage which are sub-parts of a representation being activated at a higher stage. An eighth property of the backprojection system is that it can speed the rate of learning above that possible in a simple competitive learning system.

This hypothesis of the functions of backprojections in the cerebral cortex requires a large number of backprojecting axons, as pattern-specific information (used to guide learning by providing a set of mutually orthogonal guidance signals, or to produce recall) must be provided by the backprojections. It also helps to solve the deaddressing problem, in that higher stages (such as the hippocampus) do not need to know exactly where in the cortex information should be stored. Instead, the backprojection signal spreads widely in layer 1, and the storage site is simply on those neurons which happen to receive strong (and precise) forward activity as well as backprojected activity, so that Hebbian learning by conjunction occurs there. This scheme is consistent with neocortical anatomy, in that it requires the same pyramidal cell to receive both forward and (more diffuse) backprojected activity, which the arrangement of pyramidal cells with apical dendrites which extend all the way up into layer 1 achieves (see Peters and Jones, 1984).

REFERENCES

Amaral,D.G. (1986) Amygdalohippocampal and amygdalocortical projections in the primate brain. Pp. 3-17 in Excitatory Amino Acids and Epilepsy, eds. R.Schwarz and Y.Ben-Ari. Plenum: New York.

Amaral,D.G. (1987) Memory: anatomical organization of candidate brain regions. Pp. 211-294 in Handbook of Neurophysiology. Section 1 : The Nervous System. Vol. V. Part 1. American Physiological Society: Washington, D.C.

Amaral,D. and Price,J.L. (1984) Amygdalo-cortical projections in the monkey (Macaca fascicularis). J. Comp. Neurol. 230: 465-496.

Azzopardi,P. and Rolls,E.T. (1989) Translation invariance in the responses of neurons in the inferior temporal visual cortex of the macaque. Society for Neuroscience Abstracts 15: 120.

Barlow, H.B. (1972) Single units and sensation: a neuron doctrine for perceptual psychology ? Perception 1: 371-394.

Baylis,G.C., Rolls,E.T. and Leonard,C.M. (1985) Selectivity between faces in the responses of a population of neurons in the cortex in the superior temporal sulcus of the monkey. Brain Research 342: 91-102.

Baylis,G.C., Rolls,E.T. and Leonard,C.M. (1987) Functional subdivisions of temporal lobe neocortex. Journal of Neuroscience 7: 330-342.

Cowey,A. (1979) Cortical maps and visual perception. Quart. J. Exp. Psychol. 31: 1-17.

Desimone,R. and Gross,C.G. (1979) Visual areas in the temporal lobe of the macaque. Brain Res. 178: 363-380.

Gross,C.G. (1973) Inferotemporal cortex and vision. Progr. Physiol. Psychol. 5: 77-123.

Hasselmo,M.E., Rolls,E.T. and Baylis,G.C. (1989) The role of expression and identity in the face-selective responses of neurons in the temporal visual cortex of the monkey. Behav. Brain Res. 32: 203-218.

Hasselmo,M.E., Rolls,E.T., Baylis,G.C. and Nalwa,V. (1989) Object-centered encoding by face-selective neurons in the cortex in the superior temporal sulcus of the monkey. Experimental Brain Research 75: 417-429.

Leonard,C.M., Rolls,E.T., Wilson,F.A.W. and Baylis,G.C. (1985) Neurons in the amygdala of the monkey with responses selective for faces. Behavioural Brain Research 15: 159-176.

Martin,K.A.C. (1984) Neuronal circuits in cat striate cortex. Chapter 9, pp. 241-285 in The Cerebral Cortex, Vol. 2, Functional properties of cortical

cells. Eds. E.G.Jones and A.Peters. Plenum: New York.
Mishkin,M. (1982) A memory system in the monkey. Phil. Trans. Roy. Soc. Lond. B 298: 85-95.
Perrett,D.I., Rolls,E.T. and Caan,W. (1982) Visual neurons responsive to faces in the monkey temporal cortex. Exptl. Brain Res. 47: 329-342.
Peters,A. and Jones,E.G. (1984) The Cerebral Cortex, Vol. 1, Cellular Components of the Cerebral Cortex. Plenum: New York.
Rolls,E.T. (1984) Neurons in the cortex of the temporal lobe and in the amygdala of the monkey with responses selective for faces. Human Neurobiology 3: 209-222.
Rolls,E.T. (1985) Connections, functions and dysfunctions of limbic structures, the prefrontal cortex, and hypothalamus. Pp. 201-213 in The Scientific Basis of Clinical Neurology, eds. M.Swash and C.Kennard. London: Churchill Livingstone.
Rolls,E.T. (1987) Information representation, processing and storage in the brain: analysis at the single neuron level. Pp. 503-540 in The Neural and Molecular Bases of Learning, eds. J.-P. Changeux and M.Konishi. Wiley: Chichester.
Rolls,E.T. (1989) The representation and storage of information in neuronal networks in the primate cerebral cortex and hippocampus. Ch. 8, pp. 125-159 in The Computing Neuron, eds. R.Durbin, C.Miall and G.Mitchison. Addison-Wesley: Wokingham, England.
Rolls,E.T. (1990a) The processing of face information in the primate temporal lobe. In Processing Images of Faces, eds. V.Bruce and M.Burton. Ablex.
Rolls,E.T. (1990b) A theory of emotion, and its application to understanding the neural basis of emotion. Cognition and Emotion
Rolls,E.T. (1990c) Functions of the primate hippocampus in spatial processing and memory. Ch. 12, pp. 339-362 in Neurobiology of Comparative Cognition, eds. D.S.Olton and R.P.Kesner. L.Erlbaum: Hillsdale,N.J.
Rolls,E.T. (1990d) Visual information processing in the primate temporal lobe. In Models of Visual Perception: from Natural to Artificial, ed. M.Imbert. Oxford University Press: Oxford.
Rolls,E.T., Baylis,G.C., and Leonard,C.M. (1985) Role of low and high spatial frequencies in the face-selective responses of neurons in the cortex in the superior temporal sulcus. Vision Research 25: 1021-1035.
Rolls,E.T. and Baylis,G.C. (1986) Size and contrast have only small effects on the responses to faces of neurons in the cortex of the superior temporal sulcus of the monkey. Exp. Brain Res. 65: 38-48.
Rolls,E.T., Baylis,G.C. and Hasselmo,M.E. (1987) The responses of neurons in the cortex in the superior temporal sulcus of the monkey to band-pass spatial frequency filtered faces. Vision Research 27: 311-326.
Rolls,E.T., Baylis,G.C., Hasselmo,M.E. and Nalwa,V. (1989) The effect of learning on the face-selective responses of neurons in the cortex in the superior temporal sulcus of the monkey. Experimental Brain Research 76: 153-164.
Seltzer,B. and Pandya,D.N. (1978) Afferent cortical connections and architectonics of the superior temporal sulcus and surrounding cortex in the rhesus monkey. Brain Res. 149: 1-24.
Smith,D.V. and Travers,J.B. (1979) A metric for the breadth of tuning of gustatory neurons. Chemical Senses 4: 215-229.
Squire,L. (1986) Mechanisms of memory. Science 232: 1612-1619.
Squire,L.R. and Zola-Morgan,S. (1988) Memory: brain systems and behavior. Trends in Neurosciences 11: 170-175.
Turner,B.H. (1981) The cortical sequence and terminal distribution of sensory related afferents to the amygdaloid complex of the rat and monkey. Pp. 51-62 in The Amygdaloid Complex, ed. Ben-Ari,Y. Elsevier: Amsterdam.
Van Hoesen,G.W. (1981) The differential distribution, diversity and sprouting of cortical projections to the amygdala in the rhesus monkey. Pp. 79-90 in The Amygdaloid Complex, ed. Y.Ben-Ari. Elsevier: Amsterdam.

Van Hoesen,G.W. (1982) The parahippocampal gyrus. New observations regarding its cortical connections in the monkey. Trends in Neurosciences 5: 345-350.

Acknowledgements. The author has worked on some of the experiments and neuronal network modelling described here with A.Bennett, G.C.Baylis, P.Cahusac, J.D.Feigenbaum, M.Hasselmo, R.P.Kesner, G.Littlewort, Y.Miyashita, H.Niki, R.Payne, T.R.Scott, and A.Treves and their collaboration is sincerely acknowledged. Discussions with David G. Amaral of the Salk Institute, La Jolla, were also much appreciated. This research was supported by the Medical Research Council.

Advanced Neural Computers / R. Eckmiller (Editor)

Exploration of a natural environment

W. von Seelen and H. A. Mallot

Institut für Neuroinformatik, Ruhr–Universität, D–4630 Bochum, FRG

A neural architecture that enables a system to orient in, explore, and act in a natural environment is presented. The problem is attacked by structuring the desired behavior into a hierarchy of tasks. Solutions for the modules in such a hierarchy are found in the realm of a set of neural operational principles that include two-dimensional, laterally coupled nets, topographic mappings, foveation, discrete parameter representation, and regularization. The system is endowed with flexibility by implementing associative memory on relevant levels of analysis. In this presentation we highlight selected examples that are part of an ongoing research program.

1 Introduction

The strategic aim of our work is to develop a neural architecture of an information-processing system. In this endeavour we are closely guided by biological insights to an extent far exceeding the use of formal neurons. Specifically, we use biological knowledge on the two main aspects of the problem: First, structure principles known from the neurophysiology of the visual system are used to implement solutions to information-processing tasks. Second, the information processing task itself is structured according to biologically motivated elementary behaviors.

We have chosen a concrete problem that serves as a test case for the development of such a general scheme: We aim to develop a system that is able to explore a natural environment, and, in a second step, act in this environment. The different tasks involved in this are technically well defined and ample biological information is available both on the neural structures supporting tasks of this type as well as the corresponding behaviors. The starting point is provided by the following assumptions:

1. The structures that will form the basic elements of our system are related to cortical networks.

2. Flexibility will be achieved by an associative memory on an adequate level of representation and by variation of a few parameters within the cortical network. Therefore, learning is dealt with here on the basis of networks that in their structure incorporate already a fair amount of knowledge about the problem.

3. The processing is structured by a hierarchy of tasks. The solution of subproblems on different levels is to lead to functional complexity.

Supported by the Bundesministerium für Forschung und Technologie (BMFT), Grant No. ITR8800K4. We would like to thank S. Bohrer, G. Giefing, H. Janßen, J. Kopecz, E. Schulze, S. Tölg for their contributions to the research and G. Schöner for help with the manuscript.

In the present contribution we briefly survey the system architecture and the neural structure principles and give a short status report on work in progress by highlighting exemplary modules in the general architecture.

2 The system architecure

On the functional side the difficult but important problem is to define a task hierarchy. This task hierarchy will provide a subdivision of the information-processing steps that structures the problem at hand. Therefore a good choice will be crucial to achieve functional complexity by combining and extending "simple" solutions for the individual tasks. Our preliminary proposal for the task hierarchy is as follows:

1. Picture acquisition: capability to acquire visual information, e.g., in terms of gray-scale values, velocity fields, etc.
2. Object perception: definition (if rough) of perceived objects, using the output from the picture acquisition subsystem.
3. Tracking: fixation of a moving object.
4. Fusion: relating the pictures of the two cameras and estimating stereo information.
5. Obstacle avoidance: Identification of obstacles (and estimation of their distance) by a moving observer. Elaboration of a simple 3D model of the environment.
6. Navigation: Planning of a trajectory.

We can further structure the problem in terms of processing steps. In all of the above tasks only four such steps seem to be necessary:

1. Data acquisition
2. Information processing
3. Knowledge coding
4. Action (or behavior)

These steps are, however, closely interconnected as illustrated in the diagram of Figure 1. This will become more evident as we discuss the neuronal structure principles applied in the different steps. These principles are illustrated in a number of examples in the next section.

The data acquisition is dealt with in terms of a stereo-camera system. This is an active sensor system controlled by the output of the information processing subsystem via the action subsystem, thus closing the outer feedback loop. The double camera system has three degrees of freedom and is to be mounted on an autonomous vehicle.

The main emphasis of our work is on the information processing side. Here we use the following elementary neural operations based on the structure of biological neural systems:

1. Two-dimensional laterally coupled nets are used as space-time dependent (or dynamic parametric) filters. (Example below: Fusion)
2. Topographic mappings are used as coordinate transforms. (Example below: Obstacle detection).

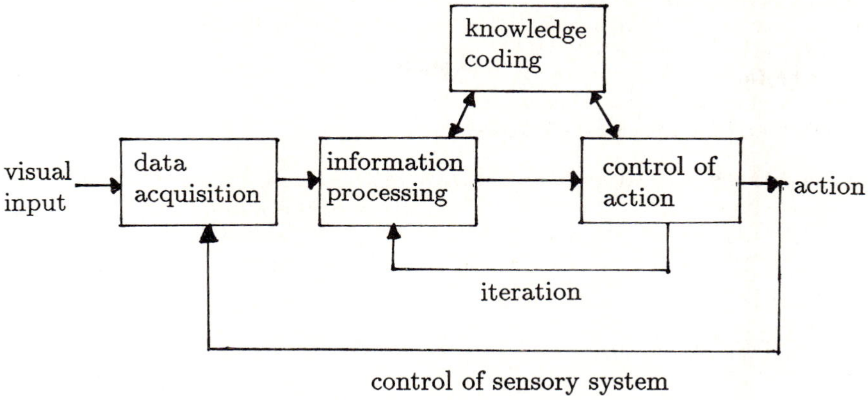

Figure 1: Processing steps of the neural architecture

3. Foveation is used to reduce the space dependent data flow as well as to organize different representations in one layer (Example below: Foveation).

4. Combination of a more than two parameter-representation in a discrete manner in one layer (Example below: Hypercolumns).

5. Regularization enables the use of continuity assumptions in reducing information (Example below: Hypercolumns).

6. Extensive use of feedback for data reduction, iteration and regularisation (all of the examples).

Knowledge coding serves to provide the system with flexibility and makes it possible to build up complexity. We use the following operations to achieve knowledge coding:

1. Adaptive variation of a limited number of simple parameters in different parts of the system. The parameters are, e.g., the thresholds and slopes of the neurons' input-output characteristics, the time constants of synapses, the latencies and amplification factors of feedback loops.

2. Associative memory (see example below).

3. Cascading of associative memories organizes the models that guide behavioral units.

3 Modules of the exploration system

We provide some examples that illustrate our approach and form the modules of the general neural architecture described above.

3.1 The camera system

We have developed a double camera system with three degrees of freedom to be mounted on an autonomous vehicle which will be used as an active sensor system: In the final stage the position of the cameras and their information flow will be controlled by the output layer of the neural system itself. We distinguish three control stages.

1. Control circuits for rotations (in hardware).
2. A system of macro-instructions in a camera related coordinate system for angles, focal length and fusion distance. Velocity control is trainable.
3. Simulation of the entire camera system in world coordinates which can be linked to the information processing system. Such simulation affords composing a trajectory and supervising the whole system.

The restricted aperture of the cameras combined with a possible fovea (see below) reduces the information flow and makes it relatively easy to realize position invariance. The caveat is that the camera system must be at the right position at the right time.

3.2 Fusion

The obvious purpose of a double camera system is to evaluate stereo information. A prerequisite for this is, however, to be able to find the horopter and to achieve fusion of the two images. In principle, this can be done with a stripe-wise representation of the different images in a neural layer and a minimalization of the energy of an appropriate filter. To gain an understanding of this processing in a biologically realistic setting we have modelled the cooperation between the geniculate body (LGN) and the visual cortex, modelled as a system of six layers, each of which is assumed homogenous. Mathematically this formulation leads to an intrego-differential equation that contains nonlinear feedback. The equation can be solved in a number of cases and exhibits a phase diagram containing regions with different types of solutions. In particular, regions with one fixed point, with a limit cycle (due to Hopf bifurcation), and with three fixed points occur. In the latter case, two fixed points are stable, one is unstable. This configuaration can be identified as the correct one, which describes fusion and reproduces a known psychophysical effect in fusion (hysteresis) [2].

3.3 Obstacle avoidance

An exploring system with given mechanical properties must avoid obstacles in its movement path. In a first approach to the problem we may view objects that are elevated over a more or less level ground as obstacles. The task is then to identify such obstacles and determine their position. The input information can be two subsequent pictures of one camera or two pictures of a double camera system. The segmentation of the pictures into ground and obstacle and the determination of obstacle position can be combined by using a special type of mapping [4,6]:

1. Inverse perpective mapping of the two images: the viewing perspective is inverted and mapped onto a defined ground plane.
2. Substraction of the two results of step one.
3. Estimation of a cube containing an area of distortion and providing the position of the obstacle.

3.4 Tracking

In a natural environment moving objects play an important role. For an active exploratory system it is desirable that is should be able to fixate visually on such moving objects. To that end three problems must ultimately be solved:

1. The object that is to be tracked must be roughly defined. In our approach a natural definition can be based on the coherent movement of parts of the visual field.

2. The object must be foveated for more detailed analysis.

3. The trajectory of the object must be estimated in order to incorporate it as a dynamic obstacle.

The first problem is the most fundamental one and has been addressed through the following sequence of operations (cf. Figure 2):

1. Filtering of the images

2. Estimation of a two-dimensional optic flow. The estimate is based on a gradient algorithm that exploits the local curvature of the brightness function.

3. Detection of objects by search for maxima of velocity histograms. Segmentation of objects and determination of their size and position is possible by backprojecting positional data stored in dynamic lists.

3.5 Foveation

A strong compression of visual information is achieved in the visual system by the space-variant resolution and sampling of the retinal image by the ganglion cells. Theoretically this can be understood in terms of retinal receptive fields, retinotopic mapping, and its area magnification factor [3]. As a result of such space-variant sampling the foveated area is particularly well-suited for pattern recognition tasks, while peripheral vision can be used to report temporal changes in the image. The latter can guide saccadic eye-movements [1]. In a new implementation a ganglion cell density can be set and the space-variance of the sampling function is adapted according to the contents of a class of relevant images by Kohonen's algorithm of self-organizing feature maps.

3.6 Hypercolumns

To further reduce visual information with the help of continuity assumptions we make use of a mapping similar to the one found in the hypercolumns of Area 17 of visual cortex. The discrete parameter orientation is mapped into cortical position (i.e., position in a cortical network model), thus producing a two-dimensional data representation that codes orientation and location of a feature into position. In this representation further data processing is possible by simply exploiting local relations of adjacent cells, e.g. as regularization of the vector field. In connection with associative memory, this mapping forms a basis for image recognition.

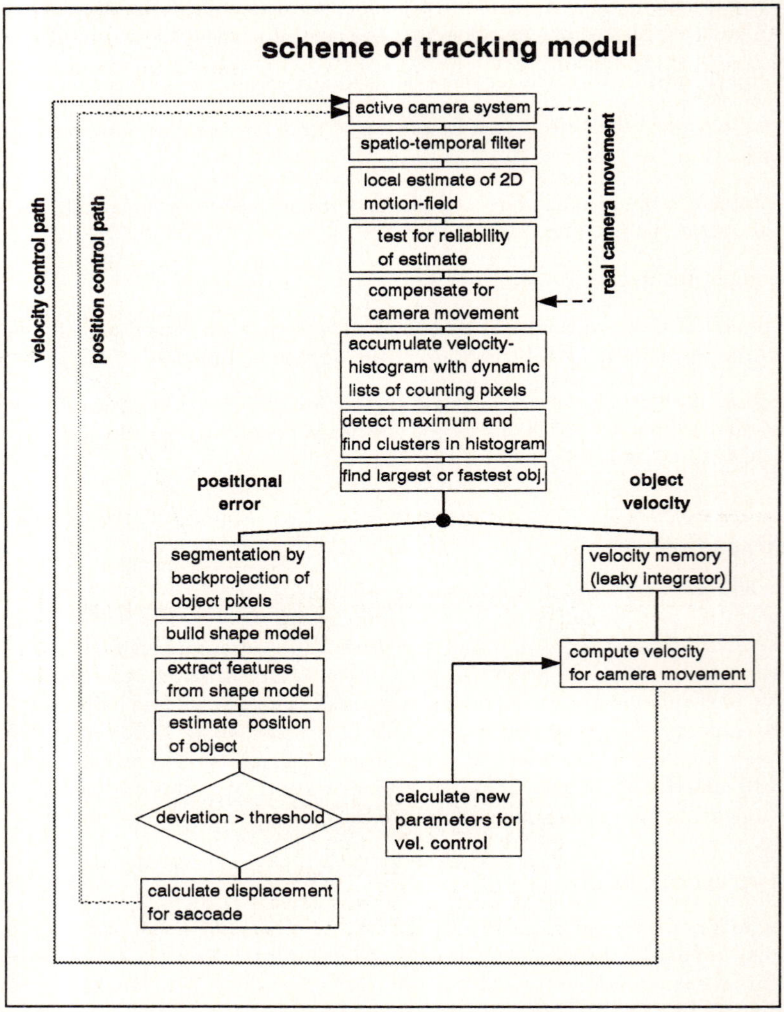

Figure 2: Scheme of the tracking modul

3.7 Associative memory

We use the advantages provided by the discrete representation of features in hypercolumns (see above) to further reduce the data for storage. The redundancy of the hypercolumn representation can be exploited by sparse binary encoding of the visual information through the locally maximal edge orientations (see Figure 3). An implementation of associative memory [5] can be made computationally highly effective in this way. The associative memory in combination with the hypercolumn representation thus performs pattern recognition in a flexible and controllable fashion and provides us with an essential module for more refined object recognition.

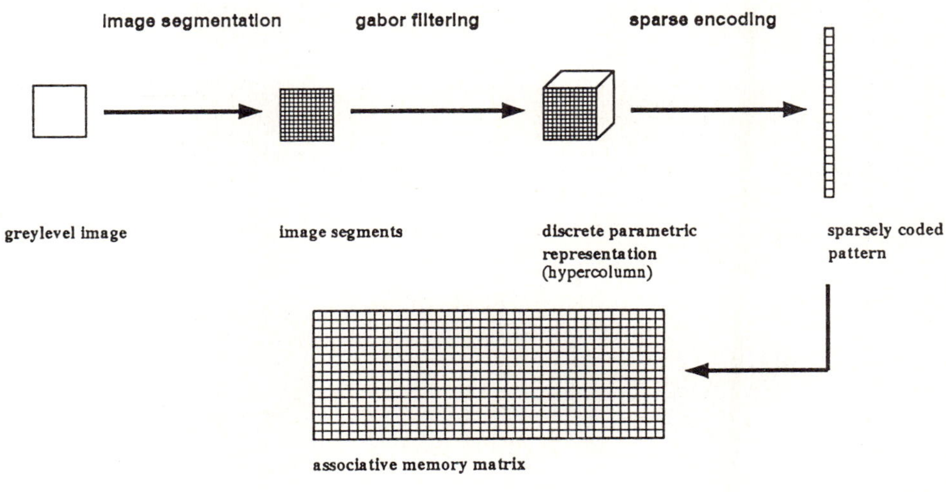

Figure 3: Pattern recognition by associative recall of discrete representations: processing scheme

4 Conclusion

We have outlined a general neural architecture to achieve information processing in the context of the task of exploring a natural environment. As we have shown in a number of examples, each of which represents a module of the global architecture, structural principles of neural organization gleaned from neurophysiology can be combined with the definition of a task hierarchy to solve the well-defined technical problems in a modular fashion.

References

[1] D H Ballard. Eye movements and spatial cognition. *Technical Report TR128, Computer Science Department, University of Rochester*, 1987.

[2] D Heinke, F Giannakopoulos, and J Best. The thalamo-cortical feedback-system: a nonlinear network model for binocular interaction. In R Eckmiller, G Hartmann, and G Hauske, editors, *Parallel Processing in Neural Systems and Computers*, pages 113–116. Elsevier Science Publishers B. V. (North Holland), Amsterdam, 1990.

[3] H A Mallot and G J Giefing. Retinal sampling grids and space-variant image compression. In R Eckmiller, G Hartmann, and G Hauske, editors, *Parallel Processing in Neural Systems and Computers*, pages 125–128. Elsevier Science Publishers B. V. (North Holland), Amsterdam, 1990.

[4] H A Mallot, E Schulze, and K Storjohann. Neural network strategies for robot navigation. In L Personnaz and G Dreyfus, editors, *Neural Networks: from Models to Applications*, pages 560–569. IDSET, Paris, 1989.

[5] G Palm. On associative memory. *Biological Cybernetics*, 36:19–31, 1980.

[6] T Zielke, K Storjohann, H A Mallot, and W von Seelen. Adapting computer vision systems to the visual environment:topographic mapping. In O Faugeras, editor, *Proc. First European Conf. on Computer Vision*. INRIA, 1990.

Advanced Neural Computers / R. Eckmiller (Editor)

MODELING VISUAL CORTEX: HIDDEN ANISOTROPIES IN AN ISOTROPIC INHIBITORY CONNECTION SCHEME

Florentin WÖRGÖTTER[1], Ernst NIEBUR and Christof KOCH[2]

Computation and Neural Systems Program
California Institute of Technology 216-76
Pasadena, CA 91125, USA

A detailed cortex model (15,000 cells) of the adult cat is presented and it is shown that a combination of unspecific inhibitory mechanisms together with input of aligned receptive fields from the LGN with little elongation (1:1.5) is able to reproduce cortical orientation selectivity and other features of cortical cell behavior. We introduce a novel isotropic intracortical connection scheme (*"circular inhibition"*) and demonstrate analytically that this mechanism results in two anisotropies: orientation tuning and a directional bias. Thus, our network shows that structurally unspecific isotropic connections can result in functionally specific behavior. Directional anisotropy introduced in this way could be the starting point for the development of the true direction specificity found in cortical cells.

1. Introduction

Two features are outstanding in cortical architecture: (1) a high degree of uniformity of the connections between cortical cells and (2) a very high sub- and intracortical convergence onto each cortical cell (Martin 1988). Although little anatomical order seems to exist, functional elements (in the visual cortex: orientation columns, ocular dominance columns, etc.) are clearly defined, and cell response characteristics show a high degree of stimulus specificity. Low structural and high functional specificity, however, seem to contradict each other and major efforts have been undertaken to resolve this problem and to establish a link between structure and function (Braitenberg 1985, Martin 1988). Probably the best studied cell property in the visual cortex is the so called *orientation specificity* or *orientation tuning* (Hubel and Wiesel 1962). Cortical cells fire most strongly when they are stimulated with an elongated contrast step (e.g. light bar) within a restricted range of orientations. Many models have been proposed (aligned convergence from the LGN, cross-orientation inhibition, iso-orientation inhibition or excitation, etc.). In fact, there is experimental evidence for all of them. The simplest solution which would resolve the apparent conflict between low structural and high functional specificity and provide an explanation for the different experimental data is to assume that "all" mechanisms exist (Ferster and Koch 1987), that they are rather unspecific, but that the combination of all of them results in the observed functional specificity.

2.1. A Detailed Model of the Visual Cortex - Methods

We model a 5×5 degree patch of the primary visual pathway of cat at a retinal eccentricity of about 4°, including retina, lateral geniculate nucleus (LGN) and layer IV of area 17.

---

[1]Present address: Institut für Neurophysiologie, Ruhr Universität Bochum, 4630 Bochum, FRG

[2]F.W. was supported by the Deutsche Forschungsgemeinschaft grant WO 388-1; E.N. by the Swiss National Science Foundation grant No. 8220-2594. C.K. gratefully acknowledges the support of the Air Force Office of Scientific Research, a NFS Presidential Young Investigator Award, and the James S. McDonnell Foundation.

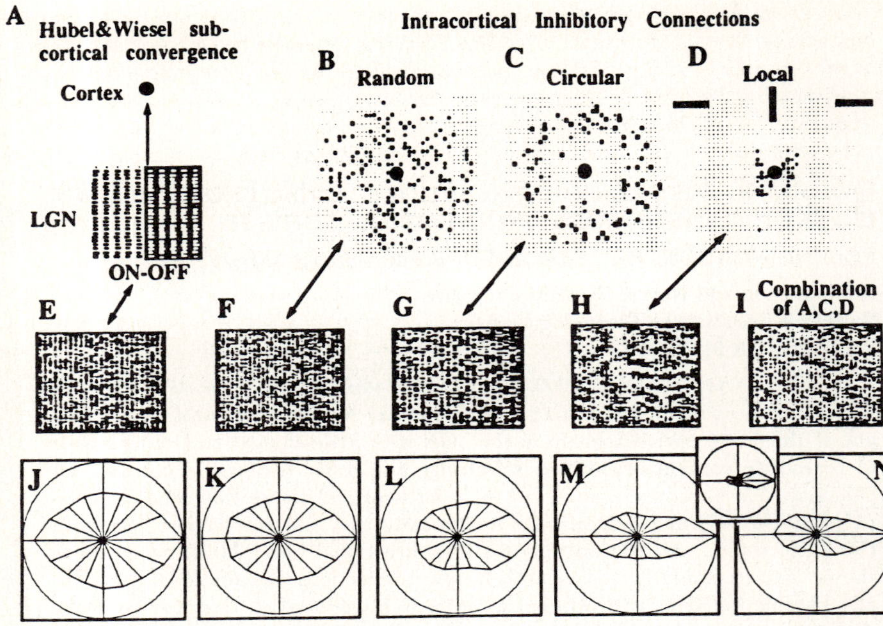

Figure 1: Detailed cortex model.
(A-D) Sub- and intracortical connection patterns. (E-I) Response of the cell population in one hypercolumn. (J-N) Average orientation tuning curves; the inset (unpublished data from Wörgötter and Eysel) shows the average tuning of real cortical simple cells.

Neurons are implemented as improved integrate-and-fire units modeling soma and axon but excluding the dendrites. The model retina is stimulated by light intensity functions that correspond to moving oriented bars. Retinal ON- and OFF-center beta-ganglion cells (n=2048) are implemented on a noisy hexagonal grid. They project with a one-to-four divergence, and preserving the topography, onto 8192 ON- and OFF-center LGN cells. In the cortex, only inhibitory cells were modeled. We implemented 4096 neurons which corresponds to approximately one quarter of all inhibitory cells in the central $2.5° \times 2.5°$ part of the patch. The projection from the LGN to the cortex is approximately linear at the chosen eccentricity and the cortical magnification factor is about 1. Thus, 2.5° roughly correspond to 2.5 mm on the cortical surface, which in turn contain about 2.5 hypercolumns (Albus 1975b). According to the model of Hubel and Wiesel (1962), each cortical cell receives input from LGN cells with receptive fields (RFs) that lie in a rectangle (Fig. 1A). On average, 5x13 LGN cells converge onto one cortical cell which corresponds to an *elongation* of about 1.5. This small elongation results in a weak orientation tuning. The angle of orientation preference continuously changes along the x-axis and was held constant along the y-axis. Thus, orientation columns resemble vertical stripes. The model neurons were implemented with realistic receptive field scatter and jitter in the orientation preferences (Albus 1975). Several inhibitory intracortical mechanisms were implemented, some of which are shown in Fig. 1B-D. The most unspecific inhibitory connections are defined by random wiring (Fig. 1B). In this case, the probability of making a connection with the cell in the center is the same for all cells within a distance of half a hypercolumn, which results in a disk-like structure of connected cells. *Circular inhibition* (Fig. 1C), which we suggest as possible intracortical connection scheme, is more specific.

Only cells whose distance from the center cell is about half a hypercolumn are connected with high probability to the center cell. The resulting structure resembles an annulus. A third scheme is shown in Fig. 1D: local inhibition can be achieved by wiring all cells with similar orientation tuning, but whose receptive fields are displaced laterally, onto the center cell (Heggelund 1981). In this case, the probability of a connection is low very close to the cell in the center and at large distances. Furthermore, this probability is lowered along the long axis of the receptive field. Our model has been implemented on SUN4 workstations; for details of the implementation see Wehmeier *et al.* (1989) and Wörgötter and Koch (1990).

2.2. A Detailed Model of the Visual Cortex - Results

The center row of Fig. 1 (E-I) shows the accumulated activity of all cells within one hypercolumn after stimulation with a moving vertical bar. Little black squares represent single neurons. The size of the squares scales with the total number of spikes elicited during one stimulus sweep. Only for the rightmost panel (Fig. 1I), a realistic separation of the columns containing cells with more horizontal (left side of the panel) or more vertical orientation preference (right) can be seen.

The bottom row (Fig. 1J-N) shows the average orientation tuning achieved using the different mechanisms. Fifty-five cells were averaged after rotating their tuning curves to 0° preferred direction; plotted is the maximal impulse rate against the direction of motion of the stimulus in a polar diagram. The narrower a polar plot, the stronger is the orientation tuning; an effect which is seen to increase with increasing specificity of the mechanism (i.e. from left to right). Only the combination of all mechanisms, however, results in a realistic orientation tuning (Fig. 1N) as compared to the tuning obtained in real cells (inset between Fig. 1M,N). Note that even for the realistical orientation tuning (Fig. 1N) the column structure (Fig. 1I) remains rather fuzzy. This reflects reality. Clearer pictures of orientation columns in the cortex can only be obtained with methods that strongly amplify the columnar organization (e.g. desoxyglucose uptake). Random inhibition served as a control situation to show if a sharpening of orientation tuning can be achieved by a completely unspecific connection scheme. With local inhibition (Fig. 1D), the average orientation tuning is also strong (Fig. 1N). However, as can be seen in the population response (Fig. 1H), the columnar structure is destroyed: quite often cells which originally (i.e. with Hubel and Wiesel convergence alone) had a horizontal orientation preference will turn and now respond best to vertical stimuli. An additional observation is that all studied intracortical mechanisms yield a directional bias which is strongest in circular- and least strong in random inhibition. This effect can easily be explained for local inhibition. Due to the small number of connected cells (≈ 20) it is likely that inhibition from one side exceeds that from the other side, thus resulting in a directional bias. This explanation, however, does not hold for circular inhibition (and random inhibition) because with over 100 connected cells random asymmetries average out.

In the first part of this paper we have demonstrated that a combination of intracortical mechanisms, all of which have only very little connection specificity, results in a realistic average orientation tuning. Two intriguing findings were made:

1) Inhibition which arises isotropically around the target cell (circular inhibition) sharpens the orientation tuning.

2) An unexpected directional bias is obtained with circular inhibition.

The question arises if these effects are specifically generated by the structure of the connections in circular inhibition. The detailed cortex simulation is much too complex to allow a straight-forward analytical description. Therefore, in the next section we will introduce a simpler model that captures all essential features and that yields a better understanding of the results of the simulation.

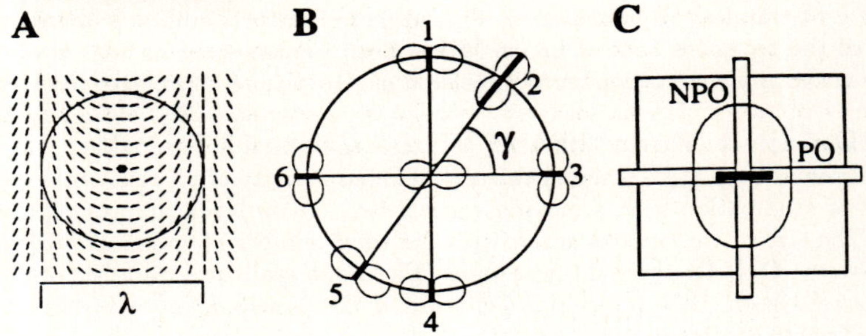

Figure 2: Structurally confined model for *circular inhibition*
(A) Idealized cortical column structure. (B) Computation of the tuning of inhibition. The orientation selective response of the cells (1-6) is given by eq. 2. (C) Average tuning of inhibition. Open bars represent the preferred (PO) and the non-preferred (NPO) stimuli.

3.1. A structurally confined model

We define a coordinate system on the cortical surface such that the y-axis is parallel to the orientation columns (vertical in Fig. 2A). As a consequence, the preferred orientation ϕ of a cell which is located at the point (x, y) is only dependent on x, $\phi = \phi(x)$, with

$$\phi(x) = \frac{\pi}{\lambda}x, \tag{1}$$

where λ is the width of one hypercolumn (Fig. 2A).

Fig. 2B shows the orientation selective response of individual cells (1-6 and center) in the simplified model. The cell activity $\mathcal{A}$ is described as a function of the stimulus angle γ relative to the preferred orientation ϕ of the cell,

$$\mathcal{A}(\gamma - \phi) = A_0 + A_2 \cos(2\gamma - 2\phi). \tag{2}$$

A stimulus bar (δ-function bar) with orientation γ (Fig. 2B) will stimulate two cells on the circle (2 and 5) and elicit responses $\mathcal{A}$ from them as depicted by the thick lines.

In an idealized circular inhibition scheme, a cell receives input from all cells that are located on the circle with radius r around the cell in the center (e.g. cells 1-6 in Fig. 2B). For the columnar structure defined in eq. (1), the total inhibitory input to the cell at the point (x, y) is then:

$$I(x, y) = 2A_0 + A_2 \cos(2\gamma)\cos(2\pi/\lambda r \cos(\gamma + 2\pi/\lambda x)) \tag{3}$$

We were concerned with the question if circular inhibition can specifically sharpen the orientation tuning. The answer is given by the average tuning of inhibition that arises throughout the whole cell population. It is calculated as (J_0 is the Bessel function of order zero):

$$\overline{I(r,\gamma)} = \frac{1}{\lambda}\int_0^\lambda I(x)\,dx = 2A_0 - A_2 J_0(2\pi r/\lambda)\cos(2\gamma), \tag{4}$$

The shape of the average inhibition tuning curve, plotted relative to a horizontal preferred orientation (black RF), is shown in Fig. 2C for $r = \lambda/2$. It is seen that inhibition is considerably more efficient perpendicularly to the preferred orientation (NPO) than along the preferred orientation (PO). This shows that *circular inhibition* does not act unspecifically but *results in a net cross-orientation inhibition effect.* This finding corresponds to experimental evidence indicating that connections contributing to cross-orientation inhibition are predominantly found at a distance of half a hypercolumn (i.e. $\lambda/2$, Matsubara *et al.* 1985).

It must be emphasized that the non-locality of the intracortical connections is essential for obtaining a net cross-orientation inhibition effect. It can be seen from eq. (4) that iso-orientation effects are obtained for $r \rightarrow 0$. Consequentially, no appreciable cross-orientation inhibition is obtained if both local and non-local interactions are taken into account by adding inhibitory inputs from within a *disc* (i.e. "random inhibition", Fig. 1B).

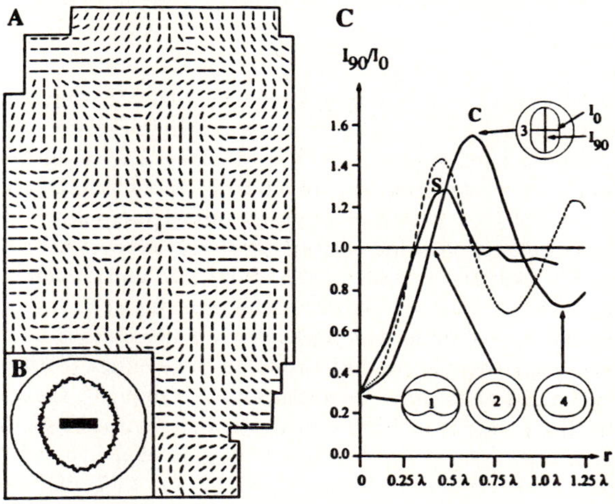

Figure 3: The effect of circular inhibition in a real cortical column structure
(A) Column structure of cat area 18 (mod. from Swindale *et al.* (1987)). (B) Average tuning of circular inhibition for $r = \lambda/2$. (C) Ratio of the two major axes of the tuning curves for different radii r. The insets show examples of tuning curves. Curve C and the dashed curve were obtained from the artificial cortices; curve S was determined from the real cortex in (A).

3.2. Circular inhibition in a real cortex

The analytical results obtained in an artificial vertical column structure are supported by results from real cortical orientation columns. Swindale *et al.* (1987) measured and analyzed a part of the column structure of area 18 in cat (Fig. 3A) and found a mean distance between hypercolumns of $\lambda = 1.25$ mm. For this cortex structure, we have determined the inhibitory input produced by circular inhibition as a function of the circle radius r,by averaging over all cells whose distance from all borders of the cortex is at least r. Most efficient circular inhibition is obtained at a radius of half a hypercolumn ($r = \lambda/2$, Fig. 3B).

Depending on the radius r of circular inhibition, tuning curves can have a vertical or horizontal elongation (insets in Fig 3C). The ratio of I_{90}/I_0 (inset 3) as a function of r gives an indication of the actual shape. Values above 1 indicate vertical elongation of the tuning curve and, thus, a net cross-orientation effect (inset 3); values below 1 show horizontal elongation, i.e. iso-orientation interactions (insets 1 and 4). The curve obtained by the analytical calculations in the previous section (curve C) reproduces most features of the curve obtained from the experimental data (curve S), except for a shift of its maximum. This shift is due to the parallel and straight column structure (see Fig. 2A) which was used for the model calculations. Implementing more realistically curved columns (see Wörgötter *et al.*, 1990) will result in identical locations for the maxima of both curves (dashed curve). This can only be demonstrated numerically, because we were not able to find an analytical expression for the integral (analog to eq. 4) for the average tuning. The tuning curve at the maximum (Fig. 3C, inset 3) is essentially identical to the tuning observed in the real cortex (Fig. 3B). Iso-orientation interactions are obtained for small radii (inset 1), as expected from eq. (4). At the distance of about a full hypercolumn ($r \approx \lambda$), a second minimum is obtained; i.e. another iso-orientation effect occurs (inset 4). In the real cortex (curve S), no clear tuning is observed for distances $r > 0.75\lambda$. This, however, is probably due to the small number of cells (n=59 for $r = \lambda$) over which averaging could be performed to avoid border effects at this large radius. The results from a real cortex confirm the observations we made for our artificial cortices.

4. Directional bias

So far we discussed the effect elicited by a δ-function flashing bar. To demonstrate the effects elicited by motion we discuss the tangential bar position shown in Fig. 4A. The corresponding tuning curve for this individual cell is plotted in Fig. 4B. Identical inhibition is obtained for movement from bottom to top and from top to bottom, provided the movement follows exactly this axis (Fig. 4A; 1,5). This, however, is an unstable equilibrium point and any deviation from this axis results in growing asymmetries. In real cortical cells the preferred orientation of a cell varies from trial to trial within about $\pm 5°$ and, in addition, orientation columns contain a jitter of $\pm 10°$. Both effects result in a breaking of the symmetry along this axis. This can be simulated by assuming that the actual inhibition along any axis of stimulus motion is not obtained from a single point but rather as the average of all inhibition-values within an angle around the axis of motion. Assuming an angle of $\pm 15°$, the average inhibition for the whole cell population results in a tuning curve as shown in Fig. 4C. Note that the amount of inhibition is plotted against the *direction* of motion of the bar which is orthogonal to its orientation. Thus, the tuning curve is rotated by 90° as compared to the tuning curve in Fig. 2C and still represents the same preferred and non-preferred orientations (PO, NPO). The average asymmetry between the preferred and non-preferred *direction* (PD,NPD) is significant and would result in a direction index (for a definition see Orban 1984) of 24% which is similar to direction indices observed in the detailed cortex simulation.

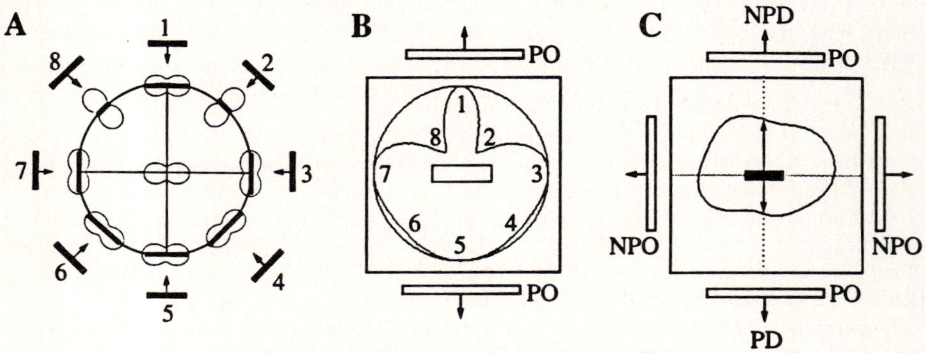

Figure 4: Generation of a directional bias.
(A) Snap-shots of a bar moving across the cortical column structure. (B) Computation of direction tuning. (C) Tuning curve for an individual cell. (D) Average tuning of inhibition for the whole cell population.

5. Discussion

Two major points have been shown in this paper.

1) A combination of very low specificity mechanism can generate cortical orientation tuning.

2) Isotropically arranged connections result in anisotropic behavior.

(1) There is substantial (but controversial) experimental evidence for a multitude of intracortical mechanisms. It is, therefore, plausible to conclude that *all* those mechanisms do in fact exist. In addition, many experimentally observed effects which support any of the discussed mechanisms are rather weak or cannot be observed in all cells. This favors the view that none of the mechanisms is highly specific. This argument is supported by the low anatomical order in the cortex that can be consistent with low-specificity connection schemes. For these reasons, the combination of low specificity mechanisms in our model might in fact reflect reality. At least, our model shows that it is possible to obtain high functional specificity with low structural specificity.

The model itself, although already quite detailed, is certainly oversimplifying the actual cortical layout. Many important features are missing (e.g. all intracortical excitatory connections), but we believe that this stage represents a valid step with interesting results in the ongoing "evolution" of this model.

(2) Circular inhibition is advantageous from a developmental point of view because only distance information is required for the connections. In addition, we expected that some kind of anisotropic behavior would be generated by this mechanism because of the periodic orientation column structure in the cortex. Consequently, we found that a net cross-orientation inhibition effect was obtained for a radius of about half a hypercolumn. The average effect is similar to that observed experimentally (Bonds 1989). The structurally confined model proved that these results are generic for circular inhibition. The change in the net effect (i.e. cross- vs. iso-) of circular connections with changing radius (Fig. 3C) is reflected in the discussions among experimental investigators about the importance of iso- vs. cross-orientation inhibition (Blakemore and Tobin 1972, Benevento *et al.* 1972, for a review see Martin 1988). Our model suggests that both effects might be mediated by the same mechanism.

The most intriguing result was the generation of a directional bias with circular inhibition. The structural model indicated that this effect is due to the different degrees of inhibition elicited along different axes of motion. Stochastic processes (e.g. jitter in the preferred orientation) will break the unstable symmetry along the preferred axis of motion and result in a directional bias.

References

Albus, K. (1975) Exp. Brain Res. *24*: 159-179 and 181-202.

Benevento, L. A., O. D. Creutzfeldt, and U. Kuhnt (1972) Nature *238*: 124-126.

Blakemore, C., and E. A. Tobin (1972) Exp. Brain Res. *15*: 439-440.

Bonds, A. B. (1989) Vis. Neurosci. *2*: 41-55.

Braitenberg, V. (1985) Charting the visual cortex. In *Cerebral Cortex, Vol. 3*, A. Peters and E. G. Jones, eds., pp. 379-414, Plenum Press, New York, London.

Ferster, D. and Koch, C. (1987) TINS, *10*: 487-492.

Heggelund, P. (1981) Exp. Brain Res. *42*: 89-98.

Hubel, D. H., and T. N. Wiesel (1962) J. Physiol. *160*: 106-154.

Martin, K. A. C. (1988) Quart. J. Exp. Physiol. *73*: 637-702.

Matsubara, J., M. Cynader, N. V. Swindale, and M. P. Stryker (1985) Proc. Natl. Acad. Sci. USA *82*: 935-939.

Orban, G. A. (1984) Neuronal operations in the visual cortex. In *Studies of Brain Function*, Springer, Berlin.

Swindale, N. V., J. A. Matsubara, and M. S. Cynader (1987) J. Neurosci 7: 1414-1427.

Wehmeier, U, Dong, D., Koch, C. and Van Essen, D. Modeling the visual system. In: *Methods in neuronal modeling*, Koch, C. and Segev, I. eds., pp 335-359, MIT Press, Cambridge.

Wörgötter, F. and Koch, C. (1990) Modeling visual cortex. Submitted.

Wörgötter, F., Niebur, E. and Koch, C. (1990) Neurocarpets: Isotropic connections generate functional asymmetrical behavior in visual cortical cells. Submitted.

Section 3
Theory of
Artificial Neural Networks

Advanced Neural Computers / R. Eckmiller (Editor)

THE LOGIC OF NEURAL COGNITION

Igor ALEKSANDER
Department of Electrical Engineering
Imperial College, London, UK.

Helen MORTON
Department of Human Sciences
Brunel University, Uxbridge, UK.

This speculative paper considers the layering that is required between the sensory and the motor if a neural system is to perform cognitive tasks. A general, hierarchical architecture is proposed. The relationship between levels of abstraction and loosely coupled auto-associative layers is considered. The way in which such a system may carry out simple planning tasks is also discussed. Throughout the paper, awareness of efficient implementation methods is maintained.

1. INTRODUCTION

A useful model of cognitive motor-sensory tasks is that well-trodden concern of AI workers in the 1970s that centered on "blocksworld" notions (as in Winograd [1]). This had the features of linguistic interaction related to a simplified "blocksworld" scene and the planning that had to be done once the input in natural language was "understood". The enterprise was not successful largely because the methodology of semantic extraction based on language parsing lacked the ability to create contexts and relate to them. Although this deficiency was later tackled by Schank and Abelson [2], who used the concept of "scripts", the feasibility of following natural language through rapid changes within a large set of scripts never appeared to be feasible in real time. More recently, Sharkey [3] has argued that neural nets could provide precisely the right medium for holding script-like schemata and, if built as hardware, might follow conversations in real time . In this paper we briefly revisit, in a speculative way, the three elements that are needed to complete the cognitive act of *understanding a naturally spoken statement* about a constrained *visual world* and *planning an action* as a result. We provide examples that may guide the design of general neural computers which exploit not only the capability of neural mechanisms, but combine this with low-level signal processing and high-level rule-based reasoning.

2. A COGNITIVE ARCHITECTURE

In a cognitive task there are three major requirements:

a) The translation of sensory signals into reliable symbols.
b) The extraction of semantic information from the symbols found in (a).
c) Reasoning and planning based on extracted semantics, leading to outward actions.

In a general-purpose architecture it is important to have sections that can be configured by the system developer to suit particular tasks. These are shown in fig. 1 and are partitioned as follows to meet the above requirements:

a sensory neural level,
a cognitive neural level,
and a conventional computing level.

Peripheral connections are made to appropriate video cameras, microphones and other electronic sensors on the input side. On the output side the system may have the ability to connect to robot arms, voice synthesizers, graphics screens and so on. The conventional computing level of the system would have provision for conventional communication with the user: keyboard, mouse, display screen and the like.

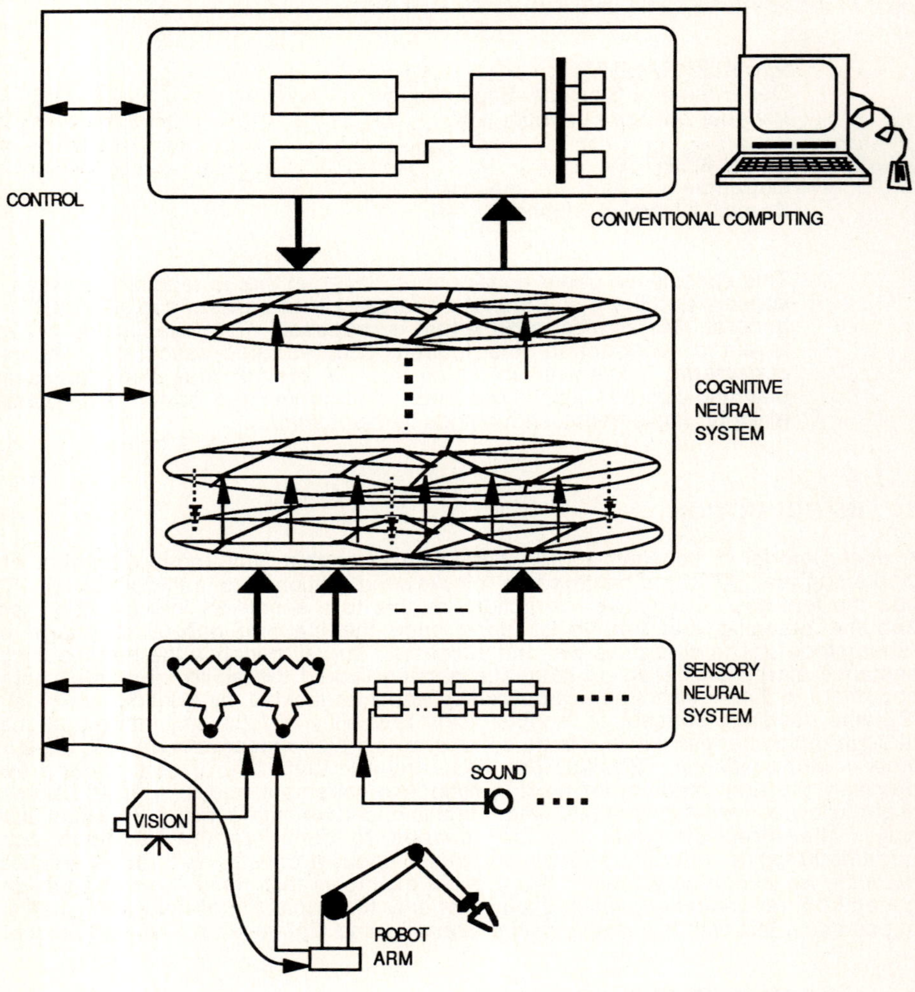

Figure 1: A general architecture, incorporating neural nets.

3. THE SENSORY NEURAL LEVEL

This is relatively well researched territory. The work of Marr [4] is relevant as far as his first three computing layers are concerned (signal capture, primal sketch, 2 1/2 D sketch). On the other hand, 3D modelling must involve learned knowledge. This does not enter Marr's considerations and must therefore be revisited as a task for the cognitive neural layer. Clearly the work of Carver Mead [5] has shown that the neural paradigm maps into silicon to achieve requirement (a) as stated above.

It should also be stressed that if the design of competent machinery is at stake, the sensory level may be achieved by the use of classical signal processing techniques (perhaps implemented in hardware, for speed). There is no point in evoking the neural when other techniques are more competent. For example, Hough transforms satisfy some of requirement (a) without having a neural basis.

4. THE COGNITIVE PROCESSING LEVEL

The major challenge for neural computer designers is the ability to coordinate various neural processes each of which is known to be feasible. We illustrate this with some specific tasks (which are described as challenges rather than recipes for a solution).

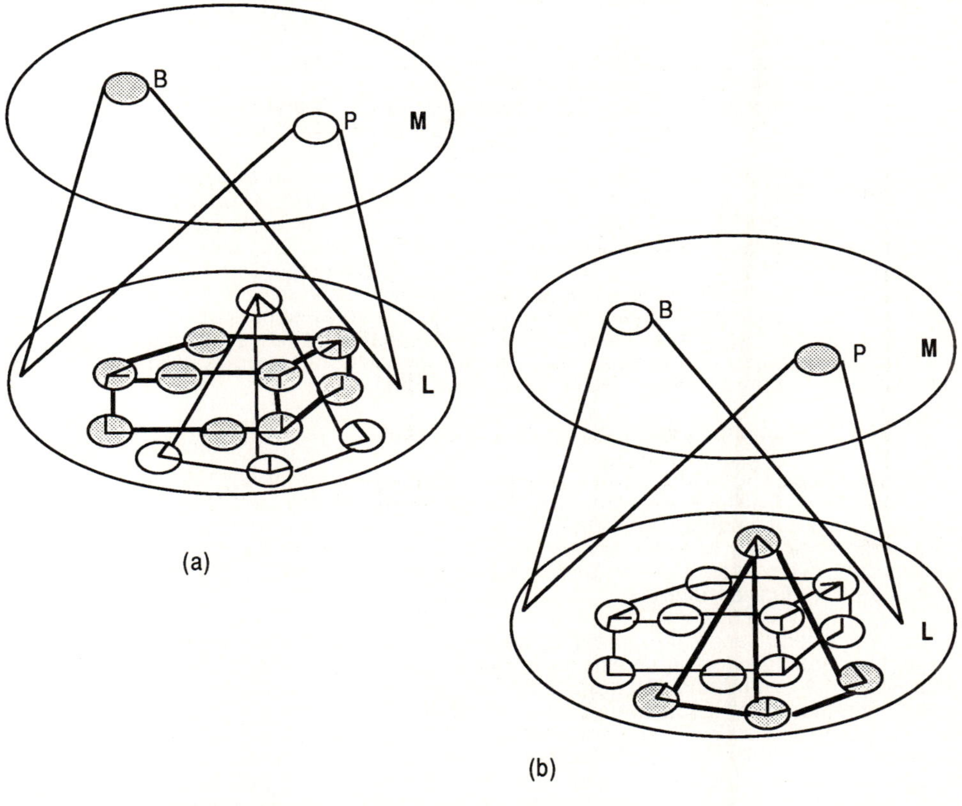

Figure 2: Schemata for the recognition of image features

4.1 Is It a Box?

The cognitive layer is responsible for taking the line features produced by a sensory layer and exclaiming: "it's a box". Here we show that this cognitive task may be broken down into a simple task for two of the cognitive layers in fig. 1. First, it is assumed that the sensory layer will extract the edges of the image and activated units in the cognitive layer irrespectively of irrelevant detail in the input image (e.g. lighting, noise). Then, as shown in fig. 2, part of the cognitive net needs to perform a pattern completion exercise. The features of the image activate a box-like schema at some layer L in the cognitive neural system (fig. 2(a)). Other arrangements of features may activate a pyramid-like schema in the same layer (fig 2(b)). The stable "box" schema in (a) leads to a localised identification at some B-neuron in a higher layer (M) while another recognition (of the pyramid, say) may lead to the activation of some P-neuron in layer M. It now remains to be said how such a recognition can be turned into an answer to the spoken phrase "What do you see?".

At the lower levels of cognitive processing, it is clear that several recognition activities must be going on in parallel. Such activities are related to the different senses: while part of the neural circuitry decodes what the eye "sees" as in fig. 2, another must be devoted to the extraction of meaning from what the ear "hears". That is, the elements "what", "you" and "see" must form a stable schema at one layer which, at a higher layer, is interpreted by the activation of one (or a few) units as "introspective description (voiced sequence) required on the vision side of the net".

In such a layer within the net, other localised representations may be:
"introspective description required on the auditory (tactile, ..) side"
"movement required of the robot arm to coordinates x,y, z"
"voice utterance required in response to state of vision side of the net"
etc. ... .

In a living organism, this process of localised interpretation in a higher net of a stable schema in a lower net must eventually lead to the appropriate actions in the organism. (Note: some of the "actions" could be internal, such as "thinking about an event"). In a man-made machine, however, there comes a point at which conventional processes of computation is triggered off by the state of the neural net. For example, the state "introspective description (voiced sequence) required on the vision side of the net" is a clear instruction for a conventional computer and a voice synthesizer. The machine would "address" the upper vision layer, discover that "box" is activated, interpret "introspective description required" as an instruction to output, via the voice synthesizer, the phrase "it's a <content of vision layer>".

4.2 "To get to Covent Garden, change at Green Park."

Sharkey [3] has suggested neural schemes for generating an appropriate description of a sequence of actions under the control of a stable schema (e.g. the actions required by the schema of catching a train). This is an example of "temporal neural processing": it requires a memory of sequences of events and the actions that would change such sequences. This aspect of neural computing is still very much in its infancy, and is a fruitful area for further research.

In a more general sense, temporal processing includes the ability of living neural systems to enable living organisms to predict sequences of events on the basis of past experience. A central and general question is how sequences of actions leading to given outcomes (like" If you change to the eastbound Piccadilly line at Green Park you will first get to Piccadilly Circus and then Covent Garden") are learnt and recalled by humans. Such ability to predict events on the basis of past experience is the focus of some psychological theories of personality (different people have different experiences and hence different personalities) and the behaviour of individuals (behaviour being dictated by the prediction of future events from individual knowledge as in Kelly, 1955). The accurate prediction of events is crucial not only in order to find one's way around the London Undrground, but generally, it underlies the ability of individuals to survive.

To illustrate what may be needed, we continue with the example of the underground journey. Consider part of the London Underground Map shown in fig. 3.

Say that a fully interconnected layer in a cognitive net is capable of learning a sequence of states by "being " in a state, and being trained to change to the next. These states could be names of underground stations. So if the state of the net is P, it could learn that the next state will be C, in the sense that if the net is clamped to P and released, it will change to C. However, a characteristic of such a layer is that one state can only lead to another specific state. Therefore merely labelling states as stations would lead to confusion as there are many states that can follow G, in our example - something else is also needed.

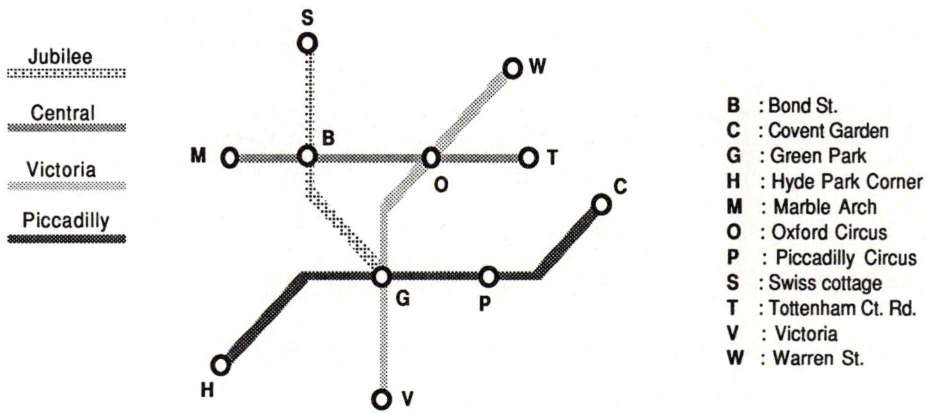

Figure 3: A simplified map of the London Underground.

Clearly, the net has to store context as a "state" (e.g. "I am on the Victoria line at O and I am trying to get to C") to determine the next state which should be "I am at G changing to the Piccadilly line towards P". The way in which these sequences are **learnt by exploration** rather than the memorization of a map is one of the open questions in neural computing. That is, the problem is not how such knowledge may be represented in neural nets (Sharkey and others provide sensible suggestions for that), but how this knowledge could get there, particularly through exploration. The challenge therefore is for a neural net to gather sufficient experience to be able to answer questions such as "How do I get from Victoria to Covent Garden?". One way of proceeding is to learn **backwards from goals** (as is postulated for explanations of animal learning) and to let the **goals** be the **context** for neural schemata.

At the early stages of learning the organism would learn single steps such as:
"If I am at Piccadilly Circus (P) and am going East on the Piccadilly line I get to Covent garden (C) next". The layer of the cognitive neural net would represent this as :

	CONTEXT/GOAL	:	PLACE /ACTION	
	C	:	P	East on Piccadilly
leads to	C	:	C	Goal achieved

At some later time in learning the state transition that needs to be learned is :

	CONTEXT/GOAL	:	PLACE /ACTION	
	C	:	G	East on Piccadilly
leads to	C	:	P	East on Piccadilly

Continuing in this way, the following state transitions could be learned:

	CONTEXT/GOAL	:	PLACE /ACTION	
	C	:	V	Initial state
leads to	C	:	V	North on Victoria
leads to	C	:	G	North on Victoria
leads to	C	:	G	Change to East on Piccadilly
leads to	C	:	G	East on Piccadilly
leads to	C	:	P	East on Piccadilly
leads to	C	:	C	Goal achieved

In other words, it is crucial that the learning should be done in the context of goals. So in the context of going to Swiss Cottage (S), instead of Covent Garden

leads to C : G Change to East on Piccadilly

we would have

leads to S : G Change North on Jubilee

which gets around the ambiguity surrounding G.

Research still needs to be done on mechanisms that lead to such learning.

5. IMPLEMENTATION ISSUES AND CONCLUSIONS.

What has been described above is the initial framework of a current research programme at Imperial College (Govt. Grant IED 1005) . This is focused on the cognitive section of the proposed architecture and its control through conventional computing techniques. The first major question is the implementation medium. This will be tackled by the use of notional weightless methods (Aleksander and Morton [7],[8]) and use memory partitioning for the low-level design (Aleksander and Morton [9]). Also, the concept of a G-Ram (Aleksander [10]) has been added to candidates for VLSI implementation.

It seems clear that if neural computing is to provide the engines that supply the cognitive competence in scene and language understanding that has eluded rule-based AI methods, a layered system is required. The layers are ordered to represent different levels of abstraction. Each layer has autoassociative properties not only for the completion of static patterns but also for the association of sequences in one part of the layer with static context in another (as in the Underground planning example shown in this paper).

Given a general-purpose architecture as described here a great deal of work needs to be done on determining the degree of reconfiguration that needs to be made available to the system developer, and what facilities can be handed to the end user.

REFERENCES

[1] Winograd, T. , Understanding Natural Language (Academic Press, New York , 1972).

[2] Schank, R. C. & Abelson, R. P., Scripts, Plans, Goals and Understanding, (Erlbaum, Hillsdale N.J. ,1977),

[3] Sharkey, N. E. , A PDP learning approach to natural language, in: Aleksander, I. (ed.), Neural Computing Architectures, (MIT press, Boston, 1989).

[4] Marr, D. , Vision, (Freeman, New York, 1982).

[5] Mead, C. , Analog VLSI Neural Systems, (Addison Wesley, New York,1989).

[6] Kelly, G. (1955):

[7] Aleksander, I. and Morton, H. B., An Overview of Weightless Neural Systems, Proc. IJNNC90, (Washington, 1990)

[8] Aleksander, I. and Morton, H. B., An Introduction to Neural Computing, (Chapman and Hall, 1990), Chapter 10

[9] ditto, (Chapter 5)

[10] Aleksander, I., Ideal Neurons for Neural Computers, Proc. ICNC (Dusseldorf,1990).

Advanced Neural Computers / R. Eckmiller (Editor)
Elsevier Science Publishers B.V. (North-Holland), 1990

Non-Lipschitzian Neural Dynamics

Jacob Barhen[+,*], Michail Zak[+], and Nikzad Toomarian[+]

[+]Jet Propulsion Laboratory
and
[*]Division of Engineering & Applied Science
California Institute of Technology
Pasadena, CA 91109

ABSTRACT

The thrust of this paper is to present a new class of dynamical systems for neural computation. Our approach is motivated by an attempt to remove one of the most fundamental limitations of artificial neural networks — their rigid behavior compared with even the simplest biological systems. It exploits the concept of terminal attractors and repellers. We demonstrate that non-Lipschitzian dynamics, based upon the failure of the Lipschitz condition at repellers, exhibits a new qualitative effect — a multi-choice response to periodic external excitations. This property enables the construction of a substantially new class of dynamical systems — the unpredictable systems, represented in the form of coupled activation and learning dynamical equations, which exhibit two pathological characteristics. Firstly, such systems have zero Jacobian. As a result of that, they have an infinite number of equilibrium points which occupy curves, surfaces or hypersurfaces. Secondly, at all these equilibrium points the Lipschitz condition fails, so the equilibrium points become terminal attractors or repellers depending upon the sign of the periodic excitation. Both of these pathological characteristics result in multi-choice responses and lead to unpredictability. We show that the unpredictable systems can be controlled by sign strings, which uniquely define the systems behavior by specifying the direction of the motions at the critical points. By changing the combinations of signs in the code strings a system can reproduce any prescribed behavior to a prescribed accuracy. That is why such unpredictable systems driven by sign strings are extremely flexible and can be exploited as a powerful tool for complex pattern recognition.

1. Introduction

The biggest promise of artificial neural networks as computational tools lies in the hope that they will ultimately enable complex information processing, comparable in sophistication to that carried out by biological systems. Notwithstanding many successes in this direction, it is rapidly becoming evident that current models are characterized by a number of severe limitations. We will analyze these limitations using the Cohen-Grossberg-Hopfiled (CGH) additive model [1,2] as a typical representative of artificial neural networks:

$$\dot{u}_i + u_i = \sum_{j=1}^{N} T_{ij} g(u_j) + I_i, \quad i = 1, 2 \ldots N \tag{1}$$

in which $u_i(t)$ is the mean soma potential of the ith neuron, T_{ij} are constant synaptic interconnections, $g(u)$ represents a sigmoid function, and I_i denotes an external input.

Firstly, the neurons performance in this model is collective, but not parallel: any small change in the activity of any neuron instantaneously effects all other neurons:

$$\frac{\partial \dot{u}_i}{\partial u_j} = \frac{dg_j}{du_j} T_{ij} \neq 0 \qquad i \neq j \tag{2}$$

In contrast to that, biological systems exhibit both collective and parallel performances. For instance, the right and the left hands are mechanically independent (i.e., their performance is parallel), but at the same time their activity is coordinated by the brain; that makes their performance collective.

Secondly, the performance of the model (1) is fully prescribed by the initial conditions. The system never "forgets" these conditions: it carries their "burden" up to $t \to \infty$. In order to change the system performance, the external input must overpower the "inertia of the past". In contrast to that, biological systems are much more flexible: they can forget (if necessary) the past, adapting their behavior to environmental changes.

Thirdly, the features characterizing the system (1) involve a single scale: they are thereby insulated from the real world where a large range of scales coexist. In contradistinction, biological systems involve mechanisms that span the entire range from the molecular to the macroscopic.[3,4]

Can these limitations be removed within the framework of classical neurodynamics? The answer is probably no. Indeed, neural systems considered heretofore are based on classical dynamics and satisfy the Lipschitz condition, which guarantees the uniqueness of the solutions subject to prescribed sets of initial conditions. For the system (1) this condition requires that all the derivatives $\partial \dot{u}_i / \partial u_j$ be bounded:

$$\left| \frac{\partial \dot{u}_i}{\partial u_j} \right| < \infty \tag{3}$$

The uniqueness of the solution

$$u_i = u_i(t, \overset{\circ}{u}_1, \ldots \overset{\circ}{u}_N), \quad i = 1, 2, \ldots N \tag{4}$$

subject to the initial conditions $\overset{\circ}{u}_i$ ($i = 1, 2, \ldots N$) can be considered as a mathematical interpretation of rigid, predictable behavior of the corresponding neural system.

Actually, limitations of the current network models mentioned above are inevitable consequences of the Lipschitz condition (3). In this paper we will discuss a new paradigm for neural nets which is free of these limitations. Our architecture is based upon some properties of non-Lipschitzian dynamics introduced in [5–7]. If the Lipschitz condition (3) fails at certain critical points of phase-space, the neural net forgets its past as soon as it approaches these points. In addition to that, it acquires the ability to be activated not only by external inputs but also by internal periodic rhythms. Such a spontaneous activity resembles the brain activity. Due to the existence of the critical points mentioned above, the neural network becomes a weakly coupled dynamical system. Its neurons (or groups of neurons) are uncoupled (and therefore, can perform parallel tasks) within the periods between critical points, while the coordination between the independent units (i.e., the collective part of the performance) is carried out at the critical points at which the neural network is fully coupled. Any infinitesimal input applied at a critical point causes a finite response of the neural network. This property appears to be an important tool for creating a chain of coupled subsystems having different scales, and whose range is theoretically unlimited. Sophisticated versions of such a neural network architecture were introduced in [8]: there the activation and learning dynamics are coupled in a way enabling the system to spontaneously change the locations and types of its attractors.

2. Unpredictable Neural Nets

Can a man-made dynamical system create new information? The answer to this question would hopfully contribute to better understanding the evolution of intelligence. So far, man-made systems such as artificial neural networks can only process information: they can learn by examples, they can memorize and recognize patterns, etc. But all these performances are fully predictable since they are prescribed in advance by the original dynamical structure.

In this section we will introduce a new paradigm for dynamical systems which enables them to acquire a large number of different structures without a specific interference from the outside: driven by a vanishingly small noise, identical dynamical systems exhibit significantly different patterns of behavior. In other words, these systems may extract information from "nothing".

Let us start with the following one-neuron dynamical system:

$$\dot{u} = \gamma \sin^{1/3} \frac{\omega}{\alpha} u \sin \omega t, \gamma = \text{ Const}, \omega = \text{ Const}, \alpha = \text{ Const}. \tag{5}$$

It is easily verifiable that at the equilibrium points

$$u_k = \frac{\pi k \alpha}{\omega} \qquad k = \ldots, -2, -1, 0, 1, 2 \ldots, \text{etc.} \tag{6}$$

the Lipschitz condition is violated:

$$|\partial \dot{u}/\partial u| \to \infty \text{ at } u \to u_k \tag{7}$$

If $u = 0$ at $t = 0$, then during the first period

$$0 < t < \frac{\pi}{\omega} \tag{8}$$

the point $u_o = 0$ is a terminal repeller since $\sin \omega t > 0$, and the solution at this point splits into two (positive and negative) branches whose divergence is characterized by an unbounded Lyapunov exponent[8]. Consequently, with an equal probability u can move into the positive or the negative direction. For the sake of concreteness, we will assume that it moves in the positive direction. Then the solution will approach the second equilibrium point $u_1 = \pi\alpha/\omega$ at

$$t^* = \frac{1}{\omega} \arccos \left[1 - \frac{B(\frac{1}{3}, \frac{1}{3})}{2^{1/3}} \frac{\alpha}{\gamma} \right] \tag{9}$$

in which B is the Beta function.

It is easy to verify that the point u_1 will be a terminal attractor [5] at $t = t^*$ if

$$t^* \leq \pi/\omega, \text{ i.e., if } \frac{\gamma}{\alpha} \leq \frac{B(\frac{1}{3}, \frac{1}{3})}{2^{4/3}} \tag{10}$$

Therefore, u will remain at the point u_1 until it becomes a terminal repeller, i.e., until $t > t_1$. Then the solution splits again: one of two possible branches approach the next equilibrium point $u_2 = 2\pi\alpha/\omega$, while the other returns to the point $u_o = 0$, etc. The periods of transition from one equilibrium point to another are all the same, are given by Eq. (9) and are shown in Fig. 1.

It is important to notice that these periods t^* are bounded only because of the failure of the Lipschitz condition at the equilibrium points. Otherwise they would be unbounded since the time of approaching a regular attractor (as well as the time of escaping a regular repeller) is infinite.[5–7]

Thus, the evolution of u prescribed by Eq. (5) is totally unpredictable: it has 2^m different scenarios where $m = E(t/t^*)$, and E denote the integer function. This is illustrated in Fig. 2.

Let us assume that the dynamical system (5) is driven by a vanishingly small noise $\varepsilon(t)$:

$$\dot{u} = \gamma \sin^{1/3} \frac{\omega}{\alpha} u \sin \omega t + \varepsilon(t), \quad |\varepsilon(t)| \ll \gamma \tag{11}$$

This noise can be ignored when $\dot{u} \neq 0$, or when $\dot{u} = 0$, but the system is stable. However, it becomes significant during the instants of instability.

Since actually a vanishingly small noise is always present, one can interpret the unpredictability discussed above as a consequence of small random inputs to which the one-neuron dynamical system (11) is extremely sensitive.

Despite the fact that the system (11) is characterized by unpredictable behavior, the locations of its critical points — terminal attractors and repellers — are prescribed in advance. Indeed, the coordinates of these points are given by Eq. (6). However, one can remove this limitation by introducing the following one-neuron-one-synapsis dynamical system[8]:

$$\dot{u} = \sin^{1/3} \alpha_o T u \sin \omega t + \varepsilon(t) \tag{12}$$

$$\dot{T} = \sin^{1/3} \alpha_o T u \sin \omega t + \eta(t) \tag{13}$$

$$\alpha_o = \text{ const } ; \varepsilon(t) \to 0, \eta(t) \to 0$$

which represents coupled activation and learning, while ε and η denote a vanishingly small noise. The system (12), (13) possesses two pathological properties.

Firstly, it has zero Jacobian:

$$J = \begin{vmatrix} \partial\dot{u}/\partial u & \partial u/\partial T \\ \partial\dot{T}/\partial u & \partial\dot{T}/\partial T \end{vmatrix} = 0 \tag{14}$$

This results in an infinite number of equilibrium points which occupy a family of hyperbolas in the configuration space u, T:

$$T_k u_k = \frac{\pi k}{\alpha_o}, \quad k = \ldots -2, -1, 0, 1, 2, \ldots \text{etc.} \tag{15}$$

Secondly, at all the equilibrium points, the Lipschitz condition fails since:

$$\left|\frac{\partial \dot{u}}{\partial u}\right| \rightarrow \infty, \qquad \left|\frac{\partial \dot{T}}{\partial u}\right| \rightarrow \infty, \text{ if } Tu \rightarrow \frac{\pi k}{\alpha_o} \tag{16}$$

As a result of that, the characteristic roots of the Jacobian (14) at the equilibrium points (16) are:

$$\lambda_1 = 0, \ \lambda_2 \rightarrow \begin{cases} \infty & \text{if } \sin \omega t > 0 \\ -\infty & \text{if } \sin \omega t < 0 \end{cases} \tag{17}$$

One should note that, strictly speaking, the formula for λ_2 in Eq. (17) can be applied only if the explicit time t in Eqs. (12), (13) is considered as a slow changing parameter, i.e., if

$$\omega \ll \lambda_2 \tag{18}$$

However, since $|\lambda_2| \rightarrow \infty$, the inequality (18) holds for all bounded ω.

Let us turn now to a global behavior of the solutions to Eqs. (12), (13) starting with some initial conditions

$$u_o = u|_{t=0}, \quad T_o = T|_{t=0}, \quad u_o T_o = 2\pi/\alpha_o \tag{19}$$

According to Eqs. (17) the point (19) is a terminal repeller for $0 < t < \pi/\omega$. In the case of precisely zero disturbances, the system would rest forever at this point. In the presence of infinitesimal disturbances $\overset{*}{u}$ and $\overset{*}{T}$ the system can "choose" an escape scenario from the four combinations:

$$u = \pm \overset{*}{u} \ e^{\lambda_2 t}, \quad T = \pm \overset{*}{T} \ e^{\lambda_2 t}, \quad \overset{*}{u}, \overset{*}{T} \rightarrow 0, \quad \lambda_2 \rightarrow \infty \tag{20}$$

Although initially the difference between the positive and the negative solutions are infinitesimal, their transient divergence is characterized by unbounded Lyapunov exponents. The escaping solution can form any angle with the curve $u_o T_o = 2\pi/\alpha_o$ in the configuration space, Fig. 3. Depending on that angle, the solution approaches a terminal attractor at one of the two curves:

$$u_o T_o = 3\pi/\alpha_o, \quad \text{or} \quad u_o T_o = \pi/\alpha_o \tag{21}$$

In the presence of infinitesimal noise $\varepsilon(t), \eta(t)$ (see Eqs. (12), (13)) the formulas (20) read:

$$u = \ \text{sgn} \ \varepsilon(0) \ \overset{*}{u} \ e^{\lambda_2 t}, \quad T = \ \text{sgn} \ \eta(0) \ \overset{*}{T} \ e^{\lambda_2 t} \tag{22}$$

and therefore,

$$\cdot \left.\frac{dT}{du}\right|_{t=0} = \frac{\varepsilon(0)}{\eta(0)} \tag{23}$$

Thus, the angle between the escaping solution and the curve $u_o T_o = 2\pi/\alpha_o$ in the configuration space u, T has an arbitrary (random) value defined by Eq. (23), and therefore, the number of possible scenarios of the escape from the terminal repeller $u_o T_o = 2\pi/\alpha_o$ is infinite. The same situation occurs each time when the system approaches a new terminal attractor and then escapes it after this attractor converts into a repeller. But an infinite number of possible behaviors of the system (12), (13) is not its only new property. In addition to that, this system unpredictably changes the location of its attractors, i.e., its dynamical structure (Fig. 3).

One can introduce more general unpredictable dynamical systems as follows. Let

$$\dot{u}_i = \tilde{u}_i \sin^{1/3} \left[\sum_{j=1}^{N} T_{ij} g(u_j) \right] \sin \omega t + \varepsilon_i(t) \tag{24}$$

$$i = 1, 2 \ldots N$$

$$\dot{T}_{ij} = \tilde{T}_{ij} \sin^{1/3} \left[\sum_{j=1}^{N} T_{ij} g(u_j) \right] \sin \omega t + \eta_{ij}(t) \tag{25}$$

in which $\tilde{u}_i =$ const $, \tilde{T}_{ij} =$ const $, \varepsilon_i, \eta_{ij} \to 0$.
All the critical points of this system occupy a family of hypersurfaces:

$$\sum_{j=1}^{N} T_{ij}^k g(u_j^k) = \pi k, \quad k = \ldots -2, -1, 0, \ldots 1, 2, .. \text{ etc.} \tag{26}$$

Thus, as in the previous case, the solutions as well as the locations of the critical points of this system are unpredictable, while the degree of the unpredictability now has the order of

$$(2N)^m \text{ where } m = E(t/t^*) \tag{27}$$

and t^* is the period of transition from one critical point (26) to another. Actually Eq. (27) corresponds to the degree of unpredictability at the vanishingly small noises $\varepsilon_i(t)$ and $\eta_{ij}(t)$, or, to be more precise, sgn ε_i and sgn η_{ij} at the critical points.

So far, the unpredictable systems (11), (12), (13) and (24), (25) were presented in a non-autonomous form, since they contain time explicitly via the periodic excitations $\sin \omega t$. However, following[8] one can represent them in an autonomous form by introducing a new variable:

$$\sin \omega t = -v_2 \tag{28}$$

with

$$\left. \begin{aligned} \dot{v}_1 &= \omega v_2 + v_1(1 - v_1^2 - v_2^2) \\ \dot{v}_2 &= -\omega v_1 + v_2(1 - v_1^2 - v_2^2) \end{aligned} \right\} \tag{29}$$

The dynamical system (29) has a stable limit cycle

$$v_1 = \cos \omega t, \qquad v_2 = -\sin \omega t \tag{30}$$

which generates periodic excitations (28). The limit cycle (30) activating the dynamical systems (11), (12), (13), (24) and (25) can be associated with the brain rhythms[9] or circardian pacemakers[10].

Numerical simulation describing unpredictable spontaneous changes of locations of equilibrium points were performed for the following equations[8]:

$$\dot{u} = -(u - T\tanh\alpha u + \varepsilon_o \cos\gamma t)^{1/3} v_2$$

$$\dot{T} = (u - T\tanh\alpha T + \varepsilon_o \cos\gamma t)^{2/3} v_2^2$$

in which $\varepsilon_o \to 0$ (but $|\varepsilon_o \lambda_2| \to \infty$) and

$$\gamma = \omega + \frac{\pi}{2}\zeta, \quad \zeta = 1, 2, \ldots, \text{ etc}$$

The additional bias can be ignored when the system is stable, but it becomes significant during the periods of instability. Different patterns of initial disturbances are simulated by different ζ, while in a real physical model they occur randomly. Figure 4 (a,b,c,d,e) demonstrates different scenarios of behavior of the system for different ζ, while in all cases $\varepsilon_o = 10^{-20}$, and $\alpha = 10$. In Figure 4(a), with $\omega = 8.10^{-3}$ the motion starts with $u = 0, T = 5$ and approaches the terminal attractor B. After resting at this point it escapes through the trajectory BC (for $\zeta = 1$) or CD (for $\zeta = 2$). Similar behaviors are demonstrated in Fig. 4(b,c,d,e) with

$$\begin{array}{rccc} \omega = 5\cdot 10^{-3}, & 5\cdot 10^{-3}, & 9\cdot 10^{-3}, & 9\cdot 10^{-3} \\ u = 1.0, & 0, & 0, & 0 \\ T = 5.0, & 0, & 3.0, & 4.0 \end{array}$$

3. Application: Modeling Brain Activity

Let us return now to the simplest unpredictable dynamical system (11) and consider a set of such systems:

$$\dot{u}_i = \gamma \sin^{1/3} \frac{\omega}{\alpha} u_i \sin\omega t + \varepsilon_i(t), \quad \varepsilon_i(t) \to 0, \quad i = 1, 2, \ldots N \tag{31}$$

These equations describe the dynamics of N identical uncoupled neurons driven by vanishingly small random noise. But since the components $\varepsilon_i(t)$ of this noise are not necessarily identical, the motions of each neuron, in general, will be different from the motions of the others. Furthermore, these differences will be finite rather than infinitesimal. Such a phenomenon can be interpreted as an "emergence from chaos" of a "society" of neurons with different "personalities" despite the fact that the initial conditions for all of them are almost identical. It is remarkable that the "character" of each "personality" has a random nature coming from the random origin of the noise $\varepsilon_i(t)$.

The next step in the development of the neurons "society" (31) can be based upon the following scenario. Let us assume that there exists an objective function to be achieved by the neurons, for instance, a functional Φ to be minimized:

$$\Phi = \int_0^t \left[u(t) - f(t)\right]^2 dt \to \min \tag{32}$$

in which $\tilde{t} =$ const > 0, and $f(t)$ is a prescribed function.

Suppose that the performance of each neuron is measured by the value:

$$\Phi_i = \int_0^{\tilde{t}} \left[u_i(t) - f(t)\right]^2 dt \tag{33}$$

and let ω_i, the frequency of the periodic excitations, evolve according to

$$\dot{\omega}_i = \left(\omega_o + \Phi_i - \frac{1}{N}\sum_{j=1}^{N}\Phi_j\right) - \omega_i \tag{34}$$

where ω_i will be different for each neuron. As follows from Eq. (34), those neurons whose performance is above the average:

$$\Phi_i > \frac{1}{N}\sum_{j=1}^{N}\Phi_j \tag{35}$$

will receive higher energy input through the frequency ω and will act faster. On the contrary, those neurons whose performance is below the average, i.e.,

$$\Phi_i < \frac{1}{N}\sum_{j=1}^{N}\Phi_j \tag{36}$$

will slow down their activity and eventually they will be out of competition.

This primitive scenario of a natural selection is only one illustration of possible developments of discrimination in the neuron's "society" (31). In addition to that, the neurons can learn from their experience memorizing useful behavior, and therefore, improving their performances. They can also cooperate and compete with each other, etc. But it is worth emphasizing that all these activities can be based upon conventional tools of information processing such as learning by examples, memorizing and recognition of patterns, local and global minimization, etc. What is most important in our scenario is the first step, the "act of creation", when identical neurons in the same environment acquired different patterns of behavior without a special interference from the outside. Such a creativity, in principle, cannot be performed by classical (Lipschitzian) dynamical systems for which the uniqueness of solutions subject to prescribed sets of initial conditions is guaranteed. Even the discovery of chaos has not shaken the rigid behavior of the Lipschitzian dynamical systems since the chaotic system are structurally stable. This means that although a particular trajectory of a chaotic motion cannot be predicted, a certain set of average characteristics of the motion as well as the global structure of the limit sets are fully predictable. It is also important to bear in mind that in the chaotic systems the unpredictability is caused by a supersensitivity to the initial conditions, while the uniqueness of the solution is still guaranteed by the Lipschitz condition. In contradistinction, in non-Lipschitzian dynamics the unpredictability is caused by the failure of uniqueness of the solution at some of the equilibrium (critical) points. That is why a set of possible trajectories in phase space is not a Cantor set (as in chaotic systems), but rather a countable set of combinatorial nature. Because of that, the global unpredictability in the non- Lipschitzian dynamics is associated with an exponential complexity (see Eq. (27)). Hence, in this respect the unpredictable systems introduced above have some connections with the "digital world".

In conclusion, it is worth emphasizing that the most important property of the unpredictable systems introduced above is the ability to change spontaneously their structural berhavior as a result of parametrical periodic excitations. Such a performance phenomenologically resembles the brain activity.[9]

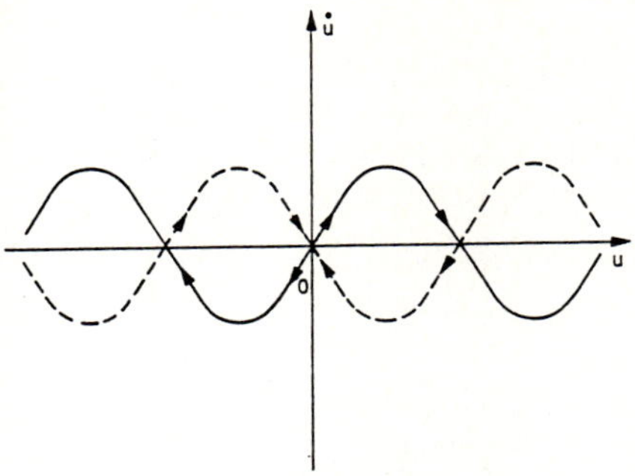

Fig. 1. Oscillations About The Attractor u = 0

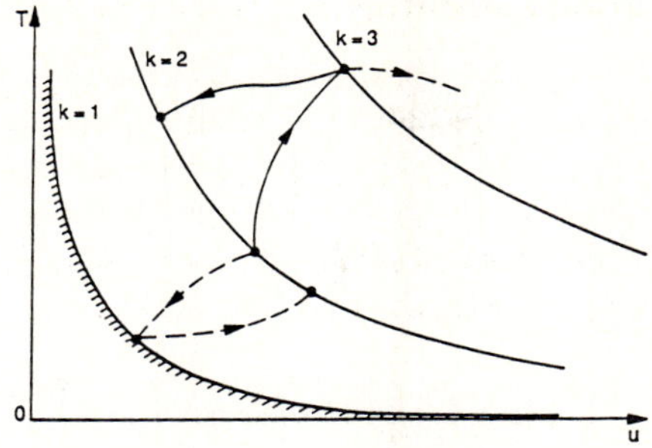

Fig. 3. Spontaneous Changes of Dynamical Structure

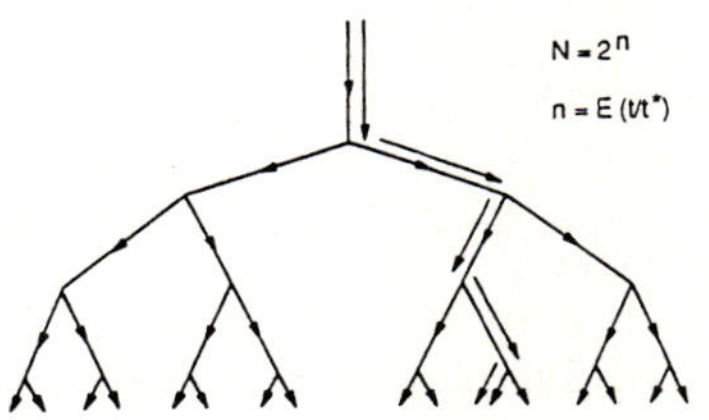

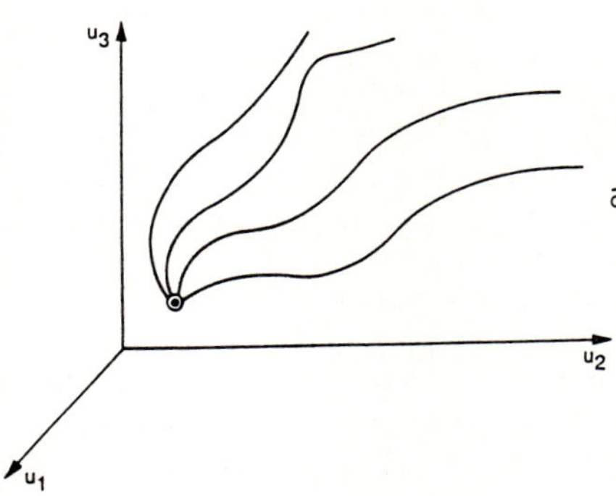

Fig. 2. Information Born in Chaos

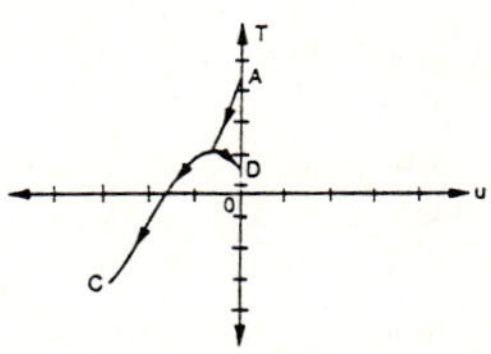

Fig. 4a

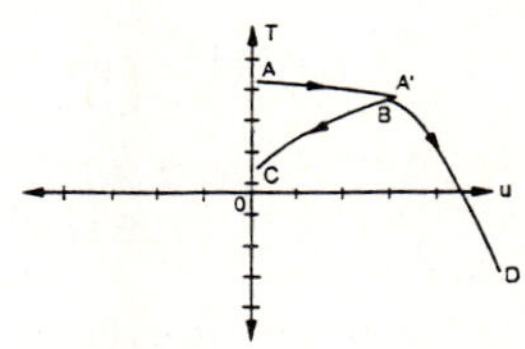

Fig. 4b

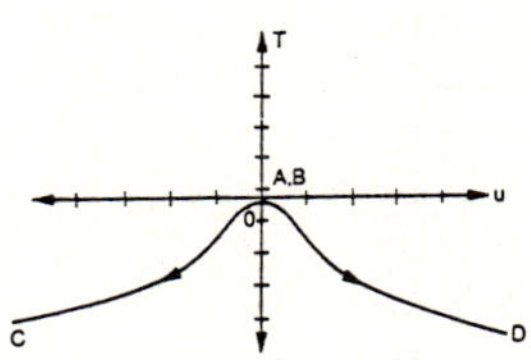

Fig. 4c

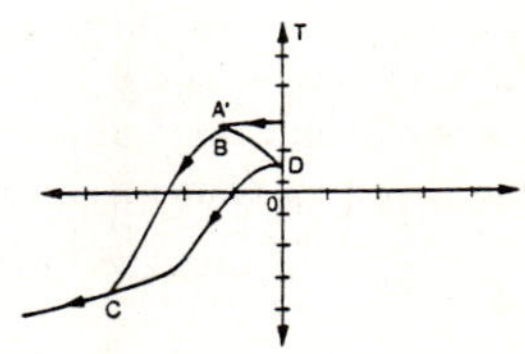

Fig. 4d

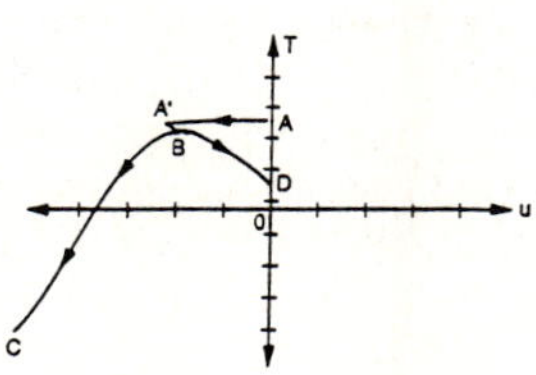

Fig. 4e
Unpredictable Motions

Acknowledgement

This research was carried out at the Center for Space Microelectronics Technology, Jet Propulsion Laboratory, California Institute of Technology. Support for the work came from Agencies of the U.S. Department of Defense, and from the Office of Basic Energy Sciences of the U.S. Department of Energy, through an agreement with the National Aeronautics and Space Administration.

References

1. Cohen, M. and Grossberg, S., 1983, "Absolute Stability of Global Pattern Formation and Parallel Memory Storage by Competitive Neural Netowrks", *IEEE Trans. Syst. Man Syber., SMC- 13*, 815-826.

2. Hopfield, J.J., 1984, "Neurons with Graded Response Have Collective Computational Properties Like Those of Two-State Neurons", *Procs. Net. Acad. Sci. USA, 81*, 3088-3092.

3. Harth, E., Csermely, T.J., Beek, B. and Lindsay, R.D., 1970, "Brain Functions and Neural Dynamics", *J. Theoret. Biol., 26*, 93-120.

4. Anninonos, P.A., Beek, B., Csermely, T.J., Harth, E. and Pertile, G., 1970, "Dynamics of Neural Structures", *J. Theoret. Biol., 26*, 121-148.

5. Zak, M., 1989, "Terminal Attractors in Neural Networks", *Neural Networks, 2*, 259-274.

6. Zak, M., 1989, "Non-Lipschitzian Dynamics for Neural Net Modelling", *Appl. Math. Letters, 2*, 69-74.

7. Barhen, J., Gulati, S., and Zak, M., 1989, "Neural Learning of Constrained Nonlinear Transformations", *IEEE Computer, 22*, (6), 67-76.

8. Zak, M. and Barhen, J., 1990, "Neural Networks with Creative Dynamics", *Math. Comp. Model.*, (in press).

9. Basar, E., 1980, *EEG-Brain Dynamics,* Elsevier, Amsterdam.

10. Daan, S., Berde, C., "Two Coupled Oscillators: Simulations of the Circardian Pacemaker in Mammalian Activity Rhythms", *J. Theor. Biol, 70,* 297-313.

Advanced Neural Computers / R. Eckmiller (Editor)

GEMINI: A PERCEPTRON-LIKE NEURAL NETWORK WITH BIOLOGICAL SIMILARITIES

Steen S. CHRISTENSEN, Rodney M.J. COTTERILL and Claus NIELSEN

Department of Biophysics
The Technical University of Denmark
Building 307, DK-2800 Lyngby, Denmark

We have studied the behaviour of a new type of neural network of the perceptron class, in which the hidden-layer neurons are arranged in pairs. Both neurons in each of these pairs simultaneously receive input from the preceding neuronal layer, but one member of each pair also receives inhibition from the other member. This makes the network particularly sensitive to well-defined regions of the input space, a discriminatory power that has useful potential for various classes of problem. By permitting temporal attenuation of the inhibitory component, it is found that the network's gradual loss of function can be spontaneously reversed upon renewed application of the input, this remarkable property being strongly reminiscent of what was observed in some of the classical conditioning experiments carried out on laboratory animals.

1. INTRODUCTION

The purpose of this short communication is to present observations made on a new type of neural network of the perceptron class, and to give an account of the way in which certain aspects of its behaviour are reminiscent of what have been observed in clinical trials on classical conditioning. The neural network in question was somewhat unusual in that the neurons of its second layer were arranged in pairs, such that one member of each pair exerted an inhibitory influence on the other member, both of these neurons being in receipt of excitatory stimuli from the cells in the input layer. A neural network with such an unusual arrangement of connections is found to possess an encouragingly high level of discrimination. It thus holds promise for certain applications in which the general goal is a brain-inspired computational strategy having the usual advantages that accrue from the parallel distributed arrangement [1].

The number of different possible configurations of the neurons in a neural network are, of course, virtually unlimited, and it puts little burden on one's powers of imagination to come up with all manner of novel connection patterns. We believe that the specific new arrangement described here distinguishes itself from many of these other possibilities in that it is capable of displaying behaviour that has been observed in conditioning experiments on laboratory animals. We have found it appropriate to arrange the subject matter of this paper in the following manner. The next section gives a brief description of the relevant conditioning experiments, and it lays particular emphasis on the phenomenon of spontaneous recovery of the conditioned response, under certain circumstances. The section after that describes the new type of neural network, and it includes investigations of its performance, demonstrating the claimed increase in discrimination. There then follows a section in which it is demonstrated that the new neural network is capable of mimicking some of the conditioning observations made on laboratory animals, and the final section is a brief evaluation of what has been achieved by this study.

2. CLASSICAL CONDITIONING

In the early part of this century, Pavlov [2] elucidated several important facets of the learning process by making a series of clinical observations on laboratory animals, particularly dogs, and he differentiated between what came to be known as unconditional and conditional effects. In a particularly noteworthy series of experiments on dogs, Pavlov noticed that these creatures would begin salivating at the prospect of being fed meat. There is nothing particularly surprising about this of course, because saliva contains enzymes which are required in the first stages of digestion of such food. Because of this, Pavlov referred to the meat as an unconditioned stimulus, and he called the salivation an unconditioned reaction.

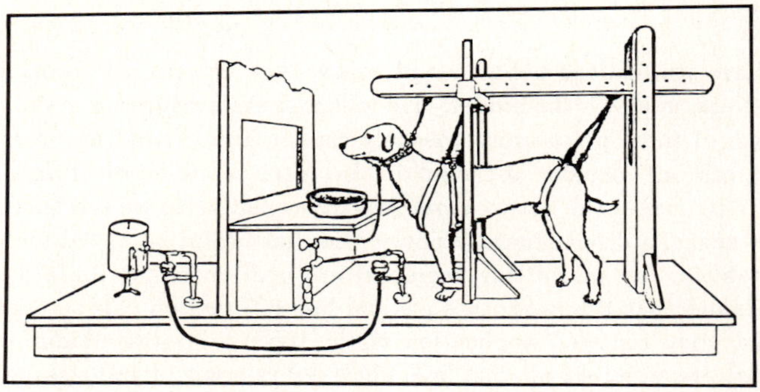

FIGURE 1

The experimental set-up for Pavlov's classic experiments which distinguished between unconditional and conditional stimuli. A compressed-air device blows powdered meat into the dog's mouth, and the observer watches for the salivation response.

In Pavlov's experimental set-up (see Fig. 1), a dog's reactions were observed under various conditions, the animal's immediate environment containing meat powder, which could be blown into its mouth, and a tuning fork. The sound from the latter was termed a conditional stimulus, because there is no obvious physical relationship between such a sound and the act of salivation; a dog's mouth would not be expected to water at the prospect of licking a tuning fork. Pavlov discovered that if the blowing of meat powder into the dog's mouth was accompanied by the sound of the tuning fork, over a sufficiently long period, subsequent sounding of the fork in the absence of the administered meat powder nevertheless produced salivation, this latter therefore becoming a conditioned response. Pavlov went on to establish the most ideal timing for conditioning, and he discovered that optimal results are obtained if the conditional stimulus precedes the unconditional stimulus by about half a second. It is interesting to note that this interval is about the time taken for consciousness of a stimulus to develop, as revealed by the experiments of Libet [3].

Pavlov went on to demonstrate that it is possible to extinguish a learned conditional response, this being achieveable by what could be called contrived disappointment. Pavlov simply subjected the trained dog to the sound of the tuning fork, that is to say the conditional stimulus, this time not coupling it to the unconditional stimulus, that is to say administration of the meat powder. Using sound durations of about eight minutes, separated by intervals of between three and four minutes, Pavlov was able to establish that the conditional response gradually diminishes; the dog's tendency to salivate merely at the sounding of the tuning fork, and in the absence of the meat powder, gradually diminished, until in the end it had virtually disappeared. The interesting point is that if, after a pause of twenty four hours, the conditional stimulus is again applied, the dog again begins to salivate, even though the sound is not accompanied by the administration of the meat powder. In fact, this sounding of the tuning fork without the coupling to the meat powder again constitutes opposition to the training conditions, so it would again tend to oppose the trained response. This is indeed what happens. But if, again after a delay of about a day, the conditional stimulus is again applied, yet again does one observe the salivation response, although this time the latter is not so strong. The entire procedure can be continued for several days, and the spontaneous reappearance of the conditioned response continues to be observed, but it simply gets weaker and weaker. Later in this paper, after presenting the new type of neural network, it will be shown that this is capable of exhibiting this spontaneous recovery of the conditioned response, if the circumstances are appropriate.

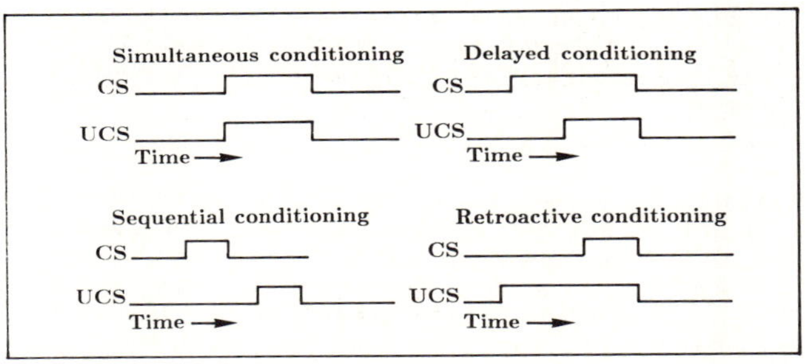

FIGURE 2

Various possibilities exist for the relative timing of the unconditional and conditional stimuli. Optimal conditioning occurs if the former precedes the latter by about half a second.

3. THE NEW TYPE OF NETWORK

The philosophy underlying the new type of perceptron was the need to inhibit undesirable activity. Moreover it was also seen as desirable that the connections within the network should reflect, as faithfully as possible, what is seen in the biological counterpart. For instance, it is a biological fact that all the synaptic contacts entered into by a given cell should have the same sign, that is to say they should either all be excitatory or all inhibitory. This is a criterion which is contravened in a surprisingly large fraction of neural networks that one encounters, and is seen, for example, in the Hopfield model and also in those described under the general heading of parallel distributed processing.

The structure of the new network is shown in Fig. 3, the symbols V_+ and V_- indicating, respectively, excitatory and inhibitory neurons. As can be seen, the second layer is comprised of pairs of cells, in which an excitatory neuron is coupled with one of the inhibitory type.

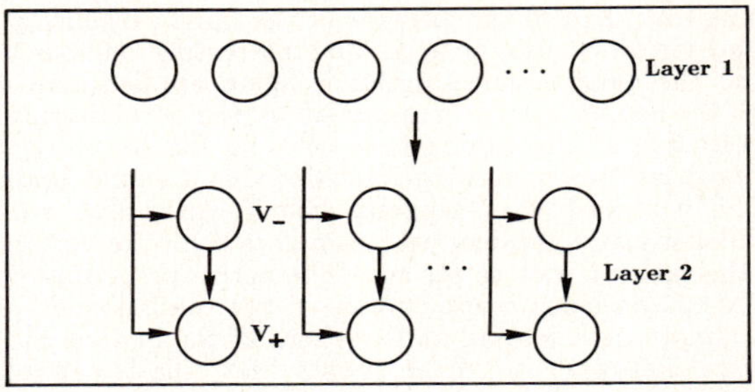

FIGURE 3

In the GEMINI network, the hidden-layer neurons are arranged in pairs, one member of each pair, V_-, inhibiting the other member, V_+. Both members receive excitation from the input layer. The V_- neurons suppress unwanted activity by inhibiting the V_+ neurons.

Now suppose that we desire a given excitatory cell to be active when the input lies within the interval A_1-A_2. It turns out that this can readily be achieved, as the following reasoning will demonstrate. If V_+ was an output cell of a perceptron, the value of the synaptic strength would be such that V_+would respond every time the input was greater than A_1, say. Likewise, if V_- was an output cell of a perceptron, the value of the synaptic strength would produce a response in this cell if the input was greater than A_2, say. Finally, if the connection between V_- and V_+ was sufficiently inhibitory, V_+ would not be able to be activated if V_- was already active.

Putting all these conditions together, we see that because V_- is only influenced by the input, it will behave as if it were an output cell for a perceptron. Similarly, V_+ will behave as a perceptron output if, and only if, V_- is inactive. In other words, a response lying within a specified interval can readily be adjusted for. Indeed, these adjustments are quite similar to those which are encountered in the back-propagation algorithm [1], in that they too employ the delta rule.

Thus, for synapses to V_+ we have the prescription for changing the synaptic weights

$$\Delta W_{ij+} = \alpha V_i(T_{j+} - V_{j+}) \tag{1}$$

T_j being a target value, in the usual way, while α is a parameter that determines the rate of learning. Similarly, for synapses to V_- we obtain

$$\Delta W_{ij-} = \alpha V_i(1 - V_{j-}) \tag{2}$$

if T_j is unity. If T_j is 0, we obtain, instead

$$\Delta W_{ij-} = \alpha V_i(0 - V_{j-}) \tag{3}$$

As can be seen from Fig. 4, reaction over a limited input interval is indeed obtained from a network of this type, adjusted according to the above rules. In this particular case, the limits of the interval were set at the integer numbers 4 and 6, and the result is a response that has a maximum centered on the integer value of 5.

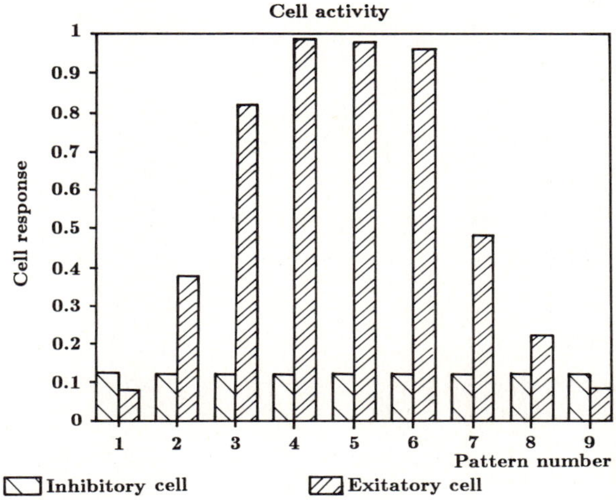

FIGURE 4

Response over a limited range of input is obtained by adjusting the synapses to specified llimits. In the case shown here, these were 4 and 6, and the response is symmetrically distributed about the value 5.

4. SPONTANEOUS RECOVERY OF DISCRIMINATION

As mentioned in the second section of this paper, extinction of the conditioned response, in laboratory animals, can be reversed by subjecting them to situations in which the conditional stimulus is not accompanied by the usual reward. But it was also noted in that section that even though such a procedure appears to totally quench the conditioned response, this reappears with full strength after a sufficiently long interval, which is usually of the order of a day or so. We have discovered that such a spontaneous recovery of the conditioned behaviour can be obtained in our model, if certain assumptions are made. These are as follows: the quenching of the conditioned response is taken to be produced by a strengthening of the synapses to V_-, whereafter activation of those neurons leads to an inhibition of the V_+ neurons. However, as time passes, the previously strengthened synapses to V_- gradually lose their potency, and after a certain time, these V_- cells no longer receive sufficient excitation to permit them to become activated. The consequence of this is that the V_- cells are no longer able to inhibit the V_+ cells, so the latter will now respond in the way they did when the conditioning was still fully in effect.

The explanation as to why one can obtain spontaneous recovery, with full strength, is thus that when the V_- cells are not activated, the V_+ cells receive exactly the same synaptic input as they did before the quenching came into effect. This entire process naturally has its constraints, the main one of these being that the time lapse that is required for the appearance of the spontaneous recovery clearly depends upon the time constant with which the synapses to the V_- cells relaxes back towards a low value, that is to say it depends upon the decay time of the synapses to those cells.

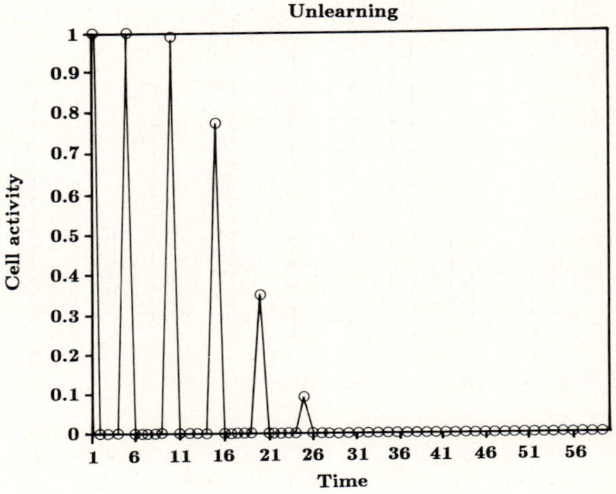

FIGURE 5

The response of the network can be quenched if the strength of the excitatory synapses that feed the V_- neurons are allowed to relax towards zero. The original response can be spontaneously recovered by reactivating the input layer. As shown, full recovery can be obtained for a few repetitions of this procedure, but the recovered response ultimately diminishes. The original situation can then be re-established only by subjecting the network to the appropriate conditioning.

As can be seen from Fig. 5, computer simulations are able to produce this general behaviour, and the figure shows the optimal effect which we obtained through appropriate adjustment of the various parameters. We cannot, at this time, and without further extensive investigations, claim that all the values of our parameters are biologically defensible, but we nevertheless feel that it is of some value that we have demonstrated that the overall behaviour observed in clinical trials can be simulated by models of the type that we have presented here.

5. CONCLUSIONS

It is encouraging that a relatively modest change to the normal perceptron configuration, namely the replacement of the single neurons in the hidden layer by twinned neurons involving an inhibitory synapse, should produce such a dramatic increase in discriminatory power. And the fact that this arrangement is also capable of displaying an emphatically non-trivial behavioral facet also observed in clinical trials on laboratory animals, suggests that this new network configuration deserves further study. It must nevertheless be pointed out that the training of the network still requires supervision, in much the same way as is the case for a traditional perceptron. The need for such supervision, in the latter case, is normally looked upon as being a deficit, in the biological context, and it would appear that the same must be said of the situation regarding this new network configuration. We are now investigating the network further, with a view to probing the possibility that both the laudable disriminatory powers and the phenomenon of spontaneous recovery might be retained even though the supervised learning can be dispensed with; we are searching for a way in which the synaptic adjustments could be made automatically through experience, without the necessary intervention of this field's persistent nemesis, the homunculus.

REFERENCES

[1] Rumelhart, D.E., Hinton, G.E. and Williams, R.J., Learning internal representations by error propagation, in: Rumelhart, D.E. and McClelland, J.L., Parallel Distributed Processing: Explorations in the Microstructure of Cognition (MIT Press, Cambridge, Mass., 1986) pp. 318-364.

[2] Pavlov, I.P., Conditioned Reflexes (Oxford University Press, London, 1927).

[3] Libet, B., Wright, E.W., Feinstein, B. and Pearl, D.K., Subjective referral of the timing for a conscious sensory experience: A funtional role for the somatosensory specific projection system in man, Brain, Vol 102, pp. 193-224 (1979).

Advanced Neural Computers / R. Eckmiller (Editor)
Elsevier Science Publishers B.V. (North-Holland), 1990

ON THE HEBB RULE AND UNLIMITED PRECISION ARITHMETIC IN A Mc CULLOCH AND PITTS NETWORK

Pietro De Pinto

Istituto per la Ricerca dei Sistemi Informatici del CNR

Francesco E. Lauria

Dipartimento di Scienze Fisiche dell' Universita'
Mostra d' Oltremare pad. 19, I-80125 NAPOLI (Italy)

Marcello Sette

Istituto per la Ricerca dei Sistemi Informatici del CNR

ABSTRACT. We present a digital and deterministic neural network, composed of linear units with threshold. First, we discuss the implementation of an Hebbian rule, as a storing device for the "programs" the system learns in its free interactions with an unpredictable evolving environment. Then, because our network can be seen as a general purpose data-flow system, we give the program to compute the algebraic sum of two numbers, each represented by a numeral with an unlimited number of digits. As we are planning to implement, in our network, many instances of each arithmetic operation, in particular of the division, so the operations here presented compute the result starting from the most significant digit. In this way the transformations, to be executed on the input data, can be automatically pipelined and, consequently, the system efficency increases.

1. INTRODUCTION

We discuss the implementation of the Hebb rule and of some arithmetic operations, with an user chosen precision, in a Mc Culloch and Pitts network [1]. This network, namely a net composed of linear units with threshold, is well known as a general purpose machine [2: pg. 65]. With the help of the Caianiello's formalism [3], we have presented the network together with the associated assembler in [4, 5, 6, 7], the network as a stored program system in [8, 9, 10, 11] and its implementation on a Transputer based MIMD architecture in [12].

The solutions to some of the problems arising with the Hebb rule implementation have been proposed in [13]. Here, we discuss the convenience, and eventually the modalities, to extend the Hebb rule, originally defined only for the excitatory connections, to the inhibitory case.

In the last chapter, we present a version of the algorithm computing the algebric sum of two relative numbers, represented by binary numerals, without any limit on the number of the digits. To this end, we program the net, suitably connecting its nodes, so to obtain a data-flow system. In other words, the digits, flowing-in through the net's input channels, are represented by the very same signals abilitating the execution of the desired arithmetic operations.

To increase speed, our algorithms compute from left to right, ie, from the most significant digit. Consequently, the pipelining of the operations is substantially facilitated and the result digits can be processed as soon as they are computed, also in the division case, one of the operations we are planning to implement next.

2. THE FAULT TOLERANT NETWORK AND ITS ASSOCIATED LANGUAGE

Our is an highly connected network, with "tau" the smallest indivisible bit of time. It has N nodes: at the time t the node h, as well as its output channel, is in one of two internal states. These are formally represented by the threshold function, f[h,t], values.

To represent a threshold function let us define:
T as a node threshold;
"redundancy" as the number of nodes R < N which, by construction, have the same input and the same threshold T, ie, which compute the same function. To simplify the presentation we suppose R to be a constant, actually it depends on the receiving node index h;
#COMB[N,R] as the number of the combinations of N objects taken R at the time;
the "combinatorial output channel" as the output channel of a set of R nodes which, by construction, have the same input channels and the same threshold T, ie, which compute the same function: because of this, their output channels carry always the same signals. Thus, they can be formally represented as one channel;
C[h,q,l] as the value associated to the l*tau-delayed monodirectional q-th combinatorial output channel connecting the q-th set of R nodes to the node number h. It is referred to as the "coupling coefficient" or C value. In the probabilistic network literature, often it is called the weight associated to a connection;
e as the constant representing the maximum number of faulty nodes, per set of R nodes. Similarly to R, it should depend upon h. It corresponds to the maximum number of errors which can be corrected in a message containing R symbols.
SUM[a=b=c]¦ g[b] ¦ as the sum of all the objects g[b], enclosed between the ¦signs¦, for b = a, ..., c;
s = [2**R]/SUM[0=i=e]¦ #COMB[R,i] ¦ as the number of available sets of R nodes, and thus of distinct Cs, for a net reliably working in presence of up to e faulty nodes, per set of R nodes.
r[h,q] as the signal threshold, with R > r[h,q];
k = {R[q]} as a variable defined over the set {R[q]} of the R integers appearing as indices in the q-th combination;
D(x) = 0 if x < 0, D(x) = 1 otherwise;
then, at the time t, the node h internal state is given by:

```
f[h,t] = D(SUM[ 1 = q = s ; 1 = l = L ]¦¦ C[h,q,l]*
          D(SUM[ k = {R[q]} ]¦ f[k,t-l*tau] ¦ -r[h,q])¦¦ -T).
```

Whenever the number of transmitting nodes k, for k belonging to the set {R[q]}, is greater or equal to the signal threshold r[h,q], then C[h,q,l] contributes one non-zero addendum to the external sum. Otherwise its contribution is zero. In other words C is a value associated no more to a single node output: it is associated to the q-th group of the R connections stemming out of a set of R nodes computing the same function.

Let "&", respectively "v", be the logical connective "and", respectively "inclusive or".

Both the positive a0[t], ..., an[t] and the negative -a0[t], ..., -an[t] boolean variables represent the internal state, at the time t, of the combinatorial output channel relative to the group of transmitting nodes a0, ..., an. Ie, a transmitting node, or channel, combination is usually represented by the very same sequence of symbols, without the temporal dependency, which denotes the variable representing its internal state.

The positive variable a0[t], ..., an[t], represents the internal state of the receiving node a0, ..., an, at the time t. As usual, when a node internal state is one, the associated variable is said to be true; false, otherwise.

Usually a receiving, respectively transmiting, node has the index h, respectively k.

Both &[a[l],a[l]] and v[a[l],a[l]] implement the monoargumental operator transforming, with a delay of one tau, any given variable into another one, not necessarily distinct from the former.

Let bi[t] be defined over the set {ai[t], -ai[t]}: in other words, bi[t] can be either ai[t] or -ai[t]. To simplify our formalism we shall write ai[li], -ai[li], bi[li] in place, respectively, of ai[t-litau], -ai[t-litau], bi[t-litau].

By definition, the elementary programs are either:

```
ai[t]: &[b1[l1], ..., bn[ln]]
```

or

```
aj[t]: v[b1[l1], ..., bn[ln]].
```

Any elementary program begins with the name of its output data flow, at present time, followed by a colon and an empty space, for readability. In turn, this is followed by a wff, in the given connectives, in which each variable depends from a past input flow, ie, with a time dependency like [t-l*tau], with l greater or equal to the number of connectives the said variable is nested in. The end period can be optional.

A program is obtained from elementary programs and programs by simply substituting a variable, either a positive or a negative one, with the, elementary, program admitting that very same variable as output flow and adding as many units to its time delay, viz to the l appearing in its argument, as nested connectives it is immersed in.

The rules to compute the Cs, corresponding to an elementary program implementation, are discussed in [7, 11], together with the assembler to allocate the network resources to the programs.

3. ON THE HEBB RULE AND THE INHIBITORY CONNECTIONS

In [14: pg. 62] the Hebb rule is defined "as follows: When an axon of cell A is near enough to excite a cell B and repeatedly or persistently takes part in firing it, some growth process or metabolic change takes place in one or both cells such that A's efficency, as one of the cells firing B, is increased.". As stated, this rule can be applied only to the excitatory case: in [2: pg.36] we find one of the many instances of its extension to the inhibitory case. As the net interacts with the environment, both rules produce a net swamped with strengthen connections: they do not accomodate for the reversibility of the actions.

To modify the Hebb rule, let us introduce a threshold M: if the cupling coefficient value is lower than M, C < M, and if A and B fire, with the right time delay, then the traditional Hebb rule holds. Otherwise, if C < M then C becomes smaller as a time function ; instead, if C is equal or greater than M, it is frozen, ie, its value is time independent. From now on, we shall call "Hebb rule" the new version.

However the extension to the inhibitory case is only a formal, not an actual, generalization of the Hebb rule, also if we introduce the threshold M. To see why, let us consider a net interacting with an unpredictably evolving environment. In these conditions, the rule applied to the excitatory connections can be made to work quite satisfactorily, depending on the value of the parameters representing the speed of change, the node threshold, the initial and final connection strengths and so on. Instead, the same rule applied to the inhibitory connections, no matter how we set its parameters, produces a net swamped, again, with strengthen inhibitory connections. In the former case only the connections in between A, the excitatory node, and B, the receiving node, are modified: the threshold and the, environment dependent, statistical fluctuations of the inputs can chek, effectively, the strengthening of the connections between A and the other excited nodes, different from B. In the latter case only A, the inhibitory node, is unambigously identified: any node, silent with the right delay, is a receiving node B. Because of this, the number of strengthened inhibitory connections increases faster than the number of strengthened excitatory connections: consequently the number of active nodes decreases whilst the number of silent nodes increases. In other words, a chain reaction is started and the end result is a network full of inhibitory connections.

Now we present the reasons enabling us to dispose of the extension of the Hebb rule to the inhibitory connections, in a general purpose McCulloch and Pitts network. In such network, there is a built-in diffuse operating system, see [9, 11], ie, the inhibitory connections, needed for an orderly working system, have been genetically implemented. To have a new program stored in the net, we need to enter, with the right repetition rate, the basic function names and the input data. It is useless, almost dangerous, either to enter or to store new inhibitions: the previously learned programs and, eventually, the diffuse operating system shall activate, autonomously, all the inhibitions needed to compute the correct result. At most, to learn to inhibit the program "a", we can strengthen the excitatory connections impinging upon the nodes activating the diffuse operating system and, thus, inhibiting the computation of the basic functions needed to compute "a".

In conclusion, either new inhibitions must not be entered, and thus stored, or only excitatory connections must be strengthened: in both cases, the Hebb rule does not need to be extended to the inhibitory connections.

4. ON UNLIMITED PRECISION ARITHMETIC

Elsewhere, see [4, 9], we have presented our network as a data-flow system, e. g. computing the addition of two binary numerals. Moreover, we have discussed it as a general purpose system, containing the elementary arithmetic operations among its basic functions. Here, we want to implement the algorithm computing the algebraic sum of two numbers, represented by binary numerals, without any constraint on the number of the digits they can have, and starting from the leftmost, ie, from the most significant digit. In the addition, subtraction and multiplication case we can start, indifferently, from the leftmost or from the rightmost digit. However, in the division case, it is more convenient to start from the most significant digit. Because of the choice made, the network can start executing the next operation on the result, as soon as the output digits are generated. As we plan to implement many instances of each operation, the possibility to pipeline them speeds-up the system.

As a fully compatible possibility to speed-up, we can batch the incoming digits: ie, we can process d digits at once. To process concurrently d digits, we need the algorithms to compute the elmentary operations, d digits at the time. Because of the limited amount of hardware available, for the time being, we have implemented the algorithm for the algebraic sum with d = 1, in a network with R = 1.

In general, we need a channel to represent the 0s and another channel to represent the 1s of each numeral: ie, to represent a number in the base two we need two channels. As d = 1, we need a pair of channels to represent the digits of the first addendum, ie, of the numeral a. And another pair of channels to represent the digits of the second addendum b. In total we need the following eleven input channels: when true, the corresponding signals admit the interpretations

a0[t] represents 0 as the digit of a, at the time t
a1[t] represents 1 as the digit of a, at the time t
b0[t] represents 0 as the digit of b, at the time t
b1[t] represents 1 as the digit of b, at the time t
aminus[t] represents - as the signum of a, at the time t
bminus[t] represents - as the signum of b, at the time t
aplus[t] represents + as the signum of a, at the time t
bplus[t] represents + as the signum of b, at the time t
point[t] represents the decimal point
sum[t] represents the sum calling sequence, at the time t
start[1] is the machine initialization signal

The output channels are: out0, out1, outpoint. They are called, respectively: the zero, the one, the decimal point output channel.

A number of temporary variables appears in the programs: to simplify the notations, we omit writing explicitly the argument t. Only the actual value of 1, appearing as the argument of the right-hand variables, has been explicity given.

The node start has value 1 at the time 0:

```
     one            : v( start(1), one(1))
```

Buffer pointers a^, b^: the node a0, a1, aminus, aplus has value 1 when pointer a^ points to the character '0', '1', '-', '+'; the node b0, b1, bminus, bplus has value 1 when pointer b^ points to the character '0', '1', '-', '+'; the node point has value 1 when either of the pointers a^ or b^ point to the character '.';

```
     a0b0           : &( a0(1), b0(1))
     a1b0           : &( a1(1), b0(1))
     a0b1           : &( a0(1), b1(1))
     a1b1           : &( a1(1), b1(1))
     aminusbminus   : &( aminus(1), bminus(1))
     aminusbplus    : &( aminus(1), bplus(1))
     aplusbminus    : &( aplus(1), bminus(1))
     aplusbplus     : &( aplus(1), bplus(1))
     eqsign         : v( aminusbminus(1), aplusbplus(1))
     neqsign        : v( aminusbplus(1), aplusbminus(1))
     endinput       : v( one(1),
                       -v( v( a0(4), a1(4)),
                           v( v( aminus(4), aplus(4)), point(4))))
```

The algebraic sum execution: the node doingadd, doingsub, has value 1 when the net is performing the addition, the subtraction.

```
     stop           : v( outstop(1), outstop(2))
     doingadd       : v( v( doingadd(2), eqsign(2)), -stop(1))
     doingsub       : v( v( doingsub(2), neqsign(2)), -stop(1))
```

The input buffer control:

```
     getinput       : v(sum(1), outright(1))
```

The calling sequence to write in the temporary buffer:

```
     writebuffer    : v( &( getinput(7),
                            v( v( neqsign(5), point(6)),
                               v( &( doingadd(6), v( a1b0(6),
                                                     a0b1(6))),
                                  &( doingsub(6), v( a1b1(6),
                                                     a0b0(6)))))),
                         v( outrightbuff(8), -outrightbuff(2)))
```

Output nodes writing in the temporary buffer:

```
     outbuffminus   : &( writebuffer(1), aminusbplus(1))
     outbuffplus    : &( writebuffer(1), aplusbminus(1))
```

```
outbuffpoint    : &( writebuffer(1), point(1))
outbuff0        : v( &( getinput(4), eqsign(2)),
                     &( writebuffer(2), v( a1b1(3), a0b0(3))))
outbuff1        : &( writebuffer(2), v( a0b1(3), a1b0(3)))
```

Nodes reading from the temporary buffer:

```
inbuffsign      : v( inbuffplus(1), inbuffminus(1))
emptybuffpos    : &( getinput(7),
                     v( v( endinput(3),
                           v( &( doingadd(6), a0b0(6)),
                              &( doingsub(6), a1b0(6)))),
                        &( &( doingsub(6), a0b1(6)),
                           inbuffsign(5))))
emptybuffneg    : &( getinput(7),
                     v( &( doingadd(6), a1b1(6)),
                        v( &( doingsub(6), a0b1(6)),
                           inbuffsign(5))))
outrightbuff    : v( v( outrightbuff(6),
                        v( emptybuffpos(3), emptybuffneg(3))),
                    -endbuffer(1))
endbuffer       : v( one(1),
                    -v( v( inbuff0(4), inbuff1(4)),
                        v( inbuffsign(3), inbuffpoint(4))))
```

Algebraic sum output nodes:

```
outchange       : &( inbuffsign(1), &( getinput(3), a0b1(2)))
outminus        : &( getinput(9),
                     v( aminusbminus(5),
                        v( &( inbuffminus(5),
                              v( a1b0(5), endinput(5))),
                           &( inbuffplus(5),  a0b1(5)))))
outplus         : &( getinput(9),
                     v( aplusbplus(5),
                        v( &( inbuffminus(5), a0b1(5)),
                           &( inbuffplus(5),
                              v( a1b0(5), endinput(5))))))
outpoint        : &( outrightbuff(2), inbuffpoint(1))
out0            : v( v( &( emptybuffpos(3), inbuff0(3)),
                        &( emptybuffneg(3), inbuff1(3))),
                     v( &( &( outrightbuff(5), inbuff0(4)),
                           v( a1b0(4), endinput(4))),
                        &( &( outrightbuff(5), inbuff1(4)),
                           a1b1(4))))
out1            : v( v( &( emptybuffpos(3), inbuff1(3)),
                        &( emptybuffneg(3), inbuff0(3))),
                     v( &( &( outrightbuff(5), inbuff0(4)),
                           a0b1(4)),
                        &( &( outrightbuff(5), inbuff1(4)),
                           v( a0b0(4), endinput(4)))))
outright        : v( v( writebuffer(2),-endinput(2)),
                     &( getinput(4), eqsign(2)))
outstop         : &( writebuffer(1), endinput(1))
```

This program has been implemented in a neural net with 116 nodes. To sum algebraically two m digit numbers, the net takes less than:

(m * 50) + 50 tau.

ACKNOWLEDGEMENTS

This research was supported in part through the MPI 40% fund and two CNR contracts: one with the "Progetto finalizzato Informatica" and another with the "Progetto finalizzato Robotica". At the moment, the following students are completing their "Tesi di laurea in Fisica" on the topics here discussed: F. Ruggero, M. Sena, C. Totaro, D. Vitale.

REFERENCES

[1] Mc Culloch, W. S. and W. Pitts - "A logical calculus of the ideas immanent in the nervous activity" Bull. Math. Bioph. 5 (1943) 115-143.
[2] Rumelhart, D. E., J. L. McClelland and the PDP Research Group - "Parallel distributed processing. Vol I Foundations" MIT Press, Cambridge (Mass.) USA (1986).
[3] Caianiello, E. R. - "Outline of a theory of thought processes and thinking machines" J. of Theor. Biol. 2 (1961) 204-235.
[4] Abbruzzese, F. and F. E. Lauria - "An assembler for a Mc Culloch and Pitts network" IEEE First Conf. on Neural Net. M. Caudill and C. Butler eds. San Diego (CA) USA IV (1987) 601-608.
[5] Lauria, F. E. - "On a learning neural network" from "Biomathematics and related computational problems" L. M. Ricciardi ed. Kluwer Acad. Pub., Dordrecht (1988) 483-496.
[6] Lauria, F. E. - "A connectionist approach to knowledge acquisition" Cyber. and Syst.: an Int. J. 19 (1988) 35-88.
[7] De Pinto, P. "The implementation of the assembler associated to a general purpose neural network". Submitted to the "Third Italian workshop on parallel architectures and neural networks" to be held in Vietri sul Mare (SA), Italy. May 15-19, 1990.
[8] Lauria, F. E. - "Learning as the high level language for a neural network". R. Trappl ed. "Cyber. and Syst. '88" Kluwer Acad. Pub., Dordrecht (1988) 383-390.
[9] Lauria, F. E. - "An universal, loops free, digital neural network" E. R. Caianiello ed. " Parallel architectures and neural networks. First Italian workshop." World Scient. Pub. Co., Singapore (1989) 274-308.
[10] Lauria, F. E. - "Learning implementation on a deterministic general purpose network" Neural Networks Supl. 1 (1988) 548.
[11] Lauria, F. E. - "A general purpose neural network as a new computing paradigm" E. R. Caianiello ed. "Second italian workshop on parallel architectures and neural networks" World Scient. Pub. Co., Singapore (1990)(in print).
[12] Sette, M. "An OCCAM simulation of a general purpose neural network". Submitted to the "Third Italian workshop on paralllel architectures and neural networks" to be held in Vietri sul Mare (SA), Italy. May 15-19, 1990.
[13] Lauria, F. E. "A cybernetic approach to the Hebb rule implementation in a McCulloch and Pitts network." R. Trappl ed. "Cyber. and Syst. '90" World Scient. Pub. Co., Singapore (1990)(in print).
[14] Hebb, D. O. "The organization of the behavior. A neurophsychological theory" J. Wiley & Sons, New York (NY) USA (1949).

Advanced Neural Computers / R. Eckmiller (Editor)

ON THE ALGEBRAIC STRUCTURE OF FEEDFORWARD NETWORK WEIGHT SPACES

Robert Hecht-Nielsen

HNC, Inc.
5501 Oberlin Drive
San Diego, CA 92121

and
Department of Electrical and Computer Engineering
University of California at San Diego
La Jolla, CA 92139

Abstract

Many feedforward neural network architectures (such as backpropagation) have the property that the weights of two units on a hidden layer can be interchanged without altering the input/output function of the network, given appropriate rearrangements of the weights on the next layer. Networks of this type are termed *permutable*. The existence of this property implies that the weight space of such a network has symmetries which could reduce the difficulty of finding a suitable set of weights for a particular application. In this paper it is shown that the set of invertible linear weight transformations that leave the input/output transfer function of the entire network unchanged form a subgroup of the group of invertible linear mappings from the weight space to itself. Further, it is shown that there exists a cone in weight space in which each weight equivalence class generated by this subgroup has an element. Thus, in searching for a suitable set of weights, only weights in this cone need to be considered. The fraction of weight space occupied by the cone is much larger than the inverse of the order of the subgroup. It is shown that much smaller weight search sets can be constructed.

1 Introduction

It has long been known that many feedforward neural networks (such as classical backpropagation [1] and backpropagation with sigma-pi units [3]) have the property that, if the weights of two units on a hidden layer are interchanged (without disturbing the internal order of the individual weights within the units), and if those weights on the next layer assigned to the inputs from these units are also appropriately interchanged, then the outputs of the network (given a fixed input vector) will remain unchanged (see Figure 1). We shall call networks with this property *permutable*. The weight spaces of permutable networks have symmetries that make many network weight vectors *equivalent*, meaning that they can be transformed into one another by one of these weight transformations. This interchangeability implies

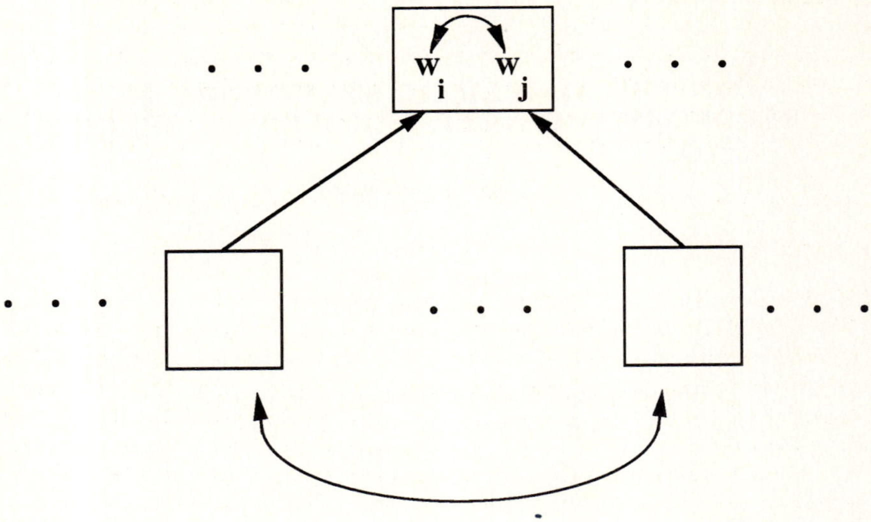

Figure 1: Transposition of the weight vectors of any two hidden layer units (which is equivalent to simply interchanging the units themselves) of a permutable neural network (and interchange of the appropriate weights within units of the next layer) leaves the output of the network unchanged.

that it is not necessary to search all of weight space to find a set of weights that meet a particular network input/output performance criterion. To investigate this issue further, we examine some algebraic issues concerning permutable networks.

2 The Algebra of Weight Equivalence

For notational convenience, we shall refer to the set of all weights of a permutable network (ordered in some regular way) as the network's *weight vector* $\mathbf{w}$. We shall assume that the network has a total of q adjustable coefficients that are real numbers. Therefore, $\mathbf{w} \in R^q$.

The set of all permutations of the elements of $\mathbf{w}$ form the non-abelian group S_q (the *symmetric group* of degree q), which will be referred to simply as S [2]. Recall that S contains $q!$ elements. Given a permutable neural network, we let T be the set of all nonsingular linear weight transformations (i.e., invertable linear mappings from R^q to R^q) that leave the input/output transfer function of the entire network unchanged.

By the definition, T must contain the set of permutations generated by exchanging the weights of pairs of hidden layer units of a permutable network (without disturbing the internal order of the individual weights within the units) and interchanging the weights assigned to the inputs to the next layer from these units. However, T can contain more than just this set of permutations. For example, in a backpropagation network, the signs of all of the weights of one hidden layer unit can be reversed and the signs of the input weights associated with the outputs of this unit at the next higher layer can be reversed and their bias weights raised by the initial value of these input weights. This transformation, which is *not* a permutation, also leaves the input/output function of the network unchanged[1]. Finally, note that, by definition, the set T associated with any permutable neural network will be a subset of the General Linear Group $GL(q, R)$ – the group of all invertible linear transformations from R^q to R^q. Given these definitions, the following theorem can be established:

Theorem 1: T is a proper subgroup of $GL(q, R)$ of order $\#T \geq \prod_{i=1}^{K} M_i!$, where M_i is the number of units on hidden layer i, and K is the number of hidden layers.

Proof: To show that T is a subgroup, we need to establish that T is closed under identity, inverse, and multiplication. Since the transformation of any element of T leaves the input/output transfer function of the network unchanged, the composition (multiplication) of such transformations will also leave it unchanged, and thus the product will be in T. T is automatically closed under inversion, since the inverse of a weight transformation in T simply restores the network to the state it was in before transformation, and thus preserves the same overall network input/output function. Thus, T is a subgroup of $GL(q, R)$. In fact, T is a proper subgroup since, for example, the permutation of two weights within a single first hidden layer unit (which is an invertible linear transformation in S – which is itself a proper subgroup of $GL(q, R)$) cannot be accomplished by any element of T.

The lower bound on the order of T can be established by considering the hidden layers sequentially from the first (the one that receives inputs from the input units[2]) to the last. Any permutation of the units of the first hidden layer can be generated by permutations (*transpositions*) between pairs of units of that layer. This follows from the fact that any permutation group is generated by its transpositions (see [2]). Thus, on the first hidden layer, T contains the group of all first hidden layer unit permutations with weight orderings left unchanged within the units. This group is of order $M_1!$.

The weight interchange permutations of the second hidden layer units (following *any* desired rearrangement of weights on the first hidden layer and the appropriate compensatory weight rearrangements on the second hidden layer) are again isomorphic to the group of all second hidden layer unit permutations, which has order $M_2!$. This process is repeated for each hidden layer through hidden layer K (the last hidden layer). Since the unit permutation selected at each hidden layer is independent of the one selected at the previous hidden layer, there will be a total of $\prod_{i=1}^{K} M_i!$ elements in T. Clearly, T will typically be larger than this, since if we did a permutation on the second hidden layer first (assuming the network has multiple hidden layers), and then did one on the first hidden layer, we would end up with a permutation in T that is different from all of those we found by following the previously described procedure. It is also possible for non-permutation transformations (such as those previously described for backpropagation) to occur in T. Thus, $\#T \geq \prod_{i=1}^{K} M_i!$. ■

---

[1]Note: this example assumes that the activation function $s(u) = (1+e^{-u})^{-1}$ is used, since $s(-u) = 1-s(u)$ for this function.

[2]See [1] for terminology

3 Weight Space Symmetries

T can be viewed as a transformation group acting on weight space R^q. As previously established, this transformation group contains certain weight permutations, which can be viewed as interchanges of the coordinate axes corresponding to the permuted weight vector coordinates — transformations that are geometrically characterized as reflections. In fact, each such permutation transformation can be expressed as a sequence of binary weight transpositions, each of which corresponds in weight space to a reflection through a hyperplane containing all of the axes (other than the two being transposed), as well as the line through the origin that is oriented at a 45 deg angle in the positive quadrant of the plane of these two axes. Thus, the geometry of this type of group action is very simple; exploiting this geometric simplicity allows us to prove the following:

Theorem 2: For each permutable neural network, there exists a cone H in its weight space (R^q) such that:

(i) H is a proper subset of R^q.

(ii) Given any $\mathbf{w} \in R^q$, there exist $\mathbf{u} \in H$ and $\sigma \in T$ such that $\sigma\,\mathbf{u} = \mathbf{w}$. In other words, every weight vector in R^q is equivalent to a weight vector in H. Thus, given any network input/output performance criterion, we need only search in H for an optimum weight vector.

(iii) H is defined by a set of linear inequalities in the weight values.

(iv) H depends on only the network architecture; not on the use to which the network is being put (such as the approximation of a function).

Proof: For our purposes, a *cone* in R^q is defined to be a set such that if $\mathbf{u}$ is in the set and $a \in R$ then $a\mathbf{u}$ is also in the set. Necessarily, the vertex of such a cone is the origin. Note also that the union of any two cones is a cone.

The proof is by construction. We begin with the cone $I = \{\mathbf{x} \in R^q \mid |x_i| \leq |x_1|,\ i = 2,3,\ldots,q\} \subset R^q$. The R^3 version of this cone is shown in Figure 2. I has the property that $SI = R^q$. This is easy to verify, because a permutation of weight w_1 into w_k will simply convert I into $\{\mathbf{x} \in R^q \mid |x_i| \leq |x_k|,\ i \neq k\}$. Since S contains all of these transpositions (and a lot more), SI contains geometrically congruent copies of I centered around each of the q coordinate axes of R^q. Clearly, the union of these sets is the entire weight space since every weight vector has the property that the magnitudes of all of its coordinates are less than or equal to the magnitude of its largest magnitude coordinate (in the cone of which the vector will lie). We now construct H from rotated copies of I.

H is defined to be the union of copies of I rotated via coordinate transposition reflections to selected coordinate axes. The coordinate axes selected are those corresponding to the weights of the first units of each hidden layer and the weights of the output layer units. Clearly, transpositions of the weight vector of the first unit of each hidden layer with the weight vectors of other units of that layer are in T and these transpositions will indeed move the copies of I around the first unit's weight axes to the weight axes of all of the weights of the other units of that hidden layer. All of the weight axes of the output layer weights are already part of H and so these axes are automatically covered. Thus, $TH = R^q$. Note that

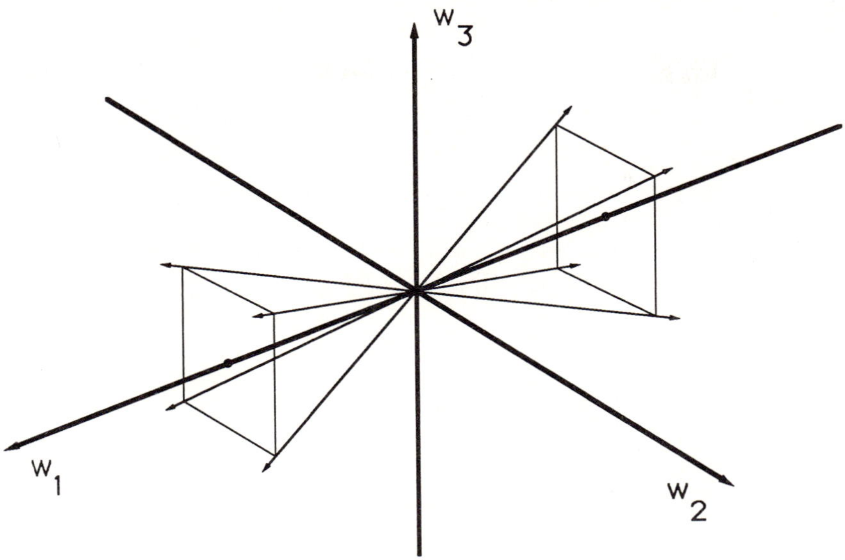

Figure 2: The cone I in R^3 (drawn narrower than it really is for clarity). I is symmetric about the w_1 axis and is bounded by the "45°" planes containing the w_2 and w_3 axes. Transposition of the w_1 axis with the w_2 axis or with the w_3 axis will simply produce a geometrically congruent cone centered about the w_2 or w_3 axis. The union of all three of these cones is the entire weight space.

for some networks (like ordinary backpropagation) H could be defined to be smaller since the intraunit permutations of weights on the second hidden layer and higher layers would distribute a copy of I on the bias and first input weight of the first unit of those layers to all other weight axes of weights belonging to units of that layer. However, for example, this scheme would have to be modified for sigma-pi backpropagation networks [3]. Thus, the H defined above works for an arbitrary permutable network, but may not necessarily be minimal in all cases.

Clearly, as shown above, each reflected copy of I is also described by a set of linear inequalities in the weight values. Thus, so is their union H. Finally, because of the way we have constructed H, it has no dependance on the use to which the network is being put. ∎

A natural question that arises in connection with Theorem 2 is whether or not this approach to constructing H can lead to a minimal search set for a particular network? In other words, if we construct H from a minimal number of copies of I for a particular network configuration, will the resulting H contain a proper subset H' such that $TH' = R^q$? We now explore the answer to this question.

First, consider the NETtalk backpropagation network [4], which has one hidden layer with 80 units. Thus, by Theorem 1, its T group is of order greater than $80! \doteq 10^{119}$. The H cone for this network is constructed in accordance with the proof of Theorem 2, using the fact that for the output layers of backpropagation networks we need only place in H the I copies corresponding to the bias and first input weights of the first unit of the output layer.

This cone occupies roughly 1% of the weight space (note that I itself occupies $(1/q)^{th}$ of weight space). Now consider a weight vector (assumed to be finite) that gives the network global minimum mean squared error performance for approximating some particular speech production input/output function. This weight vector is equivalent to at least 10^{118} other weight vectors obtained by applying the transformations of T. We can assume that at least 10^{116} of these equivalent weight vectors are in H. Thus, H is hardly free of redundancies!

Generalizing from the above example, it seems clear that a much smaller search region $H' \subset H$ must exist. One way to approach this problem is to define such minimal search regions and then explore their properties. This process is started with the following definition.

Definition 1: A *minimal search set* is a subset G of R^q for which the following two conditions hold:

(i) $T\,G = R^q$.

(ii) Given any $\mathbf{w} \in G$ and any $\sigma \in T$ (other than than the identity), then $\sigma\,\mathbf{w}$ is not in G.

Given this definition, the following theorem presents some facts about minimal search sets.

Theorem 3: Every permutable neural network has at least one minimal search set G. Also, no proper subset of a minimal search set can be a minimal search set.

Proof: To show that a minimal search set must exist, apply the axiom of choice to the orbits (equivalence classes) induced by the action of T on R^q to select one vector from each orbit. The set of these vectors is a G. With respect to subsets, let $\mathbf{w}$ be any element of G that is missing from the subset. Then, by the definition of minimal search sets, $\sigma\,\mathbf{w}$ will not be in G, for any $\sigma \in T$, *including* the identity. Thus, the equivalence class of $\mathbf{w}$ will not have a representative in G and $T\,G \neq R^q$. Thus, this subset cannot be a minimal search set. ∎

There are many questions about minimal search sets that remain open. For example: will there always be a G that is a cone? Clearly, there is much more work to be done before an understanding of minimal search sets will be achieved.

4 Discussion

Theorem 2 provides a means for significantly (but not spectacularly) reducing the volume of weight space that must be searched to find a set of weights that allow the neural network to best achieve a specified input/output performance goal. The question then becomes: how can this result be used? The answer seems to depend upon what type of learning scheme is being used. If a scheme that depends upon the smoothness of an error surface (such as ordinary backpropagation learning [1]) is being used then there seems little point in being concerned about H. This is because if we are conducting a gradient descent (or whatever), it is no disadvantage to continue following the surface beyond the confines of the set H (assuming that we started in H). The fact that this same error surface feature is also to be found somewhere in H matters little because, for one thing, it *is* the same, and for another, we don't know where to find it.

If a learning method, such as genetic learning, that does not exploit the smoothness of the error surface is being used then it may make sense to confine the search for a suitable weight vector to the set H. The simple linear inequalities that define H are easy to implement and provide a means for reducing the redundancy of the search.

References

[1] Hecht-Nielsen, Robert, "Theory of the Backpropagation Neural Network", *Proc. 1989 International Joint Conference on Neural Networks*, IEEE Press, New York, I(593-611), 1989.

[2] MacLane, Saunders, and Birkhoff, Garrett, **Algebra**, Macmillan, New York, 1967.

[3] Rumelhart, David E., and McClelland, James L., **Parallel Distributed Processing: Explorations in the Microstructure of Cognition**, Vols. I & II, MIT Press, 1986.

[4] Sejnowski, Terrence J., and Rosenberg, Charles R., "NETtalk: A Parallel Network that Learns to Read Aloud," Johns Hopkins University EE & CS Technical Report JHU/EECS-86/01, 1986.

Advanced Neural Computers / R. Eckmiller (Editor)

STATISTICAL PATTERN RECOGNITION REVISITED

Teuvo Kohonen

Helsinki University of Technology
Laboratory of Computer and Information Science
Rakentajanaukio 2 C, SF-02150 Espoo, Finland

The name "Pattern Recognition" was initially coined for a discipline, the history of which dates back to the mid-1950s. One of its basic objectives has been to categorize vectorial stochastic data into discrete classes according to simple metric relationships. The first approaches were based on either the adaptive "delta rule", which is essentially a Robbins-Monro stochastic approximation procedure, or decision-theoretic classification methods using the well-known Bayes probability formulas. Combined with other classical approaches to describe the class density functions such as the Parzen windows, the problem was thought to be solved completely long time ago. In principle it may be so, but in practice, computational aspects such as training and recognition times must be taken into account. The Neural Network hardware would also favor more straightforward operations amenable to analog computing. It has now turned out that certain new self-organizing approaches, here grouped under the title Learning Vector Quantization (LVQ), can combine theoretically near-optimal accuracy with very high speed in learning and recognition; moreover, their implementation by analog VLSI is straightforward. This presentation reports recent experiments, mainly relating to automatic recognition of speech, which demonstrate that there still exist fresh views and effective new solutions to traditional problems.

1. Introduction

Statistical Pattern Recognition is an area in mathematical statistics that deals with random, metrically relatable stochastic vectorial variables. In its purest form it constitutes a particular discipline in the statistical decision theory. Its purpose is to classify input samples.

Assume that each sample vector $\boldsymbol{x} = \boldsymbol{x}(t) \in R^n$, $t = 0,1,2,...$ belongs to some class C_i ; then the objective is to define optimal **decision surfaces** (of dimensionality n-1) that divide R^n into due class zones. A new, unknown sample is classified into C_i if its representation falls into the respective zone. In most real problems, the class distributions of the samples overlap, whereby the above classification decision is bound to commit errors: every sample that really belongs to class C_i but falls into the neighboring zone will be counted as a misclassification.

If every classification decision is provided with equal weight, it can be shown (cf., e.g., [1]) that the average misclassification cost is minimized if for every pair of "neighboring" classes C_i and C_j the decision surface is analytically defined by the following equation in $\boldsymbol{x}$:

$$p(x|C_i)P(C_i) = p(x|C_j)P(C_j) , \tag{1}$$

where $p(x|C_i)$ is the probability density function of input samples $\boldsymbol{x}$ belonging to class C_i, and $P(C_i)$ is the a priori probability of occurrence of class C_i among the samples. In other words, *the optimal decision surfaces are defined by the crossings of the class distributions.*

There exist many traditional approaches to the approximation of class distributions on the basis of available samples. In the **parametric methods**, the general form of the density function is fixed (e.g., multivariate normal distribution), and, say, the class means and covariance matrices in the analytical expressions are then estimated on the basis of training samples. An example of **nonparametric methods** is the *Parzen window* method, in which a fixed "kernel" is defined and centered around every training sample; the "kernel" must be defined everywhere in R^n, and a symmetric Gaussian is a usual choice.

A different approach altogether is the **Learning Vector Quantization (LVQ)** introduced by the present author for the first time in 1986 [2-5]. In order to drastically reduce the number of computations at every classification decision, each class C_i is only described by a relatively small number of *reference* or *codebook vectors* $\boldsymbol{m}_k$, properly placed within each class zone such that the decision borders are approximated by the nearest-neighbor rule: $\boldsymbol{x} = \boldsymbol{x}(t)$ is classified into C_i, if some codebook vector $\boldsymbol{m}_k$ of C_i is closest to $\boldsymbol{x}$. Unlike in another familiar method, namely, the *k-nearest-neighbor (kNN)* classification, the original samples are not used as codebook vectors, but they "tune" the latter. Optimal placement of the effective codebook vectors into the class zones constitutes a very subtle problem that, however, can be solved recursively. In all the methods discussed in this presentation, the $\boldsymbol{m}_k$ are defined in iterative "learning" processes. However, a common problem to all of them is "adequate" choice of the initial values of the $\boldsymbol{m}_k$. This problem will be discussed first.

2. Initialization of the Codebook Vectors

One strategy in initialization is to place a desirable number of codebook vectors into R^n such that they approximate the overall probability density function $p(\boldsymbol{x})$, and then to label them according to the majority of classes of the closest sample vectors.

As a matter of fact, in the classical (unsupervised) Vector Quantization (VQ) [6] the purpose is indeed to approximate density functions by the $\boldsymbol{m}_k$, and if $\boldsymbol{m}_c$ is the closest codebook vector to $\boldsymbol{x}$,

$$\|\boldsymbol{x}-\boldsymbol{m}_c\| = \min_k \{\|\boldsymbol{x}-\boldsymbol{m}_k\|\} , \tag{2}$$

to use $\boldsymbol{m}_c$ in place of all the $\boldsymbol{x}$ in its neighborhood. The average squared discretization error is defined by the functional

$$E = \int \|\boldsymbol{x}-\boldsymbol{m}_{c(\boldsymbol{x})}\|^2 \, p(\boldsymbol{x}) d\boldsymbol{x} \tag{3}$$

where $d\boldsymbol{x}$ denotes here a volume differential in the $\boldsymbol{x}$ space. It has been shown in [7-9] that the placement of the $\boldsymbol{m}_k$ that minimizes E also approximates the function $[p(\boldsymbol{x})]^{n/(n+2)}$. In practical problems we have usually $n>>2$ whereby, *if the $\boldsymbol{m}_k$ are placed to approximate $p(\boldsymbol{x})$, they also minimize the (initial) discretization error.*

Another effective automatic method to find the initial values of the $\boldsymbol{m}_k$ is based on the **Self-Organizing Map** algorithm introduced by this author [1], or on one of its refinements [10,11].

Although initialization is by no means a trivial problem, we shall leave it here because it mainly only optimizes the allocation of the computing resources; it is usually possible to guarantee any degree of classification accuracy by a sufficient number of codebook vectors initially placed in a suboptimal way. The final accuracy, however, centrally depends on the accurate values of the codebook vectors, and therefore we shall concentrate in the following on processes that define their asymptotic, optimized values.

3. The First Version of Learning Vector Quantization (LVQ1)

Assume now that the number of codebook vectors in each class and their initial approximate values have been selected by some "adequate" method, and a placement that is supposed to minimize the classification errors has to be determined. The first iterative algorithm LVQ1 corrects the $\boldsymbol{m}_k(t)$, $t = 0,1,2,...$ as follows: if $\boldsymbol{x} = \boldsymbol{x}(t)$ is a random input sample belonging to some known class, and the codebook vectors are similarly assigned to a number of different classes, then Eq. (2) is always used to define the closest codebook vector $\boldsymbol{m}_c$. After that, the $\boldsymbol{m}_k = \boldsymbol{m}_k(t)$ are updated according to the rule:

$$\begin{aligned}
\boldsymbol{m}_c(t+1) &= \boldsymbol{m}_c(t) + \alpha(t)[\boldsymbol{x}(t)-\boldsymbol{m}_c(t)] \\
&\quad \text{if } \boldsymbol{x} \text{ and } \boldsymbol{m}_c \text{ belong to the same class ,} \\
\boldsymbol{m}_c(t+1) &= \boldsymbol{m}_c(t) - \alpha(t)[\boldsymbol{x}(t)-\boldsymbol{m}_c(t)] \\
&\quad \text{if } \boldsymbol{x} \text{ and } \boldsymbol{m}_c \text{ belong to different classes ,} \\
\boldsymbol{m}_k(t+1) &= \boldsymbol{m}_k(t) \qquad \text{for } k \neq c \ , \qquad (4)
\end{aligned}$$

and $0 < \alpha(t) < 1$, whereby α is decreasing monotonically with time (e.g., linearly or exponentially, starting from a small value like 0.01 or 0.02).

This algorithm tends to pull the codebook vectors away from the class borders, leaving a "depletion layer" around the Bayesian decision surfaces. This can be deduced in the following way. If the steepest-descent gradient-step optimization method is first applied to minimize E in Eq. (3) on the basis of successive stochastic samples $\boldsymbol{x}(t)$, then the corrections read

$$\begin{aligned}
\boldsymbol{m}_c(t+1) &= \boldsymbol{m}_c(t) + \alpha(t)[\boldsymbol{x}(t) - \boldsymbol{m}_c(t)] \ , \\
\boldsymbol{m}_k(t+1) &= \boldsymbol{m}_k(t) \quad \text{for } k \neq c \ , \qquad (5)
\end{aligned}$$

and $\alpha(t)$ defines the relative size of the gradient step. The $p(\boldsymbol{x})$ in Eq. (3) implies what samples $\boldsymbol{x}(t)$ and with what statistical frequency there occur in the sequence defined by Eq. (5). If we then switch back to the two-class problem, Eq. (4), the minus sign in the second equation may be interpreted as *to define corrections in the same direction as if Eq. (5) were used for the class to which* $\boldsymbol{m}_c$ *belongs, but the probability density function of the neighboring (overlapping) class were subtracted from it.* In other words, we would perform a classical Vector Quantization of the function $|p(x|C_i)P(C_i) - p(x|C_j)P(C_j)|$ where C_i and C_j are the neighboring classes. The difference of the density functions of the neighboring classes, by definition, falls to zero at the Bayes border, inducing the above "depletion layer" of the codebook vectors.

One may state quite safely that the LVQ1 algorithm is *self-stabilizing* for well-behaved density functions and reasonable choice of the initial values of the $\boldsymbol{m}_k$. In practice stability means that the asymptotic state is unique although the number of iteration steps is increased without limits, provided that $\alpha(t) \rightarrow 0$ when $t \rightarrow \infty$.

4. The LVQ2

This algorithm, although so far defined only in a sketchy way, has already been adopted by many researchers (e.g., [12-13]). While in the LVQ1 only one codebook vector was updated at a time, this algorithm updates *two* vectors at each step, namely, the "winner" and the "runner-up". The purpose is to shift the midplane of these two vectors directly towards the place where the Bayes border is supposed to lie. An algorithm that can easily be seen to work in that direction is the following. First define a "window" (cf. below and Fig. 1) around the midplane of neighboring codebook vectors $\boldsymbol{m}_i$ and $\boldsymbol{m}_j$. Let $\boldsymbol{m}_i$ belong to class C_i and $\boldsymbol{m}_j$ to class C_j, respectively. The corrections are defined by

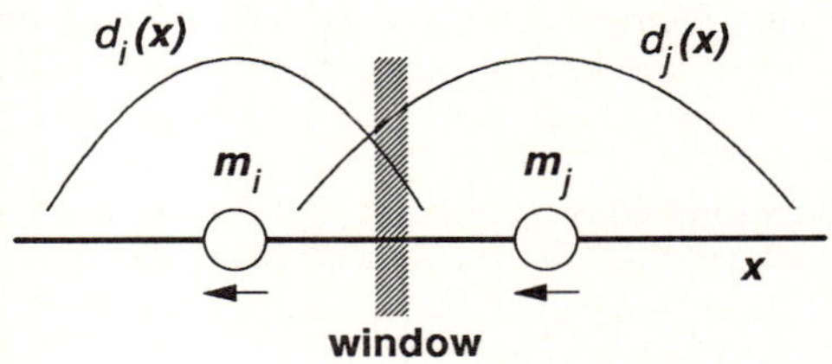

Fig. 1

$$\boldsymbol{m}_i(t+1) = \boldsymbol{m}_i(t) - \alpha(t)[\boldsymbol{x}(t)-\boldsymbol{m}_i(t)] \quad ,$$

$$\boldsymbol{m}_j(t+1) = \boldsymbol{m}_j(t) + \alpha(t)[\boldsymbol{x}(t)-\boldsymbol{m}_j(t)] \quad ,$$

if $\boldsymbol{m}_i$ is the nearest codebook vector to $\boldsymbol{x}$ and $\boldsymbol{m}_j$ the next-to-nearest one, respectively, and $\boldsymbol{x}$ belongs to C_j but not to C_i; furthermore $\boldsymbol{x}$ must fall into the "window". (5)

One question concerns the practical definition of the "window". If we are working in a high-dimensional signal space, it seems reasonable to define the "window" in terms of relative distances d_i and d_j from $\boldsymbol{m}_i$ and $\boldsymbol{m}_j$, respectively, having constant ratio s. In this way the borders of the "window" are Apollonian hyperspheres. The vector $\boldsymbol{x}$ is defined to lie in the "window" if

$$\min\,(d_i/d_j\,,\,d_j/d_i) > s\,. \tag{6}$$

If w is the relative width of the window in its narrowest point, then $s = (1-w)/(1+w)$. The optimal size of the window depends on the number of available training samples. If we had a large number of samples, a narrow window would guarantee the most accurate location of the border; but for good statistical accuracy the number of samples falling into the window must be sufficient, too, so a 20 per cent window seems a good compromise, at least in the experiments reported below.

Warning: For reasons that will be explained below, one should apply the basic LVQ2 for short-term fine tuning only: e.g., starting with $\alpha(0) = 0.01$ to 0.02, and letting it decrease to zero in no more than about 10000 training steps. If "training" is continued longer, even with a small value of α, the results may start getting worse.

5. Instabilities in the Basic LVQ2

The LVQ2 algorithm was based on the idea to *differentially* shift the decision borders towards the Bayes limits, whereas no attention was paid to what might happen to the placement of the $\boldsymbol{m}_k$ in the long run if this process were continued. Thus, although some researchers have reported good results, some have had problems, too. It has turned out that at least two different kinds of detrimental effects must be taken into account.

5.1. Mutual attraction of the corrected codebook vectors

Because the distance of $\boldsymbol{x}$ from $\boldsymbol{m}_j$ (correct class) has a larger magnitude than from $\boldsymbol{m}_i$ (wrong class) and corrections are proportional to distance, this results in monotonically decreasing distances $\|\boldsymbol{m}_i-\boldsymbol{m}_j\|$. Although this effect is not as severe with high dimensionality (where the corrections on $\boldsymbol{m}_i$ and $\boldsymbol{m}_j$ in general are not in the same direction) as when, e.g., n = 1 or 2, nonetheless it might be an improvement if the corrections on $\boldsymbol{m}_i$ and $\boldsymbol{m}_j$ had the same magnitude. A straightforward remedy would thus be to normalize the lengths of the corrections. However, this would make the learning computations significantly heavier and longer. An alternative is to compensate for the above effect, approximately at least, by other means.

The original assumption about corrections depending on *errors* only seems unnecessary, as already indicated by the LVQ1 experiments. We can accept *all the training vectors falling into the "window"*, and the only condition is that *one* of $\boldsymbol{m}_i$ and $\boldsymbol{m}_j$ must belong to the *correct* class, and *the other* to the *incorrect class*, respectively. This algorithm, dubbed "LVQ2.1" would then read

$$\boldsymbol{m}_i(t+1) = \boldsymbol{m}_i(t) - \alpha(t)[\boldsymbol{x}(t)-\boldsymbol{m}_i(t)]\,,$$

$$\boldsymbol{m}_j(t+1) = \boldsymbol{m}_j(t) + \alpha(t)[\boldsymbol{x}(t)-\boldsymbol{m}_j(t)]$$

where $\boldsymbol{m}_i$ and $\boldsymbol{m}_j$ are the two closest codebook vectors to $\boldsymbol{x}$, and $\boldsymbol{x}$ and $\boldsymbol{m}_j$ belong to the same class, while $\boldsymbol{x}$ and $\boldsymbol{m}_i$ belong to different classes; furthermore $\boldsymbol{x}$ must fall into the "window". (7)

Notice that $\|\boldsymbol{m}_i-\boldsymbol{m}_j\|$ can now both increase and decrease. At the same time more than twice as many corrections are made as in the LVQ2, which increases statistical accuracy in learning.

5.2. Drifting of the codebook vectors along the borders

The only attention in the LVQ2 was paid to the corrections of the codebook vectors perpendicular to the decision border, while there was still no control factor present that would keep the vectors steady in the direction parallel to the border. As a matter of fact, even when starting with reasonably good initial values, the corrections in Eq. (7) seem to cause drifting of the $\boldsymbol{m}_i$ and $\boldsymbol{m}_j$ away to new, nonoptimal stationary places, and after a while, the classification accuracy again starts to decrease. Apparently some effect must be added that sustains some kind of "cohesion" within each class such that the $\boldsymbol{m}_k$ keep approximating the density functions; the LVQ1 in fact contained this effect because it also corrected those codebook vectors that were not responsible for classification at the border. The simplest remedy is therefore to add these corrections to LVQ2, too, but provided with a controllable parameter ε, since the size of this effect is not quite predictable.

6. The LVQ3

Combining the ideas presented in Secs. 5.1. and 5.2., we now obtain an improved algorithm that may be called LVQ3:

$$m_i(t+1) = m_i(t) - \alpha(t)[x(t)-m_i(t)] ,$$
$$m_j(t+1) = m_j(t) + \alpha(t)[x(t)-m_j(t)]$$

where m_i and m_j are the two closest codebook vectors to x, and if x and m_j belong to the same class, while x and m_i belong to different classes; furthermore x must fall into the "window";

$$m_k(t+1) = m_k(t) + \varepsilon\alpha(t)[x(t)-m_k(t)]$$

for $k \in \{i, j\}$, if x, m_i, and m_j belong to the same class. (8)

Here the optimal value of ε depends on the size of the window. With narrow windows ε must be small. In a series of experiments, a proper value of ε was in the range 0.1 to 0.5. After introduction of this extra "cohesion", the process seemed to become self-stabilizing even over extensive periods of learning (say, hundreds of thousands of learning steps).

7. Taking More "Runners-up" into Account

The decision border is determined by those codebook vectors that are adjacent to each other over it. It then quite commonly occurs that an input vector has several neighboring codebook vectors in the same class that are almost equidistant from it. Therefore, in order to still increase the statistical accuracy of learning, the corrections might not only be restricted to the "winner" and the first "runner-up", but taking the second etc. "runners-up" also into account. An additional advantage of this is that whereas the updated "runners-up" are often also mutual neighbors in the correct class, their simultaneous correction tends to place them more smoothly.

8. Experiments with Speech Data

In a typical Neural Network Speech Recognition experiment the input pattern vectors are rather high dimensional and they may be formed, say, as a concatenation of several adjacent speech spectra (e.g., seven spectra from a 70-ms time window centered at the phoneme to be recognized [12,13]). As the purpose of the present study was *relative* comparison of algorithms, we only used *single, 15-frequency-channel spectra* of phonemes (from Finnish speech). The task was very much the same as in our real-time microprocessor-based "Phonetic Typewriter" [14]. As a matter of fact, that device was used to collect the data for this experiment. The number of statistically independent spectral vectors applied for training vs. testing (1550 + 1550) also corresponded to a typical task for which the LVQ was used, namely, quick enrollment of a new speaker after having collected about 150 to 200 words of his dictation. In Test 1, the first of the sets was used for training and the second for testing, respectively; in Test 2 the order was reversed. By and large the experimental setup corresponded to that used in our earlier reports [4,5]. The number of codebook vectors was 117. (We must emphasize, however, that for the practical design of speech recognizers, we avail about $2 \cdot 10^9$ bytes of digital speech data in our files.)

For comparison, Table 1 also contains the recognition accuracies [4,5] for the same data using the Parametric Bayes Classifier (with assumed multivariate normal distributions), the kNN classification results (identical with k = 5 and 6 neighbors), and earlier results relating to the LVQ1 and LVQ2 classifiers, respectively. The earlier differential improvements by the LVQ2 were based on rather short learning periods of about 10000 steps, but there would have been no guarantee of optimal asymptotic states, if this process had been made longer. To these, the LVQ2.1 classifier experiments using one vs. two "runners-up" to the "winner" as well as the LVQ3 results (stable for very long training) have been added.

Table 1 Speech recognition experiments. Error percentages for isolated phonemes.

	Parametric Bayes	kNN	LVQ1 (long)	LVQ2 (short)	LVQ2.1 (short) one runner-up	LVQ2.1 (short) two runners-up	LVQ3 (long)
Test 1	12.1	12.0	10.2	9.8	9.3	9.3	9.6
Test 2	13.8	12.1	13.2	12.0	11.5	11.0	11.5

Although the LVQ3 results are not best, they have been obtained safer than those of LVQ2 and LVQ2.1 ; therefore, if there exists any suspicion about how the process behaves in a particular application, one might resort to either LVQ1 or LVQ3, and use long training cycles.

9. Conclusions

Categorization of signal patterns is one of the most usual Neural Network (NN) applications. It has been demonstrated with artificial as well as natural data that the Learning Vector Quantization methods constitute a very viable alternative to the more traditional approaches: their classification accuracy is at least as high as that of any other NN algorithm, while due to the very simple computations thereby applied, their speed in learning as well as in classification can be significantly higher. Moreover they are very easy to use.

The LVQ algorithms are working explicitly in the input domain of the primary observation vectors, and their purpose is to approximate the theoretical Bayes decision borders using piecewise linear decision surfaces. This is done by optimal placement of the class codebook vectors into the signal space. As the classification decision is based on the nearest-neighbor selection among the codebook vectors, its computation is very fast, and can also be done by an analog "winner-take-all" circuit. It has turned out that the differences between the presented methods in regard to the remaining discretization error are not significant, and thus the choice of the algorithm may be based on secondary arguments, such as stability in learning.

While the classification accuracy of the LVQ algorithms has been demonstrated to be very close to the decision-theoretic Bayes limit even in difficult cases, nonetheless some minor problems have remained: one of them is optimal initialization of the codebook vectors, and another their self-stabilization during the learning process. The present work aims at providing some helpful answers to such questions and other details. Some new developments are introduced here for the first time; they perform slightly better or are more stable than the earlier versions.

References

[1] T. Kohonen, *Self-Organization and Associative Memory*, 3rd ed., Springer-Verlag, Berlin, Heidelberg, Germany, 1989.

[2] T. Kohonen, "Learning Vector Quantization for Pattern Recognition," Helsinki University of Technology, Department of Technical Physics, Laboratory of Computer and Information Science, Report TKK-F-A601, 1986.

[3] T. Kohonen, "An Introduction to Neural Computing," Neural Networks, vol. 1, pp. 3-16, 1988.

[4] T. Kohonen, "Learning Vector Quantization," Neural Networks 1, Supplement 1, p. 303, 1988.

[5] T. Kohonen, G. Barna, and R. Chrisley, "Statistical Pattern Recognition with Neural Networks: Benchmarking Studies," Proc. IEEE Int. Conf. on Neural Networks, San Diego, Cal., USA, July 24-27, 1988, pp. I - 61-68.

[6] J. Makhoul, S. Roucos, and H. Gish, "Vector Quantization in Speech Coding," Proc. IEEE, vol. 73, no. 11, pp. 1551-1588, 1985.

[7] J. Max, "Quantizing for Minimum Distortion," IRE Trans. Inform. Theory, vol. IT-6, no. 2, pp. 7-12, Mar. 1960.

[8] A. Gersho, "On the Structure of Vector Quantizers," IEEE Trans. Inform. Theory, vol. IT-28, pp. 157-166, Mar. 1982.

[9] P.L. Zador, "Asymptotic Quantization Error of Continuous Signals and the Quantization Dimension," IEEE Trans. Inform. Theory, vol. IT-28, no. 2, pp. 139-142, Mar. 1982.

[10] T. Kohonen, K. Mäkisara, and T. Saramäki, "Phonotopic Maps - Insightful Representation of Phonological Features for Speech Recognition," *Proc. Seventh Int. Conf. on Pattern Recognition*, Montreal, Canada, July 30 - August 2, 1984, pp. 182-185.

[11] J. Kangas, T. Kohonen, J. Laaksonen, O. Simula, and O. Ventä, "Variants of Self-Organizing Maps," *Proc. IJCNN 89, Int. Joint Conf. on Neural Networks*, Washington, D.C., USA, 1989, pp. II - 517-522.

[12] E. McDermott and S. Katagiri, "Shift-Invariant, Multi-Category Phoneme Recognition Using Kohonen's LVQ2," *Proc. Int. Conf. Acoust., Speech, Signal Processing*, Glasgow, U.K., 1989, pp. 81-84.

[13] H. Iwamida, S. Katagiri, E. McDermott, and Y. Tohkura, "A Hybrid Speech Recognition System Using HMMs with an LVQ-trained Codebook," ATR Technical Report TR-A-0061, August 25, 1989, ATR Auditory and Visual Perception Research Laboratories, Japan.

[14] T. Kohonen, "The 'Neural' Phonetic Typewriter," Computer, vol. 21, pp. 11-22, Mar. 1988.

Advanced Neural Computers / R. Eckmiller (Editor)

LOCAL LEARNING RULES AND SPARSE CODING IN NEURAL NETWORKS

Günther PALM

Vogt-Institut für Hirnforschung
Heinrich-Heine-Universität Düsseldorf
D-4000 Düsseldorf, F.R.Germany

In technical applications of associative neural network memories the following adjustments are optimal, if the neuron output is binary:
- the neuron output should be 0 or 1
- the local learning rule should be the Hebb rule
- the pattern vectors should be sparse, i.e. most components should be zeroe.

If these conditions are fulfilled, one can achieve an asymptotic memory capacity of $1/(2 \ln 2) \approx 72\%$ and of $\ln 2 \approx 69\%$ with a binary memory matrix.

1. INTRODUCTION

In this short note I want to discuss some recent results on the optimization of the information storage capacity of associative memories that are based on local synaptic learning rules.

I consider two essentially different memory tasks, namely hetero- and auto-association. In auto-association a set $S = \{x^1, \ldots, x^M\}$ of "patterns" (n-vectors) is stored by forming the connectivity matrix $M = (M_{ij}) = \sum_{k=1}^{M} R(x_i^k, x_j^k)$, where the function or rule $R(x,y)$ determines explicitely the amount of synaptic connectivity change for a pair (x,y) of pre- and postsynaptic activity values.
In hetero-association a set $S = \{(x^1,y^1), \ldots, (x^M,y^M)\}$ of pairs of patterns is stored by forming the matrix $M = \sum_{k=1}^{M} R(x_i^k, y_j^k)$.

The amount of information about S that can be retrieved from M is the storage capacity $H(m,n)$ for a hetero-associative mxn matrix, and $A(n)$ for an auto-associative nxn matrix. Then the asymptotic storage capacity (per synapse) is defined as the limit
$A = \lim A(n)/n^2$ and $H = \lim H(m,n)/(m \cdot n)$, for auto- and hetero-association, respectively. Similarly one defines the asymptotic

memory capacity for a specific storage and retrieval procedure by the amount of information about S that can be retrieved from M by means of that storage procedure. In particular, we shall consider one step threshold detection retrieval in this note.

We want to study the dependence of $A = A(R)$ or $H = H(R)$ on the choice of the rule R. To simplify the discussion, we restrict ourselves to network models with *two-state neurons* (as in the spin-glass literature), although many of the subsequent arguments could be extended to more general neuron models. This restriction means that the variables x and y determining the local synaptic change, can have only two values, here taken as 0 and 1, and thus a rule $R(x,y)$ is defined by 4 numbers (r_1, r_2, r_3, r_4), since there are four cases of activity combination:
(1) low pre- and postsynaptic activity,
(2) low pre- and high postsynaptic activity,
(3) vice versa,
(4) high pre- and postsynaptic activity.

2. HETERO-ASSOCIATION

In the following we assume that the pattern vector components x_i^k and y_j^k are independently generated binary random variables with $\text{prob}[x_i^k=1] = p$ and $\text{prob}[y_j^k=1] = q$ for all $i = 1,..,m$, $j = 1,..,n$, $k = 1,..,M$. Another interesting parameter is $\alpha = M/n$. The retrieval is performed by means of threshold detection as follows: Each input vector x^k is multiplied by the storage matrix M yielding the vector z with components $z_j = \Sigma_i\, x_i^k\, M_{ij}$. Threshold detection with a threshold θ is performed on each component z_j of z to obtain an estimate for y_j. In this procedure there are two kinds of error probabilities: $e_{10} = \text{prob}[z_j<\theta \mid y_j=1]$ and $e_{01} = \text{prob}[z_j \geq \theta \mid y_j=0]$.

Proposition 1: For hetero-association and threshold-detection retrieval the maximal asymptotic capacity is achieved for the optimal rule $R_0 =(pq,-p(1-q),-(1-p)q,(1-p)(1-q))$, or for any rule $R = a + b\, R_0$ with $b = 0$. For any rule R the best choice of the parameter p is given by the relation $p \rightarrow 0$, i.e. the input patterns should be *sparse*.

Apart from the optimal local synaptic rule R_0 defined in Prop. 1, there are two other important rules in the literature: the Hebb-rule H = (0,0,0,1) and the Hopfield- or correlation-rule C = (1,-1,-1,1).

Proposition 2: If $p \to 0$, i.e. if the input patterns are sparse, then the signal-to-noise ratios for the rules H, C and R_0 are
$r^2(H) = n(1-p)/[Mq(1-pq)] \approx n/(Mq)$,
$r^2(C) = 8np(1-p)/[M(p(1-q)+(1-p)q)] \approx 8np/(Mq)$ and
$r^2(R_0) = n/[Mq(1-q)]$.
Otherwise, only $r^2(R_0)$ is nonzeroe, but $r^2(H) = r^2(C) = 0$.

Proposition 3: If the condition $p \to 0$ is not fulfilled asymptotically, then every rule different from R_0 has zeroe asymptotic memory capacity for hetero-association and threshold-detection retrieval.

The obvious requirement that e_{01} and e_{10} should be small translates into the corresponding requirement that the signal-to-noise ratio r should be large. If one wants to store many patterns, i.e. if one wants to avoid that $\alpha = M/n$ goes to zeroe, then this can only be achieved for the rules H and R_0 and for $q \to 0$, i.e. for extremely sparse output-patterns.

3. HIGH FIDELITY

In the following we distinguish two asymptotically different fidelity requirements:
(i) The high fidelity (hifi) requirement $e_{10} \to 0$ and $e_{01}/q \to 0$. This requirement implies that $r \to \infty$ as $n \to \infty$. By Prop. 2 this is only possible for $q \to 0$, if we do not want to require that $\alpha \to 0$, i. e. that we can store only a very small number of patterns. Since an associative memory only makes sense, if the number of patterns that can be stored, is reasonably large, we have to require that $q \to 0$ in the cases (1) and (2), i.e. we need extremely sparse output patterns.
(ii) The low fidelity (lofi) requirement: e_{10} and e_{01} stay constant (but small) for $n \to \infty$ and thus r = constant as $n \to \infty$.

The lofi requirement was used in most calculations in the spin-glass literature. From the lofi requirement we can easily calculate M. For the rule R_0 we get $M = n/(r^2q(1-q))$ and for H we get $M = n(1-p)/(r^2q(1-pq))$.
With this value for M one can compute the asymptotic storage capacity H_0.

With the high fidelity requirement the information necessary for error correction can be asymptotically neglected, thus the retrievable information per pattern becomes $n \cdot q \cdot \log_2 q$.
The hifi requirement can just be achieved by $r = \sqrt{-2 \ln q}$, i.e. $\alpha = 1/(-2q(1-q)\ln q)$ for the rule R_0. This leads (for $q \to 0$) to an optimal asymptotic capacity of $H_0 = 1/(2 \ln 2)$.

Proposition 4: For hetero-association with the optimal rule R_0 and threshold-detection retrieval the following asymptotic memory capacity can be achieved under the hifi requirement:
$H_0 = 1/(2 \ln 2)$.
This requirement can only be achieved in the sparse limit, i.e. for $p,q \to 0$ as $n \to \infty$.

Proposition 5: For hetero-association and threshold detection retrieveal the following asymptotic memory capacities can be achieved for the rules H and C:
$H_H = H_0$ for $p,q \to 0$
$H_C = 0$ unless $p \to 0$ and $q \not\to 0$.

Proposition 6: For hetero-association and threshold detection retrieval from a binary (clipped) memory matrix the following asymptotic memory capacities can be achieved with the Hebb rule H and the correlation rule C:
$H_H{}^b = \ln 2$ for $p,q \to 0$
$H_C{}^b = 0$ unless $p \to 0$ and $q \not\to 0$.

4. AUTO-ASSOCIATION

The case of auto-association is treated in essentially the same way as hetero-association; we simply have fewer parameters, since $y^k = x^k$, $m = n$ and $p = q$. More exactly, we take as input x a pattern that is a 'subset' of one of the stored patterns x^k in the sense that every 1 in x is also a 1 in x^k.
Again we perform threshold detection on $z = x \cdot M$ to obtain an estimate for x^k. This procedure is called one-step *pattern-completion* because it is not iterated and because x contains only 1-s which are in x^k, so that the task is to complete x^k given a part or 'subset' x.

Proposition 7: If the condition $p \to 0$ is not fulfilled asymptotically, then every rule essentially different from R_0 has zeroe asymptotic memory capacity for auto-association and one-step threshold-detection retrieval. Even with the rule R_0, high fidelity can only be achieved for $p \to 0$.

Proposition 8: For auto-association and one-step threshold-detection retrieval the following asymptotic memory capacities can be achieved:
$A_0 = 2/(27 \ln 2)$ with the hifi requirement,
$A_H = A_0$ for $p \to 0$,
$A_C = 0$.

Proposition 9: For auto-association and one-step threshold-detection retrieval from a binary (clipped) memory matrix the following asymptotic memory capacities can be achieved:
$A_H^b = (\ln 2)/4$ for $p \to 0$,
$A_C^b = 0$.

5. CONCLUSION: SPARSE CODING IS NECESSARY

These results show that optimal use can be made of local learning rules and the associative memory scheme, if the following pre-requisits are fulfilled:

1) The patterns that are stored have to be sparse.
2) The local learning rule should be the optimal rule, or the Hebb rule. If the patterns are sparse the Hebb rule is almost identical to the optimal rule and much easier to implement.
3) Clipping of the synaptic weights to binary values does not hurt much, if (1) and (2) are fulfilled, and it saves computing time and memory space.

Thus sparse coding techniques will be the key to economical applications of associtive neural network memories. Such techniques will have to be investigated for each application in particular. One can speculate whether sparse coding is also used in the brain. The idea at least fits with a lot of physiological evidence.

The results presented here do fit well with the recent spin-glass literature (e.g. Gardner [1], Horner [2], Nadal and Toulouse [3], Amit et al. [4]) and with my previous calculations [5], [6]. For a more detailed discussion one should consult my review [7].

ACKNOWLEDGEMENTS

I am grateful to F. Sommer for many discussions of the subject. This work has been partly supported by the BMFT.

REFERENCES

[1] Gardner E., The Space of Interactions in Neural Network Models, Journal of Physics A (1988) 257-270.
Gardner E., Derrida B., Optimal Storage Properties of Neural Network Models, Journal of Physics A (1988) 271-284.
[2] Horner, H., Neural Networks with Low Levels of Activity: Ising vs. NcCulloch-Pitts Neurons, Z. Phys.B (1988) 1-10.
[3] Nadal, J.-P. and Toulouse, G., Information Storage in Sparsely-Coded Memory Nets, Preprint to appear in Network, Computation in Neural Systems (1990)
[4] Amit, D. J., Gutfreund, H. and Sompolinsky, H., Information Storage in Neural Networks with Low Levels of Activity, Physical Review A 35 (1987) 2239-2303.
[5] Palm, G., On Associative Memory, Biological Cybernetics 36 (1980) 19-31.
[6] Palm, G., Local Synaptic Rules with Maximal Information Storage Capacity, in: Haken H., (ed.), Neural and Synergetic Computers (Springer, 1988) pp. 100-110.
Palm, G., On the Asymptotic Information Storage Capacity of Neural Networks, in: v. d. Malsburg, Ch. and Eckmiller, R. (eds.), Neural Computers (Springer, 1988) 271-280.
[7] Palm, G. On the Information Storage Capacity of Local Learning Rules. Submitted to Physical Review A (1990).

Advanced Neural Computers / R. Eckmiller (Editor)

Speeding up Backpropagation

Fernando M. Silva - Luis B. Almeida[1]
INESC
Apartado 10105, P-1017 Lisboa Codex, Portugal
fcr@inesc.inesc.pt - lba@inesc.inesc.pt

ABSTRACT

Backpropagation is probably the best known, and most widely used learning algorithm for neural networks. It is a gradient based optimization procedure, and it suffers from the common limitations of this kind of algorithms, namely in what concerns convergence speed. In this paper, we present an improvement to the backpropagation algorithm, based on the use of an independent, adaptive learning rate parameter for each weight. We discuss the reasons for using this modification to the basic algorithm, and we give experimental results showing the improvement in learning speed obtained with this method.

1. INTRODUCTION

Backpropagation [2] is probably the best known, and most widely used learning algorithm for neural networks. In its most basic form, it is a simple gradient optimization procedure:

$$w_{ij}(n+1) = w_{ij}(n) - \eta\, \partial E/\partial w_{ij} \tag{1}$$

where E is the cost function being minimized (usually the quadratic output error), w_{ij} is a generic weight in the network, and η is the *learning rate*, or *step size* parameter.

These procedures have some well known drawbacks. The first, and simplest one, is just the difficulty in the choice of the value of η. Too small a value will result in a very slow convergence, while if the value is too large, the optimization process will diverge, instead of converging to a minimum of the cost function. In the presence of a new learning problem, the best value for this parameter is not known, and in fact it will often vary during the course of the optimization. The choice of the best value is especially hard when the problem being addressed is very large, involving perhaps a few hours of simulation for a single sweep through the whole training set.

Another, more important drawback, is the slowness of convergence when the hypersurface that represents the cost function being minimized, presents deep and narrow valleys (ravines). One of the earliest methods to be proposed for overcoming this limitation, was the use of the *momentum term* [2], which corresponds in fact to a recursive low pass filtering of the gradient of the cost function. It has the effect of attenuating "high frequency" oscillation across the ravine, and/or amplifying the "DC" component of the gradient along the bottom of the ravine. It can be quite effective for straight valleys, but when the valley presents bends, the memory effect of the recursive filtering process can be so long, that it will drive the procedure very far from the bottom of the valley.

We cannot review in detail here the various methods that have been proposed to overcome the speed limitations of backpropagation learning, but some of the most important references are [1,3,5-9]. References [6] and [7] deserve a special mention, because they propose the second-order methods that probably are simplest. Their relative simplicity stems from the fact that they both use only the diagonal terms of the Hessian matrix (in [7] these terms are computed exactly, through a backpropagation procedure, while in [6]

[1] Both authors are also with Instituto Superior Técnico, Lisboa, Portugal.

they are only evaluated in an indirect, approximate way). We will come back to a qualitative comparison with these methods by the end of this paper.

In [1,4,5] the use of a first-order method is proposed, with an independent, adaptive step size for each parameter, and this is the kind of approach that will be explored in the present paper. The rationale that we will give for doing this are somewhat different form from Sutton's, though both reasonings can be shown to be qualitatively equivalent. Let us consider, for simplicity, that we want to minimize, by gradient descent, a function of just two variables, $f(x,y)$, and assume that, at some step in the minimization process, we are at the point (x_0,y_0). The application of the simple gradient descent algorithm would yield updates given by

$$x(n+1) = x(n) - \eta\,\partial f/\partial x \quad ; \quad y(n+1) = y(n) - \eta\,\partial f/\partial y \tag{2}$$

Let us make the change of variables given by

$$x = au \quad ; \quad y = bv \tag{3}$$

where a and b are two positive constants, and consider the function

$$g(u,v) = f(au,bv) = f(x,y) \tag{4}$$

Clearly, minimizing f and minimizing g are two equivalent problems. However, if we use simple gradient descent in both cases, and if we start from corresponding points, it is easy to see that the trajectories that we will follow in the minimization process are different. In fact, assume that we are now considering function g, and that we are at the point

$$(u_0,v_0) = (x_0/a, y_0/b) \tag{5}$$

The update corresponding to gradient descent in g is given by

$$u(n+1) = u(n) - \eta\,\partial g/\partial u \quad ; \quad v(n+1) = v(n) - \eta\,\partial g/\partial v \tag{6}$$

which, expressed in terms of the original variables (x,y) becomes

$$x(n+1) = x(n) - a^2\eta\,\partial f/\partial x \quad ; \quad y(n+1) = y(n) - b^2\eta\,\partial f/\partial y \tag{7}$$

This update could be interpreted in terms of update equations (2) as the use of two *different* step sizes, one for each coordinate

$$\eta_x = a^2\eta \quad ; \quad \eta_y = b^2\eta \tag{8}$$

Therefore, using independent learning rate parameters for each of the variables in a gradient descent procedure is essentially the same as performing a simple independent rescaling of those variables. In the next section, we will discuss, in an intuitive way, how such a rescaling can be put to advantage to overcome, to a certain extent, the problem of ravines.

2. RESCALING AND RAVINES

Let us first consider, for simplicity, a two variable quadratic function, and assume that it has a narrow valley extending along the x direction (figure 1a). If we perform a suitable compression along this direction, the valley will disappear altogether, as in figure 1b (the same result could be achieved by performing a suitable expansion along the y direction, or a mixture of both). While in figure 1a the direction of the gradient points very far from the minimum, in figure 1b the gradient points directly at the minimum (which could be reached in a single iteration if the correct step size were known). Given the reasoning of the previous section, performing a compression along the x axis is equivalent to using a larger step size along that direction. This is depicted by the dashed arrow in figure 1a, which also points directly at the minimum. In general, the function being minimized won't be quadratic, and there will be no rescaling that makes the valley disappear completely. However, it still remains a fact that, given a narrow valley aligned with one of the coordinate axes, a suitable compression along that axis will make the valley become much less narrow, thus making the minimization procedure much easier.

Consider now a function with a valley that is not exactly aligned with the x axis (figure 1c). The best we can now do, is to perform a compression along the x axis, such that the direction of the valley comes to make a 45° angle with each of the axes (figure 1d). The valley will have become much less narrow, thus again making the minimization procedure easier. Of course, the gain obtained by this procedure will become smaller as the original valley direction becomes more diagonal to the coordinate axes. However, in a large neural network problem, which corresponds to a minimization in a space with many dimensions (often in the order of thousands), there will most probably exist many valleys which can gain from this compression procedure. Furthermore, as noted by Sutton [1] there are reasons to believe that in neural networks, valleys that are almost parallel to some axis will often exist[2].

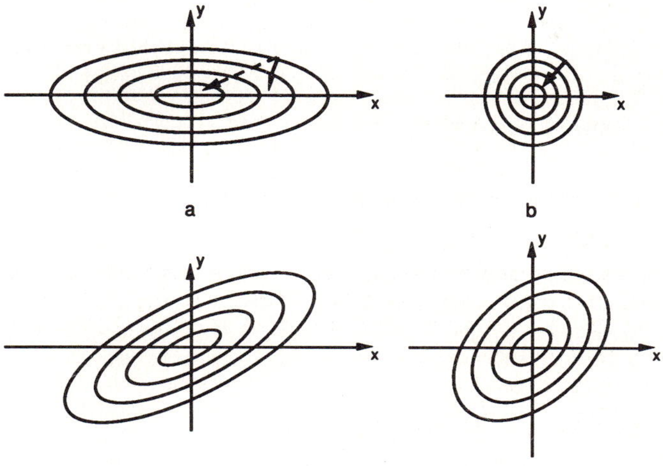

Fig. 1 - Illustration of valleys, and of the effects of compression on their widths (see text for explanation).

3. STEP SIZE ADAPTATION

The above discussion has shown the advantages of being able to use an independent step size for each weight in the network, but the question of how to choose the most appropriate step sizes remains still open. Before proceeding, note that solving this problem, effectively also solves the first difficulty that we discussed at the introduction, the choice of the (single, at the time) step size.

The basic ideas for solving this problem were given in [1,4], and a first implementation was described in [5]. Here, we will follow the same basic ideas, but we will implement a procedure that is somewhat different (and, in our understanding, better) than the one of [5]. Let us first consider a single-dimensional case: we are trying to minimize the function $E(x)$[3]. If, in two successive iterations, the updates of x (or equivalently, the gradient values) have opposite signs, that means that we have "jumped over a minimum" and that the step size is too large. On the other hand, if two successive signs are equal, it appears that we could have moved somewhat faster, while still not passing beyond the minimum. The basic heuristic for adaptation is then simply to decrease the step size if two successive updates have opposite signs, and to increase it if they have the same sign. In [5] it was proposed to use a linear step size increase, and an exponential step size decrease. According to our view, the linear increase is a major drawback of that procedure, given the very wide dynamic range of step sizes that may be needed in a single network, and we will propose using both an exponential increase and an exponential decrease of the step size. More specifically, we will update the step size according to

$$\eta(n) = u\,\eta(n-1) \qquad \text{if } \partial E/\partial x(n) \text{ and } \partial E/\partial x(n-1) \text{ have the same sign} \tag{9a}$$

[2] This reasoning also implies that there is still much to be gained if an algorithm can be found, which deals with diagonal valleys in an efficient, distributed manner.

[3] We will assume, for the time being, that the exact value of the gradient of the function to be minimized is known in each iteration of the optimization. Therefore, in the usual nomenclature of neural networks, we are performing *deterministic* or *batch* learning. Step size adaptation in the context of *stochastic* or *real-time* learning will be briefly discussed in section 6.

$$\eta(n) = d\,\eta(n-1) \qquad \text{if } \partial E/\partial x(n) \text{ and } \partial E/\partial x(n-1) \text{ have opposite signs} \tag{9b}$$

where $\partial E/\partial x(n)$ is a shorthand notation for the derivative of the error function computed at the point $x(n)$, and u and d are factors slightly above and below 1, respectively (e.g. $u=1.2$ and $d=0.7$ — we shall see later that the exact values of these factors are not critical). The update of the optimization parameter will naturally be performed by

$$x(n+1) = x(n) - \eta(n)\,\partial E/\partial x(n) \tag{10}$$

In the multidimensional case, the step size adaptation procedure is the same, *applied independently for each parameter (or weight) in the network*, i.e., the step size corresponding to each weight will be adapted according to equations (9), *based only on the sign changes of the updates of that weight.* In a simple, ideal situation, in which the optimal value of each step size were constant throughout the minimization process, the step size corresponding to a given weight would exponentially increase from its initial value, being multiplied by u in each iteration (or, alternately, it would continually decrease, being multiplied by d in each iteration), until it would just pass its optimal value. After that, it would keep in a small oscillation around the optimal value, being multiplied by d when above that value, and by u when below it. In real situations, each step size will normally have periods of exponential increase or decrease, interspersed with periods of oscillation, as the optimization process moves along ravines of different orientations and widths.

Let us come back, for a moment, to the ideal case of a constant optimal step size for each weight. We could say that, after these optimal step size values have been reached in the adaptation process, the rescaling that we are implicitly performing (which, as we have seen above, is equivalent to the use of independent step sizes) will scale the valley in such a way that the direction of its bottom is at equal angles to all coordinate axes. By doing that, it will make the valley as little narrow as possible (how narrow the valley stays, depends on its original direction and width). This is the best that can be done by a procedure that can only perform rescaling along the coordinate axes. In a more real situation, where valleys often present bends and variations in their width, the step sizes will have to adapt continuously during the optimization process, and the valleys will be in the optimal position mentioned above, only when the step sizes are essentially at their locally optimal values, i.e., when they enter the above-mentioned oscillatory periods. During the periods while step sizes are continuously increasing or decreasing, the local performance of the learning will not be optimal, though it will still be much better than could be obtained by the use of a single step size for all weights. The choice of the values of the factors u and d for the adaptation must result from a compromise between a fast adaptation (which would require values much above and below 1, respectively) and a small oscillation around the optimal step sizes (which would demand values as close to 1 as possible). In practice, we have found that values close to 1 (u in the range 1.1 - 1.3 and d in *the range* 0.7 - 0.9, approximately) generally yield good results, and that the exact values that are chosen within these ranges are not crucial in any way, as long as $d \approx 1/u$[4].

4. SOME IMPLEMENTATION DETAILS

In this section, we will describe some further details of the implementation of the adaptive step size technique, that we have used in the tests reported ahead.

4.1. Combining with the momentum term

Since, even with adaptive weights, there will still be valleys in the error surface where we are performing optimization, the use of the momentum term will still generally be of advantage. We will apply the momentum filtering to the gradient components, before multiplying by the adaptive step sizes. For example, for the single-parameter function $E(x)$ that we used in section 3, the update equation (10) would be replaced by

$$x(n+1) = x(n) - \eta(n)\,z(n) \tag{11a}$$

[4] This discussion naturally leads to the idea of also using an adaptation procedure for the factors u and d themselves, and possibly even using an independent pair of factors for each weight's step size adaptation. A simpler version of this variation of u and d would consist of starting with a relatively large u (say, in the range 2 - 10) and a correspondingly small d, and later changing them to values close to 1. In fact, in the initial iterations of learning, the step sizes normally depart from their initial values (which have usually been chosen apriori, often with the same value for all step sizes) and move towards their locally optimum values, some of which may be very far from the initial ones. This phase will be much shorter if u and d are far from 1, but after that, they should come close to 1, to allow the step sizes to stay close to their optimum values. We have not yet explored any of these possibilities.

where

$$z(n) = \partial E/\partial x(n) + \alpha\, z(n-1) \tag{11b}$$

α being the momentum parameter. The extension of these equations to the multidimensional case is straightforward.

4.2. Controlling the error evolution

Occasionally, there will be a situation during the training, in which the local shape of the error surface will be such that even the step sizes that result from the adaptive procedure will yield a weight update that leads to an increase in the total error E. Note that, since all step sizes are positive, the direction of the update is still a direction of descent in the error surface[5], but in this case we will have made too long a move in that direction. We must therefore keep control of the evolution of the error in each iteration, and we must take appropriate measures if it increases. Of course, one thing we must do in this case, is to move back to the previous point, where we were before the last iteration[6]. Then, we can simply reduce the magnitude of the weight update, keeping the same update direction. This will amount to multiplying all step sizes by the same number (smaller than *1*, e.g. *0.5*) and repeating the iteration (if the error still increases, the same procedure will be applied over and over, until the length of the weight update is small enough for the error to decrease). However, we have found it useful to still perform the step size adaptation in the way described above — equations (9) — based on the changes of sign of the gradient components between the original, and the rejected iteration point, for up to two or three "false" iterations, before resorting to the simple simultaneous reduction of all step sizes. But we should also note that this kind of situation, in which the error increases after an iteration, occurs only very seldom.

4.3. Preventing overflow and underflow

The exponential increase or decrease of the step sizes can, in some situations, lead to overflow or underflow situations. To prevent this, we have set upper and lower bounds to the step sizes. These bounds were, respectively, a few orders of magnitude below the largest representable number, and a few orders of magnitude above the smallest representable positive number, for the system where the simulation was being run.

5. EXPERIMENTAL RESULTS

5.1. Diagonal valleys

In a first experiment, aimed at evaluating the performance of the adaptive step size technique in the case of a simple, two variable quadratic valley with various orientations, we used the function

$$E = (ax_r)^2 + y_r^2 \tag{12}$$

where x_r and y_r are the coordinates along the two principal directions of the valley, and a is a parameter controlling the valley width. We have set $a=0.02$ (any value of a less than 1 yields a valley along the x_r direction). We then made a simple rotation transformation between the pair of variables (x_r,y_r) and the pair (x,y) that was used in the optimization, to be able to set the valley direction to any desired angle ϕ relative to the x axis. We always started the optimization at the (x,y) point corresponding to $(x_r,y_r) = (100,2)$, and we used as stopping criterion the condition $E<0.001$.

We have set $\eta=0.5$ for the conventional, non-adaptive gradient technique (we found this value to be nearly optimal, after some preliminary tests). In the adaptive technique, we used this same value of *0.5* for initializing the two adaptive step size parameters. In one of the cases, we also tried the value of *0.05* both for the step size of the conventional technique, and for initializing the adaptive step sizes, to be able to test the sensitivities of both methods to these values. We used, for the step size adaptation algorithm, $u=1.2$ and $d=0.7$.

---

[5] Except for the possible effect of rounding errors in the computation of the gradient.

[6] We will therefore call this a "false" iteration.

Table 1 shows the results we obtained for various valley orientations, both without momentum (α=0) and with momentum (α=0.5 and α=0.9)[7]. The results for ϕ=0 show how effective the adaptive step size technique can be when the valley is oriented along one of the coordinate axes. The improvement relative to the classical gradient technique is of more than two orders of magnitude, if no momentum is used, and is still of about 20 times with a momentum of α=0.9. Also, as we would expect, the influence of the momentum term is very strong in the classical technique, but very weak in the adaptive one, which can cope very effectively with valleys with this orientation.

Table 1 - Test on diagonal valleys. Each entry shows the number of iterations needed to reach the solution

Rotation ø (degrees)	Conventional BP				Adaptive BP			
	α=0	α=.5	α=.9		α=0	α=.5	α=.9	
	η=.5	η=.5	η=.5	η=.05	η=.5	η=.5	η=.5	η=.05
0					44	38	35	48
10					507	344	467	495
20	10367	5180	1007	10339	1904	1137	1188	1204
30					3035	2017	1182	1198
45					3853	2675	1197	1209

As ϕ increases, up to 45°, the performance of the adaptive method decreases, but even for the worst orientation, this method still outperforms the classical technique by about three times, when no momentum is used. This is because it will still dynamically adapt the step sizes to the local curvature of the surface, instead of using a single, fixed value. Only with a large momentum (α=0.9) does the conventional technique slightly outperform the adaptive one. However, note that this situation, involving a completely straight valley, is ideal for the momentum technique, and doesn't normally occur in practice. Also note that we have used an approximately optimal value for η, found from preliminary experiments, and that if this value is decreased by, say, one order of magnitude, the performance of the conventional technique will also decrease by approximately the same amount, while the adaptive technique is relatively insensitive to the initial values that are chosen for the step sizes, as shown in the table.

5.2. Other tests

A number of other, more realistic tests were performed, in order to assess the performance of the adaptive step size method. In all of these, we have used a symmetric arctangent activation function, scaled between *-1* and *1*, in the network's units, and we have set the target values for binary outputs to *-0.8* and *0.8*. For the step size adaptation algorithm, we have used the same values as above, *u=1.2* and *d=0.7*. Each test was repeated 20 times, with different initializations of the weights (always with a uniform distribution in the interval *[-1,1])*. All the tests that we report use binary target outputs. However, in some cases, instead of stopping the training when there were no binary output errors, we have used a different stopping criterion, based on a (small) RMS output error, to simulate situations in which the mapping to be learned is analog. In the tables given below, the "false" iterations mentioned in section 4.2 were always counted. In all examples, learning was performed in the *batch* mode.

The first test consisted of a simplified digit recognition task. It consisted of training the network to recognize 15 versions of each of the digits 0, 1, 2 and 3, drawn on a 5x5 pixel retina. The network had 25 input units, a hidden layer with 9 units and an output layer of 4 units, the activation of each of these indicating the recognition of one of the digits. As mentioned above, we did not use a stopping criterion based on the absence of binary output errors. Instead, we trained the system until the RMS output error, averaged over the four outputs and the whole training set, was below 0.03. Table 2 shows the results that were obtained[8]. These results show that the adaptive method performed much better than standard

---

[7] For conventional backpropagation, the results are independent of ϕ, therefore only one value is shown in the table.

[8] Both in this table and in the following ones, the value indicated for η, in the adaptive method, refers to the value used to initialize all the adaptive step sizes in the network.

backpropagation in all cases, and showed a very small sensitivity to the value used to initialize the step sizes.

The second test consisted of a standard 10-5-10 encoder problem. The network had 10 input units, a hidden layer with 5 units and an output layer with 10 units. It was required to perform an identity mapping between input and output, for input patterns in which only one unit was active at a time. We performed this test both with a digital stopping criterion (no binary output errors in the training set) and with an analog one (RMS output error lower than 0.1). We tried three different training procedures: conventional backpropagation, adaptive backpropagation as proposed here, and also the adaptive, cosine technique proposed in [3].The results are shown in Table 3. For the cosine technique, η refers to the initial value, and α refers to the *momentum factor* of this algorithm.

Table 2 - Results of digit recognition test. In tables 2, 3 and 4, entries show the mean and standard deviation of the number of iterations needed to reach the solution

η	α	Conventional BP		Adaptive BP	
		Mean	Std. Dev.	Mean	Std. Dev.
0.05	0.0	1298.2	317.1	88.4	16.5
	0.5	733.3	169.4	54.4	6.0
	0.9	836.7	375.0	75.4	19.4
0.05	0.0	10748.3	2661.8	97.5	15.3
	0.5	6219.8	1937.7	64.2	5.9
	0.9	1806.6	425.0	84.5	12.1

Table 3 - Results for 10-5-10 encoder

Stopping Crit.→			BIN		RMS < 0.1	
Method	η	α	Mean	Std. Dev.	Mean	Std. Dev.
Conv. BP	0.5	0.0	130.0	93.0	>16000	—
Conv. BP	0.1	0.8	115.8	64.6	5181.6	3790.3
Adap. BP	0.005	0.0	73.0	19.9	116.8	38.7
Adap. BP	0.005	0.8	48.9	8.7	79.1	18.2
Cosine	0.005	0.0	98.7	33.5	280.3	175.0
Cosine	0.005	0.8	48.4	15.2	129.6	73.3

The results show that both the cosine and adaptive techniques performed better than conventional backpropagation, with the adaptive technique still outperforming the cosine one. The advantage of both of these techniques over the conventional one is especially apparent in the case of the analog stopping criterion. Here, with conventional backpropagation, only 3 out of the 20 trials reached the stopping criterion in less than 20,000 iterations, and this is why statistics for this case are not shown in the table.

The last test consisted of training a 3-to-8 decoder, of the form proposed by Jacobs in [5] (he proposed this problem as one which probably involves many diagonal valley situations). The network had 3 input units, a first hidden layer with a single unit, a second hidden layer with 8 units, and an output layer with 8 units, and was trained to perform a standard 3-to-8 binary decoding operation. In this test, we used only the absence of binary errors as stopping criterion.

The results, given in Table 4, again show the better performance of the adaptive technique. The fact that the momentum term plays a more important role here than in previous cases, apparently confirms that this problem involves narrow diagonal valleys. The results obtained by us with the adaptive technique are similar to those obtained by Jacobs in the same problem, with "optimal" initial parameters. However, while his technique appears to be highly sensitive to those parameters, the one we propose here, with an exponential increase and decrease of the step sizes is very insensitive to such parameters (note that we have used for this problem the same values of η, u and d that we had been using for all the previous ones)[9]. A surprising finding, was that the cosine technique did not yield any significant improvement over conventional back-

[9] The fact that our activation function was slightly different from the one used by Jacobs probably is of very little importance here.

propagation, and sometimes even performed worse, in this problem. We have no explanation for this, apart from the fact that this technique provides very low adaptation rates.

Table 4 - Results for 3-to-8 decoder

Method	η	α	Mean	Std. Dev.
Conv. BP	0.05	0.0	5513.5	1994.3
Conv. BP	0.05	0.9	2580.9	2843.5
Adap. BP	0.005	0.0	1828.0	1119.9
Adap. BP	0.005	0.9	421.4	325.3
Cosine	0.005	0.0	7069.5	4991.0
Cosine	0.005	0.9	2419.9	1909.6

6. DISCUSSION AND CONCLUSIONS

We have presented a simple modification of the standard backpropagation algorithm, which consists of using an independent, adaptive step size parameter for each weight. The step size adaptation is performed in an exponential manner, both in the upward and in the downward direction. We have shown results that substantiate the speed-up in learning obtained by this method. Two issues still deserve mention here. One is the applicability of this method to *real-time* learning. While this case is more complex, since there are special demands that the step size variation must obey, in order for convergence to be guaranteed, we can mention that we have applied this technique in the real-time mode, to a large task of noise reduction in speech, with good results. The way we used the technique in the real-time learning mode, was to perform the weight update for every presentation of an input pattern, but to perform the step size adaptation only once per sweep over the whole training set. The step size adaptation was performed as above, except that it now was based on the signs of the *accumulated* updates of the corresponding weight (accumulated over the whole training set).

The other issue that we wish to mention, is the relationship with the "diagonal" second-order methods of Le Cun and Fahlman. Though we did not have the opportunity to perform detailed comparisons, we think that all three methods exploit essentially the same information, namely the curvature of the error surface along directions parallel to the coordinate axes. Therefore, we would guess that their performances must be grossly similar. Second-order techniques may have the advantage of a faster adaptation, but they do that at the expense of somewhat higher computational complexity, and they may present some caveats, like providing moves in an upward direction (when the surface is locally curved downwards), or yielding unreasonably large moves in cases of low local curvature.

REFERENCES

[1] Sutton, R.S., "Two Problems With Backpropagation and Other Steepest-Descent Learning Procedures for Networks", *Proc. 8th Annual Conf. of the Cognitive Science Society*, 1986, pp 823-831.

[2] Rumelhart D.E., Hinton G.E. and Williams R.J., "Learning Internal Representations by Error Propagation", in *Parallel Distributed Processing: Explorations in the Microstucture of Cognition*, Cambridge, MA: MIT Press, 1986.

[3] Chan L.W. and Fallside F., "An Adaptive Training Algorithm for Back Propagation Networks", *Computer Speech and Language*, vol. 2., Sep/Dec. 1987, pp 205-218.

[4] Kesten H., "Accelerated Stochastic Approximation", *Annals of Mathematical Statistics*, 29, 1957, pp 41-59.

[5] Jacobs R., "Increased Rates of Convergence Through Learning Rate Adaptation", *Neural Networks*, vol. 1, N. 4, 1988.

[6] Fahlman S., "Faster-Learning Variations on Back-Propagation:An Empirical Study", *Proc. 1988 Connectionist Models Summer School*, Carnegie-Mellon Univ., 1988.

[7] Becker S. and le Cun Y., "Improving the Convergence of Back-propagation Learning with Second Order Methods", *Proc. 1988 Connectionist Models Summer School*, Carnegie-Mellon Univ., 1988.

[8] Parker D. B., "Optimal Algorithms for Adaptive Networks: Second Order Back Propagation, Second Order Direct Propagation, and Second Order Hebbian Learning", *Proc. IEEE First International Conference on Neural Networks*, San Diego, California, vol. 2, June 1987, pp 593-600.

[9] Watrous R. L., "Learning Algorithms for Connectionist Networks: Applied Gradient Methods of Nonlinear Optimization", *Proc. IEEE First International Conference on Neural Networks*, San Diego, California, vol. 2, June 1987, pp 619-627.

Section 4
Neural Network Simulators

Advanced Neural Computers / R. Eckmiller (Editor)

VLSI IMPLEMENTATION OF SENSORY PROCESSING SYSTEMS

L. A. Akers, S. Haghighi, and A. Rao

Center for Solid State Electronics Research
Arizona State University
Tempe, AZ 85287-6206

The implementation of neural-network-based computational schemes in silicon is an important means of solving real-world problems in real-time. Current technology imposes severe constraints upon the nature of circuits that are implementable. It is hence necessary to design otherwise biologically-inspired schemes to conform to these physical constraints. This work describes two vision-related applications which use only local spatial information and are hence excellent candidates for VLSI implementation.

1. INTRODUCTION

Advanced lithographic techniques and the consequent increase in circuit density make the prospect of implementing neural-network-based systems very attractive. Such systems are inherently parallel and are potentially more fault-tolerant than traditional systems.

The central problem in the construction of a VLSI synthetic neural network is the high fan-in/fan-out apparent in many biological systems. However, useful processing capability can be accomplished by limited-interconnect architectures. A well-known VLSI design constraint is that communication is expensive, and transistors are cheap. Limited-interconnect systems are therefore better suited for VLSI implementation.

Akers *et al.* describe two types of analog neural cells [1, 2] which can be used as building blocks for adaptive, limited-interconnect networks. These cells incorporate programmable weights, and are compact enough to permit dense implementations.

2. A LOCAL TRAINING RULE FOR DYNAMIC SCENE ANALYSIS

In order to use cell-implementations like the ones indicated above, it is necessary that any proposed technique for sensory processing use only local information. In this section, an unsupervised adaptation rule is described which allows characterization of the correlation between the elements of a two-dimensional, time-varying input image. This function effectively performs feature selection [3], and allows the output of a node to optimally preserve joint information among inputs.

2.1 Adaptation Rule

A node consists of several inputs and one output. The output y is the weighted spatio-temporal summation of the inputs. Let x_i, $i=1...m$ denote the inputs. The weights are labeled w_i. The variance of random variable y is denoted by σ_y^2. The covariance between x_i and x_j is c_{ij} and their correlation coefficient is ρ_{ij}. The fractional variance index J is defined as the ratio of the signal to the sum of signal and noise variance, where the signal is the correlation among inputs. For simplicity, initially nodes with 2 inputs are considered. The results are then extended to multiple inputs.

Case 1: m =2

The output variance (a measure of the average power at the output) for two hypotheses H_1 (uncorrelated inputs) and H_2 (correlated inputs) is

$$\sigma_y^2 (H_1) = w_1^2 \sigma_1^2 + w_2^2 \sigma_2^2 \tag{1}$$

$$\sigma_y^2 (H_2) = w_1^2 \sigma_1^2 + w_2^2 \sigma_2^2 + 2 w_1 w_2 c_{12}. \tag{2}$$

The difference between the two output variances is due to the correlation term $2w_1w_2c_{12}$. The objective is to choose w_1 and w_2 such that the output contribution from the correlation among inputs is optimized. This is accomplished by optimizing J where

$$J = \frac{2w_1 w_2 c_{12}}{w_1^2 \sigma_1^2 + w_2^2 \sigma_2^2 + 2 w_1 w_2 c_{12}}. \tag{3}$$

For $\rho_{12} = \rho_{21} = \rho$, the values

$$w_1 = \frac{K}{\sigma_1}, \; w_2 = \frac{K}{\sigma_2} \tag{4}$$

will maximize J for $\rho > 0$, and minimize it for $\rho < 0$. On the other hand,

$$w_1 = \frac{K}{\sigma_1}, \; w_2 = -\frac{K}{\sigma_2} \tag{5}$$

will minimize J for $\rho > 0$ and maximize it for $\rho < 0$. The output variance for (4) and (5) is

$$\sigma_y^2 = 2K^2 (1 \pm \rho). \tag{6}$$

Thus, fluctuations in the output variance σ_y^2 are caused by the correlation among inputs. If the weights are selected according to (4), the output of a node will optimally indicate positively correlated input patterns. Such an adaptation mechanism will simultaneously minimize the effect of negatively correlated inputs. Adaptation rule (5) has the opposite effect.

Case 2: m ≥ 2

Adaptation rule (4) can be extended to nodes with more than two inputs. An additional requirement is that the inputs must be equally correlated and

$$\rho \geq \frac{-1}{m-1}. \tag{7}$$

(7) guarantees that the output variance is positive.

2.2 Simulation Results

The unsupervised training rule (4) was incorporated into a pyramid architecture [4] of contraction factor 2, i.e. at every layer, each node combines two inputs into a single output. The input image has 512 x 512 pixels. Each pixel is represented by 8 bits. The reference image of Fig. 1 was dynamically blurred by uncorrelated Gaussian horizontal and vertical random movements with a mean of 0, and a variance of 1 pixel. Figure 2 illustrates the output of several layers of the pyramid network after 256 movements. These outputs were expanded to the original 512 x 512 pixel size to allow comparison with Fig. 1.

3. IGORS - A VLSI SMART SENSOR

This section addresses the design of a VLSI smart sensor which emulates the following aspects of physiological vision systems:

(i) Preservation of high-resolution without using a high density of light sensors throughout the sensing area.
(ii) The capacity to recognize objects regardless of their position or size.
(iii) The compact representation of images to allow efficient storage of a large number of images.

Scale, position, and rotation invariant transformation of two-dimensional images has been the subject of considerable attention. Olshausen [5], for example, reviews some representative techniques. However, most of these techniques are computationally intensive and difficult to realize in hardware. The objective here is to design an integrated circuit which employs some of the mechanisms used in the human eye to achieve significant performance advantages over conventional techniques.

3.1. Signature Generation

The abstraction method used in this work is based upon the magnitude and orientation of the angle present in their boundaries. The signature generated is a histogram, each bin of which corresponds to one of 24 orientations. Each corner in the image adds to its bin a quantity proportional to its "sharpness" - a straight line contributes nothing, and an acute angle contributes the largest amount. The histogram thus generated is invariant with respect to scale and position. Rotational invariance can be achieved by shifting the histogram by an appropriate amount.

The technique outlined above is heuristic, and is justified on the following grounds:

(i) The scanning mechanism used by the human eye suggests that the feature detection mechanism be independent of the order in which different regions of the image are visited.
(ii) The process of detecting a curvature discontinuity is a purely local operation and hence suitable for VLSI implementation.
(iii) Corners have the important property of being invariant with respect to scale and position.
(iv) There is some evidence that operations similar to corner detection are performed by cells in the visual cortex [6].

3.2. Simulation Results

A simulation program was written to determine the feasibility of the signature generation scheme proposed above. The program performs the following tasks:

(i) *Template-set generation.* The set consists of a template each for a specified number of orientations and angles.
(ii) *Interactive image input.* This allows the user to specify a region of the screen to be used as the input image.
(iii) *"Brute-force" scan.* In this process, all pixels of the image are matched against all generated templates.
(iv) *"Smart" scan.* In this process, the image area is first scanned using a lower resolution, and then feature detection applied only to those areas which have a line passing through them.
(v) *Graphics.* This depicts the analog signature generated in a bar graph, and displays all the templates corresponding to the corners found.
(vi) *Code classification.* A leader clustering scheme is used for each scan method. The best match is returned for already stored codes, and new codes are stored for future use. Figure 3 shows the results of the simulation program for the outlines of two military aircraft. In each case, the original outline and the code generated for two different scales are shown. The bar graph represents the code, and the image displays the templates found. The program classified all the cases correctly.

4. CONCLUSION

The need for VLSI implementation of sensory processing systems makes it necessary to use architectures which utilize local information. Two examples of sensory processing which incorporate this feature are presented. The first example is based on the optimal detection of local features in a dynamic image sequence. The resulting training rule is local and highly parallel. Simulation results incorporating this adaptation mechanism into a pyramid architecture are presented. This approach reduces the amount of data processing required while retaining the underlying structure of the data.

In the second example, the angles and orientations of corners present in the boundaries of an object are used to generate a compact representation which is invariant with respect to scale and position. Once again, only local information is used for feature detection, and a significant amount of data compression is achieved. The process of signature generation is inherently parallel and will yield real-time performance when implemented in VLSI. Hardware implementation of the above schemes are currently being studied and initial results are promising.

ACKNOWLEDGEMENTS

This work was partly supported by the United States Air Force Office of Scientific Research under grant number AFOSR 89-0430.

REFERENCES

[1] L. A. Akers, M. Walker, R. Grondin, and D. Ferry, "A Synthetic Neural Integrated Circuit," *Proceedings of the IEEE 1989 Custom Integrated Circuits Conference*, San Diego, CA, 1989, pp. 12.6.1-12.6.4

[2] P. Hasler and L. A. Akers, "VLSI Neural Circuits and Systems", *Proceedings of the 9th Annual International Phoenix Conference on Computers and Communications*, 1990

[3] D. Marr, *Vision A computational Investigation into the Human Representation and Processing of Visual Information*, San Francisco: W. H. Freeman, 1982.

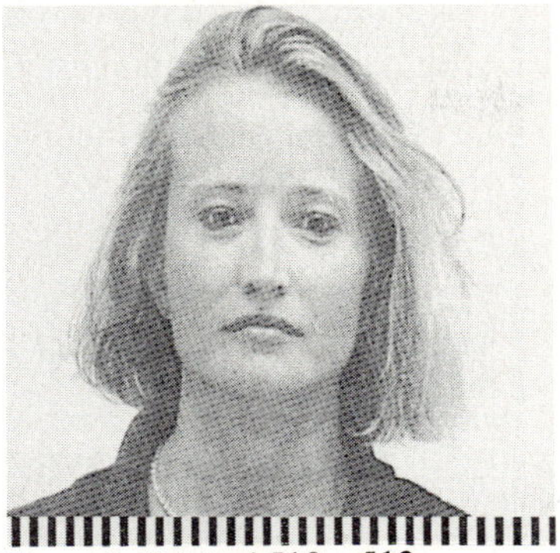

Figure 1: Original 512 x 512

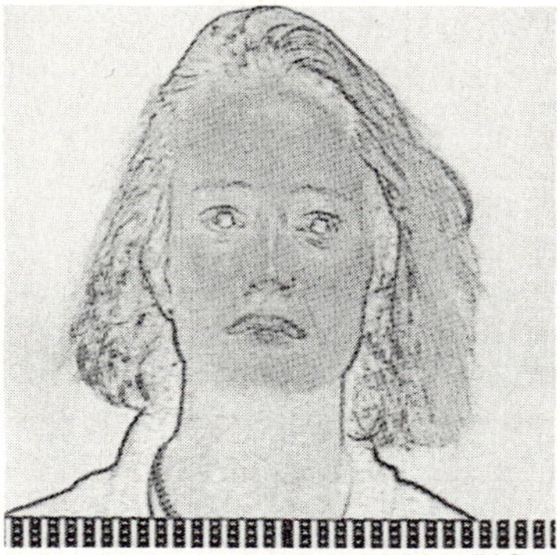

Figure 2a: layer 1 output 256 x 512

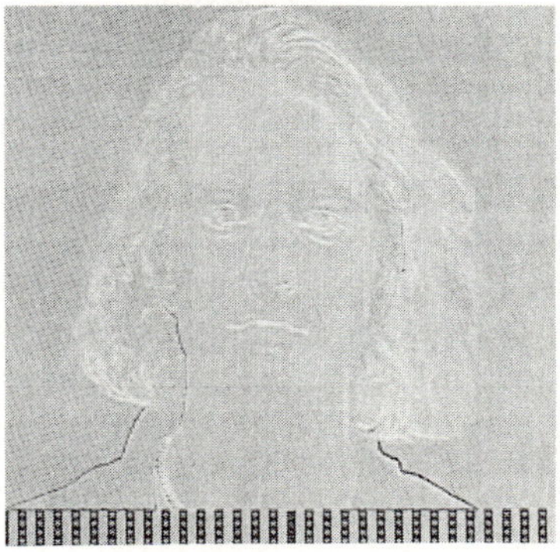

Figure 2b: layer 2 output 256 x 256

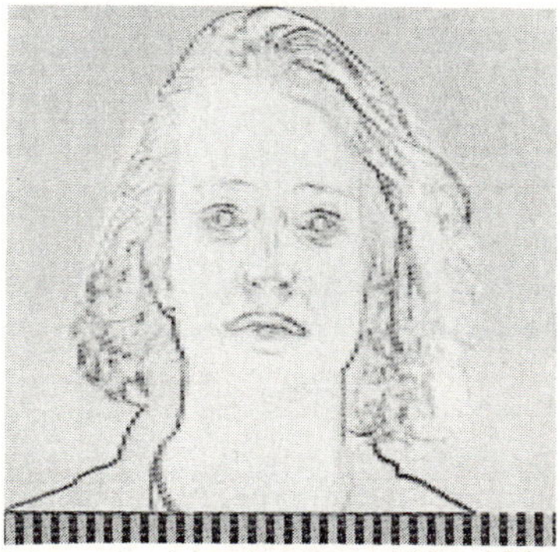

Figure 2c: layer 3 output 128 x 256

Figure 2d: layer 4 output 128 x 128

Figure 2e: layer 5 output 64 x 128

[4] *Pyramidal Systems for Computer Vision*, V. Cantoni, S. Levialdi Editors, Berlin: Springer-Verlag, 1986 .

[5] Bruno A. Olshausen, "A Survey of Visual Preprocessing and Shape Representation Techniques," *RIACS Technical Report 88.35*, Research Institute for Advanced Computer Science, NASA Ames Research Center, 1988.

[6] David H. Hubel, *Eye, Brain, and Vision*, New York: Scientific American Library, 1988.

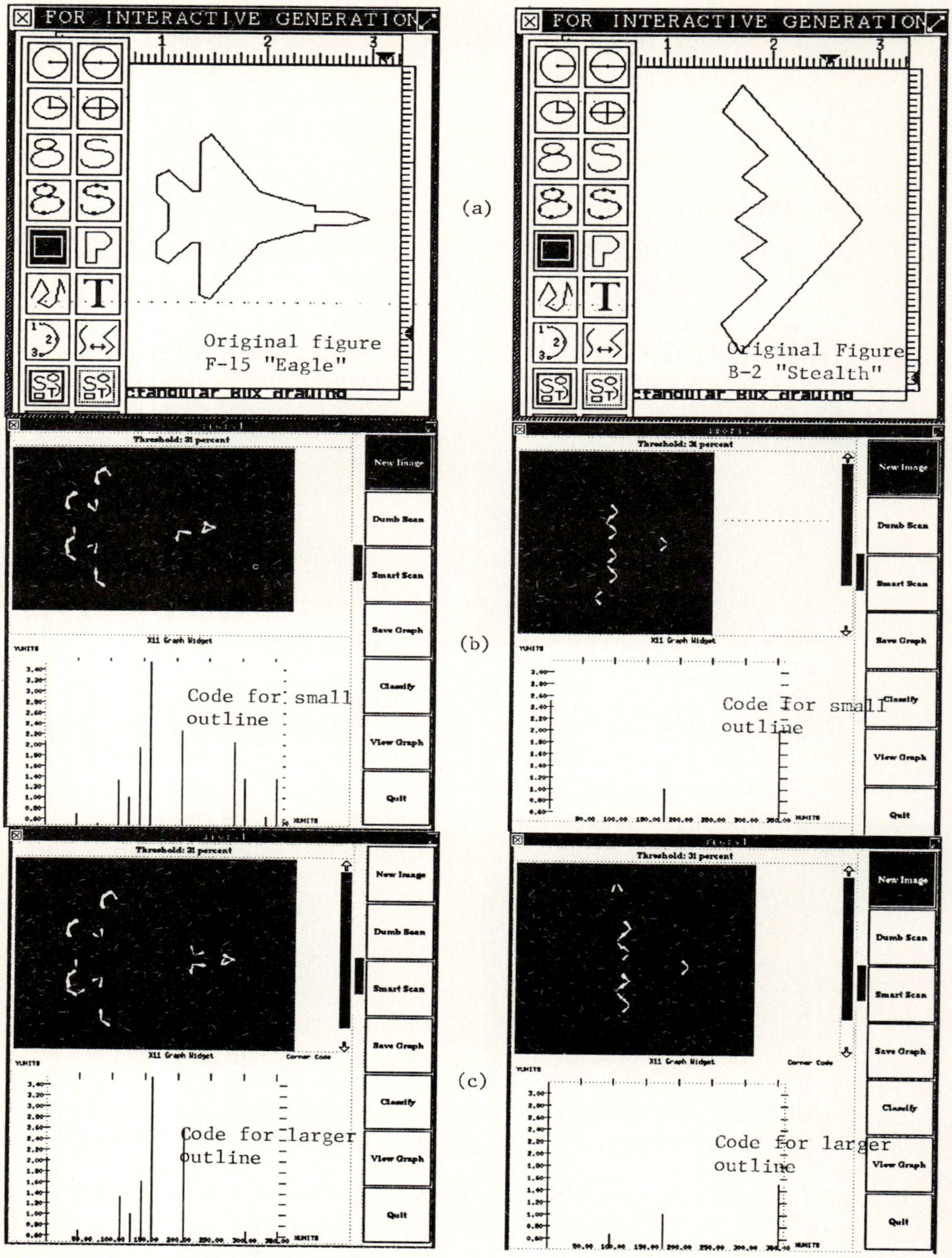

Figure 3: Codes generated for two scales of two different aircraft.

Advanced Neural Computers / R. Eckmiller (Editor)

THE PYGMALION NEURAL NETWORK PROGRAMMING ENVIRONMENT

B.Angéniol
Thomson–CSF

P. Treleaven
University College London

1. INTRODUCTION

The PYGMALION project aims to promote the application of neural networks by European industry, and to develop European "standard" computational tools for programming and simulation of neural networks. PYGMALION applications span image processing, speech processing and acousticsignal classification.
Tools for neural networks centre on a programming environment comprising five major parts:
(i) the Graphic Monitor for controlling and monitoring a networksimulation,
(ii) the Algorithm Library of common neural networks,
(iii) the high level neural programming languageN,
(iv) the intermediate level network specification language nC,and
(v) the compilers to the target machines.

Lastly, to develop a European general–purpose highly parallel neurocomputer, and to prepare the production of application–dedicated neuro–chips, future fundings will be requested.
Nevertheless, the implementation of neural algorithms in WSI (Wafer Scale Integration) is already addressed by PYGMALION. A VLSI demonstrator for such a technology is already available.

2. THE NEURAL NETWORK PROGRAMMING SYSTEM (NNPS)

2.1 GENERALITIES

A major goal of PYGMALION is to ensure the widest usage of the neural programming environment, by making it as flexible and portable as possible.The environment comprises 5 major parts:

Graphic Monitor, the graphical software environmentfor controlling the execution and monitoring of a neural networkapplication simulation. This includes a simulation command languagefor setting up a simulation, monitoring its execution, interactivelychanging values, and saving a trained network.

Algorithm Library, the parameterised library ofcommon neural networks,written in the high level language and providing the user with anumber of validated modules for constructing applications.

High Level Language N, the object-oriented programming languagefor defining, in conjunction with the algorithm library, a neuralnetwork algorithm and application, by describing the network topologyand its dynamics.

Intermediate Level Language nC, the low level machineindependentnetwork specification language for representing the partiallytrained or trained neural network applications, a format analogous toP-code for PASCAL systems.

Compilers to the target UNIX-based workstations and parallelTransputer-based machines.

This structure of the neural programming environment is illustrated by the next figure.

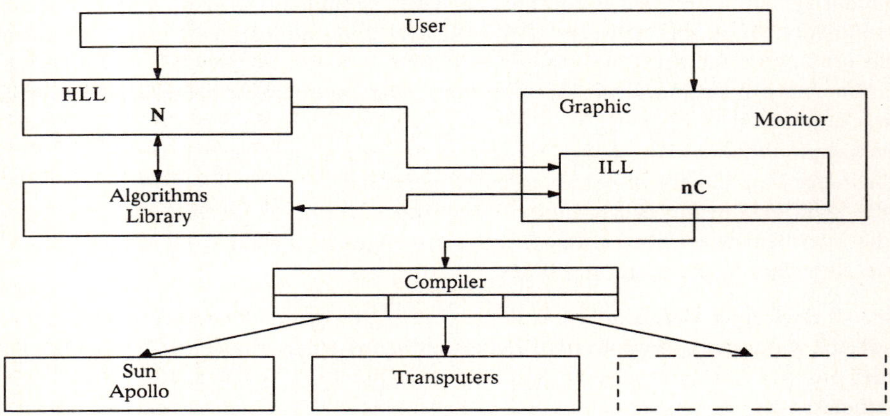

PYGMALION Neural Programming Environment

To ensure uniformity and consistency, a common interface is supported by the Graphic Monitor, Algorithm Library plus the N and nC languages. The interface has the following properties. Firstly, all components present the view of a neural system based on a hierarchical structure of networks, layers, clusters, neurons and synapses. Secondly, all algorithms are parameterised. Thirdly, all algorithms and applications share a common repertoire of data structures, function names and system variables. Lastly, the specification of an algorithm is separated from an application. The resulting, uniform, interface allows generic applications and generic algorithms; a single application may use many algorithms , and a single parameterised algorithm may be configured for many applications.

2.2 GRAPHIC MONITOR

Control of a neural network simulation is provided by the Graphic Monitor.
The view is that the Graphic Monitor will execute on a Hostcomputer and generate a specific net simulator/emulator to be executed on a Target computer. Monitoring of the simulation/emulation is done from the Host through X-windows graphic tools and the command language.

The windows environment provides pull-down menus to select and change

(i) I/O format,
(ii) network architecture,
(iii) networklearning algorithm,
(iv) network training and execution, and
(v) displays of activations, weights etc.

A neural network is initially specified using the high level language N utilising modules from the Algorithm Library. It is then translated into the intermediate level language nC. Once configured and specified in nC, the neural network can then be trained or used via the Graphic Monitor. The Graphic Monitor can be used to dynamically modify the network, to translate it to a particular Target machine or to save the trained or partially trained network for later usage, possibly on a different Target computer.

2.3 ALGORITHM LIBRARY

The Algorithm Library contains the classic neural network algorithms in a parameterised specification that can be configured for a specific user application.The popular algorithms provided are:

(i) Gradient Back propagation with or without feedback,
(ii) Hopfield,
(iii) Boltzmann machine,
(iv) Simulated Annealing,
(v) Competitive Learning
(vi) Adaptive resonance theory
(vii) Linear associative memory
(viii) Kanerva memory, etc...

In these networks the interconnection geometry and the transferequations are already specified.However, the number of PEs, their initial state and weight values,learning rates and time constants, are all user selectable.

The Library divides into five main parts:

- the Algorithm Independent Part contains the network computation subroutines, and support routines for memory and error management etc.
- the Tools Library routines for data file I/O subroutines, network architecture specificationand performance measurement
- the Algorithm Modules, specifying the parameterised algorithms
- the Algorithm Evaluation Programs for testing the Algorithm Modules
- the Application Library provides the user–taylored application modules

Pygmalion Algorithm Library

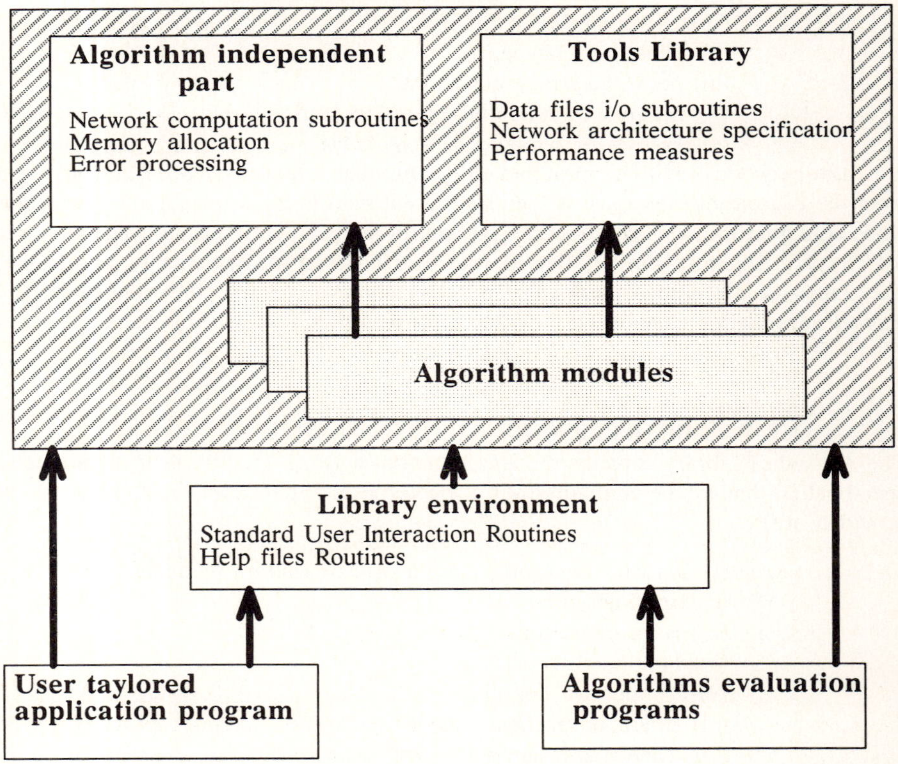

The Algorithm Library is being constructed in two stages. Initially a C version of the library is being implemented, for use by the image and speech processing applications in the Project. Then the full library will be implemented using the high level language N.

2.4 HIGH LEVEL LANGUAGE - N

N is a high level neural network programming language for both expert and naive users. It allows development of neural algorithms and use of operational algorithms in applications. Its syntax is a subset of C++ with additional neural oriented features.

It allows the description of algorithms by defining specific types having their own data and behaviour in analogy to a class in C++ and, by assembling them in a modular tree hierarchy.A library containing predefined types and parameterised algorithms (such as Hopfield, Back propagation ...) is available.
The library may also contain unprotected programmers objects:this part of the library is used in a read-write mode and is managed by programmers. The source code of both kinds of library objects is stored and thus may be easily consulted and integrated in any N program.

A typical N program consists of a list of type definitions. One type may be defined from previously defined ones.A type definition has the following structure:

```
new type xxx ( parameter-list )
    parameter declaration
   composite types declaration
    internal variables declaration
    internal function declaration
       above:
    inherited variables declarations
       plugin:
    communication fields (inputs)
       plugout:
    communication fields (outputs)
       connection:
    connections between communication fields
       public:
    inheritance variables declaration
    activation methods of the type being defined
```

Thanks to the choice made for its syntax, any program in N can be easily translated into a C++ program and consequently algorithms can be simulated on a sequential computer such as a SUN or APOLLO.

Furthermore, any neural network structure and algorithm in N can be translated into an equivalent nC structure, thus generating the nC version of any N program.

The N programming language will provide three types of facilities:

Firstly, to support the conversion of an N model (i.e.algorithm) into an abstract representation which will allows the semantic analysis and the link editing together of several algorithms in the same application.
Secondly, to allow the re–use of previously defined algorithms.
Thirdly, to provide tools and criteria to translate N applications into nC network specifications.

2.5 INTERMEDIATE LEVEL LANGUAGE - nC

The nC language acts as an intermediate level, machine–independent, representation for neural networks. A network, specified in the intermediate level language, can then be translated on to a variety of computers for training or use. After usage (ie.training) the intermediate level specification of the network is updated, so the trained network can be stored in a library, filed for later use or mapped on to a different computer. Machine independence is considered the major feature of the PYGMALION intermediate level language, and, to enhance this, we have made the language a small subset of the draft ISO standard C.

The nC intermediate level representation divides the neural network information into 4 different domains:

(i) the network topology;
(ii) the data of the system, including neuron status and synaptic weights;
(iii) the functions defining the processing in the network;
(iv) the control of the network activities.

An example of a framework for a neural network description is shown below.

```
/* Topology , Data & Function Information */
      #define system_variable constant
      struct (...) config = (...);
      typedef struct (
                float state (constant);  /* status info. */
                synapse_type *synapse;          /* status info. */
                neuron_type**input_neuron;      /* topological info. */
                neuron_type **outward_neuron; /* topological info. */
                rule_type  weight_sum;          /* functional info. */
                rule_type  weight_update; ... /* functional info. */
                    )
       neuron_type;
      struct  (
```

```
        net_def;        /***  definition of network  ***/
    ) system;

/* Control Information */
/* System function definitions */
    connect   (   ...   )
    read_weights (name_file)  (   ...   )
    main ()
    (       /* calls to system functions to control application */
            connect ()
            read_weights (file_name)
            read_states (file_name)
            learn ()
            recall () ...
    )
```

The topology information is basically described by defining the system variables (such as NETS, LAYERS, CYCLES, LEARNING_RATE, etc), using #define commands, and by completing the system and config structures. The system structure defines the central hierarchical structure in terms of nets, layers, cluster inside layers, etc,and the config structure specifies the number of elements inside the hierarchy, like number of layers inside each network, number of neurons inside each cluster, etc. The system structure also stores data information, in terms of neuron's state and weights, as well as functional information, in the form of rules. These rules are related to the functions that should be performed by a neuron, such as weight summation and weight update.

The control information is provided by some system functions definitions, which configure, initialise and train the networks,and by a list of calls to the system functions, that give the central control of the whole system.

3. HARDWARE INTEGRATION

Although a very small amount of money has been dedicated to the study of hardware integration in Pygmalion, some progress has been made and has a decentralized architecture involving a cascadable neuron processor with local control, state value circulation through a shift register, with no external control has been studied. A chip with only one neuron has been realized, and tests on it have been positive. The clock is 20 Mhz.

This architecture is customizable since the number of neurons, layers and interconnections, the state and coefficient precision, and the learning capabilities are parameters for this architecture.

The neural processor is as follows:

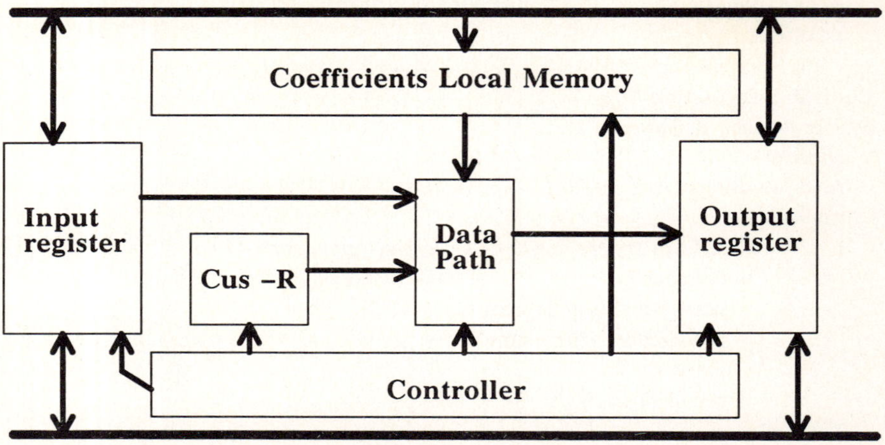

Such processors can be put together in a global architecture as in the next figure:

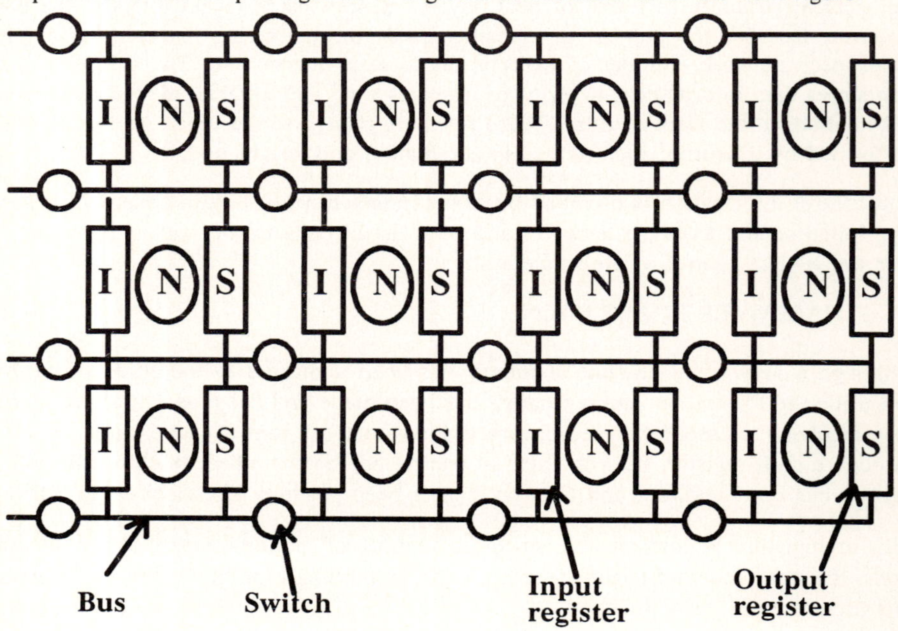

4. CONCLUSION

To conclude, the PYGMALION project has been running since January 1989.Already major progress has been made both on the applications and the environment.

For environment, the current status is that the Graphic Monitor, Algorithm Library, plus high level N and intermediate level nC languages are fully specified. Regarding implementation, a rudimentary Graphic Monitor (operating on an nC specification of a neural application) and a prototype Algorithm Library are both available for experimentation. By the end of 1990, the complete PYGMALION environment will be finished.

The Hardware integration study has proven that Neurocomputing on silicon is feasible, that dedicated ASICs can be generated in a short time starting from the building block which is the neuron processor, and that customization of neural networks through silicon compilation techniques and PROM or soft programmable switches should be studied in a future European project, namely the Galatea project.

Advanced Neural Computers / R. Eckmiller (Editor)

SIMULATORS FOR NEURAL NETWORKS

Simon C.J. GARTH

Myriad Solutions Ltd
St John's Innovation Centre
Cowley Road
Cambridge, CB2 1PZ
England

The ability to simulate artificial neural systems on computers is widely regarded as an essential part of the development process. The advent of new technology has made such simulations feasible, and in many cases preferable to building specialist hardware. In addition, the speeds available from the latest hardware are sufficient for the commercial implementation of a range of neural network applications.

1. INTRODUCTION

The development of neural network systems has centred around their simulation on digital computers. These offer high performance coupled with unrivalled flexibility and a high degree of 'observability' into the inner workings of algorithms from which more general conclusions may be drawn. Many such simulations may then be migrated into end-user applications and there are a range of such applications available to date [1].

Neural network simulations demand a range of specific requirements in addition to many of the features of conventional computers. An alternative to purchasing a general purpose computer to perform these operations is to add a dedicated accelerator to a relatively modest general purpose computer. This provides computational rates which compare favourably with many of the larger supercomputers, coupled with the familiarity and portability of low cost workstations. In addition, the solution is frequently sufficiently cost-effective and powerful for the simulator to be used directly in end-user applications.

Most simulators to date have been based around conventional digital computing methods. These include special purpose bit-slice processing equipment [2], advanced floating point coprocessor chips [3], specialist parallel processors [4, 5] and custom designed digital circuits linked to conventional computers [6]. Recently, new advances in general-purpose computing technology, coupled with the development of low cost, high density memory has led to the emergence of more general purpose accelerator products which offer simulation performance equivalent to the largest supercomputers of a few years ago (as an example, the Intel i860 processor offers performance approaching 50% of a Cray 1 supercomputer [7]).

2. NEURAL NETWORK REQUIREMENTS

Neural network simulations impose a number of requirements on computational hardware which are not commonly found in conventional computing environments. These requirements have been studied in detail by a number of workers including members of the ESPRIT project ANNIE [8] and found to be concentrated in a number of well defined categories:

1. Vector x Matrix operations

Found in a wide range of algorithms including Back-propagation, Hopfield, BAM etc, in which the vector is the input vector and the matrix contains the weights.

2. Matrix x Matrix operations

Found in a range of algorithms including the weight update phase of Back-propagation.

Each of these operations consists of a small number of arithmetic functions such as multiplication, addition, sum of difference etc.

Such operations make extensive demands on both processing power and memory. The precise nature of these demands depends on the algorithm. In particular, an important issue is the degree of resolution required in both the weight and I/O terms as these determine both the complexity of the arithmetic operations involved and the quantity of data to be processed. These parameters have been studied by a number of workers [9].

The results indicate that the majority of algorithms do not require the precision offered by floating point calculation. However, the dynamic range of the update terms may be as large as 3-4 orders of magnitude. Such values may be represented using integer arithmetic but will normally require dynamic scaling of variables. As an indication, backpropagation experiments have been successfully performed with 8 bit integers for weights in forward propagation mode, and 16 bit integers for the weight terms during learning. Such integer implementations have been attractive in the past as the integer computational performance of processors has typically far exceeded the floating point performance.

This situation is rapidly changing as processors supporting single cycle floating point performance become readily available. Such processors are able to perform most floating point operations at least as rapidly as the equivalent integer operations, eliminating the time penalty traditionally associated with floating point operations. In such systems, a 32 bit floating point representation is normally used for both weights and I/O terms. This preserves a balance between data size and flexibility.

Many of the implementations have taken advantage of the parallel nature of neural network simulations to solve problems using parallel processing hardware. However, there is a considerable programming overhead in implementing such systems efficiently on parallel machines. In addition, the dataflow requirements of such an approach are a potential limitation to the processing speed and more recent processors are capable, on their own, of exceeding the performance of many smaller parallel processing systems.

3. ARCHITECTURE OF A NEURAL NETWORK SIMULATOR

The two issues of importance to a neural network simulator are the raw processing power and the dataflow management. Modern simulators take advantage of the newly emerging range of processors which support single cycle floating point operations, for example those made by AT&T (DSP32C), Motorola (560002), Texas Instruments (TMS320C30) and Intel (i860). These processors owe a great deal of their architecture to the Reduced Instruction Set Computer (RISC) methodology. This approach recognises that computers spend a high proportion of their time executing a limited subset of the available instructions. The architecture is streamlined in such a way that only a subset of the instructions normally available on a computer are provided in hardware but that these instructions operate at the highest possible speed (usually within one clock cycle). The devices mentioned above incorporate this philosophy but add a number of instructions (such as floating point multiplication, addition and subtraction) to the list of basic instructions which operate quickly. Less frequently used operations take longer as they have to be coded in software but the overall effect is an increase in processing speed.

A follow-on from this structure is that if the peak performance is to be maintained then the data required to service these instructions must be provided at a rate which will satisfy single cycle computational rates. This frequently places unacceptable demands on the external bus bandwidth. A typical worst-case is the need to perform a multiply and sum operation. In this case the processor will need to fetch up to 5 terms (two multiplicands, two addends and an instruction) in a cycle. This can only realistically be achieved by providing several wide external buses. The popular 'Harvard' architecture goes some way towards this by offering separate external address and data buses but, in this example, the data path would need to be 128 bits wide to support the required data rate.

Such problems may be greatly alleviated by the use of internal memory and caches, in which the most recent memory accesses are stored within the chip and may be accessed at high speed without the need to access external memory. In many cases where vector operations need to be executed, the instructions are in the form of a relatively short routine which is executed in a loop. In this case, the processor will either be able to cache the instructions, maintain the short part of the program in internal memory or use a special loop operation in which the instruction need only be fetched once for the entire operation. Such practices may be used efficiently in place of the Harvard memory architecture, allowing increased external bandwidth for data accesses.

In cases such as vector x matrix multiplication, the vector may generally be stored in internal memory, and the addends stored in a register and the result of the multiplier respectively. With this arrangement, there is a need only for one external data fetch per operation which is well within the capabilities of most processors. Therefore, as this example shows, data organisation can substantially affect the available performance of the system (in this case, by a factor of 5 for processors with a single 32 bit external datapath).

It should be noted, however, that such performance requires considerable tailoring of the implementation to the characteristics of the hardware. Such tailoring is not generally available even with optimising compilers, and some work at a low level by the programmer is required to achieve peak performance. In addition, the fall-off in performance caused by not using the full range of facilities in the device may be substantial. It is not unusual for compiled C code to run an order of magnitude slower when applied to operations which may be highly optimised on a particular processor.

This problem may be alleviated by purchasing specially optimised neural network libraries from systems vendors who supply a range of primitive operations which may be used as efficient 'building blocks' from which to make simulation engines. Since most of the development time in neural network simulations is spent in the simulation itself, some additional effort in this area on behalf of the user may be rewarding.

4. THE NEXT STAGE

The majority of high performance processors function with clock frequencies of 25-50 MHz, and require data to be accessible within 1-2 clock cycles for zero wait state operation. This operating frequency is likely to increase towards 100 MHz within the next 3-5 years. In addition, there is a trend towards ever larger data spaces. The early digital signal processing microprocessors, introduced in the early 1980s, supported just 4k bytes of data. More modern devices support up to 16 MBytes, while more general purpose processors are capable of accessing up to 4 Gbytes. As neural networks are increasingly applied to more realistic tasks, data areas of 1-16M Bytes are becoming normal.

Such requirements place severe constraints on the design of the memory system. There are essentially two choices when choosing memory; static or dynamic devices. Static memories are characterised by very high speed (commercial memories are available with 12ns access times). Dynamic memories are slower and more difficult to design with, but offer a cost per bit of approximately one quarter that of static memory. In addition, speeds are increasing to the stage that fundamental electrical characteristics begin to limit performance. Consider a system in which memory access times of 10 ns are required (typical of a 50 MHz processor with single cycle access). This time may be compared to the delay passing a signal into and out of an integrated circuit package itself of approximately 3ns or the speed of electrical signals in a printed circuit board of approximately 100mm/ns.

It is clear that other, architectural, techniques are required as memory access time requirements increase. A number of techniques are available:

4.1. Internal memory

Memory internal to the processor may hold instructions or data. This may be accessed at high speed without resorting to external memory accesses. Such an approach allows repeatedly used instructions and data to be held locally on the processor, freeing the external memory manager to handle the more general accesses. This technique may be used to great effect but requires either the user or optimising software explicitly to take advantage of such memory.

4.2. Memory caching

Caching is a more general case of the use of internal memory in which the cache manager holds a copy of the last n elements of data read from the external bus. Some caches also support 'write back' in which a write to an element which is already held in cache does not access the external bus but instead updates the cache. As new elements are read into the cache, the cache controller automatically stores back the least recently used elements. The larger the caches, the more likely that a memory access request will 'hit' the cache and therefore not require an external memory access. In this way, relatively slow external memory accesses may be used while the system still retains close to peak performance.

Such techniques are highly efficient when applied to instruction caching, as many intensive operations take the form of relatively small loops (e.g. 100 or fewer instructions). The effect of data caching is more dependent on the operation in question. In particular, in many common cases (such as matrix by matrix addition) the cache will perform no useful function as data terms are not reused and are simply flushed through the cache (indeed, in some designs, such repeated cache updates will actually slow the speed of processing).

4.3 Instruction pipelining

This technique has been used for several years and is the basis of many of the most powerful computers. It allows multi-stage operations to be overlapped so that they operate in parallel. This allows the effective processing rate to be very high without forcing the entire operation to complete within the same period. Such schemes are successful on operations which are regular in nature and which do not require the result of previous operations before they have passed through the pipeline. For example, the vector operation:

p[n] = p[n] + q[n]

will be well handled by a pipelined architecture :

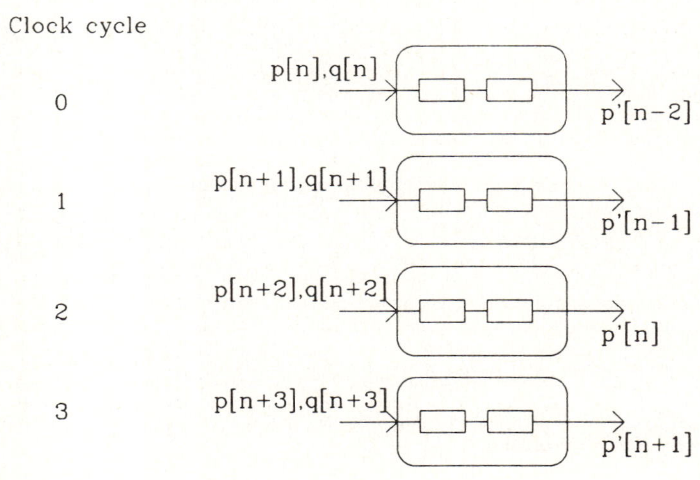

whereas

r = r + q[n]

will not be efficient as the computation must complete for each value of n before the next stage may start:

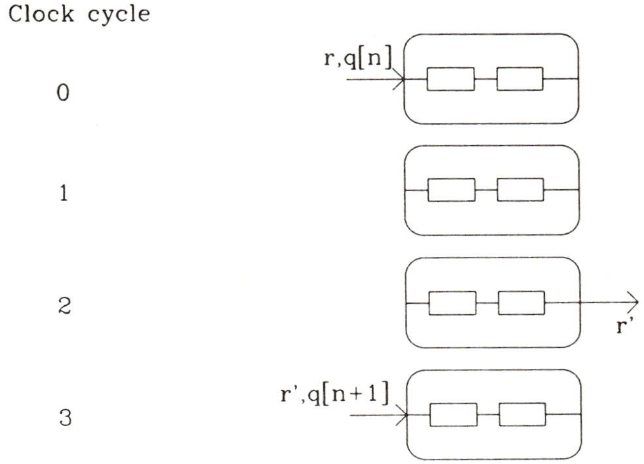

4.4. Memory pipelining

Memory pipelining is not a new technique (it has been used in mainframes for many years) but is only now beginning to be used in microprocessor systems. It involves the use of an advanced memory manager which pre-fetches up to n (typically 3) memory accesses before they are required by the program. This requires the memory manager to perform a degree of 'look ahead' in order to predict the data requirements of the program. Such methods allow the external bus manager to access several elements of data in parallel and therefore provide data to the processor at a high rate while requiring only modest data access times from the memory.

4.5. Very Long Instruction Word (VLIW) architectures

VLIW architectures are intended to alleviate the high data and instruction requirements by accessing several elements in each memory access. This is then coupled with advanced internal caching and scheduling processes to order the data so that the required data is available as the instruction demands it.

4.6. Superscalar technology

Superscalar technology is an emerging technique in which the processor fetches instructions and data at the maximum possible rate and internally schedules them to different parts of the processor. This is a form of transparent internal parallelism and tends to even out the processing requirements of the program so that as many parts of the processor as possible are functioning simultaneously.

4.7. Parallel processing

A number of parallel processors (as opposed to uniprocessors which exhibit internal parallelism) are available which offer a wide range of techniques and architectures for high performance computation. The majority of such processors are supercomputers in their own right and offer advanced software and hardware features. However, their cost is such that they are found predominantly as shared resources in larger institutions. A full review of such techniques is beyond the scope of this paper. A review may be found in [10].

5. OUTLINE OF AVAILABLE SYSTEMS

	Memory(M bytes)	MFLOPs	Cost(k$)
PC 386	1-16	0.01	1-5
PC 486	1-16	3	5-10
Sun Sparcstation	4-64	7	10-30
1st generation accelerator	4-16	5-20	10-25
2nd generation accelerator	4-100	30-80	15-25
Mini-supercomputer	4-100	50-100	100+
Supercomputer	30+	100+	300+

These figures are not definitive but are provided merely to indicate the broad classifications of systems available.

6. CASE STUDY - LOCATION OF EYES IN A FACIAL IMAGE

This project was undertaken in collaboration with British Telecom as part of the Connex project. The problem relates to data compression and requires the location of the eyes in a series of images of faces in a number of orientations, with and without glasses etc. The algorithm uses the extended restricted coulomb energy algorithm [11] as a means of detection. This is a clustering algorithm which 'grows' in response to the training data and as such is far from the regular matrix multiplication task as found in many of the early neural network systems (e.g. Hopfield, Back propagation networks). A typical solution consists of ~600 neurons organised in clusters of ~9. The data is a 256 x 256 image which is compressed to 64 x 64 and then a 'template' of 8 x 8 pixels is passed over the entire image. Simulation times of 7 hours were recorded using a conventional 10 MHz PC 286. This time was reduced to 150 seconds using a second generation accelerator based on the Texas Instruments TMS320C30 processor running unmodified C code. Further optimisations were applied including storing sections of the code and data in internal memory. This reduced the processing time to approximately 45 seconds. It is clear that with further algorithmic enhancements and data manipulation, processing times of the order of 15 seconds will be achievable. Such speeds are sufficient to consider commercial implementations of the technology..

7. CONCLUSION

Neural network simulations impose a range of challenging requirements on computational hardware. In addition, there is a need to balance computational power and the ability of the user to readily program and understand the simulations. Specialist simulators are able to boost the performance of conventional processors to the level of mini-supercomputers for the purposes of neural network simulations, at a fraction of the cost of high performance general computers. Advances in processor and memory technology and the corresponding reductions in cost are leading to the situation in which such simulators may be employed in a range of end user-applications. This offers advantages to the developer as the simulation vehicle may be used with a range of diagnostic software during the evaluation phase and then deployed with a stripped-down version of the software in the end application. This allows the final implementation to be updated readily as further developments occur and eliminates the need for a complicated porting process from the simulator to dedicated hardware.

REFERENCES

[1] SAIC application note 1989

[2] Kraft T., 1990 Artificial Neural Systems - Technology of Today. Proc. 'Neural computing - the marketplace' IBC Technical Services Ltd London

[3] Hecht-Nielsen Corporation promotional literature

[4] Hecht-Nielsen R., 1987 TRW Inc. Internal technical report

[5] Garth S.C.J., 1987. A dedicated computer for simulation of large systems of neural networks. Neural Computers, NATA ASI series. pp435-444 Springer-Verlag

[6] Mackie S., 1987. Implementation of neural network models in silicon. Neural Computers, NATA ASI series. pp467-477 Springer-Verlag

[7] i860 performance brief. Intel Corporation. 1990.

[8] Williams P. & Gittins M., 1989 Review of neural network simulators. In press.

[9] Debenham R.M. & Garth S.C.J., 1988 Investigations into the effect of numerical resolution on the performance of back propagation. Neural networks from models to applications. pp752-755. IDSET, Paris

[10] Duncan R., 1990 A survey of parallel computer architectures. IEEE Computer Vol. 23, No. 2 pp5-17

[11] Debenham R.M. & Garth S.C.J., 1990 The application of radial basis functions to image recognition. In press.

Advanced Neural Computers / R. Eckmiller (Editor)

Dynamics and VLSI Implementation of Self–Organizing Networks*

Dan Hammerstrom
Todd Leen
Eric Means

Department of Computer Science and Engineering
Oregon Graduate Institute
19600 Von Neumann Drive
Beaverton, Oregon 97006-1999

1 Introduction

Present artificial neural models encounter severe degradation in economy as larger, more complex perceptual and cognitive problems are approached. In particular, several fundamental scaling problems arise that need to be overcome before artificial neural technology can provide real-time solutions to the large, complex problems solved by biological systems.

The high dimension of many data representations severely impact the cost of neural classifiers through three factors. The first factor, of primary importance for hardware implementation, is the scaling of VLSI implementation costs with increased node fan-in. It has been shown [1] that, for a general computational model, the required chip area, and hence the cost, increases cubically with the node fan-in.

The second scaling problem concerns learning time. Simply stated, the time required to train a classifier grows with the number of free parameters available. For neural algorithms, the number of links and nodes, and thus the number of free parameters, grows with increasing input dimension.

Third, recent advances in learning theory [2, 3] suggest that the required number of training examples may be expected to grow linearly with the number of network links. A by-product

*This work was supported in part by the Semiconductor Research Corporation contract no. 86–10–097, and by the Office of Naval Research, ONR contract no. N00014 88 K 0329, and ONR contract no. N00014-90-J-1349.

of this growth in training examples is increased data storage requirements. Again, large-dimensional input representations contribute to the problem.

It is our belief that the solution to the scaling problem in Artificial Neural Networks requires the construction of modular neural networks from smaller components. Certainly ample evidence exists to show that nature uses such constructions; the ubiquitous limited receptive field structures and the cortical columns of neocortex provide two such examples.

In this paper we present a survey of two complementary research areas at the Oregon Graduate Institute that support our ultimate goal of building the large neural network systems required to solve complex cognitive problems.

2 Scaling and Feature Discovery

One way to create such modular structures is to encode the input in terms of a set of features, thus reducing the dimension of the input space. Unsupervised, self-organizing neural networks are able to perform this reduction. Models based on Hebbian (and here, anti-Hebbian) learning rules discover statistical regularities in the data, and eliminate redundancy in the original input. Such models are also interesting from a biological point of view since they describe how physiologically motivated, local learning rules respond to the statistics of the environment to form specific receptive field structures [4, 5, 6].

2.1 Unsupervised Feature Discovery

Dimension reduction must be carried out without loss of information. Geometrically, the key idea is that data originally represented in an N dimensional space (the naive feature space) may lie in or near a submanifold of lower dimension, M. The goal is to find such a submanifold and place coordinates on it. The new coordinates then serve as a set of M-dimensional features that encode the original patterns.

If we restrict the search for the submanifold to linear subspaces, then principal component analysis (PCA) provides the desired transformation. The projection of the pattern vectors, x, onto the eigenvectors, e_i, of the input's auto-correlation matrix serve as the new pattern coordinates. Assuming that the eigenvalues, λ_i, of the correlation matrix have been ordered according to $\lambda_1 > \lambda_2 > \cdots > \lambda_N$, dimension reduction is achieved by retaining the leading, high variance projections $x \cdot e_i$, $i = 1, \ldots M$, and discarding the rest. We have applied neural network implementations of PCA to encode signals for speech recognition [7]. The technique achieves a two to five-fold decrease in network size and training time with no loss in performance relative to training with raw spectrograms [8].

2.2 Neural Network Implementations

In a classic paper, Oja [9] draws the connection between Hebbian learning and PCA. Oja treats a single linear neuron with weights that develop according to a Hebbian learning rule.

Denoting the vector of synaptic weights by ω, the neuron response to the input pattern, x, is given by $y = x^T\omega$. The learning rule takes the form

$$\delta\omega = \gamma(xy - y^2\omega) \tag{1}$$

where $\delta\omega$ is the change in ω on presentation of the input pattern x, and γ is the learning rate. The first term on the right hand side of (1) is the usual Hebbian co-occurrence term. The second term may be regarded as an active decay, which prevents the synaptic weight vector from becoming unbounded. As Oja shows, stochastic approximation theory [10] provides a correspondence between the discrete update in (1) and the ensemble-averaged differential equation

$$\dot{\omega} = < xy > - < y^2 > \omega = Q\omega - \omega\,(\omega^T Q\omega) \equiv f(\omega) \tag{2}$$

where $< \cdots >$ indicates the average over the ensemble of input patterns, and $Q \equiv < xx^T >$ is the auto-correlation matrix of the input patterns. Under the dynamics of (2) the weight vector converges to e_1, and the neuron output is proportional to the first principal component.

Several authors have proposed extensions to perform complete PCA based on projection-like feedback processes [11], or additional nodes [12]. Here we discuss extensions based on lateral connections between the output cells with attention to the dynamical properties of the networks.

2.2.1 Lateral Connections for Feature Selection

We define the matrix of forward weights, $\omega : R^N \mapsto R^M$. The ith row of ω corresponds to the weight vector ω_i from the input, to the ith output cell. The system of forward weights is augmented by lateral connections between the output cells. The $M \times M$ matrix of lateral connection strengths is denoted η. This matrix is symmetric so the output cells are fully interconnected, and has zeroes on the diagonal (no self-connections). With the inclusion of the lateral connections, the output vector $y \in R^M$ is given by $y = u\,\omega\,x$, where $u \equiv (1 - \eta)^{-1}$.

The ensemble-averaged, continuous time form of the learning rule for the forward weights takes the form

$$\begin{aligned} \dot{\omega} &= < yx^T > - \, Diag < yy^T > \omega \\ &= u\,\omega\,Q - Diag\,(u\,\omega\,Q\,\omega^T u^T)\,\omega \end{aligned} \tag{3}$$

where $Diag$ takes the diagonal elements of its argument. The lateral connection strengths are developed according to the anti-Hebbian rule

$$\begin{aligned} \dot{\eta}_{ij} &= d\,\eta_{ij} - e\,\eta_{ij}{}^3 - C < yy^T >_{ij} \\ &= d\,\eta_{ij} - e\,\eta_{ij}{}^3 - C(u\,\omega\,Q\,\omega^T\,u^T)_{ij}\,, \quad 1 < i \neq j < M \end{aligned} \tag{4}$$

The last term on the right-hand-side of (4) acts to de-correlate the activities of the output cells, thus forcing the forward connections to tune to different statistical features in the input space. The anti-Hebbian learning rule in (4) differs from the usual form [13, 14, 15] by the addition of the linear and cubic terms. The linear term is necessary to stabilize the desired equilibrium and the cubic term improves the behavior when C is reduced below the critical value for stability.

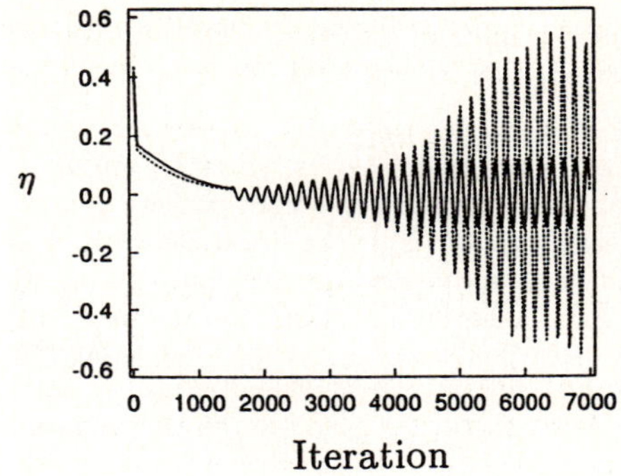

Figure 1: Oscillations in the model both with (solid line), and without (dotted line) the η^3 term of equation (4).

2.2.2 Bifurcation Behavior

Equations (3) and (4) have an equilibrium at $\omega_i = e_i,\ i = 1 \ldots M;\ \eta = 0$. This equilibrium is stable provided $d > 0$ and

$$C > C_0 \equiv \frac{d}{\lambda_i + \lambda_j} + \frac{(\lambda_i - \lambda_j)^2}{\lambda_i^2 + \lambda_j^2}, \quad 1 < i \neq j < M. \tag{5}$$

Since the stability conditions in (5) depend explicitly on the (unknown) eigenvalue spectrum of Q, one cannot be assured that an arbitrarily chosen value of C will lead to convergence. This point is not sufficiently stressed by previous authors [13, 15] who discuss similar networks.

Given this, it is helpful to understand the behavior under violation of (5). If (5) is violated for a single pair of indices (i, j), then the conditions for a Hopf bifurcation are satisfied; a set of periodic solutions emerge near C_0. A Liapunov-Schmidt reduction [16] shows that the bifurcation can be sub- or super-critical depending upon (λ_i, λ_j). The bifurcation direction can be changed by adjusting the coefficient of the η^3 term in (6).

Figure 1 shows the evolution of the lateral connection strength between two cells, obtained by numerical integration of (3) and (4). Early in the simulation, $C > C_0$ and the connection strength converges towards zero. At 1500 iterations, C is dropped below C_0 and η begins to oscillate. The two curves show the behavior with and without the η^3 term of (4).

2.2.3 Approximations and Relations to Other Models

The model in (3) and (4) contains several other models as approximations and special cases. Expanding u to first order in η eliminates the matrix inversion required to obtain y from x. The system can be further reduced, retaining only the lowest order terms in η and ω. The resulting model exhibits quite different bifurcation behavior [17] and contains, as a special case, Yuille's model for the development of receptive fields in visual cortex [5].

Rubner et al. [15] propose a model in which the ith cell receives signals along the lateral connections only from cells j with $j < i$. This inhomogeneous structure is implausible biologically, and could potentially lead to inefficient parallel implementation. The present model demonstrates that a more natural structure can serve the same purpose.

Finally, the bifurcations can be largely avoided by modulating the lateral learning rate according to the cell activities. This result may be generally useful.

3 Self-Organizing Biological Networks and VLSI

Neural algorithms which recursively estimate the eigenvectors of the input's autocorrelation seem to be fundamentally related to clustering algorithms. Suppose that the linear neural response is changed to a bistable response with possible outputs (0,1). Then, under the learning rule in (1), the weight vector will converge to the centroid of the subset of input vectors for which the response is unity. Arrays with competition between the neurons partition the input space into clusters. These networks build an encoding of the input based on metric clustering rather than on principal components. Surprisingly, anatomical and physiological evidence suggests that just such a function is carried out in piriform cortex.

3.1 The Piriform Model

Our investigation of VLSI architectures that could implement cortical models has led to detailed analysis of biologically–derived neural networks that perform such a clustering. One such model is the Lynch–Granger model of piriform cortex (the piriform model) [18]. This model describes a layered, feed–forward unsupervised network that performs a hierarchical clustering of training data. Feedback paths from a cortical network synchronously cancel out successively dominant components of the network input, allowing the network to form clear representations of progressively weaker input vector elements. Overall network response is a sequence of individual responses to the various components that constitute a single input vector.

Our research has focused on architectural implementations of piriform layer II, the most well–developed portion of the overall model. Inputs to this portion of the network enter as signals on the LOT, the Lateral Olfactory Tract. The LOT consists of axons originating in the olfactory bulb that sparsely contact dendrites of layer II neurons. These neurons are arranged in a linear sequence of "patches", each composed of 20 to 100 neurons. On every network input, each neuron forms a scalar product of its own synaptic weight vector with a sparse subset of the LOT. Each patch performs a winner–take–all function; only the most strongly activated neuron that exceeds a minimum threshold is allowed to fire. The remainder of the patch is quiescient.

Each neuron's output axon rejoins the LOT, replacing a randomly chosen axon from a prior source. The composition of the LOT therefore changes as it progresses from the rostral (upstream) portions of the network to caudal (downstream) regions. The effect is that caudally–located neurons contact more highly–processed signals than do rostrally–located neurons.

The piriform model describes a synchronous network where processing proceeds in distinct cycles, or "sniffs". Feedback inhibition and post–activation refractory periods combine to cause the network to form different outputs on successive samples of a single LOT input. It is hypothesized that this series of responses establishes a hierarchical categorization of inputs; similar inputs initially elicit similar network outputs, but with each successive sniff the elements common to each input are removed and the network responds to progressively dissimilar components. Hence, network outputs diverge in later sniffs.

3.2 VLSI Architectural Issues

Three issues dominate VLSI architecture for neurocomputers: connectivity, weight storage, and neural computation. Of these, connectivity poses the most challenging implementation problems. Neurons in layer II piriform contact between 5% and 20% of the available axons in the LOT; such sparse connectivity is one advantage cortical models possess for VLSI implementation. Nevertheless, the n^2 relationship between connection count and interconnect area severely limits the maximum size attainable in a direct implementation. In fact, for a 10,000 neuron network with a LOT width of 1000 lines, 97% of the estimated silicon area would be consumed by metal interconnect.

3.3 The Sparse Digital Architecture

We have studied an architecture dubbed "SD" (for "Sparse Digital"), because it offers an efficient match to the requirements of the piriform model. Connectivity is encoded in binary decoders on every neuron rather than directly in metal wires. A single binary–encoded communication bus represents the LOT, and spans the entire linear array of processors; each neuron receives input data from this bus exclusively. Two salient features of the model prevent the single LOT bus from becoming a communication bottleneck. Due to the winner–take–all character of each patch, only a single winning neuron in each patch is active. This organization imposes sparse *temporal* activation on network communication; on each sniff, only 1% to 5% of the total neuron population requires use of the bus. In the SD architecture, rather than dedicating expensive interconnect area to every potential communication path, scarce communication resources are only used by the minority of active neurons that need it.

Patches in the SD architecture are organized into dedicated processors called Physical Nodes (PNs). (See Figure 2). PNs would be layed out in a linear array consistent with the layout of patches in the piriform model. Each PN contains arrays of decoders to decode LOT transmissions for each neuron's active inputs. Calculations indicate that while decoder area would be the primary consumer of silicon in the SD architecture, it offers significant savings over dedicated metal interconnect. Decoder area increases at a rate proportional to the $\log_2$ rather than the square of LOT width, as would connectivity area in a direct implementation.

Arbitration between the hundreds or thousands of patch winners for access to the single LOT bus would be greatly eased because of the sequential nature of processing in the piriform model. In piriform cortex, a wave of neural activation proceeds from the rostral to the caudal region of the network as more neurons have their inputs excited; similarly, in the SD architecture, transmission access to the LOT would begin with the most rostrally–located patches and proceed downstream. Every neuron in the network would receive and decode the LOT transmissions in parallel, but actual transmission would proceed serially.

An attractive feature of biologically–inspired neural networks is the inherent low precision of the components. Four–bit precision in synaptic weight memory is assumed in the SD architecture. Weights would be stored in DRAM, and each PN would time–multiplex a collection of digital adders between the subset of neurons that receive active inputs. Large numbers of low–precision adders could be integrated into the architecture in this way.

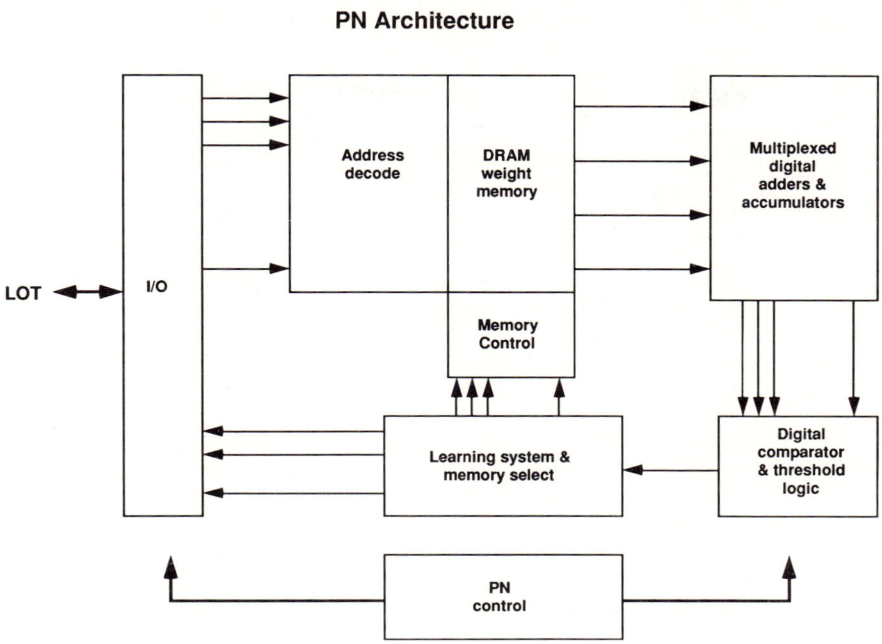

Figure 2: Block diagram of a single PN in the SD architecture.

The combination of multiplexed interconnect, individual address decoders, low–precision digital adders and dense DRAM weight storage would enable large networks to be integrated on a single ULSI silicon wafer. Biological evidence [19] indicates that the ratio of layer II neurons to LOT axons is approximately 10:1. We estimate that a 10,000 neuron network with a 1000-element LOT input could be fabricated on 4.1cm^2 of silicon. A similarly proportioned 6–inch wafer scale network could host a network consisting of approximately 64,000 neurons, over 6,000 LOT inputs, and over 40 million synaptic connections. Performance is estimated at approximately 30,000 LOT input vectors per second for the smaller network. These estimates describe a digital VLSI architecture occupying an order of magnitude less area than an equivalent direct (analog) implementation of the piriform model. Given comparable interconnect structures and functionality, this performance is comparable to an analog implementation. Preliminary analysis [20] indicates that this network model is sufficiently fault–tolerant such that typical silicon defect densities would provide acceptable yield even at such large die sizes.

References

[1] Jim Bailey and Dan Hammerstrom. Why VLSI implementations of associative VLCNs require connection multiplexing. In *Proceedings of the 1988 International Conference on Neural Networks*, June 1988.

[2] Eric Baum and David Haussler. What size net gives valid generalization? *Neural Computation*, 1:151–160, 1989.

[3] Yaser S. Abu-Mostafa. The Vapnik-Chervonenkis dimension: Information versus complexity in learning. *Neural Computation*, 1:312–317, 1989.

[4] R. Linsker. Self–organization in a perceptual network. *IEEE Computer*, 21:105–117, March 1988.

[5] A.L. Yuille, D.M. Kammen, and D.S. Cohen. Quadrature and the development of orientation selective cortical cells by Hebb rules. *Biol. Cyb.*, 61:183–194, 1989.

[6] H. Barrow. Learning receptive fields. In *Proceedings of the IEEE First International Conference on Neural Networks*, volume IV, pages 115–121, 1987.

[7] R. Cole, Y. Muthusamy, L. Atlas, T.Leen, and M. Rudnick. Speaker-independent vowel recognition:comparison of backpropagation and trained classification trees. In *Proceedings of the IEEE Hawaii International Conference on System Sciences*, 1990.

[8] T. Leen, M. Rudnick, and D. Hammerstrom. Hebbian feature discovery improves classifier efficiency. In *Proceedings of the IJCNN*, 1990, submitted.

[9] E. Oja. A simplified neuron model as a principal component analyzer. *J. Math. Biology*, 15:267–273, 1982.

[10] L. Ljung. Analysis of recursive stochastic algorithms. *IEEE Trans. Automatic Control*, 22:551–575, 1977.

[11] T. Sanger. An optimality principle for unsupervised learning. In *Advances in Neural Information Processing Systems*. Morgan-Kauffman, 1989.

[12] E. Oja. Neural networks, principal components, and subspaces. *International Journal of Neural Systems*, 1:61–68, 1989.

[13] P. Foldiak. Adaptive network for optimal linear feature extraction. In *Proceedings of the IJCNN*, pages I 401–405, 1989.

[14] T. Kohonen. *Self-Organization and Associative Memory, 2nd Edition*. Springer-Verlag, Berlin, 1988.

[15] J. Rubner and K. Schulten. Development of feature detectors by self-organization: A network model. *Biol. Cyb.*, 1990, in press.

[16] M. Golubitsky and D. Schaeffer. *Singularities and Groups in Bifurcation Theory, Vol. 1*. Springer-Verlag, Berlin, 1984.

[17] Todd K. Leen. Weight dynamics of recurrent Hebbian networks. In *Proceedings of the International Society for the Systems Sciences*, to appear 1990.

[18] Richard Granger, Jóse Ambros-Ingerson, Ursula Staubli, and Gary Lynch. Memorial operation of multiple, interacting simulated brain structures. In M. Gluck and D. Rumelhart, editors, *Neuroscience and Connectionist Models*. Erlbaum Associates, 1989.

[19] Gordon M. Shepherd. *The Synaptic Organization of the Brain*. Oxford University Press, New York, 1979.

[20] Norm May and Dan Hammerstrom. Fltsim detailed description and operation. Technical Report CS/E-88-021, Oregon Graduate Institute, May 1988.

Advanced Neural Computers / R. Eckmiller (Editor)

HARDWARE FOR NEURAL-NET OPTICAL CHARACTER RECOGNITION

L. D. Jackel, B. Boser, J. S. Denker, H. P. Graf, Y. Le Cun, I. Guyon, D. Henderson, R. E. Howard, W. Hubbard, O. Matan, and S. A. Solla

AT&T Bell Laboratories, Room 4D-433
Holmdel, NJ 07733

Through a series of experiments in optical character recognition, an understanding is beginning to emerge of the general nature of the hardware required. Rather than the fully-connected layered neural nets conceived by most hardware researchers, many machine perception tasks require local connectivity and repeated weight patterns between layers to support computing of convolutions. No current-day hardware is available to evaluate in parallel all the connections in a character recognition system. Fortunately, the repetitive nature of the convolution operation makes time-division multiplexing of the hardware possible and even efficient. To avoid I/O bottlenecks, the hardware must contain substantial input data buffers and shift registers. I/O requirements are further relaxed if several layers of the net are processed in a pipelined fashion without recourse to external storage. This paper will discuss hardware architectures for character recognition and will outline choices for possible circuits. An advanced (and working) reconfigurable neural-net chip, that mixes analog and digital processing, will be described.

1. INTRODUCTION

Neural-net hardware designers have been plagued by the following dilemma: with currently available electronics technology, it is impossible to design hardware that is flexible enough to encompass all possible network architectures and, at the same time, have enough resources to accommodate the large networks needed for many real-world applications. Designers typically guess that the ultimate users of the hardware will want several fully-connected layers of neurons with as many neurons and connections as will fit in the system. This high connectivity cannot be scaled to large networks because the number of connections between fully interconnected layers of neurons grows as the product of the number of neurons in the layers. Even in a small image-processing problem, the input field is at least 16 x 16. If the number of neurons in the next layer of the net is the same size as the input field (it is usually larger), then (16x16) x (16x16) = 64,000 connections are needed. The largest neural-net chip made so far [1] has 32,000 1-bit connections, so it falls short of the needs of this apparently minimal network. In practice, single-bit connections are likely to be insufficient for our needs, and several 1-bit connections would have to be combined to provide composite connections with the required analog depth, pushing the arrival of a completely parallel, one-chip network toward the beginning of the next millennium.

The prospects for the near-term availability of really useful hardware are not as bleak as the previous paragraph might suggest. Through our work on various systems to recognize characters we have discovered, that at least for this class of problem, constraints imposed on the network to improve classification accuracy result in an architecture that has limited connectivity and replicated weights, leading to an ideal structure for time-multiplexing the hardware. We will describe several architectures for character recognition, stressing the characteristics they have in common. We will then discuss the hardware options available to implement these architectures, including how the most compute-intensive parts of the network can be mapped onto a new, (and fully-tested) neural net chip.

2. THE CHARACTER RECOGNITION TASK

In optical recognition, a character must be identified from its image pixels. Depending on the nature of the image, this task ranges from being extremely difficult to being fairly straightforward. If the image includes only cleanly printed, fixed-font symbols, simple template matching does an excellent job of classification. When multiple fonts are used, or when the image is noisy, template matching is not as successful, and more sophisticated methods, usually including feature extraction, must be used. Nevertheless, it is still possible to read a full page of poorly printed text with variable fonts and make only a few errors. Many of these can be eliminated using contextual information from syntax and semantics [2].

The problem becomes much more difficult with hand-printed characters. For this problem simple template matching does not work because of the variability of writing styles. When there are breaks within a character, or when characters are touching, the task becomes even more difficult. Here, the job of segmenting the image to determine which pixels belong to which characters becomes both the time and accuracy rate-limiting processes. Currently, to read 5-digit hand-printed zipcodes buried in the confusion of all the writing on a typical envelope, the best systems must reject about 60% of the images to insure that the zipcodes in the remaining images are read correctly with 99% confidence. Machine reading of unformatted, hand-*written* script is a dream we are unlikely to see come true since many of us can't even read our own writing.

3. FEATURE EXTRACTION

We can think of designing a neural net for the recognition task as equivalent to creating a mapping from an input space whose dimension is the size of the image bit-array (say 16x16 = 256) to a 10-dimensional output space. If the mapping were regular, so that points near each other in input space (in a simple metric such as Euclidean distance) also mapped to the same point in output space (same category), then simple techniques, such as learning with a small, fully-connected backprop net, would do the job. Alas, accurate mappings for this task are much nastier: even characters that appear essentially the same to a human can be far apart in a simple metric where the distance between character images within a class is often greater than distances between character images in different classes. In this case, backpropagation through an unstructured net can't provide acceptable results. This is because in such a general network, an enormous amount of training data is needed to determine the huge number of free parameters that set the network weights. With limited data, these free parameters make it easy to "learn" the training data, but result in poor "generalization" when the network has to classify characters not in the training set. Even if sufficient data could be found, the learning time would be prohibitively long.

The "classical" solution of this problem is to change the input representation of the input data to bring elements of the same category closer to each other than to members of different categories. This is called feature extraction. In a series of character recognition experiments, we used a set of hand-crafted feature extractors to provide feature map representations. In an other solution, we designed a network architecture, also based on feature maps, but where the features were learned.

4. A PRE-PROGRAMMED FEATURE EXTRACTION SYSTEM

In an early attempt at hand-printed digit recognition, we used a series a heuristic methods, and hints from biological vision systems to develop feature extractors. The original grey-scale images were thresholded and size normalized to provide a 32 x 32 binary image. Next, we "skeletonized" the images, reducing the stroke width to one pixel. We then convolved the skeletonized images with 49 feature extraction kernels that were chosen by hand. These included families of oriented line and arc detectors, repeated at several scales. The resultant 49 maps were thresholded and combined by logical operations to produce 18 32 x 32 maps. To reduce the amount of data, each feature map was coarse-blocked into a 3 x 5 array by simply OR-ing neighboring bits in the larger maps. (The coarse blocking also has the advantage of building a fair amount of translation, rotation, and distortion invariance into the processing.) The 18 3 x 5 maps then constituted a 270-bit vector that was used for classification. We used statistical techniques, such as Parzen windows, or a small backpropagation network with one hidden layer for the classification step. The backprop net had slightly higher accuracy than the other methods we tried, but its prime advantage was that it ran quickly on our workstation.

The above recognition system had state-of-the-art classification accuracy. The classifier was trained on feature maps extracted from images of 7300 zipcode digits taken from envelopes by a U. S. Postal Service contractor. It was then tested on 2000 different digits obtained in the same way. On the test set, the system achieved a substitution error rate of 1% while rejecting 11% of the digits as unclassifiable. Although this level of correct classification may, at first glance, not seem very remarkable, inspection of typical digits taken from the test set and shown in Figure 1, illustrate how hard the task really is. Many of the digits are poorly formed, have extraneous markings, or are in other ways so ambiguous that it is hard even for a human to classify them with confidence.

The major computing tasks in the above system were the skeletonization and the feature extraction. Both these tasks can be reduced to a series of convolutions of the image, where only a small part of the input data is processed at any given time. For this task, we used a custom chip to convolve simple kernels across the image at high speed [3] and threshold the output. In fact, the kernels were chosen to be compatible with the chip design which allowed kernels up to 7 x 7 in size with 3-valued coefficients. This feature extraction process was equivalent to the evaluation of a network with five layers of weights: three for skeletonization and two for the actual feature extraction and coarse-blocking. Although this equivalent network has about 4,000,000 connections, most of the processing fits on a chip with only 3,000 weights. This was possible because, at most, only a 7 x 7 region of the image was needed at any one time to determine the value of a unit in the next layer.

The time bottleneck for this system was the formatting of the data sent to the chip. The chip was designed as a general pattern-matching circuit without much thought of how it might be used in a large image-processing problem. In evaluating a convolution, the kernel is scanned serially across the image, with the center of the kernel passing over each pixel location. Thus, for a 7 x 7 kernel, the same pixel is presented 49 times, each time in a different location in a 7 x 7 array. In a chip designed as a convolver, shift registers are provided, so that the same data need not be passed onto the chip more than once. Our general purpose chip had no such register, and to evaluate the convolutions we had to pass 49 times more input data than algorithmically required. Furthermore, the chip had no convenient way of storing intermediate results, so the data from the evaluation of each layer had to pass off the chip and on again before the next evaluation. Learning from this experience, our new chips include both these features.

Despite the inefficiencies in this system, it could classify about one character/sec (including preprocessing), evaluating over 8 million connections/sec. A workstation, doing all the same

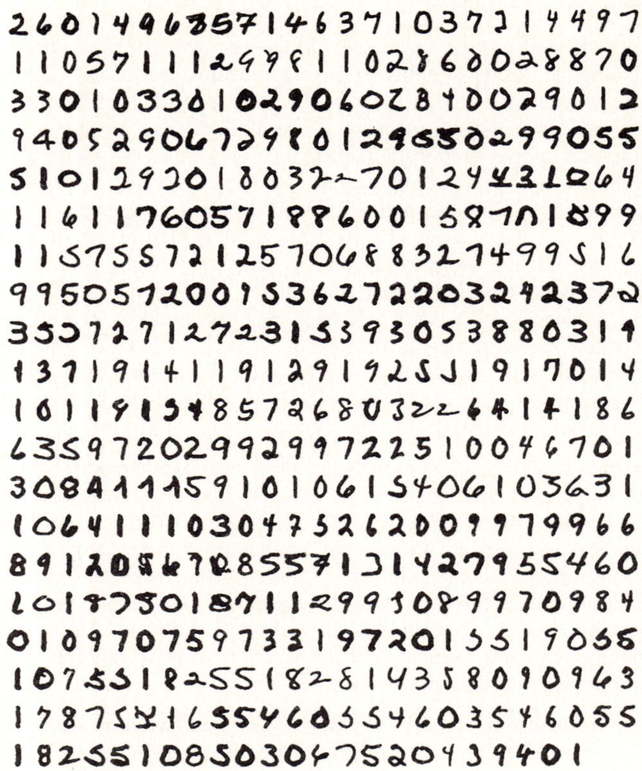

FIGURE 1.
Typical examples from the U.S. Postal Service handwritten digit database. Notice that many of the digits are poorly formed and hard to classify, even for a human.

processing in software ran about 30 times slower. In fact, without the chip to help us devise the feature extraction process, limits to our patience would have prevented us from ever designing a high-performance recognizer.

5. A DIGIT RECOGNIZER FOR LEARNED FEATURE EXTRACTION

The success of the chip-based system with hand-crafted feature extraction and the poor performance of systems which attempted to do recognition using backpropagation learning directly on a pixel image might lead to the conclusion that there is no particular advantage to a neural-net approach, except as a language for describing a hardware accelerator. Being even more critical, the chip itself is really just used as an image convolver with a thresholded output.

Such a conclusion, it turns out, would have been premature. Recently, Le Cun [4], working with a small database of digits, showed that a network could be *trained* to develop its own feature extraction kernels. He designed a small network with a limited connectivity where the first few layers performed multiple convolutions. This was guaranteed by constraining the weights in the net to take the form of convolution kernels, but *not fixing* these weights. Le Cun's network had many fewer connections than a fully-connected net with comparable computing power. The constraints on the network drastically reduced the number of free parameters thereby improving generalization. These ideas were refined and applied to a larger network that was trained on the Postal Service data with astonishing results: the classification accuracy was about the same as the net with the hand-crafted feature extraction, but the new net required less than 70,000 connections (a factor of 30 less than the hand-crafted net) and had only 10,000 free parameters [5]. It is shown schematically in Figure 2. With this number of connections, the system could process one digit per second on a Sun 3 workstation. Using an AT&T DSP32C Digital Signal Processor in conjunction with either the Sun or a 386PC, the rate increased to 10 digits per second. Evaluation of the network took only 30msec; most of the computing time was taken by the scaling of the images. The network was refined by deleting low-importance weights [6], and replacing many low-resolution feature maps by a few higher-resolution maps followed by adaptive coarse-blocking. This net, which had only 2500 free parameters, gave even better performance, rejecting 9% of the test digits to attain a 1% substitution error[7]. When the net the training set was expanded to include 20,000 more digits obtained from another source, the reject rate was reduced to 7%.

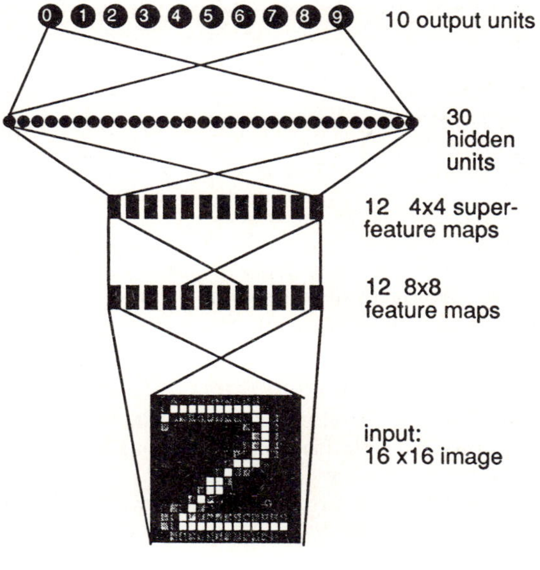

FIGURE 2.
A network architecture for classifying handwritten digits. All the connection weights between layers are learned using the backpropagation algorithm. Two layers of feature extraction are followed by an addition layer of 30 neurons (here labeled hidden units). In later networks these 30 neurons were eliminated, and the first layer of 12 feature maps was replaced by a layer of 4 higher-resolution maps.

6. COMMON CHARACTERISTICS OF THE RECOGNIZER NETWORKS

After looking at the example systems just described, common themes in the architecture emerge. While we can't make the leap to say that they *must* be common to all machine perception systems, it's a good bet that they will be important.

Here is what we find: the early layers of the network have limited receptive fields. The units (or neurons) in these layers can be grouped so that their outputs form maps whose dimensionality is the same as the input field (obviously 2D for vision problems). Most important, units within a map perform the same operation as their neighbors, only they operate on a shifted input. Explicitly, it seems that the right thing to do is to take convolutions followed by a non-linear function on each output component. Since high-level features require less precision in their location, the networks also tend to have contractions of the feature maps, so that the maps have less spatial resolution than their inputs.

That biology seems to have come up with the same principles in animal vision systems, where numerous feature maps are formed for the visual field, gives us confidence in our approach. But biological neurons are much "cheaper" than silicon neurons; our brains cram 10^{15} synapses into a two liter volume. Even if we knew how to hook them up, that many silicon connections, stacked as chips 1 cm apart, would fill a room 10 meters square and a few meters high.

Silicon neurons, however are fast, perhaps 100,000 times faster than biological neurons. Clearly, systems using electronic neurons would do well to compensate for their limited parallelism with time-multiplexing to take advantage of their high speed. This tradeoff will not work if all the connections of a network have different, random values since we would have to load every neuron's unique set of input connection weights onto the chip, creating an enormous I/O load on the system. A fortunate result of our character recognition experiments is that in order to learn effectively from examples or even to do feature extraction with fixed, unlearned kernels, we need a highly regular, locally connected network with repetitive use of the same weights. This is precisely the kind of network that lends itself to multiplexing.

Another feature of our recognition networks that aids multiplexed processing is that even with the coarse-blocking of the feature maps, successive layers of feature extraction still just require input data whose origin can be traced to a restricted region of the image input field. This means that if we provide some modest on-chip storage, we can serially process portions of the image several layers deep through the net before requiring new input data, significantly reducing I/O, and easing a potential bottleneck.

An additional result, confirmed both empirically and theoretically, showed that as we move closer to the input of the network, the connections can have fewer and fewer bits of analog depth and still preserve the accuracy of the classifier. This means that at the front-end of the net, which has the greatest share of connections, we can use hardware with only a few bits of precision. Here, a high-density analog processor is appropriate. As we near the output layer, there are relatively few connections, but they need high precision. At this point, a good choice for hardware is a digital signal processor (DSP) which has high precision and is still an order of magnitude faster than a general purpose microprocessor.

7. AN ADVANCED NEURAL-NET CHIP FOR MACHINE VISION

In this section we describe a second generation neural-net chip [1], designed by H. P. Graf that includes support circuitry that makes it efficient for image processing. The chip, which combines analog and digital processing, is reconfigurable, so that the number of "neurons" can be varied as well as the number of connections per neuron. The 32,000 programmable 1-bit connections on the chip can be combined to form fewer connections with greater analog depth.

Figure 3 is a photograph of this chip which measures 4.5 mm by 7.0 mm. It was fabricated by AT&T in 0.9 micron CMOS. It can evaluate all 32,000 connections in parallel (with 4% accuracy on the weighted sums) every 100nsec, giving a rating of 300 billion connections/sec. The connections, which appear as the rectangular blocks on either side of the chip, each take up a cell 23 microns by 17 microns and contain 9 transistors. The block in the center of the chip contains thresholding circuitry, multipliers, switches to set the network architecture, and decoders. At both ends of the chip are input and output shift registers to control the data flow. The shift registers can also be used to store intermediate results, passing the output of one neuron to the input of another. Digital methods are used to store the 1-bit connection weights. Each connection is evaluated locally using a digital NXOR. Outputs from the NXORs are connected to current sources to permit efficient analog summing. The chip has now been used to do edge extraction from images and is being incorporated into a machine vision system.

In our most advanced character recognizer, the DSP evaluates the network, but it spends most of its time scaling the image. Therefore, using the high-speed chip to evaluate the network would only result in a small speed improvement. However, with the chip's high speed, we may be able to avoid scaling the image; we can extract features across the entire input field at all scales. Furthermore, the image segmentation, which is also a computational bottleneck, need not be done explicitly. We can have many networks scanning portions of the image, attempting to recognize whatever appears in their field of view.

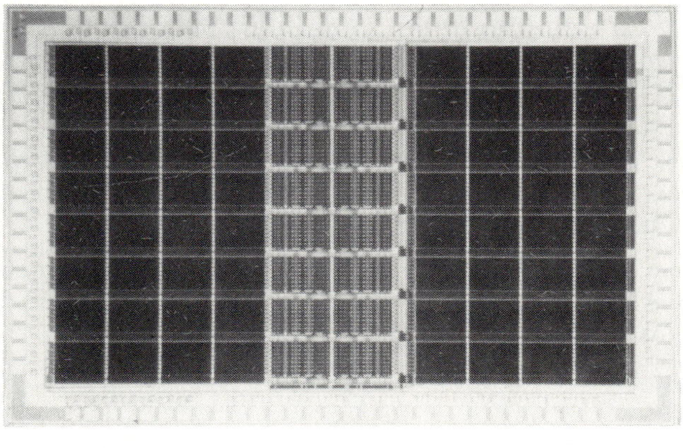

FIGURE 3.

A photograph of a new 32,000 connection neural net chip. The chip size is 4.5 mm by 7 mm and can process 300 billion connections/sec.

8. CONCLUSIONS

We have found that different approaches to image recognition often lead to neural-net architectures that have limited connectivity and repeated use of the same set of weights. This architecture is ideal for time-multiplexing (a combined parallel-serial processing) on hardware systems that would be too small to evaluate the entire network in parallel. To make this process efficient, a chip needs to have shift-registers to format the input data, and additional registers to store intermediate results. Within this framework, it is possible to design chips that have broad utility, large connection capacity, and high speed. This was demonstrated by a new chip with 32,000 reconfigurable connections.

ACKNOWLEDGEMENT

We thank the U.S. Postal Service for providing us with a database of handwritten digits.

REFERENCES

[1] H. P. Graf and D. Henderson, "A reconfigurable CMOS neural network", to appear in Technical Digest of International Solid-State Circuits Conference, IEEE, 1990.

[2] S. Kahan, T. Pavlidis, and H. S. Baird, "On the Recognition of Printed Characters of Any Font or Size", IEEE trans. on PAMI, **PAMI-9** pp. 274-288 (1987).

[3] J. S. Denker, W. R. Gardner, H. P. Graf, D. Henderson, R. E. Howard, W. Hubbard, L. D. Jackel, H. S. Baird, and I Guyon, "Neural Network Recognizer for Hand-Written Zip Code Digits, in *Advances in Neural Information Processing Systems 1,* David S. Touretzky, ed., Morgan Kaufmann, San Mateo, CA, pp. 323-31 (1989).

[4] Y. Le Cun, "Generalization and Network Design Strategies" in *Connectionism in Perspective,* R Pfeifer, Z. Schreter, F. Fogelman, and L. Steels, eds. Elsevier, Zurich (1989).

[5] Y. Le Cun, B. Boser, J. S. Denker, D. Henderson, R. E. Howard, W. Hubbard, and L. D. Jackel, "Back-Propagation Applied to Handwritten Zipcode Recognition" to appear in Neural Computation **4** January, 1990.

[6] Y. Le Cun, J. S. Denker, and S. A. Solla, "Optimal Brain Damage", to appear in *Advances in Neural Information Processing Systems 2,* D. S. Touretzky, ed. Morgan Kaufman, San Mateo, CA, 1990.

[7] Y. Le Cun, B. Boser, J. S. Denker, D. Henderson, R. E. Howard, W. Hubbard, and L. D. Jackel, "Handwritten digit recognition with a backpropagation network" to appear in *Advances in Neural Information Processing Systems 2,* D. S. Touretzky, ed. Morgan Kaufman, San Mateo, CA, 1990.

Advanced Neural Computers / R. Eckmiller (Editor)
Elsevier Science Publishers B.V. (North-Holland), 1990

THE ROLE OF TIME IN NATURAL INTELLIGENCE: IMPLICATIONS FOR NEURAL NETWORK AND ARTIFICIAL INTELLIGENCE RESEARCH*

A. HARRY KLOPF and JAMES S. MORGAN

Wright Research and Development Center
Wright-Patterson Air Force Base, Ohio 45433-6543
U.S.A

Abstract. Real-time, closed-loop interactions between biological systems and their environments appear to be fundamental to the mechanisms that underlie natural intelligence. Such a theoretical view has given rise to neuronal models that predict a wide range of Pavlovian animal learning phenomena and to neural networks that may model instrumental conditioning phenomena. The theoretical framework that is emerging suggests an alternative to the current paradigms for neural network and artificial intelligence research.

1. INTRODUCTION

Neural network researchers have pursued a variety of theoretical approaches in recent years. Some have been inspired by analogs of theoretical models in physics and have investigated Boltzmann machines [1-3] and what are sometimes called Hopfield networks [4-8]. Others, employing supervised learning mechanisms that involve the feedback of error signals from a teacher, have studied perceptrons [9-10], adalines [11] or, more recently, back-propagation networks [12-17]. Still others have paid special attention to the theoretical and experimental results of animal learning research [18-30]. Among the latter group, some of us have devoted particular attention to the question of what kind of basic element, possibly corresponding to a model of single-neuron function, should be assumed in neural network research. It is to this research on alternative basic elements for neural network modeling that we turn our attention first, because a principle is emerging from this research that may have implications for our understanding of natural and perhaps artificial intelligence.

First we state the principle and then note some of the evidence that has drawn us to it. In a very general form, the principle may be stated like this: real-time considerations are fundamental to natural intelligence. This is to say that when it comes to understanding memory, learning, and intelligence as manifested by biological systems, precise temporal relationships among stimuli and between stimuli and responses may be crucially important. Such a principle has been emerging from the neuronal modeling efforts of Klopf [18-21] and Sutton and Barto [22-23]. If the principle turns out to be valid, it may have substantial implications for neural network and artificial intelligence research because it has generally been assumed by both neural network and artificial intelligence researchers

*This research was supported under Task 2312 R1 by the Life Sciences Directorate of the United States Air Force Office of Scientific Research. This is a revised version of a paper presented at the International Joint Conference on Neural Networks, Washington DC, 18-22 June 1989.

that real-time considerations are not a fundamental dimension of the problems they are addressing. In essence, artificial intelligence researchers have assumed that symbolic or cognitive relationships having the character of IF-THEN statements could serve as building blocks for the synthesis of intelligent information processing systems. Cognitive psychologists have adopted a similar approach. In general, such a formulation does not model real-time aspects of a system's interaction with its environment. Likewise, most neural network models do not capture real-time aspects of a system's interaction with its environment. The dominant paradigm in neural network research has been what might be called the spatial neural network paradigm. Within this paradigm, a central question has been how to construct neural networks that can be trained to classify sets of spatial patterns. In essence, the artificial intelligence paradigm and the spatial neural network paradigm deal with what but not when. The spatial dimension is present but not the temporal. We suggest here that a paradigm that deals with what and when may be essential for modeling natural intelligence. We call such a paradigm a spatio-temporal neural network paradigm. Such a paradigm, which emphasizes real-time, closed-loop interactions between a learning system and its environment (see Figure 1), is emerging from research on alternative models of single-neuron function [18-23]. Next, we briefly review this research.

2. REAL-TIME LEARNING MECHANISM MODELS

The research began with the assumption that animal learning theory and experiments could be relevant to neuronal modeling [18-19]. Some of us who have turned to animal learning research for clues as to how to construct neuronal and neural network models have discovered this century's animal learning research to have yielded a gold mine of theory and experiments. In particular, the theoretical and experimental results of studies of classical conditioning have importantly shaped some of our recent neuronal modeling efforts [21-22]. In fact, when we as neural network researchers turned to the study of classical conditioning, we learned something that animal learning researchers had known from the beginning: real-time considerations are fundamental to natural intelligence [31].

Hebb [32] exhibited an appreciation of this principle in the neuronal model he proposed, and that was really the beginning of what we have come to call real-time learning mechanism models. Hebb suggested that the efficacy of a modifiable synapse increased whenever the synapse was active in conjunction with activity of the postsynaptic neuron. Thus, Hebb was proposing that learning (i.e., changes in the efficacy of synapses) was a function of correlations between approximately simultaneous pre- and postsynaptic levels of neuronal activity. Real-time learning mechanism models such as Hebb's emphasize the temporal association of signals: each critical event in the sequence leading to learning has a time of occurrence associated with it and this time plays a fundamental role in the computations that yield changes in the efficacy of synapses. It should be noted that "real-time," in this context, does not mean continuous time as contrasted with discrete time; nor does it refer to a learning system's ability to accomplish its computations at a sufficient speed to keep pace with the environment within which it is embedded. Rather, a real-time learning mechanism, as defined here, is one for which the time of occurrence of each critical event in the sequence leading to learning is of fundamental importance with respect to the computations the learning mechanism is performing. Real-time learning mechanisms may be contrasted with non-real-time learning mechanisms such as the perceptron, adaline, or back-propagation learning mechanisms for which error signals follow system responses and only the order of the inputs, outputs, and error signals is important, not the exact time of occurrence of each signal, relative to the others.

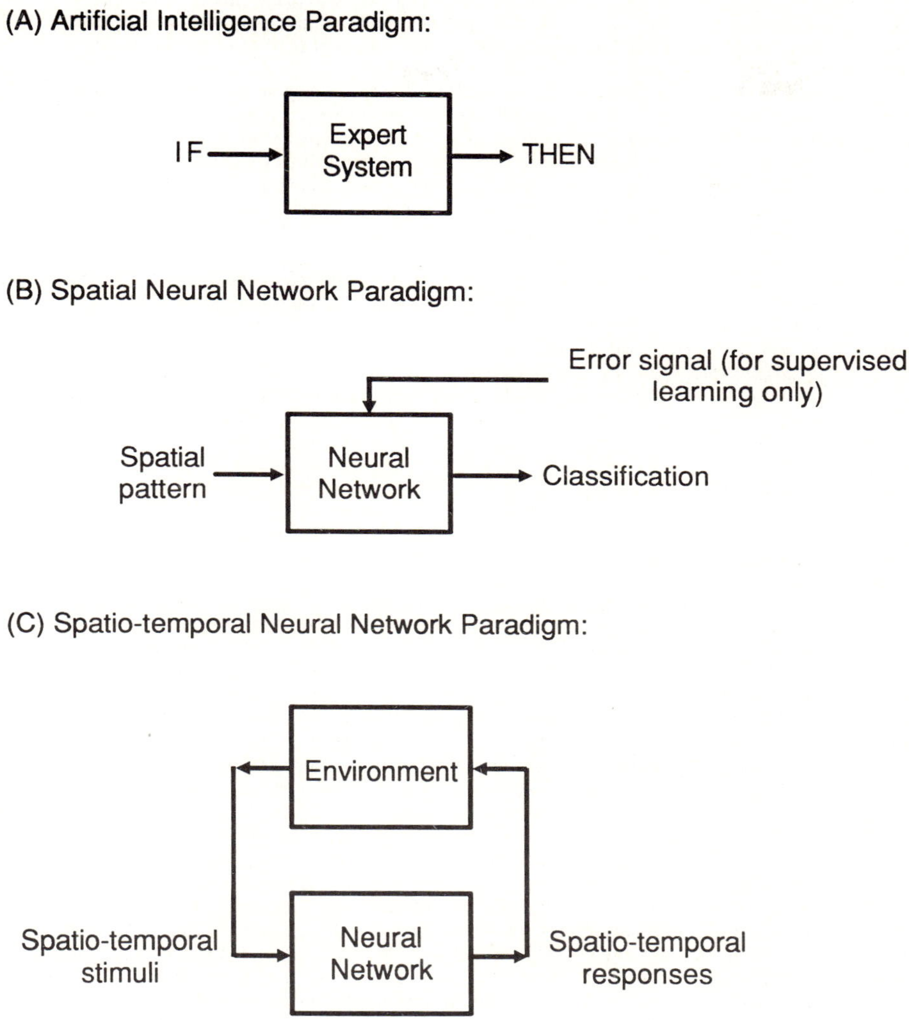

Figure 1. Three paradigms that are employed in artificial intelligence and neural network research. In the artificial intelligence paradigm (A), it is assumed that symbolic or cognitive relationships having the character of IF-THEN statements can serve as building blocks for the synthesis of, for example, expert systems. In the spatial neural network paradigm (B), neural networks are trained to classify spatial stimuli. The temporal dimension of the neural network's relationship to its environment is absent, as is also generally the case in the artificial intelligence paradigm. In the spatio-temporal neural network paradigm (C), a neural network interacts with its environment in a real-time, closed loop fashion that is of fundamental importance, with respect to the learning mechanisms that are employed, and perhaps with regard to the neural network's function, in general.

Hebb's model, while it is a real-time learning mechanisms model, utilizes time in a way that may not be valid. Hebb assumed that neurons correlate approximately simultaneous signals. Both the assumption of simultaneity and the assumption that signals are correlated by single neurons can be called into question in that it has now been demonstrated that much stronger contact with the experimental results of classical conditioning studies is obtained if one adopts two alternative assumptions: first, that neurons are correlating sequential rather than simultaneous events as a basis for learning [18-19] and second, that neurons are correlating changes in signal levels (first derivatives with respect to time) rather than the signal levels themselves [21-22]. These alternative assumptions yield a real-time learning mechanism model that correlates earlier changes in presynaptic signal levels with later changes in postsynaptic signal levels. This class of differential real-time learning mechanism models was independently discovered by Klopf [20] and Kosko [33]. One result of this theoretical approach has been a neuronal model that predicts a wide range of classical conditioning phenomena [21-22]. This neuronal model, termed a drive-reinforcement model of single-neuron function, is serving as a basic element for the synthesis of neural networks that interact with their environments in a real-time, closed loop fashion.

3. EXPERIMENTAL TESTS

Simple one- and two-layered networks of two or four drive-reinforcement neurons have been tested in two kinds of environments. Klopf [34] and Klopf and Morgan [35] have reported that a simulated robot controlled by a network of drive-reinforcement neurons will learn to approach one class of objects and avoid another class of objects after a limited amount of real-time, closed-loop experience involving the robot interacting with objects in a room. The robot or learning system operated in an environment containing two spatially separated objects, an "attractant" and a "repellent." The learning system could locomote and could sense objects by tactile and visual means. Innate behaviors (relexes) were built into the learning system. Changes in the behavior of the learning system were then observed and recorded during real-time, closed-loop learning. In order to accomplish the behavioral tests, the learning system, the neural network that controlled the learning system, and the environment within which the learning system operated were realized in the form of a computer simulation. Other examples of computer simulations of real-time, closed-loop interactions between a neural network-controlled learning system and its environment are those due to Barto and Sutton [36], and Barto, Sutton, and Anderson [37].

Morgan, Patterson, and Klopf [38] have reported that an unsupervised network of two simulated drive-reinforcement neurons learned a solution to a simple version of a classic dynamic control problem without experiencing failure. The control problem was that of balancing a pole attached by a hinge to a cart which was free to move horizontally along an infinite track. The pole was free to swing in the plane of motion of the cart. Each trial began with the pole dislodged from vertical by a force of 0.1 newton applied to the cart. A trial ended with failure when the angle of the pole from vertical exceeded twelve degrees. To facilitate comparison with other research, the cart-pole simulation was identical to that reported in a study due to Barto, Sutton, and Anderson [37]. The magnitude of the force applied to the cart was determined by the difference between the output signal frequencies of two simulated neurons. The direction of the force was determined by the neuron which had the greater output signal frequency. The goal of balancing the pole was conveyed to the network through a sensor which had an output signal frequency proportional to the pole angle. The network was provided with sensors which decoded the physical state space of the cart-pole system into pole angle and pole angular velocity regions. The network, utilizing hardwired feedback loops that crudely approximated the required control system, proceeded to refine the hardwired feedback loops by means of the drive-reinforcement neurons such that the network was able to learn to balance the pole in less than one trial and then keep the pole balanced for hours. When the network was denied the use of the learning mechanisms in the drive-reinforcement neurons so that only the hardwired feedback loops were available, the network was then able to keep the pole balanced for only about two seconds.

4. CONCLUSIONS

Neuronal models of classical conditioning phenomena and neural network models of instrumental conditioning phenomena suggest to us that, as a general principle, real-time considerations may be fundamental to natural intelligence. More specifically, we are investigating the hypothesis that learning in biological systems consists of acquired positive and negative real-time feedback loops built on a foundation of innate positive and negative real-time feedback loops [35]. In some respects, this theoretical approach is taking us back to an approach to the modeling of the mechanisms of memory, learning, and intelligence not unlike that pioneered by Wiener [39], Ashby [40], and Powers [41].

REFERENCES

[1] D. H. Ackley, G. H. Hinton, & T. J. Sejnowski, "A learning algorithm for Boltzmann machines," Cognitive Science, 9, 147-169, 1985.

[2] G. E. Hinton, & T. J. Sejnowski, "Learning and relearning in Boltzmann machines," In E. E. Rumelhart & J. L. McClelland (Eds.), Parallel distributed processing: Explorations in the microstructure of cognition: Vol. 1. Foundations (pp. 282-317), Cambridge, MA: Bradford Books/MIT Press, 1986.

[3] G. E. Hinton, T. J. Sejnowski, & D. H. Ackley, Boltzmann machines: Constraint satisfaction networks that learn (Tech. Rep. No. CMU-CS-84-119), Pittsburgh: Carnegie-Mellon University, Computer Science Department, 1984.

[4] M. A. Cohen, & S. Grossberg, "Absolute stability of global pattern formation and parallel memory storage by competitive neural networks," IEEE Transactions on Systems, Man, & Cybernetics, SMC-13, 815-826, 1983.

[5] J. J. Hopfield, "Neural networks and physical systems with emergent collective computational abilities," Proceedings of the National Academy of Sciences USA, 79, 2554-2558, 1982.

[6] J. J. Hopfield, "Neurons with graded response have collective computational properties like those of two-state neurons," Proceedings of the National Academy of Sciences USA, 81, 3088-3092, 1984.

[7] J. J. Hopfied, & D. W. Tank, "Neural computation of decisions in optimization problems," Biological Cybernetics, 52, 141-152, 1985.

[8] J. J. Hopfield, & D. W. Tank, "Computing with neural circuits: A model," Science, 233, 625-633, 1986.

[9] F. Rosenblatt, Principles of neurodynamics, New York: Spartan Books, 1962.

[10] M. L. Minsky, & S. A. Papert, Perceptrons: An introduction to computational geometry, expanded edition. Cambridge, Massachusetts: MIT Press, 1988.

[11] B. Widrow, "Generalization and information storage in networks of adaline neurons," In M. C. Yovits, G. T. Jacobi, & G. D. Goldstein (Eds.), Self-organizing systems-1962 (pp. 435-461), Washington, DC: Spartan Books, 1962.

[12] P. J. Werbos, Beyond regression: New tools for prediction and analysis in the behavioral sciences, Unpublished doctoral dissertation, Harvard University, Cambridge, MA, 1974.

[13] D. B. Parker, Learning Logic, (Invention Report No. 581-64, File 1), Stanford, California: Stanford University, Office of Technology Licensing, 1982.
[14] D. B. Parker, Learning-logic (Tech Rep. No. 47), Cambridge, Massachusetts: Massachusetts Institute of Technology, Center for Computational Research in Economics and Management Science, 1985.
[15] Y. Le Cun, "Une procedure d'apprentissage pour reseau a seuil asymetrique [A learning procedure for an asymmetric threshold network]," Proceedings of Cognitiva, 85, 559-604d, 1985.
[16] D. E. Rumelhart, G. E. Hinton, & R. J. Williams, Learning internal representations by error propagation (ICS Report No. 8506), San Diego: University of California, Institute for Cognitive Science, 1985.
[17] D. E. Rumelhart, G. E. Hinton, & R. J. Williams, "Learning internal representations by error propagation," In D. E. Rumelhart & J. L. McClelland (Eds.), Parallel distributed processing: Explorations in the microstructure of cognition. Vol. 1: Foundations (pp. 318-364), Cambridge, MA: Bradford Books/ MIT Press, 1986.
[18] A. H. Klopf, Brain function and adaptive systems - A heterostatic theory (Rep. No. 133 [AFCRL-72-0164]), L. G. Hanscom Field, Bedford, MA: Air Force Cambridge Research Laboratories, 1972. (DTIC Report AD 742259, available from the Defense Technical Information Center, Cameron Station, Alexandria, VA 22304-6145).
[19] A. H. Klopf, The hedonistic neuron: A theory of memory, learning, and intelligence, Washington, DC: Hemisphere, 1982.
[20] A. H. Klopf, "A drive-reinforcement model of single neuron function: An alternative to the Hebbian neuronal model," In J. S. Denker (Ed.), AIP Conference Proceedings 151: Neural networks for computing (pp. 265-270), New York: American Institute of Physics, 1986.
[21] A. H. Klopf, "A neuronal model of classical conditioning," Psychobiology, 16(2), 85-125, 1988.
[22] R. S. Sutton, & A. G. Barto, "Toward a modern theory of adaptive networks: Expectation and prediction," Psychological Review, 88, 135-170, 1981.
[23] R. S. Sutton, & A. G. Barto, "A temporal-difference model of classical conditioning," Proceedings of the Ninth Annual Conference of the Cognitive Science Society (pp. 355-378), Hillsdale, NJ: Erlbaum, 1987.
[24] S. Grossberg, "Pavlovian pattern learning by nonlinear neural networks," Proceedings of the National Academy of Sciences USA, 68, 828-831, 1971.
[25] S. Grossberg, Studies of mind and brain, Boston: Reidel, 1982.
[26] S. Grossberg, The adaptive brain (Vols. 1 & 2), New York: North-Holland, 1987.
[27] A. Gelperin, J. J. Hopfield, & D. W. Tank, "The logic of Limax learning," In A. Selverston (Ed.), Model neural networks and behavior (pp. 237-261), New York: Plenum Press, 1985.
[28] D. E. J. Blazis, J. E. Desmond, J. W. Moore, & N. E. Berthier, "Simulation of the classically conditioned nictitating membrane response by a neuron-like adaptive element: A real-time variant of the Sutton-Barto model," In Proceedings of the Eighth Annual Conference of the Cognitive Science Society (pp. 176-186). Hillsdale, NJ: Erlbaum, 1986.
[29] G. Tesauro, Simple neural models of classical conditioning, Biological Cybernetics, 55, 187-200, 1986.
[30] M. A. Gluck, & R. F. Thompson, "Modeling the neural substrates of associative learning and memory: A computational approach," Psychological Review, 94, 176-191, 1987.
[31] I. P. Pavlov, Conditioned reflexes, Oxford: Oxford University Press, 1927 (Dover Edition, 1960).
[32] D. O. Hebb, The organization of behavior, New York: Wiley, 1949.
[33] B. Kosko, "Differential Hebbian learning," In J. S. Denker (Ed.), AIP Conference Proceedings 151, Neural networks for computing (pp. 277-282), New York: American Institute of Physics, 1986.

[34] A. H. Klopf, "Drive-reinforcement learning: A real-time learning mechanism for unsupervised learning," in Proceedings of the IEEE First Annual International Conference on Neural Networks, San Diego, California, 21-24 June 1987.
[35] A. H. Klopf and J. S. Morgan, "The role of time in natural intelligence: Implications of classical and instrumental conditioning for neuronal and neural network modeling," In: Learning and Computational Neuroscience (M. Gabriel and J. Moore, eds.). Cambridge, Massachusetts: MIT Press, in press.
[36] A. G. Barto, & R. S. Sutton, "Landmark learning: An illustration of associative search," Biological Cybernetics, 42, 1-8, 1981.
[37] A. G. Barto, R. S. Sutton, & C. W. Anderson, "Neuronlike elements that can solve difficult learning control problems," IEEE Transactions on Systems, Man, & Cybernetics, SMC-13, 835-846, 1983.
[38] J. S. Morgan, E. C. Patterson, and A. H. Klopf, "A network of two drive-reinforcement neurons that learns a solution to a real-time dynamic control problem," in Abstracts of the First Annual International Neural Network Society Meeting, Volume 1, Supplement 1 of Neural Networks, Boston, Massachusetts, 6-10 September 1988.
[39] N. Wiener, Cybernetics, Cambridge, Massachusetts: MIT Press, 1948/1961.
[40] W. R. Ashby, Design for a Brain, New York: Wiley, 1952/1960.
[41] W. T. Powers, Behavior: The Control of Perception, New York: Aldine, 1973.

Advanced Neural Computers / R. Eckmiller (Editor)

HARDWARE CONCEPTS FOR NEURAL NETWORKS

Ulrich Ramacher

SIEMENS AG, Corporate Research & Development
D-8000 Munich, F.R. Germany

1. INTRODUCTION

The response and the characteristics of present models of artificial neural nets are primarily investigated by simulation on vector computers, workstations, special coprocessors or transputer arrays. The fundamental drawback of such simulators is that the spatio-temporal parallelism in the processing of information that is inherent to the neural net is lost entirely or partly and that the computing time of the simulated net especially for large associations of neurons (tailored to application-relevant tasks) grows to such orders of magnitude that a speedy acquisition of "neural" know-how is hindered or made impossible. Figure 1 shows the performance obtainable with commercially available

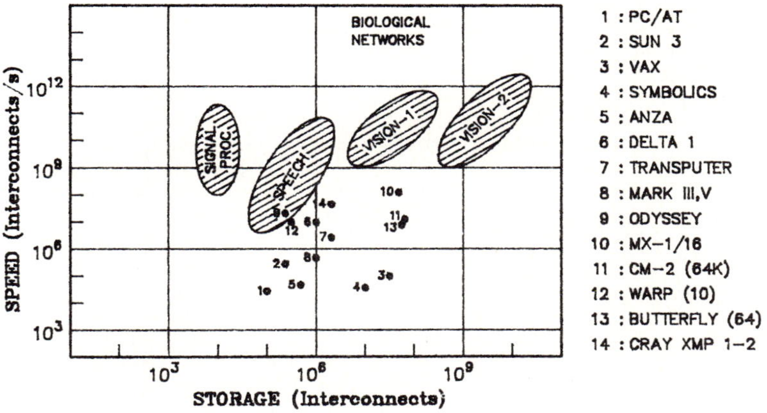

Figure 1 Computational capabilities of neural network simulators versus computational requirements of some applications

simulators [1] in terms of weights and weights per second. This must be confronted with the applicational needs. It becomes obvious that today's hardware capabilities are limiting the development of neural network research.

Consequently, a great number of technologies have been tried for direct implementation of neural nets, and a dozen chips built [2]. Since the applications may require quantities of neurons that allow for single-chip integration or overtax the single-chip integration potential of present technology as well as that of future 0.3-µm technology by whole orders of magnitude (see figure 1), these chips fall into either of two categories: single-chip integration of a complete neural net, or chip integration of function blocks that emulate the compute-intensive pieces of the neural algorithms, in particular those of the learning mode. In the latter case, the specially designed chip must be assisted by a standard one, be it a micro-processor, a transputer or an ASIC, which performs the rest of the neural computations.

This paper reviews both opportunities and presents a guide line to neural chip design taking into consideration applicational needs, technological constraints and the system environment.

2. SINGLE-CHIP INTEGRATION OF NEURAL NETS

Single-chip integration includes on-chip storage of a sufficient number of weights. Consequently the amount of information a neural chip can process is limited in size. This means in turn that the application must match the implementation potential of the technology.
Because the pad-bandwidth problem for the weights is avoided with on-chip storage of the weights, a potentially higher number of weights can be processed per second as compared to off-chip. To get an idea of what processing speed and net size can be achieved by singe-chip implementation some typical examples are reviewed next.

An example for mostly digital design is presented by the configurable CMOS neural network chip described recently by H. P. Graf [3]. Binary input/output signals (instead of continuously varying ones) and coarse-grain weighting (≤ 4bits) are considered appropriate for low-level recognition of pre-processed images. The chip provides 256 synaptic building blocks each of which consists of 128 parallel 1bit-multiply-accumulate units and a subsequent multiplier and comparator. The comparator is the only analog piece, all other components are designed digital. Configuration of the chip is possible with regard to the number B (≤8) of synaptic building blocks per neuron, and the degree D of resolution (1to 16 steps) for the weights. The number of neurons is 256 / ($B \cdot \log_2 D$) and the number of weights processed per second is 320 billion / ($B \cdot \log_2 D$). Since the chip´s bus width is 128 bit, the latter number assumes an input interface capable of a data rate of up to 16 x 80 = 1280 Mbit/sec.
In terms of the coordinates used in figure 1 the chip´s performance ranges from (32768,320G) for 256 neurons, each with 128 binary pixels, to (8192,10G) for 8 neurons, each with 1032 4bit-pixels. Consider then a video environment with 50 pictures recorded per second, each carrying 512x512 4bit-pixels. Depending on the selected configuration the chip would run 100 to 3 times faster than needed. Thus the chip´s computational performance is well balanced with respect to the applicational requirements and system environment met in low-level image recognition, and leaves a sufficient reserve for pictures with 10^6 pixels (25 to 0.8).

Two other chips have recently been realized [4,5]. The one uses CCD and floating-gate technology, allowing for analog input which is weighed digitally (6 bits) by a multiplying D/A converter. This chip has 2016 programmable weights and performs about 3 billion weights per second. The other chip uses EEPROM and NMOS technology, all functional blocks are realized in analog design with about 4bit analog depth of resolution. The number of synapses amounts to maximally 10240 and the performance is expected to reach 10 billion weights per second with a 64 bit wide bus. In contrast, Graf´s CMOS chip, if configured for 4 bit resolution, performs 80 billion weights per second (see table 1) . The lower speed of [5] is mainly due to the floating gate device used for storage of weights.

Comparing the synaptic density obtained either with digital design and 0.9 µm CMOS process [3] or with analog design and 1 µm NMOS technology [5] , it turns out that both approaches can achieve about 50 000 4bit-weights per cm^2. Future 0.3 µm CMOS processes will allow for chip areas of about 4 cm^2, giving a "digital" upper limit of about 2 million 4bit-weights. As analog design does not scale linearly with structure size, digital design seems to be going to dominate neural chip design. However, analog design of neural networks will be carried on because the integration of analog sensors and neural pre-

approach	synaptic density	# of 4bit weights processed per second
[3] digital 0.9µm	32 000 x 1bit at 0.15cm^2	80 billion (128 bit bus)
0.3 µm	ca.500000 x 4bit per cm^2	
[5] analog 1µm	10 000 x 4bit at 0.2 cm^2	10 billion (64 bit bus)
0.3µm	?	

Table 1 Comparison of the analog and digital approach

processing is of outmost importance to many applications [6,7] and brings about performance advantages at the system level (like reduced costs for interfaces).

Generally, single-chip integration of a neural net expresses itself in a comparatively small number of synapses corresponding to not more than a thousand fully interconnected neurons today (see table 1). Thanks to this, simulation of the learning algorithms is accessible by existing computers, with the result that the applicational task under consideration is well defined and the hardware can be matched optimally to the task. Thus, the weights can be computed in advance, and there is no extra circuitry required other than for programmable storage or hard-wiring of the weights.

The task of the architecture developer consists in this case of putting as many synapses as possible on a chip for a particular application, because the computing time reduces linearly with the number of implemented synapses. It will depend on the number of pads available and the required processing time (realtime conditions) of the neural net to what extent it is possible to deviate from the ideal massive parallel networking of a neural net and, thus, avoid the interconnection problem. Together with the decision as to whether analog or digital signal processing concepts are to be applied and the selection of a technology, there results an initial architecture draft [8-11] .

2.1. Analog Design Issues

Particularly for analog realization, the emphasis of circuit design is on the exploitation of the functional properties inherent in basic circuit elements. An important requirement is the compactness of the connection element, because the cell size mainly determines the overall area of the network.

An advantage of analog circuits in comparison to digital circuits is that they can "process more than 1 bit per transistor". If this benefit is to be made use of, however, the following problems have to be mastered:

-- Nonvolatile storage of analog weights provides very high synaptic density, but may be not sufficiently often programmable.

-- The design of a synapse, the size of a neural network and the degree of analog resolution are dependent on each other.

-- A major design problem with analog circuits is the relation of accuracy to chip area. The more precisely one wishes to control the matching of the analog components, the more chip area is needed. An analog depth of not more than 8 bit is recommendable. Crosstalk and susceptibility to coupled-in interference make special precautions necessary for analog signal processing.

-- The minimal chip area is also influenced by factors like noise and current consumption. Low current consumption calls for high-valued resistors in resistor-capacitor circuitry. Low noise creates certain limits for minimal transistor Q surfaces and capacitors; this applies to switch-capacitor as well as to resistor-capacitor technique.

-- The temperature dependence, clock feed-through and process-parameter dependence can be reduced in analog circuits so that they no longer interfere, but this is done at the expense of circuit complexity and has an effect on the chip area.

-- With future 0.3-µm transistor channel length, a lower supply voltage than 5 V must be expected, so questions of low-voltage design have to be considered. Accurate transistor modelling, innovative circuit techniques and design cleverness will be significant here like in the cases above.

The limited precision in grading the weights (realised, for example, in the form of ohmic resistances or switched capacitors) means, on the one hand, limited computing accuracy for an analog implementation and therefore influences the number and complexity of the patterns that can be reliably processed with an analog net. This applies equally to the selection of the discriminator: the computing accuracy of the entire analog chip has to be considered. The limited precision in processing information by the analog neural net means, on the other hand, that the information may be encoded in a fuzzy fashion, i.e. only as sharply defined as is necessary for secure recognition. Therefore it is the task of the user concerned with problem analysis and modelling to characterize those tasks of pattern processing in which deviations of the actual weight values from the pre-computed ones can be tolerated and where it is possible to make do, for example, with ternary weighting of binary input/output signals. For, the latter poses the least problems to the analog designer.

In the analog implementation of neural nets it is consequently a matter of bringing together the application-oriented problem analysis and the circuit architecture; this is the only way to determine the application spectrum that can be implemented with analog hardware. Isolated definition of the effort for analog multiplication, for instance, would be just as inappropriate on the part of the chip architect as determination of the weights by simulation, without allowing for the computing accuracy that can be achieved, on the part of the user.

2.2. Digital Design Issues

What is of clear advantage here is that the application-oriented problem analysis and modelling of net characteristics can be made independently of circuit design. For by simulation one can determine the computation accuracy (word width) for each function bloc before implementing it.

It is the task of the chip designer then to implement the neural algorithms in accordance to the state-of-the-art in Digital Signal Processing [12] . A point to be tackled, for instance, is the problem of the so-called limit cycles, i.e. parasitic oscillations. These can appear in recursive digital structures (which show up in the learning phase or in feedback nets) as a result of amplitude quantization. The problem of limit cycles can be eliminated by appropriate effort in computing accuracy and numeric range (floating point). If this effort becomes unsupportable, it will be necessary to check whether such limit cycles appear and whether they can have a disturbing effect.

The finer resolution of the weights, which is easy to implement in digital architecture, allows more individual weighting of the input signals than in analog processing. Thus it can be concluded from a structural point of view that digital neural ICs take on a field of application in their own right.

3. CHIP INTEGRATION OF COMPUTE-BOUND NEURAL ALGORITHMS

Neural hardware can be tailored

-- for an application asking for a single neural network fixed in size and topology,
-- for an application which calls for a set of different neural networks which are programmable as to size and concatenation,
-- or be designed to serve general-purpose neurocomputing.

The first applicational species amounts mainly to single-chip integration as described in section 2; the second overtaxes in most cases the single-chip integration potential of present technology as well as that of future 0.3-μm technology by whole orders of magnitude, and a fortiori does the third species. Applicational domains like speech or vision (see figure 1) can not be implemented by a single chip, and unbearable costs and volume prevent taking sufficiently many (other than pure RAM chips) so that the total number of weights add up to what the application calls for. Thus the weights need to be stored off the chip.

With off-chip storage of weights the chip area is reserved for neurocomputing circuitry. The main task then is to provide a sufficient communication bandwidth between the memory bank and the processor chip(s). A thorough analysis of what to realise at chip or board level must be conducted before bothering the chip architect.

Contrary to the situation of single-chip implementable neural nets, the size of such a net will not permit simulation (especially of the learning phase) within a reasonable period of time and therefore the weights cannot be determined by simulation, which means that it is essential for the learning algorithm to be implemented in hardware. In consideration of the resulting lack of neural engineering know-how for applications as vision or speech, it is a matter of designing a system and circuit architecture that supports in optimal fashion the massive parallel networking of the neural net and produces a sufficient measure of flexibility and expansion capacity for coping with the known paradigmas, and prepare for those to come.

As the use of analog concepts is detracted from, besides others, by the low computing accuracy of only a few percent, and application-oriented problem analysis and modelling of neural network characteristics can not be made independently of circuit design, digital design is believed to be best suited for neurocomputers, i.e. for machines with which to cross into an unknown region and study in breadth and depth the potential of neural networks.

3.1. Algorithmic Analysis Of Neural Paradigmas

Generally, a versatile neurocomputer architecture must absorb in silicon the elementary algorithmic strings shared by all known neural paradigma. In addition, a set of universal substrings has to be derived from those algorithmic strings which are not common to all the models. Elementary strings and substrings would compose the functional blocks, which have to be implemented in silicon, whereas concatenation of strings or substrings would be initiated by instructions. As the variety of models can be created to a large extent by dedicated sequences of such instructions, the design of a neurocomputer splits into three parts: 1. design of the functional blocks, 2. design of corresponding control and communication blocks, 3. generation of an associated micro-programme. The variables of the latter are ruled by a host which carries the programming environment for neural networks.

The analysis of today's neural paradigmas [13,14] brings to light a set of elementary compute-intensive algorithmic strings which are shared by all neural models and, thus, make sense to be implemented in hardware. To give an example of the compute-bound algorithmic kernel of a fairly large class of neural networks consider these three equations [15,16]:

$$y_{ip} = f_i\left(\left[\sum_{j=0}^{N} W_{ij} y_{jp} + Y_i \right] \cdot \lambda_i \right) \quad , i = 1 \,..\, N,\ p \varepsilon P \ ; \qquad \text{(1a)}$$

$$z_{jp} = D(f_j) \cdot \left| \sum_{i=0}^{N} W_{ij} z_{ip} + \mathrm{E}(t_{jp}, y_{jp}) \cdot \chi_j \right| \quad , j = 1 \,..\, N,\ p \varepsilon P \ ; \qquad \text{(1b)}$$

$$\delta W_{ij} = \alpha \cdot \sum_{p \varepsilon P} z_{ip} \cdot y_{jp} \quad , i,j = 1 \,..\, N \ . \qquad \text{(1c)}$$

A neuron's individual input is denoted by Y_i, the parameter λ_i controls the slope of the neuron's discriminator function f_i or the temperature in case that a Boltzmann-type net is to be generated. $D(f_i)$ denotes the derivative of f_i, t_i the reference output in case of supervised learning by means of some error function E, and χ_i the characteristic function of the output neurons. N designates the number of neurons and P the set of patterns.

A network described by formula 1 can conduct supervised or unsupervised learning, the latter one not representing the most general case. It can be structured arbitrarily, be of pure feed-forward type or include feedback structures. In case of feedback, equations 1b-1c represent infinitely recursive equations which need to be checked for stability [17] and convergence on finite grids.

It is seen that the matrix-matrix operation is the one only compute-bound operation shared by the learning and search mode. By concatenating this operation with a few more "low cycle" operations (like adding "noise" to an updated weight) it is possible to create a large variety of neural models including for example Hopfield and Boltzmann-type neural networks, or Multi-layer Perceptrons.

3.2. Systolic Emulation Of Neural Algorithms

There exist various ways to implement formula (1) . Which one will be chosen depends on the applicational needs, technological constraints, the functional balance between chip and board architecture and the system environment [18-20].

The elementary structure common to formulas 1a-1c is the scalar product operation: accumulation over the index j, i, and the pattern index p. An implementation which is very effective in view of the mentionned communication bottleneck between memory and processor chip(s) is by way of a linear systolic array of multipliers and accumulators as depicted by figure 2. Circles indicate registers, a number x in a circle a x-stage shift register.

During the search phase (formula 1a) the chain is fed by the sequence of weights W_{1j}, W_{2j}, ... , W_{8j} and by the sequence of inputs y_{j1}, y_{j2}, ..., y_{j8} , respectively; as mentionned above, y_{jp} denotes the j-th pixel of the p-th image. The i-th multiplier picks up W_{ij} and holds it for 8 cycles until the j-th pixel of all 8 images has been computed and separately stored, then proceeds by picking up W_{ij+1} and computing the (j + 1)-th pixel of all 8 images and adding these separately to the previous ones, and so on. After completion of the weighting of the first 8 neurons, the accumulator registers are queued-up and read out. Then the procedure is repeated with the weights for the next 8 neurons in the network, and so on.

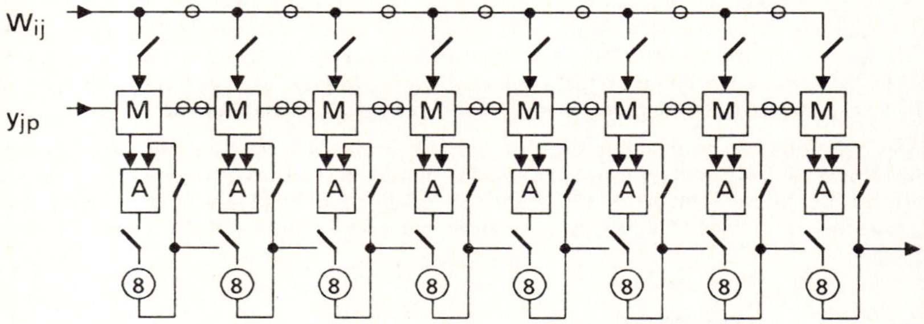

Figure 2 Systolic chain in the search mode

The chain can be used for learning, too, by re-arranging the formulas 1b and 1c, respectively:

$$\sum_{i=0}^{N} W_{ij} \cdot z_{ip} = \sum_{i=0}^{N} W^t_{ji} \cdot z_{ip} = \sum_{i=0}^{N} z^t_{pi} \cdot W_{ij} ; \quad \text{(2a)}$$

$$\sum_{p \varepsilon P} z_{ip} \cdot y_{jp} = \sum_{p \varepsilon P} y_{jp} \cdot z^t_{pi} = \sum_{p \varepsilon P} z_{ip} \cdot y^t_{pj} . \quad \text{(2b)}$$

It is left to the memory control and bus circuitry, apparently, to transpose the weight matrix (middle expression of (2a)) or to change from row-wise to column-wise read-off (right expression of (2a)), respectively. This is not a problem if on-chip storage of weights is possible or affordable. With off-chip storage of weights, however, the design of the memory control and bus circuitry gets complicated, especially for large memory banks. In this case it is desirable to use a fixed schedule for serving the weights and, instead, have some extra circuitry added to the chain.

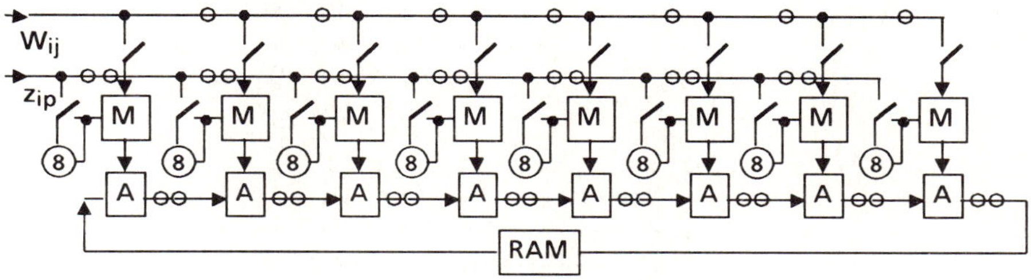

Figure 3 Systolic chain in the learning mode

Figure 3 shows how the chain must be modified for learning if the weights are fed into the chain in the same order as in figure 1. As the first weight index is distributed along the chain, the accumulation must be distributed in the same manner, according to (2a). The 8-stage shift register of the i-th multiplier is loaded with z_{ip}, p = 1..8, and repeatedly used for multiplying W_{ij}, j = 1..N. Note that there is a summation rippling along the chain for every pair of indices (j,p). Accordingly, the size of the (off-chip) RAM is at most proportional to the number of neurons and patterns, respectively. The content of the RAM is fed back to the chain in order to continue the accumulation along the next 8 rows of the weight matrix, together with the next block of 8 pixels of the same set of 8 patterns.

To calculate a weight update by means of the learning configuration as shown in figure 2 the following identity is to be observed:

$$\sum_{p \varepsilon P} z_{ip} \cdot y_{jp} = \sum_{p \varepsilon P} y^t_{pj} \cdot z^t_{pi} = \sum_{p \varepsilon P} z^t_{pi} \cdot y^t_{pj} . \qquad (2c)$$

As the right expressions of (2c) are structurally equal to the left expression of (2a) it follows that the systolic chain shown in figure 3 can be used for weight updating as well.

3.3. Configurable Arrays Of VLSI-Array Processors

The systolic structure of figure 2 and 3 may be absorbed by a configurable functional block FuncBloc which contains a multiplier, an adder, a shift register and some switches. This block is then repeatedly implemented. Note that the longer the chain is the more

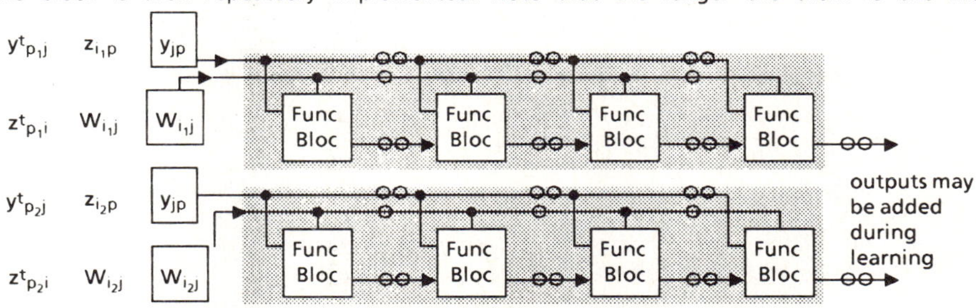

Figure 4 Parallelizing 2 elementary chains in the row index

weights can be processed per second. It means also that more pixels of patterns need to be interleaved for the search mode because the number of interleaved patterns is equal to the length of the chain. The degree of interleaving can be reduced, thus, by parallelizing chains of reduced length. According to formula 1a this is done, for instance, by serving a

parallel set of weights (W_{i_1j}, W_{i_2j}), but one set of pixels y_{jp} of half the number of patterns (figure 4).
With 1µm CMOS technology 16 functional blocks configured as 1- or 2-dimensional array according to figures 2-4 may be implemented at chip site allowing for 640 million 16 bit connections per second. It is notable that the processing power does not require sophisticated chip packages like pin-grid arrays; a mere 64 pins for the weights suffice if 4-fold interleaving is chosen.

To increase the processing power further, a 1- or 2-dimensional array of such VLSI array processors can easily be arranged for, since the systolic structure provided at the chip

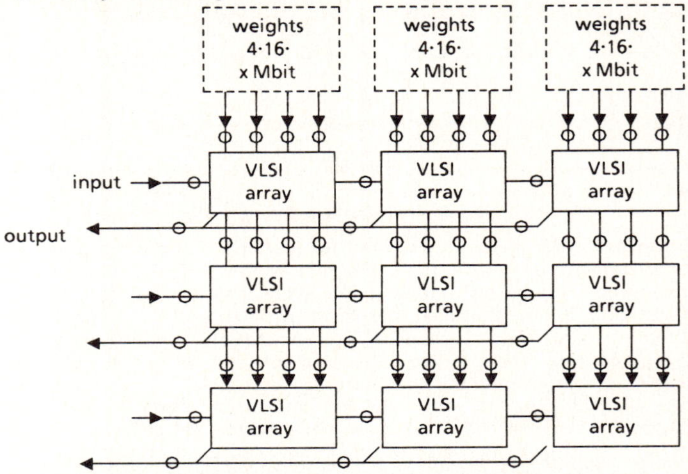

Figure 5 Economic use of weight memory in a 2-dimensional systolic array of VLSI array processors

level is hereditary to the board level (figure 5) . In order that this processor array´s computational performance be reached an adequate controller and interface architecture must be designed that handle the data flow taking place at the chip and board site, respectively. This part of the neurocomputer design is reported in [21] .

4. CONCLUSIONS

In consideration of the applicational needs indicated in figure 1, two important opportunities for neural hardware can be envisaged: 1. single-chip integration of a neural net; 2. implementation of compute-bound neural algorithms on dedicated array processors.

ad 1. MOS technology provides sufficient computational speed for the search phase, but is limited in its applicational range by the number of synaptic weights that can be stored on-chip. Support for learning is not needed, as the neural net size that can be implemented on a chip allows for simulation on conventional computers. Whether analog or digital design will have to be chosen is mainly decided by considering the costs for interfacing a neural chip to the system environment, and not by a clear performance advantage of the one over the other.

ad 2. Because of the size of the application, support for learning is now indispensible; also, on-chip storage of the weights is no longer manageable. Digital design turns out to be the prevailing concept for neurocomputers. It appears that 1 or 2-dimensional arrays composed of a systolic neural signal processor module that integrates the elementary strings as hard-wired functional blocks present a favourable solution to the interconnection problem, i.e. to the architectural problem of mapping neural parallelity and adaptivity into silicon. Throughput rates at the chip site of the order of 10^3 MC/sec (1 Connection = 16 bit) are to be expected with 0.8μm CMOS technology. By systolic extension to the board level a system performance of 10^5 MC/sec should be attainable which will enable the user to access real-world applications in reasonable time. In addition, the proposed neurocomputer concept is sizeable to the applicational domain in terms of processing power, memory and flexibility.

Since MOS technology comes up against limits in terms of synaptic density (in case 1) and processing power for learning algorithms (in case 2) there is a request for competing technologies [22] , particularly optics. Nevertheless, CMOS technology will continue to be an economic choice for the implementation of neural networks, as it is a standard technology.

ACKNOWLEDGEMENTS

I like to thank Prof. B. Hosticka for valuable discussions on the design issues concerning the analog implementation of neural networks.

REFERENCES

[1] DARPA Neural Network Study, pp.34 (figure 2.14-15), pp.330 (figure 28.5), AFCEA International Press, Nov. 1988

[2] ibid. pp.372 (table 33.1-5)

[3] H.P. Graf, "A Reconfigurable CMOS Neural Network", Digest of Technical Papers of the Int. Solid State Circuits Conf., vol.33, pp.144, San Francisco, Febr. 1990

[4] A. Chiang et al., "A Programmable CCD Signal Processor", Digest of Technical Papers of the Int. Solid State Circuits Conf., vol.33, pp.146, San Francisco, Febr. 1990

[5] M. Holler et al., "An Electrically Trainable Artificial Neural Network (ETANN) with 10240 Floating Gate Synapses", pp. II-191, Proceedings of the IJCNN-89, Washington DC, June 1989

[6] J. Harris et al., "Resistive Fuses: Analog Hardware for Detecting Discontinuities in Early Vision", pp. 27-56, in Analog VLSI Implementation of Neural Systems, edited by C. Mead and M. Ismail, Kluwer Academic Publishers 1989

[7] R.F. Lyon, C. Mead, "An Analog Electronic Cocchlea", IEEE Transactions on Acoustics, Speech and Signal Processing, Vol. 36, No. 7, July 1988

[8] C.A. Mead et al.,"VLSI-Architectures for Implementation of Neural Networks", California Institute of Technology, Pasadena, USA. AIP Cof. Proc. Neural Networks for Computing, nowbird, Utah, 1986

[9] Y.P. Tsividis, D. Anastassiou, "Switched-Capacitor Neural Networks", Electronic Letters, Vol 23 No. 18, August 1987

[10] U. Rückert, K. Goser, "VLSI Design of Associative Networks", Int. Workshop on VLSI for Artificial Intelligence, Uni. Oxford, July 1988

[11] A.P.Thakoor, A. Moopenn, "Electronic Neural Network with Optically Modulated Variable Strength. Resistive a-Si:H Interconnects for Analog Computation", MRS Spring Meeting, paper E 7.5 , Reno, Nevada, 1988

[12] M. Duranton, J.A. Sirat, "Learning on VLSI: A General-Purpose Digital Neurochip", pp. II-613, Proceedings of the IJCNN-89, Washington DC, June 1989

[13] R. P. Lippmann, "An introduction to computing with neural nets", IEEE ASSP Magazine, pp. 4-22, April 1987

[14] P.K. Simpson, " A Review of Artificial Neural Systems", part I&II, CRC Critical Reviews in Artificial Intelligence, 1988

[15] L.B. Almeida, "Backpropagation in Non-Feedforward Networks", pp. 74, Neural Computing Architectures, edited by I. Aleksander, MIT Press, 1989

[16] F.J. Pineda, "Generalization of Backpropagation to Recurrent and Higher Order Neural Networks", pp. 602-611, Proceedings of IEEE Conf. on Neural Information Systems, Denver, Colorado, 1987

[17] B. Schürmann, "Stability and Adaptation in Artificial Neural Systems", Phys. Rev. A40 (1989) 2681.

[18] S. Y. Kung, J. N. Hwang, "Parallel architectures for artificial neural nets", vol.2, IEEE Int. Conf. on Neural Networks, San Diego, July 1988

[19] U. Ramacher, J. Beichter, "Architecture of a Systolic Neuro-Emulator", vol.2, p. 59-63, Int. Joint Conf. on Neural Networks, Washington D.C., January 1990

[20] H. Kato et al., "A Parallel Neurocomputer Architecture towards Billion Connection Updates per Second", vol.2, p. 47-50, Int. Joint Conf. on Neural Networks, Washington D.C., January 1990

[21] U. Ramacher, W. Raab, "Fine-grain System Architectures for Systolic Emulation of Neural Algorithms", to be published

[22] "Microelectronics for Artificial Neural Nets", editors H. Klar, U. Ramacher, VDI-Verlag, Düsseldorf, 1989

Advanced Neural Computers / R. Eckmiller (Editor)

Rapid Prototyping for Neural Networks

David E. Van den Bout and Wesley Snyder and Thomas K. Miller III *
Department of Electrical and Computer Engineering
North Carolina State University
Raleigh, NC 27695-7911

Abstract

A massively parallel, all-digital, stochastic architecture — TInMANN — is described which performs competitive and Kohonen types of learning at rates as high as 145,000 training examples per second. TInMANN is composed of very simple neurons and is very amenable to VLSI implementation, but rapid advances in IC technology and neural network theory reduce the rewards of such an endeavor. As an alternative, we discuss the rapid-prototyping of a bit-serial version of TInMANN using commercially available logic cell arrays and RAMs.

1 Introduction

Massively parallel architectures composed of highly interconnected, simple processing elements — neural networks — form a different paradigm of computing in the hopes of rapidly solving problems while adapting to a changing environment. For example, vector quantization of images normally requires specialized programming to detect and encode the meaningful clusters of vectors, but a Kohonen self-organizing map [1] can adaptively form the necessary codebook using a simple, general learning algorithm.

Uniprocessor simulation of neural networks has been the norm, but the parallelism in neural networks cannot be utilized without specialized hardware. Most current hardware-based neural network simulators use 1) a single high-speed ALU [2] or 2) multiple DSP chips connected through communication buses [3]. Unfortunately, the first approach does not allow the effects of parallelism to be adequately explored, while the use of complex processors in the second approach hinders investigations into the minimal hardware needs of an implementation. In order to gain such knowledge, it is desirable that an implementation possess the same characteristics as a neural network — i.e. that it be built from a large number of simple, cooperating processing elements.

However, the large number of processing elements (or *neurons*) and their highly interconnected nature affects another desirable trait: practicality of construction. Highly-connected, densely-packed analog neurons can be practically realized on a single chip using VLSI technology [4]. Difficulties arise when interconnecting several such chips to solve a larger problem since the number of analog signals exceeds the available I/O while external parasitic capacitances and noise can affect the reliable operation of the network. Therefore, it is desirable to build neural systems based upon digital signals which can be multiplexed to reduce I/O requirements and which are relatively immune to noise.

We have previously described all-digital versions of a Hopfield neural network (STONN [5, 6]) and a Kohonen Self-Organizing Feature Map (TInMANN [7, 8]) in which the analog signals are replaced by binary signals that randomly assume either the value 0 or 1. The mean value of such a *stochastic signal* [9] can be viewed as an analog signal in the range $[0,1]$. This signal representation allows pseudo-analog computations to be performed using very space-efficient digital logic. Multiplication of stochastic signals, for example, can be done using only a simple AND gate. In addition to the massive parallelism made possible by such compact circuitry, stochastic networks also possess high execution speeds and can be cascaded to implement larger networks. Unfortunately, our experience in realizing STONN in VLSI showed that a large amount of time is required to do the layout, simulate

*The authors wish to acknowledge the support they have received from the Neural Engineering Group, the Computer Systems Lab, and the Center for Communications and Signal Processing at NCSU.

the design, create a test plan, and finally fabricate the chip. By the time the chip was available, the rapid theoretical advances occurring in the field of neural networks revealed desirable new features which should have been included in the design [10, 11, 12]. Therefore, the ability to be rapidly prototyped is another desirable trait of neural network hardware.

This paper describes the basic theory behind the TInMANN neural network and its re-design using standard RAMs and a recent rapid-prototyping device — electronically-reconfigurable logic cell arrays (LCAs). The use of LCAs speeds construction, increases system flexibility, and creates new design possibilities.

2 TInMANN Algorithm and Architecture

In the competitive learning algorithm [13], training vectors of length W, $\mathbf{v}=(v_1, v_2, \ldots, v_W)$, are presented to a winner-take-all network of N neurons. Each neuron i possesses a weight vector of length W, $\mathbf{w}_i = (w_{i1}, w_{i2}, \ldots, w_{iW})$, and a winning neuron k is selected as the one whose weight vector is closest to the current training vector. Neuron k is then moved closer to the training vector by modifying its weights as follows

$$w_{kj} \Leftarrow w_{kj} + \epsilon \cdot (v_j - w_{kj}) \quad 0 < \epsilon < 1, \quad 1 \leq j \leq W \,.$$

If the network is trained with a set of vectors which are naturally clustered into N groups, then each neural weight vector will eventually reside in the center of a different group. Thereafter, an input vector applied to the network will activate the neuron which has been sensitized to the group containing the input, thus performing an encoding.

Kohonen's self-organizing feature maps are trained using a generalization of competitive learning where each neuron i is provided with an additional X-element vector, $\mathbf{x}_i = (x_{i1}, x_{i2}, \ldots, x_{iX})$, that defines its topological position with relation to the other neurons in the network. As before, neuron k of the N neurons wins if it is the closest to the current training vector, but the weight adjustment now affects *all* neurons as determined by a decreasing function f of their topological distance from neuron k and a threshold distance d_T:

$$w_{ij} \Leftarrow w_{ij} + \epsilon \cdot f(||\mathbf{x}_k - \mathbf{x}_i||, d_T) \cdot (v_j - w_{ij}) \quad 0 < \epsilon < 1, \quad 1 \leq j \leq W, \quad 1 \leq i \leq N \,.$$

This function allows the winning neuron to *drag* its neighbors toward a given section of the input space so that topologically close neurons will eventually react similarly to closely spaced input vectors.

The integer Markovian learning algorithm of Figure 1 simplifies the Kohonen learning procedure by noting that the neuron weights slowly *integrate* the effects of environmental stimuli. This integration can be done by stochastically updating the weights with a probability proportional to the neural input. The stochastic update of the neural weights is accomplished by generating two uncorrelated random numbers on the interval $[0, d_T]$, R_1 and R_2, which each neuron compares to its distance from the current training vector and its topological distance from the winning neuron, respectively. A neuron will try to increment or decrement the elements of its weight vector closer to the training vector if the absolute value of the intervening distance is greater than R_1, thus creating a total movement proportional to the distance when averaged over many cycles. This movement is inversely modulated by the topological distance to the winning neuron k via a comparison with R_2. The total effect produced by these two stochastic processes is equivalent to that produced in the previous learning algorithms, but only simple additive operations are now needed. Figure 2 demonstrates the results of applying this algorithm to two problems which have often been solved using Kohonen networks.

The integer Markovian learning algorithm is practical to implement since only simple neurons are needed to perform the additive operations and the interneuron communications can all be handled using broadcast transmissions. The high-level architecture for such an implementation is shown in Figure 3. TInMANN consists of a global controller coupled to an array of simple neurons. The controller performs all the serial operations and coordinates the actions of the neurons. The neurons contain circuitry for comparing and updating their weights, and for enabling and disabling themselves during the conditional portions of the algorithm. The topological structure of the network is

```
for( i ⇐ 1; i ≤ N; i ⇐ i + 1 )
        c_i ⇐ 0
        for( j ⇐ 1; j ≤ W; j ⇐ j + 1 )
                w_ij ⇐ random()
for( v∈ {training set} )
        parallelfor( all neurons i )
                d_i ⇐ c_i
                for( j ⇐ 1; j ≤ W; j ⇐ j + 1 )
                        d_i ⇐ d_i + |v_j − w_ij|
        k ⇐ 1
        for( i ⇐ 1; i ≤ N; i ⇐ i + 1 )
                if( d_i < d_k )
                        k ⇐ i
        parallelfor( all neurons i )
                d_i ⇐ 0
                for( j ⇐ 1; j ≤ X; j ⇐ j + 1 )
                        d_i ⇐ d_i + |x_ij − x_kj|
        for( j ⇐ 1; j ≤ W; j ⇐ j + 1 )
                R_1 ⇐ random(d_T)
                R_2 ⇐ random(d_T)
                parallelfor( all neurons i )
                        /* stochastic weight update */
                        if( |v_j − w_ij| > R_1 and d_i ≤ R_2 )
                                w_ij ⇐ w_ij+ sign(v_j − w_ij)
        d_T ⇐ α_d · d_T
```

Figure 1: The integer Markovian learning algorithm.

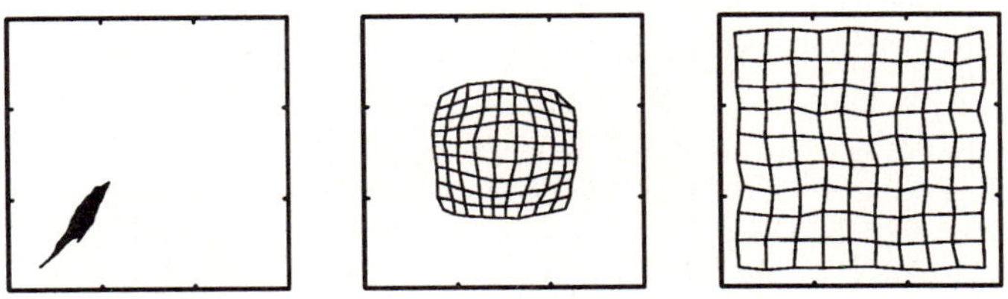

(a)

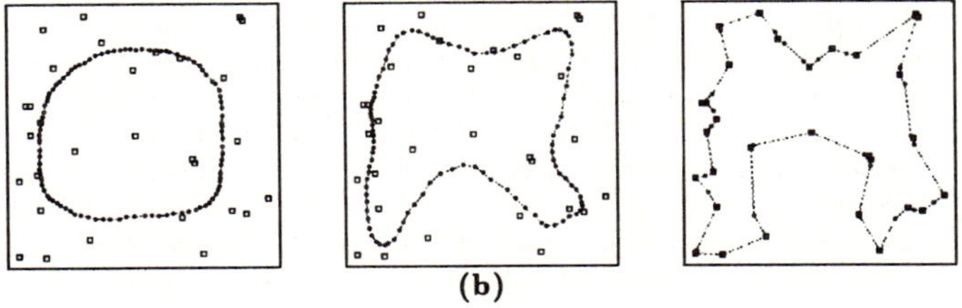

(b)

Figure 2: The evolution of 100 neurons when using the integer Markovian learning algorithm to **(a)** encode a uniform 2-dimensional distribution and **(b)** solve a 30-city Traveling Salesman Problem.

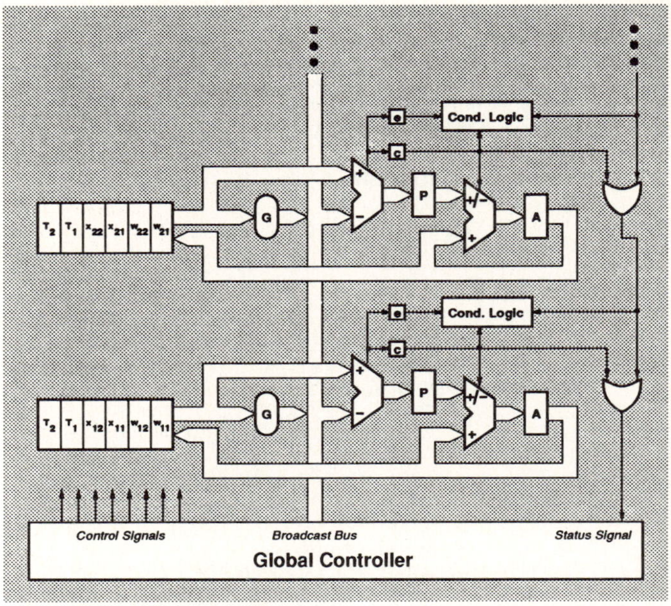

Figure 3: The TInMANN architecture.

represented by properly arranging the neurons in an X-dimensional space rather than by attempting to represent a graph structure in the hardware. This allows the calculation of the topological distance between neurons using the same circuitry as is used in the weight calculations. As each training vector **v** is presented to TInMANN, the system performs the following operations:

1. The global controller broadcasts the W elements of **v** while each neuron accumulates in A the absolute value of the difference between the elements of its weight vector (stored in the small, local RAM) and those of the training vector.

2. The global controller does a binary search for the neuron closest to the training vector by broadcasting distance values bisecting the range containing the winning neuron. The neurons do a comparison with their stored distances and signal on the wired-OR status line if their distance is less than the broadcast value (i.e. the carry bit c is set). Neurons with distances greater than the broadcast value are disabled by resetting their e flags. However, if no neuron is left enabled, the global controller can restore the enable bits from the previous comparison and adjust its search region (this action is needed on $\approx M/2$ of the search steps, where M is the machine word length used by TInMANN). The last neuron left enabled is the winner of the competition (ties are resolved by the conditional logic in each neuron).

3. The gate G of the winning neuron is opened so that it may broadcast the elements of its topological vector, X, to the remainder of the neural array. The other neurons accumulate into A the absolute value of the difference between their topological vectors and that of the winning neuron. This topological distance is stored in temporary register T_1.

4. Those neurons are disabled which have topological distances in T_1 greater than the random number R_2 broadcast by the global controller. The remaining neurons each compute the distance between a component of their weight vector and that of the training vector broadcast by the global controller. All neurons whose calculated distances are greater than random number R_1 broadcast by the controller will increment or decrement their weight elements

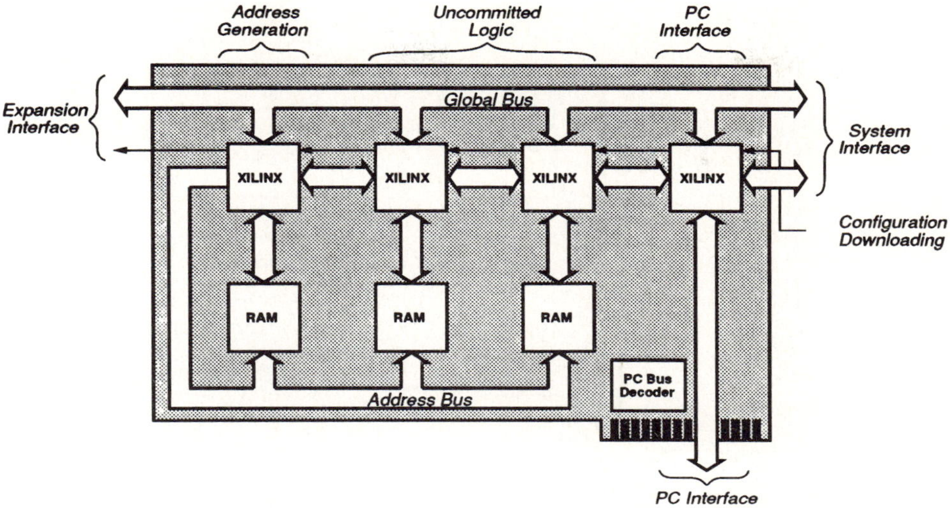

Figure 4: The XILINX card for use in the Anyboard rapid prototyping environment.

depending upon the carry bits left in the c flags during the distance calculations. All neurons are then re-enabled and this step is repeated for the remaining $W-1$ elements of the training vector.

Provided all additive operations are performed in a word-parallel fashion, a single training vector can be processed in $11W + X + 2.5M + 15$ clock cycles using the procedure just described [7, 8]. A word-width, M, of 12-bits and a clock cycle of 10 MHz would allow TInMANN to learn at a rate of 145,000 2-dimensional vectors per second.

3 Rapid Prototyping of TInMANN

TInMANN could be efficiently implemented using VLSI techniques since each neuron requires only 1,000 transistors. However, building a custom TInMANN chip would eventually make us victims of progress in VLSI technology and neural network theory. Since commercial chip speeds are doubling every 18 months, we would be forced to continually modify and re-implement TInMANN in order to keep it competitive with alternative methods of performing Kohonen types of learning. Additional design modifications would be needed to keep up with improvements in Kohonen learning algorithms (see, for example, [14]).

For the above reasons, it is advantageous to construct TInMANN using electronically-reprogrammable logic cell arrays whose VLSI technology is kept continuously up-to-date by the commercial vendors. XILINX LCAs, for example, provide as many as 9,000 logic gates which are quickly and flexibly reconfigured merely by loading data into an on-chip RAM [15]. A development environment for the LCAs consists of an IBM-PC into which is inserted an Anyboard rapid-prototyping card [16] containing four to eight XILINX chips (Figure 4). Two of the LCAs have dedicated functions while the remainder contain uncommitted logic that will be used to implement the TInMANN neurons. Adjacent XILINX chips are connected to each other through local buses, while all the chips have access to a bus through which global signals are broadcast. Connections are made between chips by programming the appropriate pins on the XILINX chips as inputs or outputs. If no connection is desired, then an I/O pin can be left unprogrammed so that it remains tri-stated. A byte-wide RAM is also connected to each XILINX chip for applications requiring more storage (as in TInMANN).

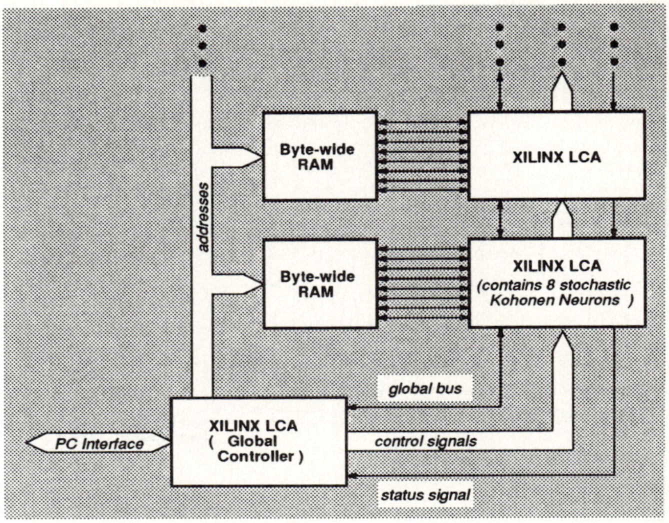

Figure 5: Implementing the TInMANN architecture with RAMS and XILINX chips.

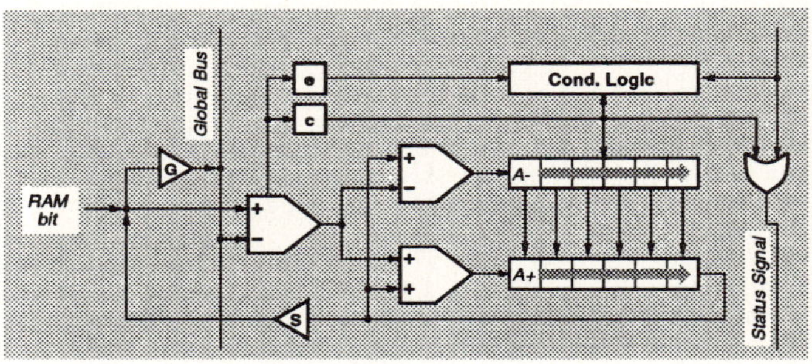

Figure 6: Bit-serial TInMANN neuron.

RAM addressing is done by the last XILINX chip in the array, which limits flexibility but saves I/O pins and logic on the remaining LCAs.

The TInMANN architecture shown in Figure 5 will be embedded in the Anyboard. Each XILINX chip contains 8 neurons except for the LCA responsible for global control. In order to save space on the LCAs, weights are stored on the external RAMs and the global controller generates the addresses necessary to pass data to and from the neurons at the appropriate times. Additional space and complexity are eliminated by designing bit-serial TInMANN neurons (Figure 6). The main difference between the neuron in Figure 6 and those shown in Figure 3 is the presence of two accumulators. The old contents of the accumulator plus or minus the comparator output is stored in shift-register/accumulators $A+$ or $A-$, respectively. If the sign of the comparator result is negative at the end of the comparison, then $A-$ is transferred into $A+$ which allows absolute values to be easily computed. $A+$ is considered the main accumulator and its value can be shifted into the external RAM through the additional tri-state gate S.

Implementing TInMANN using XILINX chips and the Anyboard card provides these advantages:

- The system can be dynamically reconfigured. For example, initializing the external RAMs will be accomplished using logic specialized for ease in loading the RAMs. The TInMANN configuration will then be loaded into the XILINX chips and learning will commence. This overlay feature makes the neurons simpler and denser since they do not have to include extra RAM initialization circuitry.

- The bit-serial design and the reconfigurable nature of the XILINX chips permits adjustment of the TInMANN data width, M, without changing the hardware. Applications demanding higher precision can then be handled merely by downloading a new configuration file which creates fewer neurons each with longer $A+$ and $A-$ accumulators. Arbitrary-length data is also facilitated by the decision to use the data stream from each byte-wide external RAM as 8 individual bitstreams, one for each serial neuron on a XILINX chip.
- The circuitry can be modified as easily as is software in order to reflect changes in the underlying neural algorithms.

Of course, the rapid-prototyping system described above does not run as fast or use as few chips as a full-custom VLSI implementation. However, if applying neural nets to a problem using the Anyboard card shows enough promise, then VLSI technologies can always be used to get even more performance with the added confidence brought on by having an initial working prototype.

References

[1] T. Kohonen. Self-organized formation of topologically correct feature maps. *Biological Cybernetics*, 43:56–69, 1982.

[2] G. Works. The creation of Delta: A new concept in ANS processing. In *IEEE International Conference on Neural Networks*, pages II:159–II:164, 1988.

[3] P. Penz and R. Wiggins. Digital signal processor accelerators for neural network simulations. In *American Institute of Physics Conference Proceedings No. 151*, volume 151, pages 345–355, 1986.

[4] M. Maher, S. DeWeerth, M. Mahawold, and C. Mead. Implementing neural architectures using analog VLSI circuits. *IEEE Transactions on Circuits and Systems*, 36(5):643–652, May 1989.

[5] D. E. Van den Bout and T. K. Miller III. A digital architecture employing stochasticism for the simulation of Hopfield neural nets. *IEEE Transactions on Circuits and Systems*, 36(5):732–738, May 1989.

[6] W. Wike and D. E. Van den Bout. STONN: A stochastic neural network chip. In *Proceedings of the Sixth MIT Conference on Advanced Research in VLSI*, April 1990.

[7] D. E. Van den Bout and T. K. Miller III. TInMANN: The integer markovian artificial neural network. In *Proceedings of the IEEE International Conference on Neural Networks*, pages II:205–II:211, 1989.

[8] D. E. Van den Bout and T. K. Miller III. TInMANN: The integer markovian artificial neural network. Accepted for publication in the *Journal of Parallel and Distributed Computing*, 1989.

[9] B. Gaines. Uncertainty as a foundation of computational power in neural networks. In *IEEE International Conference on Neural Networks*, pages III:51–III:57, 1987.

[10] G. Bilbro, R. Mann, T. Miller III, W. Snyder, D. E. Van den Bout, and M. White. Mean field annealing and neural networks. In *Advances in Neural Information Processing Systems*, pages 91–98. Morgan-Kaufmann Publishers, Inc., 1989.

[11] D. E. Van den Bout and T. K. Miller III. Graph partitioning using annealed neural networks. *IEEE Transactions on Neural Networks*, 1(2), June 1990.

[12] D. E. Van den Bout and T. K. Miller III. Improving the performance of the Hopfield-Tank neural network through normalization and annealing. *Biological Cybernetics*, 62(2):129–139, December 1989.

[13] D. Rumelhart and J. McClelland. *Parallel Distributed Processing: Explorations in the Microstructure of Cognition*, chapter 5. MIT Press, 1986.

[14] J. Kangas, T. Kohonen, and J. Laaksonen. Variants of Self-Organizing Maps. *IEEE Transactions on Neural Networks*, 1(1):93–99, March 1990.

[15] R. Freeman. User-programmable gate arrays. *IEEE Spectrum*, pages 32–35, December 1988.

[16] T. Peterson and D. E. Van den Bout. A simple rapid-prototyping environment. Submitted to the *1990 International Workshop on Rapid System Prototyping*, 1990.

Section 5
Pattern Recognition with Neural Networks

Advanced Neural Computers / R. Eckmiller (Editor)

ANIMATE VISION USES OBJECT-CENTERED REFERENCE FRAMES*

Dana H. Ballard
University of Rochester
Rochester, NY 14627

Animate vision systems have gaze control mechanisms that can actively position the camera coordinate system in response to physical stimuli. Compared to passive systems, animate systems show that visual computation can be vastly less expensive when considered in the larger context of behavior. The most important visual behavior is the ability to control the direction of gaze. This allows the use of very low resolution imaging that has a high virtual resolution. Using such a system in a controlled way provides additional constraints that dramatically simplify the computations of early vision. An additional source of economy is introduced when behaviors are learned. Because errors are rarely fatal, systems using learning algorithms can amortize computational cost over extended periods. Further economies can be achieved when the learning system uses indexical reference, which is a form of dynamic variable binding. Animate vision is a natural way of implementing this dynamic binding.

1. VISION AS BEHAVIOR

A paradigm that we term *animate vision* argues that vision is most readily understood in the context of the visual behaviors that the system is engaged in, and that these behaviors may not require elaborate categorical representations of the 3-D world. Animate visual systems have anthropomorphic features such as binocularity, foveas, and most importantly high speed gaze control. While it is possible to build many different kinds of visual systems, such as those that have more than two cameras or use active sensing, what we are calling animate vision is directed towards specific computational advantages of having anthropomorphic features. We argue that the animate visual system can use its gaze control ability to choose exocentric frames of reference,as shown in Figure 1. The main purpose of this paper is to stress the advantage of using dynamic, exocentric frames of reference.

One of the most central aspects of animate vision is the use of an exocentric coordinate frame termed the frame of fixation. This frame provides direct access to information from a small region near the fixated point. Of particular importance is the information associated with *early vision* [1]. Early vision builds retinotopically-indexed maps of important environmental features such as depth, color, and velocity. Despite extensive work in this area over the past decade, the construction of such maps with computational models has proven to be very difficult. A primary reason for this may have been the assumption of a passive vision system. In an animate vision system, the degrees of freedom of the cameras are under the control of the animal. Aloimonos et al. [2] show in a general way how such assumptions can stabilize the computation of those features but their analysis misses the following vital point. A passive vision system is more or less constrained to use the coordinate system dictated by the camera optics. In contrast, an active system that can fixate an environmental point can use an object-centered frame of reference centered at that point. The calculations of early vision are greatly simplified given this ability.

Note that this is a very different assertion than that of Marr [1], who emphasized that the calculations were in viewer-centered coordinates. We assert that the calculations are more correctly represented as being in world-centered coordinates. As shown in Figure 1, the world-centered frame is viewer-oriented, but not viewer-centered. The origin of this frame is at the point of intersection of the two optical axes. To orient this frame one axis can be parallel to the line joining the two camera centers; the other can be chosen as the optical axis of the dominant eye.

---

*This research was supported by NSF Grant No. DCR-8602958 and NIH Grant No. R01 NS22407-01.

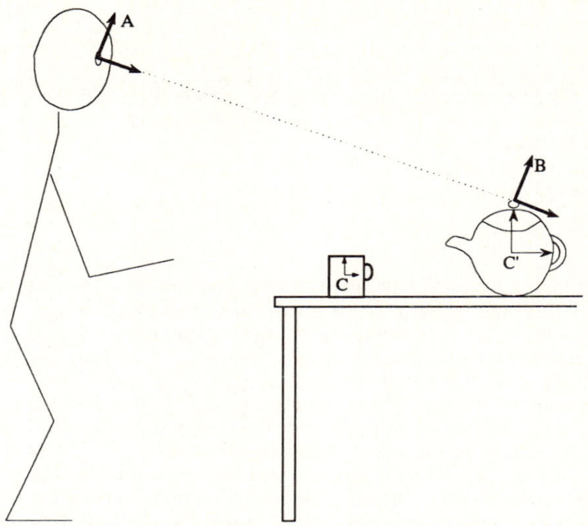

Figure 1 Much previous work in computational vision has assumed that the vision system is passive and computations are performed in a viewer-centered frame (A). Instead, biological and psychophysical data argue for a world-centered frame (B). This frame is selected by the observer to suit information-gathering goals and is centered at the fixation point. The task of the observer is to relate information in the fixation point frame to object-centered frames (C).

2. USING THE FIXATION FRAME

The small size of the fovea, together with the rapid movements humans can make, places a premium on gaze stabilization mechanisms. Perhaps for this reason a number of separate mechanisms for human gaze control have evolved. As Table 1 shows, the eye movement system has a number of different systems that function to control gaze under different circumstances. In addition there is the accommodation system that acts to focus the lens.

The University of Rochester's animate vision system was built to simulate these movements. The "robot head" has three motors and two CCD high-resolution television cameras providing input to a DataCube MaxVideo® image-processing system. One motor controls pitch of the two-eye platform, and separate motors control each camera's yaw. The motors have a resolution of 2,500 positions per revolution and a maximum speed of 400°/second. The robot "neck," a Unimation 762, has a workspace consisting of most of the volume of a sphere with a two-meter radius, and a top speed of about one meter/second. Currently we use a "dominant eye" control protocol whereby the dominant camera controls the system pitch and its own yaw coordinate using a simple correlation tracking scheme [3]. The non-dominant camera uses a novel vergence correction algorithm [4] based on the cepstral filter [5] to correct its own yaw error. Brown [6, 7, 8] has recently shown how these and other components can work together synergistically. These components run in real time. At the moment there are many differences with a reasonable human model, but the performance is sufficiently good to allow us to explore vision while fixating in real time. Details may be found in [3].

To illustrate the advantages of using the fixation frame, we developed a computational model of motion parallax. Motion parallax, or kinetic depth, is the sensation of depth obtained by moving the head while fixating an environmental point in a static scene. If the observer has little forward motion, objects in front of the fixation point appear to move in the opposite direction to the motion while objects behind the fixation point move in the same direction. (For a more general analysis that includes forward motion, see [9].) The apparent velocity is proportional to the distance from the fixation point [10]. Under these conditions it is easy to compute scaled depth (depth / fixation depth), which is a monotonic function of spatial and temporal derivatives of the image intensity function and has a zero value at the fixation point. By implementing this strategy on our robot we verified that a depth estimate can be obtained in real time over a 400×400 pixel image without iteration [11]. This result shows that the early vision computations of animate vision , at least in the case of kinetic depth, are decidedly simpler than fixed camera vision, as first noted by Aloimonos [2].

Table 1 Summary of Primate Gaze Control Systems

<table>
<tr><td rowspan="4">Hold Gaze</td><td rowspan="2">Fixed Target</td><td>Vestibular-Ocular Reflex (VOR). A system that uses knowledge of accommodation and vergence state together with head accelerations to stabilize the gaze vector.</td></tr>
<tr><td rowspan="2">Vergence. A binocular system for locking both foveas over the same three-dimensional target.</td></tr>
<tr><td rowspan="2">Moving Target</td></tr>
<tr><td>Pursuit. A system for tracking moving objects by generating smooth velocity control signals.</td></tr>
<tr><td>Change Gaze</td><td colspan="2">Saccades. High speed precomputed movements that rapidly change gaze over small to very large visual angles.</td></tr>
</table>

3. RELATIVE VISION

The kinetic depth computation naturally produces a relative result; for absolute depth the calculations must include direction of gaze. Since the relative result is easier to obtain, it motivates the question as to whether other visual behaviors might in fact use relative vision. In fact many examples can be found that suggest that relative quantities are used and that their computation is simpler. For example, many psychophysical tasks suggest that the way the image is interpreted depends on occlusion cues such as shown in Figure 2 [12]. It is not easy to make such judgements from an arbitrary viewing position, as would be required by a viewer-centered hypothesis. The kinetic depth result suggests that the notion of a fixation point may be implicit behind the analysis even though we might not be aware of it. Our perceptual system is structured to make accurate judgements relative to an object-centered frame at the fixation depth. Simplistically, imagine that one keeps two maps: one for structures that are judged to be in front of or at the fixation depth, and one for structures that are behind the fixation depth. The different interpolation rules can be fixed for each map. This structure is much simpler than that which would be required for viewer-centered maps. Such maps would have to be able to make corrections based on comparisons of all possible pairs of depth values.

The notion that the computational results of early vision are intrinsically relative can be challenged by obvious counter-examples. We can reach to places in space that we have recently seen but are not currently looking at. So at least in this example the information from the gaze system must be cast in three-dimensional coordinates. However it may well be the case that the behavior that controls reaching under these circumstances is separate from behaviors that use relative visual data. One example of the latter comes from experiments done by Erkelens and Collewijn [13]. Subjects fixated a visual stimulus of random dot targets arranged in a fronto-parallel plane on an display. Changing the disparity of the dots created a situation similar to that which would have been produced by a real target moving back and forth in depth. In fact the subjects' vergence movements showed that they were tracking the simulated movement. In spite of this they reported no depth change in the perception of the plane. So even though the vergence state could in principle have been used to create a three dimensional percept of a moving plane it was not done in this case. However when another disparity was introduced into the display that remained fixed, subjects immediately saw the movement of the plane. The experiments of Olson and Potter [4] hint at why this might be the case. They used the central disparity target as a servo error signal to make the vergence system work. Owing to the small spatial extent of the binocular foveas, the vergence system must continually control the gaze so that both foveas are verged on the same target. This means that the logical zero for this system is at the fixation point, in the same way that the logical zero for the kinetic depth system was at the fixation point.

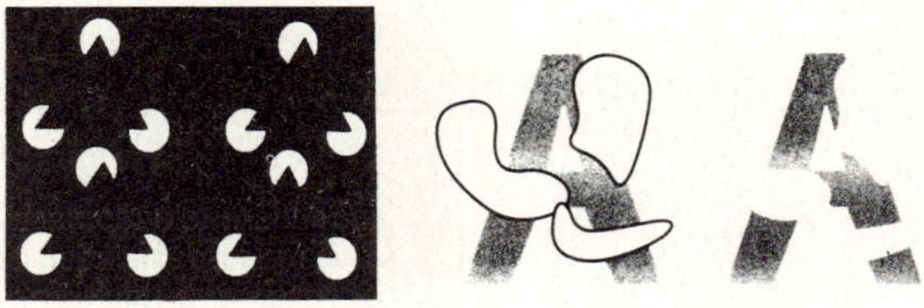

a b

Figure 2 (a) Ken Nakayama's illusion of subjective contours using stereo (not to scale). When fused, if the relative disparities are such that the triangle is in front of the circles, subjective contours are seen; if behind, then they are not. (b) The letter "A" is easier to see if its components result from real occluding boundaries. This can be explained if the occluders can invoke a fixation depth that is in front of the plane of the A's components.

The relative system has the virtue of requiring much less mathematical precision than the computations done in absolute coordinates. This is because the foveas provide the best precision only at the fixation point and an animate vision system can control the location of its fixation point. In contrast, to provide the same resolution everywhere, a fixed resolution system would have to be at least ten thousand times larger. This system would require even greater increases in computational costs, which scale by at least a low order polynomial factor [14]. To see how the relative measurements could be used for three-dimensional positioning, consider visually guided reaching. An arm out of the plane of fixation can be guided in depth to a target at the fixation plane by using only relative disparities of the manipulator as seen by the visual system. This scheme has the virtue of using the natural output of the stereo system which is in terms of fixation-relative coordinates.

4. LEARNING COORDINATED BEHAVIORS

The fixation frame with its small fovea allows the animate system to simplify its access to the environment. The idea is that, at any given instant only a relatively small number of features of the external world are registered but through perceptual actions the system can actively control the features that are registered. This is done naturally by virtue of the binocular foveal system, that provides high resolution coverage of targets of a few degrees but can also be done dynamically as shown in Figure 3.

A consequence of this ability is that with animate vision or more generally animate perception, systems can be built which learn to operate in a complex task domain without the associated explosion in the input feature vector required to represent all the elements of the domain.Steven Whitehead has applied reinforcement learning ideas to the study of animate vision [15, 16]. Whitehead has been studying bock stacking tasks. On each trial, the system is presented with a pile of colored blocks. A pile can consist of any number of blocks and they can be arranged in any configuration. Each block is uniformly colored and can be either red, green, or blue. The system can manipulate the pile by picking and placing objects. An object can be picked up only if its top in clear, and an object can be placed on another object only if the target object's top is clear. When the system arranges the blocks into a *successful configuration*, it receives a positive reward and the trial ends. A successful configuration is some predefined set of states which represents a desired outcome. For example, one extremely simple block stacking task is for the system to learn to pick up a green block. In this case, the successful configurations consist just of those states where the system is holding a green object. The objective of the system is to learn algorithms for arranging arbitrary configurations of blocks into successful configurations.

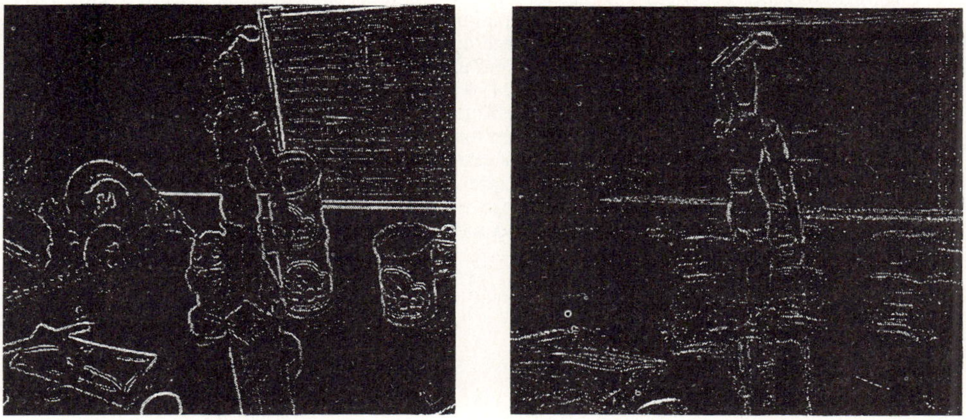

Figure 3 (left) An image of the contrast edges of a cluttered scene containing a central figure of a wooden doll. (right) Moving while fixating on the doll tends to blur the contrast edges that are out of the plane of fixation creating an automatic figure ground segmentation. Figure courtesy of C.M. Brown and R. D. Rimey.

The key to the success of this system is to use the fixation frame to create object centered representations [16]. The system does not attempt to maintain an accurate representation of every item in the universe, but instead should only register objects and aspects (features) that are relevant to the task at hand [17]. For the block stacking problem, the system only registers objects (and their features) according to the functional roles they play in solving the task, such as "THE-GREEN-BLOCK-I-AM-FIXATING." Whitehead's system uses both a fixation frame and an *attention frame* as shown in Figure 4. Details may be found in [16].

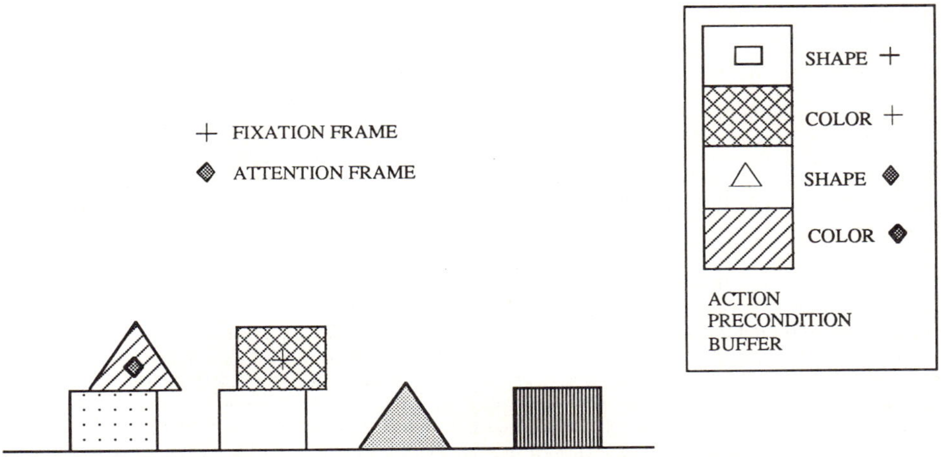

Figure 4 The active perceptual system is divided into two parts: the fixation frame and an attention frame. The information registered in the fovea (or fixation point) can be actively controlled by executing perceptual and gaze control "acts." For example, fixating the block as shown causes its features to be registered in the state vector; attending to the triangle as shown causes its features to appear in the state vector. The two degrees of freedom in the state vector that can be independently controlled correspond to "markers." One can think of placing a special marker on an object causing its properties to appear in the appropriate place in the state vector. The system used by Whitehead is slightly more complex but still only uses twenty bits total to represent the state of the world.

Over a number of trials the system can learn to solve particular tasks. Figure 5 shows the number of steps used to solve the problem of picking up a green block. There are many pros and cons associated with this scheme and these are discussed in [16]. In this paper we stress the advantage this kind of learning derives from the use of object centered representations that are created by fixating. This allows (a) the access of items by property instead of by category, and (b) run-time indexing. Access by property is very efficient in the following way. Consider the problem of hanging a picture where a nail has to be driven into a wall. We do not really need a hammer, but something that could serve as a hammer. Plan access by category forces the identification of image items, followed by a check to determine the appropriate properties. Access by properties short circuits this process. Also, the fact that these properties are determined by what is in the environment at the moment filters out the consideration of strategies that would require unavailable items.

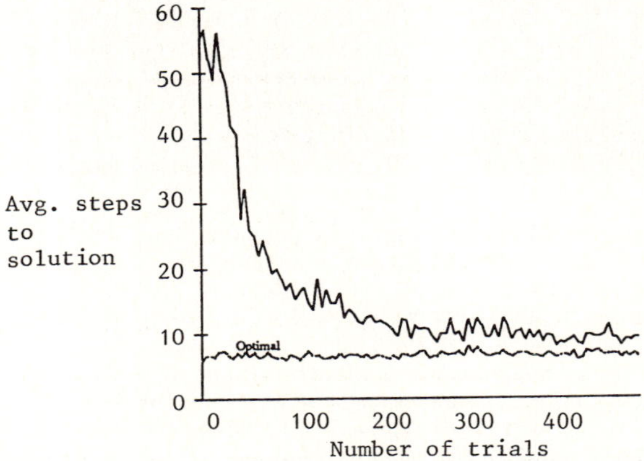

Figure 5 The results of applying reinforcement learning to a simple block stacking task: Pick up the green block. The system uses its fixation and attention frames to register features dynamically and thus avoid the combinatorial cost of representing large state spaces. The lower trace shows the smallest number of steps needed to solve the problem computed as the running average of the last three presentations. The upper trace shows the time taken to solve the problem, also averaged over three presentations.

5. CONCLUSIONS

In this paper we have argued that animate vision systems use exocentric frames of reference for almost all aspects of visual behavior, and we have attempted to outline the advantages of such a system. Table 2 summarizes these developments comparing animate vision with fixed camera vision.

As humans we have the compelling experience of living in a three-dimensional visual movie. The world appears vividly colorful and stable. One temptation is to propose models of perception that capture this phenomenon in very explicit ways, say as a pictorial memory buffer. If the explicit buffer seems too crude, one can posit elaborate data structures that are equivalent in the sense that they contain the information necessary to construct such a picture. However, when one examines the detailed *mechanisms* of human and animal visual perception, or tries to build anthropomorphic robots, it quickly becomes apparent that the way the apparatus works at this level of abstraction, e.g., the fast sequential saccadic searches, is very incompatible with phenomenological notions of invariance and stability. Instead, we content that the visual system achieves this virtual permanence in a way analogous to a computer's use of virtual memory: The visual system keeps track of a representation that has high fidelity at the point of fixation and encodes the location of objects in the world relative to that point. The ability to change the gaze point rapidly, plays the role of "paging" and contributes to the illusion of stable perception.

The ability to have behaviors that learn to adapt to the local environment will have a profound effect on the design of animate vision algorithms. The discussion on learning introduced the notion of a personalized representation: That is, associating features with an object that make its behaviors concerning it especially easy to execute. One can think of many other cases that challenge traditional notions of invariance. For example, we do not think of our coats as being rigid objects, yet they appear to be to our visual systems while they are hanging on coat racks, and this limited invariance can be exploited. The hope is that such algorithms may be able to discover which combinations of such features work in each problem instance. It could be the case that the general assumptions that define categories are almost never as useful as these special assumptions found by adaptive algorithms.

Table 2 A Comparison of the Computational Features of Fixed Camera Vision and Animate Vision

Fixed Camera Vision	Animate Vision with Exocentric Fixation
Local constraints that relate physical parameters to photometric parameters are underdetermined	Local constraints are sufficient when used in a behavioral context
Minimalist constraints such as smoothness used to regularize the solution	Maximalist constraints such as specific behavioral assumptions used to obtain solution
Algorithms require parallel iterations over the retinally-indexed array	Algorithms are local and has a constant time solution
Frame of reference is camera-centered (egocentric)	Frame of reference is fixation point centered (exocentric)
Figure ground segmentation requires the use of many different static occlusion cues	Movements can create figure ground segmentation
Isolated views of the scene are extremely limiting	The fixation frame can be used to create object centered representations that can be part of learned behaviors

Acknowledgements

I would like to thank my colleagues Christopher Brown and Randal Nelson for critiquing these ideas. I am also especially grateful to the University of Rochester team of researchers, Tim Becker, David Coombs, Nat Martin, Tom Olson, Robert Potter, Ray Rimey, Michael Swain, Dave Tilley, Steve Whitehead, Lambert Wixson, and Brian Yamauchi, all of whom have greatly helped refine the ideas herein. The learning example comes from a research project headed by Steve Whitehead. Peggy Meeker is responsible for the pleasing format of this manuscript.

References

[1] Marr, D.C. *Vision*. W. H. Freeman and Co., 1982.

[2] Aloimonos, J., A. Bandopadhay, and I. Weiss. Active vision. In Proc., *1st Int'l. Conf. on Computer Vision*, pp. 35-54, June 1987. Also in *Int'l. J. Computer Vision 1*, 4, pp. 333-356, 1988.

[3] Brown, C.M. (Ed.), with D.H. Ballard, T.G. Becker, R.F. Gans, N.G. Martin, T.J. Olson, R.D. Potter, R.D. Rimey, D.G. Tilley, and S.D. Whitehead. The Rochester Robot. TR 257, Computer Science Dept., U. Rochester, August 1988.

[4] Olson, T.J. and R.D. Potter. Real-time vergence control. TR 264, Computer Science Dept., U. Rochester, November 1988.

[5] Yeshurun, Y. and E.L. Schwartz. Cepstral filtering on a columnar image architecture: A fast algorithm for binocular stereo segmentation. Robotics Res. TR 286, Courant Inst., New York U., March 1987.

[6] Brown, C.M. Gaze controls with interactions and delays. To appear, *IEEE Trans. on Systems, Man, and Cybernetics 20*, 2, March 1990a.

[7] Brown, C.M. Prediction and cooperation in gaze control. To appear, *Biological Cybernetics*, 1990b.

[8] Rimey, R.D. and C.M. Brown. Selective attention as sequential behavior: Modelling eye movements with an augmented hidden Markov model. TR 327, Computer Science Dept., U. Rochester, February 1990.

[9] Raviv, D. and M. Herman. Towards an understanding of camera fixation. Technical Report, Robot Systems Division, National Institutes of Standards and Technology, December 1989.

[10] Cutting, J.E. Motion parallax and visual flow: How to determine direction of locomotion. *4th Meeting, Int'l. Soc. for Ecological Psychology*, Hartford, CT, 1982.

[11] Ballard, D.H. and A. Ozcandarli. Eye fixation and early vision: Kinetic depth. *Proc., 2nd IEEE Int'l. Conf. on Computer Vision*, December 1988.

[12] Nakayama, K. Presentation. *Woods Hole Workshop on Computational Neuroscience*, Woods Hole, MA, August 1988.

[13] Erkelens, C.J. and H. Collewijn. Eye movements and stereopsis during dichoptic viewing of moving random-dot stereograms. *Vision Research 25*, pp. 1689-1700, 1985.

[14] Tsotsos, J. A complexity level analysis of vision. In *Proc., IJCCV*, London, June 1987.

[15] Whitehead, S.D. and D.H. Ballard. A role for anticipation in reactive systems that learn. *Proc., 6th Int'l. Workshop on Machine Learning*, Cornell U., Ithaca, NY, June 1989.

[16] Whitehead, S.D. and D.H. Ballard. Active perception and reinforcement learning. Submitted for conference publication, 1990.

[17] Agre, P.E. and D. Chapman. Pengi: An implementation of a theory of activity. *Proc., AAAI 87*, pp. 268-272, 1987.

Advanced Neural Computers / R. Eckmiller (Editor)

A Performance Evaluation of ALIAS for the Detection of Geometric Anomalies on Fractal Images

Peter Bock, Richard Rovner, and C. Joseph Kocinski

Research Institute for Applied Knowledge Processing (FAW)*
University of Ulm
7900 Ulm, West Germany

Based on Collective Learning Systems Theory and a versatile general-purpose architecture for massively parallel networks of processors, a Transputer-based parallel-processing image-processing system, known as ALIAS (Adaptive Learning Image Analysis System), has been applied to a difficult image processing task: the phase, translation, and scale invariant detection of anomalous features in otherwise "normal" images. ALIAS consists of a three-layer hierarchical network of 32 learning cells and 33 non-learning cells. This paper presents an evaluation of ALIAS for the detection of anomalies which are square sections of a class of geometric images (called Manhattan) placed on binary fractal images belonging to one of three distinct "normal" equivalence classes (called Islands, Plateaus, and Wheatfields). Results indicate that the ability of ALIAS to detect and discriminate Manhattan anomalies improves with increasing area of the anomaly, although positive discrimination is only achieved with large anomalies. The ability of ALIAS to localize Manhattan anomalies exhibits a positive maximum when the area of the anomaly is 25 pixels, illustrating the Franz-Josef Syndrome.

1. PROJECT ALIAS

An alternative to pre-programmed rule-based Artificial Intelligence is a hierarchical network of learning cellular automata (learning cells) which acquire their knowledge through a series of trial-and-error interactions with an evaluating Environment, much as humans do. The input to the hierarchical network is provided by a set of sensors which perceive the external world. Based upon this perceived information and past experience (memory), the learning cells synthesize collections of trial responses. Periodically the learning cells estimate the effectiveness of these collections using either internal evaluations (unsupervised learning) or external evaluations from the Environment (supervised learning), modifying their memories accordingly. Known as Collective Learning Systems Theory, this paradigm has been applied to many sophisticated gaming problems, demonstrating robust learning and dynamic adaptivity. [5,6,9,10,11]

A difficult vision task, not handled well by classical image processing algorithms, is the detection of anomalous features in images: "What's wrong with this picture?". Using a non-symbolic, non-algorithmic approach, Project ALIAS (Adaptive Learning Image Analysis System) is applying Collective Learning Systems Theory to this task. [1] ALIAS requires a three-layer network consisting of 33 non-learning cells and 32 learning cells and processes images, each of which is a 252 by 252 matrix of binary pixels (e.g., black or white). After being trained on a set of normal images, ALIAS is capable of detecting images corrupted with anomalies, and responds with an estimate of the location and severity of the anomaly.

The first layer of ALIAS is the **Analysis Layer**, consisting of 32 non-learning cells operating in parallel. Each of these cells receives an identical copy of the input image (**normal** or **anomalous**), and produces a **transformed** image for its particular **rank**. For the experiment reported in this paper, the

*Project ALIAS is sponsored and partially funded by Robert Bosch GmbH

Analysis Layer uses a phase-invariant transformation scheme, called **Overlap** [3]. This scheme computes the ratio of white to black pixels within a square matrix, called a **Transformation Token**, which is scanned across the entire image from left to right and from top to bottom in a fully overlapped manner. If the number of white pixels within the Transformation Token exceeds the number of black pixels, the central pixel in the transformed image is set to white; otherwise it is set to black, as illustrated in Figure 1. The Overlap transformation acts as a spatial filter, producing transformed images whose spatial resolution decreases as the size of the Transformation Token increases, where this size is defined as the rank number.

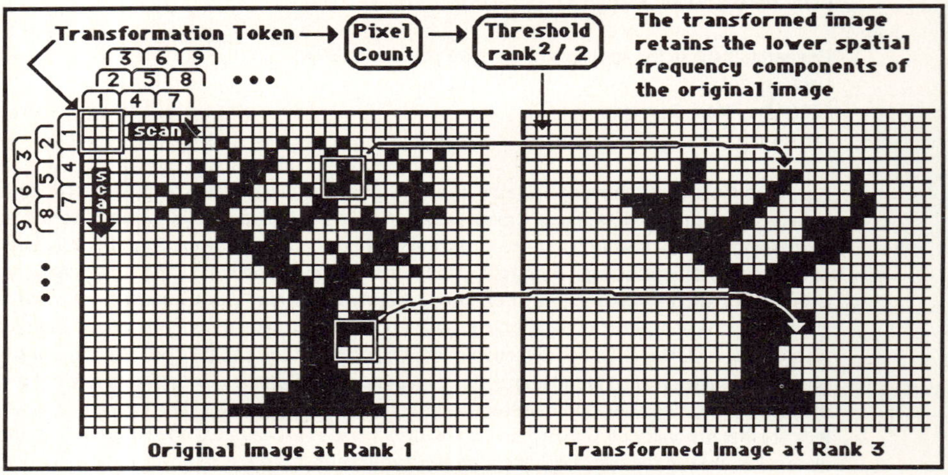

Figure 1 - Overlap Transformation Scheme

Following the transformation of the original image, each cell (rank) in the Analysis Layer scans the transformed image in a fully overlapped manner, producing a stream of **Analysis Tokens**, as illustrated in Figure 2. The Analysis Token captures a 4 by 4 matrix of pixels; the 16-bit row-major encoding of the contents of this matrix is called an **Analysis Pattern**. As they are produced, the Analysis Patterns for each rank are sent to the learning cells at the corresponding rank in the second layer, the Hypothesis Layer.

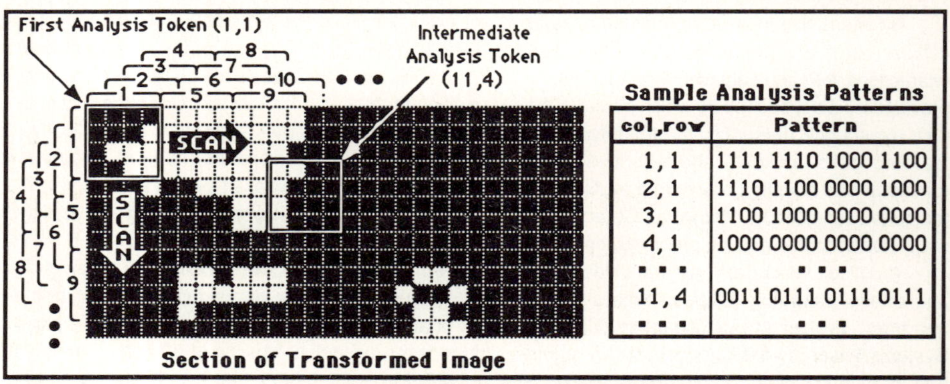

Figure 2 - Analysis Token Production

The **Hypothesis Layer** of ALIAS consists of 32 learning cells operating in parallel, one for each rank. The Analysis Pattern captured by each Analysis Token arriving from the Analysis Layer is a stimulus for the learning cell at the corresponding rank in the Hypothesis Layer. Since there are 65536 possible Analysis Patterns (2^{16}), the stimulus domain of the State Transition Matrix (STM) for each learning cell consists of 65536 stimulants (Analysis Patterns). Each stimulant has a single respondent associated with it, the Pattern Normality. Each time a stimulus appears, the cell responds with the corresponding Normality.

Each pixel in the transformed image is captured by 16 different overlapping Analysis Tokens. As a learning cell in the Analysis Layer receives the 16 Analysis Tokens, the 16 Pattern Normalities in the STM for the corresponding Analysis Patterns are averaged to form a single estimate of the Normality of the corresponding pixel in the transformed image. These Normality estimates are truncated to 8-bits and assembled into a matrix of estimates which is spatially isomorphic with the transformed image, called a **Rank Hypothesis**. This Rank Hypothesis is then transmitted to the third layer, the Synthesis Layer.

The Rank Hypothesis functions as an estimate of the normality of the transformed image at the particular rank, i.e., whether or not each of the component Analysis Patterns "belongs" in images of the particular class at the given rank. ALIAS can display the Rank Hypothesis for each rank as an "image" in which the intensity of each pixel represents the average of the 16 Pattern Normalities corresponding to the 16 overlapping Analysis Patterns which included the corresponding pixel in the transformed image.

At the conclusion of the processing of each image, every learning cell at every rank modifies all of its Pattern Normalities using a linear multiplicative compensation policy and an additive update policy. For those Analysis Patterns which *were* encountered in the transformed image (**Discovery**), the Pattern Normality is *increased* in proportion to its distance from maximum Normality (+32767); as the Pattern Normality approaches the maximum, therefore, the update converges to zero. Likewise, for those Analysis Patterns which *were not* encountered (**Extinction**), the Pattern Normality is *decreased* in proportion to its distance from maximum Normality. The current update policy does not allow the Pattern Normality to become negative, which restricts the effect of Extinction to a **Normality Floor** of zero.

The single non-learning cell in the **Synthesis Layer** computes the average of the *non-normal* pixels through all 32 Rank Hypotheses, producing a single **Super Hypothesis**, a summarial estimate of the Normality of each pixel in the original image. ALIAS displays both the Rank and Super Hypotheses on a color graphics monitor. As the memories of the learning cells converge to homeostasis during training with normal images, the displays of the Rank and Super Hypotheses mirror this process by converging to an all-white image. When anomalies have been introduced into normal images of the learned class, if ALIAS can detect them, the Rank and Super Hypotheses will indicate their presence as colored areas of various intensities in and around the location of the anomalous features.

The physical architecture of ALIAS is a network of 33 Transputers operating in parallel. Thirty-two Transputers comprise the Analysis and Hypothesis Layers, with each performing the required tasks for both layers for a single rank. The 33rd Transputer performs the functions of the Synthesis Layer. [4,7] The Environment for ALIAS resides in a Macintosh IIx, which submits the input images to the Transputer Subsystem (where it is pipelined to all 32 Transputers), evaluates and displays the Rank and Super Hypotheses, and monitors the operation of the entire system.

2. EXPERIMENT PROCEDURE AND PERFORMANCE MEASURES

2.1 Definition of Scores

A **score** is an experiment-specific raw data value obtained by measuring the output of ALIAS in some specified fashion. The scores used for the experiment described in this paper are defined below. Each score is calculated for some region of an Hypothesis*. The region may be the entire Hypothesis.

Overall Average (OVA): the average of all pixel Normalities in a region
Non-Normal Average (NNA): the average of *only* those pixel Normalities less than +127 in a region
Minimum Non-Normal (MNN): the minimum pixel Normality in a region
Number Non-Normal (NNN): the number of pixels whose Normality is less than +127 in a region

2.2 Experiment Procedure

For a given experiment ALIAS is first presented with a Training Set of images. The Training Set consists of a specified number of images which are consistently "normal", i.e., images which do not intentionally contain anomalies, are believed to belong to the same equivalence class, and which exhibit

* The term "Hypothesis" refers to either a Rank Hypothesis or a Super Hypothesis

the same statistical characteristics. The three fractal-based image classes used in the experiment reported in this paper (see Section 3.1) are examples of such classes. Learning is enabled during the Training Phase, with ALIAS using a specified memory modification policy, such as the one described in Section 1.

After completion of the Training Phase it is necessary to establish a baseline performance level to be used for statistical analysis. This requires a Control Set consisting of images of the same equivalence class as those in the Training Set, but disjoint from the Training Set. The images in the Control Set are presented to ALIAS with learning disabled. For each of these images ALIAS synthesizes a Super Hypothesis, from which each of the scores listed in Section 2.1 are calculated. The behavior of the entire Control Set can be summarized using various statistics, such as the mean, standard deviation, etc.

The sample size for the Control Set is determined by computing the *final* standard deviation of the Non-Normal Average over 500 control images. This final standard deviation is compared to the *running* standard deviation of the Non-Normal Average over the same set. The image number at which the running standard deviation converges to the final standard deviation determines the Control Set sample size. Note that this process can result in different Control Set sizes for different image classes.

Once the Control Set has been processed, the Test Phase commences. As before, the Test Set is based upon images belonging to the same equivalence class as the Training and Control Sets, but disjoint from them. The Test Set sample size is the same as the Control Set sample size. Unlike the Training and Control Sets, however, the Test Set images are the images on which the anomalies will be placed. Once again, the Test Set results will produce a set of sample statistics for each score of interest. For a particular score, the Control Set statistics can be compared to the Test Set statistics to identify differences between the two sets, if any. This allows performance to be quantified.

2.3 Performance Metrics

A **metric** is a normalization of one or more scores for the purpose of identifying levels and trends of performance, as well as allowing meaningful comparisons of performance across different experiments. Three metrics were used to evaluate the performance of ALIAS for the experiment reported in this paper: **Detection**, **Discrimination**, and **Localization**.

Detection for ALIAS was evaluated using two different but related metrics: a *summary* metric to assess the ability of ALIAS to detect anomalies over a *sample* of images (**Sample Detection**), and a *transient* metric to assess the ability of ALIAS to detect anomalies in a *single* image (**Unit Detection**). [8]

The summary metric Sample Detection, D_s, is a statistical comparison of the Overall Average of the response of ALIAS to normal images versus anomalized images. Below is an explanation of the statistical procedure and how the comparison was made.

Typically, one performs a parametric or non-parametric statistical test to determine if two independent samples were drawn from different populations. Such a statistical test produces a level of significance (α) which indicates the strength of the difference between the two samples. This α may be interpreted as the probability that these two samples could have been produced from a single population strictly by chance. As α decreases, the confidence that the two samples come from different populations increases.

Consider the Test Set of images presented to ALIAS *without* anomalies. When the resulting score sample is compared to the score sample from the Control Set, the α from this test (called α_b where b denotes the baseline) should be close to 0.5, providing evidence of little difference between the samples.

Now consider the same Test Set of images presented to ALIAS *with* anomalies. As before, the score sample is compared to the Control Set score sample. If the presence of the anomalies was detected by ALIAS, the α from this test (called α_t where t denotes Test Set) should be *less than* α_b. For this case, a measure for *positive* detection may be derived by comparing the actual value of α_t with the *best* possible case, which would be an α_t of zero. Alternatively, for the case where α_t is *greater than* α_b, a measure for *negative* detection may be derived by comparing the value of α_t with the *worst* possible case, which would be an α_t of one. Normalizing each of these measures yields two formulas for computing the Sample Detection metric, D_s, bound in the interval [-1, 1].

$$\text{Positive Detection } (\alpha_t \leq \alpha_b) \rightarrow D_S = \frac{\alpha_b - \alpha_t}{\alpha_b} \qquad \text{Negative Detection } (\alpha_t > \alpha_b) \rightarrow D_S = \frac{\alpha_b - \alpha_t}{1 - \alpha_b}$$

The *t*-test, typically used to compare two independent samples, requires that the populations be normally distributed and analysis of the data has shown that this criterion is not always met. Therefore, the statistical test used for analyzing ALIAS performance data was the Wilcoxon Rank-Sum Test, a non-parametric alternative to the *t*-test which does not require normally distributed populations [12]. The values for α resulting from this test were used to calculate Sample Detection, D_S.

Another measure of the detection capability of ALIAS derives from industrial requirements, in which an automatic inspection system must accept or reject samples produced from some process in accordance with some rejection criterion. ALIAS can perform this task once the Control Set data has been gathered by using the mean of the Non-Normal Averages from the Control Set as a standard of comparison. A Test Set image is *accepted* (considered normal) if its Non-Normal Average is higher than the Control Set mean, or *rejected* (considered not normal) if it is lower. The metric Unit Detection, then, is simply the fraction of the anomalous Test Set images that are rejected, and is bound in the interval [0, 1].

When an anomaly is placed on an otherwise normal image, the anomalous region should exhibit Normalities significantly less than normal regions. The strength of this difference is measured with the Discrimination metric. The Minimum Non-Normal pixel provides a sound basis for measuring this difference, because this pixel will always survive a reasonable threshold applied to an Hypothesis. For a specified threshold, pixels exceeding (more normal than) the threshold would be ignored, a process which could prove useful for *discriminating* the anomaly. Ideally, the Minimum Non-Normal pixel in the anomaly (MNN^A) will be significantly less than the Minimum Non-Normal pixel external to the anomaly (MNN^X).

The Discrimination metric, Z, is the normalized difference between MNN^A and MNN^X in an Hypothesis, averaged over the entire Test Set, and is thus bound in the interval [-1, 1], as shown below.

$$Z = \frac{\sum_{i=1}^{n} \left(\frac{MNN_i^X - MNN_i^A}{127 - N_f} \right)}{n}$$

where n is the number of Test Set images and N_f is the normality floor.

Localization, L, is a measure of the spatial accuracy of the response of ALIAS. The metric is the normalized difference between the Number Non-Normal per unit area in the anomaly (NNN^A) and the Number Non-Normal per unit area external to the anomaly (NNN^X), averaged over the entire Test Set, and is thus bound in the interval [-1, 1], as shown below.

$$L = \frac{\sum_{i=1}^{n} \left(\frac{NNN_i^A}{m_i^A} - \frac{NNN_i^X}{m_i^X} \right)}{n}$$

where n is the number of images in the Test Set, m^A is the total number of pixels in the anomaly, and m^X is the total number of pixels external to the anomaly.

3. GEOMETRIC ANOMALIES EXPERIMENT

The experiment described in this paper measured the ability of ALIAS to detect, discriminate, and localize geometric anomalies placed on fractal images. Performance was evaluated using metrics described in Section 2.3.

3.1 Images and Anomalies

In an effort to imitate spatial geometries which occur in nature, the images presented to ALIAS for this experiment were 2-dimensional samples of 3-dimensional fractal objects. The fractal objects were algorithmically derived from uniform and non-uniform power distributions in the frequency domain, subjected to inverse-frequency filtering, and moved to the spatial domain by the application of the inverse discrete Fourier transform, producing instances of fractional Brownian motion. The images for ALIAS were then created by extracting 2-dimensional samples of these fractal objects (e.g., slices). The equivalence and spatial complexity of these images can be theoretically predicted and verified, assuring rigorous parametric control of the feature detection capabilities of ALIAS [2].

Three different equivalence classes of fractal images were used for this experiment, known as **Islands, Plateaus**, and **Wheatfields**, so named because of their resemblance to aerial images of these naturally occurring geographical features. The images in the classes Islands and Plateaus were samples of fractal objects derived from *uniform* power distributions. For the image class Islands, the fractal objects were thresholded at a specified value, with all pixels above that value set to white and all pixels below set to black, resulting in an image with large homogeneous all-white and all-black regions. A section of a typical Islands image is exhibited in Figure 3a. The images in the class Plateaus were created by taking several horizontal slices through the fractal objects, setting only the pixels at the selected levels to black, resulting in images with several contour lines. Figure 3b shows a section from a typical Plateaus image. The images in the class Wheatfields were samples of fractal objects derived from *non-uniform* power distributions, produced by introducing four discrete frequency components into an otherwise uniform power distribution. The resulting fractal objects were then thresholded in a similar manner to Islands, this time resulting in an image with large areas of dither and repetitive spatial features, as exemplified in Figure 3c.

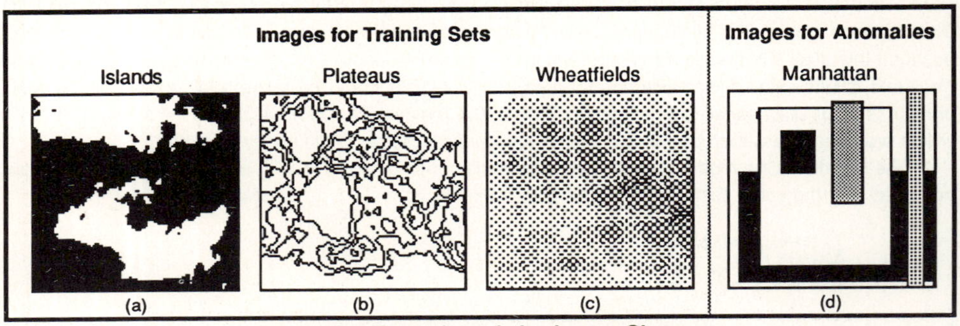

Figure 3 - Examples of the Image Classes

Using the method described in Section 2.2, the Control Sets for Islands and Wheatfields were each set at 150 images, while the Control Set for Plateaus was set at 300 images.

The anomalies for this experiment were small sections of a completely different class of images generated in a completely different fashion. Each of the images in this class contains a random number (≤ 40) of randomly placed rectangles of random size, each randomly filled with one of three patterns: all-white, all-black, or a simple symmetrical dither. Rectangles may overlap, and the only condition in placing rectangles is that a rectangle must fit entirely in the image frame. This class of images was dubbed "Manhattan", because of its faint resemblance to a bird's-eye-view of the borough of New York City. A section of a typical Manhattan image is shown in Figure 3d.

The anomalies are square regions selected from Manhattan images and placed on the fractal images. The square sizes (in one dimension) are 1, 3, 5, 7, 11, 15, and 23. For a given image class, each Test Set image receives a single square anomaly. This square is taken from one Manhattan image by starting in the center of the Manhattan image and searching for the first square region with the same pixel density (percentage of black pixels) as the entire image within some epsilon of accuracy (typically 5%). The selected square is then randomly placed on a fractal image. Each Test Set image receives a square anomaly from a different Manhattan image. Thus, the 150 images in the Islands Test Set require sections taken from 150 different Manhattan images.

3.2 Hypotheses

There are three main hypotheses associated with this experiment.

Hypothesis 1: ALIAS will *detect* Manhattan anomalies of all seven sizes placed on fractal images.
Hypothesis 2: ALIAS will *discriminate* Manhattan anomalies placed on fractal images.
Hypothesis 3: ALIAS will *localize* Manhattan anomalies placed on fractal images.

3.3 Results

Figure 4 displays the results of the experiment for both Sample Detection and Unit Detection. It is clear that Sample Detection performance improves monotonically with increasing anomaly area.

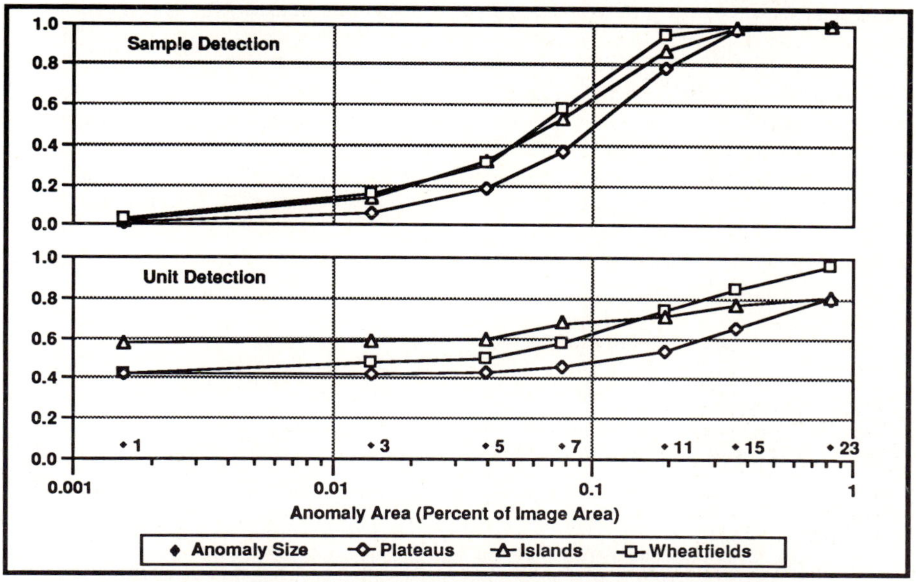

Figure 4 - DETECTION of Manhattan Anomalies on Fractal Images

A 1x1 anomaly (a single pixel) is not detected for any fractal image class. This anomaly is a special case since it is the only anomaly size which is always completely uniform (all-white or all-black). It is therefore possible to place a white pixel onto a white section in the fractal image (or, alternatively a black pixel on a black section). In this case, the Test Set image would simply not exhibit an anomaly. Moreover, an isolated black pixel (i.e., completely surrounded by white pixels) appears frequently in normal images for all three image classes (although, this is not true for an isolated white pixel in the case of Islands and Plateaus). Essentially, in many of the Test Set images containing a 1x1 anomaly there is nothing abnormal for ALIAS to detect, and the results confirm that.

As the anomaly area increases, Sample Detection consistently improves. At a 23x23 anomaly Sample Detection is 1.00 for all three cases. Since a 23x23 anomaly comprises only 0.08% of the total image area, this is indeed strong evidence of robust detection.

In general, it appears more difficult for ALIAS to detect Manhattan anomalies on Plateaus than on Islands or Wheatfields. Many Manhattan anomalies contain some portion of the dither pattern characteristic of Manhattan images, and with the small anomalies this dither resembles sections of contours found in Plateaus, causing ALIAS to consider them normal.

Unit Detection, also shown in Figure 4, behaves differently, remaining constant from a 1x1 anomaly through a 5x5 anomaly. Only at the 7x7 anomaly does Unit Detection start to increase, eventually reaching 0.81 for Islands and Plateaus and 0.96 for Wheatfields for the 23x23 anomaly. While Unit Detection is constant up to a 5x5 anomaly, ALIAS is still rejecting approximately 50% of the Test Set images, a remarkable figure considering that a 5x5 anomaly comprises less than 0.04% of the image area.

Figure 5 presents the results for both Discrimination and Localization. In almost every case Discrimination is negative, meaning that, on the average, the Minimum Non-Normal pixel was not found in the anomaly, but rather in the region external to the anomaly. For Islands, Discrimination does not become positive for any anomaly size, while for Wheatfields ALIAS produces positive Discrimination for the 11x11 anomaly and beyond. Manhattan anomalies are positively discriminated on Plateaus for the 23x23 anomaly. Although Discrimination is almost always negative it does improve with increasing anomaly area.

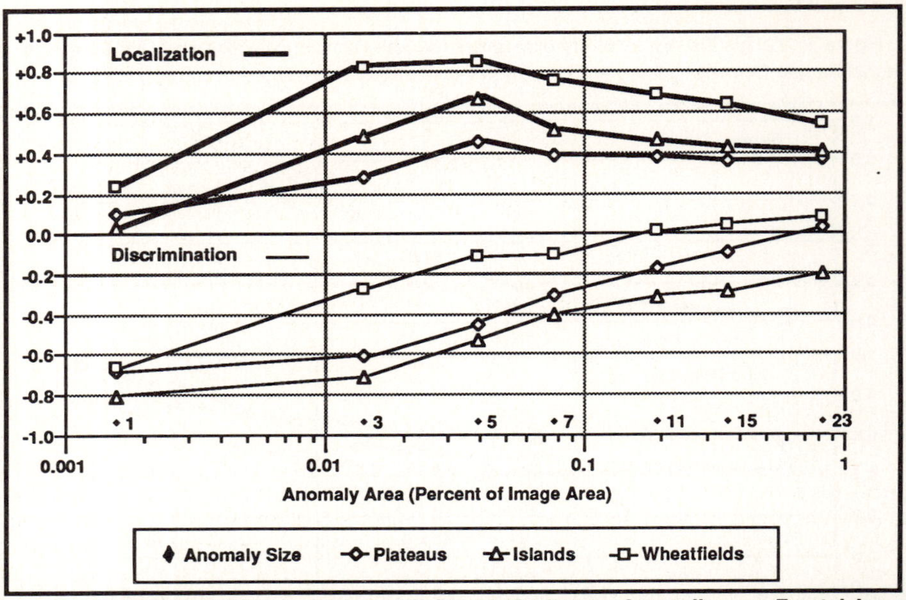

Figure 5 - DISCRIMINATION & LOCALIZATION of Manhattan Anomalies on Fractal Images

An important factor in discrimination is the Normality Floor. An inspection of the data reveals a large number of Minimum Non-Normal pixels in the anomaly with Normalities of zero (the Normality Floor), and this number increases with increasing anomaly area. This is true for all three image classes. Thus, lowering the Normality Floor to -32767 should improve Discrimination, since the Normalities of the Analysis Patterns associated with these pixels will be able to descend to lower values due to extinction.

Localization, also exhibited in Figure 5, produces extremely interesting results. The graph indicates the presence of a local maximum at the 5x5 anomaly. This characteristic is evidence of the Franz-Josef Syndrome, the name given to the situation where the teacher believes that an anomaly is *entirely* abnormal, when in fact it is not. In this scenario, the teacher, a.k.a. Franz-Josef, places an anomaly on an image belonging to a class which ALIAS has learned. After ALIAS responds with its Super Hypothesis, the teacher then evaluates the response of ALIAS, penalizing ALIAS for every pixel in the anomalous region which ALIAS does *not* detect as non-normal. Franz-Josef is proceeding under the assumption that *every* pixel in the anomaly is non-normal. Unfortunately, this is not always true. A 1x1 anomaly is rarely non-normal. As shown in Figure 6, as the size of a Manhattan anomaly increases to 5x5, the anomalies slowly acquire the characteristic of an entire Manhattan image, and the teacher's assumption of total non-normality begins to acquire more validity. The 5x5 anomaly produces exactly 4 Analysis Tokens, whose corresponding Analysis Patterns will *not* generally be found in the fractal images. However, as the anomaly size continues to increase, and the anomaly begins to look more and more like a complete Manhattan image, the Analysis Patterns in the anomaly have a greater chance of being normal, i.e., being found in fractal images. For example, a section of a typical Manhattan image may well have large all-black regions, and so does an Islands image. Likewise, a section of a typical Manhattan image may have large all-white regions, and so do Islands, Plateaus, and Wheatfields images. Thus, when the anomaly becomes large enough, some of its Analysis Patterns will undoubtedly be patterns normally found in the fractal images. These regions of the anomaly are actually normal, and while Franz-Josef has assumed that the *entire* anomaly is non-normal, he is *wrong*, and ALIAS is telling him so!

Therefore, Localization is influenced not only by ALIAS, but also by the teacher. Errors on the part of the teacher, either in constructing the Training Set images or in evaluating the performance of ALIAS, will degrade Localization performance. It is incumbent upon the teacher to present ALIAS with a Training Set that belongs to an equivalence class that is statistically consistent and largely free of anomalies. Nevertheless, ALIAS is robust enough to overcome all but the most serious errors of this kind.

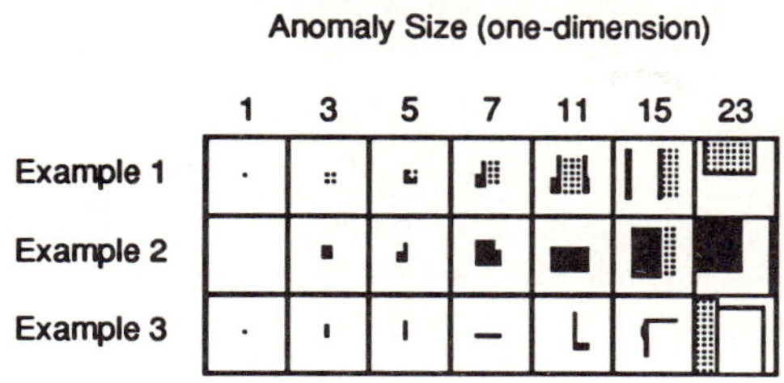

Each square in this figure is 23x23 pixels. Note that as the anomaly size increases the anomaly tends to contain more homogeneous regions of all-white and all-black, resulting in the Franz-Josef Syndrome.

Figure 6 - Examples of Manhattan Anomalies

4. CONCLUSIONS

The experiment reported in this paper uses an *internal* evaluation policy to drive learning, which assumes by default that every image in the Training Set is *completely normal*, a potentially dangerous assumption as pointed out in Section 3.3. It is tempting to characterize such a learning policy as *unsupervised*. However, since the Training and Control Set images were *carefully constructed* in an attempt to minimize the effect of the Franz-Joseph Syndrome, this in itself implies a kind of *supervision*. This process might be designated "textbook learning", and textbooks are rarely error-free!

With real images, the quality control of the Training Set images will be even more difficult, and it is expected that *external* evaluations will be necessary to minimize the effects of the Franz-Joseph Syndrome due to unavoidable inconsistencies and anomalies in the Training Images. It should be noted, however, that external evaluations *also* invite the Franz-Josef Syndrome, since real teachers are generally no more in possession of the truth about the normality of the images, than real images are totally free of inconsistencies and anomalies.

Despite the strict control possible with the generation of *fractal* images, such images are very complex, as exemplified by the large number of Analysis Patterns which they produce [2]. For this reason, when only an *internal* evaluation policy is used, it is extremely difficult to achieve an Hypothesis from the Control Set that is completely normal, i.e., in which the Normality of every pixel is 127. Typically, a Super Hypothesis for a Control Set image will exhibit several thousand *non-normal* pixels (Normalities less than 127), but those Normalities are generally *very close* to completely normal (Normality of 127). The Overall Average of a Super Hypothesis is typically greater than 125.

Certainly, a hard-limiting modification policy would eventually result in every Analysis Pattern being completely normal, but no anomalies would ever be detected; the gradual application of Discovery and Extinction is necessary to overcome the inconsistencies and capture the essential consistencies in the images. External evaluation may also be helpful in this respect by allowing a knowledgeable teacher to evaluate individual Hypotheses during training, penalizing ALIAS precisely and accurately when the Hypothesis contains large numbers of non-normal pixels, and rewarding ALIAS whenever the Hypothesis improves (becomes more normal). In this manner, the number of non-normal pixels appearing in the Hypotheses for the Control Set images will be greatly reduced. Therefore the objective is to develop methods for applying both internal and external evaluation in conjunction with an appropriate modification policy, such that the Control Set Hypotheses are as close to normal as possible, while still maintaining an acceptable level of anomaly detection. Experience with Collective Learning shows conclusively that a judiciously chosen modification policy can accelerate learning by several orders of magnitude. [13,14]

Even using only internal evaluations, ALIAS demonstrates robust detection of Manhattan anomalies placed on fractal images, with the detection capability improving with increasing anomaly area. The ability of ALIAS to consistently reject a high percentage of corrupted images is also a function of anomaly area once the anomaly area begins to contain more than a single Analysis Token. Using external evaluations, it is expected that ALIAS will exhibit improved detection of small anomalies.

While ALIAS strongly detects anomalies of size greater than 1x1, its ability to discriminate these anomalies from background clutter is poor at best, and often not discriminated at all. This, of course, is partially a function of the complexity of the fractal images, a problem which cannot be prevented and must be faced squarely. However, simply lowering the Normality Floor to -32767 should improve discrimination dramatically. In addition, external evaluations will help to drive the Hypotheses corresponding to normal sections of images toward complete normality, and anomalous sections toward the Normality Floor.

Localization dramatically illustrates the Franz-Josef Syndrome, in which the teacher believes an entire section of an image to be abnormal, when in fact, that section exhibits the same statistical characteristics as the Training Set of normal images. Clearly, this phenomenon demonstrates the importance of truth and accuracy when training and testing students.

Even without the benefit of external evaluations, and under the unavoidable influence of the Franz-Josef Syndrome, ALIAS demonstrates a remarkable ability to detect anomalies smaller than 1% of the entire image area with virtual certainty, even displaying positive discrimination in some cases. ALIAS also has the ability to tell us, the teachers, that we are sometimes wrong. Hopefully we are intelligent enough to listen to our student. As ALIAS grows and is guided by accurate and truthful supervision, the viability and utility of Collective Learning Systems Theory as a powerful paradigm for signal processing will continue to evolve.

REFERENCES

[1] P. Bock, G. Becker, H. Holz, C. J. Kocinski, R. Rovner, "An Application of Collective Learning Systems Theory to an Adaptive Learning Image Analysis System: Project ALIAS", Proc. of the International Workshop Neuro Nimes 89 on Neural Networks and Their Applications, Nimes, France, Nov 1989.

[2] P. Bock, C. J. Kocinski, R. Rovner, "The Determination of a Fast Metric for Specifying the Spatial Complexity of Binary Images" (tbp).

[3] P. Bock, R. Rovner, C. J. Kocinski, "On the Transformation of Binary Images for the Extraction of Spatial Characteristics" (tbp).

[4] P. Bock, G. Becker, "A Design Tool for Modeling Large Networks of Simple Parallel Processors", with G. Becker, proceedings of the Nineteenth Annual Pittsburgh Conference on Modeling and Simulation, May 1988.

[5] P. Bock, "Observation of the Properties of a Collective Learning Stochastic Automaton", Proc. International Information Sciences Symp, Patras, Greece, Aug 76.

[6] P. Bock, "A Perspective on Artificial Intelligence: Learning to Learn", Annals of Operations Research, v16, Apr 88.

[7] P. Bock, "A Massively Parallel Architecture for Collective Learning Systems", Journal of the Latin American Society on Artificial Intelligence, Mar 88.

[8] P. Bock, "Proposed Performance Metrics and Behavioral Norms for Collective Learning Automata", Proc. International Symp New Directions in Computing, Trondheim, Norway, Aug 85.

[9] P. Bock, F. Weingard, and J. White, "A Universal Model for the Structure and Function of Collective Learning Systems", Proc. International Symp New Directions in Computing, Trondheim, Norway, Aug 85.

[10] S. Lakshmivarahan, Learning Algorithms Theory and Applications, Springer-Verlag, 1981.

[11] K. S. Narendra, Editor, "Special Issue on Learning Automata", Jour of Cybernetics and Info Sci, v1 #2-4, 1977.

[12] L. Ott, An Introduction to Statistical Methods and Data Analysis, Duxbury Press, 1984.

[13] R. Plourde, "A Progressive Compensation Policy for Collective Learning Automata", Masters Thesis under Professor Peter Bock for the Department of Electrical Engineering and Computer Science at the George Washington University, Washington DC, 1978.

[14] J. White, "A Modification Policy that Accelerates the Convergence of Collective Learning Systems' Optimality", Doctoral Dissertation under P. Bock, George Washington University, Washington DC, 1989.

Advanced Neural Computers / R. Eckmiller (Editor)

HOW CONNECTIONIST MODELS COULD IMPROVE MARKOV MODELS FOR SPEECH RECOGNITION

Hervé A. Bourlard

Philips Research Laboratory Brussels
Av. Van Becelaere 2, Box 8
B-1170 Brussels - Belgium.

Abstract

The statistical and sequential nature of the human speech production system makes speech recognition difficult. *Hidden Markov Models (HMM)* have provided a good representation of these characteristics of speech, and were a breakthrough in speech recognition research. However, the a priori choice of the model characteristics (e.g. statistical distributions), strong hypotheses and weak discriminative power limit HMM capabilities.

Recently, connectionist models, and more particularly *Multilayer Perceptrons (MLP)*, have been recognized as an alternative tool for pattern classification problems such as speech recognition. Their main advantages are their discrimination-based learning, their flexible architecture (which permits easy use of contextual inputs), their weak hypotheses (about statistical distributions) and their highly parallel architecture. Using the interpolative capabilities of the MLP, statistical pattern recognition can be performed over an undersampled pattern space [18] without many restrictive simplifying assumptions. However, connectionist models are not tailored for time sequential input (such as speech) and it is still impossible to recognize continuous speech with MLPs only. As an alternative, hybrid approaches exploiting the advantages of connectionist models while using HMM formalism to integrate over time and to segment continuous speech have been proposed. Such approaches are explained here; it is discussed under which conditions and to what extend these approaches could improve standard HMMs.

1. Introduction

Hidden Markov Models (HMM) [7] are widely used for automatic speech recognition and inherently incorporate the sequential and statistical character of the speech signal. However, their discriminant properties are weak if they are trained along the *Maximum Likelihood Estimate (MLE)* [5]. An algorithm based on another criterion, *Maximum Mutual Information (MMI)* [5] provides more discrimination but the mathematics become trickier, and many constraining assumptions must be made. Moreover, the a priori choice of the model characteristics (i.e. first-order HMM assumption, number of states, statistical distributions) limit HMM capabilities. Finally, the incorporation of acoustic or phonetic contextual information requires a complex HMM and a large (possibly prohibitive) storage capacity.

On the other hand, connectionist architectures, and more particularly *Multilayer Perceptrons (MLP)* [20], have recently been recognized as an alternative tool for pattern classification problems such as speech recognition. Their main advantages are their powerful discrimination-based learning, their flexible architecture (which permits easy use of contextual inputs), their weak hypotheses (about statistical distributions) and their highly parallel architecture. Using the interpolative capabilities of the MLP, statistical pattern recognition can be performed over an undersampled pattern space [18] without many restrictive simplifying assumptions. However, the temporal aspect remains difficult to handle with connectionist models and MLPs are generally restricted to classification of static inputs where no sequential processing is involved. Good results for isolated speech units (words or phonemes) have already been reported [2,10,19] where the patterns to be recognized are treated as a whole at the input of a network, e.g. in a fixed time window representing time-power spectra. However, this approach does not seem to be appropriate to the recognition of connected speech units. If the connections are supplied with delays, feedback loops can be added providing dynamic and implicit memory. Along this line, several authors [6,8,14,22] have proposed original architectures where the speech signal enters the network sequentially. These architectures have been proved useful in recognizing isolated speech units. However, in the framework of continuous speech recognition, it is still impossible to recognize a sentence in terms of sequence of speech units with MLPs only, which is very efficiently solved in the HMM approach by the well known *"Dynamic Time Warping"* algorithm [17]. As an alternative, hybrid approaches exploiting the advantages of connectionist models while preserving HMM formalism to integrate over time and to segment continuous speech have been proposed [1,11,12]. The purpose of this paper is to review such approaches and to discuss under which conditions and to what extend they could improve on standard HMMs.

2. Hidden Markov Models

In the *Hidden Markov Model (HMM)* formalism, the speech signal is supposed to be produced by a particular finite state automaton built up from a set of states $\mathcal{Q} = \{q_1, q_2, \ldots, q_K\}$ governed by statistical laws. In that case, each speech unit (e.g. each vocabulary word or each phoneme) is associated with a particular HMM made up of L states $q_\ell \in \mathcal{Q}$, with $\ell = 1, \ldots, L$, according to a predefined topology. A preprocessor extracts vectors of acoustic parameters from the speech waveform at regular intervals, typically every 10-ms. In this way, the speech signal is transformed into a sequence of acoustic vectors $X = \{x_1, x_2, \ldots, x_N\}$.

The training and recognition criteria are based on the *Maximum a Posteriori Probability (MAP)* $P(M_i|X)$ that the acoustic vector sequence X has been produced by M_i. If X is a sentence, M_i is the Markov model obtained by concatenating elementary HMMs corresponding to a particular sequence of words or phonemes. Using Bayes' rule, $P(M_i|X)$ can be written as

$$P(M_i|X) = \frac{P(X|M_i)\, P(M_i)}{P(X)} \quad . \tag{1}$$

During recognition, $P(X)$ is a constant as the model parameters are fixed. However, during training, this probability depends on the parameters of all possible models; that is made explicit by the notation $P(X|\lambda)$, where λ is the parameter set. Since the models are mutually exclusive, we have:

$$P(M_i|X,\lambda) = \frac{P(X|M_i,\lambda)\, P(M_i)}{P(X|M_i,\lambda)\, P(M_i) + \sum_{k\neq i} P(X|M_k,\lambda)\, P(M_k)} \quad . \tag{2}$$

where the summation extends over all model sequences. Maximization of $P(M_i|X,\lambda)$ as given by (2) is usually restricted to the subspace of the M_i parameters only, which leads to the *Maximum Likelihood Estimate (MLE)* criterion. If M_i stands for a sequence of word models, the a priori probability $P(M_i)$ is provided by a language model independently of the acoustic decoding [7]. If M_i stands for a sequence of HMM states, the priors $P(M_i)$ are fixed by the model topology. This "model by model" optimization allows important simplifications in the training algorithms by avoiding computation of all rival sequences but at the cost of a weak discriminative power.

On the other hand, maximization of $P(M_i|X,\lambda)$ with respect to the whole parameter space leads to discriminant models since it implies that the contribution of the correct model should be enhanced while that of the rival models should be reduced. This maximization has been shown equivalent to the *Maximum Mutual Information (MMI)* criterion; it provides more discrimination but the mathematics become trickier, and many constraining assumptions must be made.

Besides its weak discriminative power, MLE also suffers from further hypotheses which are reviewed now. Let q_ℓ^n denote the state q_ℓ observed at time $n \in [1, N]$. Events q_ℓ^n are mutually exclusive so that probability $P(X|M_i)$ can be written for any arbitrary n:

$$P(X|M_i) = \sum_{\ell=1}^{L} P(q_\ell^n, X|M_i) , \tag{3}$$

where $P(q_\ell^n, X|M_i)$ represents the probability that X is produced by M_i while associating x_n with state q_ℓ. Maximization of (3) can be performed by the forward-backward recurrences of the Baum-Welch algorithm [5]. However, it is sometimes preferred to replace the maximization of the actual MLE by a *Viterbi criterion* which is an approximation where only the most probable state sequence capable of producing X is taken into account. In that case, probability (3) is then approximated by:

$$\overline{P}(X|M_i) = \max_{\ell_1,\ldots,\ell_N} P(q_{\ell_1}^1, \ldots, q_{\ell_N}^N, X|M_i) . \tag{4}$$

In both cases (MLE and Viterbi), it can be shown that probabilities $P(X|M_i)$ and $P(M_i|X)$ can be expressed in terms of $p[q_\ell^n, x_n|Q_1^{n-1}, X_1^{n-1}, M_i]$, where X_k^n is the acoustic vector sequence $\{x_k, x_{k+1}, \ldots, x_n\}$ and Q_k^n a particular state sequence $\{q_{\ell_k}^k, \ldots, q_{\ell_n}^n\}$. In the following, only the Viterbi criterion will be considered. In that case, if we assume that HMMs are first order Markov chains (i.e. the influence of past states on the current state is restricted to the immediately preceding state alone), (4) can be computed by the following *Dynamic Programming (DP)* recurrences [17] of the Viterbi algorithm:

$$\overline{P}(q_\ell^n, X_1^n|M_i) = \max_k \left[\overline{P}(q_k^{n-1}, X_1^{n-1}|M_i)\, p(q_\ell^n, x_n|q_k^{n-1}, X_1^{n-1}, M_i)\right] . \tag{5}$$

In order to reduce the number of free parameters, a further necessary simplification is to assume that the acoustic vectors are not correlated. In that case, probability $p(q_\ell^n, x_n|q_k^{n-1}, X_1^{n-1})$ in (5) reduces to $p(q_\ell^n, x_n|q_k^{n-1})$ and are referred to as *local probabilities* (or also *emission on transition probabilities* in [7]). Also, those local probabilities are often split into a product of a *transition probability*, which is assumed independent of time and is denoted $p_{k\ell} = p(q_\ell|q_k)$, and an *emission probability* $p(x_n|q_\ell^n, q_k^{n-1})$ which is assumed dependent on the current state only and becomes then $p(x_n|q_\ell^n)$.

If the models are trained by using this formulation of the Viterbi algorithm, no discrimination is taken into account. Actually, the discrimination problem results from the fact that the training criterion is based on MLE and not on MAP which is the optimal criterion minimizing the decoding error rate at the word level. That issue was discussed in [16] and also in [1] where it was shown how to compute the MAPs $P(M_i|X)$ with a particular form of the Viterbi algorithm.

In conclusion, notwithstanding their undoubted efficiency, standard HMMs suffer from several weaknesses, namely:

- Poor discrimination due to the training algorithm which maximizes MLE instead of MAP.
- A priori choice of model topology and statistical distributions, e.g. assuming the the emission probabilities $p(x_n|q_\ell)$ associated with each state q_ℓ can be described as a multivariate Gaussian density or, more recently, as a mixture of multivariate Gaussian densities.
- Assumption that the state sequences are first-order Markov chains.
- No contextual information is taken into account and the possible correlation of the successive acoustic vectors is thus overlooked.

3. Connectionist models and time sequential inputs

The common property between HMM and connectionist models as *Multilayer Perceptrons (MLP)* [20] is their learning ability. However, the first advantage of MLPs is their discriminating power. It has indeed been proved that MLPs are able to approximate any kind of *nonlinear discriminant functions* [13]. In fact, by performing nonlinear and nonparametric regression, they extract input features that are relevant to classification without any assumption about the underlying statistical distributions. If the training set is large enough to determine the correct discriminant features, these connectionist models will exhibit "generalization" properties, i.e. they will be able to correctly classify unseen data. Another advantage of MLPs is their flexible architecture which permits to deal with contextual inputs and recurrences quite easily. However, connectionist formalism is not tailored for time sequential input patterns (like speech).

One popular way to attack the temporal pattern recognition problem is to turn it into a spatial recognition problem in which the entire input sequence to be recognized is stored in a buffer at the input of the MLP [10,19]. In that case, each speech unit of the lexicon is associated with a particular output unit of the MLP. However, this approach does not seem to be appropriate to the recognition of connected speech units or, in other words, to find the best explanation of an input pattern in terms of a sequence of output classes. Moreover, the buffer must be large enough to accommodate the longest possible input sequence, which increases the number of parameters and, consequently, the number of required training examples. Thus, the buffer model is not a viable solution to continuous speech recognition.

Recurrent networks have also been proposed for sequential processing and speech recognition. In [22], sequential processing is tackled with the an MLP where delayed selfloops are added to the hidden and output units. It can easily be observed that the system described in [6] is an alternative (even more general) implementation of this network. In both cases, feedback is easily implemented by extending the input field with an additional vector containing the hidden unit values generated by the preceding input. Another recurrent model was also proposed in [8] where output values are fed back to the inout field. Initially used as a production model, it can also be designed for the classification of sequential inputs and was shown equivalent [1] to a particular form of HMM. A solution halfway between the spatial input model and recurrent models has been proposed in [21] in which recurrent networks are approximated over a finite time period by a feedforward network where the loops are replaced by the explicit use of several preceding activation values.

All those models have been shown yielding good performance (sometimes better than HMMs) on short isolated speech units (like E-set). By their implicit dynamic, they include some kind of time warping effects or, at least, some integration over time. However, training and recognition of connected speech units are still impossible with MLPs only. From the training point of view, a very serious problem remains with training connectionist networks using supervised learning algorithm. Indeed, a target function has to be defined, which is difficult if the training is carried out on connected speech units where the segmentation is generally unknown. Even for training isolated units, there is no principled method for selecting the target function which is usually chosen as a linear ramping function [22]. That problem does not appear in the HMM approach where only the sequence of speech units must be available. From the recognition point of view, *Dynamic Time Warping (DTW)* [7,17] does not tackle the variability of speech pronunciation only, but is also an efficient tool for connected speech recognition and segmentation. This property seems to be difficult to achieve using a connectionist architecture only. Indeed, even assuming a perfect dynamical system taking the entire past into account, the output values would still represent the scores for states (or output classes) at the current time but would not give any idea about the underlying segmentation. Avoiding explicit DTW for a continuous speech recognition task remains thus a challenging problem (even for HMMs where the actual MLE is usually replaced by the Viterbi criterion). On the other hand, it is also questionable whether it is even desirable to replace the DTW algorithm, as this process is very effective, and also has efficient hardware implementations [15]. On the other hand, a neural net architecture, called the "Viterbi Net", that can implement a DTW decoder, has been defined in [12].

To circumvent those problems, an hybrid approach using MLP to estimate local probabilities of HMMs and DTW to integrate over time has been proposed in [1,2]. It is shown in the following how this approach allows us to overcome some of the HMM's drawbacks; but it is also discussed under which conditions and to what extend the proposed hybrid model could improve standard HMMs.

4. Hybrid approaches: HMM + MLP

Let q_k, with $k = 1, \ldots, K$, be the output units of an MLP associated with Q and let us assume that the training set consists in a labeled sequence of N acoustic vectors $\{x_1, x_2, \ldots, x_N\}$. At time t, the input pattern of the MLP is the acoustic vector x_t and is associated with a particular state (or class) q_k^t. In classification mode, the training of the MLP parameters is usually based on the minimization of the following *Mean Square criterion (MSE)*:

$$E = \frac{1}{2} \sum_{n=1}^{N} \sum_{k=1}^{K} [g_k(x_n) - d_k(x_n)]^2 \ , \tag{6}$$

where $g_k(x_n)$ represents the output value of unit k (associated with state q_k) given x_n at the input and $d_k(x_n)$ is the associated target value and is equal to $\delta_{k\ell}$ (Kronecker delta) if the input is known to belong to class q_ℓ. It has been shown in [1] that, if the MLP contains enough parameters and if the training does not get stuck at a local minimum, the optimal output values of the MLP are estimates of the probability distribution over classes conditioned on the input:

$$g_k^{opt}(x_n) = p(q_k|x_n) \ . \tag{7}$$

The outputs of the MLP approximate thus local a posteriori probabilities, which are known leading to the optimal classification; they are discriminant by nature and minimize the classification error rate. This conclusion has also been observed experimentally in [3] and was the necessary link between HMMs and the connectionist approach. Moreover, if $2c + 1$ frames are used as input to provide context to the network, the output values of the MLP were shown to be good estimates of

$$p(q_k|x_{n-c}, \ldots, x_{n+c}) \ . \tag{8}$$

In [1], it was shown possible to compute the global MAPs $P(M_i|X)$ given in (1) by a particular form of Viterbi algorithm using local probabilities as (8). However, while this helped frame performance, it hurt word performance [4]. This may be due (at least partly) to a mismatch between the relative frequency of classes in the training sets and the prior class probabilities forced by the topology of the Markov models.

Using Bayes' rule, the effect of the priors on the DTW may be prevented by dividing the activation values obtained at the output of the MLP by the prior class probabilities as estimated from the training set. In that case, instead of (8), we are now estimating (within a constant independent of the classes) probabilities like $p(x_{n-c}, \ldots, x_{n+c}|q_k)$ which can be used in (5) as local probabilities in a DP algorithm to estimate $P(X|M_i)$. This was shown leading to a small decrease in frame classification performance, but a large improvement in word recognition performance [4]. The main advantage of this approach is the possibility to extract more powerful emission probabilities (relying on contextual information) without particular assumptions about the underlying statistical distributions. It was shown in [4] that, provided some additional modifications (cross-validation, optimization of word transition costs, segmentation of training data), such an approach was yielding correct word recognition scores (on a 1000 word vocabulary, speaker dependent, continuous speech recognition task) at least as good and sometimes slightly better than standard HMMs. However, it is still difficult to reflect good frame performance at the word level and to improve significantly on standard HMMs. Of course, MLPs can make better frame level discriminations than simple statistical classifiers, because they can easily incorporate multiple sources of evidence (multiple frames, multiple features) without simplifying assumptions. However, what is overlooked now and may pose problems is that the DP recurrences (5) are no longer valid with that kind of local probabilities. It can be shown that it is impossible to get $P(X|M_i)$ simply by replacing standard local probabilities in (5) by those "contextual" probabilities. It is indeed important to keep in mind that DP recurrences of the Viterbi algorithm as (5) are valid only if *instantaneous* features appear on the left side of the conditional in the local probabilities. Another argument is to observe that, assuming independence of the acoustic vectors within a contextual window, the Viterbi algorithm does not restore the correct MLE if emission probabilities are estimated from the outputs of an MLP (even divided by the priors). Indeed, in that case, the probability to observe a sequence of acoustic vectors $\{x_1, x_2, \ldots, x_N\}$ on a particular HMM state q_k is estimated as:

$$\prod_{n=1}^{N} p(x_{n-c}, \ldots, x_n, \ldots, x_{n+c}|q_k) ,$$

where Bayes' rule has already been used to convert the MLP outputs into MLE probabilities. If independence is assumed, and if boundary effects (context extending before frame 1 or after frame N) are ignored, this becomes:

$$\prod_{n=1}^{N} \prod_{i=-c}^{c} p(x_{n+i}|q_k) = \prod_{n=1}^{N} [p(x_n|q_k)]^{2c+1} ,$$

where the latter probability is just the classical MLE solution, raised to the power $2c + 1$. Note that, in the case where dependencies exist between frames, the optimal exponential will be less than $2c+1$, down to a minimum of 1 for the case in which frames are completely dependent (e.g., same within a constant factor). This could also explain why it was necessary to increase word transition costs in [4] to get acceptable word recognition performance.

5. Another hybrid approach

As shown in the previous Section, it is not so easy to interface properly MLPs and HMMs to take advantage of what are believed to be the strong points of each of the two approaches while preserving the theory of HMMs and the optimality of DP. Another example of that problem is given in the case of recurrent neural networks where the output classifications may depend on several previous classifications. Indeed, while this may improve local performance, it is no longer equivalent to a first order Markov model, hence problems with standard DP.

Another approach, related to autoregressive HMMs [9], is to use the MLP as a nonlinear predictor [11]. The basic idea of this approach is to assume that, for each class q_k, the observation vectors are drawn from a particular autoregressive process described by a function F_k. During training, if the order of prediction is assumed to be p, the parameters of the functions F_k (each of them being associated with a particular q_k, $k = 1, \ldots, K$) are determined such as to minimize, for each acoustic vector x_n observed on q_k, the error

$$E = \sum_{k=1}^{K} \sum_{x_n \in q_k} \| \hat{x}_n - x_n \|^2 , \tag{9}$$

where

$$\hat{x}_n = F_k(X_{n-p}^{n-1}) , \text{ with } X_{n-p}^{n-1} = \{x_{n-p}, \ldots, x_{n-1}\} .$$

It can be shown that, if the prediction error $e_n = \hat{x}_n - x_n$ is assumed to be a Gaussian noise with zero mean and unity variance, minimization of E in (9) is equivalent to estimation of

$$\prod_{k=1}^{K} \prod_{x_n \in q_k} p\left(x_n | q_k^n, X_{n-p}^{n-1}\right) = \prod_{k=1}^{K} \prod_{x_n \in q_k} (2\pi)^{-d/2} \exp\left[-\frac{1}{2} \| x_n - F_k(X_{n-p}^{n-1}) \|^2\right], \quad (10)$$

if $x_n \in R^d$, which is perfectly compatible with the DP recurrences (5) and which is nothing else but a generalization of the standard emission probabilities taking the correlation of the acoustic vectors into account. In standard autoregressive models [9], $F_k(X_{n-p}^{n-1})$ is assumed to be a linear function ($\hat{x}_n = \sum_{i=1}^{p} a_{ki} x_{n-i}$). If an MLP with X_{n-p}^{n-1} at the input is trained to minimize e_n (where the desired output vector associated with X_{n-p}^{n-1} is x_n), $F_k(X_{n-p}^{n-1})$ is a nonlinear predictor and, consequently, (10) may be better estimated (but is still limited to a Gaussian distribution). In that case, each state q_k must be associated with a particular MLP. An alternative approach, as proposed in [11], is to have a single MLP with additional "control" input units coding the state q_k being considered. During DTW (for training or recognition), the local distance associated with class q_k at time n is simply the Euclidian distance between x_n and its predictor $F_k(X_{n-p}^{n-1})$, and minimization of the accumulated distance is equivalent to maximization of $P(X|M_i)$ as in (5).

Using the results presented in Section 4 (in classification mode, MLP's outputs are estimates of the a posteriori probabilities), it is possible to generalize the former approach and to avoid the Gaussian hypothesis. It is indeed easy to prove (by using Bayes' rule with an additional conditional X_{n-p}^{n-1} everywhere) that:

$$p(x_n | q_k^n, X_{n-p}^{n-1}) = \frac{p(q_k^n | X_{n-p}^{n})\, p(x_n | X_{n-p}^{n-1})}{p(q_k^n | X_{n-p}^{n-1})}. \quad (10)$$

As $p(x_n | X_{n-p}^{n-1})$ in (10) is independent of the classes q_k it can overlooked in the DP recurrences (5). Based on (7), it is then interesting to observe that, without any assumption about mean and covariance of the driving noise, the same correlated local probabilities $p(x_n | q_k^n, X_{n-p}^{n-1})$ can be expressed as the ratio of the output values of two "standard" MLPs (as used in Section 4), respectively with X_{n-p}^{n-1} and X_{n-p}^{n} as input, and trained according to (6). This approach is currently under investigation and could throw new light on the previous attempts to incorporate time correlation between successive observations in HMMs [23].

6. Conclusions

In conclusion, we can say that MLPs have attractive properties for speech recognition problems. However, simple feedforward networks are not tailored for sequential and time-varying input patterns. While recurrent networks seem to be better suited to temporal domains, they are still unable to deal with connected speech recognition problems. The alternative solution is to consider hybrid approaches where MLPs are used to improve standard HMMs, taking advantage of what are believed to be the strong points of each of the two approaches. Indeed, while HMMs have very nice time-alignment capabilities, MLPs could contribute to the improvement of HMM approaches by providing them with potential solutions to the problems of poor discrimination, a priori choice of probability density functions and correlation of successive acoustic events. Such an approach has already been shown yielding word recognition performance at least as good and sometimes slightly better than standard HMMs [4]. However, it is still difficult to improve significantly on standard HMMs. As shown in this paper, this problem could be due to the difficulty to interface properly MLPs with HMMs. An potential solution to that problem could be to use MLPs as nonlinear predictor [11]. Although this method is quite attractive, it is still under investigation.

Thus, for the moment, connectionist models have not yet proved definitive superiority versus standard approaches and further work will be required before we can conclude that there is any real advantage to using connectionist models for continuous speech recognition.

References

[1] Bourlard, H., & Wellekens, C.J. (1988). Links between Markov Models and Multilayer Perceptrons, *Advances in Neural Information Processing 1*, Ed. D. Touretzky, Morgan Kaufmann, pp. 502-510.

[2] Bourlard, H., & Wellekens, C.J. (1989). Speech Pattern Discrimination and Multilayer Perceptrons, *Computer, Speech and Language*, **3**, pp. 1-19.

[3] Bourlard, H., Morgan, N., & Wellekens, C.J. (1989). Statistical Inference in Multilayer Perceptrons and Hidden Markov Models with Applications in Continuous Speech Recognition, to appear in *Neuro Computing, Algorithm, Architectures and Applications*, NATO ASI Series.

[4] Bourlard, H. & Morgan, N. (1989). A Continuous Speech Recognition System Embedding MLP into HMM, to appear in *Proc. of the Neural Information Processing Systems Conference*, Denver, CO.

[5] Brown, P. (1987). *The Acoustic-Modeling Problem in Automatic Speech Recognition*, Ph.D. Thesis, Comp. Sc. Dep., CMU.

[6] Elman, J.L. (1988). Finding Structure in Time, *CRL Tech, UCSD, Tech. Report.*

[7] Jelinek, F. (1976). Continuous Speech Recognition by Statistical Methods, *Proceedings of the IEEE*, vol. 64, no. 4, pp. 532-555.

[8] Jordan, M.L. (1986). Serial Order: A Parallel Distributed Processing Approach, *UCSD, Tech. Report 8604.*

[9] Juang, B.H. & Rabiner, L.R. (1985). Mixture Autoregressive Hidden Markov Models for Speech Signals, *IEEE Trans. on ASSP*, vol. 33, no. 6, pp. 1404-1412.

[10] Landauer, T.K., Kamm, C.A., & Singhal, S. (1987). Teaching a minimally structured back propagation network to recognize speech, *Proc. of the Ninth Annual Conference of the Cognitive Science Society*, pp. 531-536.

[11] Levin E. (1990). Speech recognition using hidden control neural network architecture, *Proc. of the IEEE Int. Conf. on ASSP*, New Mexico.

[12] Lippmann, R.P., & Gold, B. (1987). Neural Classifiers Useful for Speech Recognition, *First Int. Conf. Neural Networks*, pp. IV-417, San Diego, CA.

[13] Lippmann, R.P. (1987). An Introduction to Computing with Neural Nets, *IEEE ASSP Magazine*, **3**, pp. 4-22.

[14] Mozer, M.C. (1988). A Focused Back-Propagation Algorithm for Temporal Pattern Recognition, *University of Toronto, Tech. Report CRG-TR-88-3.*

[15] Murveit, H., & Brodersen, R.W. (1986). An Integrated-Circuit-Based Speech Recognition System, *IEEE Trans. ASSP*, vol. 34, no.6, pp. 1465-1472.

[16] Nadas, A., Nahamoo, D. & Picheny M.A. (1988). On a Model-Robust Training Method for Speech Recognition, *IEEE Trans. on ASSP*, vol. 35, no.9, pp. 1432-1436.

[17] Ney, H. (1984). The use of one-stage dynamic programming algorithm for connected word recognition, *IEEE Trans. on ASSP*, vol. 32, pp. 263-272.

[18] Niles, L., Silverman, H., Tajchman, G. & Bush, M. (1989). How Limited Training Data Can Allow a Neural Network Classifier to Outperform an 'Optimal' Statistical Classifier, *Proc. IEEE Int. Conf. on ASSP*, Vol. 1, pp. 17-20, Glasgow, Scotland.

[19] Peeling, S.M., & Moore, R.K. (1988). Isolated digit recognition experiments using the multi-layer perceptron. *Speech Communication*, **7**, pp. 403-409.

[20] Rumelhart, D.E., Hinton, G.E., & Williams R.J. (1986). Learning Internal Representations by Error Propagation, *Parallel Distributed Processing. Exploration of the Microstructure of Cognition. vol. 1: Foundations*, Ed. D.E.Rumelhart & J.L.McClelland. MIT Press.

[21] Waibel, A., Hanazawa, T., Hinton, G., Shikano, K., & Lang, K. (1988). Phoneme recognition Using Time-Delay Neural Networks, *Proc. IEEE Int. Conf. on ASSP*, New York.

[22] Watrous, R.L., & Shastri, L. (1987). Learning Phonetic Features Using Connectionist Networks: an Experiment in Speech Recognition, *1st Int. Conf. Neural Networks*, pp. IV-381-388, San Diego, CA, 1987.

[23] Wellekens, C.J. (1987). Explicit Time Correlation in Hidden Markov Models for Speech recognition", *Proc. of the IEEE Int. Conf. on ASSP*, pp. 384-386, Tokyo, Japan.

Advanced Neural Computers / R. Eckmiller (Editor)

AN ALGEBRAIC APPROACH TO BOOLEAN FEEDFORWARD NETWORKS

Wolfram Büttner

Siemens AG, Corporate Research and Development
D-8000 Munich, F. R. Germany

ABSTRACT

A layered boolean feedforward network N classifies input with respect to containment in certain regions, also called classes, of the input space $\mathbb{R}^n$.

By placing a sufficiently large number m of basic geometrical objects H_i - typically halfspaces - in $\mathbb{R}^n$ the first hidden layer L_1 of N generates a decomposition of $\mathbb{R}^n$ into cells. It thereby assigns to an input x a binary address, segm x, describing the position of x with respect to H_i $(1 \leq i \leq m)$. False classification occurs if x, y belong to different classes but obtain the same address, or if x, y are in the same class and obtain different addresses. Only errors of the first type will be tolerated. These are caused by L_1. It is the role of subsequent layers L_i $(i > 1)$ to correct errors of the second type by implementing suitable boolean mappings $\Pi_i := (\Pi_{i1,} \ldots, \Pi_{ir_i})$ from the r_{i-1}-dimensional state vectors of L_{i-1} to the r_i-dimensional state vectors of L_i.

We will show that $(\Pi_i \circ \ldots \Pi_2 \circ \mathrm{segm})(x)$ is the address of input x with respect to 'new' geometrical objects $H_s^{(i)} := (\Pi_{i_s} \circ \Pi_{i-1} \ldots \circ \Pi_2)(H_1, \ldots, H_m)$ $(1 \leq s \leq r_i)$ $(1 \leq t \leq m)$. Here boolean operators in Π_i are interpreted as set operations. Classification is achieved at level i_0 iff classes arise as subsets of cells with respect to the basic geometrical objects $H_s^{(i0)}$ $(1 \leq s \leq r_{i_0})$. This result provides a geometrical semantics of the layered activity of the net.

In order to suppress errors of the first type m might have to be chosen quite large. Therefore the task of computing the map class = $(\Pi_i \circ \ldots \circ \Pi_2)$ is closely related to logic minimization and hence computationally complex.

In the worst case this complexity is linear in the number of cells generated by L_1. This may still be too large. However, when the classification focusses on restricted 'interesting' regions of the input space the problem turns out to be tractable. With an example we provide evidence for the claim that learning the mapping class will be best achieved by specialized logic minimization techniques.

1 INTRODUCTION

Generally, the role of a specific subset of neurons for the task performed by a neural network is quite mysterious. More is known about the functioning of the various layers L_i $(1 \leq i \leq i_0)$ of a feedforward net N of boolean neurons.

A network N implements a mapping $\Pi_N : \mathbb{R}^n \rightarrow \{0, 1\}^r$. N thereby induces a finite partition of $\mathbb{R}^n$ via preimages i. e. $\mathbb{R}^n = \bigcup_{0 \in \mathrm{im}\Pi_N} \Pi_N^{-1}(0)$.

Conversely, assume we are given a criterion which groups every vector into one out of r disjoint classes. Given a test sample we then wish to find a suitable feedforward network N of boolean neurons such that with high probability each class is contained in a preimage of Π_N.

In order to achieve this classification of test data, essentially two tasks 2 (1) must be solved: Input vectors belonging to the same (different) class(es) must be mapped by Π_N to the same (different) output(s).

Task 1 is the job of the first hidden layer L_1. Each neuron t in L_1 ($1 \leq t \leq m$) is capable of making a hard decision about containment of an input x in a basic geometrical object H_t. For standard boolean neurons which sum up weighted input and compare this sum with a threshold, the geometrical objects are halfspaces. But we might as well replace the weighted sum by the defining equation of, say, a circle and use the neuron to test an input for containment in this circle.

In any case L_1 assigns to an input x a binary vector of length m - its address segm(x). The i-th component of segm(x) equals 1 iff x is contained in H_i. Hence every address corresponds to a cell, i. e., an m-fold intersection of H_i, $\mathbb{R}^n \backslash H_i$ respectively.

For r classes one often chooses $t = \frac{r \cdot (r-1)}{2}$. On the basis of earlier results by Schläfli [1], Makhoul et al. [2] have shown that the number of cells dramatically increases with t.

Task 1 is achieved if for testpattern $x \neq y$ we have segm(x) $\neq$ segm(y). There is a variety of approaches to solving this task, among these are the fast linear programming techniques as suggested by Strobach [3].

In this paper we will be concerned mainly with task 2. Errors of type 1 (corresponding to task 1) cannot be corrected by subsequent layers. It is the role of layers $L_2, \ldots, L_{i_0}$ to 'repair' errors of type 2.

In Section 2 we will define the basic algebraic machinery needed later on.

As an immediate consequence we obtain in Section 3 an algebraic characterization of the various actions performed by the network:

Every layer L_i ($i > 1$) implements a boolean mapping $\Pi_i := (\Pi_{i_1}, \ldots, \Pi_{ir_i})$ from the set of state vectors of L_{i-1} to the set of state vectors of L_i. Interpreting the boolean operations $+ . \cdot, -, 0, 1$ in Π_i as union, intersection, complementation, empty set, $\mathbb{R}^n$ respectively the boolean expressions $H_s^{(i)} := (\Pi_{i_s} \circ \Pi_{i-1} \ldots \circ \Pi_2)\ (H_i), \ldots, H_m)$ ($1 \leq s \leq r_i$) specify subsets of $\mathbb{R}^n$.

We then have: $(\Pi_i \circ \ldots \circ \Pi_2 \circ \mathrm{segm})(x)$, the state vector of layer i with x at the input, is the address of x with respect to the 'new' geometrical building blocks $H_s^{(i)}$. Classification is achieved at level i_0 iff classes arise as subsets of cells with respect to $H_s^{(i_0)}$ ($1 \leq s \leq r_{i_0}$).

This characterization holds as well for layered feedforward networks of neurons with continuous output ranging over [0, 1].

Here the j-th component of $(\Pi_i \circ \ldots \circ \Pi_2 \circ \mathrm{segm})(x)$ measures whether the input x is contained in the interior of $H_j^{(i)}$, outside of $H_j^{(i)}$ or near the boundary of $H_j^{(i)}$.

Section 4 relates task 2 to logic minimization. How can we represent and compute a boolean mapping class $:= \Pi_i \circ \ldots \circ \Pi_2$ which depends on a very large number t of

boolean variables ? A 20-class-problem for example requires at least
$t := 190\ (= \frac{20 \cdot 19}{2})$ neurons in layer 1.

Let p be the number of all cells which will be considered in the recognition phase. p may be a small fraction of the number of all cells generated by L_1. We will show that in the worst case task 2 requires up to p computations, However if classes are not too small, much less effort is required. It is not the aim of this paper to discuss the quite elaborate techniques developed in the field of logic minimization.
We use an example to provide evidence for the claim that learning the mapping class will be best achieved with specialized logic miminization techniques.

Although we will provide the basic algebraic framework a certain familiarity with algebraic reasoning will be required. Proofs will only be sketched.

2 AN ALGEBRAIC FRAMEWORK FOR BOOLEAN FEEDFORWARD NETWORKS

Let $X_1, ..., X_s$ be subsets of $\mathbb{R}^n$. By finitely often applying the set operations $\cup$, $\cap$, $\mathbb{C}$, $\emptyset$, $\mathbb{R}^n$ to $X_1, ..., X_s$ we obtain a finite set algebra $M(X_1, ..., X_s)$. Every element in this algebra can be written as a boolean combination of the generators X_i, but alternative building blocks exist.

Def. 2.1

An element a of a boolean algebra A with operators $+, \cdot, -, 0, 1$ is an atom if $0 \neq a = x + y$ implies $x, y \in \{0, a\}$

The atoms in $M(X_1, ..., X_s)$ are all nonempty sets taking the form $f(X_1) \cap ... \cap f(X_s)$ where $f(X_i) \in \{X_i, \mathbb{C}(X_i)\}$. Atoms in set algebras will also be called real cells. Every element in $M(X_1, ..., X_s)$ can be written uniquely as a union of all real cells contained in this element. The following examples show some of the phenomena occuring in these algebras.

Ex. 2.2

a) Let $n = 2$ and $X_1 = \{(x, y) \mid x \geq 0\}$, $X_2 = \{(x, y) \mid y \geq 0\}$
Then $M(X_1, X_2)$ contains 2^{2^2} elements and the real cells are the 4 quadrants.

b) Let $M(X_1, X_2, X_3, X_4, X_5)$ be the set algebra defined in Fig. 1
There are "closed" real cells a_1, a_2, a_3, a_4, a_5, a_6, "open" real cells as a_7, a_8, and imaginary cells. Imaginary cells take the general form of cells but evaluate to the empty set if intersection is performed.
$X_1 \cap \mathbb{C}(X_2) \cap X_3 \cap \mathbb{C}(X_4) \cap X_5$ is an imaginary cell.

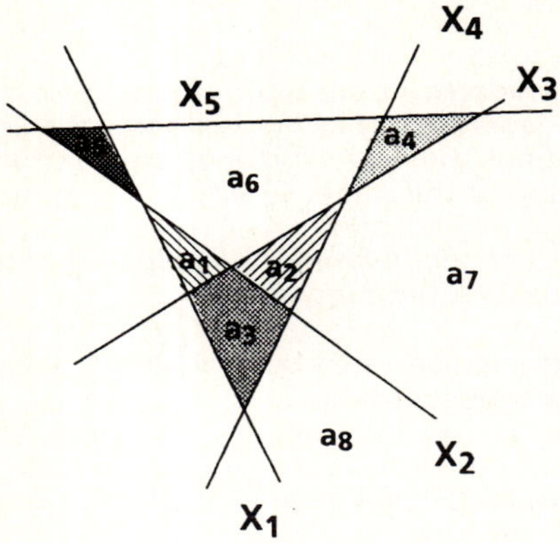

$adr(a_1) = (0, 1, 0, 0, 0)$
$adr(a_2) = (0, 0, 1, 0, 0)$
$adr(a_3) = (0, 1, 1, 0, 0)$
$adr(a_4) = (0, 0, 0, 1, 0)$
$adr(a_5) = (1, 0, 0, 0, 0,$
$adr(a_6) = (0, 0, 0, 0, 0)$
$adr(a_7) = (0, 0, 1, 1, 0)$
$adr(a_8) = (0, 1, 1, 1, 0)$
$cl_1 = a_1 \cup a_2 \quad cl_2 = a_3 \cup a_4 \cup a_5$

Fig. 1 The set algebra generated by 5 halfplanes

Cells (i. e. real or imaginary cells) can be represented by binary vectors (s. Fig. 1).

Def. 2.3

For every cell c in $M(X_1, ..., X_s)$ the address - adr(c) - is the unique binary vector of length s whose i-th component equals 1 iff $c \subseteq X_i$.

We have listed in Fig. 1 the addresses of 8 real cells of the set algebra defined there. (1, 0, 1, 0, 1) ist the address of an imaginary cell.

In the following we will inspect the relation between geometrical objects and boolean functions.
We will need some basic results from boolean algebra which will be applied to networks in the next section.

Lemma 2.4

Let $M(x_1, ..., x_s)$ be the set of all s-ary functions with arguments and values in {0, 1}. Furthermore we set $x + y := \max\{x, y\}$, $x \cdot y := \min\{x, y\}$, $\bar{x} := 1 - x$ and extend these operations to $M(x_1, ..., x_s)$. Then the following holds:

i) $M(x_1, ..., x_s)$ equipped with +, ·, - and constants 0, 1 is the free boolean algebra in s generators.
ii) Let $S \subseteq \{0, 1\}^s$ and $M_S(x_1, ..., x_s) := \{f \in M(x_1, ..., x_s) \mid f(a_1, ..., a_s) = 0$ for $(a_1, ..., a_s) \notin S\}$. $M_S(x_1, ..., x_s)$ is a boolean algebra if +, ·, -, 0, 1 are suitably modified.

Via $M_S(x_1, ..., x_s)$ we can deal with partially defined functions.
The following proposition will be useful.

Proposition 2.5

Let A, B be finite boolean algebras with operators +, ·, -, 0, 1 and let At(A), At(B) be the set of atoms of A, B respectively. Then the following holds:
Every surjection f: At(A) → At(B) ∪ {0} with $f(a) \cdot f(b) = 0$ for $a \neq b$ and $\sum_{a \in At(A)} f(a) = 1$ uniquely extends to a homomorphism from A onto B.

From proposition 2.5 we obtain the following lemma.

Lemma 2.6

For $a = (a_1, \dots, a_s) \in \{0,1\}^s$ and sets $X_1, \dots, X_s \subseteq \mathbb{R}^n$ we let $X^a := X_1^{a_1} \cap \dots \cap X_s^{a_s}$ where $X_i^{a_i} = \begin{cases} X_i & \text{for } a_i = 1 \\ CX_i & \text{for } a_i = 0. \end{cases}$

Let concr : $\{0,1\}^s \to M(X_1, \dots, X_s)$ be defined as concr$(a) := X^a$.

i) The homomorphic extension of concr defined by concr $(f(x_1, \dots, x_r) = f(X_1, \dots, X_r)$ for $f \in M(x_1, \dots, x_r)$ establishes a surjective homomorphism concr: $M(x_1, \dots, x_s) \to M(X_1, \dots, X_s)$.
ii) concr $(x_i) = X_i$
iii) ker (concr) = {imaginary cells in $M(X_1, \dots, X_s)$}
iv) For $S = \{0,1\}^s \setminus$ {addresses of imaginary cells} we have $M_S(x_1, \dots, x_s) \simeq$ concr $(M_S(x_1, \dots, x_s)) = M(X_1, \dots, X_s)$.
v) Every mapping $\Pi : \{0,1\}^r \to \{0,1\}^s$ extends to a homomorphism, also called Π, from $M(x_1, \dots, x_r)$ to $M(y_1, \dots y_s)$.
The assignment $\hat{\Pi}$ $(f(X_1, \dots, X_r) :=$ concr $(\Pi\ (f(x_1, \dots, x_r)))$ defines a homomorphism $\hat{\Pi} : M(X_1, \dots, X_r) \to M(Y_1, \dots, Y_r)$.

3 A GEOMETRICAL SEMANTICS OF LAYERED NETWORK ACTIVITY

Let L_i be i-th layer of the network N introduced in section 1. We wish to geometrically interpret state vectors ($\in \{0,1\}^{r_i}$) of L_i. This is straightforward for L_1. For input x the associated state vector segm(x) specifies the position of x with respect to halfspaces $H_k^{(1)}$ $(1 \le k \le r_1)$.

In the following we will provide a recursion for computing $H_l^{(i)}$ from the basic geometrical objects $H_k^{(1)}$ and from the mappings $\Pi_i : \{0,1\}^{r_{i-1}} \to \{0,1\}^{r_i}$ implemented by N.

We assume that we have already computed sets $H_j^{(i-1)}$ $(1 \le j \le r_{i-1})$ such that $\{0,1\}^{r_{i-1}}$ equals the set of addresses of the cells of M $(H_1^{(i-1)}, \dots, H_{r_{i-1}}^{(i-1)})$. Let Π_i have components $\Pi_{i1}, \dots, \Pi_{ir_i}$. For $a \in \{0,1\}^{r_{i-1}}$ we denote by $a \in \Pi_{ij}$ the fact that the atom a is contained in the atomic decompositon of Π_{ij}, i. e. $\Pi_{ij}(a) = 1$.

Recall from Lemma 2.5 that for $a = (a_{1r}, \dots, a_{r_{i-1}}) \in \{0,1\}^{r_{i-1}}$ the expression $(H^{(i-1)})^a$ stands for the set $(H_1^{(i-1)})^{a_1} \cap \dots (H_{r_{i-1}}^{(i-1)})^{a_{r_{i-1}}}$ where $(H_j^{(i-1)})^{a_j} = \begin{cases} H_j^{(i-1)} & \text{for } a_j = 1 \\ CH_j^{(i-1)} & \text{for } a_j = 0. \end{cases}$

We claim that the appropriate geometrical objects associated with layer L_i are the sets $H_t^{(i)} := \bigcup_{a \in \Pi_{it}} (H^{(i-1)})^a$ $(1 \le t \le r_i)$.

For $\alpha \in \{0,1\}^{r_{i-1}}$ we then have to show that $(H^{i-1})^\alpha \subseteq$ concr $(\Pi_i(\alpha))$ i. e. the cell with address α on the (i-1)st level is contained in the cell with address $\Pi_i(\alpha)$ on level i.

From lemma 2.5 we derive concr $(\Pi_i(\alpha)) = (\bigcup_{a \in \Pi_{it}} (H^{(i-1)})^a)^{\Pi_{i1}(\alpha)} \cap \dots \cap (\bigcup_{a \in \Pi_{ir_i}} (H^{(i-1)})^a)^{\Pi_{ir_i}(\alpha)}$.

Hence $(H^{(i-1)})^\alpha$, i. e. the cell with address α on level i is contained in $(\bigcup_{a \in \Pi_{it}} (H^{(i-1)})^a)^{\Pi_{it}(\alpha)}$ $(1 \le t \le r_i)$.

This settles the claim and by computing the recursion we have proven the following theorem:

Theorem 3.1

Let N be a layered feedforward network of boolean neurons and let L_i ($1 \le i \le k$) be the i-th layer of N of size r_i. $\Pi_i := (\Pi_{i1}, \dots, \Pi_{ir_i})$ with $\Pi_{ij} : \{0, 1\}^{r_{i-1}} \to \{0, 1\}$ denotes the boolean mapping between i-1-th and i-th layer implemented by N.
Assume that $\{0, 1\}^{r_1}$ equals the set of addresses of all cells in $M(H_1^{(i)}, \dots, H_{r_1}^{(i)})$.
Then $\{0, 1\}^{r_i}$ ($i \ge 2$) equals the set of addresses of all cells in $M(H_1^{(i)}, \dots, H_{r_1}^{(i)})$
where $H_t^{(i)} = \Pi_{it} \circ \Pi_{i-1} \circ \dots \circ \Pi_2 (H_1^{(i)}, \dots, H_{r_1}^{(i)})$.

Note that the geometrical objects H'_t are contained in the set algebra $M(H_1^{(i)}, \dots, H_{r_1}^{(i)})$. This is due to the fact that Π_2 (similarly for Π_i ($i > 2$)) performs set operations on $H_1^{(i)}, \dots, H_{r_1}^{(i)}$ and therefore produces elements in $M(H_1^{(1)}, \dots, H_{r_1}^{(1)})$ which are more complex than the basic building blocks $H_j^{(1)}$.

Fig. 2, 3 illustrate Theorem 3.1.

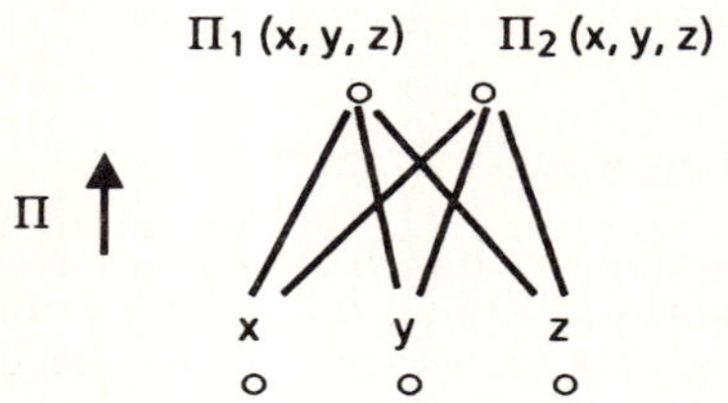

$$\Pi_1 (x, y, z) = x \cdot \overline{y}$$

$$\Pi_2 (x, y, z) = y \cdot \overline{z}$$

Fig. 2 A boolean mapping Π between adjacent layers

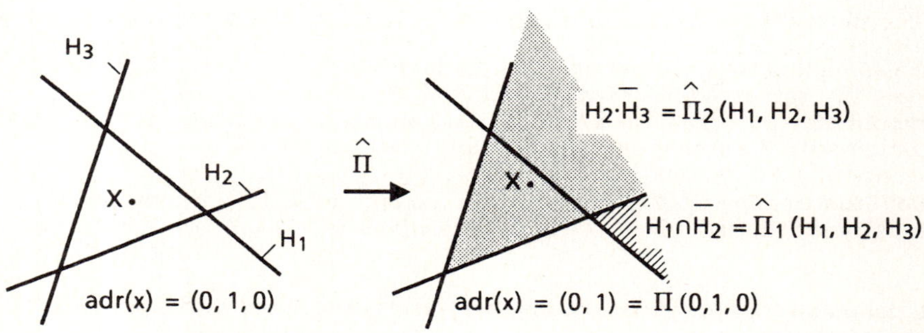

Fig. 3 Geometrical interpretation of Π

4 LEARNING IN BOOLEAN FEEDFORWARD NETWORKS

In this section we assume that the neurons of the first layer haven chosen their thresholds and weights and thereby compute a mapping segm: $\mathbb{R}^n \to \{0, 1\}^m$. This process defines basic geometric objects $H_1, \dots, H_m$. There are 2 reasons for potential false classification of given testpatterns.

1 - patterns x, y belong to different classes, but segm(x) = segm(y)
2 - patterns x, y are from the same class, but segm(x) $\neq$ segm(y).

Errors of type 1 cannot be 'repaired' on subsequent layers. However, errors of type 2 can be suppressed. We require that the boolean mapping class : $\{0, 1\}^m \to \{0, 1\}^r$ ($r := \#$ {classes}) achieves complete suppression of errors of type 2. Apparently, the question of learning the map class from examples is independent from learning the map segm.

Assume that classification focusses on a certain 'interesting' region R of $\mathbb{R}^n$ containing $p = 2^q-1$ cells of $M(H_1, \ldots, H_m)$. All testpattern are supposed to be elements of R.
The 2-power requirement is no severe restriction, since given a number of cells we may always add cells in order to achive $p = 2^q-1$. The map class is only partially specified by testpattern. In order to reduce the potentially large number m of variables of class, we introduce two auxiliary mappings compr(ession) : $\{0, 1\}^m \rightarrow \{0, 1\}^q$ and class* : $\{0, 1\}^q \rightarrow \{0, 1\}^r$ with the following properties:

$$\text{compr} \mid \{\text{addresses of cells in R}\} \text{ is a bijection onto } \{0,1\}^q \setminus \overbrace{(0, \ldots 0)}^{q}.$$

$$\text{compr(a)} = \overbrace{(0, \ldots 0)}^{q} \text{ for all addresses of cells outside R.}$$

$$\text{class* (compr(a))} = \begin{cases} \text{class (a)} & \text{if a is the address of a cell containing a testpattern} \\ \overbrace{(0, \ldots 0)}^{r} & \text{if the cell with address a contains no testpattern.} \end{cases}$$

class* ∘ compr agrees with class on the testpattern and is taken as approximation of class.
Computing class* and compr under various restrictions is called logic minimization. We will demonstrate with a 5-dimensional example that class can be learned rapidly with techniques from this field.

Ex. 4.1

We consider the cell decomposition of Fig. 1. There we have 5 'interesting' cells a_1, a_2, a_3, a_4, a_5 grouped in 2 classes $cl_1 = a_1 \cup a_2$ and $cl_2 = a_3 \cup a_4 \cup a_5$. We add 3 further auxiliary cells a_6, a_7, a_8

and let $R = \bigcup_{i=1}^{8} a_i$.

We approximate class : $\{\text{adr}(-a_i) \mid 1 \leq i \leq 5\} \rightarrow \{0, 1\}^2$ by class* ∘ compr.
We set compr: $a_1 \rightarrow (1,1,1)$, $a_2 \rightarrow (1,1,0)$, $a_3 \rightarrow (0,1,1)$, $a_4 \rightarrow (0,1,0)$,
$a_5 \rightarrow (0,0,1)$, $a_6 \rightarrow (1,0,1)$, $a_7 \rightarrow (1,0,0)$, $a_8 \rightarrow (0,0,0)$
$a \rightarrow (0,0,0)$ for every address a of a cell outside of R.

and let class* $(a, b, c) = (a \cdot f_1(b, c), \ \overline{a} \cdot f_2(b, c))$.

The tree

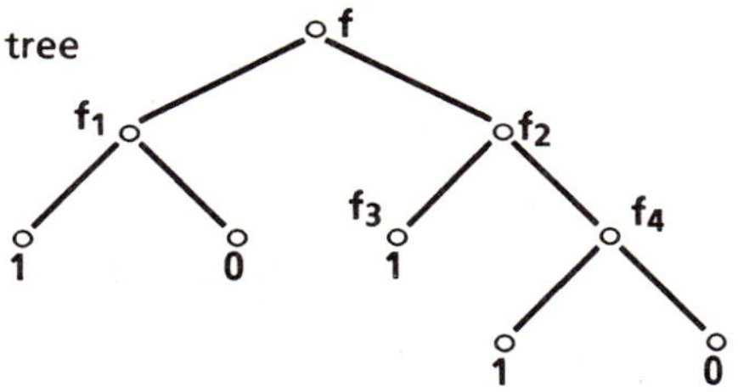

recursively defines functions on 3, 2, 1 variables respectively: $f(a, b, c) = a \cdot f_1(b, c) + \overline{a} \cdot f_2(b, c)$, $f_1(1, c) = 1$, $f_1(0, c) = 0$

$$f_2(b, c) = b \cdot f_3(c) + \overline{b} \cdot f_4(c)$$

$$f_3(1) = f_3(0) = 1, \ f_4(1) = 1, f_4(0) = 0.$$

Obviously these computations can quite well be done on sequential computers.

If a neural net would do the task, it has to compute 2 output functions depending on m variables (m = 5 in the example). In order to obtain weights and thresholds the net must compute these functions symbolically. Such a task may require effort exponential in m. This computational burden is avoided in the approach as sketched in Ex. 4.1.

5 CONCLUSIONS

We have given a geometrical interpretation of state vectors for an arbitrary layer of a layererd feedforward network. This naturally extends the interpretation of the states of the first hidden layer as positional descriptions with respect to certain geometrical building blocks. We then split the task of learning the mapping that is defined by a classification problem in 2 independent learning of the mappings, segm(entation) and class(ification). Learning class is closely related to logic minimization. We argue that techniques emerging from this field are well suited to achieve the learning task.

6 REFERENCES

[1] L. Schäfli (1814-1895), Gesammelte Mathematische Abhandlungen, Vol. 1, Birkhäusser-Verlag, Basel, 1950.

[2] J. Makhoul, R. Schwartz and A. El Jaroudi, "Classification, capabilities of two-layer neural networks", in Proc. ICASSP-89, pp. 635-638, Glasgow, Scotland, May 1989.

[3] P. Strobach, "A neural network with Boolean output layer", in Proc. ICASSP-90, Albuquerque, NM, April 1990

7 ACKNOWLEDGEMENTS

The author wishes to thank his colleague Peter Strobach for his helpful suggestions and stimulating discussions.

Advanced Neural Computers / R. Eckmiller (Editor)

ALPHANUMERIC CHARACTER RECOGNITION BY THE NEOCOGNITRON

Kunihiko FUKUSHIMA and **Nobuaki WAKE**

Department of Biophysical Engineering, Faculty of Engineering Science
Osaka University
Toyonaka, Osaka 560, Japan

A neural network model of visual pattern recognition, called the "neocognitron", was previously proposed by the author. It is capable of deformation-invariant visual pattern recognition. In this paper, we discuss a pattern-recognition system which works with the mechanism of the neocognitron. The system has been trained to recognize thirty-five handwritten alphanumeric characters. The ability to correctly recognize deformed characters depends highly on the choice of the training pattern set. This paper offers some techniques for selecting training patterns useful for deformation-invariant recognition of a large number of characters.

1. INTRODUCTION

A neural network model for visual pattern recognition called the "neocognitron" has been previously proposed by the author [1]-[3]. It is capable of deformation-invariant visual pattern recognition. The neocognitron is a hierarchical network consisting of many layers of neuron-like cells. There are forward connections between cells in adjoining layers. Some of these connections are variable, and can be modified by learning. The neocognitron can acquire the ability to recognize patterns by learning, and can be trained to recognize any set of patterns. After learning, it can recognize input patterns lobustly, with little effect from deformation, changes in size, or shifts in position.

The ability of the neocognitron has already been demonstrated in various experiments. As an example, the author and his group constructed a pattern recognition system with the mechanism of the neocognitron. The system was trained to recognize handwritten numerals, and operates on several kinds of computers: from microcomputers to parallel computers [3]-[5].

There were only ten numeric characters that were recognized by the above system. In order to show that the neocognitron works well when the categories of recognized patterns is large in number, we have expanded the scale of the previous system, and constructed a new system [6]. The new system has been trained to recognize not only numeric characters but also alphanumeric characters for a total of thirty five characters (where the alphabetic character O and numeral 0 are treated as the same pattern). Although the number of characters to be recognized is increased by a facter of 3.5, the number of cells in the new system is only 1.8 times as large as that of the previous one. This paper discusses the new system in detail.

The ability to correctly recognize deformed characters depends highly on the choice of local features to be extracted in intermediate stages of the hierarchical network. These local features are determined by training patterns given to the network. This paper offers some techniques for selecting training patterns useful for deformation-invariant recognition of a large number of characters.

2. THE STRUCTURE OF THE NETWORK

The hierarchical structure of the network is illustrated in Fig. 1, in which each rectangle represents a two-dimensional array of cells. The lowest stage of the network is the input layer U_0, and consists of a two-dimensional array of receptor cells. Each succeeding stage has a layer U_S consisting of cells called "S-cells" followed by another layer U_C of cells called "C-cells". Thus, in the whole network, layers of S-cells and C-cells are arranged alternately. S-cells are feature-extracting cells. The C-cells are inserted in the network to allow for positional errors in the features. The layer of C-cells at the highest stage is the recognition layer, representing the final result of the pattern recognition by the neocognitron.

Each layer of S-cells or C-cells is divided into subgroups, called "cell-planes", according to the feature to which they respond. The connections converging to the cells in a cell-plane are homogeneous: all the cells in a cell-plane receive input connections of the same spatial distribution, in which only the positions of the preceding cells shifts in parallel with the position of the cells in the cell-plane.

The present system for alphanumeric character recognition has four stages of layers containing S- and C-cells. The number of S- or C-cells in each layer is indicated in Fig. 1. Incidentally, each layer of S-cells contains subsidiary inhibitory cells, called "V-cells", but they are not indicated explicitly in Fig. 1.

The density of cells in each layer is designed to decrease with the order of the stage. Figure 2 shows how the cells of different cell-planes are spatially interconnected. This figure, in which only one cell-plane is drawn for each layer, illustrates a one-dimensional cross section of the connections between S- and C-cells.

Connections converging to feature-extracting S-cells are variable and are reinforced by training (or learning). After finishing the training, S-cells, with the aid of the subsidiary V-cells, can extract features from the input pattern. In other words, an S-cell is activated only when a particular feature is presented at a certain position in the input layer. The features which the S-cells extract are determined by training patterns given to the input layer.

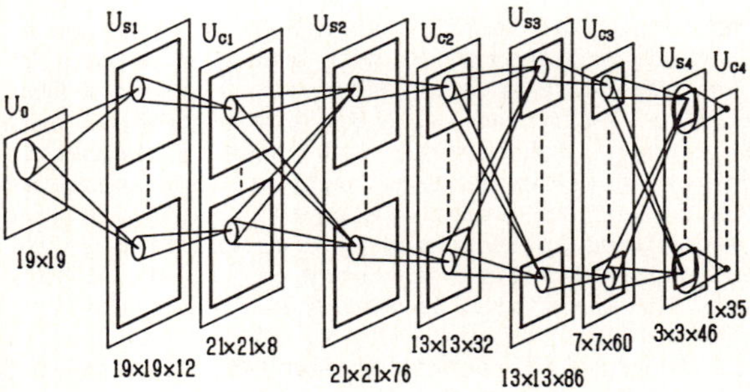

Fig. 1. Hierarchical network structure of the neocognitron.

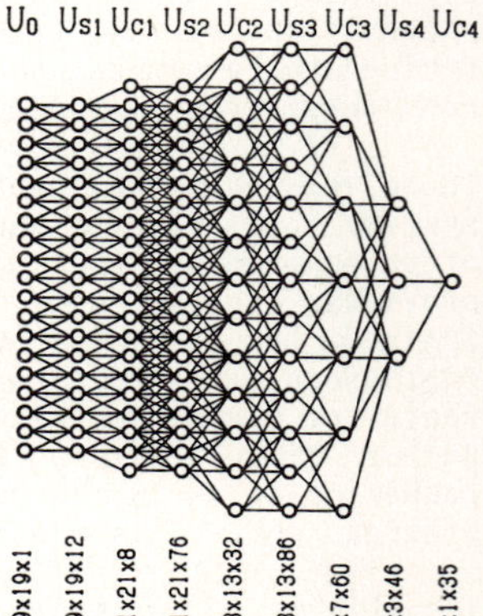

Fig. 2. One-dimensional cross section of interconnections between cell-planes.

C-cells have the function of tolerating positional errors of the features extracted by the S-cells. Connections from S-cells to C-cells are fixed. Each C-cell receives signals from a group of S-cells which extract the same feature, but from slightly different positions. The C-cell is activated if at least one of these S-cells is active. Hence, the C-cell's response results in lower sensitivity to shifts in position of the input pattern.

In the entire network, with its alternate layers of S-cells and C-cells, the process of feature-extraction by the S-cells and toleration of positional shift by the C-cells are repeated. During this process, local features that are extracted in a lower stage are gradually integrated into more global features. Finally, each C-cell of the recognition layer at the highest stage integrates all the information of the input pattern, and responds only to one specific pattern. In other words, only one C-cell is activated, corresponding to the category of the input pattern.

In the present system for alphanumeric character recognition, the recognition layer U_{C4} has 35 cell-planes, each of which contains only one C-cell. These 35 C-cells corresponds to 35 alphanumeric patterns: namely, 26 uppercase alphabetic characters and 10 Arabic numerals, where the alphabetic character O and numeral 0 are treated as the same pattern.

3. TRAINING THE NETWORK TO RECOGNIZE HANDWRITTEN ALPHANUMERIC CHARACTERS

3.1 Training the Network

The neocognitron can be trained either by supervised learning or by unsupervised learning. The present system for alphanumeric character recognition is trained by supervised learning (or learning-with-a-teacher) [3].

The variable input connections of the S-cells are reinforced by the training. Their initial values before training are all zero. Training is performed step by step from the lower stages to the higher stages. In other words, training of a higher stage is performed after completely finishing the training of the preceding stages.

All of the stages are trained with the same process. Let us consider a case of training a certain stage. From the layer of S-cells in the stage, a "teacher" (or a trainer) first chooses a cell-plane to be trained. He then presents a training pattern to the input layer U_0, and indicates which cell in the cell-plane should be the "seed cell". The seed cell is pointed to by the position of its receptive field center.

The amount of reinforcement of each input connection to the seed cell is proportional to the intensity of the response of the cell from which the relevant connection is leading. The response of the latter cell is obtained (or can be calculated) by simply presenting the training pattern to the input layer, since the training of the preceding stages has already been completed. Thus, the seed cell comes to acquire the ability to extract the feature of the stimulus which has been presented during the training period.

The seed cell works like a seed in crystal growth: all the other S-cells in the cell-plane follow the seed cell and have their input connections reinforced by having the same spatial distribution as those of the seed cell. Thus, the homogeneity of connections within cell-planes is always preserved.

3.2 A Strategy for Selecting Features

When recognizing a pattern consisting of line drawings by the neocognitron, the cells in a lower stage extract local features such as line segments in a particular orientation, intersections of lines, corners of a bent line, curvature of lines, end of lines, and so on. Among these features, line segments show peculiar characteristics different from others.

Suppose an intermediate layer of the neocognitron, say layer U_{S2}, contains cell-planes that extract line segments, as well as other cell-planes extracting corners, crossing, and so on. Let a pattern like 'L' be presented to the input layer. Many cells will be activated in the cell-plane which extracts horizontal line segments, as well as in the cell-plane which extracts vertical line segments. However, only one cell (or at most a few cells around it) will be activated in a cell plane which extract corners. The same is true for each end of the bent line. If the output signal from these cell-planes are treated under the same criterion, the influence of the line segments becomes extremely strong because of the large number of activated cells. To make matters worse, the number of activated cells varies considerably with the change in size of the input pattern, depending on the length of the straight lines in the pattern. This makes deformation-invariant recognition difficult.

Ignoring the line-extracting cells in the intermediate layers can be effective for size- and deformation-invariant recognition of line drawings. Readers might feel that a pattern consisting of only a straight line, for example, cannot be recognized without detecting line segments. However this is not the case. In order to recognize a straight line, it is enough to detect the existence of both ends of the line, and also to detect the absence of all other features between them. If the input pattern is not a straight line, some other features must be detected between both ends of the line.

Therefore, intermediate layers U_{S2} and U_{S3} are trained to extract local features other than line segments. This does not mean, however, that line extracting cells are completely eliminated from all stages of the network. On the contrary, the first layer U_{S1} of the present system consists of cell-planes that extract line segments only, and no other features are extracted in this stage. All the other features are extracted indirectly in the higher stages using the output of layer U_{S1}.

3.3 Training Patterns

Training Patterns for Layer U_{S1}: Layer U_{S1} is trained to extract line component of different orientations. Figure 3 shows the 12 training patterns used to train the 12 cell-planes of layer U_{S1}. Each of the training patterns is presented to the network only once. The cell at the center of the cell-plane to be trained is always appointed as the seed cell. As can be seen from Fig. 2, each cell of this layer has a receptive field of 3×3 in size. Hence, only the central 3×3 area of each training pattern is effective during training, and only this central area is shown in Fig. 3.

Since the size of the receptive fields of S-cells is as small as 3×3, it is difficult to extract all parts of a line by only one cell-plane when the line has an inclination ratio of 1:2. Therefore, two cell-planes are used to extract such a slanted line component, and the output from these two S-cell-planes are joined together and made to converge to a single C-cell-plane. Each bracket drawn to the left of the training patterns in Fig. 3 indicates how the outputs of the corresponding S-cell-planes are joined together.

The orientation selectivity of S-cells has been adjusted in such a way that the S-cells respond not only to optimally oriented lines, but also to lines of slightly different orientations. For example, S-cells trained with the training pattern shown at the top of the left column of Fig. 3 respond to a small degree to the second and the third patterns of the same column, and also to the fifth and the sixth pattern in the right column.

Training Patterns for Layer U_{S2}: Figure 4 shows the training patterns used to train the 76 cell-planes of layer U_{S2}. Only the central 9×9 areas of the training patterns are shown here, because the S-cells of this layer have receptive-fields 9×9 in size. Again, the cell at the center of the cell-plane to be trained is appointed as the seed cell.

As can be seen in Fig. 4, each training pattern generally consists of a part of an alphanumeric pattern which is supposed to appear during the process of pattern-recognition. In other words, typical examples of deformed patterns are presented to the network as training patterns.

Sometimes, a single cell-plane is trained with more than one training pattern. This is effective in increasing the S-cell's ability to extract deformed features. A group of patterns arranged in a horizontal line in Fig. 4 represents such a set of training patterns. When superimposing these kinds of training patterns, the adjustment of their relative positions is important. The position of the training patterns presented to the same seed cell are adjusted in such a way that they overlap at the center as precisely as possible, and that the offset occurs only in the peripheral parts.

In handwritten character recognition, considerably different shapes have to be treated as the same feature. If the difference in shape among such features is too large to be extracted by a single cell-plane, they are extracted separately by several S-cell-planes in parallel, and the output from these S-cell-planes are joined together at the input of a C-cell-plane. Similarly to layer U_{S1}, the brackets in Fig. 4 indicate how the cell-planes are joined.

Another important factor which determines the ability of feature extraction is the decision of which part of the training pattern should come at the receptive field center of the seed cell. For example, the corners of the L-shaped training patterns in the 20th line in the left column of Fig. 4 are not placed at the center, but are placed to the upper right of the center. This kind of offset is useful for detecting the absence of line components in the lower left part of the receptive field, and consequently increases the ability to discriminate L-shaped patterns from, say, cross-shaped patterns.

There are some features which are difficult to be detected directly in one step in layer U_{S2}. An example of such features is the central part of 'X', where many lines cross with each other. Because of a large excitatory effect from many lines, the absence of only one of them is difficult to be detected by a single S-cell. Therefore, the cell might erroneously be activated even if one of the lines is missing. In the present system, several features are extracted around such a crossing point separately by a number of cell-planes in layer U_{S2}, and these features are integrated into one at the succeeding stage U_{S3}. If we try to detect the difference only with layer U_{S2} by increasing the selectivity of the S-cells, this simply results in a decreased ability to extract deformed features.

Training Patterns for Layer U_{S3}: Figure 5 shows the training patterns for layer U_{S3}. Since the receptive fields of S-cells of this layer are larger in size than the input layer U_0, the cell at the center of a cell-plane cannot always be appointed as the seed cell. Therefore, the position of the seed cell (that is, the receptive-field center of the seed-cell) is marked by a cross in each training pattern in Fig. 5.

In order to prevent confusion between characters that resemble each other, it is important to choose features which emphasize the difference between them. To discriminate 'E' and 'F', for example, we use features which are contained in only one of them, as shown in the 17th and the 18th patterns in the middle column of Fig. 5.

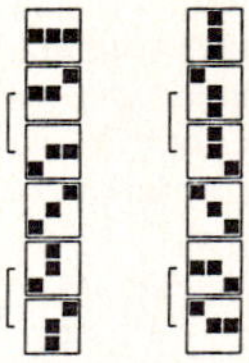

Fig. 3. Training patterns for layer U_{S1}.

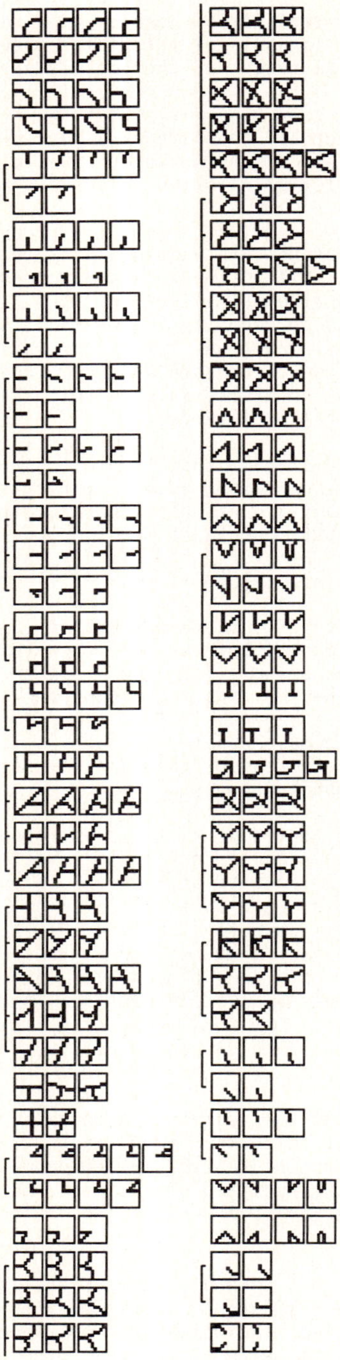

Fig. 4. Training patterns for layer U_{S2} [6].

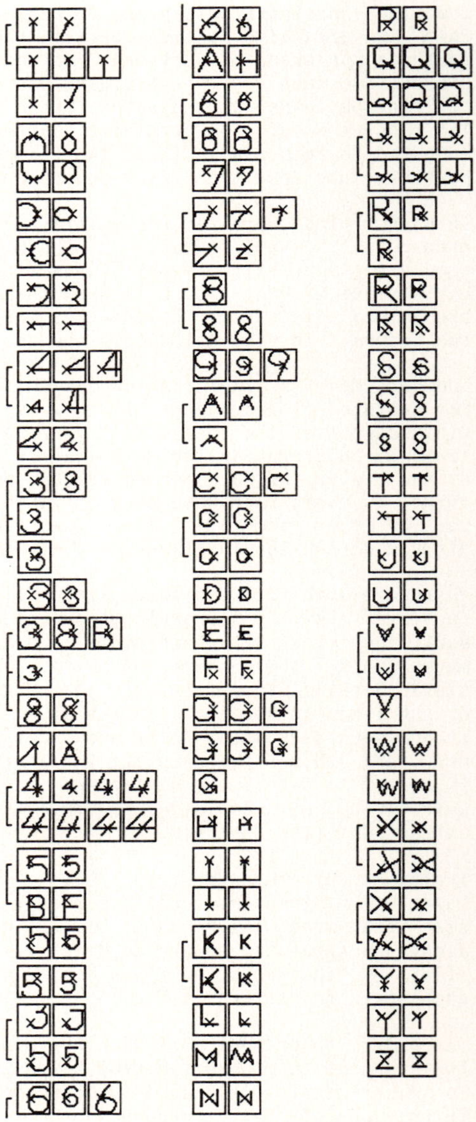

Fig. 5. Training patterns for layer U_{S3} [6].

Generally speaking, we tried to select features to be extracted in layer U_{S3} in such a way that the same number of cell-planes are always activated in layer U_{S3}, independent of the categories of the input patterns.

Training Patterns for Layer U_{S4}: Figure 6 shows the training patterns used to train layer U_{S4}. The cell at the center of each cell-plane is appointed as the seed cell.

Some characters have two or more different styles of writing, which are difficult to be detected by single cell-planes. In this case, two S-cell-planes are used to detect the single character, and their outputs are joined together to a single C-cell in the recognition layer U_{C4}. As can be seen in Fig, 6, however, it was only a few characters that actually needed such a joining operation.

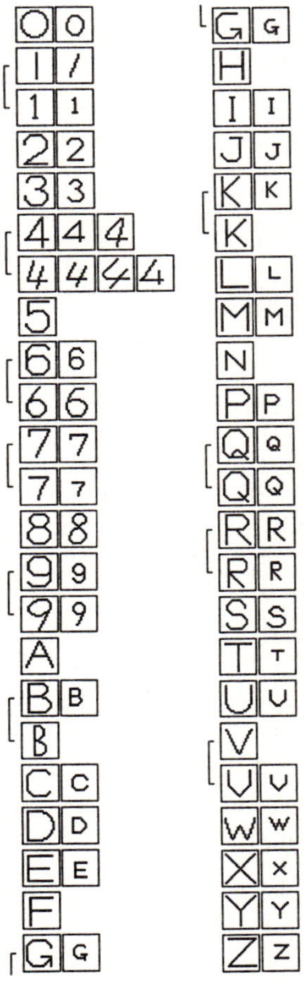

Fig. 6. Training patterns for layer U_{S4} [6].

Fig. 7. Examples of deformed patterns which the neocognitron has recognized correctly [6].

3.4 Response of the Network

Figure 7 shows some example of deformed input patterns which the neocognitron has recognized correctly. As can be seen from this figure, the neocognitron recognizes input pattern correctly without being affected by deformation, changes in size, shifts in position, or contaminating noise.

4. DISCUSSION

The present system which can recognize thirty-five alphanumeric characters is somewhat larger in scale than a previously reported system [3]-[5], which can recognize only ten handwritten numerals. However, the increase in scale is not so great: the number of cells in the present system is 66,048 (including S-, C-, and V-cells, as well as the receptor cells), while that of the previous system is 36,321. The number of characters to be recognized is increased 3.5 times, but the number of cells is increases only around 1.8 times. To be more specific, the number of cell-planes for U_{S1}, U_{S2} and U_{S3} in the present system is 12, 76, and 86, respectively, while the number of the previous system is 12, 38, and 35. The numbers are increased only by 1.0, 2.0, and 2.5 times, respectively. This is because the local features to be extracted in the lower stages are common, and usually are contained in many patterns of different categories.

The readers might feel that the possibility of confusion between similar patterns increases with the increased number of characters to be recognized, but this is not always the case for the neocognitron. It is possible to discriminate between similar patterns of different categories through a skillful choice of training patterns as discussed in this paper.

This system is working on a SUN workstation (SPARCstation 370). The program is written in FORTRAN. The computation time to recognize one alphanumeric character is 3.0 seconds on average.

REFERENCES

[1] Fukushima, K.: "Neocognitron: a self-organizing neural network model for a mechanism of pattern recognition unaffected by shift in position", Biological Cybernetics 36[4], pp. 193-202 (April 1980).

[2] Fukushima, K. and Miyake, S.: "Neocognitron: a new algorithm for pattern recognition tolerant of deformations and shifts in position", Pattern Recognition 15[6], pp. 455-469 (1982).

[3] Fukushima, K.: "Neocognitron: a hierarchical neural network capable of visual pattern recognition", Neural Networks 1[2], pp. 119-130 (April 1988).

[4] Fukushima, K., Miyake, S., Ito, T. and Kouno, T.: "Handwritten numeral recognition by the algorithm of the neocognitron -- an experimental system using a microcomputer", (in Japanese), Trans. Information Processing Society of Japan 28[6], pp. 627-635 (June 1987).

[5] Ito, T., Fukushima, K. and Miyake, S.: "Realization of a neural network model neocognitron on a hypercube parallel computer", International Journal of High Speed Computing, to be published (1990).

[6] Fukushima, K., and Wake, N.: "Handwritten alphanumeric character recognition by the neocognitron", Neural Networks, to appear (1990).

Advanced Neural Computers / R. Eckmiller (Editor)

STORING AND PROCESSING INFORMATION IN CONNECTIONIST SYSTEMS

Hans Geiger

Kratzer Automatisierung GmbH
Maxfeldhof 5-6
D-8044 Unterschleissheim

1.0 Introduction

In our group we are concerned mostly with solving problems in the realm of industrial automation that have not been satisfactorily solved with conventional means so far. After analysing typical problems of this sort, it seemed practical to sacrifice generality for the sake of reducing the complexity of the problem. Since automation is primarily concerned with in some way controlling processes taking place in the physical universe (as opposed to the abstract world of general information theories), it seemed appropriate to describe this universe by the physical state variables and the natural laws governing their interactions. Reducing the tremendous amount of data available to a degree where it can be handled by relatively simple computing algorithms is achieved by segmentation of parts of this universe into disjunct subsets describing discrete "objects". These subsets can be associated with real physical objects or a combination of physical parameters called "features", that have symbolic (semantic) meaning.

Our system is defined to "know" something about this universe if it correctly predicts changes in physical parameters (position and speed of an object, temperature or pressure during a chemical reaction etc.). If the system is able to acquire this knowledge by observing the physical universe for some time, it can then be used for self-organizing construction of arbitrary control circuits.

Another kind of knowledge is knowledge about objects. Objects are defined by features in some way computable from the subset of physical attributes that define this object. Recognizing an object is thus achieved by first detecting the features associated with this objects (this includes segmentation, figure-ground-problems etc.) and then finding the objects whose description is most similar to the features present. In order to obtain a practically useful system showing non-trivial capabilities while reducing the complexity of the problem as far as possible, the function of the system described here is reduced to the two tasks mentioned above. In this paper I would therefore like to restrict myself to information relating to problems of the real, physical world, and process this information in a connectionist system (or Neural Network).

This implies the following assumptions:

- Input consists of numerical data (visual, acoustic, pressure, temperature etc) representing physical variables.

- For classification tasks the output consists of one of a finite number of predefined reactions in response to an arbitrary input, possibly replacing part of the output with variable values. One example might be classification of objects, where the output consists of the identfier assigned to the object, another example is the generation of a database query (e.g. using a formal language like SQL) in response to a natural language input, replacing part of this query with actual values obtained from the input statement.

- For control tasks the output would be interpreted as a direct physical variable (e.g. voltage, current etc.).

- It is not generally possible to isolate a subset of physical variables and process them independently of the others. Frequently there are dependencies between practically all significant variables.

- No problem-dependent mathematical function should be used explicitly, since this can not be integrated into NNs in a natural way. Rather functional dependencies between variables should be expressed in the language of NNs, i.e. the setting of synaptic efficacies.

- For integrating conventional algorithms, on the other hand, the information in the network must at every stage be interpretable. The coding of numerical values must allow extraction into conventional formats.

- In order to use approved methods for applying rules to a given situation, the input information must be transferred into a symbolic subspace. This transformation is coupled with a significant reduction of the amount of information. This necessary reduction, however, is not without risk, since it is quite frequently not known beforehand, what information is pertinent to the problem at hand.

In general the system forms a hypothesis about the most probable output dependent on the available data, then by feedback tests the input data against this hypothesis and modifies its assumption until the contradictions between hypothesis and input data are minimized. This approach also uses a feedback component to modify the preprocessing of the data (e.g. first-stage feature detectors) in order to extract more information pertinent to the decision process.

2.0 The model

For reasons mentioned below, we decided on using an enhanced neuronal model for our network. Our neurons are single-spike rather than state neurons, thus opening the possiblity of coding continuous values in the frequency domain. This implies a number of additional properties for describing a single neuron:

- Neurons must "remember" their history in order to modify their firing frequency as a function of the inputs from their presynaptic elements. This is necessary since two neurons as a rule are not active at exactly the same time. We use a modification of the capacitor-model for this purpose (e.g. [3]).

- There are additional parameters governing the behaviour of the neurons. Most of these have the function of time constants for decay and activation characteristics.

- Plasticity must be redefined, since simple Hebb-like rules, generalized delta rule and others are not applicable in this model.

- It is convenient to introduce a stochastic factor into the neurons behaviour. While being compatible with the notion of single-spike neurons, some kind of probabilistic factor (reminiscent of "temperature" in other models) is absolutely necessary for some salient properties (e.g. associative recall of information, trial-and-eror forming of hypotheses etc.).

- Representation of numerical, continuous data must be redefined. The simple frequency coding has too many drawbacks in a practical application (see below).

2.1 Theoretical and practical requirements for an intelligent system

In order to meet these assumptions, a system must, irrespective of the model used, adhere to a few limiting conditions. Some are imposed by theoretical considerations, others must be met to satisfy the requirements of the man-machine-interface.
Theoretical requirements are:

- Processing of data must be knowledge based. Most of the problems to be solved require a priori knowledge about the physical world, its constituent objects and the relations between these objects.

- Procedural als well as factual knowledge must be represented in a "fuzzy" way, enabling the inclusion of probabilities and default reasoning etc.

- Retrieving information must be done associatively: New situations are treated as representations of (possibly a combination of) "similar" known situations.

Practical considerations include:

1. Automatic acquisition of knowledge. The system must be "trained on the job" analogous to a human worker. This implies that the physical environment describes itself through the time-dependent evolution of the observable physical variables. The law of gravitation, for example, should be "learned" by a system if it observes position, speed etc. of several objects during a free fall experiment. If the objects used are significantly different e.g. in their mass/surface ratio and this information is also fed into the system, this should then also learn about the role of aerodynamics during free fall.

2. The system must be able to trade speed for accuracy both during learning and the functional phase. If the system begins generating useful outputs, however inaccurate, as soon as it is supplied with the first training examples, it also has the ability to react to continuous changes of the environment in a reasonable way. If, on the other hand, a constant number of examples is required (e.g. for generation of a spline interpolating function) before the first output can be obtained, the system cannot cope with changes in a timescale slower than a single measurement but faster than a complete set of training examples. The same principle holds true for the "doing" phase. Very often a quick, inaccurate answer is acceptable, whereas a slow, accurate one is not. An ideal combination is a system that begins to generate a "best guess" output immediately after the input data arrives, while it increases the accuracy of its output with every time step and/or every additional measurement.

3. A given system should be able to solve a whole class of problems rather than one specific problem. It is desireable to adapt an existing production line quickly and efficiently to a new product. Software development times in the order of several man-months simply to exchange one type of car against a slightly modified one are becoming more and more unacceptable. Having once been trained e.g. to fit a wheel to a carriage, the system should be retrained much in the manner of a human worker, i.e. by once (or very few times) being shown the new type of wheel. It should then be able to cope with this assignement by using most of its knowledge built up while learning to "fit wheels to a car" in a very general way.

2.2 Representation of information in this model

The single-spike model described above lends itself readily to representing binary information. It is thus quite straightforward to represent symbolic information as well as the rules governing interactions between this data. The system must, however, also cope with continuous values representing not only physical variables but also parameters modifying symbolic information such as "beliefs", probabilities, confidence factors etc (e.g. Pao 1989). In addition contextual knowledge and information about internal bindings between numerical values as well as symbolic features must be encoded. A simple method for this is to describe the state of a neuron by a real number that is interpreted as the element's mean firing frequency. While this simple frequency coding is adequate for some purposes (such as representing brightness distributions in a model retina), this method, however, has several disadvantages:

1. The precision for numerical values necessary for even simple tasks requires a high precision for the measurement of time intervals on the postsynaptic site. Using averaging techniques to increase the precision leads to unacceptably long transfer times.

2. The Hebbian concept of coupling two elements that are "active at the same time", which has shown its merits in numerous applications, is very hard to implement in a frequency coded model. (What is "active at the same time"?)

3. The additional values for probabilites, confidence factors etc. must be processed and transferred via additional units. This increases the size of the networks and also makes it necessary to include additional circuits to use this information in processing the original data, leading to difficultites in identifying the relations between sets of data (which probability for which variable?).

4. One of the main tasks our system should solve is finding an internal representation for arbitrary functional dependencies between two (or more) physical values (e.g. speed and height in free fall). Coding these variables in the firing frequency of a neuron severely limits the possible functions that can be represented. Only linear combinations of the functions used to describe the input/output behaviour of a neuron can be represented. Even then, learning rules for this kind of task are not easily found.

It seemed desireable therefore to retain the single-spike-approach but look for alternative ways to encode continuous values within this framework. We thus modified our model to include additional degrees of freedom for the "language" used to code the information. The first step was to use the phase information for our spikes, i.e. the exact point of time a neuron generates a spike is used to convey additional information to its postsynaptic partner (see [1]). Evaluating this information, however proved to be extremely critical as to the size and position of the time window used at the postsynpatic site. Fortunately there has been experimental evidence for a way to circumvent this problem ([2]): The "language" of neurons consists of microburst with a repetition frequency of appr. 20 to 60 Hz. Every microburst (provided it consists of more than 2 spikes) is sufficient for the postsynaptic neuron to extract the frequency and hence the amplitude information it needs. In addition, the relative (instead of absolute) phase of the microbursts yields information about internal correlations of different amplitude values. This method allows straightforward application of Hebb-like learnig rules by substituting correlations of bursts (irrespective of the amplitude coded in these bursts) for correlations of single spikes (which would imply identical firing frequency). There are, however, even more channels for transferring information:

- Introducing a variation of the mean time between two spikes in a micro burst by adding a stochastic component to the neurons threshold function shows a natural way to add information about "confidence" or the probability of a hypothesis. This information can be evaluated by the postsynaptic neuron without additional circuitry and without leaving the domain of the "natural language" for the neurons in this model.

There still remains the problem mentioned above of representing quantitative functional dependencies between continuous variables. This can be solved by coding this kind of information in a different way, somewhat similar to the way acoustic information is coded in the cochlea of mammals:

- For every variable x we use a number of neurons ordered along a onedimensional axis. A value x1 is encoded by activating these neurons according to their "receptive fields". If these fields consist of overlapping Gaussian curves, it can be shown that a high precision can be accomplished with relatively few elements. Thus numerical values can be coded in topological information. Functional dependencies can then be represented by the topological distribution of connections instead of by input/output functions of a single neuron. Standard learning procedures (Hebb-like, forced learning etc.) can be applied to self-organize such a problem-dependent topology.

A topology thus gained can mirror either natural laws, thereby forming an environment for simulation and control tasks, equally well it can also solve classification tasks for numerical and symbolic data. Using the additional information coded independently in other channels (firing rate, standard deviation of firing rate, phase information etc.) allows the application of neural networks to a whole class of problems that were so far untractable by conventional means.

3.0 Conclusion

Extending the "vocabulary" of a neuron also extends the network's information-handling capacity wihout unduly increasing its size and the complexity of its algorithms. Representing natural laws and classifying objects by combining numerical and symbolic information can be self-organised by using the self-descriptive properties of natural environments. These principles will in future be applied to a greater number of tasks.

REFERENCES

[1] v.d.Malsburg, C., The Correlation Theory of Brain Function Internal Report 81-2, (1981) Goettingen

[2] Singer, W., Gray, C.M., Engel, A., Koenig, P., Spatio-temporal distribution of stimulus-specific oscillations in the cat visual cortex; (1988) Neuroscience Abst. Vol.14/362.13

[3] Pao, Y.H., Adaptive Pattern Recognition and Neural Networks (Addison-Wesley, 1989)

Advanced Neural Computers / R. Eckmiller (Editor)

THE CLOSED LOOP ANTAGONISTIC NETWORK (CLAN)

G. HARTMANN[1]

Fachbereich 14 Elektrotechnik
Universität - GH - Paderborn, Pohlweg 47-49
D-4790 Paderborn, West Germany

A set of adaptive neurons is embedded in a special architecture providing excitatory input from an antagonistic feature space, normalizing inhibitory input, and global feedback. A neuron adapted to this representation of a pattern responds to a non-familiar pattern proportional to a quality measure rewarding match and punishing mismatch. Adapted and non-adapted neurons compete within a global feedback loop comparing their quality of response. A familiar pattern recalls the neuron adapted to the presented class. A non-familiar pattern is learnt by the best responding non-adapted neuron and a new class is formed. By this mechanism patterns are parsed into sets, and categories are formed without a teacher. The decision between learning and recall is due to the dynamics of the feedback loop defined by the parameters of the pulse coded model neurons.

1. INTRODUCTION

A "Closed Loop Antagonistic Network" (CLAN) provides fast learning as it is known from biological systems. It parses input patterns into sets and forms categories without a teacher. This cannot be performed by networks implementing supervised learning e. g. by error back-propagation /1/, /2/, /3/. Competitive learning /4/ in its well known variations is usually slow and may be temporally instable /5/. The adaptive resonance theory /6/ provides features similar to those of a CLAN, the implementation of a CLAN, however, is less expensive. Some principles of the CLAN architecture are well known from previous research. Antagonistic representations have been used by Willshaw et al. /7/ twenty years ago and representations with positive and negative components have been described by Kohonen /8/. Competition in networks with interlaced inhibitory neurons has been proposed by von der Malsburg /9/ and competition in a closed loop architecture has been investigated by Palm /10/. We will show that the benefits of our network result from a combination of these well known principles within the CLAN architecture.

2. A QUALITY MEASURE FOR PATTERN MATCHING

The quality of a match between a pattern L and a pattern P is said to be high if a high percentage of L matches with a high percentage of P. This is a very simple statement, but a measure like this is not at all easily evaluated by a neuron.

Let *f* neurons form a feature space, spanned by feature vectors $\mathbf{f} = (f_1, f_2, \ldots f_i \ldots)$. The set of components f_i is called $F = \{f_i\}$. For simplicity we confine ourselves to binary neurons for a

---

1. This work was supported by a BMFT-grant ITR 8800 D/0

moment with $f_i \in \{0,1\}$. A pattern with $p = |P|$ active neurons is described by the set $P = \{f_i^{(P)} | f_i^{(P)} = 1\}$ of non-zero components in $\mathbf{f}^{(P)}$. Similarly, a pattern with $l = |L|$ active neurons is described by $L = \{f_i^{(L)} | f_i^{(L)} = 1\}$ of non-zero components in $\mathbf{f}^{(L)}$.

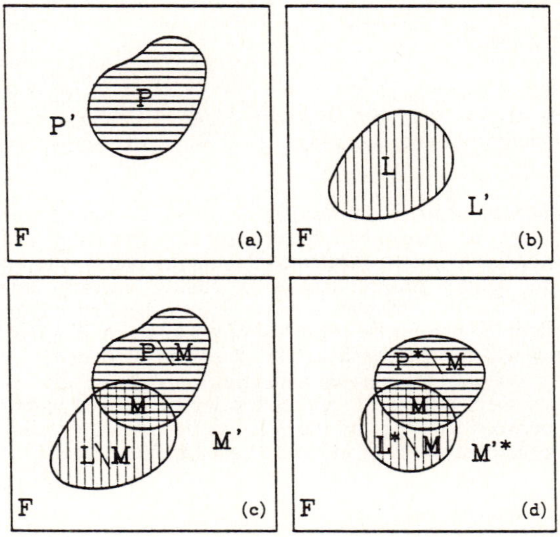

Fig. 1. F is the set of feature neurons, P ⊂ F the set of active neurons, and P' the set of active antagonistic neurons. A pair P, L of patterns (a), (b) may have the same match M (c) as a different pair P^*, L^* of patterns (d). A good measure is to punish mismatch P\M and L\M

For visibility, the set F and its subsets P⊂F and L⊂F are plotted in a two dimensional representation in fig. 1. The set of matching non-zero features between P and L is $M = P \cap L$ with $m = |M|$ elements (fig. 1c). Obviously, m is not a good measure, as $M = P \cap L = P^* \cap L^*$ provides the same $m = |M|$ for different pairs of patterns (fig. 1c, d). The intuitively better quality of match between P^* and L^* in fig. 1d is due to the smaller mismatch $P^* \backslash M$ and $L^* \backslash M$ compared to the mismatch P\M and L\M in fig. 1c. Consequently, a good quality measure should not only count the number m of matching active neurons, but also punish the number $(p\text{-}m) = |P \backslash M|$ and $(l\text{-}m) = |L \backslash M|$ of non-matching active neurons. In the simplest case, a quality measure q(P,L) is given by

$$q(P,L) = m - [(p-m) + (l-m)] = \mathbf{f}^{(L)} \cdot \mathbf{f}^{(P)} - [\mathbf{f}^{(L)} - \mathbf{f}^{(P)}]^2 \qquad (1)$$

This measure is high, if a high percentage of pattern L matches with a high percentage of pattern P, as expressed by the initial statement.

3. EVALUATION OF THE QUALITY MEASURE BY A NEURON

A quality measure is not only to be intuitively good, it is also to be evaluable by neurons. We can show that a single neuron will respond according to q(P,L), if it is embedded in a special network architecture.

We start with the very simple architecture of fig. 2a. The set of F-neurons, representing the feature space by feature vectors **f**, has been discussed in the previous section. This set F of neurons is fully interconnected with a set A of adaptive neurons. The weights w_{ij} connecting the F-neurons to a neuron A_j form the weight vector $\mathbf{w}_{AF}$. The non adapted weights of an A-neuron are $w_{ij} = w$. As soon as an A-neuron is adapted to a previously learnt pattern L, all weights connected with active F-neurons are saturated at $w_{ij} = W > w$, all the other weights are $w_{ij} = 0$. All the active F-neurons in pattern L, however, are denoted by the non-zero components of the corresponding feature vector $\mathbf{f}^{(L)}$. Hence we can write the weight vector $\mathbf{w}^{(L)}$ of an A-neuron adapted to pattern L as $\mathbf{w}^{(L)} = W \cdot \mathbf{f}^{(L)}$. According to (1) a neuron A_j adapted to a (learnt) pattern L will respond to a (presented) pattern P with an activity

$$a_j(P|L) = \mathbf{w}_{AF}^{(L)} \cdot \mathbf{f}^{(P)} = W \cdot \mathbf{f}^{(L)} \cdot \mathbf{f}^{(P)} = W \cdot m \tag{2}$$

So neuron A_j can only evaluate the matching term of the quality measure (1), but not the mismatch term. Of course, a neuron A_j will provide different signals, if it is embedded in a different network architecture. The antagonistic network (AN) in fig. 2b additionally provides f antagonistic F'-neurons, described by an antagonistic feature vector **f'**. An F'-neuron is off, if its F-counterpart is on, and vice versa. So a pattern represented by a set P of non-zero components in $\mathbf{f}^{(P)}$ is additionally represented (fig. 1a) by a set P' = F\P of non-zero components in $\mathbf{f'}^{(P)}$. From now on we combine $\mathbf{f}^{(P)}$ with $\mathbf{f'}^{(P)}$ to a feature vector $(\mathbf{f}^{(P)}, \mathbf{f'}^{(P)})$ with $2f$ components.

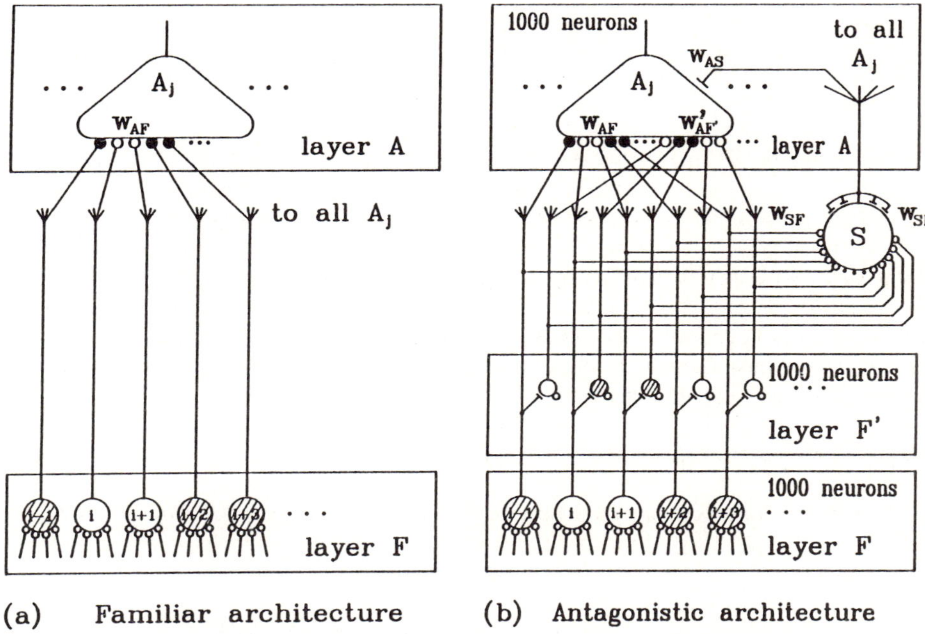

Fig. 2. In a familiar architecture (a) a neuron A_j adapted to a pattern L can only evaluate the match M with a presented pattern P. In an antagonistic architecture (b) it can evaluate a measure rewarding match and punishing mismatch.

The weights connecting neurons F' with neuron A_j form the vector $\mathbf{w'}_{AF'}$, which is very similar to $\mathbf{w}_{AF}$. The components $w'_{ij} = w_{ij} = w$ of both vectors are equal, as long as A_j is not yet adapted. As soon as A_j is adapted to a pattern L, all weights connected with active F'-neurons will become $w'_{ij} = W$, and we can write $\mathbf{w'}^{(L)}_{AF} = W \cdot \mathbf{f'}^{(L)}$. Before we also combine the weight vectors, we double the weights of $\mathbf{w}_{AF}$ and yield a weight vector $\mathbf{w}^*_{AF} = 2\mathbf{w}_{AF}$. So the composed weight vector is $(\mathbf{w}^*_{AF}, \mathbf{w'}_{AF'}) = (2\mathbf{w}_{AF}, \mathbf{w'}_{AF'})$ and neuron A_j responds with

$$a_j(P|L) = (2\mathbf{w}^{(L)}_{AF}, \mathbf{w'}^{(L)}_{AF'}) \cdot (\mathbf{f}^{(P)}, \mathbf{f'}^{(P)}) = \tag{3}$$
$$= 2W \cdot \mathbf{f}^{(L)} \cdot \mathbf{f}^{(P)} + W \cdot \mathbf{f'}^{(L)} \cdot \mathbf{f'}^{(P)} = 2W \cdot m + W \cdot m'$$

The term $2W \cdot m$ corresponds with (2), while the antagonistic part $W \cdot m'$ counts the matching non-zero components in $\mathbf{f'}^{(L)}$ and $\mathbf{f'}^{(P)}$. Fig. 1c shows how to evaluate the number of elements $m' = |M'|$ in set M'. As $M' = (F\backslash P) \cap (F\backslash L) = F\backslash(P \cup L) = F\backslash(P \cup L\backslash M)$, the number of elements $m' = |M'|$ is $m' = f - (p+l-m)$. Replacing m' in (3) by this term we get

$$a_j(P|L) = W \cdot [m - (p-m) - (l-m)] + W \cdot f = W \cdot q(P,L) + W \cdot f \tag{4}$$

As long as we assume the neurons to be binary, the term $W \cdot f$ is constant and we could eliminate it by a threshold. However, the term $W \cdot f$ can also be subtracted by inhibitory input from S-neurons. In fig. 2b one S-neuron is shown, receiving input from all the neurons F and F'. As these neurons form antagonistic pairs, f neurons will always provide input to each neuron S_k and the response s_k will be proportional to f. The set of S-neurons is described by a vector $\mathbf{s} = (s_1, \ldots s_k \ldots)$ and the weights w_{kj} form a weight vector $\mathbf{w}_{AS}$. These inhibitory weights at neuron A_j are again adaptive, saturating from $w_{kj} = -w$ to $w_{kj} = -W$. The contribution of S-neurons to the activation of A_j can be adjusted to be $\mathbf{w}_{AS} \cdot \mathbf{s} = -W \cdot f$, compensating the term $W \cdot f$ in (4). Hence, a neuron A_j embedded in the complete antagonistic network (fig. 2b) responds according to the previously defined quality measure (1) with

$$a_j(P|L) = (2\mathbf{w}^{(L)}_{AF}, \mathbf{w'}^{(L)}_{AF'}, \mathbf{w}^{(L)}_{AS}) \cdot (\mathbf{f}^{(P)}, \mathbf{f'}^{(P)}, \mathbf{s}) = W \cdot q(P,L) \tag{5}$$

4. THE CLOSED LOOP ANTAGONISTIC NETWORK (CLAN)

Before we discuss competition between differently responding neurons in a closed loop, we are to compare quantitatively the response of adapted and non-adapted neurons. According to (1) and (5) the response of a neuron A_j is

$$a_j(P|L) = W \cdot [m - (p-m) - (l-m)] = W \cdot q(P,L) \tag{6}$$

If the learnt pattern L is the presented pattern P, the response is

$$a_j(P|P) = W \cdot p \tag{7}$$

as $l = m = p$ in (6). Remembering the components of the weight vector in (5) to be w in the case of a non-adapted neuron, the response will be

$$\begin{aligned} a_j(P|0) &= (2\mathbf{w}_{AF}, \mathbf{w}'_{AF'}, \mathbf{w}_{AS}) \cdot (\mathbf{f}^{(P)}, \mathbf{f}'^{(P)}, \mathbf{s}) = \\ &= 2\mathbf{w}_{AF} \cdot \mathbf{f}^{(P)} + \mathbf{w}'_{AF'} \cdot \mathbf{f}'^{(P)} + \mathbf{w}_{AS} \cdot \mathbf{s} = \\ &= 2\mathrm{w} \cdot p + \mathrm{w} \cdot (f\text{-}p) - \mathrm{w} \cdot f = \mathrm{w} \cdot p \end{aligned} \tag{8}$$

Comparison of the response of an adapted neuron (6) with the response of a non-adapted neuron (8) provides the normalized quality measure $Q(P,L) = q(P,L)/p$

$$a_j(P|L) \;/\; a_j(P|0) = (3m/p - l/p - 1) \cdot W/w = Q(P,L) \cdot W/w \tag{9}$$

This measure will be $Q(P,P) = 1$, if the learnt pattern is presented ($P = L$), and $Q(P,L)$ may even become negative, if there is no similarity between L and P (e. g. $m = 0$). On the other hand, according to (9), the normalized quality of a non-adapted neuron is $Q(P,0) = w/W$ independent of the pattern.

In an adaptive system, we want a pattern to be recalled if it is familiar, and a pattern to be learnt if it is not yet familiar. In our system this decision is very simple. If there are adapted neurons with $Q(P,L) > Q(P,0) = w/W$, that with the highest value of Q will be the winner and there will be a recall. If there are no neurons with $Q(P,L) > w/W$ a non-adapted neuron will learn the presented pattern. So we call $Q(P,0) = w/W$ the learning threshold of our system. This decision between recall and learning will automatically happen, if we introduce a closed loop. All the output signals of the A-neurons are fed to a group of C-neurons (fig. 3) and these control neurons provide additional inhibitory input to the A-neurons.

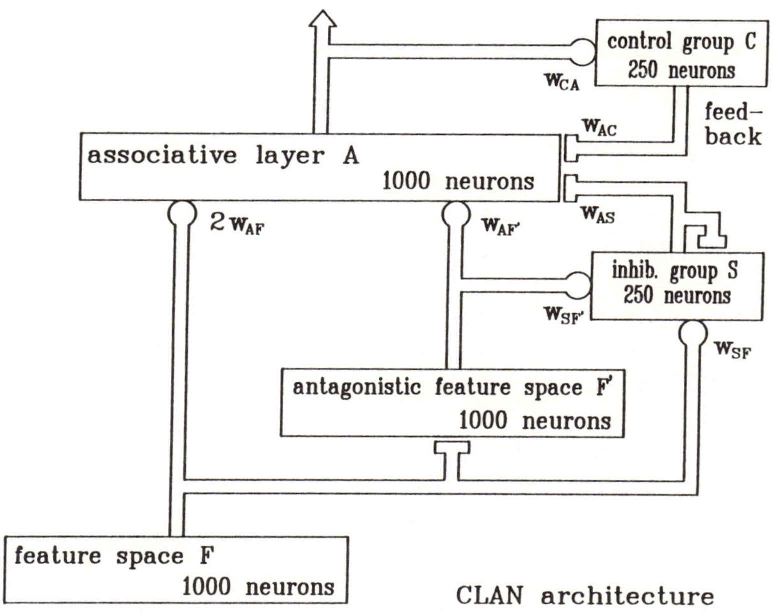

Fig. 3. The complete "Closed Loop Antagonistic Network" as it is used in simulations. A group of control neurons (C) provides global feedback and allows competition between adaptive neurons (A).

While the response of a single neuron A_j can be quantitatively described by simplified model neurons, the collective behaviour of the Closed Loop Antagonistic Network (CLAN) is strongly dependent on the features of more realistic neurons. In our simulations we use pulse coded model neurons of the type described by French and Stein /11/. The threshold of the model neurons is essential for the control of the learning mechanism, while other parameters like time constants are responsible for the dynamics of the CLAN. It is out of the scope of this short presentation to describe the closed loop behaviour of this network quantitatively.

In a qualitative analysis of the closed loop behaviour, we start from the assumption, that neuron A_j provides the highest response of all A-neurons to a pattern P. Its membrane potential $V_j = V_j(net_j\text{-}netf)$ is a function of the difference between the pattern driven weighted input net_j and the weighted feedback netf.

If the membrane potential exceeds a threshold T, the neuron is supraliminal and the response is $a_j(P|L) \sim (V_j\text{-}T)$ if $V_j > T$. A neuron with $V_j < T$ is subliminal and does not respond. As neuron A_j was above assumed to be the winner, $V_j > V_{j'}$ will hold for all the other neurons $A_{j'}$. As the membrane potential V_j depends on netf it can be shifted by the gain of the feedback loop to fulfil the condition $V_j(net_j\text{-}netf) > T > V_{j'}(net_{j'}\text{-}netf)$ for all $j' \neq j$. In this case only the one neuron A_j is active while all the other neurons $A_{j'}$ are silent. The feedback loop driven by this single neuron provides just a weighted feedback signal netf $\sim a_j(P|L)$ fulfilling the above condition.

5. LEARNING AND ASSOCIATIVE RECALL IN A CLAN

Before we discuss learning rules, we must release the simplifying assumption, that all weights of a non-adapted A-neuron are exactly equal. In our simulations we initialize these weights according to a distribution with mean value $w = 0{,}7 \cdot W$ where W is the saturation value.

If we switch from a familiar pattern L to a non-familiar pattern P, the normalized quality measure of this neuron changes from Q(L,L) to Q(P,L). This Q(P,L) may become less than the quality Q(P,0) of the non-adapted neuron with the best match. Consequently the activity of the previously matching neuron decays and with it the negative feedback signal netf. The membrane potential $V_{j'} = V_{j'}(net_{j'}\text{-}netf)$ of all the other previously subliminal neurons increases with decreasing netf until the best matching non-adapted neuron becomes supraliminal. This neuron, however, can only hold the feedback loop, as soon as it provides a sufficiently high rate, exceeding the threshold of the C-neurons. So in this equilibrium, the winner A-neuron is not only supraliminal, it is distinctly responding.

This equilibrium is an optimal condition for Hebbian learning: the best matching non-adapted neuron is distinctly active while the antagonistic pattern is presented to its adaptive synapses. All synapses in ($\mathbf{w}_{AF}$, $\mathbf{w}'_{AF'}$, $\mathbf{w}_{AS}$) interconnected with active neurons will saturate to W, all the other synapses will decay to zero. Our very simple learning rule combines a decay term dw/dt with a positive increment Δw per action potential at supraliminal neurons:

$$\left.\begin{array}{l} dw/dt = -\alpha \\ \Delta w/\text{spike} = \beta \end{array}\right\} \text{ if } 0 < w < W \text{ and } V_j > T \qquad (10)$$

$$dw/dt = \Delta w/\text{spike} = 0 \qquad \text{otherwise.}$$

With increasing adaption the quality measure and the weighted input net_j increases, while the membrane potential V_j and the closed loop response are approximately constant. As the membrane potential $V_j = V_j(net_j\text{-}netf)$ is constant, the feedback signal netf is to increase with increasing net_j. By this mechanism, however, the neurons with lower learning rate and the subliminal neurons are pushed down by increasing netf more and more. Learning stops as soon as all weights are either W or zero. If a new pattern is presented now, not yet familiar to the CLAN, the same procedure will begin. If the new pattern is already familiar, the adapted neuron will immediately respond and hold the feedback loop.

6. CONCLUSION

A CLAN with 1000 adaptive neurons and with a feature space of 1000 antagonistic pairs has been implemented at a SUN4-workstation. First simulations show the expected realtime behaviour and good dynamical features. New patterns are learnt within 700 time slots while an adapted neuron responds to a pattern of its class within 300 time slot. If our model neurons are interpreted as biological neurons, they learn a pattern within 0.7 seconds and respond to a familiar pattern within 0.3 seconds. We could show that a CLAN is able to form categories without a teacher. A transputer version of a CLAN with extended capacity and increased speed is in progress. There are many structural similarities between the CLAN architecture and cortical architectures requiring detailed analysis.

REFERENCES

/1/ D. E. Rumelhart, G. E. Hinton, R. J. Williams, Learning internal representations by error propagation. In: Parallel Distributed Processing: Explorations in the Microstructures of Cognition, Vol. 1, Cambridge MA, MIT-Press, 318-362, (1986)

/2/ Y. Le Cun, Learning in an asymmetric-threshold network. In: Disordered Systems and Biological Organization, E. Bienenstock, F. Fogelmann Souli, G. Weisbuch (Eds.) Berlin, Springer (1986)

/3/ D. Parker, Learning Logic, Technical Report TR-87, Center for Computational Research in Economics and Management Science, MIT Cambridge MA, (1985)

/4/ F. Rosenblatt, The Perceptron: a probalistic model for information storage and organization in the brain. Psychological Review 65, 386-408, (1958)

/5/ G. A. Carpenter, S. Grossberg, Neural Dynamics of category learning and recognition: Attention, memory consolidation, and amnesia. In: J. Davis, R. Newburgh, and E. Wegmann (Eds.), Brain structure, learning, and memory. AAAS Symposium Series, (1987)

/6/ S. Grossberg, Adaptive pattern classification and universal recoding, II: Feedback expectation, olfaction, and illusions. Biological Cybernetics 23, 187-202, (1976)

/7/ D. Willshaw, H. C. Longuet-Higgins, P. Buneman, A simple network capable of inductive generalization. Proc. R. Soc. London B, 182, 233-247 (1972)

/8/ T. Kohonen, Self-Organization and Associative Memory, Berlin, Springer-Verlag, (1984)

/9/ C. von der Malsburg, Self-organization of orientation sensitive cells in the striate cortex, Kybernetik 14, 85-100, (1973)

/10/ G. Palm, private communications

/11/ A. S. French, R. B. Stein, A flexible neural analog using integrated circuits. IEEE Trans. Biomed. Eng., 17, 248-253 (1970)

Advanced Neural Computers / R. Eckmiller (Editor)

Adaptive Resonance Structures in Hierarchical Receptive Field Pattern Recognition Machines

Kenneth Johnson
Rockwell International Science Center
1049 Camino Dos Rios Mail Stop A-18
Thousand Oaks, CA 91360
kbj@risc.com / 805-373-4487

Abstract

Machine vision researchers have long recognized the need for feedback in pattern recognition systems. Two excellent examples of feedback pattern recognition systems are the Adaptive Resonance Theories (ART) of Grossberg and Carpenter [1987a, 1987b, 1990] and the Selective Attention Neocognitron (SAN) of Fukushima [1987]. Several researchers have reported the incorporation of ART into the Neocognitron [Li and Wee, 1990; Rajapakse et al., 1990]. However, explicit comparisons of the relationship between the two models were not presented. In this paper I will examine the functional, architectural, and implementational relationships between several ART variants and the SAN. This comparison will show that the SAN and ART models are conceptually and architecturally similar. In some instances the similarities are equivalent equations and structures, in other instances the similarities are functional. The primary differences between the two models involve specific definitions and re-routing of the mismatch mediated neuron reset and gain controls.

Three ART Architectures

The ART model shown in Figure 1 is a self organizing neural model that uses feedback during the organization of its long term memory (LTM). The architecture is comprised of two layers of neurons termed F1 and F2 which are connected by the weights of the LTM. Not shown is a reset subsystem which computes the match between the top-down and bottom-up data paths in F1 and resets F2 neurons accordingly. The equations are shown in the figure. The neurons in F1 are defined as x_i and the F2 neurons as x_j. The index i is between $1 < i < N$ and the index j is between $N < j < M$. J^+ and J^- represent excitatory and inhibitory inputs to the F1 and F2 neurons and are computed as indicated. The weights z_{ij} and z_{ji} are called long term memory traces (LTM) because they are adjusted according to the learning rules given in the figure.

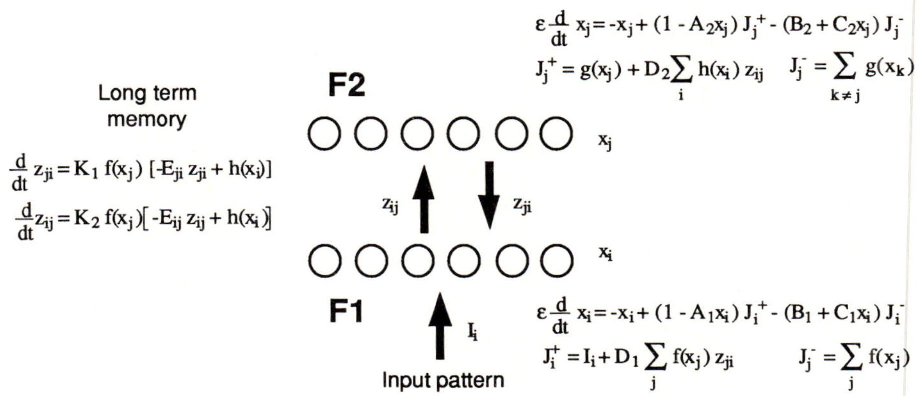

Figure 1: ART I system architecture and equations

The above system of equations shows that the x_i responses in F1 depend on the external input I_i and the product of z_{ji} and the x_j activities in F2. Similarly, the activities of the x_j neurons in F2 depend on the activities in F1. The reset mechanism operates by computing a match ratio which indicates how many neurons receiving external input are also receiving top-down input. If the match ratio falls below a preset criterion the currently active neuron in F2 is reset by adding a constant to its inhibitory input J^-.

Unlike ART I which processes binary input patterns, ART II introduces the concept of analog pattern processing into Adaptive Resonance Theory. In ART II, shown in Figure 2, the neurons in F2 are identical to those in ART I. However, the F1 neurons are replaced by a system comprised of several types of neurons which serve two purposes. First, they compute a dot product match between the vectors representing the top-down and bottom-up patterns. Secondly, they isolate the top-down and bottom-up sections so that the readout of the top-down vector does not upset the bottom-up data driving F2.

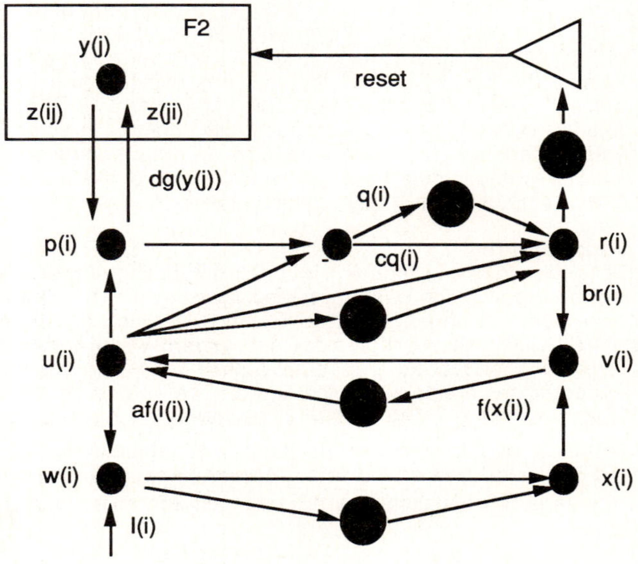

Figure 2: ART II system for processing analog patterns

Finally, there is the most recent version of ART known as ART III. In this model the reset mechanism for F2 was modified so that several F2 neurons could simultaneously respond to the input pattern and thereby form a distributed code vector. The primary modifications of ART II required to achieve this involve modifying the efficacy of the LTM synapses before they are used to compute the excitatory input to the F2 neurons. This is done by introducing a set of first order decay equations, given in Figure 3, which modify the effectiveness of z_{ij} over time if the reset system is active.

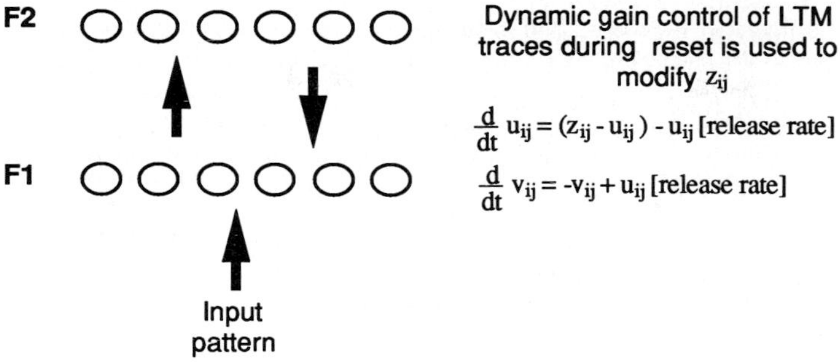

Figure 3: ART III system possessing LTM gain control

Hierarchical Receptive Field Architectures

The original Neocognitron model [Fukushima, 1980], shown in Figure 4, builds an internal representation of a two dimensional pattern using a feedforward multi-layer structure. The neurons at each layer use weighted receptive field masks to extract features from the previous layer of neural activity. Because the neurons are arranged into 2D planes (arrays) the location of the activity on the plane implies the position of the feature in the input pattern. In this manner the machine forms a representation of the input pattern that is distributed across the planes of each u_S layer.

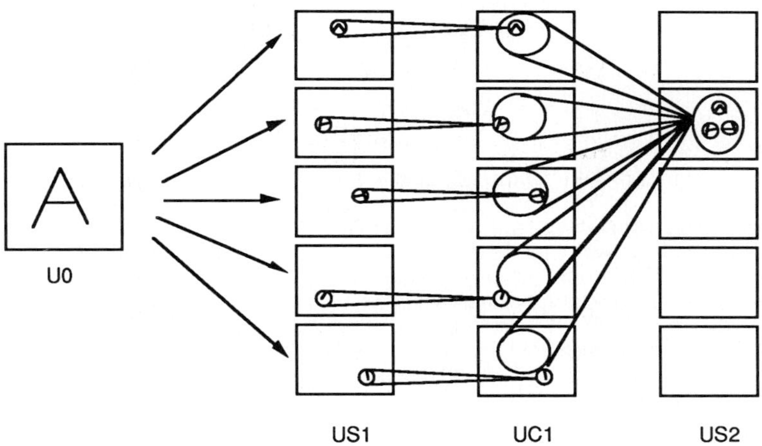

Figure 4: Hierarchical receptive fields as feature extractors

As features are extracted by each succeeding layer the representation becomes more abstract because each layer's features are combined at the next layer. At level u_{S1} the features extracted from the input image u_O are things like corners, curves, and oriented line segments. At level u_{C1} the features are slightly blurred versions of the features at u_{S1}. The blurring reduces the sensitivity of the recognition process to moderate variations in the input image. At u_{S2} the features are combinations of the blurred features at u_{C1}. This process is repeated at each succeeding layer until the output layer is reached. Thus, at the output layer neural activity represents the spatial relationships of earlier primitive features.

ART and Receptive Fields

As depicted in Figure 5, one can view the NxN features in the u_o input pattern as equivalent to the 1-D vector of neurons in the F1 layer of ART. Furthermore, the **A** masks of the Neocognitron can be thought of as the LTM traces of ART and the vector of neurons at position (i,j) in the different planes of u_{s1} can be viewed as a vector of F2 neurons. Therefore, if we can convert the current feedforward feature extraction process of the Neocognitron into a feedback ART III model of feature extraction and duplicate the structure at each (i,j) position in the US1 plane we have created a convolutional, or receptive field Adaptive Resonance Theory pattern recognition machine.

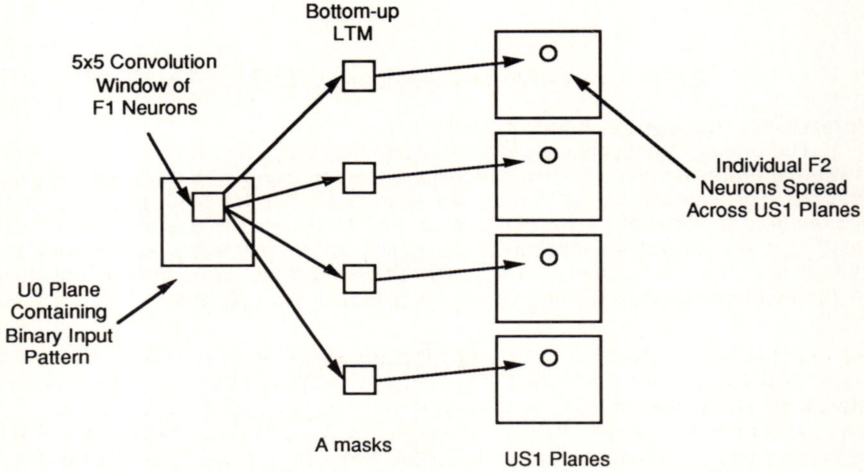

Figure 5: ART receptive fields in the Neocognitron architecture

Selective Attention Neocognitron (SAN)

The SAN, shown in Figure 6, is a significant extension of the feedforward Neocognitron (FFN) model which embodies the basic principles of the Neocognitron while simultaneously incorporating those of ART. The main system equations are given in equations (1-9). It is quite obvious that there are both feedforward (FF) paths and feedback (FB) paths within the system. LTM is denoted by the **A** masks in the two paths. Cross coupling of the FF and FB paths is apparent and implements gain and threshold control on the u_s and u_c cells.

Modification of system coefficients and parameters in the FF paths of the SAN by data flowing through the FB paths produces significant new behaviors in the SAN. The backward flow is guided by threshold gating signals received from the FF paths. When components of the input pattern are missing, the features are not present in the FF path, and thereby prevent signals from flowing backward. This condition is detected by the w_{cx} cells which lower the threshold $r_l(\mathbf{n},k)$ which in turn allows the u_s cells to extract vague remnants of the features in the input pattern, thereby unlocking the backward flow of signals. The propagation and gating of feedback signals continues until they reach the input layer and completely reconstruct the input pattern. When an input pattern is activating the network, those u_c cells that are not activated

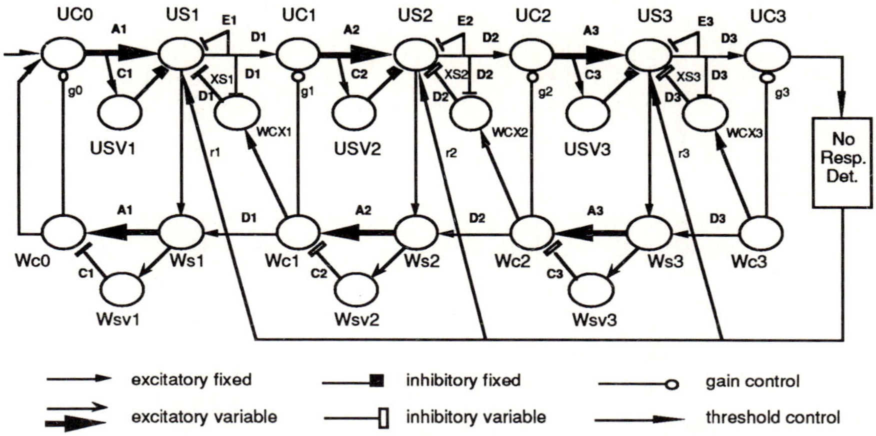

Figure 6: The Selective Attention Neocognitron (SAN)

begin to lose their ability to respond while those that are activated have an increased level of response. This is done using the gain control mechanism, $g_l(\mathbf{n},k)$. Thus, the network begins to selectively respond to subcomponents of the input pattern. The selection is further enhanced by the competitive nature of the u_S responses which try to force a decision. When a change of attention signal is initiated, the network leaves its current state and reduces the gain of those u_C cells that were active. The change of attention represents a type of neural fatigue or tetanus which biases the network's response and allows other subpatterns in the input pattern to begin activating the neurons in the SAN.

The SAN and Hierarchical ART

Figure 7 shows two versions of a hierarchical ART III system using the concept of mismatch mediated reset. It is important to note that in an ART III system reset modifies the efficacy of synaptic influence using a set of coupled differential equations which decrease the gain on mismatched synapses. The structure on the left indicates that in a conventional ART system mismatch computations at one level reset responses at the level above them. Using this scheme the reset/gain mechanism helps produce stable self-organizing LTM traces. In the figure on the right, computed mismatches are used to reset the level below. This is the structure the SAN uses to associatively recall stored patterns.

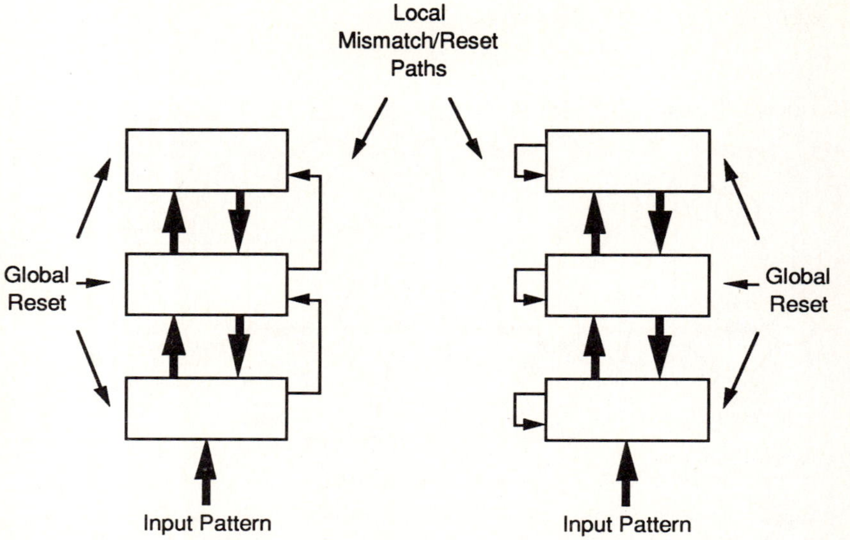

Figure 7: Two examples of mismatch/reset paths in a hierarchical system

Figure 8 shows the cells of the SAN organized into functional blocks. The cells and their functional groupings can be shown to implement all the computation performed by an ART III model with the structure shown on the right side of Figure 7. One can see similarities between the two models beginning with the mismatch/gain mechanism. The w_{CX} cells (eq. 1) compute the difference between the top-down w_C responses and the bottom-up u_S responses and thereby compute the mismatch between the top-down and bottom-up signals. The w_{CX} response is then used by the x_S and r_l cells (eq. 2 and 3) to develop a gain control signal $r_l(\mathbf{n},k)$ which is used by

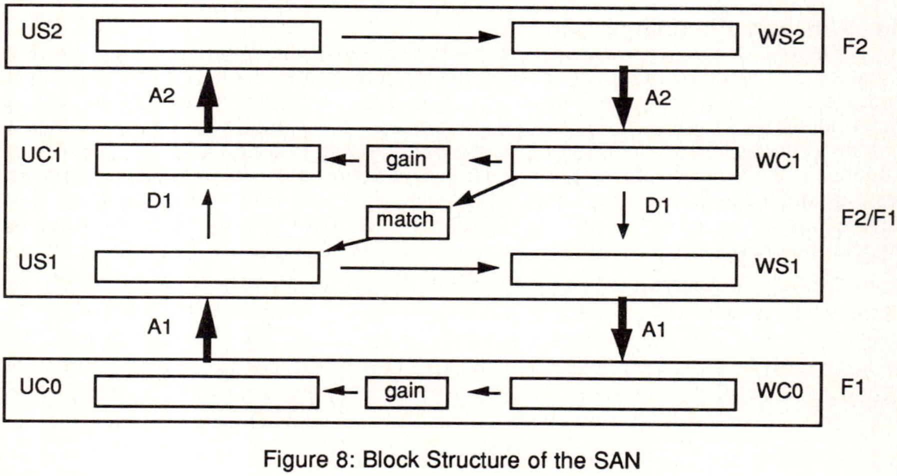

Figure 8: Block Structure of the SAN

$$w^t_{CXl}(\mathbf{n},k) = \varphi\left[w^t_{Cl}(\mathbf{n},k) - \sum_{\mathbf{v}\in D_l} d_l(\mathbf{v})\, u^t_{Sl}(\mathbf{n}+\mathbf{v},k)\right] \tag{1}$$

$$x^t_{Sl}(\mathbf{n},k) = -\beta_l\, x^{t-1}_{Sl}(\mathbf{n},k) + \beta_l \sum_{\mathbf{v}\in D_l} d_l(\mathbf{v})\, w^{t-1}_{CXl}(\mathbf{n}-\mathbf{v},k) \tag{2}$$

$$r^t_l(\mathbf{n},k) = \frac{r^0_l}{1 + x^t_{Sl}(\mathbf{n},k) + x^t_{Xl}} \tag{3}$$

$$u^t_{Sl}(\mathbf{n},k) = r^t_l(\mathbf{n},k)\, \varphi\left[\frac{\partial_l + \sum_{k=1}^{K_{l-1}} \sum_{\mathbf{v}\in A_l} a_l(\mathbf{v},k,K)\, u^t_{Cl-1}(\mathbf{n}+\mathbf{v},k)}{\partial_l + \frac{r^t_l(\mathbf{n},k)}{1 + r^t_l(\mathbf{n},k)}\, b_l(k)\, u^t_{SVl}(\mathbf{n})} - 1\right] \tag{4}$$

$$u^t_{Sl}(\mathbf{n}+\mathbf{v},k) := \varphi\left[u^t_{Sl}(\mathbf{n}+\mathbf{v},k) - \sum_{\mathbf{v}\in E_l} e_l(\mathbf{v})\, u^t_{Sl}(\mathbf{n}+\mathbf{v},k) - \sum_{k=1}^{K_l} \sum_{\mathbf{v}\in E_l} \bar{e}_l(\mathbf{v})\, u^t_{Sl}(\mathbf{n}+\mathbf{v},k)\right] \tag{5}$$

the feature extraction u_S cells (eq. 4) as an inhibitory gain control signal. Thus, the mismatch between the top-down signals represented by w_C, and the bottom-up signals represented by u_S, adjusts the gain of the inhibition used in computing the bottom-up signals. This mechanism, represented in Figure 8 as the 'match' box, represents the mismatch mediated reset of the hierarchical ART III system depicted on the right side of Figure 7. Note that unlike an ART system the mismatch is a direct difference. However, like ART III, the gain term is a first order differential equation (eq. 2) which modifies the inhibitory gain term $r_l(\mathbf{n},k)$ used in the computation of the F2 like u_S cells. In a previous paper Johnson et al. [1988] showed that modification of the inhibitory gain term r in the FFN indirectly influenced the efficacy of the LTM traces contained in the **A** masks.

Another important consideration in the comparison of the SAN and ART is that the u_S cell responses, which are similar to the F2 cells, use competition to contrast enhance their responses. This is done using the recurrent surround inhibition given in equation 5. Thus, the u_S cells have a competitive mechanism which is identical to the competitive mechanism used by the F2 neurons in ART models. Finally, there is a gain mechanism which affects the response of the network when patterns are presented sequentially. Carpenter notes that because of the dynamic modification of LTM synapse efficacy used in ART III, the responses of F2 neurons are biased away from their response to the pattern that was previously driving the system. The mechanism in the SAN which implements this process is denoted in Figure 8 as the 'gain' block. The mechanism begins with the w_C cells (eq. 9) which are processing the flow of top-down information from the bottom-up gated w_S cells (equation not given). Thus, when a feature is present in the bottom-up signals the w_C cells are enabled. This in turn causes $g_l(\mathbf{n},k)$ to increase according to the first order decay equation given in equation (7). The result of the increase in gain is that the u_C system (eq. 6) responds more strongly to the feature that gated the top-down signal. However, when

$$u^t_{Cl}(\mathbf{n},k) = g^t_l(\mathbf{n},k)\, \psi\left[\sum_{\mathbf{v}\in D_l} d_l(\mathbf{v})\, u^t_{Sl}(\mathbf{n}+\mathbf{v},k)\right] \tag{6}$$

$$g_l^t(\mathbf{n},k) = \gamma_l\, g_l^{t-1}(\mathbf{n},k) + (1-\gamma_l)\, \psi\left[\gamma_l\, w_{Cl}^{t-1}(\mathbf{n},k)\right] \tag{7}$$

$$g_l^t(\mathbf{n},k) = \frac{1}{1 + \gamma_l\, g_l^{t-1}(\mathbf{n},k)} \tag{8}$$

$$w_{Cl}^t(\mathbf{n},k) = \Psi\left[\alpha_l\left(\sum_{k=1}^{K_{l+1}} \sum_{\mathbf{v}\in A_{l+1}} a_{l+1}(\mathbf{v},k,K)\, w_{Sl+1}^t(\mathbf{n}-\mathbf{v},k) - \sum_{\mathbf{v}\in A_{l+1}} c_{l+1}(\mathbf{v})\, w_{SVl+1}^t(\mathbf{n}-\mathbf{v})\right)\right] \tag{9}$$

a new pattern is presented, or attention is switched, the gain term $g_l(\mathbf{n},k)$ is biased away from the previously presented pattern. Furthermore, if the attention is switched by externally changing from the gain equation given in (7) to the gain equation given in (8) those gains that were previously large due to facilitation now become small due to reciprocal fatigue. Thus, we again have behaviors that are identical to those used in the various versions of ART.

Conclusions

In this paper I presented a review of the three main variants of Adaptive Resonance Theory and the Selective Attention Neocognitron and shown that the ART concept of feedback could be incorporated into a hierarchical receptive field pattern recognition model. Next, I examined the relationship between the various mechanisms used in ART I, ART II, and ART III, and shown that the SAN had identical mechanisms and processes. These similarities include the mismatch mediated reset, attentional gain control, and competitive pattern enhancement. Furthermore, I have shown that the reset/gain mechanism, while connected differently in the two models, operates in a similar fashion and is used not to produce stable self-organizing memory but to associatively recall stored patterns.

References

[Carpenter, G., and Grossberg, S., 1990] ART 3 hierarchical search: chemical transmitters in self-organizing pattern recognition architectures, Proc. International Joint Conference on Neural Networks 1990, Vol. II, pp. 30-33.

[Fukushima, 1980] Neocognitron: A self-organizing neural network model for a mechanism of pattern recognition unaffected by shift in position, Biol. Cybernetics, Vol. 36, pp. 193-202.

[Fukushima, K., 1987] Neural network model for selective attention in visual pattern recognition and associative recall, Applied Optics, Vol.. 26, No. 23, pp 4985-4992.

[Grossberg, S., and Carpenter, G., 1987a] A massively parallel architecture for a self organizing neural pattern recognition machine, Computer Vision, Graphics, and Image Processing, Vol. 37, pp. 54-115.

[Grossberg, S., and Carpenter, G., 1987b] ART 2: self-organization of stable category recognition codes for analog input patterns, Applied Optics, Vol. 26, No. 23, pp. 4919-4936.

[Johnson, K., Daniell, C., and Burman, J., 1988a] Feature extraction in the Neocognitron, Proc. IEEE International Conference on Neural Networks, Vol. 2, pp. 117-127.

[Li, D., and Wee, W., 1990] A new Neocognitron structure modified by ART and backpropagation, Proc. International Joint Conference on Neural Networks 1990, Vol. I, pp 420-423.

[Rajapakse, J., Jakubowicz,, O, and Acharya, R., 1990] A real time ART I based vision system for distortion invariant recognition and autoassociation, Proc. International Joint Conference on Neural Networks 1990, Vol. II, pp 298-301.

Advanced Neural Computers / R. Eckmiller (Editor)

RECEPTIVE FIELD TAXONOMY

Jan J. KOENDERINK and Andrea J. VAN DOORN

Buys Ballot Laboratory
Utrecht University
Utrecht, The Netherlands

Given very general constraints, only a few receptive field types are admissible. These can be characterized completely through a certain second order partial differential equation. Families of receptive fields satisfying certain symmetry conditions can be constructed that are both orthonormal and complete.

1 INTRODUCTION

Since the early work by *e.g.*, Kuffler[12] in the fifties many varieties of *visual receptive field structures* (abbreviated RFS's) of the mammalian visual system have been reported, with perhaps a temporary culmination in Hubel and Wiesel's discovery[5] of "bar detectors" in the visual cortex, leading to the award of their Nobel prize. These RFS's are localized spatiotemporal structures that may assume a bewildering variety of forms. A large class is closily approximated by various derivatives of an isotropic Gaussian profile[6,7,13]. At the time there exists no *principled* taxonomy of such structures. The usual taxonomies are based on anatomical, physiological, or hypothetical functional characteristics. Nothing like a "periodic system" or such exists, nor are there formal theories of a *general* nature that require the RFS's discovered so far or that predict the existence of novel ones, although many *specific* theories exist, basically *ad hoc* attempts at the interpretation of bodies of empirical data, or based on functional considerations. (A simple example is the center/surround opponency required in models of contrast detection.) It is not even clear how "general theories" could play much of a rôle in this field which has the general flavor of "butterfly collecting". Yet the repeated occurrence of specific RFS's shapes over many species and subsystems is striking and can hardly be coincidental.

We report here on a general framework for the description of linear spatial RFS's. The framework is based on a few general assumptions, and yet permits only certain very specific classes of RFS's. For a given level of geometrical expertise it actually *requires the existence* of specific families of RFS's. Moreover, not only do you obtain a taxonomy, the framework also allows for various relations between RFS's of different families and determines the possible functional rôles of the members. Thus it predicts certain generic types of neural circuitry.

2 BASIC ASSUMPTIONS

One basic assumption is that the RFS's are *abundant*, such that the sampling density leads to a negligible bandlimited interpolation error. The upshot is that a continuous field theory is an apt approximation.

Two other assumptions are needed that are more specific. They address the problem of *scale* and *resolution.* The RFS size determines the level of resolution at which the RFS "sees" the retinal irradiance field (RIF). The RIF is a scalar field. To the visual system it is only available in sampled form. A class of RFS's with sizes within a restricted range yields a set of samples that represents the RIF at a level of resolution set by that size. When many different size classes are present, then the RIF can be said to be represented at that many different resolutions *simultaneously*. Such a collection of representations is like a geographical atlas in which the earth's surface is represented on maps of various scales.

Given two maps at different scales that represent the *same* part of the earth, one may expect relations between them. These relations are of a curiously *directed* nature: One expects to be able to find the "cause" of detail on a coarse map in the fine grained map, but not *vice versa*. The atlas has the structure of a continuous tree ("tree" in the sense of datastructures), branching occurs only in the direction of increasing resolution. (Indeed, bifurcations are typical of geographical atlases. Cartographers speak of "generalization" for the inverse of a bifurcation.) This "causality for blurring", or "absence of spurious resolution" appears to be a necessary constraint on a multiresolution representation[8]. We assume it to hold for the multiresolution representation of the RIF by RFS's of various size classes. There exists psychophysical evidence[1].

This assumption has important consequences. It can be shown that the only structures that satisfy the causal atlas constraint satisfy a certain partial differential equation (PDE). This PDE has the structure of a *diffusion equation*: If you pass from a high to a low resolution you blur the detail via diffusion of the RIF. Thus you require

$$\Delta\mathcal{I}(x,y;s) = \partial\mathcal{I}(x,y;s)/\partial s,$$

where $\mathcal{I}(x,y;s)$ denotes the RIF as a function of location (x,y) and the resolution parameter s. The amount of diffusion determines the resolution of the resulting representation. The propagator of the PDE is a Gaussian kernel. You obtain a low resolution version of the RIF by convolution with a Gaussian kernel, it is a sampling with a very simple RFS. The Gaussian is unique in many respects, for instance it remains Gaussian under concatenated convolutions, and it is the unique rotationally symmetric kernel that is also separable in Cartesian coordinates.

Since the Gaussian kernel keeps its shape under blurring, except for a size change and an amplitude scaling, it fits nicely into schemes that encompass *size invariance*. This is indeed something one would like in general: RFS's at different resolutions must be equal except for size and amplitude. We accept this as a final assumption. It makes the visual system *selfsimilar* under scale changes. (Within limits of course.)

3 RECEPTIVE FIELD STRUCTURE

These assumptions suffice to put a strong constraint on the possible RFS's. If you require that the RFS be a resolution dependent amplitude scaling times a size scaled spatial distribution, you may use the PDE that governs the atlas structure to derive a PDE in *normalized spatial coordinates* that has to be satisfied by all RFS's that comply with the assumptions. Only such RFS's yield size invariance without spurious resolution.

The PDE governing the RFS can be solved with the usual methods of mathematical physics. Indeed, a simple mathematical trick transforms the PDE into that of the time independent

Schrödinger equation of the quantummechanical harmonic oscillator: You write

$$A(x, y; s) = \frac{e^{-\frac{x^2+y^2}{8s}}}{8\pi s};$$

$$\psi_n(x, y; s) = (\frac{1}{\sqrt{4s}})^n \varphi(\frac{x}{\sqrt{4s}}, \frac{y}{\sqrt{4s}}) A(x, y; s),$$

where $A(x, y; s)$ denotes an aperture function (basically a "fuzzy characteristic function") and the scaling with the resolution parameter is taken to depend on the "order" n. The significance of the order will appear below. Then the PDE becomes

$$\Delta \varphi_n(\xi, \eta) + (2n + 2 - \xi^2 - \eta^2)\varphi_n(\xi, \eta) = 0,$$

where ξ and η denote the scaled coordinates $x/\sqrt{4s}$ and $y/\sqrt{4s}$. Thus one may turn to physics texts to find the solutions in various coordinate systems all worked out.

4 SPECIFIC FORMS

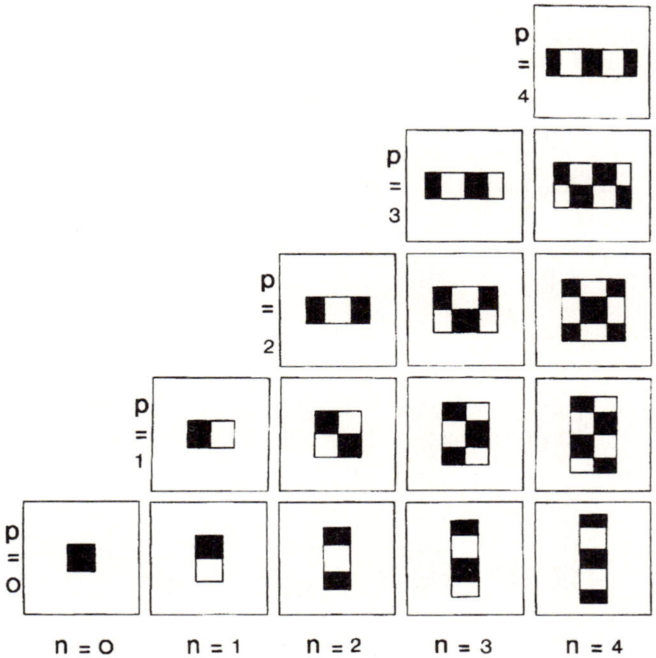

FIGURE 1.
The Cartesian RFS's up to (and including) the fourth order. The order is n, whereas p denotes the order in the horizontal direction. The order in the vertical direction is just $q = n - p$. The boundary of the oscillatory region was taken as the boundary of of the RFS's, whereas the internal structure is given by the regions of positive or negative sign. Of course the RFS's are in reality smooth functions extending to infinity!

4.1 Cartesian Fields

The solutions C_{pq} in Cartesian coordinates (Figure 1) are (in terms of the φ)

$$\varphi_{pq}(\xi,\eta) = \frac{H_p(\xi)H_q(\eta)e^{-\frac{\xi^2+\eta^2}{2}}}{\sqrt{2^n p! q! \sqrt{\pi}}},$$

with $p + q = n$, whereas the H_n denote Hermite polynomials. It is especially interesting because the solution C_{pq} with wavenumbers (p, q) proves to be the mixed partial derivative of the Gaussian kernel, p times with respect to x, q times with respect to y. This is so interesting because the RIF as sampled by these RFS's is the exact $[p, q]$-order mixed partial derivative of the RIF at the level of resolution of these RFS's. This enables us to characterize the nature of the activity assembly of RFS's with integral order less or equal than n (that is $p + q \leq n$, $p, q = 0, 1, \ldots, n$) at a given location: It is the equivalence class of all RIF's that agree in the nth order Taylor expansion at that location for that resolution. Technically it is the "n-jet" of the RIF at that location, and the totality of these RFS's at all locations are the "n-jet bundle". This immediately reveals the exact power of the representation: The RFS representation of the RIF allows exactly those geometrical computations that rely on the n-jet of the RIF[9,10]. For instance, you can only compute boundary curvature[11] (curvature of an isophote of the RIF) at a point if $n \geq 2$.

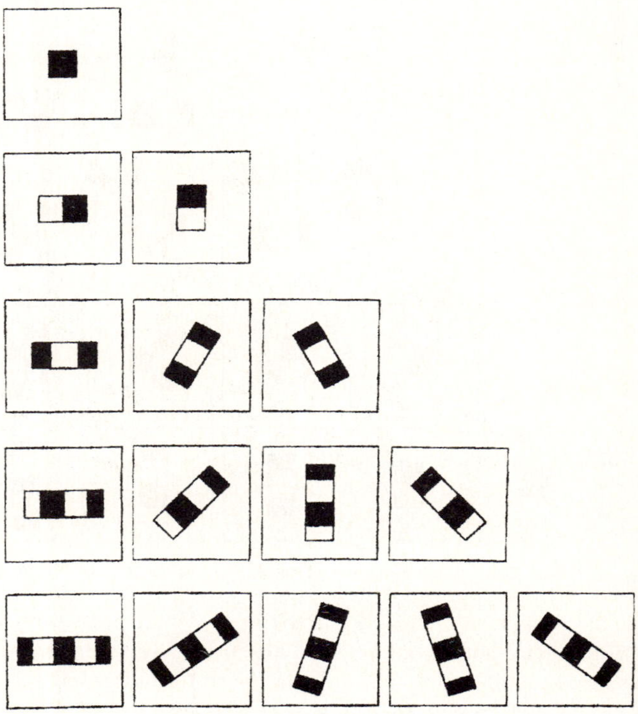

FIGURE 2.

The wavelets up to and including the fouth order. Wavelets of any orientation exist: Here a possible (minimal) basis is shown. Refer to legend of figure 1 for further details.

These RFS's or very similar structures are also popular in image processing. For instance the $(1,0)$–type is the well known "Canny edge detector"[2].

Many different representations of the nth order RFS's are possible. Two classes are especially interesting because of their specific symmetry properties. These are the "wavelets", that are the Cartesian solutions $W_n = C_{n0}$, and the polar RFS's P_{km} ($n = 2k + \|m\|$, $k = 0, 1, 2\ldots$, m integer $0, \pm 1, \pm 2, \ldots, \pm k$).

4.2 Wavelet Fields

The wavelets (Figure 2) are so named because they look like Gabor wave trains. (However, the number of zero crossings is not infinite, but equals the order. A wavelet of order n in the direction ϑ is simply $W_n(x, y; \vartheta) = C_{n0}(x\cos\vartheta + y\sin\vartheta, -x\sin\vartheta + y\cos\vartheta)$.) A complete basis of wavelets needs at least $n+1$ different orientations (spaced at intervals $\pi/(n+1)$ say). These functions yield samples of nth order directional derivatives.

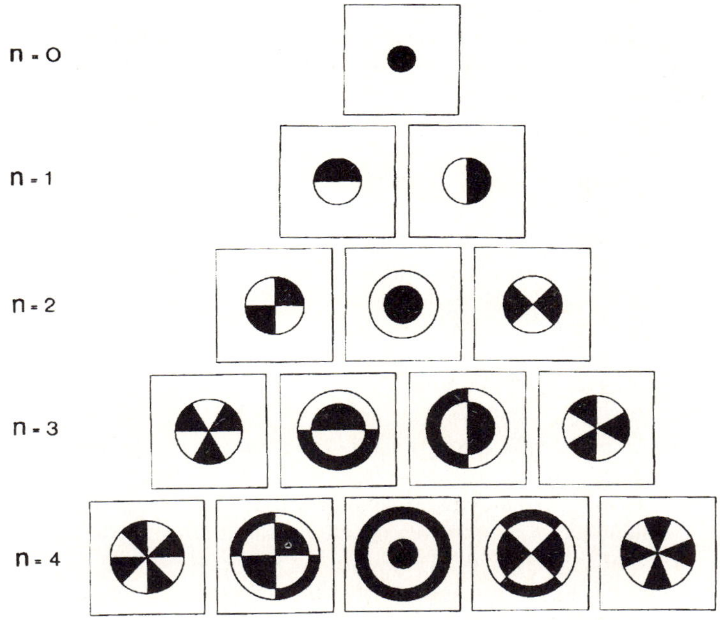

FIGURE 3.
The polar RFS's up to and including the fourth order. The order is n. Notice that the rotationally symmetric RFS's occur only as unique specimen for a given order, whereas the RFS's with azimuthal modulation occur in pairs with mutual phase shift of $\pi/2$. Refer to legend of figure 1 for technical details.

4.3 Polar Form

The polar RFS's (Figure 3) are of interest because of their peculiar symmetry. Their structure is

$$\varphi_{km}(r,\alpha) = \frac{r^m L_k^m(r^2) e^{-r^2/2} e^{\pm i m \alpha}}{\sqrt{m! \binom{k+m}{k} \pi}},$$

with $n = m + 2k$, $k = 0, 1, 1, \ldots$ and $m \geq 0$, whereas $\xi = r\cos\alpha$, $\eta = \sin\alpha$, and the L_k^m are associated Laguerre polynomials. (Of course, we only consider real linear combinations.) For even orders the RFS's P_{k0} are isotropic. The simplest nontrivial RFS is the center/surround opponent field. It samples the Laplacean of the RIF. The RFS's $P_{0,m}$ display a m-fold rotational symmetry. They are "windmill" shaped forms. These RFS's are also used in image processing applications[3,4].

5 TRANSFORMATIONS AND COMBINATIONS

Because of the linearity of the fundamental PDE there exist linear transformations between the various RFS families. For instance, the center/surround opponent RFS equals the sum of two crossed (orthogonally) bar detectors, a property that is not *a priori* obvious and results from the fundamental assumptions. The nth order subfamilies are closed under linear combination. Thus all RFS's can be obtained from linear combination of the wavelets. This is important because the wavelets are in certain respects the simplest representation. (There is only a single RFS for a given order if you disregard orientation. The Cartesian and polar families are much richer, the number of distinct RFS's increases asymptotically with the square of the order.) Many other interrelations exist, *e.g.*, the RFS's behave simply under blurring and concatenation.

6 BRAIN CIRCUITRY

A linear combination of RFS's can be regarded as a *change of representation*. For instance, you can shift or rotate RFS's, or change from Cartesian to polar coordinates. For a given RIF there are certain "canonical representations" for which the RIF structure assumes a particularly simple form. A suitable representation thus allows a "tuning" to specific input structures. Such a tuning might well be directed by a "hypothesis", or top down command to the RFS assembly. Such a "command" would take the form of a set of coefficients to define the linear transformation.

Certain nonlinear algebraic combinations of RFS assembly activity have immediate *geometrical significance*. One may conceive of such combinations as being implemented in local circuitry within the assembly. For a given order the geometry of the RIF can be represented by a finite number of geometrical invariants. (*E.g.*, for $n = 1$, the local value and the gradient.) These invariants can easily be prewired into the assembly.

Acknowledgements

This work is part of the ESPRIT program Insight.

References

[1] Bijl, P. and J. J. Koenderink, *Visibility of blobs with a gaussian luminance profile.* Vision Res. **29**, 447–456, 1989.

[2] Canny, J. F., *Finding edges and lines in images.* MIT AI lab Technical Report No. 720, 1983.

[3] Coggins, J. M. and A. K. Jain, *A spatial filtering approach to texture analysis.* Pattern Recognition Letters **3**, 195–203, 1985.

[4] Coggins J. M., F. S. Fay and K. E. Fogarty, *Development and application of a three-dimensional artificial visual system.* Computer Methods and Programs in Biomedicine **22**, 69–77, 1986.

[5] Hubel, D. H. and T. N. Wiesel, *Receptive fields of single neurons in the cat's striate cortex.* J. Physiol. **148**, pp. 574–591, 1959.

[6] Jones, J. P. and L. A. Palmer, *The two-dimensional spatial structure of simple receptive fields in cat striate cortex.* J. Neurophysiol. **58**, 1187–1211, 1987.

[7] Jones, J. P. and L. A. Palmer, *An evaluation of the two-dimensional Gabor filter model of simple receptive fields in cat striate cortex.* J. Neurophysiol. **58**, 1233–1258, 1987.

[8] J. J. Koenderink, *The structure of images.* Biol. Cybern. **50**, 363–370, 1984.

[9] Koenderink, J. J. and A. J. van Doorn, *Representation of local geometry in the visual system.* Biol. Cybern. **55**, 367–375, 1987.

[10] J. J. Koenderink, *Operational significance of receptive field assemblies.* Biol. Cybernet. **58**, 163–171,1988.

[11] Koenderink, J. J. and W. Richards, *Two-dimensional curvature operators.* J. Opt. Soc. Am. **A5**, 1136–1141, 1988.

[12] Kuffler, S. W., *Neurons in the retina: Organisation, inhibition and excitation problems.* Cold Spring Harbor Symp. on Quant. Biol. **17**, pp. 281–292, 1952.

[13] Young, R. A., *The gaussian derivative theory of spatial vision: Analysis of cortical cell recptive field line-weighting profiles.* General Motors Res. Tech. Rep.**GMR-4920**, May, 1985.

Advanced Neural Computers / R. Eckmiller (Editor)

CONSIDERATIONS FOR A VISUAL ARCHITECTURE

Christoph von der Malsburg[1]

Computer Science Dept. and Section for Neurobiology
University of Southern California, Los Angeles

Many aspects of the visual process are beginning to be understood, through the efforts of neuroanatomy, neurophysiology, psychophysics and computer vision. What is needed now is the integration of all components into one coherent functional whole: the definition of a visual architecture. It is argued here that this problem is nearing a threshold. We are able to define it with greater and greater clarity; most of the pieces of the jigsaw puzzle are on the table, they only have to be put together; many misconceptions have been identified and are being put out of the way; massively parallel machines promise to soon give us the necessary processing power; and the motivation and man-power directed at the issue are rapidly increasing. My paper intends to focus attention on the problem.

What figures are produced when a cube is cut by a plane? The question lets us mentally create a cube and a plane, we move the plane around to cut the cube at various angles, we create line segments and vertices where the plane cuts faces and edges of the cube, our attention focuses in to attend to this or that detail. When the limits of our imagination are reached we take a pencil and sketch out particular configurations. Eventually we pronounce and explain our answer in words. What marvellous machine is it that allows us to perform such operations?

I think it is time we took aim at an answer to this question. Much progress has been made recently, providing constraints on the structure of the visual architecture, putting out of the way false solutions and distracting prejudices, and providing us with a technological basis for experimental realizations.

THE VISUAL PROCESS

Our visual system creates for us imagined scenes which, we believe, are true mirror images of the reality surrounding us. Indeed, our head creates for us a model world which, it seems, differs from the outside reality only by being less detailed and less complete, and by being restricted to the particular perspective of the individual. The simple question I will discuss here is, what is the stuff from which this model world is built, and what is the mechanism that creates and forms that stuff? This question is of enormous practical, theoretical and philosophical importance. The visual system constitutes more than a third of our brain. Our thinking is to a large extent visual imagery. All navigation and manipulation is guided directly by vision or by imagined geometry. Our intelligence is curiously restricted to things that can be formulated as scenes, which are largely visual in substance. Language only makes sense by continuous reference to visual imaginations. Understanding vision very likely will mean understanding the brain and the mind.

Our visual system is a geometrical engine that allows us to create geometrically shaped objects, to compose them into more complex objects and scenes, to decompose them into subobjects, to rotate, manipulate, deform, intersect them, and to turn, whatever we create, into a number of different representations that can relate to our motor system, especially to our hands, to language, and to

[1]This work has been supported by grants from the German Ministry for Science and Technology (ITR-8800-H1) and from the AFOSR (88-0274) and from the BRAIN Initiative of the European Community (ST2J - 0416 - C (EDB)).

abstract symbols. The imaginations in our visual system autonomously grow, apparently generated by a general mechanism of organization, just as clouds grow in the sky. Our visual machine is incredibly efficient, creating, whatever it creates, effortlessly and fast. This effortlessness is the source of three illusions, those of *simplicity*, of *passive observership*, and of *omnipresence.* These illusions have misled efforts ot understand the visual architecture.

Simplicity. When communicating, we designate objects and relations by symbols. Our symbols are parsimonious and simple. It is a misconception that our brain manipulates just such symbols. Symbols have no meaning in themselves. Our brain turns communication symbols into complex imaginations, manipulates these, and turns the result into simple symbols again. Let me give an example. A circle can symbolically be designated by giving the length of its radius and the location of its center. A circle drawn on a piece of paper is a large ensemble of molecules of ink, layed out in circular arrangement. A circle as a visual imagination may well contain as part of it an extensive array of data elements that actually form a circle by their arrangement in some space. Imaginations are rich and detailed. They are the natural playground for mechanisms of organization. Symbols can only be handled with the help of independent insight into the domain at hand, that is, with recurrence to their expansion in a human mind. This fact is camouflaged by the phenomenon, extensively exploited in Artificial Intelligence, that some systems of manipulation can themselves be put into the form of parsimonious symbols and rules that can be run autonomously on a computer. Given the problem of finding points of intersection of line figures, a symbolic approach represents the line objects by cartesian equations and finds the coordinates of intersection points as solutions of the simultaneous set of equations. The symbolic approach is fundamentally misleading, because it is dependent on the imagination in the programer's mind, and because it is limited to a set of fortuitous application domains, which are of measure zero in the space of all problems. With our ink-on-paper example it is a trivial step of generalization to go from a circle to some irregular ovoid and determine its intersection points with another line. For the symbolic approach different ovoid curves are very different beasts, and their symbolic manipulation quickly loses its simplicity. *In order to be a substrate for general mechanisms of organization, the objects in our brain are formed as vast arrays of data elements isomorphic in some sense to the objects they represent.* This type of representation has been termed “natural representation” [1].

Passive observership. In a camera, light simply imprints a picture on film. The process of seeing is so effortless and reliable that we have the impression that it likewise is a simple passive process of impression of a picture on us. Massive psychophysical evidence, however, shows that the process of seeing is one of active construction, relying more on stored knowledge and experience than on passive intake of visual information. Indeed, there is evidence that the rate of visual data acquisition is only about 50 or 100 bits per second. The bulk of the structure in a visual scene comes from within, not from the eyes! It is suggestive here that from among the fibers entering primary visual cortex only about 1% are visual afferents. *Scenes are constructed by a process of autonomous active organization, on the basis of stored patterns and knowledge.* In the course of this process, decision points are reached. At these points, the visual system performs active tests on the sensory information. In this process, *structure lying dormant in memory is activated and turned from potential existence into actual existence.*

Omnipresence. You are looking out of the window at a complex scene. All of the myriads of little details are simultaneously present, aren't they? Do the obvious test, go through a quick sequence of arbitrary checks, and you find, whatever you check, it is there. This leads to the illusion of simultaneous presence in your mind of all detail in the scene. In reality, the different chunks of structure appearing in your flashes of attention are instantly created and much of their structure disappears again with the next shift in fixation. When looking at a lawn, there are a billion blades of grass, and they seem all to be there in your mind. In reality you create them with your flashes of attention. The sequence itself carries no objective reality, it is not worth remembering or even noticing. Our conscious experience shuts out fixation sequences and concentrates on the more permanent structure accumulated in the process. Thus, in spite of our impression of a still, or slowly evolving, picture in our mind, *seeing is a complex sequential temporal process of organization and decay.*

Two important conclusions are suggested by the discussion in the last two paragraphs. One is that the process of seeing takes the form of an extremely rich and quick process of self-organization. The other is that the data in our visual system are arranged as a gradient from latent to overt structure. Self-organization pulls structure from a deeper layer and turns it into more concrete, explicit form. A number of stages can be distinguished. The most concrete, most narrow and fleeting is the flash of attention. It is at present under extensive study [2] and it is described in more detail by Nakayama [3], whose term for the structure concretized in an individual flash of attention is "icon." During a given eye fixation several flashes of attention may take place. The amount of detail in each of them has been characterized as being equivalent to an array of 30×30 pixels (C. Anderson, personal communication), spread out over a large part of the visual field or concentrated in one part of it. Actual eye fixations — foveations on different parts of a scene — take place at a somewhat slower time scale. Each eye fixation provides high visual resolution in a new location in the scene and thus offers the potential for a new range of flashes of attention. Conversely, eye movements are guided by the information picked up from earlier attention flashes, as the result of which interesting parts of a scene have been identified.

The next level of the hierarchy in the direction of the less concrete, more comprehensive may be the object description or scene description. The description has to pay the price for comprehensiveness by leaving out detail, by having to summarize structure in a parsimonious way. But this summary description is evidently capable to control and constrain a pattern formation process when attention is fixed on any one part of the scene to quickly produce that part of it in clear detail.

One more stage of the hierarchy from the concrete to the latent is reached when a concrete scene is absorbed into long-term memory. In memory, many scenes are superimposed upon each other and none of them is present explicitely. But it is possible, with closed eyes, to conjure structure up from memory, turn it into concrete descriptions of concrete scenes, with any level of detail desired, going up the hierarchy we just descended (leaving out only the stage involving eye movements). In this process, arbitrary decisions are to be met, presumably influenced by contact with other parts of the brain, say, language, and the resulting scene has the flavor of being just that, arbitrary. With open eyes, this process is guided by the constraints furnished by visual input, but the two processes are actually very similar in nature.

One may object that the description of the visual process just given relies too much on self-organization and on sequential processing and too little on the actual simultaneous availability of visual information in the form of the retinal image. There is, however, a wealth of psychophysical work corroborating the view given. Here is not the place to review it all, but let us discuss some constraints that may be responsible for this apparent limitation of our visual system (the style discussed is a limitation because it laboriously produces structure by self-organization that apparently could be available directly, and because it is sequential and slow where it perhaps could be parallel and fast). One reason may be hardware limitation: the same machinery is used for the representation of different potential scenes from long-term memory, and for the representation of different foci of attention within one scene. So, you may say, why doesn't the visual system do it the fashion of a cinema film, which records different scenes on physically different strips of celluloid. Economy comes to mind. But a much more important reason for recording different structures in a physically overlapping fashion is the need to generalize: to learn from one scene for many others. If you have a tool-and-model box that allows you to fluently create scenes typical for an environment, you have much more than just a collection of previously scenes — you have the statistical an physical laws that govern the range of phenomena, you can deal with entirely new scenes! This is very important in our world that never repeats a visual scene in a lifetime. Generalization is the benefit that you gain when using the same tool, the same model over and over again in different contexts: the structure you absorb into a model in one context can be used in many others. The price you pay is having the tool only once, and you have to deal with the different contexts one at a time in a sequential manner.

A related but distinct reason for going sequential is the binding problem. Imagine you have a red A and a green B in a scene, and you want to represent the situation with tools that talk about redness, greenness, A-ness and B-ness separately. Having them all active at the same time may create the illusory conjunction of a red B or a green A [2]. An easy way out of the problem is to keep the red A and the green B separate in time, as actually proposed by Treisman. A more expensive solution would be the introduction of specialized pieces of hardware for dealing with red As and green Bs (and green As and red Bs). But whatever you learn about redness in connection with a red A you wouldn't transfer automatically to red Bs and you would have to relearn it for them.

One of the most puzzling aspects of our visual system is its vast power of generalization and its enormous flexibility. Part of the answer must lie in the style we just outlined: structures are not stored in any literal sense as copies of images but rather in the form of models, rules and tools from which the structures can be created again by self-organization. This wouldn't be possible in a world without general laws and structure. The deep mystery of epistemology must have its solution in the existence of powerful organic laws in the structure of the world we see and in the visual system by which we see it, and in a pre-established harmony between them, pre-established by evolution.

THE ARCHITECTURE APPROACH

The classical AI style addresses individual problems with specialized data structures and algorithms. When a large problem, such as vision, is to be handled, the problem is first decomposed into sub-problems, these are solved, and finally an integration of the different subsystems is attempted. A perfect example of this style is office automation. We already have components such as text editors, typesetting, file systems, email and fax, printers, graphic systems, spread-sheets and databases, but we are still waiting for these components to talk to each other. There is no fundamental problem, but it turned out that the effort needed to integrate simple component systems by far transcends the original effort in developing those components. Out of this painful process has emerged the realization that for the construction of large systems it is both necessary and possible to devise architectures. Architectures are standardized flexible formulations of data structures and processes. Examples are ASCII characters and bus structures, domain-specific programming languages, communication protocols, Postscript and TeX, PHIGS and expert systems. In the architectural approach a specific structure is specified in two stages. First the general structure of a field of individual problems is encapsulated in the form of protocols for data and processes, thereby restricting the degrees of freedom of the original system. Then a specific structure is created by playing just on those degrees of freedom. Indeed, all natural and artificial production processes are dominated by the architectures that are implicit in tools, design methods, materials and building elements. The essence of the evolutionary progress of life and of human industry lies in the development of more and more powerful architectures. In the context of Artificial Intelligence the tremendous effectiveness of architectures lies in the fact that they restrict the programmer in his degrees of freedom very tightly to those that are natural to the domain of application, thus keeping him from making mistakes and from creating misunderstandings between different subsystems.

DATA STRUCTURE

When I show you an object you have never seen before you can nevertheless decompose it into elementary shapes, you can describe it to me in words, you can grasp it, forming your hand appropriately, and you can make a drawing of it. All of this could not be performed by a system that was just capable of putting out simple symbols or modes of reaction for the objects it has seen before, as implicit, for instance, in the perceptron architecture [4]. The capabilities of our visual system can only be explained on the basis of its power of creating representations for objects that somehow are isomorphic to their real structure (whatever that is). What can be the format of this representation?

The general requirements of visual scene representation have been discussed in [5, 6]. It seems obvious that representations of complex, variable entities are assembled from simpler, more rigid and more general parts in a hierarchical fashion. This is illustrated in a most instructive way by the results of psychophysical work by I. Biederman [7]. He shows that complex objects and scenes are parsed, by our visual system, into an alphabet of two or three scores of shape-primitives ("geons"), and are represented as data objects consisting of these geons and their spatial relationships. Objects that are naturally described in this way can quickly be recognized, memorized and handled, whereas objects that are not easily parsed into a small array of geons (such as a ball of crumpled paper) cannot. Geons themselves are represented and recognized as structured arrays of line elements. The basis for grouping the many line elements in a visual stimulus into shape primitives are non-accidental relations such as collinearity, symmetry, parallelism, and cotermination. More generally, a visual scene can be thought of as a large array of data elements which are assembled and attached to each other. More complex structures are formed in a herarchical way by assembling simpler structures. This hierarchy extends on the lower end to simple visual features, like local grey levels, edge elements or stereotyped objects, and extends on the higher end to rich descriptions of individual scenes.

A complete scene is described by representing the objects in the scene, complete with description of their shape and properties as well as their roles and biological significance (e.g., obstacle, object-to-grasp, food, prey, source of danger, social partner, self). The scene desription further represents the spatial relationships of objects, as well as their temporal trajectory. And the scene description represents the application of organizing schemas, such as "street scene," or "peeling an orange" or "killing a prey animal." Many object types, like "vehicle" or "house" are complex flexible schemas.

When talking about a hierarchy of complexity in scene representation it is important to avoid confusion between the complexity of an object to be represented and the complexity of the representing data object. An object of any complexity (pixel, object, complete scene) can still be designated by a single data element, although this data element cannot reflect variable structure. On the other hand, a data object composed of many data elements can flexibly reflect the structure of the object represented and, moreover, can represent structural relationships to other objects in terms of partial identity. To give an example, a particular human face could be represented with the help of just one data element that selectively responded to that face; but the data element could not reflect variable facial expression, and it could not express relations to other faces in terms of common traits. On the other hand, if a face was represented by a data object that was composed of many data elements, different components of the data object could represent different aspects of facial structure, facial expression, for instance, and could take part in the representation of other faces such that structural relationships between them are truthfully represented.

It is natural to assume that individual data elements are (relatively) fixed in their meaning. It is further natural to assume that the flexibility required for the representation of variable objects and scenes stems from the variable combinatorics of data elements combined into complex data objects. This architectural trait —constant data elements, variably composed data objects— is common to most symbolic systems and reflects a very fundamental aspect of the world we live in.

The defininition of a combinatoric system requires a means to assemble parts into wholes. Different symbol systems have different means to do so. All paper-and-pencil based systems use spatial contiguity to this end. This text, for instance, uses letters as data elements, and it combines them into words by stringing them up. Blanc spaces, punctuation marks, paragraph markings and chapter heads are used to create higher levels of a hierarchy of data objects. The programming language Lisp uses brackets to assemble elementary symbols into a hierarchy of data objects.

Neural networks conform to a certain extent to the characteristic discussed here. Neurons are data elements. They acquire their stable symbolic meaning in terms of their connections to other neurons and to inputs and outputs. They can be assembled into comples data objects by co-activation. A major draw-back of the neural network architecture, however, is its inability to form hierarchically structured data objects, as has been pointed out before [1, 8]: All co-active neurons merge into one structure-less object.

Our physical world conforms to the scheme just outlined: it is composed of elements —atoms, molecules— that are hierarchically composed into complex objects. This is the ultimate reason for the usefulness of combinatoric symbol systems. There is, however, a fundamental difference between the physical world out there and the symbolic world in our mind: the elements of the physical world form rather stable assemblages, whereas we require the data elements in our minds to flexibly fall into ever changing patterns. This is due to the fact that we actively move around and are presented with a changing scene, so that we have to require our mind to rapidly fall into different patterns. As mentioned before, we couldn't survive with a mind based on separate data elements for separate scenes, because such a system couldn't absorb structure from one scene and make it available for other scenes.

Here are a few considerations regarding the complexity level represented by individual data elements. The number of possible data elements grows quickly with their complexity. Not all possible data elements above a trivial level can be present in a system, and choices have to be made. These choices are made by evolution-ontogeny and by learning in contact with a particular invironment. It is costly, in terms of evolutionary or learning time, to create the information implicit in a rich set of high-level data elements. On the other hand it is costly in terms of processing time to create complex data objects from very simple data elements. A compromize is dictated by economy. Presumably our visual architecture starts out, at births, with a primordial set of data elements which are relatively simple and structured in terms of simple symmetries; there are mechanisms in place to create complex data objects, although these mechanism must be slow. For those data objects (of any complexity) that frequently recur literally new data elements are created. Thus, the structural complexity of data objects, and the time to produce them, is reduced as much as possible. It is important to stress, though, that it has to be possible to represent a given object in terms of a combination of low-level data elements *before* the decision can be met whether it is worthwhile to dedicate a new data element to it. If this condition is violated (as is the case with neural networks), the system would have to tentatively represent all possible combinations of the previously existing data elements over a stretch of time before it could make the decision which of them are worthwile to keep. This would put severe constraints on the level of complexity of possible input scenes and of possible data elements, which is indeed a major difficulty with neural networks.

It seems fair to assume that data elements in our visual system are to be identified with neurons. What can be said about the structure of data elements in the visual architecture? We already know that many neurons have receptive fields localized in retinal space and that they respond to certain combinations of visual quality within those receptive fields, e.g., local spatial frequency, movement, stereo depth, color. We also know that it is advantageous to have a resolution hierarchy and that such a hierarchy is in fact realized in our visual system. There is evidence that there are neurons that are highly specific to complex objects such as faces [9]. It is inimaginable that evolution has equipped us with specific neurons for many different complex patterns (faces may be an exception, for their biological relevance). It seems likely that heavily overlearned patterns such as letters and common words are represented directly in terms of data elements. It is an important research issue to find out whether there are complex data elements beyond local feature detectors in our visual system at birth and after learning and what their structure could be. It is not inconceivable that initially there are only local feature detectors, since it is possible to represent and recognize complex visual objects directly in terms of assemblages of local feature detectors [10].

What is the data format to express the assembly of data elements into structured data objects? This issue is riddled with misconceptions. Most man-made symbol systems use mobile letters or icons that can be assembled into local groups in some space, like in a two-dimensional graphical space or the one-dimensional temporal extent of spoken language. It the data elements in our visual system are indeed neurons, then they cannot be moved around to be assembled into groups. One misconception is the idea of assembling a group of neurons into a higher unit by representing it by a new data element. This idea has been criticised before [1, 8] and the main arguments have already been mentioned here. Another misconception is the idea of using registry in visual space as the tool for binding data elements. Although visual topology is an important source of information for the definition of useful data objects, visual registry is too special a system, since it is often necessary to bind data elements which are not neighbors in visual space.

Serious candidates for binding systems are based on the idea of tagging: tags of some sort are attached to data elements and all elements that carry the same tag are thereby assembled into a group. A tagging system based on temporal signal structure has been proposed as part of a cognitive architecture [1, 8, 11, 12]. Another tagging system, based on real-valued tags, has recently been proposed [13]. Tagging systems can be furnished with hierarchical structure and can thereby express hierarchically structured data objects.

What is the type of assemblages of data elements that are required in a visual architecture? More research is required here, but a few observations may already capture essential aspects. When visual information hits our eyes it is in two-dimensional form. It is certainly important and useful to favor assemblages of sets of neurons forming neighborhoods in visual space. This can be naturally implemented in a tagging system, by connecting neigboring data elements such that they tend to have similar tags. A related issue is the segmentation of visual scenes into segments that may correspond to physically coherent objects out there. This is not a simple corrolary to a topological binding scheme since segments may be formed by non-contiguous parts of visual space (e.g., when we see an object through foliage or a fence). Another important structure to be represented is the hierarchical structure in a scene composed of objects composed of sub-objects composed of elementary features. It seems plausible that at least three levels are required in this hierarchy. Still another important structure is the attachment of descriptors, e.g. functional roles or colors or form descriptors, to objects. Any tagging system should be able to provide a basis for these binding structures, if organization mechanisms can be found to naturally create those structures.

The visual system has to transform visual data as they appear on the retinae into other representations that are useful as a basis for operations to be performed by other parts of the brain. As part of this job it has to give identity and role of objects in the scene, it has to describe their spatial coordinates in appropriate frames (object centered, body centered, scene centered), it has to provide shape information that can be used by the motor system to preshape the grasping hand, it has to predict trajectories of moving objects, and it has to describe the reliability of the data it provides. Much of this information may be implicitely present in the original retinal signal. It has to be made explicit by projecting the data onto appropriate data structures. As an important example, visual data are evaluated as to their "what" (identity of objects) and their "where" (location of objects). These different partial aspects have to be cross-referenced in order to create an unambiguous and explicit representation of the scene.

There are at present two well-established general types of data structures in vision theories. In Computer Vision, there are precise numbers, arrays, lists and graphs. These certainly have all the versatility needed, but they are too weakly defined to form the basis of an architecture; different concrete data structures need very different algorithms, between which there is no commong ground. In Neural Networks, there is a very coherent data structure, vectors of neural activity, which forms the basis for coherent processes of organization (exchange of excitation and inhibition, relaxation to stationary states; mechanisms of synaptic plasticity), but that data structure is not powerful enough to support important visual processes, the missing piece being a means to express grouping of elements into hierarchically structured wholes, a means to express cross-indexing between different descriptors.

A candidate data structure for a visual architecture is based on dynamic graphs in the Dynamic Link Architecture [1, 8, 11, 12, 14, 15, 16]. In these graphs, nodes are neurons, as in Neural Networks, and links are rapidly switching synapses. There are three types of variables — neural signals, rapidly switching synaptic weights and slowly changing synaptic weights (the slow weights constrain the dynamic weights). Neural signals fluctuate rapidly (in distinction to Neural networks, where they relax to stationary states). On neural signals, temporal correlations can be observed. Correlations express grouping, cross-indexing and binding. Rapid synaptic strengths are controlled by signal correlations: synapses are switched on by positive correlations, and are switched off by negative correlations. In the context of vision, useful graph structures are block structures, to express segmentation of a scene into objects, or topological graphs, which can represent the lay-out of local features over the face of an object [10, 16], or super-graphs: graphs formed by cross-linking of sub-graphs, to express the composition of a complex scene out of sub-patterns. An important process in the Dynamic Link Architecture is the "discovery" by the system that two graphs are isomorphic in structure [16, 17], and the matching of those graphs by activating the appropriate links between them [16].

ORGANIZATION

The most profound revolution has taken place, or is taking place at present, with respect to the issue of organization. The old view, aptly dubbed hetero-organization, is based on a perceived clear separation between two processes, which we may call the logical process and the creative process. The two processes are coupled by mechanisms of execution and transmission. One prime example for this mode of thinking is the idea of algorithmic control. The logical process is the one in the machine. The creative process is the one in the programmer's mind. The program serves as interface. This is a poor model for intelligence since the essential process, the creative one, is shut out from the field of view. In the context of the visual system, the philosophy of hetero-organization sees the existing structures as realization of pre-existing plans (in the genes) which define wiring diagrams and signal codes and specific mechanisms. Furthermore, according to this philosophy the task of the visual system is to process the input (this being the logical process) and present the result to an interpreting and integrating agent (the creative process) that is always beyond the field of view. (This agent is often called homunculus.) The visual system can only be understood if also the creative processes of structure formation and interpretation are made explicitly subject to study.

The new view of organization is that of auto-organization or self-organization. The subject of study are complex, non-linear, self-interacting systems, governed by relatively simple rules of interaction. These systems are usually rather homogeneous and fine-grained in formulation. In these systems, specific organized structures arise as the result and at the end of a complex and usually chaotic process, there being no explicit plan ahead of time. Prime examples for self-organization are crystallization, reaction-diffusion systems, convection, and star formation. For the visual system the essential processes of organization are evolution, ontogenesis, learning, and the process of establishment of a scene representation. In self-organization there is still a trace of the algorithmic scheme, in the form of the rules of the game, established ahead of time. But these rules are usually of an extremely elementary nature and do not refer explicitly to any specific structure. A more detailed description of self-organization in ontogenesis and function of the visual system has been given in [14, 18]. The physical structure of a mature visual system and the process of representing a visual scene are much too complex and variable and too dependent on the specific environment of the animal to be described directly in their specific form in the genome or in the design plans of an engineer. What can be designed by the human engineer or the big engineer evolution is the set of rules and structures that define the visual system as a self-organizing system. These rules and structures are exactly what you would call an architecture. This architecture and this set of rules are to set up the pre-established harmony we spoke of earlier.

Here is a hard barrier to progress with present visual science and engineering. It is already possible to describe many important sub-processes in the visual system, such as feature extraction, low-level vision (structure from motion, shape from shading, structure from stereo, color vision, texture analysis, segmentation), pattern recognition, shape description, co-ordinate transformation, geometrical manipulations, learning from examples, and parameter estimation. It is clear, however, that none of these processes works perfectly by itself. It is clear that all these component processes have to be combined, each contributing its own incomplete set of constraints. There is wide recognition now that the visual system (or any intelligent system for that matter) has to be constructed in this multiplicity-of-agents style. On a high level of complexity this is, for instance, formulated in Arbib's schema theory, each schema being a component process-and-structure. On a low level this is attempted in many laboratories in the form of Markov random field formulations in which the interaction between component processes (such as a motion estimation mechanism and an edge detection mechanism) are coupled by specific ernergy terms. The problem with this program of combining sub-processes lies in the fact that the complexity of any such system quickly grows beyond any manageable level if more than two processes are involved. It is evident from this that a next-generation visual architecture has to be based on the formulation of a homogeneous (that is, simple) system of abstract coupled processes which can be differentiated and adapted with the help of learning mechansisms when coupled with visual input. The architecture would start with a large number of initially uncommitted variables and terms which, at the end of a learning period would define and implement specific mechanisms and their interactions. This style seems to be in reach with layered Neural Networks or Markov random field formulations, but is at present plagued with diverging learning times. Apparently some more potent rules have to be found to reduce search spaces and to formulate a more design-independent visual architecture.

The cutting edge of the architectural approach is the formulation of rules and structures that fit the intended problem space like a tight glove. The architecture has to strike the right combination of generality (for optimal design simplicity and flexibility) and parsimony. The learning time problem of Neural Networks is caused by their data structure that doesn't capture important structural traits of the world, for our purposes the visual world. Prominent among those structural traits are segmentation and symmetry. The word segmentation refers to the fact that our world is composed of coherent, fairly stably structured, objects that tend to vary in their relative arrangement (which is due to actual relative movement or to change in perspective). The most prominent symmetries in the visual world are caused by a relatively stable environment viewed under relatively fluid perspective. It is absolutely mandatory that a visual architecture has inherent data structures and mechanisms to deal with segmentation and symmetry, that is, to detect and represent the distinction between stable relations within objects and less stable relations between objects (segmentation) and to generalize from one view or arrangement of a scene to others (symmetry). In our visual world it is easy to pick up the information relevant to segmentation (e.g., homogeneity in texture and depth, common fate, structural relationships, spatial contiguity, of the points within a figure). The visual architecture should process and represent this information and absolutely should make use of it during learning, not even attempting to relate points in a scene by a rule if these points evidently form an accidental arrangement. In this way the search space of potentially useful relations can be drastically reduced. Likewise, it is disastrous to learn several pattens independently if they are related by a symmetry. These are the motivations that lead to the development of the Dynamic Link Architecture, which does process and represent segmentation information, which does restrict learning to relations within segments, and which can detect and make use of the relations between symmetric figures.

In summary, although much conceptual work has yet to be done, the vision problem begins to be sharply enough formulated to enter a critical stage. The problem is worked on with growing intensity, we will soon have the necessary processing power on massively parallel machines, and I feel that we have the essential experimental facts in our hands. The vision problem is one of the most exciting challenges of our time, and within a decade we may see a break-through in the form of a functional vision architecture.

References

[1] C. von der Malsburg. Am I thinking assemblies? In G. Palm and A. Aertsen, editors, *Proceedings of the Trieste Meeting on Brain Theory, October 1984*, pages 161–176. Springer, Berlin, Heidelberg, 1986.

[2] A. Treisman. Preattentive processing in vision. *Computer Vision, Graphics and Image Processing*, 31:156–177, 1985.

[3] K. Nakayama. The iconic bottleneck and the tenuous link between early visual processing and perception. In C. Blakemore, editor, *Vision: Coding and Efficiency.* Cambridge Universtiy Press, 1990.

[4] F. Rosenblatt. *Principles of Neurodynamics.* Spartan Books, Washington, D.C., 1962.

[5] C. von der Malsburg. Goal and architecture of neural computers. In R. Eckmiller and C. von der Malsburg, editors, *Neural Computers*, pages 23–28. Springer, Berlin, 1988.

[6] C. von der Malsburg. A neural architecture for the representation of scenes. In J.L. McGaugh, N.M. Weinberger, and G. Lynch, editors, *Brain Organization and Memory: Cells, Systems and Circuits.* Oxford University Press, New York, 1990.

[7] I. Biederman. Recognition-by-components: A theory of human image understanding. *Psychological Review*, 94:115–147, 1987.

[8] Christoph von der Malsburg. The correlation theory of brain function, internal report, max-planck-institute for biophysical chemistry. Postfach 2841, Göttingen, FRG, 1981.

[9] D.I. Perrett, E.T. Rolls, and W. Caan. Visual neurones responsive to faces in the monkey temporal cortex. *Experimental Brain Research*, 47:329–342, 1982.

[10] Joachim Buhmann, Jörg Lange, and Christoph von der Malsburg. Distortion invariant object recognition by matching hierarchically labeled graphs. In *IJCNN International Conference on Neural Networks, Washington*, pages I 155–159. IEEE, 1989.

[11] Christoph von der Malsburg. Nervous structures with dynamical links. *Ber. Bunsenges. Phys. Chem.*, 89:703–710, 1985.

[12] C. von der Malsburg and E.Bienenstock. Statistical coding and short-term synaptic plasticity: A scheme for knowledge representation in the brain. In E. Bienenstock, F.Fogelman, and G.Weisbuch, editors, *Disordered Systems and Biological Organization. Nato advanced research workshop*, pages 247–272. Springer, Berlin, Heidelberg, 1986.

[13] T.E. Lange and M.G. Dyer. High-level inferencing in a connectionist network. *Connection Science*, 1, 1989.

[14] Christoph von der Malsburg. How are nervous structures organized? In E. Başar, H. Flohr, H.Haken, and A.J. Mandell, editors, *Synergetics of the Brain, Proceedings of the International Symposium on Synergetics*, pages 238–249. Springer, Berlin, Heidelberg, New York, May 1983.

[15] Christoph von der Malsburg and Elie Bienenstock. A neural network for the retrieval of superimposed connection patterns. *Europhysics Letters*, 3:1243–1249, 1987.

[16] Elie Bienenstock and Christoph von der Malsburg. A neural network for invariant pattern recognition. *Europhysics Letters*, 4:121–126, 1987.

[17] Christoph von der Malsburg. Pattern recognition by labeled graph matching. *Neural Networks*, 1:141–148, 1988.

[18] C. von der Malsburg and W.Singer. Principles of cortical network organization. In P. Rakic and W. Singer, editors, *Neurobiology of Neocortex*, pages 69–99. John Wiley, 1988.

Advanced Neural Computers / R. Eckmiller (Editor)

NEURAL MODELLING OF VISION AND OLFACTION

John G. TAYLOR

Department of Mathematics
King's College London
Strand, London WC2R 2LS, U.K.

1. INTRODUCTION

Both invertebrates and vertebrates have evolved, by the well-knowm process of "survival of the fittest", various neural nets which allow the animal to function efficiently in it's environment. Both the retina and the later layers of neurons, such as primary and associative cortex in mammals, have been evolved so as to form a remarkable vision machine. If we could understand the working of even only parts of that machine it should be possible to duplicate them in hardware. Standard neural nets could then be used to fill in the gaps in the processing chain to give what might be expected to be a much more succesful device.That method of approach has already been started for auditory processing [1] where the activity of the cochlea has even been modelled in hardware [2]. Similar study has been going on for quite some time in vision, as described, for example in [3] and has begun to be set in a mathematical framework [4]. Work has also commenced on similar lines in olfaction, where modelling has been performed of the early (nasal receptor) [5] and olfactory bulb [6] processing. Attempts have also been made to model the olfactory cortex [7].The purpose of this article is to describe contributions to such modelling in both vision and various types of olfaction (with hippocampal activity attempted to be included in the latter).

Understanding the neurophysiology of vision has proved difficult to obtain. There is still incomplete knowledge of the wiring diagram of cells involved at the various stages, nor is the mode of action of a single visual cortical cell yet completely understood [8]. However, progress is being made in these various areas, and the time will come when the detailed models of the visual cortex presently being slowly constructed will be successful. A similar situation occurs in audition and olfaction.

The nature of retinal processing will be considered in the next section. That will be followed by an analysis of various transformations that are performed on the retinal output by the primary visual cortex. Olfaction will be considered in the following section, and the activity of the hippocampus in the penultimate section; brief conclusions will be drawn in the final section.

2 THE RETINA

Much has been understood about the retina of a wide range of animals and about the principles underlying the processing of visual information which it performs [9]. There are considerable differences in detail between different species, however, so that a certain amount of simplification will be used here to avoid missing the wood for the trees. In particular only the vertebrate eye will be considered in any detail. The retina is composed of an outermost sheet of receptors (the rods and cones), an adjacent sheet (the outer plexiform layer) of horizontal cells, and a further sheet of amacrine cells (the inner plexifom layer). The outer and inner plexiform layers are connected by a set of cells at right angles to the two layers; these cells are called bipolar (from the fact that they have two ends). Finally the inner plexiform layer feeds into the final or output cells of the retina; these are called the ganglion cells. In all, then, the flow chart in the retina is as follows

$$\begin{aligned} &\text{Light} \rightarrow \text{Rods and Cones} \rightarrow \text{Outer Plexiform layer} \rightarrow \\ &\text{Bipolar Cells} \rightarrow \text{Inner Plexiform layer} \rightarrow \text{Ganglion Cells.} \end{aligned} \tag{1}$$

The nature of the retinal transformation may be described by means of the receptive field (RF) of the ganglion cell, this being the region in visual space that when illuminated causes a response in the ganglion cell concerned. The specification of a ganglion cell solely in terms of RF's clearly leaves to one side the temporal response, even to the gross difference between transient and permanent.

Light absorbtion by rods and cones causes a change of photo-recepter membrane potential, which is transmitted by means of a chemical synapse into a similar change of the horizontal and bipolar cell membranes. The horizontal cells are themselves connected together through electrical synapses, in which there is a direct transfer of electrical energy, without any chemical intermediary. This leads to the outer plexiform layer acting as a resistive sheet, in which each horizontal cell is connected through resistors (the electrical synapses) to several nearest neighbouring similar cells. These cells also possess a capacatative membrane surface, which gives the cells the ability to store charge up to the time-constant of the membrane, of the order of tens of milliseconds. This allows both memory of the local illumination to be stored and also a lateral spread of the input to more distant areas of the retina (as determined by the conductances between the cells). For a given connectivity between the horizontal cells it is possible to write down the equations describing the response of these cells to an arbitrarily varying input in both space and time [4]. These equations may be solved by computer simulation. Alternatively the outer plexiform layer may be approximated as a continuous sheet, when the resulting equations reduce to a linear system of second order in space and first order in time. The transfer function may then be obtained in analytic form by means of Laplace or Fourier methods [4].

The output of the outer plexiform layer is given by taking away from the input illumination, as transferred directly to the bipolar cells from the rods and cones, the horizontal cell activity, since the horizontal cells act in an inhibitory manner on the bipolar cells. The transfer function of the net response can now be obtained in analytic form as above in the continuum limit. The results of this analysis compare well with the experimental features of the cells in, say, the mud-puppy retina. The response is composed of an initial one from direct transmission through the bipolar cells, with a later phase bringing in the inhibition from more distant regions of the retina by means of the horizontal cell layer. This latter corresponds to a mean level of illumination over the retina, and acts as a background level against which the ongoing activity is to be compared. Such a subtractive process leads to an explanation of various psychophysical anomalies such as Mach bands, etc. In particular it also leads to extraction of changes of illumination, both in space and in time.

There are considerable differences between the inner plexiform layer in different animals. It possesses cells sensitive to motion in the case of lower vertebrates, such as the rabbit or pigeon. In the primate there are few cells with such properties. so that motion analysis must be performed in the cortex in the latter case. There appears to be greater use of the amacrine cells in the lower vertebrates, with bipolar cells connected to amacrines, which then connect to motion-sensitive ganglion cells as their main sourse of input. It has been suggested [10] that motion detection is achieved in this system, as in invertebrates such as the fly, by a veto action of one cell onto the output of another cell nearby. If the two cells are neighbours then they can be connected up to a further cell in such a way as to make the input to this latter cell depend crucially on the direction of motion of a moving spot of light. However the manner in which a cell may become sensitive to motion over a small fraction of its RF, and with sensitivity that is the same over the whole RF is not presently understood.

It is usual to describe the RF of a retinal ganglion cell by means of suitably chosen parameters in a difference of two Gaussians (DOG's); in one dimension this would have the form

$$A\mathrm{ex}(-x^2/a^2) \quad - B\exp(-x^2/b^2) \tag{2}$$

where a is the width of the positive central region in an ON-cell and b the inhibitory surround. An OFF-cell would have an over-all minus sign multiplying (2). It is possible to obtain a response approximately equal to (2) by connecting the outputs of bipolar cells in a suitable manner to later ganglion cells. For the sustained X-cells with a small receptive field only a few nearby ON-bipolar cells need be used to construct an ON-ganglion cell (and similarly for OFF-cells). The transient response, and larger RF of Y-cells may be constructed from the addition of many (in the hundreds) of bipolar cell responses. The larger RF is seen to arise from the addition of many bipolar cell responses, before the horizontal cell inhibition can enter. When this latter does arrive at the bipolar cells their response is reduced in total almost to zero. Given that the above connectivity succeeds in producing the correct static RF for the ganglion cells one would hope that it would lead to the correct response when there is temporal dependence. That will depend, however on the detailed temporal responses of the amacrine and ganglion cells as well as the various synapses. In particular the latter between the bipolar and amacrine cells have an interesting reciprocal form. This may allow the synapses to act as time differentials on the output signal [11]. However more analysis must be made of the possible modes of action of such synapses, especially their effects on various types of input signal [12]. It is necessary to include in the output function of the Y-cells a certain level of non-linearity, as is found in their response to modulated gratings [13]; this can be done [4].

3 THE PRIMARY VISUAL CORTEX

Information travels from the ganglion cells, in the form of nerve impulses, to a centre in the thalamus called the lateral geniculate nucleus (LGN). There is some sharpening and modifying of information in the LGN, although details of that have not been fully understood. We will turn our attention to the visual cortex, where an important feature occurs. It is found, by direct measurement of the response of a cortical cell when light is shone onto the retina, that the RF of a cortical cell may be classified as simple or complex (following the classic work of Hubel and Wiesel). The former RF is now that of an elongated ellipse, the latter RF is larger, but the complex cell now has motion sensitivity. In the case of a simple cell it has been suggested [14] that the RF in both space and wave-number space i.e. in Fourier space may be described by a two-dimensional Gabor function. In one-dimension this has the form of a Gaussian multiplied by a cosine or sine wave with an obvious extension to the two-dimensional case. Given this RF the connectivity between ganglion cells and these cortical cells which can result in such a Gabor function-type of RF (neglecting effects from the LGN) may be determined by using the DOG approximation to the RF of the retinal ganglion cell [4]. A sum of DOG's, with displaced centres, and modulated by a cosine or sine will lead to a difference of two Gabor's, which reduces approximately to a single Gabor for DOG widths small compared to the range of centres [4]. Thus the correct response can roughly be achieved by summing the outputs of ganglion cells with RF's centred at x_0 over values of x_0 chosen with a Gaussian distribution of width c and modulated by a cosine of wavelength $2\pi/w$. This gives a direct physical interpretation of c as the range (in receptive field space) over which inputs to the simple cell feed, when that range is much larger than the range of the DOG's in the simple cells. The variable $2\pi/w$ can be considered as the distance, in receptive field space, over which inputs from ON X-cells are being summed (from $-\pi/2w$ to $\pi/2w$). The next range of $x_0(\pi/2w<x_0 <3\pi/2w)$ has contributions from OFF X-cells, and so on. The model predicts there to be a juxtaposition of ranges of ON and ranges of OFF X-cells in this interpretation of the modulation function cos(wx). Complex cells may also be modelled in a similar manner, but now with half-wave rectification, as noted by Pollen et al [15]. This leads to a complex response which depends on the energy of the incident light. Such a response is regarded as a possible mechanism for motion and for texture discrimination [15], and is clearly of interest. It has, however, been shown [16] that pure Gabor functions do not appear to give a satisfactory description of RF's of all simple cells, but that differences of off-set DOG's can do so. It is known that tens of active input lines are necessary to cause a cortical cell to fire [17]. If we denote the DOG (2) with centre x_0, by DOG (x,x_0,A,B,a,b), then the RF is expected to be given by an expression of form

$$\int dx_0 dA dB da db f(x_0,A,B,a,b,) DOG(x,x_0,A,B,a,b) \tag{3}$$

The choice for f as a sum of 3 terms, each involving a δ-function for each of the variables x_0,A,B,a,b, gives the form used succesfully in [16]; it

is clear that more details of connectivity are needed here to determine the functional form of DOG (2).
It is not known in such detail how information is processed at higher levels in the visual cortex, although a great deal of effort is presently being expended on finding it out.

4 OLFACTION

The corresponding flow chart for olfaction is

$$\text{Nose}\rightarrow\text{nasal receptors}\begin{cases}\rightarrow\text{accessory olfactory bulb(AOB)}\leftrightarrow\text{amygdala, hypothalamus}\\ \rightarrow\text{olfactory bulb(OB)}\leftrightarrow\text{Olfactory cortex(OC)}\leftrightarrow\text{hippocampus}\end{cases} \quad (4)$$

It should be noted that some of the arrows in (4) involve feed back as well as feed forward. Two channels are accessible to odor information (for mammals). The first of these is through a set of nasal receptors (constituting the vomeronasal organ) which are distinct from those used in the other (main) channel. The AOB has a rather similar structure to the OB, yet does not require the hippocampus in order to encode odor memories as does the main channel [18]. It therefore appears simpler to model, and work on this has begun [19], which will be described shortly. As noted in (4), the OB does need the hippocampus, so is a decidedly more complex system. There does not appear to be any detailed structure at the nasal receptor stage. Both OB and AOB have, as main output neurons, the so-called mitral cells. There are also granule cells, which play an inhibitory role, as well as periglomerular and tufted cells which give further transformation of the output. The response of the OB has been known for some time to possess an oscillatory component from the work of Freeman and co-workers [6]. But it has not been clear that the oscillations are involved in information coding in the OB. It may be that these oscillations are just epiphenomena associated with the activity of the leaky integrator neurons of the OB, and that coding is done in terms of the gross modulation of the higher frequency response. This slower effect follows faithfully the time course of the input odor; the detailed analysis of [6] can be interpreted in that manner. It is not known in detail how it is possible to use frequency as a code, although the amplitude distribution of this high frequency across the OB may also be used. This question has already been raised in [6], without a satisfactory answer being given. This problem may be related to the presence of phase locking of coupled oscillatory circuits in the visual cortex [20].

The nature of memory coding in the AOB has been studied by various workers [21]. As an example, imprinting may be established in a female mouse, at the time of mating, to the odors (pheromones) of the stud male. This memory prevents pregnancy loss on subsequent exposure of this male's pheromones; pheromones from strange males do cause pregnancy block. The memory is established during a critical 4-hour period after mating and lasts for the reproductive life of the female. It's formation depends on intact noradrenergic projections from the locus coerulus to the AOB. These latter are thought to be active during the imprint phase. The experimental findings are consistent with the theory that memory is imprinted when sensory input is coincident with high noradrenergic transmission at biologically significant times.

How is the transform function of the AOB expected to be modified by the above learning process? We will model the activities of the various cells as leaky integrators, using the membrane potential value as the essential parameter describing the activity of each neuron. The output will be taken as the mean firing rate, which we will take for simplicity as a linear function of the membrane potential. It will also be assumed that the AOB is 2-dimensional, and that all cells can be labelled uniquely by their position $\underline{r}$ in the plane. We also neglect off diagonal connections.Let the membrane potential of the mitral cell at position $\underline{r}$ be $M(\underline{r})$, and that of the granule cell be $G(\underline{r})$. Let $I(\underline{r})$ be the input signal at $\underline{r}$ to the glomerulus there. The input on each mitral cell will consist of that from the glomerulus at $\underline{r}$, along with feedback inhibition from granule cells. Thus the equation for M is

$$\dot{M}(\underline{r}) = -M(\underline{r}) - K(\underline{r})\, G(\underline{r}) + I(\underline{r}) \tag{5}$$

The factor $K(\underline{r})$ is the connection matrix at the appropriate dendro-dendritic synapse. The granule cell input is that from the nearby mitral cells, which are connected both by the dendro-dendritic synapses, as in (5), and by axon collaterals. Thus the granule cell dynamical equation is

$$\dot{G}(\underline{r}) = -G(\underline{r}) + H(\underline{r})\, M(\underline{r}) \tag{6}$$

where H is the connection matrix for the mitral cell excitation on the granule cell at $\underline{r}$. The solutions of (5) and (6) can be written down immediately by transforming to the Fourier domain in time. If a tilda above a function is used to denote the Fourier transform in the time variable, the solution to (5) and (6) is

$$\tilde{M} = \tilde{I}\ /[(iw+1) + K.H./(iw+1)] \tag{7}$$

$$\tilde{G} = \tilde{I}.H/[(iw+i) + K.H(iw+1)][iw+1] \tag{8}$$

Such response functions have already been discussed in [6] and especially [22]. From (7) the input-output transfer function may be obtained. We will consider two extremes of the parameters in (7) to make the analysis concrete. These will be

(i) H=0
(ii) H=00

The former of these may be regarded as an approximation to the completely unexperienced system, whilst the latter could be considered the totally trained state. The value (ii) be valid at the positions $\underline{r}$ on the AOB at which incoming activity occured conjointly with feedback inhibition so as to allow H to increase for such mitral cells. The case (i) will be at the remaining positions on the AOB. In case (i) the transform function is peaked at w=0, with peak height 1. In the second case the peak has been shifted to $w=[H.K+1]^{1/2}$ and the peak height is now 1/2. The value of the transfer function (7) for small values of w is of order 1/[1 + K.H.]. For case (ii) this value is much less 1. What is to be learned from these results, modulo the imperfections of the model? It is that the OAB can act as an adaptive filter, with the central frequency being raised by the learning experience. There is also a reduction by 50% of the response at the peak; that may not be a crucial feature in the learning process. We conclude that the coding performed by this very simple model of the AOB (and we might suspect also of the OB and olfactory cortex) involves use of the peak frequency of the response function of the system. It has been suggested by Keverne [24] that there is a process of masking of the input of the learnt odour by the AOB, in that the granule cells involved in the leaning process are turned on even more actively by their associated mitral cells after the mitral-granule cell excitatory synapses have been made more effective. This then turns off the associated mitral cell output, so that it cannot cause any pregnancy block by input to the amygdala and then to the hypothalamus. This proposal may be seen as an extreme case of the more general result described by (7). Indeed this 'masking' will be the result of the transform function (7) if the amygdala or hypothalamus respond only to frequencies considerably below the new peak frequency at about H.K. Addition of periglomoruler cells, correct conductance changes, use of non - PDP blobs and non-linear mitral cell feed back to granule cells does not change the general features of the above 'generalised masking' hypotheses [19].

We thus conclude that AOB imprinting could occur by a generalised form of masking. Since there is also central noradranergic distribution feedback to granule cells in the OB 'generalised masking' in the modified OB transfer function could occur there, and could lead to some of the activity pattern variations with odor observed in the OB. A similar masking phenomenon could also occur in the olfactory cortex (like the OB, it receives comparable centrifugal noradrenergic inputs). Excitatory synapses on the feedforward or feedback inhibitory interneurons in olfactory cortex may be potentiated when disinhibition occurs on the neurons.

5 HIPPOCAMPUS

It appears necessary to analyse the manner in which the hippocampus (HC) acts in order to have a full understanding of (episodic) memory storage. There are many proposals as to the function of the hippocampus. The position taken here is that the hippocampus acts, among other things so as to encode and store (ultimately in associative cortex) temporal sequences of events, and not just single patterns as does an associative net (as in various recent HC models). The structure of the hippocampus is schematically

$$\Rightarrow \mathrm{EHC} \Rightarrow \mathrm{DG} \Rightarrow \mathrm{CA3} \Rightarrow \mathrm{CA1} \Rightarrow \mathrm{SUB} \Rightarrow \mathrm{EHC} \Rightarrow \qquad (9)$$

Associative cortex inputs to the entorrhinal cortex (EHC), which mainly inputs to the HC formation proper at the dentate gyrus (DG), whilst a lesser amount enters the cell fields CA3 and CA1. The main flow (as indicated by the double arrows) then continues to CA1, subiculum (SUB) and finally returns to the EHC. The system therefore forms a multi-synaptic loop with return time of about 20 msec ; there are also smaller sub-loops, although their significance is not clear.

There are basically three models for temporal pattern storage: time delay lines, feedback loops, or use of time summation on neurons. Let us consider activity of the HC in the light of the three types of model in turn. The sets of input fibres for EHC → CA3 and EHC → DG → CA3 (the perforant path and the mossy fibres) are thin and unmyelinated, and have the same conduction velocity of about 1m/sec [24]. The only time delay between the two pathways is thus the synaptic one at dentate granule cells, so will not be very long (<1msec). There may be relative time delays between different synapses on mossy fibres, but these will also be less that 1msec. Therefore it does not seem easy to use such short time delays to store sequences seconds or more in length.

The feedback loop approach may be used, in which the total HC is used to feedback EHC activity to itself. Such a model requires error propagation of some sort in order to give an output equal to the preceeding input [25], [26]. There is no clear evidence that an error signal is sent from the EHC back back into the HC in order to achieve that effect.

The third class of models uses time delays inherent in the action of the neurons themselves. The possibility of modifying weights for earlier traces [27] may produce a useful artificial system, but does not have any neurophysiological basis [28]. The use of the leaky integrator features of pyramidal neurons [8] allows a neurophysiologically feasable model of HC to be proposed [29]. The outlines of this [30] are that patterns $P^{(k)}$ input on a set of leaky integrator neurons in a net N_1 are then input on a net N_2. The connection weights $w_{i\ell}$ for input from neuron ℓ of N_1 to i of N_2 are modified by

$$\delta w_{i\ell} \alpha (P_i{}^{(k)} - P_i{}^{(k)1})\ \mathrm{act}(\ell) \tag{10}$$

where $P_i{}^{(k)}$ is the activity in the ith fibre in the input pattern $P^{(k)}$ on N_1, $P_i{}^{(k)}$ that in the output pattern $P^{(k)1}$ of the ith neuron of N_2, and act(ℓ) the activity of the ℓth neuron in N_1. It is assumed that there is a 1:1 relation between input lines to N_1 and output neurons in N_2 (such as may occur between the EHC input to, and output from, the HC in (9)). Such a model gives an effective way to store sequences of patterns [30].

Its realisation in HC is proposed as being by identification of DG with the net N_1 and CA3 with N_2, so that the error signal (10) is achieved by feedback inhibition of CA3 pyramidal cells to themselves (the term $P_i{}^{(k)1}$) subtracted from the direct EHC to CA3 input (the term $P_i{}^{(k)}$). This is only effective provided there is a simultaneous activation of the mossy fibre input (the factor act ℓ) from DG to CA3. Feedforward and -back inhibition may also occur in DG and CA3 to achieve cleaning up the signal; leaky integrator summation in CA3 should enhance the temporal sequence storage, as would time delays from long-lasting ionic channels, etc. Further 'cleaning up' may occur in CA1 before it is output. Further details are given in [29], [30].

6. CONCLUSIONS

This paper has surveyed ongoing work modelling vision and olfaction, including in the latter the hippocampus for pattern sequence storage. Some of this work is still at a very preliminary stage, and needs much detailed theoretical analysis and simulation. However it would appear that when more subtle properties of neurons are included (leaky integrator and other delay effects) various aspects of memory can be approached with hope of success. Allied to the use of pRAM technology [31], with especial emphasis on stochastic features or by other hardware approaches it appears that these models may be expressed in hardware form in the near future.

What of the hope of improving on the brain? Already at retinal level this may be achievable, for example by having further inner or outer plexiform layers, or extra areas in primary or associative visual cortex. There is no reason, in principle, why higher levels of natural intelligence cannot be improved on, although that is still some distance away.

7. ACKNOWLEDGEMENTS

The author would like to thank the organizers of the Conference, especially Prof R. Eckmiller, for financial support enabling him to attend.

8. REFERENCES

[1] S.A. Shamma, J.Acoust, Soc.Am. 78(5), 1622-1632, (1985)
[2] J. Lazzaro and C. Mead, Neural Computation 1, 47 (1989)
[3] M.A. Arbib, The Metaphorical Brain 2, John Wiley, (1989)
[4] J.G. Taylor, Neural Networks (in press); ibid, pp 231-253, in Models of Brain Function, ed R. Cotterill, Camb. Univ. Press, (1989)
[5] D. Schild, Biophys. J. 54, 100 (1988)
[6] B. Baird, Physica 22 D 150 (1986); Z li and J. Hopfield, Biol. Cybern 61 379 (1989); Y. Yao and W.J. Freeman, Proc. Int.J.Conf. Neural Nets, Washington D.C., I-699 (1989)
[7] R. Grayer, J. Ambros-Ingerson and G. Lynch, J. Cogn. Neuroscience 1, 61 (1989)
[8] K. Stratford, A. Mason, A. Larkman, G. Major and J. Jack, 296-321 in The Computing Neuron, ed Durbin, Miall and Mitcheson, Addison-Wesley (1989)
[9] J. Dowling, The Retina: An approachable part of the brain, Harvard Univ. Press, Cambridge MA, (1987)
[10] J.C. Koch, T. Paggio and V. Torre, Trends in Neurosciences 7, 204-211 (1986)
[11] J. Richter and S. Ullman, Biol. Cybernetics, 43, 127-145, (1982
[12] J.M. Terasawa, M.T. Sukuda and G. Hauske, Biol. Cybernetics, 60, 239-246, (1989)
[13] J.C. Enroth-Cugell and J. Robson, J. Physiol. 187, 517-552, (1966)
[14] J. Daugman, 233-250, in New Developments in Neural Computing, ed J.G. Taylor and C.L.T. Mannion, Adam Hilger, (1989)
[15] D.A. Pollen, J.P. Gaska and L.D. Jacobson, in Models of Brain Function, ed R. Cotterill, Camb. Univ. Press, (1989)
[16] M.J. Hawken and A.J. Parker, Proc. Roy Soc B (Lond), 251 (1987)
[17] K.A. Martin, Quart J. Exp. Physiol. 73 637-702 (1988)

[18] U. Staubli, G. Ivy and G. Lynch, Proc. Nat. Acad. Sci. 81, 588S (1984)
[19] J.G. Taylor and B. Keverne, "Accessory Olfactory learning", King's College preprint, (1990), C.M. Gray and W. Singer, Soc. Neurosci. Abstr. 404 3 (1987);
[20] C.M. Gray, P. König, A.K. Engeland and W. Singer, Nature 338 334 (1989); R. Eckhom et al, Biol. Cybern. 60 121 (1988)
[21] E.B. Keverne and C. de la Riva, Nature 296 148 (1982)
[22] S.L. Bressler, Brain Res. 409, 285, 294 (1987)
[23] B. Keverne, private communication
[24] A. Tielen, F. da Silva and W. Mollevanger, Exp. Brain Res. 42 231 (1981)
[25] J.L. Elman, "Finding Structure in Time", CLR Technical Report 8801, UC San Diego, April 1988; N. Chater "Learning to respond to structure in time", UC, London preprint, (Oct 1989)
[26] T. Kohonen Self-Organization and Associative Memory, Springer (1984)
[27] J.G. Taylor, "Temporal Patterns and leaky Integrator Neurons", submitted to ICANN'90, Paris (1990).
[28] G. Barrioneuvo et al, J. Neurophysiol. 55 540 (1986)
[29] J.G. Taylor and M. Reiss, Does the Hippocampus store temporal patterns?
[30] M. Reiss and J.G. Taylor, in preparation
[31] See the contribution of D. Gorse and J.G. Taylor, this conference.

Advanced Neural Computers / R. Eckmiller (Editor)

Neural Computers for Foveating Vision Systems

Yehoshua Y. Zeevi[1] *and Ran Ginosar*[1]

Department of Electrical Engineering
Technion - Israel Institute of Technology
Haifa 32000, Israel

1. Introduction

Most currently-available schemes of, and systems for, image acquisition and processing for the purpose of visual communication and/or high-level computer vision, sample and process the visual data in a uniform manner. Such systems do not adapt automatically to the specific structure of the visual environment and/or the task to be accomplished. Consequently, such vision systems do not allocate efficiently the available acquisition and computational resources. Since biological and man-made vision systems have to accomplish similar tasks, and they confront similar problems, it is instructive to consider the design of the human visual system which suggests methods for accomplishing sufficiently complicated tasks with limited computational resources.

Analysis of cell density, neural circuitry, receptive field physiology and the rules that govern the retinotopic mapping, reveals some basic principles of organization, and the functional architecture of the early stages of the visual pathway [1]. In particular it becomes apparent that the visual system is spatially inhomogeneous in that only a small area near the center of the retina, the so-called fovea, affords acute vision, and that the rate of both spatial sampling and processing decreases toward the periphery ([1], Fig. 1a). Certain low level processing such as the detection of blobs and edges is executed in parallel by a relatively large number of self-similar localized operators which are scaled, nested and distributed over a wide field-of-view. Families of functions which well represent one important family of such self-similar receptive fields, and which are generated from a single function by the operations of translation and dilation, have recently attracted a great deal of interest in the context of multiresolution image representation by the Gabor scheme [3,4,5] and other types of wavelets [6]. The map resulting from this effortless, preattentive [6,7], projection conjoins any a-priori available information and/or internal representation of the environment, to determine the oculomotor control signal which superimposes in turn the more powerful processing mechanisms, associated with foveal vision, on the focus of attention. Thus, subsequent to the low level mode of parallel preattentive processing, the visual system appears to implement a serial mode for shift of focal attention [8]. The end result is a series of computationally-intensive operations, each being performed over a relatively small area of interest. The sequencing and distribution of foci of attention, elicited by visual stimuli during the execution of various tasks, have been studied by recording the eye movement scan paths ([9,10], Fig. 1b).

2. Foveating Vision Systems

Our approach to the development of adaptive systems for visual information acquisition and processing has been motivated by the above-described design of biological visual systems. The main emphasis has been on data reduction by focal plane processing, implementing both sensitivity control [17, 18] and data selection algorithms which automatically match to image structure, or which are alternatively determined by some a-priori information regarding the structure of the visual scenario and the task.

Since visual acquisition is in most cases mediated by a sensor which transforms a two-dimensional array of pixels into a one-dimensional sequence of bytes, whereas images are highly correlated

[1]This work was conducted at the Technion. R. Ginosar is presently on Sabbatical leave at the University of Utah, and Y.Y. Zeevi at the CAIP Center of Rutgers University and at Harvard University on a leave of absence from the Technion.

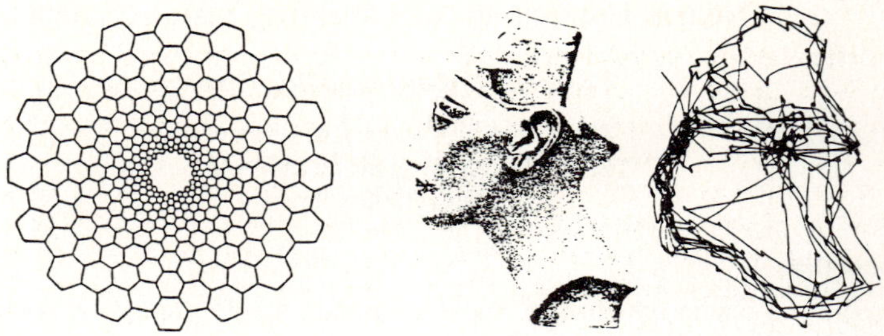

(a) (b)

Figure 1. (a) Inhomogeneous distribution of sampling and processing resources in the early stages of vision. (b) Transitions of the foci of attention as depicted by eye movement scan paths [9].

along the spatial and temporal variables (as well as chromatically, but this attribute is not dealt with in the context of the present paper although it is an integral part of the vision system we developed), the reduction from two- to one-dimensional data structure raises the following problem. How can the two-dimensional relationships be preserved over the characteristic "mean-free-path" of highly correlated information, in order to perform neighborhood operations in real time as the data are acquired? One possible solution is afforded by the Peano-Hilbert scan or by other scanning trajectories of the proper fractal dimension ([11], Fig. 2).

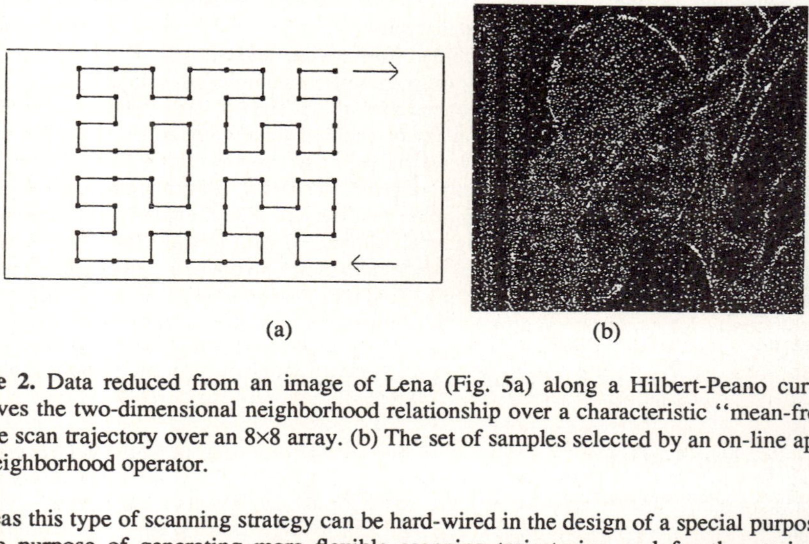

(a) (b)

Figure 2. Data reduced from an image of Lena (Fig. 5a) along a Hilbert-Peano curve which preserves the two-dimensional neighborhood relationship over a characteristic "mean-free-path." (a) The scan trajectory over an 8×8 array. (b) The set of samples selected by an on-line application of a neighborhood operator.

Whereas this type of scanning strategy can be hard-wired in the design of a special purpose sensor, for the purpose of generating more flexible scanning trajectories, and for the attainability of adaptive control of reconfigurable areas of interest in terms of their number, positions and sizes, it is required to have a random-access array of pixels (see Sect. 3). Having such random access, combined serial-parallel capability, what kind of low-level local operations can be instrumental in selection of the areas of interest? We have been working on several algorithms of neighborhood operations which are instrumental in the identification and selection of conspicuous loci. These algorithms, which are based on a set of local relations, are readily implementable in a neural network operating in the focal plane. We have also developed a theoretical approach to the definition of information distribution over the image [12,13]. This approach is based on the concept of "local bandwidth", defined over the expansion in the combined position-frequency space [3,13].

The simplest neighborhood relation is defined by intensity differences. This type of relation can be extracted by a network of mutually inhibitory neurons. As was previously shown [14], the performance of such a network can be significantly enhanced by the incorporation of a nonlinear feedback loop. Such a network automatically adjusts the local gains in a way that the resultant functional connectivity becomes best matched to the image structure. The effective space and time constants of the inhibitory signals are then determined by both of the hard-wired network with its synaptic weights, as well as by the input. The same principle of organization is further elaborated in the context of the neural networks for foveating vision systems, by the incorporation of multiple feedback loops operating over higher order set of relations at the levels of shape analysis (proximity of features) and even at the level of symbolic concepts.

3. A Foveating Sensor

A special imaging sensor was developed for foveating vision [16]. Like in most conventional semiconductor imaging devices, in this device too each cell consists of a light sensitive component and a charge storage component. In contrast with conventional devices, data readout is not carried out in a sequential raster-scan manner. Rather, each cell is individually addressable, and may or may not be read during any specific operational cycle.

While raster-scan devices are designed such that the read-out cycle is tightly coupled with the light sensing and sampling cycle, our foveating sensor maintains two independent and asynchronous activities - periodic light sampling and arbitrary readout according to "random addresses" provided externally. Thus, overall system design is decoupled from the inherently synchronous nature of image acquisition. While the complete set of light detectors stares at the image and samples the data, only a subset of these data are extracted off the sensor.

As will be explained in subsequent sections, the foveating sensor is designed for the most general configuration of a multi-foveae system. While the human eye has only one fovea and can thus direct its attention only towards one area which affords acute vision, although there is evidence for a parallel tracking mechanism [19], the foveating sensor can practically multiply the number of its functional "foveas", and can dynamically adapt the resolution of acquisition as appropriate over each and every small part of its visual field. Moreover, since only a small fraction of the total number of pixels is required (as will be demonstrated below), the effective "frame", as determined by the time required to serially extract all the necessary information, lasts for only a small fraction of the time of a complete, raster-scan frame. Thus, successive frames may be started much sooner, resulting in a highly enhanced frame rate. In normal imaging applications we have witnessed up to twenty-fold frame rate acceleration, indicating new applications were acquisition and processing of sequences of images was too slow before.

The basic cell architecture is shown in Figure 3a. A simple layout of our first experimental sensor-chip is provided in Figure 3b. We have subsequently experimented with additional sensors, including an 80x80 array. Recently, others have also developed similar "random-access" sensors [20].

4. A Foveating Image Acquisition System

The Foveating Image Acquisition System (FIAS) consists of three main building blocks (Fig. 4): The foveating sensor, the Foveal Position Controller (FPC), and the Area-of-Interest Selector (AIS). The sensor requires a stream of *x-y* addresses, which are generated by the FPC. The FPC accepts a sequence of area-of-interest specifications, as produced by the AIS and as specified by other elements of the system (to be discussed below). Initially, in the absence of any a-priori information about the image, whenever such is not available, the FPC generates a predetermined low resolution scene coverage. Inside the AIS, an image processor (e.g.,

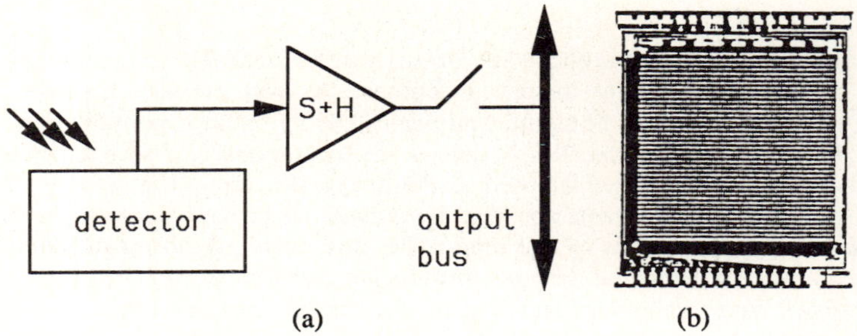

Figure 3. (a) Architecture of the Foveating Sensor. (b) Chip Layout of an Experimental Foveating Sensor.

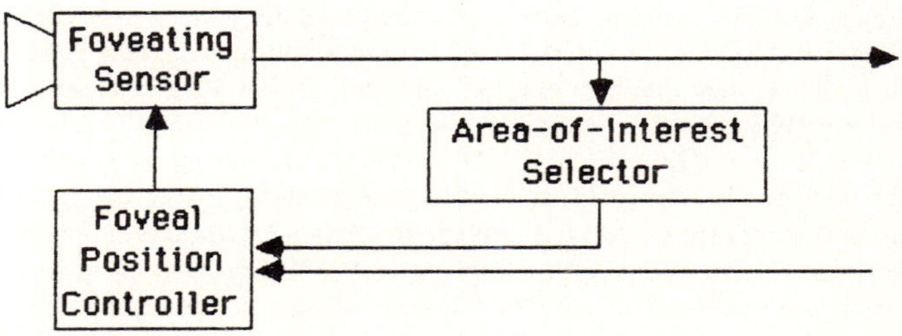

Figure 4. Architecture of the Foveating Image Acquisition System

based on the kind described in Section 6 below) extracts feature information, as appropriate for the task at hand, and creates a dilated binary image representing areas where higher resolution is called for. These areas are identified and fed back to the FPC. This process continues at increasing levels of resolutions while at the same time improving the selectivity. This cyclic repetition ends when the highest level of resolution is achieved, and the whole process is restarted.

The FPC also receives input from higher levels which are involved in control of low level foveation. Such inputs may either override, eliminate, or introduce additional areas-of-interest. For instance, certain areas of the image which appear to be very interesting from the local AIS viewpoint, may be determined unimportant to the high-level controller. These inputs are combined at the FPC, which reconciles conflicts based on programmed priorities.

It should be noted that the foveating sensor and system described above, are not always essential for foveating vision. Indeed, for applications which do not require a high bandwidth, we have developed Foveating Filters, which take normal raster-scan video, apply mechanisms similar to those of the system, and produce the equivalent foveating signal.

5. Example of a Foveated Image

Consider the image shown in Figure 5a. Several alternative models exist to determine the areas-of-interest in this and other types of images. One of these models is chosen arbitrarily, and the image is sampled at each of the "interesting" pixels, as shown in Figure 5b. Less than 7% of the pixels are included in the sample-set of this example. The data reduced from an image by the foveating system provides partial information which is sufficient for direct application in computer vision (e.g., pattern recognition and classification). This type of data reduction is also useful in management of data prior to compression for the purpose of efficient visual communication. In the latter case it is necessary, however, to reconstruct the image at the receiver. Such reconstruction is

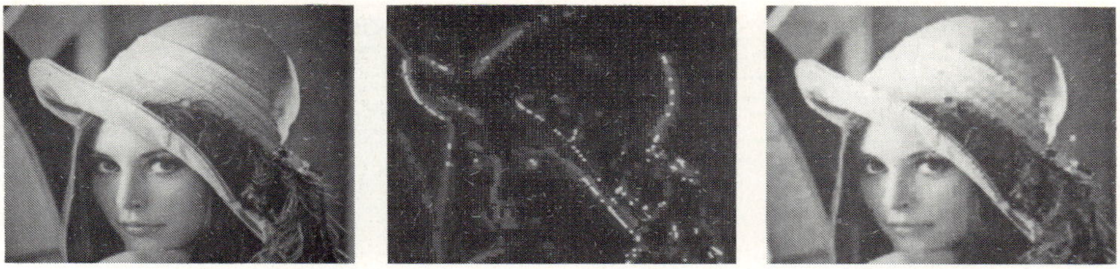

(a) (b) (c)

Figure 5. (a) Original image. (b) Foveated Image. (c) Interpolated Foveated Image.

also useful in the assessment of the informational content of the reduced data set. We have been working on aliasing-free techniques, using the local bandwidth framework of analysis [12,13], as well as on simple methods of diffusion and interpolation. In Figure 5c we demonstrate a result obtained from the data of Figure 5b, using the simplest interpolation (i.e., zero order).

It should be reemphasized that application of the foveating vision method results in a lossy *reduction*, rather than compression, of the original (i.e., uniformly sampled) data set. It is *not* intended for lossless reconstruction of the original; its purpose is to significantly reduce the amount of data necessary to process for higher level vision. Unlike compression, the foveated reduced data need not be expanded prior to further processing. It is only for demonstration purposes that Fig. 5c was generated. Note that conventional (possibly lossless) compression techniques may be applied post-foveation. However, the effect of the two techniques does not necessarily add up linearly.

6. Image Processing of Foveated Images

Reconsider the foveated image of Figure 5b. Note how scattered and sparse the pixels are. This is indeed typical of data acquired by the foveating system. On the other hand, conventional image processors require that the data be presented on a uniform grid, and hence cannot be applied to the data format associated with the foveating vision system.

The scattered pixels of Figure 5b are actually organized in overlapping, rectangular, uniform-resolution *windows*. The foveating sensor is usually programmed to produce these windows sequentially. Thus, while the complete image data do not come in a dense matrix form, each of the individual windows does. Each such window is preceded by a header, specifying its position, dimensions, and resolution.

Normal small-neighborhood image processors, such as convolvers, consist of a multi-tapped delay line and a transform operator. The delay line provides the required neighborhood of (e.g. 3×3) pixels, and the operator performs the required transform (e.g. linear combination in the case of convolution) on the neighborhood, usually in a pipelined fashion (Fig. 6a). For foveated images, the transform operators remain largely intact, but the delay line is replaced by an involved ***neighborhood generator*** [21]. The neighborhood generator provides, in the simplest case, a flexible delay line for the incoming variable-size neighborhoods (Fig. 6b). The delay line has multiple alternative sets of taps, and it selects one according to the size (width) of the incoming neighborhood. Thus, one major obstacle to foveating vision is removed. Small-neighborhood image processing of foveated images encounters one additional difficulty. In normal raster-scan images the off-frame neighborhood of boundary pixels is undefined and is usually ignored, resulting in slight ambiguity around the periphery of the image. This approach can no longer be tolerated with foveated images, due to the high portion of boundary pixels in

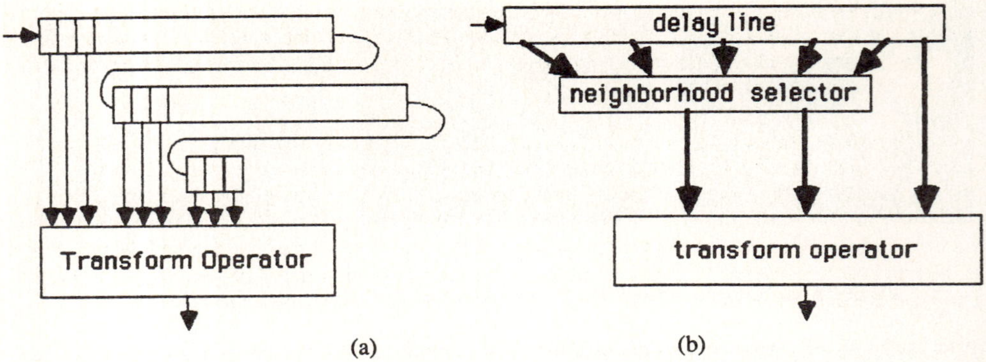

Figure 6. Small-Neighborhood Image Processor: (a) Raster-Scan images. (b) Foveated images.

multiple small windows. Consequently, we have developed a method to extrapolate each small window beyond its boundary in a transform-dependent neutral manner, so that the result of each neighborhood transform is equivalent to applying the transform on an infinite plane. The neighborhood generator of Figure 6b accomplishes this neighborhood extension automatically.

We have also designed other versions of the FIAS and the image processors, operating under different principles, which allow non-rectangular neighborhoods to be acquired and processed [21,22]. Such neighborhoods are not necessarily convex and may even contain holes. Certain special applications may require the added advantages of such more advanced systems.

7. Viewing Foveated Images

As was explained in Sect. 5, foveated data are proper for machine processing, but not for display at the receiving end of a visual communication network. A real-time architecture for image interpolation was therefore developed ([2], Fig. 7). Each incoming window is decomposed into individual pixels and the *x-y* coordinates of each pixel are generated. The interpolator maintains an image in the Frame Buffer *(FB)*, of which some of the pixels are input and all others are interpolated. The Distance Buffer *(DB)* stores, for each pixel, the distance from the pixel from which it was derived. This distance is of course zero for input pixels.

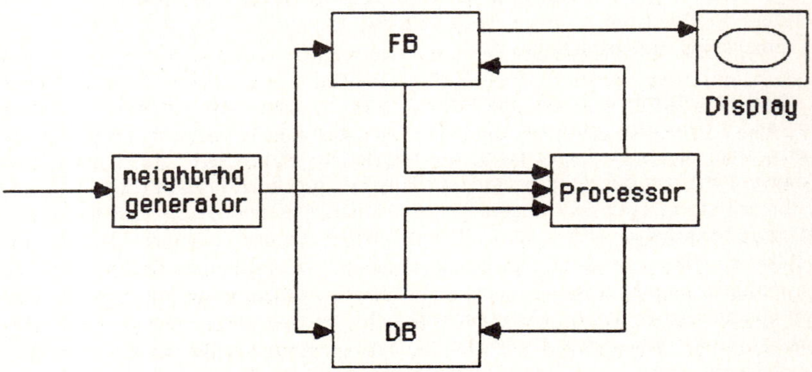

Figure 7. Foveated Image Incremental Interpolator

Upon the arrival of a new input pixel, it is first stored in *FB* and the corresponding element of

DB is cleared. Then, each element over a reasonably small area around the input pixel, for which its stored distance in *DB* is larger than its distance from the new input pixel, is replaced in *FB* with the new input and the distance is updated as well. Simultaneously, the image stored in *FB* is continually read out for display.

Thus, the interpolator is incremental in the sense that updates occur on-line, even while the image is being displayed. Consequently, it enables *successive refinement* of image resolution. If and when all 100% of a full raster-scan image pixels are provided, the interpolated image converges to the original. This method and system have been applied to intelligent image retrieval and reception, where the viewer gets to see the essence of the image much earlier than its full arrival or retrieval [2]. It is further applied to video sequences of moving images, as explained in the next Section.

8. Temporal Foveation Control Method

The efficient transmission (or storage) of live video sequences usually requires very wide bandwidth. Effective compression techniques often entail heavy computational delays, and consequently are difficult to exploit in this environment, due to the real-time nature of the application. The data reduction and selective attention featured by foveating vision promise to offer a practical solution to this problem.

Spatial foveating vision, of the type discussed in previous sections, may be applied as is to image data reduction prior to image transmission. The foveating control method can be adapted to direct attention at the task-dependent more interesting parts of the images, so that maximal rendition quality is maintained over the communication channel. At the receiving end, image interpolation as described above is used to reconstruct images for display. Moreover, the transmitting end sorts the data according to prioritizing algorithms, which take advantage of the successive refinement feature of the interpolator to provide for the most time-efficient image reconstruction.

The video sequences can be further coded based on inter-frame differences. With this technique only the differences between successive frames are transmitted, taking advantage of the low levels of variations between frames in many applications, such as video-teleconferencing. However, such methods usually do not provide sufficiently effective data compression. Moreover, with foveating vision the problem is even worse, because additional variations are created due to pixels which are selected for sampling in one frame and are ignored in the next frame. Thus, a more effective, temporal foveation method has been developed.

In temporal foveation, differences are measured not between two successive video frames, but between the most recently acquired frame at the transmitting end and the current frame at the receiving end. The differences are dynamically sorted in order of importance, and only the most important differences are transmitted. Some differences which are suppressed continue to accrue and eventually become large enough to be considered most important and get transmitted.

In addition to this method of cumulative differences, spatial foveating control method is superimposed to influence the algorithm which determines the spatial importance of each pixel. Thus, not all equal differences are really equal, as different weights are associated with different segments and edges of the image. Naturally, like all other foveating techniques, this is task-dependent and is determined by higher level computer vision algorithms. Without them, no brute force video sequence compression can be expected to yield such effective results as to enable real-life visual communication over, say, conventional telephone lines.

With such complicated signals, the spatial interpolator described above needs to be modified to reflect temporal effects as well. We have designed a temporal interpolator, which dynamically determines how to interpolate each pixel based not only on spatial distances but also on temporal differences [2].

References

1. R.E. Kronauer and Y.Y. Zeevi, "Reorganization and Diversification of Signals in Vision," IEEE Trans. SMC, Vol. 15, pp. 91-101, 1985.
2. R. Ginosar, Y.Y. Zeevi and O.A. Hilsenrath, "A Dynamic Image Representation System," Patent Application, 1988.
3. M. Porat and Y.Y. Zeevi, "The Generalized Gabor Scheme of Image Representation in Vision," IEEE Trans. PAMI, Vol. 10, pp. 452-468, 1988.
4. I. Gertner and R. Tolimieri, "A Group Theoretic Approach to Image Representation," to appear in J. Visual Communication and Image Representation.
5. S. Mallat, "A Theory for Multiresolution Signal Decomposition: The Wavelet Representation," IEEE Trans. PAMI, Vol. 11, pp. 674-693, 1989.
6. B. Julesz, "Toward an Axiomatic Theory of Preattentive Vision," in Dynamic Aspects of Neocortical Function, G. Edelman, M. Cowan, and E. Gall, Eds., Wiley, NY, 1984.
7. A. Treisman, "Preattentive Processing in Vision," Comp. Vision, Graphics and Image Proc., Vol. 31, pp. 156-177, 1985.
8. D. Sagi and B. Julesz, "Where and What in Vision," Science, 228, pg. 1217, 1985.
9. A.L. Yarbus, "Eye Movements and Vision," Plenum Press, New York, 1967.
10. D. Noton and L. Stark, "Scanpaths in Eye Movements During Pattern Perception," Science, Vol. 171, pp. 308-311, 1971.
11. N. Sorek and Y.Y. Zeevi, "On-Line Visual Data Compression along a One-Dimensional Scan," in Proc. SPIE, Vol. 1001, pp. 764-770, 1988.
12. Y.Y. Zeevi, N. Peterfreund and E. Shlomot, "Pyramidal Image Representation in Nonuniform Systems," Proc. SPIE, Vol. 1001, pp. 563-570, 1988.
13. E. Shlomot and Y.Y. Zeevi, "Nonuniform Sampling and Representation of Images which are not Band limited," to appear in IEEE Trans. ASSP.
14. Y.Y. Zeevi and R. Ginosar, "Neural Computers in Vision," in Neural Computers, , R. Eckmiller and C. v.d. Malsburg Eds, Springer-Verlag, Berlin, 1988.
15. Y.Y. Zeevi and O.A. Hilsenrath, "Random Scan System," U.S. Pat. 4,858,014, 1989.
16. R. Ginosar, Y.Y. Zeevi and O.A. Hilsenrath, "Intelligent Scan Image Sensor," Patent Application, 1987.
17. R. Ginosar, Y.Y. Zeevi and O.A. Hilsenrath, "A Wide Dynamic Range Imaging Sensor and Camera," Patent Applications, 1988.
18. R. Ginosar, Y.Y. Zeevi and O.A. Hilsenrath, "Adaptive Sensitivity / Intelligent Scan Imaging Sensor Chips," Proc. SPIE Vis. Comm. Image Proc., Camb., MA, Nov. 1988.
19. Z. W. Pylyshyn and R. Storm, "Tracking Multiple Independent Targets: Evidence for Parallel Tracking Mechanism," Spatial Vision, Vol. 3, pp. 179-197, 1988.
20. S.C. Tanaka, H.F. Tseng, and W.L. Wang, "A 512 x 512 Random Access Photodiode Array for Industrial Applications," Proc. Electronic Imaging, pp. 868-873, Boston, Oct. 1989.
21. R. Ginosar, Y.Y. Zeevi and O.A. Hilsenrath, "Intelligent Scan Image Processors," Patent Application, 1988.
22. R. Ginosar and R. Telishevski, "Intelligent Scan Image Processors," Technical Report, Dept. of Electrical Engineering, Technion, 1988.

Advanced Neural Computers / R. Eckmiller (Editor)

On the Neural Computations Underlying Curve Detection

Steven W. ZUCKER[*+]*

Allan DOBBINS[*] & *Lee IVERSON*[*]

[*]Research Center for Intelligent Machines
McGill University, Montreal, P.Q., Canada
and
[+]The Canadian Institute for Advanced Research

1. The Dilemma of Curve Detection

The initial measurement of orientation information is broadly tuned, which suggests the averaging necessary to counteract retinal (sensor) sampling, quantization, and noise. However, the end result of curve detection is unexpectedly precise: corners can be distinguished from arcs of high curvature, and nearby curves can be distinguished from one another to a hyperaccurate level, even though they might pass through the same receptive field.

An analogous dilemma exists for computer vision systems, even with the spectacular numerical precision of which computers are capable: quantization and noise imply smoothing, but smoothing blurs corners, endpoints, and nearby curves into confusion (Zucker, 1986). At the foundation is a chicken-and-egg problem: if the points through which the curve passed, together with the locations of discontinuities, were known, then the actual properties of the curve could be inferred. But initially they are not known, so any smoothing inherent in the inference process is potentially dangerous.

2. Two Stages of Curve Detection

We have discovered a computational solution to this dilemma, which involves decomposing the full problem into two stages, each of which has a rather different character (Fig. 1). Our approach differs significantly from previous ones in that no attempt is made to match curves directly against the image, or even against measurements (i.e., "curve operators") evaluated over the image. Instead we stress the organizational point that a stable, reliable, but *coarse* description should be computed as an intermediate between the image (measurements) and the global curves. A particular intermediate representation—the discrete tangent field—is proposed.

The second stage of the algorithm synthesizes the global curves through the tangent field. The novel idea behind our approach is to recover the global curve by computing a *covering* of it; i.e., a set of objects whose union is equivalent to the original curve, rather than attempting to compute the global curve directly. The elements of the covering are unit-length dynamic splines, and global curves are recovered to sub-pixel accuracy.

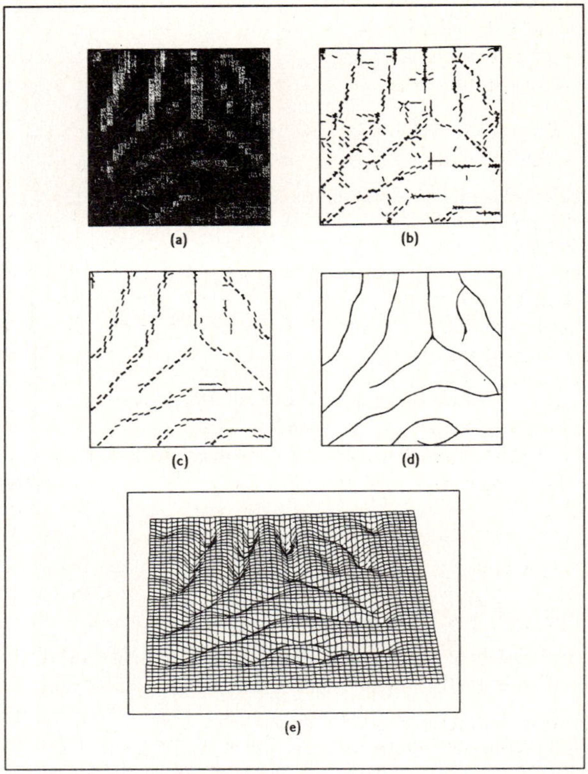

Figure 1 An illustration of the different stages of curve detection. In the first stage, a reliable, but coarse, description (tangent field) of the local structure of curves is computed, while global structure is computed in the second. This is illustrated for the small fingerprint image (a); note the smooth curves and discontinuities around the "Y" in the center. The first stage is broken into two steps. In the first step, initial measurements are performed to estimate what the local curvature and orientation might be (b). In the second step these initial measurements are refined by a relaxation labeling process and (c) shows the final tangent field after 2 iterations; note that most of the spurious initial responses have been eliminated. There are also two steps in the second stage, first the construction of a potential distribution from the entries in the tangent field (e), and second, the covering of the global curve by a family of short curves, or snakes (d).

3. The Model of Curve Detection

We define orientation selection to be the inference of a local description of the curve everywhere along it, and postulate orientation selection as the goal of our first stage. In the second stage, global curves are inferred through this local description. The various stages of our process are shown in Fig. 1, and expanded below.

3.1 Stage 1: Inferring the tangent field

Formally orientation selection amounts to inferring the trace of the curve, or the set of points (in the image) through which the curve passes, its (approximate) tangent and curvature at those points, and their discontinuities [Zucker, 1986]. We refer to such information as the *tangent field*, and note that, since the initial measurements are discrete, this will impose constraints on the (inferred) tangents, curvatures, and discontinuities [Parent and Zucker, 1988].

This first stage of orientation selection is in turn modeled as a two step process:

Step 1.1. *Initial Measurement* of the local fit at each point to estimate orientation and curvature. These estimates derive from a model of simple cell receptive fields instantiated at multiple scales and orientations at each image position. Non-linear differences between orientation estimated over different extents provides the curvature estimate, and is related to the physiological property of endstopping [Dobbins, Zucker, and Cynader, 1987; 1989]. We thus propose that endstopped neurons in the visual cortex represent joint hypotheses about orientation and curvature, and that their firing rate along an (endstopped) orientation hypercolumn represents how well these hypotheses match the local image structure. However, such local measurements are inherently inaccurate (e.g., broadly tuned), so we require

Step 1.2. *Interpretation* into an explicit distributed representation of tangent and curvature by establishing consistency between the local measurements. Consider an arc of a curve, and observe that tangents to this arc must conform to certain position and orientation constraints for a given amount of curvature; we refer to such constraints geometrically as *co-circularity* (Fig. 2a). Discretizing all continuous curves in the world that project into the columnar space of coarse (orientation, curvature) hypotheses partitions these curves into equivalence classes, (Parent and Zucker, 1989; Zucker and Iverson, 1988). Interpreting the (orientation, curvature) hypotheses as endstopped neurons, such co-circularly-consistent relationships are expected between endstopped neurons in nearby orientation hypercolumns given such a curve as stimulus.

Such inter-columnar interactions can be viewed physiologically as excitatory and inhibitory projections between endstopped cells at nearby positions (adjacent hypercolumns), and can be used as follows. Since curvature is a relationship between tangents at nearby positions, two tangents should support one another if and only if they agree under a curvature hypothesis, and co-circularity provides the measure of such support. In addition, two tangents that disagree with the curvature estimate should detract support from one another. Relaxation labeling provides a formal mechanism for defining such support, and for specifying how to use it [Hummel and Zucker, 1983]. Mathematically it amounts to gradient descent; physiologically it can be viewed as the computation implemented by pyramidal neurons as they combine information from adjacent (endstopped) orientation hypercolumns. Since only 2 - 3 iterations are required for convergence (empirically), it is natural to propose that these are accomplished by the forward- and back-projecting pyramidal neurons connecting areas V1 and V2 [Zucker *et al.*, 1989].

One specific model of the physiology could be as follows: initial orientation estimates are obtained by the small (layer 4) simple cells in V1; the difference required for curvature estimation can be built up from a layer 6 to layer 4 back projection, and the first iteration of the relaxation process can be implemented by a pyramidal neuron with dendritic inputs from nearby (endstopped) orientation hypercolumns. Such neurons project to V2, where a similar computation takes place; the backprojection to V1 then provides a final iteration. The tangent field is represented by those neurons whose firing rate is maintained, with tangent corresponding to preferred orientation, and curvature to percentage endstopping.

3.2 Stage 2: Inferring a Covering of the Curve

Since the tangent is the first derivative of a curve (with respect to arc length), the global curve can be recovered as an integral through the tangent field. Such a view typically leads

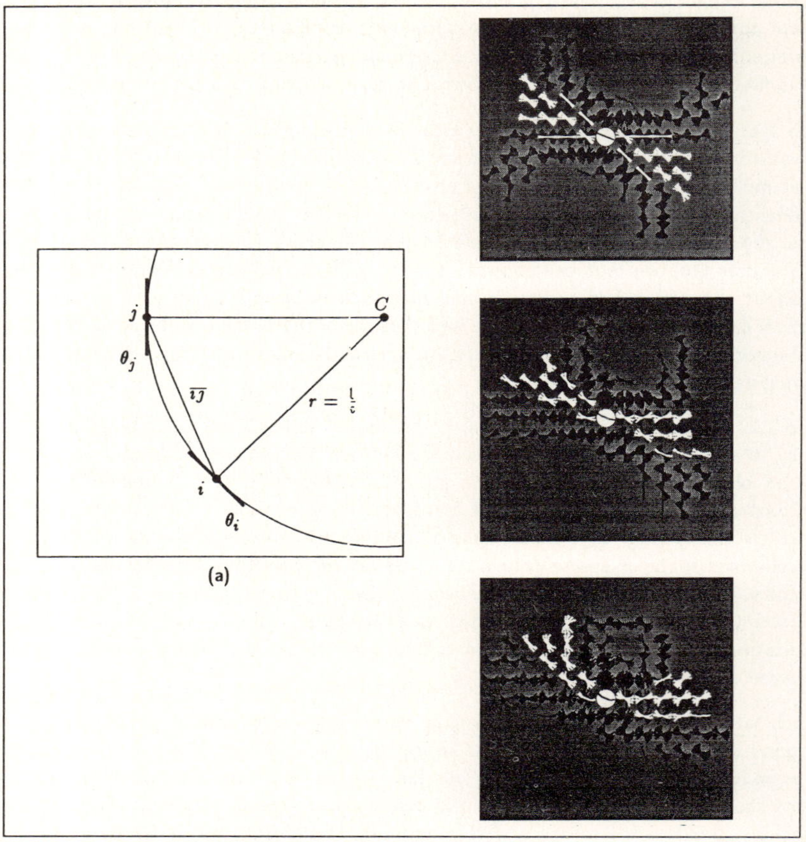

Figure 2 (a)The geometric relationships necessary for defining the compatibilities between two label pairs at nearby points $i = (x_i, y_i)$ and $j = (x_j, y_j)$. (b) Compatibilities between coarse (orientation, curvature) hypotheses at nearby positions. 8 distinct orientations and 7 curvatures were represented, and 3 examples are shown. (top) The labels which give positive (white) and negative (black) support for a diagonal orientation with no curvature; (middle) positive and negative support for a small curvature class; (bottom) positive and negative support for the maximum curvature class. The magnitude of the interactions varies as well, roughly as a Gaussian superimposed on these diagrams. The values were obtained by numerically solving a 6-dimensional closest point problem (Zucker *et al.*, 1988). Physiologically these projective fields could represent inter-columnar interactions implemented by pyramidal neurons.

to sequential recovery algorithms (e.g., Kass and Witkin [1987]). But these algorithms require global parameters, starting points, and some amount of topological structure (i.e., which tangent point follows which); in short, they are biologically implausible. In contrast, we propose a novel approach in which a collection of short, dynamically modifiable curves ("snakes" in computer vision; see Kass, Witkin and Terzopoulos [1988]) move in parallel.

Recovering the global curve by computing a *covering* of it; i.e., a set of objects whose union is equivalent to the original curve, avoids the prerequisite global problems. Let the elements of the covering be unit-length dynamic splines, initially equivalent to the elements of the tangent field, but which then evolve according to a potential distribution constructed from the tangent field. The evolution takes two forms: (i) a migration in position to achieve smooth coverings; and (ii) a "growth" to triple their initial length.

Again, there are two conceptually distinct steps to Stage 2 of the algorithm:

Step 2.1. *Constructing the Potential Distribution* from the discrete tangent field. Each entry in the tangent field actually represents a discretization of the many possible curves in the world that could project onto that particular (tangent, curvature) hypothesis. Now these pieces must be put together. Assuming the curves are continuous but not necessarily differentiable everywhere, each contribution to the potential can be modeled as a Gaussian (the Wiener measure) oriented in the direction of the tangent field entry. The full potential distribution is their pointwise sum; see Fig. 3.

Step 2.2. *Spline Dynamics* The discrete entities in the tangent field are converted into unit splines initialized in the valleys of the potential distribution. They evolve according to a variational scheme that depends on spline properties (tension and rigidity) as well as the global potential (Fig. 3).

The potential distribution is created by adding together contributions from each element in the tangent field; see Fig. 3. Changing the representation from the tangent field to the potential distribution changes what is explicit and what is implicit in the representation, and local information is combined into global information. In Stage 1 there were discrete coarse entities; now there are smooth valleys that surround each of the global curves, with a separation between them. The "jaggies" imposed by the initial image sampling have been eliminated, and interpolation to sub-pixel resolution is viable.

To recover the curves through the valleys, imagine creating, at each tangent field entry, a small spline of unit length oriented according to the tangent and curvature estimates (Fig. 4). Since each spline is born in a valley of the tangent field potential distribution, they are then permitted to migrate to both smooth out the curve and to find the true local minima. The union of these local splines is the global cover. But the the splines must overlap, so that each point on every curve is covered by at least one spline. We therefore let the splines extend in length while they migrate in position, until they each reach a prescribed length. The covering is thus composed of these extensible splines which have grown in the valleys of the tangent field potential. Their specific dynamics and properties are described more fully in Zucker *et al.* (1988); David and Zucker (1988).

It is difficult to interpret these ideas physiologically within the classical view of neurons, in which inputs are summed and transformed into an output train of action potentials. Dendrites simply support passive diffusion of depolarization. Recently, however, a richer view of neuronal processing has emerged, with a variety of evidence pointing to active dendritic computation and dendro-dendritic interaction [Schmitt and Worden, 1979]. Active conductances in dendrites functionally modify the geometry, and dendro-dendritic interactions suggest that the output transformation is not uniquely mediated by the axon. Taken together, these facts imply that patterns of activity can be sustained in the dendritic arbor, and that this membrane could be the substrate of the above potential distribution computations.

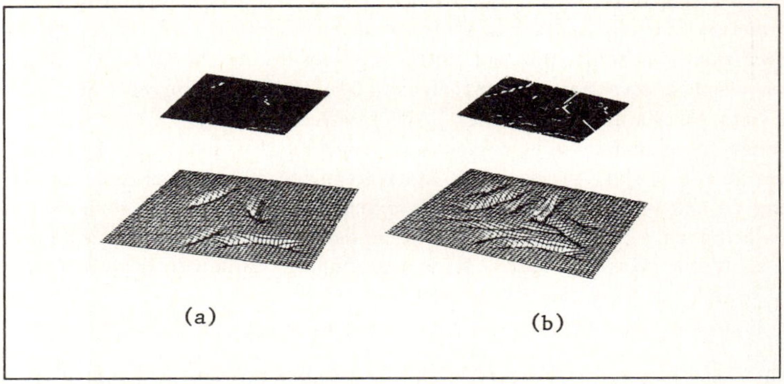

Figure 3 Illustration of how a potential distribution is constructed from tangent field entries. (a) A small number of tangents, showing the individual contributions from each one. (b) As more tangents are included, long "valleys" begin to form when the individual entries are added together. The complete tangent field and potential distribution are shown in Fig. 1. Physiologically one might think of such potentials as being mapped onto local clusters of neuronal membranes, and supported by localized dendric or dendro-dendritic interactions.

The large constructed potential distributions may bear some resemblance to the large receptive fields observed in areas V4 and IT [Maunsell and Newsome, 1987]. While any such relationship is clearly speculative at this time, it should be noted that they have two key similarities: (i) extremely large receptive fields (potential distributions) have been created, but they maintain about the same orientation selectivity as in V1; (ii) their structure can change. We have stressed how structure is controlled by upward flowing information, but it should also be modifiable by "top-down" attentional influences as well [Maunsell and Newsome, 1987; Moran and Desimone, 1985]. Attention could easily "gate" the tangent field entries at the creation of the potential.

4. References

David, C., and Zucker, S.W., Potentials, valleys, and dynamic global coverings, Tech. Rep. TR-CIM-89-1, McGill Research Center for Intelligent Machines, Montreal, 1989.

Desimone, R., Schein, S., Moran, J., and Ungerleider, L., Contour, color, and shape analysis beyond the striate cortex, *Vision Research*, 1985, **25**, 441 - 452.

Dobbins, A., Zucker, S.W., & Cynader, M.S. (1987) Endstopping in the visual cortex as a substrate for calculating curvature. *Nature*, **329**, 438-441, 1987.

Dobbins, A., Zucker, S.W., and Cynader, M., Endstopping and curvature, *Vision Research*, 1989, **29**, 1371 - 1387.

Nelson, J.J. & Frost, B.J. (1985) Intracortical facilitation among co-oriented, co-axially aligned simple cells in cat striate cortex. *Exp. Br. Res.*, **61**: 54-61.

Hummel, R., and Zucker, S.W., On the foundations of relaxation labelling processes, *IEEE Trans. PAMI* **5**, 1983, pp. 267–287.

Kass, M., Witkin, A., and Terzopoulos, D., SNAKES: active contour models, *Int. J. Computer Vision*, 1988, **1**, 321 - 332.

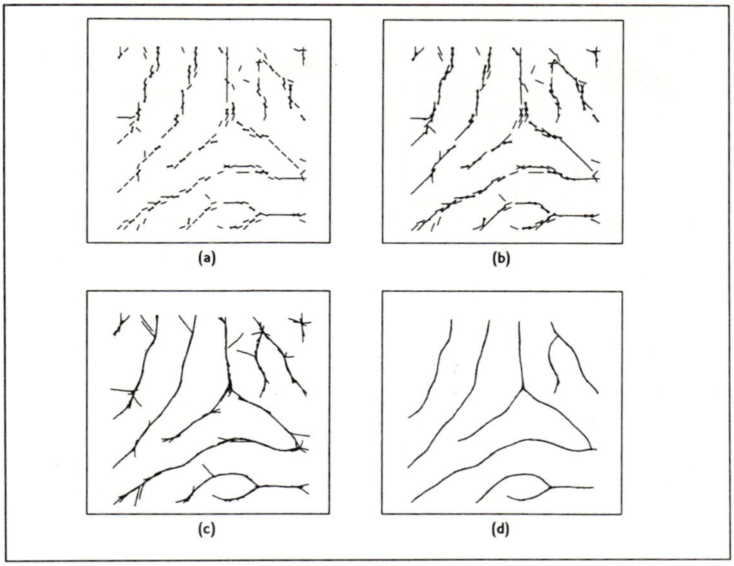

Figure 4 Illustration of the splines in motion. Initially, each spline is born at a tangent field location, with unit length. Then, according to the potential distribution shown in Fig. 1e, the splines migrate in position (to find minima in the distribution) and in length, so that they overlap and fill in short gaps. At convergence, the length of each spline has tripled.

Maunsell, J., and Newsome, W., Visual processing in monkey extrastriate cortex, *Ann. Rev. Neuroscience*, 1987, **10**, 363 - 401.

Moran, J., and Desimone, R., Selective attention gates visual processing in the extriastriate cortex, *Science*, 1985, **229**, 782 - 784.

Parent, P. and Zucker, S.W., Trace Inference, Curvature Consistency, and Curve Detection, *IEEE Trans. Pattern Analysis and Machine Intelligence*, 1989, **11**, 823 - 839.

Schmitt, F., and Worden, F. (eds.), *The Neurosciences: Fourth Study Program*, MIT Press, Cambridge, 1979.

Zucker, S.W., David, C., Dobbins, A., and Iverson, L., The organization of curve detection: Coarse tangent fields and fine spline coverings, *Proc.* 2nd *Int. Conf. on Computer Vision*, Tarpon Springs, Fla, 1988.

Zucker, S.W., and Iverson, L., Computational networks in early vision: From orientation selection to optical flow, in Eckmiller, R., and v.d. Malsberg, C. (eds.), **Neural Computers**, Springer, New York, 1988.

Zucker,S.W., Dobbins, A., and Iverson, L., Two stages of curve detection suggest two styles of visual computation, *Neural Computation*, 1989, **1**, 68 - 81.

Section 6
Motor Control
with Neural Networks

Advanced Neural Computers / R. Eckmiller (Editor)

Network Based Autonomous Robot Motor Control: from Hormones to Learning

Rodney A. Brooks and Paul A. Viola
MIT Artificial Intelligence Lab*
Cambridge, MA, *USA*

Abstract

Network models have started to be used to control physical robots. A major problem is how to control the selection of grossly different high level behaviors and how to express that selection down at the motor level. In this paper we show how to extend the subsumption architecture [**Brooks 86**] inspired by a model of behavior selection of [**Maes 89**], and incorporating a model of hormonal control [**Kravitz 88**]. In robotic terms a hormonal control system enables global control of a distributed system with only a very low bandwidth global communication system. This has important implications concerning the ability to fabricate intelligent silicon controllers for tiny microfabricated micro robots [**Flynn, Brooks and Tavrow 89**].

1 Introduction

We have been using the subsumption architecture [**Brooks 86**] to control mobile robots. While the subsumption architecture can be described as a model that is built on parallel distributed processing we feel that one can in addition claim that it is neurally inspired. Conceptually, it is a network of computational units sending messages along connections between units. It differs from many other neural models however in that the computational units that comprise the network are by no means uniform thoughout the network. Each one is carefully designed by hand, a separate augmented finite state machine.

The subsumption architecture is in part a response to the classical action selection paradigm in AI, namely planning. It addresses the problem of selecting appropriate actions for particular environments. Unfortunately as a alternative to planning, the subsumption architecture exists at the same level of output abstraction, a world of atomic actions. As such, it does not specifically address the questions of action performance and motor learning. Any reasonably complex creature must perceive the world, learn to select correct actions and learn to perform actions correctly. These goals can not be attained seperately, they must, as in all biological systems, exist in a unified and integrated whole.

We have seen the beginning of isolated perceptual systems, isolated action selection stategies, and isolated motor learning strategies. The subsumption architecture is a response to the challenge of integrating perception and action selection systems into a complete and

*Support for this research was provided in part by the University Research Initative under Office of Naval Research contract N00014–86–K–0685, in part by the Advanced Research Projects Agency under Office of Naval Research contract N00014–85–K–0124, in part by a contract from Hughes Research Labs Artificial Intelligence Center, and in part by a gift from Siemens.

functioning system. We now feel that a creature is not truly complete unless it can i) flexibly apply differing action strategies, ii) learn to select actions within these strategies, and iii) learn to perform those actions correctly. We address the question of flexible behavioral strategies here by introducing a mechanism for hormonal control. [**Maes and Brooks 90**] have suggested a technique for learning how to "do right thing" that fits within the distributed architecture proposed in the subsumption architecture. Towards the third requirement, we are beginning research into the adaptation of actions performed by the motor system; this work has as its root the work of Viola [**Viola 89**] on adaptation in an artificial oculomotor system.

We will describe in detail recent experiments with a model hormonal control system. These experiments have been performed on the mobile robot group's six-legged research robot, Ghenghis[**Angle 89**]. As part of our description of Ghenghis we will quickly describe resarch into the process of learning how to select appropriate actions with respect to behavioral goals and environmental structure [**Maes and Brooks 90**]. Finally we will briefly describe an "architectural" addition that will allow for the incorporate motor control and motor learning into the subsumption architecture.

2 Hormonal Control

As with other PDP systems the subsumption architecture is difficult to analyze and, more importantly, difficult to direct towards global goals. The hormonal control structure we propose, is a mechanism for modulating between alternative behavoir patterns. [**Kravitz 88**] describes a model of hormonal control of behavior. Following his own summary the major points of this model are:

1. Sensor inputs enhance the release of hormones.
2. A hormone may be released from tissues or neurons and may act in isolation or in concert with other substances.
3. The hormone finds receptors where it either stimulates a new behavior pattern or either enhances or diminshes an existing pattern.
4. The things effected by hormones may include sensory elements, groups of neurons in higher processing centers, and motor or hormonal output systems.
5. The method of stimulation is a gain setting mechanism biasing the output of the organism in particular directions.
6. The change is apparent in that the organism now responds to particular sensory inputs with altered outputs.
7. Individual organisms may respond to particular hormones with different levels of effectiveness—determined by genetic or environmental influences.
8. The effected circuit may itself further enhance or diminish the release of the hormonal substance.

Kravitz uses the lobster as his primary instantiation of this model. In this paper we demonstrate a robotic instantiation of this model which successfully demonstrates 7 of the listed 8 properties (number 7 being the only one not accounted for).

3 A Robot Implementation

We have implemted a model of Kravitz' hormonal control system on a six legged walking robot. We had carried out a number of previous experiments with that robot—the hormonal model gives us a method for controlling the gross behavior of the robot, whereas previous work had concentrated on lower level motor issues.

3.1 The Subsumption Architecture

A subsumption program is built on a computational substrate that is organized into a series of incremental layers, each, in the general case, connecting perception to action. In our case the substrate is networks of finite state machines augmented with timing elements.

The subsumption architecture was described initially in [**Brooks 86**] and later modified in [**Brooks 89**] and [**Connell 89**]. The subsumption compiler compiles augmented finite state machine (AFSM) descriptions into a special-purpose scheduler to simulate parallelism and a set of finite state machine simulation routines. This is a dynamically retargetable compiler that has backends for a number of processors, including the Motorola 68000, the Motorola 68HC11, and the Hitachi 6301. The subsumption compiler takes a source file as input and produces an assembly language program as output.

The behavior language [**Brooks 90**] was inspired by [**Maes 89**] as a way of grouping AFSMs into more manageable units with the capability for whole units being selectively activated or de-activated. In fact, AFSMs are not specified directly, but rather as rule sets of real-time rules which compile into AFSMs in a one-to-one manner. The behavior compiler is machine-independent and compiles into an intermediate file of subsumption AFSM specifications. The subsumption compiler can then be used to compile to the various targets.

The original subsumption was used to control a number of robots including a sonar based wandering robot [**Brooks 86**], a soda can collecting robot [**Connell 89**], a visually guided navigating robot [**Horswill and Brooks 88**], and the original experiments with the six legged walking robot [**Brooks 89**]. The newer behavior language has been used for a sonar based robot which builds totally distributed maps of the world [**Mataric 90**] in a very robust way, and for experiments in learning to walk [**Maes and Brooks 90**].

3.2 Genghis

Genghis [**Angle 89**] is a 1Kg six legged robot which walks under subsumption control and has an extremely distributed control system. The robot successfully walks over rough terrain using 12 motors, 12 force sensors, 6 pyroelectric sensors, one inclinometer and 2 whiskers. It also follows cooperative humans using its pyroelectric sensors.

In the original experiments with Genghis [**Brooks 89**] the subsumption layers successively enable the robot to stand up, walk without any sensing, use force measurements to comply with rough terrain, use force measurements to lift its legs over obstacles, use inclinometer measurements to selectively inhibit rough terrain compliance when appropriate, use whiskers to lift feet over obstacles, use passive infrared sensors to detect people and to walk only when they are present, and to use the directionality of infrared radiation to modulate the backswing of particular leg sets so that the robot follows a moving source of radiation.

In contrast, one could imagine a control system which had a central repository which modeled the robot's configuration in translation and orientation space. One could further imagine high level commands (for instance from a path planner) generating updates for the robot's coordinates. These high level commands would then be hierarchically resolved into instructions for individual legs.

The original control system on Genghis has no such repository. Indeed there is not even a central repository for each leg—separate motors on the legs are controlled quite separately in different parts of the network. While there is some semblance of a central control system for each individual motor, these controllers receive messages from diverse parts of the network and simply pass them on to the motors, without any attempt at integration. The only central control in the system is a central AFSM that sequentially tickles the legs to lift them up (and induce a walking cycle) and a servo system that tries to keep the sum of the outward point angles of the legs at zero. The effect of this servo is that when one leg swings forward the others (which are most likely on the ground) push backwards enabling the robot to walk.

The control system was also very easy to build. It was built incrementally, with each new capability being a simple of addition (no deletion, no change to previous network) of new network structure. The debugged existing network structure was never altered.

The resulting control system is elegant in its simplicity. It does not deal with coordinate transforms or kinematic models. It is not at all hierarchical. It directly implements walking through many very tight couplings of sensors to actuators. It is very distributed in its nature, and we believe its robustness in handling rough terrain comes from this distributed form of control.

Recently [**Maes and Brooks 90**] have used Genghis for experiments in learning. Each leg has a number of behaviors (written in the behavior language) which together are capable of operating the basic step cycle of the leg. Instead of a central leg controller the initiation of the appropriate lifting behavior the network of behaviors learn to activate themselves based on the activity of neighboring legs. This learning is done in a totally distributed and local way, and uses negative feedback from touch sensors on the robot's belly as an evaluation function. The walking gait emerges from the interactions of behaviors within the network. The only gobal communication left is the sum-to-zero leg angle servo.

In the experiments for this paper we have eliminated this last vestige of central control. We follow much more closely the model of six legged insect walking presented by [**Wilson 66**]. The primary change is the inclusion of a stroke behavior on each leg whose speed is hormonally controlled. Different gaits then arise under different hormonal conditions.

3.3 The Hormonal Model

In our model sensory conditions do not directly release hormones. Rather we use a two stage mechanism so that summation of hormone quantities can be centralized—this is clearly different from the way it might be implemented in a biochemical system.

3.3.1 Conditions and Releasers

Any computational process can *excite* a *condition.* Labels we have used for conditions in our programs include such character strings as *fear* and *trepidity.* Multiple processes can (pseudo) simultaneously excite a single condition—their effects are additive. In our model the excitation level of a condition is an integer in the range 0 to 15. A processes can excite a condition with any increment to this level that it chooses.

The excitation level of a condition decays naturally. As it happens the default decay rate is linear and one twelth of a unit per second. The programmer can specify the decay rate as a bilinear function. The semantics are such that above a specified threshold it is possible to have a negative decay rate so that a condition can become self sustaining. The decay rates are set at program compile time and cannot be altered dynamically.

Releasers correspond more directly to hormones. These are the things that actually influence behaviors. A releaser's value at any point in time is an instantaneous function of the current levels of excitement of some set of conditions. There are no a priori restrictions on the value that can be taken by a releaser. For the experiments described in this paper the labels used for releasers in our programs include such character strings as *fearomone* and *confomone*.

3.3.2 Activation of Behaviors

Behaviors are implemented as a collection of augmented finite state machines. Each AFSM is a computational process. A behavior can be *active* or *inactive*. The difference between these states is that different computational processes are allowed to run. A behavior can have three clasess of processes:

- **Regular processes:** These processes always run, and any messages they send out reach their destinations.
- **Haltable processes:** These processes only run when the behavior is active. Otherwise they do not run, do not process their inputs and do not send out any messages.
- **Inhibitible processes:** These processes always run but when the behavior is inactive their outputs are inhibited or blocked. They still receive all their inputs however and can retain and change internal state.

Following [**Maes 89**] each behavior has an activation level, and the behavior becomes active when it passes some threshold[1]. It is a continuously recomputed value and does not decay in any sense. The original idea of activation was that it should be spread from behavior to behavior as a behavior tried to get certain preconditions met by activating other behaviors. For the hormonal model we have made it so that activation level can also be a function of releasers. In fact in the experiments with Genghis that is the only component used in activation.

3.4 Implementation on Genghis

We have implemented a walking program on Genghis that includes the use of hormones.[2] The program runs on a Hitachi 6301 with 8K of PROM and 640 bytes of RAM. This same processor is the master of a 62.5 Kbaud token ring that supplies position commands to two servo processors and listens to crude force, inclinometer and whisker sensor readings from a fourth processor.

The robot uses a totally distributed walking algorithm such as that described in [**Wilson 66**]. As the robot walks a condition of "trepidity" rises whenever the leggs encounter a non-flat surface (sensed by reading the forces on the two axes of motion). A releaser that is inversely depedent on this condition controls the backward swing rate of the legs, and hence the robot speed and gait.

A second condition, "fear", is stimulated by rapid touching of the whiskers. A releaser which inhibits walking is directly dependent on fear and also, with a smaller weight coefficient, is dependent on "trepidity". Thus if the robot has been walking over rough terrain, it is more pre-disposed to a fearful reaction (stopping) and can be made with less whisker manipulation than is necessary when the robot has been walking over a flat surface.

[1] There is some user controllable hystersis in the system as the activation level falls below the threshold once again.

[2] As of March 1990, actual testing of the program has been complicated by the fact that the robot has no real position feedback. In earlier experiments [**Brooks 89**] use of most-recently-commanded position was used to simulate position feedback, but in the current application a time dependent estimator had to be added to this measure to ensure reasonable performance—still there are problems. We are currently constructing a much higher performance six legged walking robot with over 150 sensors on board—we believe experiments with this robot will be much simpler.

4 Critique

We are now in a position to compare how our implentation on the six legged robot compares with Kravitz' model of hormones.

1. *Sensor inputs enhance the release of hormones.* In our experiment, behaviors which process sensor readings can excite a condition, which in turn can contribute to the level of a releaser (or hormone).

2. *A hormone may be released from tissues or neurons and may act in isolation or in concert with other substances.* Any behavior is free to excite a condition and hence change a releaser level. Furthermore, activation levels of behaviors can be functions of many releasers, and thus a releaser may be acting by itself or it may be acting in concert with other releasers.

3. *The hormone finds receptors where it either stimulates a new behavior pattern or either enhances or diminshes an existing pattern.* If a releaser pushes a behavior's activation level beyond its threshold then a new behavior pattern can indeed by initiated. Furthermore, since activation levels are accessible to behaviors it is possible to have this control certain parameters of a behavior, for instance the walking speed of the robot.

4. *The things effected by hormones may include sensory elements, groups of neurons in higher processing centers, and motor or hormonal output systems.* In our system all such things are controlled by behaviors, and these can be effected by the hormone system.

5. *The method of stimulation is a gain setting mechanism biasing the output of the organism in particular directions.* This was the original idea borrowed from [**Maes 89**]. By having releasers change the activation level of behaviors it can mean that either less or more spreading of activation from another behavior will be needed in order for this behavior to activate. Thus indeed the releasers can bias whether a particular behavior is activated, and thus bias the overall behavior of the robot.

6. *The change is apparent in that the organism now responds to particular sensory inputs with altered outputs.* This is the point of behavior activation. For instance in the example programmed for this behavior when the robot has been walking over rough terrain, it is much more likely to become "fearful" from having its whiskers stimulated.

7. *Individual organisms may respond to particular hormones with different levels of effectiveness—determined by genetic or environmental influences.* This aspect of the model is not included in our experiments.

8. *The effected circuit may itself further enhance or diminish the release of the hormonal substance.* There are two ways in which our implementation can do this. First, it is possible to make a condition decay negatively above some threshold, effectively keepnig the condition's value at its maximum level.

5 Grounding Out in Motor Control

[**Viola 89**] describes a complex autonomous sensory motor system that performs useful visual information processing. The system, A-eye, has the same chronic need for calibration that all sensory motor systems require. But A-eye, instead of relying on complex calibration routines, evaluates its own performance and learns to correctly perform its processing. The learning

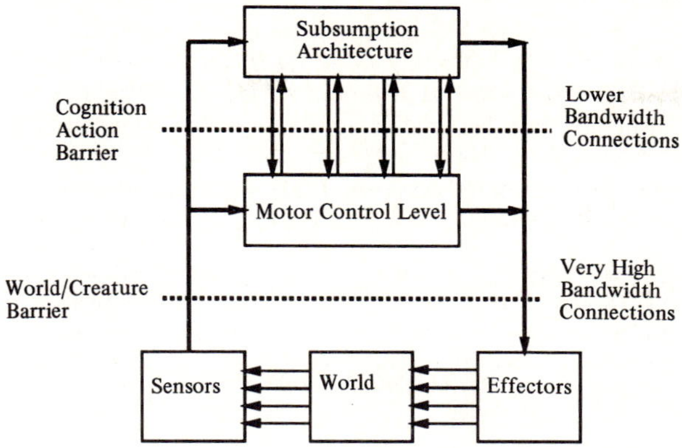

Figure 1: **An augmented subsumption architecture most often effects the world by controlling the activity of a motor control layer. The meat of the subsumption architecture remains firmly in the action level of abstraction, while the motor control layer causes joints to servo at particular velocities with stability. The motor control layer is comprised of "motor control boxes" that perform particular motor control functions (e.g., non-linear velocity control) and can learn to accurately perform tasks using a low bandwidth error signal.**

process requires only the sign of the performance error and it need not be available at the servo rate. While this type of autonomous motor learning is good when it is practical, most sensory motor systems are incapable of evaluating their own performance. We have begun to investigate a division of labor that capitalizes on this readily available motor learning. On one side lies existing subsumption architectures and its capability to perform action selection; on the other lies a "motor control layer" that adaptively performs these actions (see figure 1). Actions are now triggered by enabling particular "motor control boxes" that perform the correct motor control action (e.g., "apply torque to the elbow" or "position the wrist at 10"). These motor control boxes can adapt appropriately through the use of low bandwidth error signals that result for a high level evaluation of performance.

6 References

[**Angle 89**] "Genghis, a Six Legged Autonomous Walking Robot", Colin M. Angle, *MIT S.B. Thesis in Electrical Engineering and Computer Science*, March.

[**Brooks 86**] "A Robust Layered Control System for a Mobile Robot", Rodney A. Brooks, *IEEE Journal of Robotics and Automation*, RA-2, April, 14–23.

[**Brooks 89**] "A Robot that Walks: Emergent Behavior from a Carefully Evolved Network", Rodney A. Brooks, *Neural Computation 1:2*, Summer, 253–262.

[**Brooks 90**] "The Behavior Language; User's Guide", Rodney A. Brooks, *MIT AI Memo*, April.

[**Connell 89**] "A Colony Architecture for an Artificial Creature", Jonathan H. Connell, *MIT AI Lab, TR–1152*, June.

[Flynn, Brooks and Tavrow 89] "Anita M. Flynn, Rodney A. Brooks and Lee S. Tavrow", Twilight Zones and Cornerstones: A Gnat Robot Double Feature, *MIT AI Memo 1126*, July.

[Horswill and Brooks 88] "Situated Vision in a Dynamic World: Chasing Objects", Ian D. Horswill and Rodney A. Brooks, *AAAI-88*, St Paul, MN, August, 796–800.

[Kravitz 88] "Hormonal Control of Behavior: Amines and the Biasing of Behavioral Output in Lobsters", Edward A. Kravitz, *Science 241*, September 30, 1775–1781.

[Maes 89] "The Dynamics of Action Selection", Pattie Maes, *IJCAI-89*, Detroit, MI, 991–997.

[Maes and Brooks 90] "Learning to Coordinate Behaviors", Pattie Maes and Rodney A. Brooks, *submitted to AAAI-90*, draft.

[Mataric 90] "Environment Learning Using a Distributed Representation", Maja J Mataric, *IEEE Robotics and Automation, to appear in May*, Cincinatti, OH.

[Viola 89] "Neurally Inspired Plasticity in Oculomotor Processes", Paul Viola, *1989 IEEE Conference on Neural Information Processing Systems–Natural and Synthetic*, Denver, CO, Nov.

[Wilson 66] "Insect Walking", Donald M. Wilson, *Annual Review of Entymology 11*, reprinted in *The Organization of Action: A New Synthesis*, C. R. Gallistel, Lawrence Erlbaum, Hillsdale, NJ, 1980.

Advanced Neural Computers / R. Eckmiller (Editor)

SPINAL NETWORK COMPUTATIONS ENABLE INDEPENDENT CONTROL OF MUSCLE LENGTH AND JOINT COMPLIANCE

Daniel Bullock† and Stephen Grossberg‡

Center for Adaptive Systems, Boston University
111 Cummington Street, Boston, MA 02215 USA

1. AN OPPONENT NEUROMUSCULAR DESIGN FOR INDEPENDENT CONTROL OF MUSCLE LENGTH AND MUSCLE TENSION

How can an organism continuously vary the compliance of its joints without inadvertently changing joint angle? Such behavior is remarkable because muscle length remains invariant during a rescaling of muscle force, despite the natural tendency for muscle force to covary with muscle length. Here we summarize our model [1,2] of the neural network that helps ensure independent control of muscle length and force. Called FLETE, for Factorization of LEngth and TEnsion, the model (Figure 1) has allowed us to advance several novel hypotheses regarding functional computational properties of known spino-muscular anatomy. Mathematical analysis shows that if muscle tissue is subject to yielding at high force levels, then achieving a wide force range at each muscle length requires that motor units behave according to the size principle of motor unit recruitment. In a system that obeys the size principle, attempting to vary joint compliance by adding the same co-contractive signal to both opponent muscle control channels disrupts invariant muscle length control, but the disruption may be preemptively compensated by an efference copy feedback pathway. A pathway with appropriate properties is provided in the spinal cord by Renshaw cells and Ia interneurons, and our simulations verify the compensatory properties of such a pathway. Further simulations show how a gradual learning process based on stretch feedback can allow the system to achieve feedforward compensation for changes, associated with joint rotations, in muscle mechanical advantage. In summary, the FLETE model explicates the neural bases of compensation for several intrinsic sources of variability in the realization of central motor commands, and thereby provides a rationale for many incompletely understood properties of the neuromuscular system.

2. WIDE FORCE RANGE AT EACH MUSCLE LENGTH REQUIRES SIZE PRINCIPLE

Consider the forces, F_i, $i = 1,2$ developed by two muscles operating on different sides of a joint. In a springy tissue like muscle, developed force depends on the amount of stretch beyond the resting length. Because muscle can actively contract, muscle has a *variable* threshold length for force development [3]. These properties can be approximated by

$$F_i = g\left([L_i - \Gamma_i + C_i]^+\right) \tag{1}$$

where L_i is muscle length, Γ_i is the resting muscle length, C_i is the amount of contraction, and function $g(w)$ is monotone increasing. Notation $[w]^+$ means $\max(w,0)$. Thus equation (1) says that whenever the sum of L_i and C_i exceed Γ_i, the muscle generates a force whose magnitude increases as L_i or C_i become larger.

Because contracted fibers relax after each neurally elicited twitch and *yield* when the force acting to stretch them is sufficiently large [9], a simple law for C_i is

$$\frac{d}{dt}C_i = \beta_i\left[(B_i - C_i)M_i - \delta C_i\right] - [F_i - \Gamma_F]^+ \tag{2}$$

† Supported in part by the National Science Foundation (NSF IRI-87-16960).

‡ Supported in part by the National Science Foundation (NSF IRI-87-16960) and the Air Force Office of Scientific Research (AFOSR F49620-86-C-0037 and AFOSR F49620-87-C-0018).

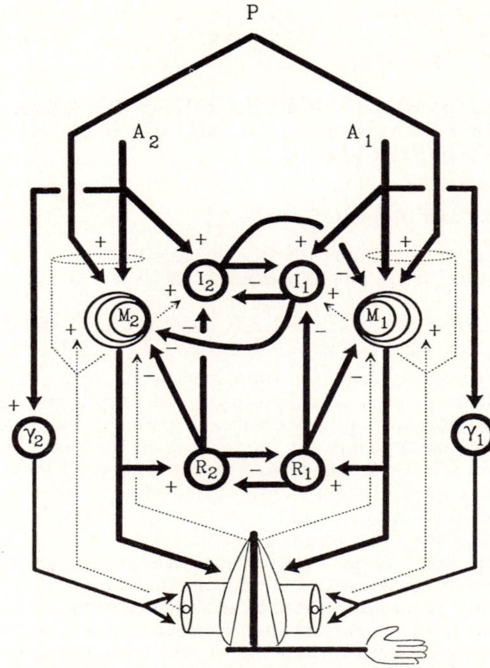

Figure 1. FLETE model components: Neuron populations comprising two channels control opponent muscles acting on a joint. Descending signal P to both channels allows co-contraction and joint stiffening. Adjusting the balance between descending signals A_1 and A_2 allows reciprocal contractions and joint repositioning. Medially drawn feedback (dotted) pathways arise from Golgi tendon organs; lateral feedback pathways arise from spindle organs associated with small intrafusal muscles, shown to be in parallel with large muscles. Key: I_i = Ia interneuron population in channel $i, i = 1,2$; γ_i = gamma motoneurons; M_i = alpha motoneurons; R_i = Renshaw cells; + = excitatory input; − = inhibitory input.

where $0 < \beta_i < 1$ and M_i is the output signal of the ith alpha-motoneuron pool. As M_i grows, it activates more contractile fibers up to the limit set by B_i. Parameter δ specifies the fiber relaxation rate. When force F_i exceeds threshold Γ_F, which may happen when an external or antagonist muscle's force opposes muscle shortening, it reduces contraction. By constraining β_i to be between 0 and 1, contraction caused by neural input M_i is assured to be slow relative to the decontraction or "yielding" produced by external or already developed antagonist muscle forces.

At equilibrium, $\frac{d}{dt}C_i = 0$ in (2), so the equilibrium value of C_i is

$$C_i = \frac{M_i B_i - \dfrac{[F_i - \Gamma_F]^+}{\beta_i}}{M_i + \delta}. \tag{3}$$

Given (3), how is it possible to generate and sustain forces much larger than Γ_F at a fixed muscle length? By (1), greater force at a fixed length L_i can be generated only by increasing C_i. However, if β_i is constant and less than 1, then (3) shows that the negative force feedback will cancel the effects of increasing M_i, and C_i will not grow large. To overcome this deficiency, let the contraction rate parameter β_i and the number of contractile fibers B_i increase with M_i. Such a relation corresponds to a law known empirically as the *size principle* of motor unit organization [6]: As total excitatory input to the alpha motoneuron population grows, it recruits additional, progressively larger motoneurons which have faster conducting axons, whose collaterals reach many more motor fibers and whose potentials evoke more rapid muscle contractions. Equation (3) provides a more complete functional perspective on the size principle by emphasizing the importance of contractile rate for the achievement of large force magnitudes.

3. SIZE PRINCIPLE WITH CO-CONTRACTION THREATEN POSITION-CODE INVARIANCE

However, the size principle, which helps decouple length and force variation, can pose a threat to position-code invariance. To see how, suppose that the CNS controls equilibrium muscle lengths by setting the relative sizes of inputs A_1 and A_2 to motoneurons in opponent muscle control channels 1 and 2, respectively. If a limb segment is initially at equilibrium with $F_1 = F_2$, then by (1),

$$g\left([L_1 - \Gamma_1 + C_1(A_1)]^+\right) = g\left([L_2 - \Gamma_2 + C_2(A_2)]^+\right), \tag{4}$$

where $C_i(A_i)$ denotes the equilibrium value of C_i when $M_i = f(A_i)$ in (2). To hold the limb at the same position, but more rigidly, increase the level of muscle contraction on both sides of the joint. The simplest way to co-contract is to add a constant P to each motoneuron input [8]. Then $M_1 = f(A_1 + P)$ and $M_2 = f(A_2 + P)$. However, in a system that obeys the size principle, (4) implies

$$g\left([L_1 - \Gamma_1 + C_1(A_1 + P)]^+\right) = g\left([L_2 - \Gamma_2 + C_2(A_2 + P)]^+\right) \tag{5}$$

for arbitrary P and the same initial values of L_i only if $A_1 = A_2$. For example, with $A_1 > A_2$, co-contractive signal P can cause the total input $A_1 + P$ to exceed the big cell threshold while input $A_2 + P$ remains below the big cell threshold. Then part of the signal P is subjected to greater amplification in channel 1 than in channel 2. This would create a force imbalance. Thus a co-contractive input P aimed at stabilizing limb position could instead cause a large limb rotation. This would constitute a failure to factorize length and tension.

If left uncompensated by the spino-muscular system, a *different* pair of signals A_1 and A_2 would have to be learned to specify the *same* joint angle for every distinct value of the nonspecific compliance control signal, P. We now suggest how the spino-muscular system may compensate for position distortions created by the size principle. It thereby avoids a combinatorial explosion in the learning required for limb stabilization across a wide range of joint compliance settings.

4. AUTOMATIC COMPENSATION BY THE RENSHAW-IaIN PATHWAY FOR UNEQUAL AMPLIFICATIONS OF CO-CONTRACTIVE SIGNALS

Renshaw cells (see Figure 1), which receive efferent copies of motoneuronal outputs as their inputs [11], are well situated to play a compensatory role. In [1], we hypothesized that opponent Renshaw populations R_1 and R_2 measure the output of their respective alpha-motoneuron populations, α-MN_1, and α-MN_2, and compare those outputs via mutually inhibitory signals (Figure 1). A consensus emerges regarding which MN channel to inhibit via Renshaw feedback, and which to *dis*inhibit via feedback along the Ia interneuron (IaIN) pathway. Suppose that a co-contractive input, P, to α-MN_1 and α-MN_2 occurs when input A_1 exceeds A_2 and that the activity of α-MN_1 is consequently multiplied by a larger factor than that of α-MN_2 due to the size principle. Then R_1 also becomes much more active due to a size-correlated synaptic weighting on α-MN_1 axon collaterals to R_1 [10]. Because the opposing R_2 has not experienced as large an input increment, R_1 will transiently become more active than R_2 by an amount that scales with the *difference* between the α-MN output increments due to the change in P. Thus, this system calculates a *predicted error* due to unequal amplifications of co-contractive inputs. This predicted-error signal directly inhibits α-MN_1 and, by inhibiting $IaIN_1$, indirectly activates α-MN_2. Both actions work to zero the error signal, and thereby pre-empt occurrence of an actual rotation error, without negating either the shared increment in α-MN_i activation required to increase joint stiffness, or the joint angle setting determined by the different descending inputs, A_1 and A_2, to opponent α-MN and IaIN populations.

This conjecture has been supported by our computer simulations, which assumed an elbow-like rotary joint affected by two opponent muscles, each of which is inserted in the moving segment one unit from the axis of rotation. The distance from muscle origin to the axis of rotation was 20 units, and the midpoint of the limb's 180° excursion was stipulated to be at joint angle $\Theta = 0°$. Origin-to-insertion muscle lengths, L_i, were thus functions of Θ:

$$L_1 = \sqrt{(\cos\Theta)^2 + (20 - \sin\Theta)^2}, \quad L_2 = \sqrt{(\cos\Theta)^2 + (20 + \sin\Theta)^2} \tag{6}$$

Because these simulations concerned only large-scale effects on equilibrium joint angle, we ignored force-velocity effects and chose a simple linear force law

$$F_i = k[L_i - \Gamma_i + C_i]^+ \tag{7}$$

where $k = .5, \Gamma_i = 20.9$ and $i = 1, 2$. Limb dynamics were governed by equation

$$\frac{d^2}{dt^2}\Theta = \frac{1}{m}(F_1 - F_2 - n\frac{d\Theta}{dt}) \tag{8}$$

where m represents mass and n is a damping coefficient. We use forces rather than torques in (8) to illustrate the compensatory properties of the Renshaw-IaIN network. This network is not able to compensate for the moment-arm variation that creates a discrepancy between the muscle force balance and the torque balance within the opponent system. In Section 5, we describe a learning process capable of providing moment-arm compensation.

Contractile state C_i was governed by (2) with $\Gamma_F = 1$. Variables β_i and B_i were defined by:

$$\beta_i = .05 + .02(A_i + P), \quad B_i = 2 + 20(A_i + P) \tag{9}$$

Both variables grow as a function of total descending input $A_i + P$ to the MN pools in channel i, but β_i grows with a smaller slope. Use of β_i and B_i in Equations (2) and (9) approximates α-MN recruitment effects that occur as a result of the size principle.

Recruitment of larger motoneurons causes larger inputs to the Renshaw cells [10]. In our lumped model, this effect was absorbed into a single variable, z_i, which increases with recruitment extent, approximated by $A_i + P$. The equations for opponent Renshaw populations were thus

$$\frac{d}{dt}R_i = \phi(\lambda B_i - R_i)z_i M_i - R_i(1 + R_j) \tag{10}$$

$$z_i = .2 + .8(A_i + P) \tag{11}$$

where $\{i, j\} = \{1, 2\}$, $\phi = .2$, and $\lambda = 5$. Equation (10) represents a membrane equation embedded in a shunting competitive network [4].

We modeled the opponent alpha-motoneuron populations via the shunting competitive network

$$\frac{d}{dt}M_i = \phi\left[(\lambda B_i - M_i)(A_i + P + \chi E_i)\right] - M_i(\delta_i + \Omega R_i + \rho F_i + I_j) \tag{12}$$

where $\{i, j\} = \{1, 2\}, \delta_i = 1, \chi = 0, \rho = 0$ or 1, and $\Omega = 0$ or 1. Inhibitory inputs I_j come from the IaINs (Figure 1) and excitatory inputs E_i from the muscle spindles. Inhibitory input ρF_i allowed study of the role of the force feedback known to originate in Golgi tendon organs and to be passed to α-MNs via IbINs. IaIN dynamics were modeled without direct dependence on B_i, and without a co-activating input P:

$$\frac{d}{dt}I_i = \phi(10 - I_i)(A_i + \chi E_i) - I_i(1 + \Omega R_i + I_j) \tag{13}$$

In our simulations, variables A_1, A_2, and P were independent variables and variables L_i, F_i, and Θ were dependent variables. Spindle feedback signals E_1 and E_2 in Equations (12) and (13) were gated off in our simulations by setting $\chi = 0$. This allowed us to test the ability of the Renshaw-IaIN-MN feedback circuit to achieve position code invariance without assistance from stretch reflexes. When Renshaw feedback was absent ($\Omega = 0$), changing

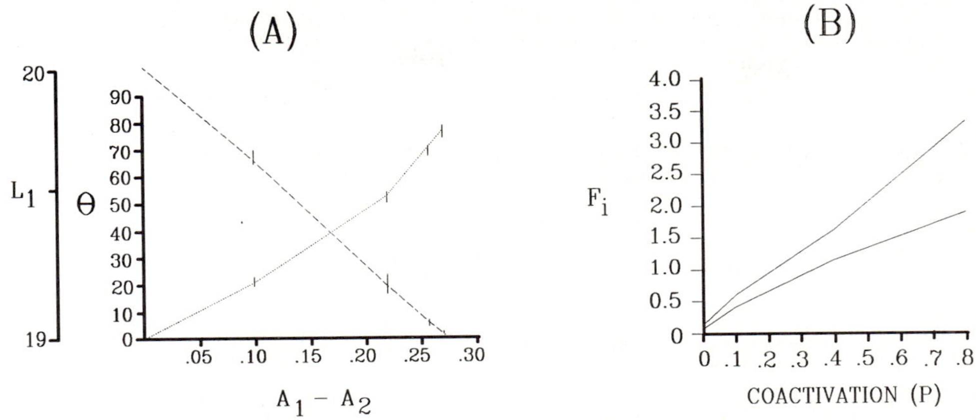

Figure 2. **A.** Summary of simulations demonstrating independent control of length and tension in the FLETE model. Muscle length L_1 (dashed line) is a linear function of $A_1 - A_2$ and varies little despite large changes in co-contractive signal P. Joint angle Θ (solid line) is shown for comparison. See text for details. **B.** Force rises more quickly as a function of co-contractive signal P with mutual Renshaw inhibition (upper curve) than without it (lower curve).

P while A_1 and A_2 remained fixed led to large rotations. When Renshaw feedback was present ($\Omega = 1$), rotations due to changing P with fixed A_1 and A_2 were small. Generally, when the system was not operating in the saturation range, excursions were $< 1°$. On the other hand, the forces F_i, which were monotone increasing in P, varied over a large range. This was the invariance property we sought.

Figure 2A plots L_1 and Θ versus $A_1 - A_2$ for half of a full range of limb excursions. The half not shown, for $A_1 - A_2 < 0$, is symmetrical. The small residual effect on position of changing P in the range 0–.8 is shown by the vertical bars, which indicate the full range of variation, not standard deviations. Figure 2B illustrates the importance of including mutual inhibition, via term $-R_iR_j$ in (10), between opponent Renshaw cell populations. Without it, increments in P produce diminishing returns of force output from each muscle in the system. With it, force development is approximately linear in P.

5. LEARNED AND REACTIVE COMPENSATIONS FOR VARIABLE MOMENT-ARMS USING SPINDLE ORGAN ERROR SIGNALS

Because joint rotations depend on muscle torques rather than muscle forces as such, equation (8) must be replaced by equations

$$\frac{d^2}{dt^2}\Theta = \frac{1}{m}\left(T_1 - T_2 + T_e - n\frac{d\Theta}{dt}\right) \tag{14}$$

and

$$T_i = D_iF_i, \quad i = 1, 2. \tag{15}$$

D_i is the moment-arm of force F_i, T_i is the torque associated with muscle i, and T_e is an external torque (see next section). The moment-arm is the perpendicular distance between the line of action of F_i and the axis of joint rotation. Equation (15) says that the torques T_i are a function of both the forces F_i and the moment-arms D_i. The latter are in turn functions of joint angle Θ:

$$D_1 = \frac{20}{\sqrt{\left(\frac{\sin\Theta - 20}{\cos\Theta}\right)^2 + 1}} \tag{16}$$

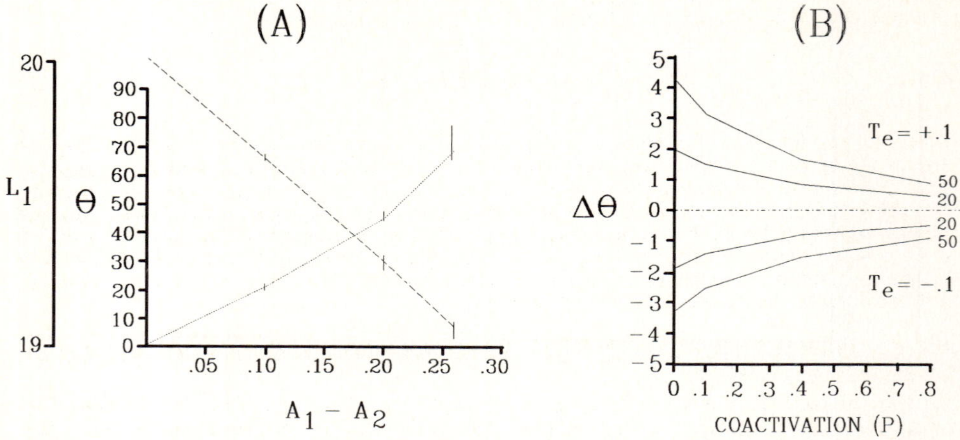

Figure 3. A. Immediate reactive compensations and long-term adaptation of coefficients in feedforward signal pathways, both mediated by spindle-organ feedback signals, allow the FLETE model to ensure independent control of muscle length and tension despite angle-dependent variations in muscle mechanical advantage. Key given in Figure 2A caption. **B.** A demonstration of compliance control in the FLETE model. Angular displacements $\Delta\Theta$ caused by imposed torques $T_e = .1$ and $T_e = -.1$ are decreasing functions of co-contractive signal P. Starting Θs were 20° and 50°.

$$D_2 = \frac{20}{\sqrt{\left(\frac{\sin\Theta+20}{\cos\Theta}\right)^2 + 1}} \tag{17}$$

Variables D_i introduce yet another threat to position-code invariance. However, because of the factorization properties already described, moment-arm compensation may take an especially simple form in a system based on the FLETE module. Recent simulations [2] show how adaptive gains $g(A_1, A_2)$ may be learned and applied with opposite sign to alter the coefficients of total descending signals, $A_i + P$, to the opponent alpha motoneuron populations. In particular, the new descending signals become:

$$S_1 = \left[1 - g(A_1, A_2)\right](A_1 + P) \tag{18}$$

$$S_2 = \left[1 + g(A_1, A_2)\right](A_2 + P) \tag{19}$$

In our theory the adaptive gains $g(A_1, A_2)$ in equations (18) and (19) are learned with the aid of collateral ascending projections that arise from muscle spindle organs. These pathways carry muscle-length error signals. In equations (12) and (13), these error signals cause fast reactive corrections in motoneuron activation via the inputs E_i. Here we assume that they also cause slower adaptive corrections via a learning process which affords predictive elimination of positional errors on future performance trials. In particular, the muscle-length error signals change the adaptive gains $g(A_1, A_2)$ in such a way that the spindle error signals eventually approach zero. This learning process is assumed to occur in the cerebellum. When the learned gains $g(A_1, A_2)$ are used to bias the descending signals $A_i + P$ in equation (12), and when $\chi = 1$ in equations (12) and (13), then moment-arm effects are compensated and position-code invariance is restored, as shown in Figure 3A. Because these gains are independent of the compliance control signal P, the factorization property that gives the FLETE model its name is preserved.

Grossberg and Kuperstein [5] have shown how different activation patterns (A_1, A_2) can be converted into different locations in a spatial map. Each map location activates different pathways, which can learn a distinct adaptive gain. The learning rule that we used started with zero initial gains $g(A_1, A_2)$. For patterns (A_1, A_2) learning caused $g(A_1, A_2)$ to increase if $E_2 > E_1$ and to decrease if $E_1 > E_2$. In particular,

$$\frac{d}{dt}g(A_1, A_2) = \epsilon(E_2 - E_1). \tag{20}$$

Here the magnitude of ϵ controls learning rate. This adaptive gain control process used an opponent organization in two different senses. First, the error signals E_1 and E_2 change the gains g via an opponent error term $E_2 - E_1$. Second, the gains g have an opponent effect, via terms $(1 - g)$ and $(1 + g)$ in (18) and (19), upon the output signals of the opponent movement channels. Such an opponent organization is reminiscent of the opponent action of Renshaw feedback at the spinal level: the net signal emerging from the Renshaw stage competition between opponent channels simultaneously decrements one channels' output and increments the opposing channel's output.

6. CO-CONTRACTIVE AND STRETCH FEEDBACK CONTROL OF LOAD COMPENSATION

For the simulations of Figure 3, we used a simple model of the subsystem composed of γ-MNs, intrafusal muscles, and spindle organs (Figure 1). Our model includes only those aspects needed to test factorization of position and compliance at equilibrium. We modeled γ-MN activity N_i by

$$\frac{d}{dt}N_i = \phi\big[(10 - N_i)A_i\big] - N_i(1 + A_j) \tag{21}$$

intrafusal muscle contraction U_i by

$$\frac{d}{dt}U_i = 4N_i - U_i \tag{22}$$

and spindle organ response via

$$\frac{d}{dt}W_i = [U_i + L_i - \Gamma_i]^+ - W_i. \tag{23}$$

Equation (21) embodies the ideas that the γ-MNs do not participate in the size principle—unlike the α-MNs in (12)—do not receive a co-contractive input P, and that the effect of inputs A_1 and A_2 is normalized by the shunting term $-N_i(1 + A_j)$. Equation (22) says that the intrafusal muscle contraction U_i is proportional to the γ-MN activation level N_i. Equation (23) says that the spindle organ responds to intrafusal muscle contraction U_i and extrafusal muscle stretch $L_i - \Gamma_i$. In addition, χ in equation (12) was set equal to 1 and E_i was defined by

$$E_i = W_i. \tag{24}$$

Because χE_i was non-zero in these simulations, we replaced equation (9) by

$$\beta_i = .05 + .02(S_i + \chi E_i), \quad B_i = 2 + 20(S_i + \chi E_i) \tag{25}$$

with S_1 and S_2 defined by (18) and (19), to assure that stretch feedback E_i played a role in rescaling parameters of active motor units, as occurs *in vivo* [8]. Because a nonlinear force law also contributes, we replaced the linear law in (7) by

$$F_i = k\Big([L_i - \Gamma_i + C_i]^+\Big)^2. \tag{26}$$

Compliance control by this model is summarized in Figure 3B, which shows that the angular displacement $\Delta\Theta$ induced by an external torque T_e applied to the model arm varies inversely with P. This shows that increases in co-contractive signal P reduce arm compliance in the FLETE model. Full load compensation is not achieved for any P value because the stretch reflex feedback gain of the network as a whole was less than unity.

The simulations summarized in Figure 3B were run with $\delta_i = 0$ in (12). Then the model α-MNs behave as neural integrators. With $\delta_i = 1$, as in previous simulations, leaky integrator behavior was modeled. Both parameter choices are consistent with the observation that α-MNs exhibit plateau potentials *in vivo* [7]. Further details regarding this research and its place within our more general theory of invariances under rescaling in sensory-motor control may be found in [1,2,5].

REFERENCES

[1] Bullock, D. and Grossberg, S. (1989). VITE and FLETE: Neural modules for trajectory formation and postural control. In W.A. Hershberger (Ed.), **Volitional action**. Amsterdam: North-Holland/Elsevier, 253–297.

[2] Bullock, D. and Grossberg, S. (1990). Adaptive neural networks for control of movement trajectories invariant under speed and force rescaling. *Human Movement Science*, **9**.

[3] Feldman, A.G. (1986). Once more on the equilibrium-point hypothesis (λ model) for motor control. *Journal of Motor Behavior*, **18**, 17–54.

[4] Grossberg, S. (1973). Contour enhancement, short-term memory, and constancies in reverberating neural networks. *Studies in Applied Mathematics*, **52**, 217–257.

[5] Grossberg, S. and Kuperstein, M. (1989). **Neural dynamics of adaptive sensory-motor control: Expanded Edition**. New York: Pergamon Press.

[6] Henneman, E. (1985). The size-principle: A deterministic output emerges from a set of probabilistic connections. *Journal of Experimental Biology*, **115**, 105–112.

[7] Hounsgaard, J., Hultborn, H., and Kiehn, O. (1986). Transmitter-controlled properties of α-motoneurones causing long-lasting motor discharge to brief excitatory inputs. *Progress in Brain Research*, **64**, 39–50.

[8] Humphrey, D.R. and Reed, D.J. (1983). Separate cortical systems for control of joint movement and joint stiffness: Reciprocal activation and coactivation of antagonist muscles. In J.E. Desmedt (Ed.), **Motor control mechanisms in health and disease**. New York: Raven Press, 347–372.

[9] Partridge, L.D., and Benton, L.A. (1981). Muscle, the motor. In **Handbook of physiology: The nervous system II**. Bethesda, MD: American Physiological Society, 43–106.

[10] Pompeiano, O. (1984). Recurrent inhibition. In R.A. Davidoff (Ed.), **Handbook of the spinal cord, Vols. 2 and 3. Anatomy and physiology**. New York: Marcel Dekker.

[11] Renshaw, B. (1946). Central effects of centripetal impulses in axons of spinal ventral roots. *Journal of Neurophysiology*, **9**, 191–204.

Advanced Neural Computers / R. Eckmiller (Editor)

Neural Computers for Motor Control

Rolf Eckmiller[1]

Department of Biophysics
Heinrich-Heine-Universität Düsseldorf (FRG)

The complexity of biological motor control is first demonstrated with the surprising lack of precision in 2-dimensional blind pointing movements (without vision of the pointing arm) in human subjects and with several deficits in the blind pointing performance of trained monkeys following a unilateral lesion of the parietal cortex. Subsequently, several novel approaches to designing neural networks for motor control of a redundant robot arm for 2-dimensional movements are described. A comparison of these biological and technical motor systems under neural net control clearly demonstrates the importance of an internal representation of space with continuous updating from various sensors regarding targets, obstacles, and the controlled arm in space.

Biological Motor Control

The most important concept sources for neural computers are various disciplines of neuroscience (Eckmiller, 1990c; Georgopoulos, 1986; Houk and Gibson, 1987; Lemon, 1988).
For this reason I will first briefly describe two studies on the control of arm movements in humans and in trained macaque monkeys. Subsequently I will describe some of our recent efforts to control a redundant robot arm with 4 joints (4-joint machine) for 2-dimensional movements by means of several neural net modules.
Fig. 1 gives a scheme for the experimental basic paradigm we used for our studies in monkeys and human subjects.

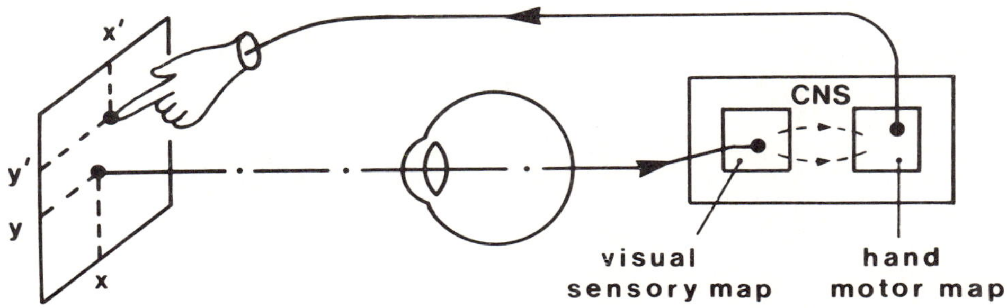

Fig. 1 Blind pointing paradigm for mapping visual target onto pointing positions without vision of the pointing arm.

[1]Supported by Ministry for Research and Technology(BMFT) and by German Science Foundation (SFB-200)

A visual target appears at location x/y within the grasping space in front of the primate (human subject or trained monkey). The task is to generate a pointing movement at this target without seeing the pointing arm. This blind pointing paradigm requires a sensorimotor mapping operation based on various internal representations of the point in space as indicated here for a neural sensory map and a neural motor map. Many neurophysiological and neuroanatomical details of such sensorimotor functions in primates are still unknown (Berkinblit et al., 1986; Biguer et al., 1984; Eckmiller, 1989b, 1990a; Flash and Hogan, 1985; Soechting et al., 1986). However, we tend to think of these maps as cortical areas with layered neural net topologies. The spatial coordinates on the map surface may encode various parameters such as locations in space, movement velocities, or movement directions. The primate brain performs this task surprisingly poorly in that the spatial difference between target x/y and blind pointing location x'/y' typically exceeds several centimeters on the pointing plane at about 20 cm distance (Bock and Eckmiller, 1986; Ott and Eckmiller, 1988).

Fig. 2 shows 2-dimensional blind pointing data (Eckmiller, 1990a) of a normal human subject sitting in an upright position for the paradigm "oculomotor" on the left and for the paradigm "retinal" on the right. Open symbols at straight ahead (marked by an open star) and at 10, 20, or 30 degrees in one of the eight directions indicate the visual target locations for both paradigms. Blind pointing was performed with the right hand to the outside of a hemisphere with targets visible on the inside. The corresponding blind pointing positions are given as filled symbols and are averages from three random measurement sequences for each direction.Tactile feedback was provided only at the straight ahead position in order to provide a common reference for the four separately measured blind pointing characteristics. During the "oculomotor paradigm", the subject was asked to fixate the visual target and then point at it from the outside. Therefore the retina gives no clue as to the location of the target in space. The brain has to re-establish the spatial information from efference copy signals of the oculomotor system. Please note, that the blind pointing 'spider-shaped' set of data indicates a sensorimotor mapping operation full of nonlinear distortions, gain changes, rotations, and shifts.

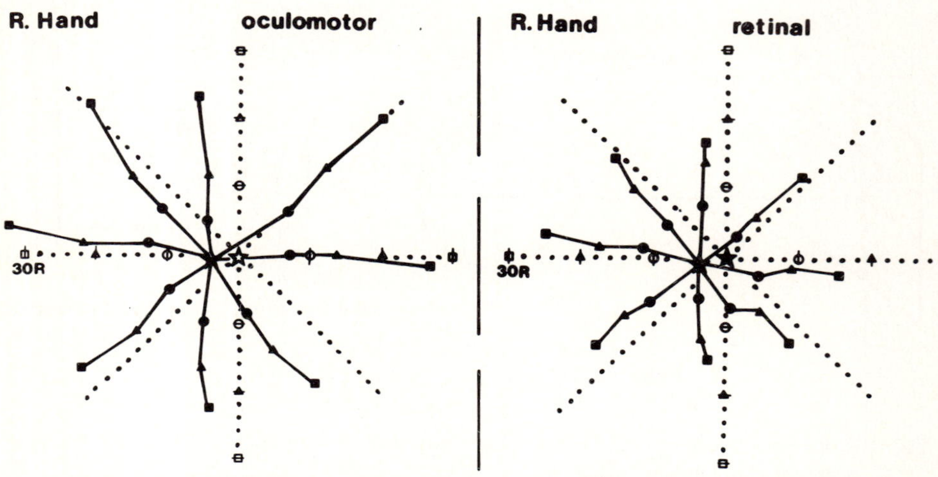

Fig. 2 Two-dimensional blind pointing a human subject. Oculomotor paradigm (left): eyes fixate the target. Retinal paradigm (right): eyes fixate a point at straight ahead, while target for blind pointing appears extrafoveally (except for target at straight ahead, open star).

For the "retinal" paradigm on the right of Fig. 2, the subject was asked to always fixate a stationary green target at the straight ahead location. Simultaneously a red target appeared at one of the locations as during the 'oculomotor' paradigm. The subject had to point at the red target without looking at it and without seeing the pointing arm. In this case, the only source of spatial information regarding the red target is the retina. An internal representation of the visual map in retinotopic coordinates can be assumed here to provide the necessary input for the pointing movement.

Please, note that the 'blind pointing spider' (set of data) on the right is also far off the corresponding set of target locations and on the other hand quite different from the 'blind pointing spider' on the left. Appearantly the two sensory inputs provide very different spatial information, both insufficient, however, for a reasonably accurate pointing movement. These data were in principle similar to those for other normal human subject but quite different for certain patients.

The next set of experiments, which was performed in collaboration with Richard Anderson (MIT) and Otmar Bock (York University), deals with the question, how the blind pointing paradigm depends on an intact posterior parietal cortex. Several lines of neurobiological evidence suggest that parts of the posterior parietal cortex are involved in the internal representation of spatial coordinates for visual inputs as well as oculomotor and arm motor outputs (Anderson et al., 1985; Georgopoulos, 1988; Doman et al, 1989).

Macaque monkeys were trained for several weeks to fixate small visual targets at various locations inside a cylindrical screen just above a horizontal dividing plate. Simultaneously the monkey moved a lever under the dividing plate so as to position his right hand under the currently lit visual target.

Microlesions in the left posterior parietal cortex at the border between area 7a and 7b were generated by microinjection of a small amount of a neurotoxin called Ibotenic acid. Evidently, this neurotoxin forces all cortical cells in the vicinity of the injection site to irreversibly degenerate while leaving traversing nerve fibers intact.

Fig.3 gives a summary of some really surprising deficits, which one would have hardly been able to predict.

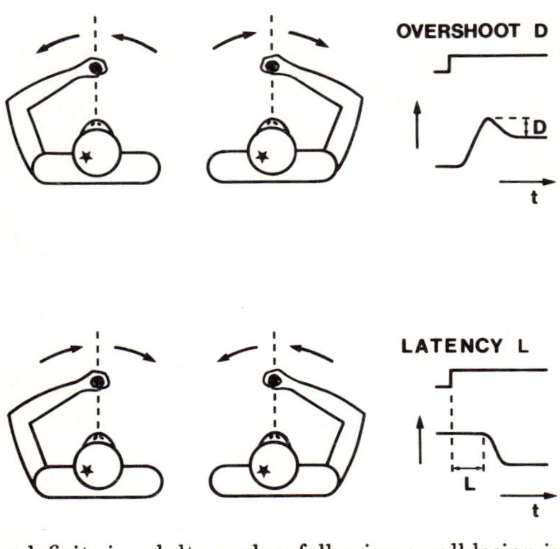

Fig. 3 Blind pointing deficits in adult monkey following small lesion in left posterior parietal cortex (star). Top half: bilaterally symmetrical dynamical overshoot D. Botton half: bilaterally symmetrical reaction time latency L for movements in opposite directions.

The lesion in the left parietal cortex is marked as star. The upper portion of Fig. 3 indicates that blind pointing with the left arm leftwards or with the right arm rightwards consistently led to a pathological dynamic overshoot D before the pointing arm reached its final position. D had a typical size of several degrees quite independant of the overall pointing amplitude and pointing direction.
In contrast, blind pointing movements in the opposite directions, with the left arm rightwards or with the right arm leftwards was started with a pathologically increased latency L as indicated in the lower half of Fig. 3.
Please, note that both significant deficits in this sensorimotor mapping operation were not unilateral as would be expected from a unilateral cortical lesion. Instead both deficits were bilaterally symmetrical. Recently a model for the underlying neural network was proposed (Bock, 1989).
In summary of these biological data it follows that primates obviously do not rely entirely on sensori-motor mapping functions previously acquired during a learning phase. In addition they seemingly use continuous sensory updating of the sensori-motor mapping net and the corresponding internal representation (Eckmiller, 1990a) via various sensory inputs (Held and Bauer, 1974), which were not available during our experiments.
Accordingly, autonomous vehicles or redundant robots under neural net control may require internal representations of space and spatio-temporal events (trajectories) to assure sufficiently precise movements (Bullock and Grossberg, 1988; Eckmiller, 1989; Kawato et al., 1988; Kuperstein, 1988; Massone and Bizzi, 1989).

Neural Networks for Control of a Redundant Robot Arm
Based on these and other neurobiological studies we began a project on controlling a redundant 4-joint machine by means of neural networks (Eckmiller et al., 1989; Goerke et al., 1990; Hakala et al., 1990), which includes the design of pulse-coded neural net hardware (Beerhold et al., 1990).

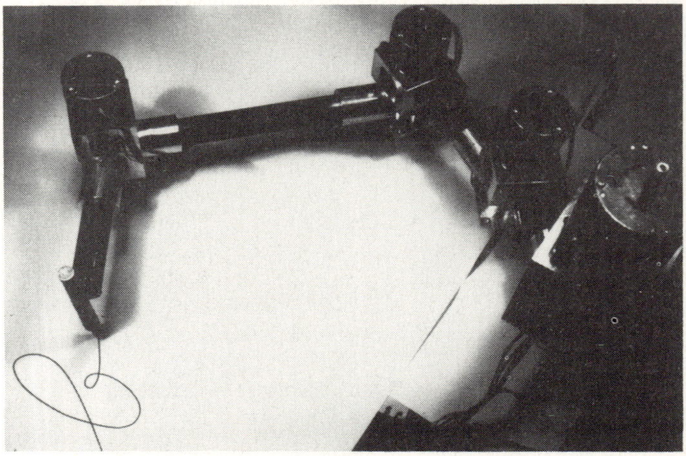

Fig. 4 Early version of our 4-joint machine as redundant robot arm for 2-dimensional movements. Hand link: 15cm; lower arm link: 30cm. Actuators: stepping motors.

Fig. 4 shows the 4-joint machine with the capability of generating various 2-dimensional trajectories at the fingertip while the individual contributions of the 4 joints can be continously changed in real time during the movement.

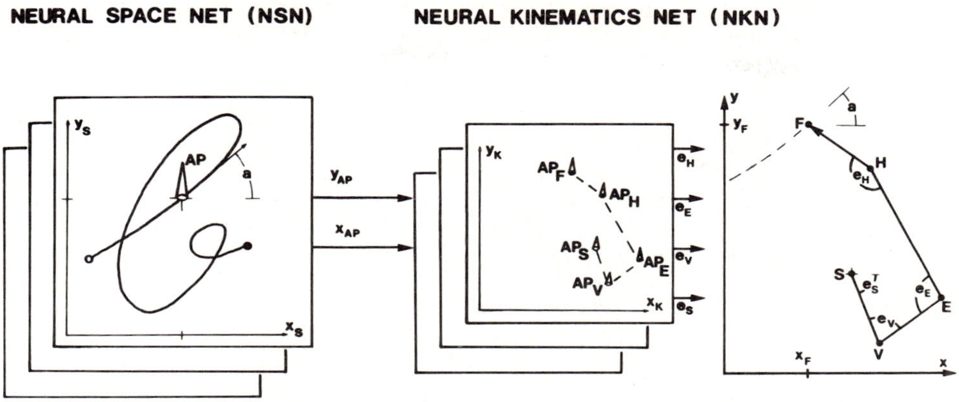

Fig. 5 Scheme for neural net control of 4-joint machine. NSN: Storage of various trajectories (one shot learning); generation of desired trajectories by means of travelling activity peak (AP) on a neural lattice. NKN: Mapping of desired trajectory $(x_{AP}(t), y_{AP}(t))$ onto four simultaneous time functions for the rotatory control signals of the four actuatores.

Fig. 5 compiles the two required neural net modules, the neural space net (NSN) (Eckmiller, 1989b; Eckmiller, 1990c) and the neural kinematics net (NKN) as well as the 4-joint machine on the right side.

In short, NSN on the left is supposed to store desired trajectories, such as the trajectory for hand-written letter b. When b is being called, an activity peak AP travels along the path of b on a neural lattice (Eckmiller, 1989b). The NSN output provides time functions for the 2-dimensional coordinates of the activity peak while AP travels. These time functions y_{AP} and x_{AP} form the input for the neural kinematics net NKN (Eckmiller, 1989a; Eckmiller et al., 1989; Hakala et al., 1990). NKN is assumed to consist of several neural net components in order to perform the required mapping operation, thus generating time functions for the four actuators indicated here as angle signals e_H, e_E, e_V, and e_S for hand, ellbow, virtual joint, and shoulder.

In principle, NKN operates locally in that it receives the current direction angle a from NSN for the next trajectory element and finds the corresponding combination of actuator control signals on the basis of its internal position model (POM) of the 4-joint machine. POM can be thought of as a continuously updated bookkeeping system for all geometric parameters of the 4-joint machine (Eckmiller, 1989a).

We are currently approaching the various problems of the neural space net, NSN, (including real-time obstacle avoidance) and of the neural kinematics net, NKN, which is also dealing with certain types of obstacle avoidance, from several quite different directions. Some approaches emphasize self-organization of a neural net to find its desired mapping function. Other approaches assume no self-organization and try to find successful network topologies by different means.

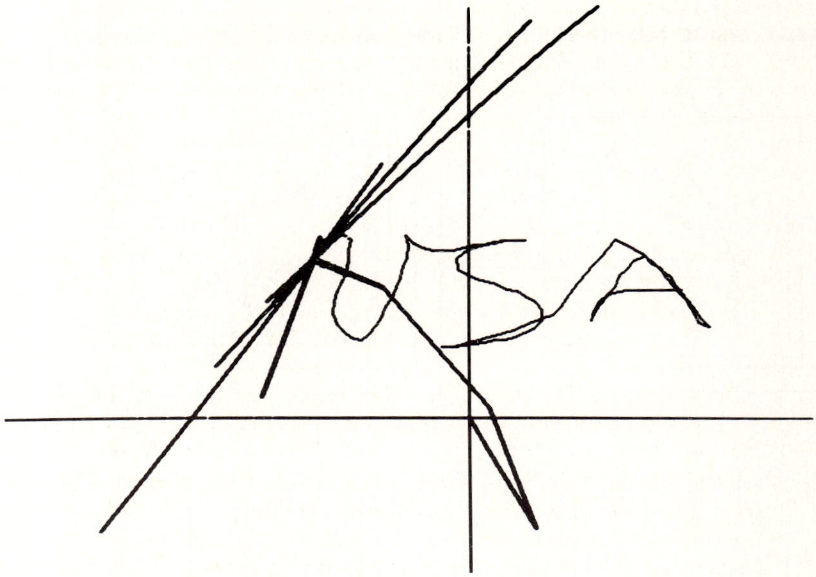

Fig. 6 Computer simulation of the 4-joint machine in the process of drawing a trajectory. Lines at fingertip F indicate the possible vector components of the four actuators in F for the assumed rotation of 1 degree in either direction.

Fig.6 showes a simulation of the 4-joint machine in the process of drawing a previously inserted hand-written trajectory. For each trajectory element like for the immediately following one, NKN has to decide by how much and in which direction the individual 4 actuators have to be rotated. The lines at the fingertip indicate the possible movement vectors of the actuators if each actuator would rotate by only 1 degree in either direction. The length differences for opposite directions represent the fact that an additional incentive is provided for each joint to stay as close as possible to its neural position. NKN selects the best movement directions in a non-iterative feedforward process and adjusts the individual vector components in such a way, that their geometrical vector addition in the corresponding neural net component yields exactly the next trajectory-element. For every new trajectory-element the relative contribution of each actuator can be changed in terms of gain, neutral position, range of operation, and so on. This feature seems to be very useful, since a technical robot often encounters unexpected problems, such as joint friction or mechanical obstacles during a real time movement. While the cost function may dynamically change throughout trajectory generation, the fingertip moves undisturbed, as is also possible in primate motor control.
The described example of embedding the inverse kinematics of a redundant robot arm (Fig. 6) was not achieved by self-organization of a neural network, but rather by developing a sequence of geometrical operations, which can be implemented with certain neural net topologies (Eckmiller, et al., 1989; Eckmiller, 1990b; Hakala et al., 1990; Pellionisz, 1988). At this point we have not delt with 3-dimensional movements nor have we incorporated dynamics. These two challenges obviously form part of our future research.

References

Anderson, R.A., Essick, G.K.,Siegel, R.M.: The encoding of spatial location by posterior parietal neuron, Science, 230, pp. 456-458, 1985

Beerhold, J.R., Jansen, M., Eckmiller, R.: Pulse-processing neural net hardware with selectable topology and adaptive weights and delays, Proc. IEEE IJCNN San Diego, Vol. II, pp. 569-574, 1990

Berkinblit, M.B., Feldman, A.G., Fukson, O.I.: Adaptability of innate motor patterns and motor control mechanisms, Behavioral and Brain Sciences, 9, pp. 585-638, 1986

Biguer, B., Prablanc, C., Jeannerod, M.: The contribution of coordinated eye and head movements in hand pointing accuracy, Exp. Brain. Res., 55, pp. 462-469, 1984

Bock, O.: A neural network predicting posterior parietal cortex function in the control of goal-directed arm movements, Neural Networks, 2, pp. 351-358, 1989

Bock, O., Eckmiller, R.: Goal-directed arm movements in absence of visual guidance: evidence for amplitute rather than position control, Exp. Brain Res., 62, pp. 451-458, 1986

Bullock, B., Grossberg, S.: Neural dynamics of planned arm movements: emergent invariants and speed-accuracy properties during trajectory formation, In: Neural Networks and natural intelligence, Grossberg, S. (ed.), MIT Press, Cambridge, pp. 553-622, 1988

Doman, D., Bock, O., Eckmiller, R.: Interaction of visual and non-visual signals in the initation of smooth pursuit eye movements in primates, Behav. Brain Res., 32, pp.95-99, 1989

Eckmiller, R.,: Neural Networks for generation of eye and arm movement trajectories, In: Neural programming, Ito, M.(ed.), Karger, Basel, pp. 173-187, 1989a

Eckmiller, R.,: Neural nets for sensory and motor trajectories, IEEE Control Systems Magazine, 9, pp. 53-60, 1989b

Eckmiller, R.,: Internal representation of space in neural networks of primates and other sensorimotor mapping machines, Proc. IEEE IJCNN Washington, Vol. I, pp.165-168, 1990a

Eckmiller, R.: Concerning the emerging role of geometry in neuroinformatics, In: Parallel processing in neural systems and computers, Eckmiller, R., Hartmann, G., Hauske, G. (eds.), Elsevier, Amsterdam, pp. 5-8, 1990b

Eckmiller, R.: The design of intelligent robots as a federation of geometrical machines, In: An Introduction to neural and electronic networks, Zornetzer, S., Davis, J., Lau, C. (eds.), Academic Press, Orlando, pp. 109-128, 1990c

Eckmiller, R., Beckmann, J., Werntges, H., Lades, M.: Neural kinematics net for a redundant robot arm, Proc. IEEE IJCNN Washington, Vol. II, pp. 333-339, 1989

Flash, T., Hogan, N.: The coordination of arm movements: An experimentally confirmed mathematical model, J. Neurosci., 5, pp. 1688-1703, 1985

Georgopoulos, A.P.: On reaching, Ann. Rev. Neurosci., 9, pp. 147-170, 1986

Georgopoulos, A.P.: Neural integration of movement: Role of motor cortex in reaching, Faseb Journal, 2, pp.2849-2857, 1988

Goerke, N., Schöne, M., Kreimeier, B., Eckmiller, R., : A network with pulse processing neurons for generation of arbitrary temporal sequences, Proc. IEEE IJCNN San Diego, Vol. III, pp. 315-320, 1990

Hakala, J., Steiner, R., Eckmiller, R.: Quasi-local solution for inverse kinematics of a redundant robot arm, Proc. IEEE IJCNN San Diego , Vol. III, pp. 321-326, 1990

Held, R., Bauer, J.A.,: Development of sensorially-guided reaching in infant monkeys, Brain Res., 71, pp. 265-271, 1974

Houk, J.C., Gibson, A.R.: Sensorimotor processing through the cerebellum, In: New Concepts in Cerebellar Neurobiology, King, J.S. (ed.), Alan Liss Inc., pp. 387-416, 1987

Kawato, M., Uno, Y., Isobe, M., Suzuki, R.: Hierarchical neural network model for voluntary movement with application to robotics, IEEE Control Systems Magazine, 8, pp. 547-561, 1988

Kuperstein, M.: An adaptive neural model for mapping invariant target position, Behav. Neurosci., 102, pp. 148-162, 1988

Lemon, R.: The output map of the primate motor cortex, TINS, 11, pp. 501-506, 1988

Massone, L., Bizzi, E.: A neural network model for limb trajectory formation, Biol. Cybern., 61, pp. 417-425, 1989

Ott, D., Eckmiller, R.: Dynamic adaption of the blind pointing characteristic to stepwise lateral tilts of body, head,-and trunk, Behav. Brain Res., 30, pp. 99-110, 1988

Pellionisz, A.: Tensor geometry: A language of brains & neurocomputers. Generalized coordinates in neuroscience & robotics, In: Neural Computers, Eckmiller, R., v.d. Malsburg, C. (eds.), Springer, Heidelberg, pp. 381-391, 1988

Soechting, J.F., Lacquaniti, F., Terzuolo, C,A.: Coordination of arm movements in three-dimensional space. Sensorimotor mapping during drawing movement, Neuroscience, 17, pp. 295-311, 1986

Advanced Neural Computers / R. Eckmiller (Editor)

Feedback-Error-Learning Neural Network for Supervised Motor Learning

Mitsuo Kawato
Cognitive Processes Department
ATR Auditory and Visual Perception Research Laboratories, Kyoto

Abstract

In supervised motor learning, where the desired movement pattern is given in task-oriented coordinates, one of the most essential and difficult problems is how to convert the error signal calculated in the task space into that of the motor command space. We proposed the feedback-error-learning approach where the feedback motor command is used as an error signal to train a neural network which then generates a feedforward motor command. We successfully applied this approach to learning control in joint space of PUMA, an industrial manipulator, trajectory control in visual coordinates even when PUMA was given an extra degree of freedom, and Softarm with muscle-like actuators (manufactured by Bridgestone Co.). I mathematically show that the feedback-error-learning approach can be considered a Newton-like method in functional space. Mathematical proof of the convergence of the feedback-error-learning control scheme is provided both for trajectory stability and learning stability. The feedback-error-learning neural network was originally proposed as a model for the lateral cerebellum and the parvocellular part of the red nucleus. It will be shown that functions of other parts of the cerebellum, such as the vermis or the flocculus, can also be understood from the feedback-error-learning scheme.

1 Introduction

One of the features of the central nervous system (CNS) in its control of movement is the capability of motor learning. For higher mammals, especially humans, supervised learning is probably the most important class of motor learning. In nearly every case, the teacher can not directly show the correct motor command to the student, but only can show the desired movement trajectory.

Consider a neural network which receives a desired motor pattern and outputs a motor command to realize the desired movement. The motor command is transmitted to the musculoskeletal system and some particular movement is realized. The realized trajectory is measured by various sensory systems, and compared to the desired movement pattern (teaching signal). If the teacher were to able to give the difference between the ideal motor command and the actual motor command, various supervised learning rules could be used to train the motor control network. However, since this is not possible, the problem of converting the error from task-oriented coordinates to the motor command space is an essential and difficult one. This problem was addressed by Jordan and Rumelhart [2] and termed, "supervised learning with a distal teacher". They proposed the forward and inverse modeling approach to resolve the problem.

We proposed the *feedback-error-learning* neural network as a model of the lateral cerebellum and the parvocellular part of the red nucleus [5,6]. This model constitutes one possible answer to the above error conversion problem. In the next section, three representative computational schemes to resolve the problem are reviewed and compared. We then mathematically formulate the feedback-error-learning approach as a Newton-like method in functional space. Mathematical proof of the trajectory and learning convergence of feedback-error-learning will be given. Finally, functional roles of various parts of the cerebellum are examined based on the feedback-error-learning.

2 Computational schemes to convert trajectory error into motor command error

A perfect feedforward control can be realized if the feedforward controller provides an inverse model of the controlled object. Let us formulate this statement. θ denotes an n-dimensional vector which represents the body coordinates, such as joint angles or muscle lengths, of a controlled object. τ represents an m-dimensional vector of motor commands such as joint torque or muscle tension. The state change of the controlled object is described by the following ordinary differential equations.

$$\begin{aligned} d\theta/dt &= \dot{\theta} \\ d\dot{\theta}/dt &= f(\theta, \dot{\theta}, \tau), \end{aligned} \tag{1}$$

here f is an n-dimensional nonlinear vector function. x denotes a k-dimensional vector representing the task-oriented coordinates of the controlled object, for example, the retinal coordinates of the hand position. x is uniquely determined from θ according to the following nonlinear equation: $x = G(\theta)$, here G is a k-dimensional nonlinear vector function.

The problem of feedforward control is to find the motor command $\tau_d(t)$ which realizes the desired movement pattern $x_d(t)$. First, the desired trajectory in body space is calculated from that in task space: $\theta_d(t) = G^{-1}(x_d(t))$. Second, the necessary motor command is calculated from the desired trajectory, velocity and acceleration $(\theta_d(t), \dot{\theta}_d(t), \ddot{\theta}_d(t))$ as a solution of the second equation of (1). Although this is an implicit equation with respect to τ, it is rewritten in explicit form as follows: $\tau_d(t) = h(\theta_d(t), \dot{\theta}_d(t), \ddot{\theta}_d(t))$. Consequently, in this case, the motor learning problem is equivalent to acquisition of the conjoined inverse kinematics model (IKM) and inverse dynamics model (IDM) $h \cdot G^{-1}$ in the feedforward controller.

In Fig. 1, I compare three computational approaches for learning the inverse model of a controlled object. The simplest approach is shown in Fig. 1a. The controlled object receives the torque input $\tau(t)$ and outputs the resulting trajectory $x(t)$. The inverse model is oriented in the input-output direction opposite to that of the controlled object, as shown by the arrow. That is, it receives the trajectory as an input and outputs the torque $\tau_i(t)$. The error signal $s(t)$ is given as the difference between the actual torque and the estimated torque: $s(t) = \tau(t) - \tau_i(t)$. This approach to acquiring an inverse model is referred to as direct inverse modeling [2]. Fig. 1b shows the method of combining a forward model and an inverse model, proposed by Jordan and Rumelhart [2]. First, the forward model of the controlled object is learned by monitoring both the input $\tau(t)$ and the output $x(t)$ of the controlled object. Next, the desired trajectory $x_d(t)$ is fed to the inverse model to calculate the feedforward motor command $\tau(t)$. The resulting error in the trajectory $x_d(t) - x(t)$ is back propagated through the forward model to calculate the error in the motor command, which is then used as the error signal for training the inverse model.

Fig. 1c shows the *feedback error learning* approach [5]. The total torque $\tau(t)$ fed to the controlled object is the sum of the feedback torque $\tau_{fb}(t)$ and the feedforward torque $\tau_{ff}(t)$,

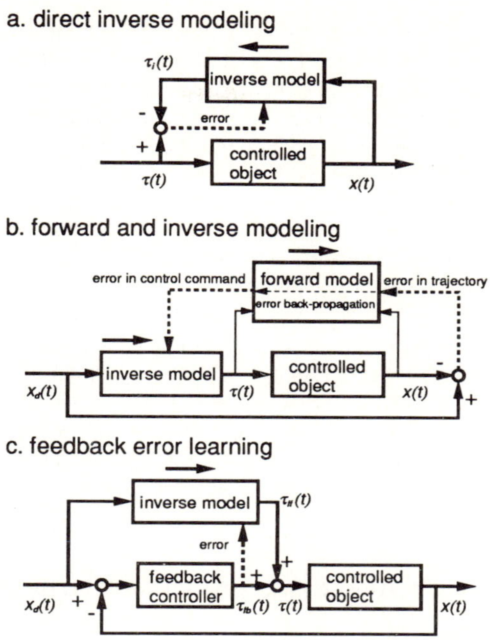

Figure 1: Three computational schemes for learning inverse model of a controlled object: a) Direct inverse modeling. b) Forward and inverse modeling. c) Feedback error learning scheme.

which is calculated by the inverse model. The inverse model receives the desired trajectory x_d and monitors the feedback torque $\tau_{fb}(t)$ for the error signal. It is expected that the feedback signal tends to zero as learning proceeds. We call this learning scheme *feedback error learning* to emphasize the importance of using the feedback torque (motor command) as the error signal of the heterosynaptic learning.

In summary, the direct inverse modeling approach avoids the error conversion problem by reversing the input and the output. The forward and inverse modeling approach converts trajectory error into motor command error by backpropagation through the forward model. In the feedback-error-learning approach the feedback controller converts trajectory error into motor command error.

Direct inverse modeling does not seem to be used by the central nervous system. The main reason is that after the inverse model is acquired, before it can be input from the desired trajectory instead of the actual trajectory, large-scale connection changes must be carried out while preserving minute one-to-one correspondence. In engineering applications, one drawback of the direct inverse modeling approach seems to be that it does not necessarily achieve a particular target trajectory $x_d(t)$, even when the training period is sufficiently long. In this sense, the learning is not "goal-directed" [2]. The forward and inverse modeling approach of Jordan & Rumelhart is goal-directed because the error for learning is defined as the square of the difference between the desired trajectory and the realized trajectory. I will provide a mathematical proof that the feedback error learning approach is also goal-directed.

The direct inverse modeling method can not cope with the learning control of a redundant controlled object. Jordan [2] clearly explained the reason for this in the one-to-many inverse kinematics problem. The forward and inverse modeling approach can resolve the ill-posedness of the problem by learning performance index as synaptic weights in the inverse model. Any feedback controller selects one specific motor command even for redundant controlled objects. However, the desired trajectory can not be exactly realized by the feedback control alone. Because of the above-mentioned desirable characteristics inherent in the feedback controller, the feedback error learning approach can realize the learning control of controlled objects which are redundant either at the kinematics or dynamics level [3,4].

Kano et al. succeeded in learning trajectory control within the stereo camera coordinates even when PUMA was given an extra degree of freedom [3]. In this study, the feedback controller calculated the feedback motor command by multiplying the error in the visual coordinates with the Moore-Penrose pseudoinverse of the coordinate transformation. Because the pseudoinverse matrix finds the solution with the smallest norm, this method is closely related to our minimum motor-command change criterion.

Katayama et al. solved the ill-posed inverse dynamics problem for an arm-like manipulator (Bridgestone SoftArm) with rubbertuators which are air driven, muscle-like actuators. Because each joint contains agonist and antagonist rubbertuators, there is no unique solution to determining tensions to realize a particular joint angle movement. In this experiment, we obtained a roughly minimal muscle-tension change trajectory with the feedback-error-leaning scheme [4].

3 Feedback-error-learning as a Newton-like method in functional space

The inverse dynamics problem is to calculate the required motor command $\tau_d(t)$ so that the desired trajectory $\theta_d(t)$ in the body space is realized. The dynamics of the controlled object is described by (1). The Newton method is first described. It is more convenient to restrict the inverse dynamics problem to that in a finite time interval $[0,T]$. A functional $F(\tau) = \theta_d - \theta(\tau)$ is defined as a mapping from a function space $\Xi = C[0,T]$ of the motor command to a function space $\Theta = C^2[0,T]$ of the body space trajectory. The first derivative of F can be computed through the solution of the following variational equation:

$$F'(\tau)\delta\tau \equiv J\delta\tau = \delta\theta. \tag{2}$$

$$\begin{aligned} d(\delta\theta)/dt &= \delta\dot{\theta}, \quad \delta\theta(0) = 0, \\ d(\delta\dot{\theta})/dt &= \partial f(\theta,\dot{\theta},\tau)/\partial\theta \cdot \delta\theta + \partial f(\theta,\dot{\theta},\tau)/\partial\dot{\theta} \cdot \delta\dot{\theta} \\ &\quad + \partial f(\theta,\dot{\theta},\tau)/\partial\tau \cdot \delta\tau, \quad \delta\dot{\theta}(0) = 0. \end{aligned} \tag{3}$$

According to the Newton method, we can calculate the motor command error from (3) as follows:

$$\begin{aligned} \delta\tau &= F'^{-1}(\tau)\delta\theta \\ &= (\partial f(\theta,\dot{\theta},\tau)/\partial\tau)^{-1}\{-\partial f(\theta,\dot{\theta},\tau)/\partial\theta \cdot \delta\theta - \partial f(\theta,\dot{\theta},\tau)/\partial\dot{\theta} \cdot \delta\dot{\theta} + \delta\ddot{\theta}\}. \end{aligned} \tag{4}$$

Although this equation looks quite complicated, it must be emphasized that all calculation can be done by differentiation of the body space error $\delta\theta = \theta_d - \theta$ and matrix calculation. However, because we do not know the dynamics of the controlled object (i.e. f), we can not use this Newton method. A quite general solution to this difficulty is the Newton-like method which approximates F'^{-1} by some simpler operator M. One apparent candidate is the following:

$$\delta\tau = M(\delta\theta) = K_P(\theta_d - \theta) + K_D(\dot{\theta}_d - \dot{\theta}) + K_A(\ddot{\theta}_d - \ddot{\theta}). \tag{5}$$

This approximation is validated since the product factor $(\partial f(\theta,\dot{\theta},\tau)/\partial\tau)^{-1}$ in the third term of (4) corresponds to the inertia matrix which is symmetrical, and positive definite. Furthermore, in the simplest case, the product factor $-(\partial f(\theta,\dot{\theta},\tau)/\partial\tau)^{-1}\partial f(\theta,\dot{\theta},\tau)/\partial\dot{\theta}$ of $\delta\dot{\theta}$ in the second term of (4) corresponds to a viscosity coefficient. Similarly, the product factor $-(\partial f(\theta,\dot{\theta},\tau)/\partial\tau)^{-1}\partial f(\theta,\dot{\theta},\tau)/\partial\theta$ of $\delta\theta$ in the first term of (4) corresponds to the stiffness of a virtual spring. Thus, all three factors can be approximated by positive diagonal matrices K_P, K_D and K_A, which can be regarded as gains of proportional, differentiation and acceleration feedbacks, respectively. Thus, the PDA feedback controller can calculate $\delta\tau$ as a Newton-like method. The feedback error learning which uses the feedback motor command as the error signal to modify the feedforward motor command was originally proposed by us [5,6].

In the forward and inverse modeling, the forward model provides a dynamical model of the controlled object. Thus, the backpropagation through the forward model is also a dynamical process which is described by differential equations. On the other hand, the feedback-error-learning scheme utilizes a linearized approximation of the inverse dynamics model (i.e. feedback controller) which can convert trajectory error into motor command error by relatively simple computation.

4 Stability of feedback-error-learning scheme

In this section, stability of the feedback-error-learning scheme is proved for a learning control system shown in Fig. 1c. The dynamics of the controlled object is described by (1). In this section, we consider only the inverse dynamics problem without kinematics. Further, we treat a simple case where f is invertible for clarity. Hence, the dynamics of the controlled object can be described as follows: $\tau = h(\theta,\dot{\theta},\ddot{\theta})$. The total torque fed to the controlled object is the sum of the feedback torque τ_{fb} calculated by a PDA feedback controller and the feedforward torque τ_{ff} calculated by the neural network IDM.

$$h(\theta,\dot{\theta},\ddot{\theta}) = \tau = \tau_{fb} + \tau_{ff} = K_P\xi + K_D\dot{\xi} + K_A\ddot{\xi} + \tau_{ff}, \tag{6}$$

here $\xi = \theta_d - \theta$. The neural network IDM calculates τ_{ff} from the desired trajectory θ_d and the synaptic weights w:

$$\tau_{ff} = \psi(w,\theta_d,\dot{\theta}_d,\ddot{\theta}_d). \tag{7}$$

The shape of the function ψ depends on the kind of neural network model used for the IDM. Here, I assume that an appropriate neural network model is chosen and that it can realize the exact inverse dynamics for an optimal set of synaptic weights $\tilde{w}$:

$$h(\theta,\dot{\theta},\ddot{\theta}) = \psi(\tilde{w},\theta,\dot{\theta},\ddot{\theta}). \tag{8}$$

The synaptic modification rule of the feedback-error-learning scheme is represented in a general manner as follows:

$$dw/dt = (\partial\tau_{ff}/\partial w)^T\tau_{fb}. \tag{9}$$

Because this expression is quite general, it includes several learning rules for a prepared-nonlinearity neural network and MLP which we used in previous studies [3,4,5,6].

Substituting (7) and (8) into (6), we obtain the following equation.

$$\begin{aligned}
\tau_{imag} &\equiv \tilde{\tau}_{ff} - \tau_{ff} \\
&= \psi(\tilde{w},\theta_d,\dot{\theta}_d,\ddot{\theta}_d) - \psi(w,\theta_d,\dot{\theta}_d,\ddot{\theta}_d) \\
&= \psi(\tilde{w},\theta_d,\dot{\theta}_d,\ddot{\theta}_d) - h(\theta,\dot{\theta},\ddot{\theta}) + \tau_{fb} \\
&= h(\theta_d,\dot{\theta}_d,\ddot{\theta}_d) - h(\theta,\dot{\theta},\ddot{\theta}) + \tau_{fb} \\
&\equiv \Delta h(\theta_d,\xi,\dot{\xi},\ddot{\xi}) + \tau_{fb},
\end{aligned} \tag{10}$$

here τ_{imag} is an imaginary torque which is fed to an imaginary dynamical system described by the last expression of (10). The imaginary torque τ_{imag} is generated by an estimation error of $\tilde{w}$ by w. If $w = \tilde{w}$ then $\tau_{imag} = 0$ for any θ_d. The last expression defines an imaginary dynamical system which is a combination of the variational system of the controlled object around the desired trajectory θ_d and the feedback controller with the input τ_{imag}:

$$\Delta h(\theta_d, \xi, \dot{\xi}, \ddot{\xi}) + K_P\xi + K_D\dot{\xi} + K_A\ddot{\xi} = \tau_{imag}. \tag{11}$$

This equation (11) defines an imaginary nonautonomous dynamical system with respect to ξ with the input τ_{imag}. Here, I make the first assumption about the stability of this imaginary dynamical system.

Assumption 1 *If $\tau_{imag} = 0$, then the solution ξ of (11) will tend to 0 as t goes to infinity.*

Thus, global asymptotic stability of the origin of (11) for zero input is assumed here. We make the second assumption about the feedback motor command τ_{fb}.

Assumption 2 *τ_{fb} is approximately proportional to $\lambda\tau_{imag}$ with $0 < \lambda < 1$.*

This assumption can be justified in two different ways. Let us consider an expansion of the imaginary dynamical system (11).

$$\begin{aligned}(K_A + \partial h(\theta_d, \dot{\theta}_d, \ddot{\theta}_d)/\partial\ddot{\theta})\ddot{\xi} \;&+\; (K_D + \partial h(\theta_d, \dot{\theta}_d, \ddot{\theta}_d)/\partial\dot{\theta})\dot{\xi} + (K_P + \partial h(\theta_d, \dot{\theta}_d, \ddot{\theta}_d)/\partial\theta)\xi \\ +o(\xi, \dot{\xi}, \ddot{\xi}) \;&=\; \tau_{imag},\end{aligned} \tag{12}$$

here $o(\xi, \dot{\xi}, \ddot{\xi})$ is a higher order term in ξ, and hence a small order compared with the linear terms for small ξ. If the feedback gains are sufficiently large compared with the partial derivatives of h, then Assumption 2 holds with $\lambda \cong 1$. If these feedback gains are chosen as in (4) so that the feedback-error-learning scheme becomes a good approximation of the Newton method as described in the previous section, then Assumption 2 holds with $\lambda \cong 1/2$. The following function V is examined as a candidate of the Liapunov function.

$$V = 1/2 \cdot \tau_{imag}^T \tau_{imag} \geq 0. \tag{13}$$

The equality of (13) holds only when $w = \tilde{w}$ for nontrivial θ_d. It is quite natural to assume that θ_d is not always zero. I calculate the time derivative of V.

$$\begin{aligned} dV/dt \;&=\; \tau_{imag}^T \partial\tau_{imag}/\partial w \cdot dw/dt + dV/d\hat{t} \\ &=\; \tau_{imag}^T\{-\partial\tau_{ff}/\partial w\}(\partial\tau_{ff}/\partial w)^T\tau_{fb} + dV/d\hat{t} \\ &=\; \tau_{imag}^T\{-\partial\tau_{ff}/\partial w\}(\partial\tau_{ff}/\partial w)^T\lambda\tau_{imag} + dV/d\hat{t} \\ &=\; -\lambda\{(\partial\tau_{ff}/\partial w)^T\tau_{imag}\}^T\{(\partial\tau_{ff}/\partial w)^T\tau_{imag}\} + dV/d\hat{t}, \end{aligned} \tag{14}$$

here $dV/d\hat{t}$ is the partial derivative of V with respect to the time t while fixing w constant. Thus, it can be expressed as follows:

$$dV/d\hat{t} = \partial V/\partial\theta_d \cdot \dot{\theta}_d + \partial V/\partial\dot{\theta}_d \cdot \ddot{\theta}_d + \partial V/\partial\ddot{\theta}_d \cdot d\ddot{\theta}_d/dt \tag{15}$$

Now, I average the rate of change of V for a time interval which is shorter than the time constant of change of w but much longer than the mixing rate of the desired trajectory θ_d. Thus, the rate of change of w is assumed much slower than that of θ_d. Then, if θ_d is a strongly stationary stochastic process, the time average of the second term of (14) vanishes since V is regarded as a Baire function of the strongly stationary process.

$$\overline{dV/d\hat{t}} = d\overline{V}/d\hat{t} = 0. \tag{16}$$

This is because, when w is constant, V is a function of θ_d alone. Then, from the definition of the strongly stationary stochastic process, the average of V is constant. Consequently we obtain:

$$\overline{dV/dt} = -\lambda\overline{\{(\partial\tau_{ff}/\partial w)^T\tau_{imag}\}^T\{(\partial\tau_{ff}/\partial w)^T\tau_{imag}\}} \leq 0 \quad (17)$$

The equalities of (17) and (13) hold only when $w = \tilde{w}$ for nontrivial θ_d. Consequently, I can conclude that w asymptotically converges to the optimal set of synaptic weights $\tilde{w}$. Then, because $\tau_{imag} = 0$ for $w = \tilde{w}$, θ asymptotically converges to θ_d based on Assumption 1.

5 Feedback-error-learning neural network as models of different parts of cerebellum

The cerebellum is divided into separate sagittal regions with distinctive anatomical connections although the cellular organization of the cerebellar cortex is simple, regular and uniform. These divisions form three functionally distinct parts of the cerebellum: the vestibulocerebellum, the spinocerebellum, and the cerebrocerebellum [1].

The cerebrocerebellum is the lateral zone of the cerebellum. Its inputs originate exclusively in pontine nuclei that relay information from the cerebral cortex, and its output is conveyed by the dentate nucleus to the thalamus and then to the motor cortex. The feedback-error-learning neural network was originally proposed as a model for the cerebrocerebellum and the parvocellular part of the red nucleus [5,6]. Fig. 2c shows this model of the lateral part of the cerebellar hemisphere. In this figure, the feedback controller and the summation of the feedforward and feedback command reside in the motor cortex of the cerebrum. The feedback loop is the transcortical loop. The desired trajectory is sent to the cerebellum and the motor cortex from the association cortex. The output of the cerebellum is sent back to the motor cortex via the thalamus.

The spinocerebellum includes the vermis at the midline and the intermediate zone of the hemispheres. These two regions are the areas of the cerebellum that receive sensory information from the periphery. The vermis is related to control of posture. Gomi and I are now proposing a closed loop control system based on the feedback error learning as shown in Fig. 2b. It can be considered as a model of the vermis.

The vestibulocerebellum occupies the flocculonodular lobe. Flocculus is known to play a role in adaptive modification of the vestibulo-ocular reflex [1]. Its circuit diagram is shown in Fig. 2a. Although this circuit does not contain any feedback controller, the visual system measures the combined eye and head velocity and plays a role in converting trajectory error into the motor command error. Consequently, the function of the flocculus can also be understood from the feedback-error-learning concept.

Acknowledgment

The author wishes to express his thanks to Drs. E. Yodogawa and K. Nakane of ATR Auditory and Visual Perception Research Laboratories for their continuing encouragement.

References

[1] Ito M (1984) The cerebellum and neural control. Raven Press, New York

[2] Jordan MI (1988). Supervised learning and systems with excess degrees of freedom. *COINS Technical Report 88-27*, 1–41.

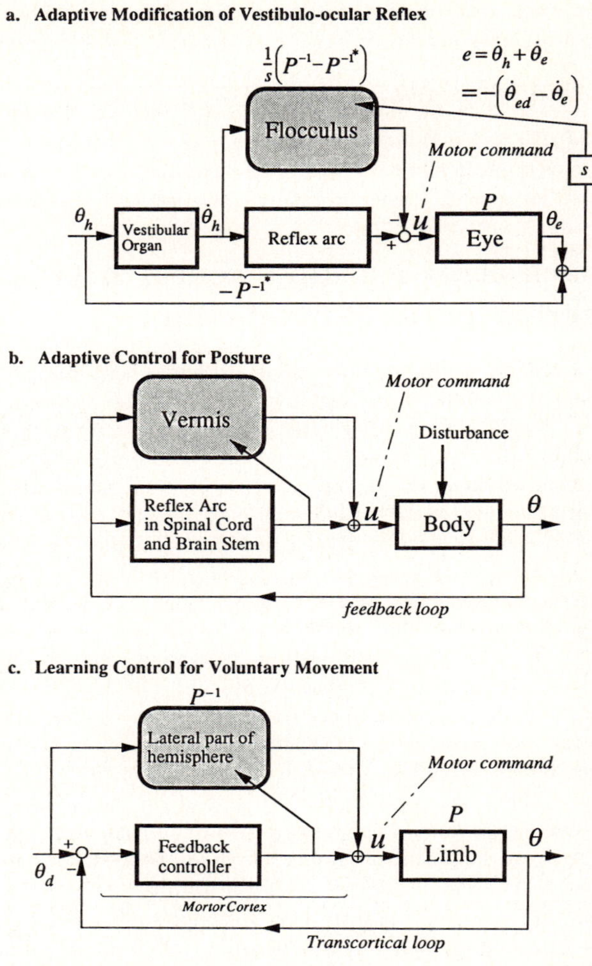

Figure 2: Functional roles of different parts of cerebellum interpreted based on the feedback error learning scheme: a) Flocculus for adaptive modification of the vestibulo-ocular reflex. b) Vermis for adaptive control of posture. c) Lateral hemisphere for learning of voluntary motor control.

[3] Kano M, Kawato M, Suzuki R (1989) Acquisition of inverse-kinematics and inverse-dynamics model of a redundant arm by feedback error learning. *Jpn IEICE Tech Rep* **MBE88-171**, pp 91–96 (in Japanese)

[4] Katayama M, Kawato M (1989) Learning control of a redundant controlled-object by feedback error learning. *Jpn IEICE Tech Rep* **MBE89-76**, pp 83–90 (in Japanese)

[5] Kawato M, Furukawa K, Suzuki R (1987) A hierarchical neural-network model for control and learning of voluntary movement. *Biol Cybern* **57**:169–185

[6] Tsukahara N, Kawato M (1982) Dynamic and plastic properties of the brain stem neuronal networks as the possible neuronal basis of learning and memory. In: Amari S, Arbib MA (eds) Lecture notes in biomathematics, **45** *Competition and cooperation in neural nets.* Springer-Verlag, Berlin Heidelberg New York, pp 430-441

Advanced Neural Computers / R. Eckmiller (Editor)

DAS LERNFAHRZEUG
NEURAL NETWORK APPLICATION FOR AUTONOMOUS MOBILE ROBOTS

Rigobert OPITZ

IBP PIETZSCH GmbH
Hertzstr. 32-34
D-7505 Ettlingen
Tel. 0049-7243-709-134

SUMMARY

Using Neural Network Technology for information representation and information processing opens a wide and promising field of application in the control area for mobile robot vehicles and for driving support systems. Features like supervised learning and self-learning during the training phase (LERNPHASE) and associations combined with very short response times in the operation phase (KANNPHASE) improve the chance of realizing a high degree of autonomous cooperation with the unexpected. Three steps of investigating Neural Network application for the LERNFAHRZEUG (automatic guided vehicle) using the bottom-up approach will be presented:
1. Sensor/Motor associations with trained obstacle primitives
2. Complex driving ground behavior
3. Dynamic cooperative behavior.
Using a developed application simulation system the process of engineering Neural Networks and improving their performances will be discussed including paradigms and architectural evaluations.

Future technical real time tasks of automatic guided vehicles in real environments consisting of environment space, event space, system space, reaction space and task space will demand information processing techniques with high tolerance and the ability to handle complex cybernetical situations and processing tasks. Numerical processing techniques with bottleneck effects and programming problems in cooperation and interaction are insufficient. In addition, isomorphic representations in form of transfer chains from the physical situation using adequate sensor configurations, preprocessing techniques, input vectors, network topologies, paradigms, and output vectors for locomotion are important for high performances in autonomy.
The background of the LERNFAHRZEUG (autonomous mobile robot) was to create a simulation system for Neural Network integration and testing in application fields with a high degree of relevance to realistic situations. Using a sensor system for object contour lines and a locomotion set, various neural network types were applied and investigated.

TARGET

The overall aim and purpose of simulation was to implement and investigate the following performances:
(1) learning strategies to avoid collision with complex obstacles
(2) control of robot vehicle movements in a structured environment, subject

to local perturbations; operation in unknown environments with reflex behavior
(3) performing cooperative behavior of multiple mobile robot vehicles
(4) training by supervised learning with input/output vector fields without algorithms for programming or mathematical models
(5) clear separation of LERNPHASE (training of network) and KANNPHASE (recall of network) for investigation of learning and recall performances using bottom-up approach with realistic sensors and neural software simulators on PC level

Several problem classes in the field of autonomous systems appeared to be applicable for neural network processing:

OBSTACLE AVOIDANCE / REFLEX BEHAVIOR
- move parallel to obstacle with fixed distance
- move around obstacle in trained manner (pass close, maximize distance to obstacle)
- move through doorways

DRIVING AID /NEAR RANGE NAVIGATION
- parking aid
- shunting in narrow environment
- overtake warnings
- warning on backward movements based on obstacles

OBSTACLE SITUATION RECOGNITION
- scan contours of obstacle
- detect moving obstacles
- classify obstacles (with scattering methods)

SYSTEM ARCHITECTURE

The following figure shows the conceptual layout of the system.

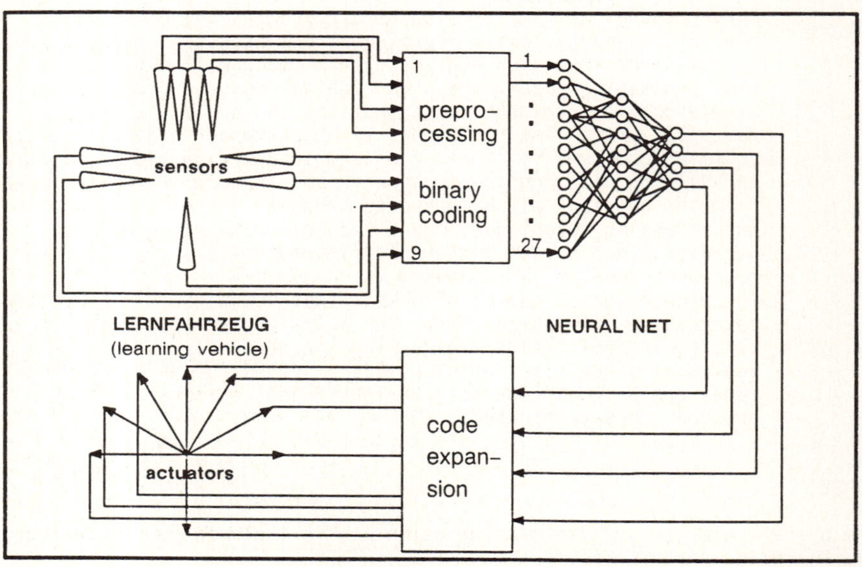

PROCESS OF NEURAL APPLICATION SIMULATION

Sensor data of the vehicle are preprocessed and fed into a chosen neural network. The output of the neural net controls the vehicle's actuator system that moves the vehicle to a different location by overlay of translatory and rotatory components.
The new sensor values are acquired and sent back to the neural net which responds with actuator control corresponding to the new sensor data and its internal associations. It is supposed that physical control of the actuator part of the vehicle will be provided by a conventional control system. Applying neural net simulators to real applications requests time constants greater than 10msec. In future, special purpose hardware will be available that allows for response times in milliseconds.
A complete simulation run consists of a few phases. Firstly, a proving ground has to be configured which will be used in learning and recall phase. Subsequently, a learning file has to be created. This is done by leading the vehicle around obstacles several times. With every movement, the sensor data and the appropriate moving data are written into a file. In the learning phase, this file will be presented to the neural network. If the neural network converges to a desired global error (<1) the net is trained and can be used in recall mode. Now the vehicle can be positioned arbitrarily on the proving ground. The vehicle will drive around obstacles controlled by its abstracted reflexes. Two interacting processes for application ground and network simulation are combined and executed in the following procedure:

1. Configuration of proving ground and learning (LERNPHASE)

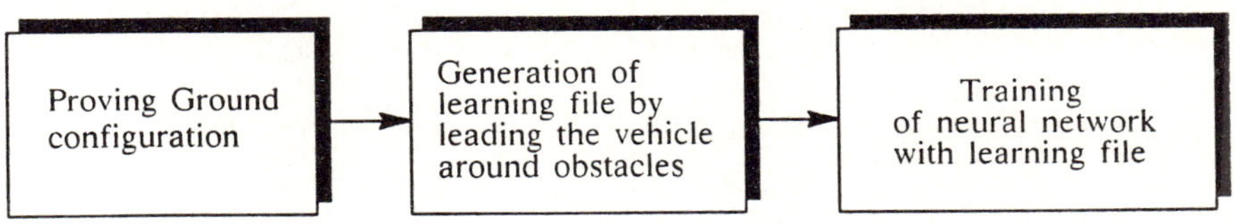

2. Recall mode (KANNPHASE)

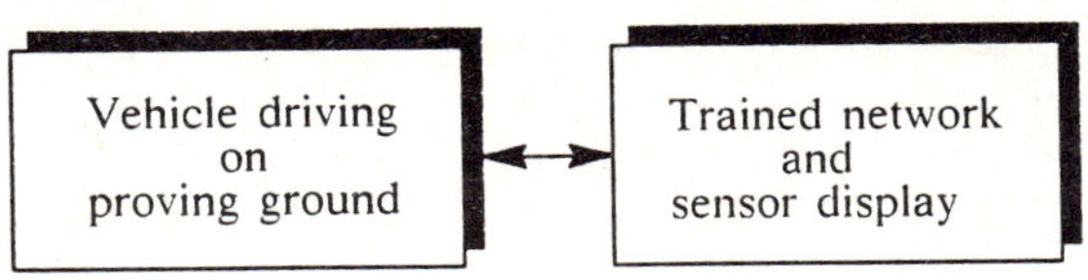

Optimization of the network structures by comparing paradigms like backpropagation (analog and digital inputs), Palm nets, counterpropagation, that simulation performance in response time of neural networks could be higher than in conventional AI-Systems. The simulation system presented implements basic functions for training and recall of a neural network, including creation of a proving ground where the user may design the vehicle's moving environment or only special elements (obstacle primitives) like crossings, pillars etc. that will be used to train the vehicles's desired 'behavior'. Created proving ground can be stored on disk and reloaded for further training or recall sessions. Creation of learning data files is realized by simply moving the vehicle on the proving ground with mouse clicks. By start of the recall operation of a neural net the vehicle's initial position on the proving ground can be defined by the user. Starting the recall session moves the vehicle around on the proving ground only controlled by the applied network output.
While learning a neural network model, several data of interest are displayed on screen and important parameters are supervised.

LERNFAHRZEUG I

For the initial acquisition of training data (LERNFAHRZEUG I) with obstacle primitives, we used a discretisized moving ground and created the data sets. The vehicle was equipped with 9 ultrasonic sensors.
As locomotion vector, 8 different moving actions were defined: stop, fast forward, slow forward, turn right 45, turn left 45, turn right 90, turn left 90, slow backward.

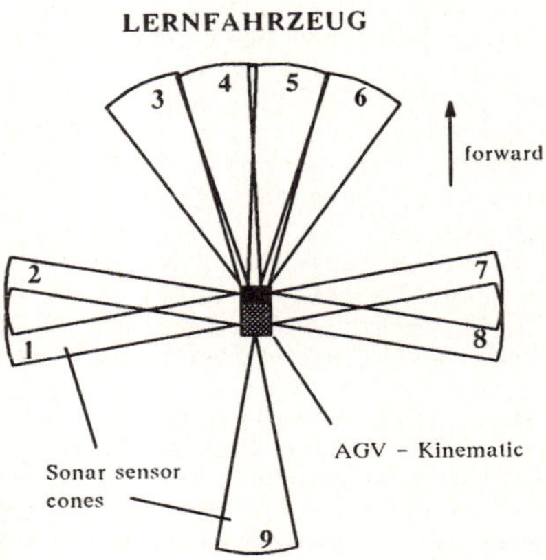

Logarithmic Resolution
$y = 12 - \log(16-x) * 9.96$

Area	Distance (m)	Coding
15	12	0001
14	9	0010
13	7.245	0100
12	6	1000
11	5.034	0101
10	4.245	1001
9	3.578	1010
8	3	1100
7	2.490	0110
6	2.034	0011
5	1.622	0111
4	1.245	1011
3	0.899	1101
2	0.578	1110
1	0.279	1111

Sensor resolution and coding of sensitivity areas

To limit the amount of sensor data we partitioned every sensor cone into 15 blocks. The corresponding distances were assigned logarithmically in correspondence with the sensitivity to near range obstacles.
We designed a coding of the sensor blocks in which the code of block n differs only by one bit from the code of block n+1 and block n-1.
For 8 movements, we used 3 bits for binary mapping. The network we used was a backpropagation network. It consists of 36 input nodes, 8 hidden nodes in 1 hidden layer and 3 output nodes.

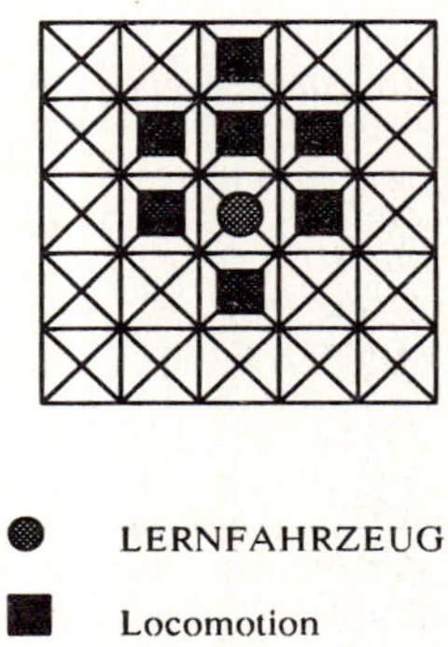

-> 7 directions + stop

Output nodes of neural network

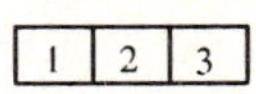

Bit 1	2	3	
0	0	0	-> Stop
0	0	1	-> Backward
0	1	0	-> forward slow
0	1	1	-> forward fast
1	0	1	-> turn left 90 °
1	0	0	-> turn left 45 °
1	1	0	-> turn right 45 °
1	1	1	-> turn right 90 °

The network did learn to move around 10 different obstacles in 10 different training sessions with about 10,000 presentations per obstacle-course. Finally we combined all training sets of the 10 obstacles into one training set and taught the network with little more than 20,000 presentations.

Some of the 10 predefined obstacle primitives are shown below. The vehicle was trained to avoid the primitive and to reach the upper right corner of the simulation screen.

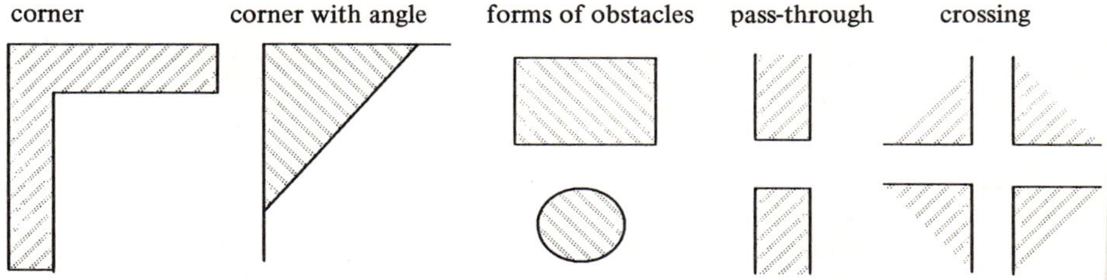

- A wide range of fault-tolerance could be proved.
- It is possible to see which primitives are learned in a stable way, and those having a few unstable vectors.
- Obviously 10 percent is the greatest amount of noise our trained net is able to resist because with a ten percent noise factor frequently only slow/fast errors occured, which means that the car is mostly driving correct directions. The vehicle is turning the direction correctly, but in different distances to the obstacle.

LERNFAHRZEUG II

The next generation of autonomous mobile robots was investigated and based on the previously described closed loop simulation system. Proving ground configuration, learning file generation were supported by a simulator. Various trained networks were compared, including different sensor representations and learning file assemblies.

The following figure shows some networks trained with data generated on a proving ground. The training was stopped after 800,000 presentations and the learning file consisted of 1,000 patterns. The networks were initialized with small random values between 0.1 and -0.1.

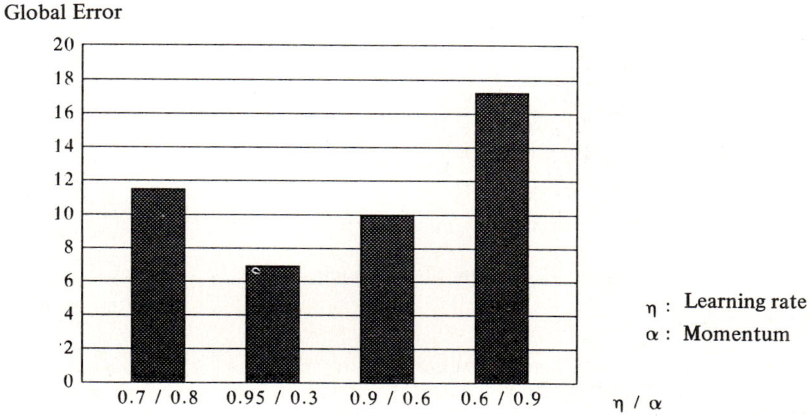

The speed and quality of convergence depends on different factors. Good convergence rates can be reached if the training pattern have no contradictions.

The impressive results:
- o nucleus area (KERNFELD) with over 1000 accurately learned representations
- o a wide associative space of identical behavior (FANGFELD) for not accurate but similar input constellations
- o no programming work during training (LERNPHASE)
- o short response time in the recall mode (KANNPHASE)
- o ability to drive in unknown environments

demonstrate very obviously the performance of neural network technology in sensor/motor association, control and learning.

ADVANCED CONCEPTS FOR NEURAL NETWORKS

One of the most impressive aspects of information processing with neural networks beside their functional performances are the abilities to create and adapt architecutes. The general performances of neural networks can be classified in contrast to classical information processing techniques with the Von Neumann Machine as follows:

Recall and Association

of complex data sets, non linear functions and informations used for relatively simple tasks like sensor motor associations, signal classification and in general for input/output vector recall and association. The process is clearly separated into LERNPHASE (learning mode) and KANNPHASE (recall mode). Network behavior in the training areas (KERNFELD) is up to 100 % predictable and accurate. Associations (FANGFELD) depend on training sets and representative data choice.

Classification

The second type of networks has to solve classification tasks in the area of pattern recognition in single and multidimensional space like binary vectors and images. Two levels of performances are existing: passive and active classification.
Passive classification means, to allocate patterns or data sets in prelearned classes and clusters seen or not seen before in addition to the previously learned and predefined data sets.
The process of classification tasks (Signal classification) may be described as follows:

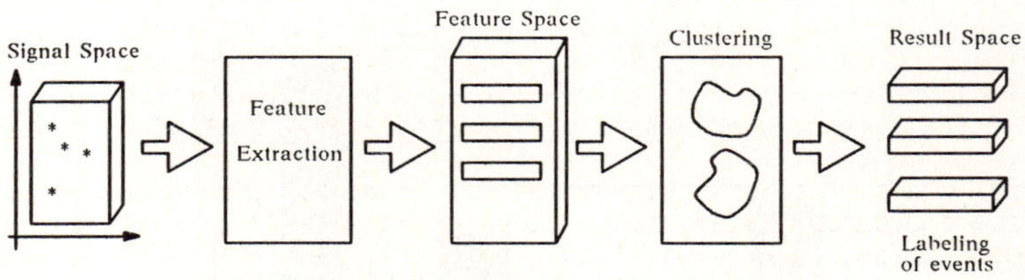

Signal Classification

Sensor Fusion

A special case of combining signals or information derived from different origins or physical processes or data files is the problem of sensor fusion with subsequent classification processes.

Learning and Adaptation

All networks are able to learn, however, they learn in different forms, formats, and on different levels. On the lowest level one will find learning modes like HEBBIAN LEARNING, BACKPROPAGATION and COMPETETIVE LEARNING. Learning means to compare a desired vector on a simple base (neuron) from the output side with a realized vector (by the network), and to use the differences for modification of weights (backwards). Normally the modification is calculated by an error function not considering parallel, historical and future aspects, and not considering general and strategic aspects. In our point of view, this is a wide field of improvement to increase performance of neural networks. Based on the previous work and the experience in realistic application tasks, the following approaches will be proposed to reach higher performances in learning and association:

1. REINFORCEMENT LEARNING NETWORKS (SELBSTLERN NETZE)

Reinforcement learning means to use high level learning strategies and learning sets to generate the desired behavior and performances without apriori information and experience by trial and error modules. This may incorporate surveyed driving of networks between learning and recall mode depending on failure rates and degrees of performance. The problem is a consistent definition and architecture of spaces for environment, system state, and learning aims to represent a learning process. The strategic aspects of storage, adaptation, exchange and reactivation are not considered in most learning system definitions.

2. TIME FUNCTION NETWORKS (VORGANGS NETZE)

For technical applications, individual association of discrete points in input and output space are usually not sufficient. More information is included in procedures and time-dependent functions. Time function networks will include both: historical and previous states in consideration of the actual state and projections into the future by apperception and anticipation influenced by desired behavior.

3. HERARCHICAL NETWORKS (NETZWERK BAUSTEINE)

Complex systems cause complex network assemblies with architectures, breaking general strategies into low level associations by cooperation of topdown projected strategies and local situative operations of networks.

4. AUTOPOIETIC NETWORKS (SELBSTAUFBAUENDE NETZE)

Backpropagation procedures will be replaced by more flexible and locally independent operations with learning procedures and self-referring mechanisms including architectural growing of the network size with connection drivers depending on the motivation and information pressure. Anabolic and catabolic processes will create an adequate network structure for optimal pragmatism.
The dynamic aspect of using autocatalytic elements with perspectives to chaotic and ordered system states is of great interest. Dramatic system structure exchanges in combination with impressive metamorphosis procedures challenge new approaches on the way to optimal pragmatism and self-organization.

Advanced Neural Computers / R. Eckmiller (Editor)

Motor Learning by "Charge" Placement with Self-organizing Maps

H. RITTER

Beckman Institute and Department of Physics
University of Illinois at Urbana-Champaign
Urbana IL 61801, U.S.A.

Adaptively learned sensory-motor mappings are useful for describing fixed or slowly varying characteristics of a motor task. If interactions with variable objects are important, a more flexible representation scheme is needed. In this contribution we suggest to combine the "method of charges" with adaptive networks, such as self-organizing maps, to provide a flexible and powerful approach to tasks of motor learning. As an example, we discuss this approach for the task of learning grasp movements for planar objects of variable shape and report simulation results using a self-organizing map learning the proper placement of the charges.

1 Introduction

Biological neural networks manage to control movements, using neurons that are intrinsically slow and of only moderate reliability. Despite these "hardware limitations", biological motor systems are able to control even very fast movements and in addition excel with their high degree of flexibility and their capability of learning.

These are compelling reasons to investigate neural network-based artificial algorithms as promising candidates for the synthesis and control of robot movements. Although current neural network approaches cannot yet supplant more conventional algorithms developed over decades in the past, they have reached a level were low-level robot control has become feasible and most of their control capabilities need not be programmed but can be learned during operation.

Most of this work so far has centered on the learning of various sensori-motor mappings required for execution of simple movements or compensation of nonlinearities in the control path of e.g. a robot manipulator (see e.g. [2,6,7,8,10,12].) Such mappings describe fixed or slowly varying characteristics of the robot arm itself, such as its kinematic and dynamic properties.

However, most movements involve the interaction between the manipulator and external objects, such as target objects or obstacles. Refs. [6] and [9] provide two different approaches to address this issue if the task is to grasp cylinders of variable location and orientation. However, both approaches still rest on the assumption of a stereotyped shape of the target object.

Obviously, the next step needs to address the situation of objects of variable shape and the possible presence of obstacles. Such tasks probably can no longer be well solved by a single, monolithic network, but instead need to be subdivided into simpler subtasks solved by several, cooperating modules (the approach of [9], using a hierarchy of networks, is already a step in this direction.) In addition, the solution of such tasks will greatly benefit from more efficient representations of the movement itself.

2 The "Method of Charges"

A very appealing and still natural representation for movements is provided by the "method of charges" (see e.g. [1,3,11]): target objects are considered as carrying an "attractive" charge, and obstacles are considered as carrying a "repulsive" charge. Corresponding charges are also attached to the robot arm itself, and the movement then is generated by the free dynamics of the robot arm in the force field generated by the charges. For the case of only few degrees of freedom, the method can be implemented in the configuration space of the robot and the formation of a successful trajectory (if one exists) can then be guaranteed. Usually however, the configuration space is too high-dimensional and the method can only be implemented in the (lower dimensional) task space of the robot. As a price of this simplification the resulting movements may become trapped in local minima or occasionally still encounter an obstacle. Therefore, the method does not fully solve the problem of trajectory planning. However, if placement and magnitude of the charges are properly chosen, the method will generate in many cases a very satisfactory trajectory. Fig.1 shows two examples of trajectories obtained for a planar redundant robot arm with gripper. In both diagrams, the target position was specified by a pair of locations for the tips of the two gripper jaws, and the "diamonds" acted as repulsive obstacles.

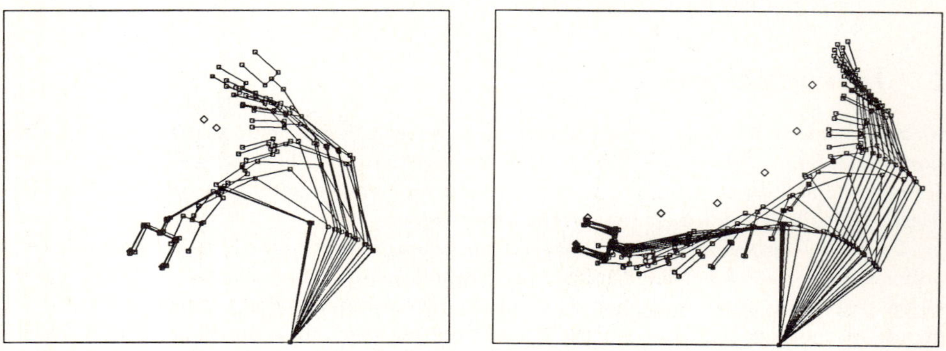

Fig.1 Trajectories for a planar, redundant robot arm, generated by the "method of charges".

While the "method of charges" in itself is not yet an adaptive method, it greatly reduces the number of cases requiring intervention of some higher control level and facilitates the task of the latter. However, good results require a suitable positioning and specification of the charges. We suggest for this part of the method the use of an adaptive neural network. The task of the network then is *to gradually achieve the ability to place charges that effect the desired movement.* In this way, the virtues of the method of charges and of adaptive neural networks can be combined in a very efficient way: the network uses the positioning of the charges as a flexible and powerful representation of the intended movements. The considerable degree of "low-level intelligence" already inherent in that representation then can make the learning of even quite sophisticated movements possible.

In the next section we shall explore this idea in the context of a still simple, but concrete and interesting task: the task of grasping planar objects of variable shape.

3 Learning to Recognize Stable Grasp Points

We consider the situation depicted in Fig.2: A robot arm with a parallel jaw gripper shall grasp a planar object placed somewhere on a table in front of it. Following the previous discussion, this task is split into two parts: (*i*) charge placement and (*ii*) subsequent trajectory generation by the "method of charges". We will use four charges, two of which are permanently attached to the tips of the two gripper jaws in the manner shown in Fig.2, while the positions for the remaining two charges will determine the two grasp points and have to be chosen for each task instance individually. In the following, we will focus on this part of the task exclusively. A "good" choice shall lead to a stable grasp and, therefore, has to take into account several factors, such as limited friction between gripper and object boundary, location of object centroid relative to grasp points, and limited maximal width of gripper opening. Below we report results of an idealized simulation taking into account only one of these factors, namely limited (and constant) friction between gripper and object boundary. In this case, a stable grasp requires that the line passing through the two grasp points lies within two "stability cones" whose width is a function of the angle subtended by the two edges meeting at the point of contact between gripper jaw and object boundary, and of the friction coefficient between gripper jaw and object surface (Fig.3).

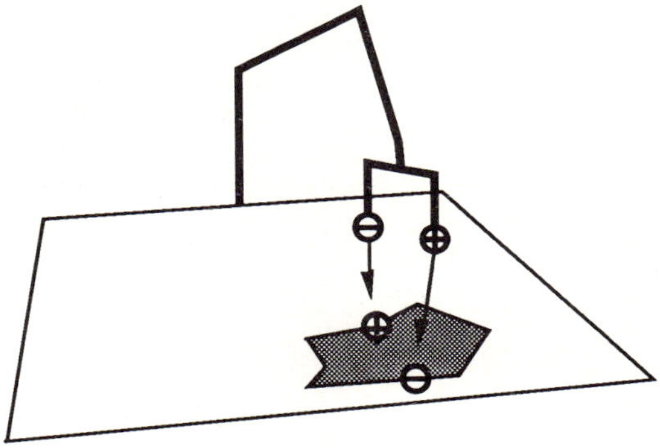

Fig.2 Robot arm and target object with attached "charges".

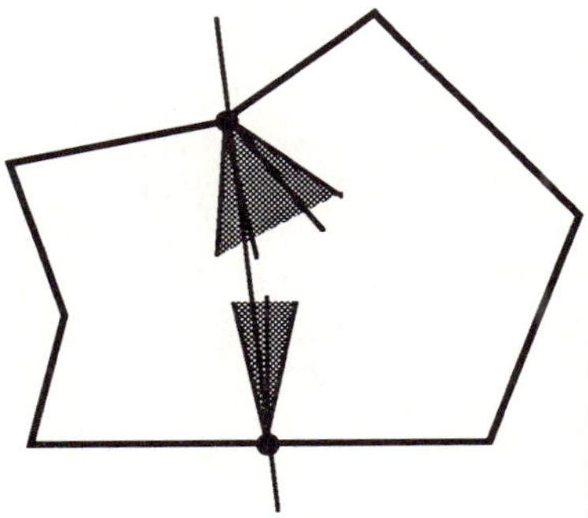

Fig.3 "Stability cones" for stable grasps.

We will employ a neural network whose task shall be to gradually learn a measure of the "goodness" of a suggested pair of grasp points. This measure shall be based on the direct visual appearance of the grasp locations in a perspective camera image of the scene, i.e. on information that can be extracted directly and readily from the visual image, without any knowledge about the viewpoint of the camera or the laws of perspective distortion. The network shall acquire its ability by being presented with a training sequence of good grasp point pairs for various sample objects.

In the simulation, each grasp point p was represented for the network by an eight-dimensional input vector $\vec{x}(p)$. The first two components were the cartesian coordinates of the grasp point in the image plane. The remaining six components encoded the directions of the two edges converging at point p and the direction to the other grasp point, respectively (Fig.4). Each of these three directions was encoded by a pair of values, namely the horizontal and vertical (in image coordinates) components of a "mask" consisting of a line of unit length

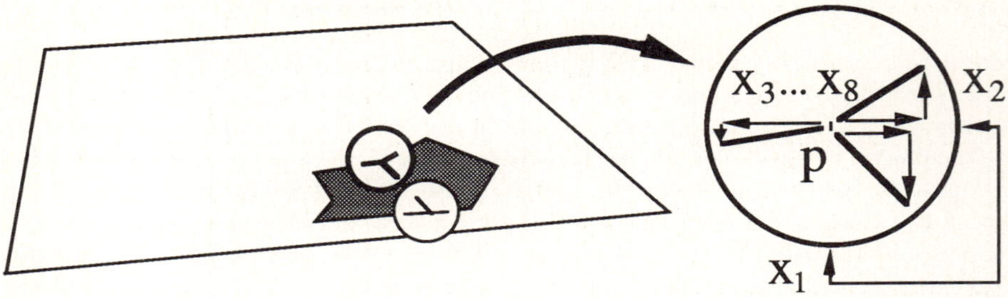

Fig.4 Visual features used for representation of grasp points.

oriented along the respective direction (this encoding was chosen to meet the requirement that all input information be readily available from the raw two-dimensional scene image.) Note that a grasp point p is always specified only with respect to its second partner: this partner defines the third direction encoded by the last two components of the representation vector $\vec{x}(p)$.

The set of all possible grasp points thus forms a five-dimensional manifold M (the eight-dimensional encoding is redundant with respect to the encoding of the three directions), of which all stable grasp points form a subset S. The training examples provide a discrete subset T of S. The network shall construct an approximation of the subset S, based on the examples T. This kind of task can be very well accomplished with a type of network known as "Kohonen self-organizing map" ([4,5]). For the task at hand, a square array of 36 units was used. Each unit $\mathbf{r}$ carries an 8-dimensional "reference vector" $\vec{w}_\mathbf{r}$ and, therefore, corresponds to some point in the manifold M. A random sequence of training examples provides a sequence of sample vectors $\vec{x}(p) \in T$ representing stable grasp points. Each sample vector gives rise to an adaptation step (actually, each example provides two grasp points p and, therefore, gives rise to two successive adaptation steps)

$$\Delta\vec{w}_\mathbf{r} = \epsilon \cdot h_{\mathbf{r},\mathbf{s}}(\vec{x} - \vec{w}_\mathbf{r}). \tag{1}$$

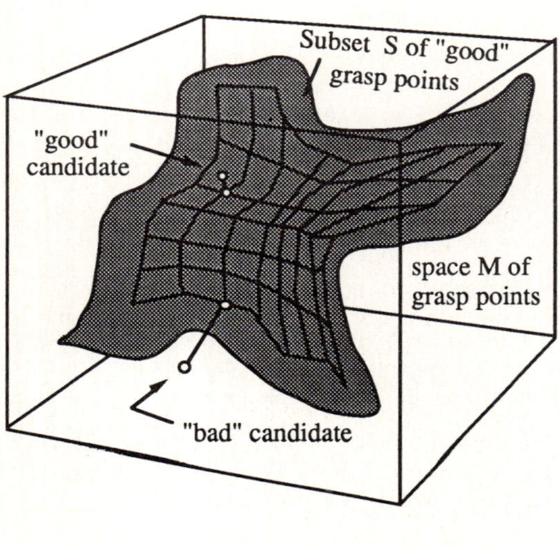

Fig.5 Subset S (shaded) of "good" grasp points, embedded in the space of all possible grasp points M (schematically indicated by the bounding cube). After learning, the self-organizing map (mesh) provides an approximation to the set S, so that the suitability of a grasp point can be judged by its distance to the closest reference vector (mesh-point) of the self-organizing map.

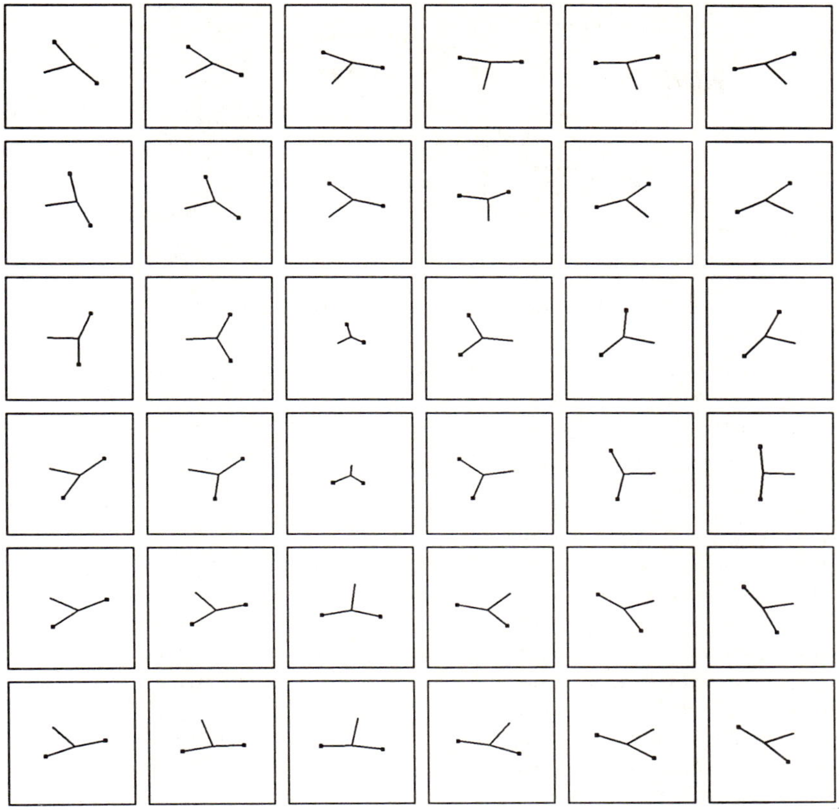

Fig.6 Topographic feature map for "good" grasp points, obtained after 3,000 training steps (for explanation see text).

Here, ϵ scales the learning step size and $h_{\mathbf{r},\mathbf{s}}$ is a Gaussian of the distance between units $\mathbf{r}$ and $\mathbf{s}$ in the lattice. In eq. 1, $\mathbf{s}$ is determined by

$$\mathbf{s} = \arg\min_{\mathbf{s}} ||\vec{w}_{\mathbf{s}} - \vec{x}|| \qquad (2)$$

(for a motivation of this learning rule, see e.g. [4,5,12]). The effect of sufficiently many such adjustments is to gradually "distribute" the reference vectors of the units over the subset of stable grasp points. This is schematically depicted in Fig.5, where the shaded surface represents the subset of stable grasp points and the mesh surface the approximation furnished by the self-organizing map. After training, the sum of the distances of the two grasp points of a candidate pair can be used as the desired (inverse) measure of the "goodness" of the choice: only if both grasp points are stable, both distances and, therefore, their sum will be small.

The training examples were obtained using a set of 25 different polygonal shapes. Each shape was, together with a pair of stable grasp points, presented many times and in many different orientations and locations, to the network of 36 units. In addition, before presenting a new training example, the chosen shape was partially distorted by a randomly generated

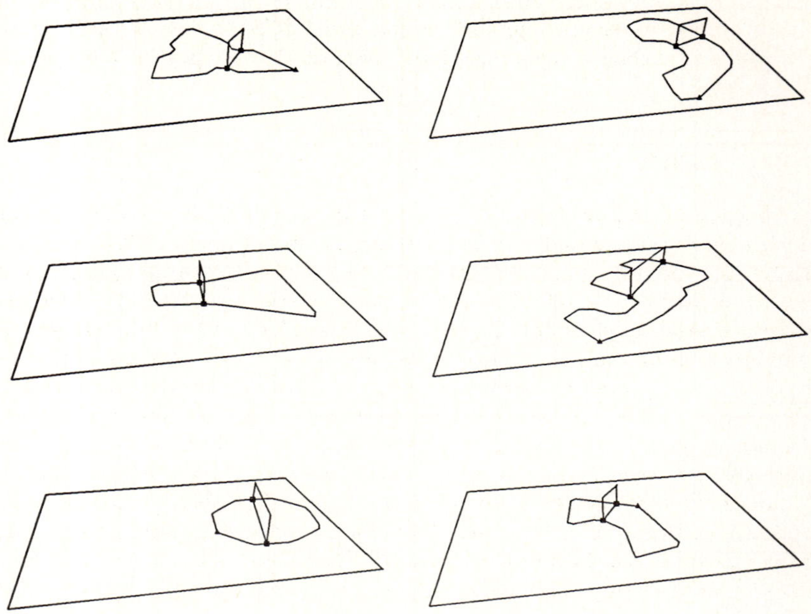

Fig.7 Some grasp choices made using the map of Fig.6.

(with restricted variance) affine transformation. The friction coefficient between gripper jaw and object boundary was assumed to be 0.1 (corresponding to very "slippery" objects). Starting from a randomly initialized network, Fig.6 shows the state of the array after 3000 training steps. Each unit has come to represent a particular combination of three directions characterizing a stable grasp point. For each unit, these three directions are indicated by three line segments in Fig.6: the plain line indicates the direction towards the second grasp point, and the two marked lines indicate the directions of the two edges converging at the grasp point. The combinations found by the units can be interpreted as different perspective views of "concave corners" such that the direction to the second grasp point tends to bisect the angle between the two converging edges, thus maximizing the stability of the grasp point. The combinations of different directions are distributed in a continuous fashion across the array, yielding a "topographic" map of the visual features pertaining to perspective views of good grasp points. Remarkably, the order found by the network is such that the "more concave" corners, indicating very stable grasp points, are discretized only coarsely and are represented near the center of the array, using only few units. Combinations pertaining to grasp points with less stability are represented in finer discretization steps, using the larger number of units available in the periphery of the array.

Finally, Fig.7 shows a few grasp points selected by means of the trained network. For each selection, the network was used to select the best candidate among a set of 240 candidate pairs, obtained by considering all possible pairings of 32 equidistant points along the periphery of the shape considered. Without any further refinements, the success rate (i.e. suggested grasp point pairs that proved stable) of the small network for the 25 training shapes, together with 75 "new" shapes never presented before, was about 85%. In view of the small number of units (N=36) and the fairly high-dimensional space (d=5) this appears to be a reasonably good result.

4 Conclusion

It was the purpose of this contribution to suggest combination of adaptive maps and the "method of charges" as a new and promising approach to motor learning. We reported results of a computer simulation studying such combination for the task of learning grasp movements, which by this method can be solved in a very simple setting. However, the simulation still contained several idealizations which should be removed in future work. Important extensions will be the inclusion of additional influence factors in the choice of grasp points, such as centroid position and limited range of gripper opening and the use of more realistic visual input information. Further, in the current simulation the network only learnt to choose among a set of externally given grasp point alternatives; clearly it would be more desireable if the network generated a solution entirely on its own. However, the purpose of the presented simulation was not to present a final algorithm, but to provide a working example illustrating the general idea put forward in this paper. Much further work will be needed to develop this approach into an efficient and competitive method. Further interesting issues on this way will be a study of adaptive charge placement for trajectory optimization and for the avoidance of local minima.

References

[1] Hwang Y.K. (1988) Robot Path Planning Using Potential Field Representation. Thesis, Univ. of Illinois at Urbana-Champaign.

[2] Kawato M., Fusukawa K., Suzuki R. (1987) A hierarchical neural network model for control and learning of voluntary movements. Biological Cybernetics 57:169-185.

[3] Khatib 0. (1986) Real time obstacle avoidance for manipulators and mobile robots. Int. J. Robotics Res. 5:90-98.

[4] Kohonen T. (1982) Self-organized Formation of Topologically Correct Feature Maps. Biol Cybern 43:59-69

[5] Kohonen T. (1984) Self-Organization and Associative Memory. Springer Series in Information Sciences 8, Heidelberg.

[6] Kuperstein M. (1988) Neural network model for adaptive hand-eye coordination for single postures. Science 239:1308-1311.

[7] Martinetz T., Ritter H., Schulten K. (1990) Three-dimensional Neural Net for Learning Visuomotor Coordination of a Robot Arm. IEEE Transactions on Neural Networks 1:131-138.

[8] Martinetz T., Ritter H., Schulten K. (1990) Learning of Visuomotor Coordination of a Robot Arm with Redundant Degrees of Freedom. In: Parallel Processing in Neural Systems and Computers (Eckmiller R., Hartmann G., Hauske G. Eds.), pp.431-434 (North Holland, Amsterdam).

[9] Martinetz T., Schulten K. (1990) Hierarchical Neural Net for Learning Control of a Robot's Arm and Gripper. IJCNN-90, San Diego (submitted)

[10] Mel B.W. (1988) Building and Using Mental Models in a Sensory-Motor Domain: A Connectionist Approach. Proc. of the 5th Int. Conf. on Machine Learning, Ann Arbor, pp.207-213 (Morgan Kaufman Publishers Inc., San Mateo).

[11] Ritter H., Schulten K. (1986) Planning a Dynamic Trajectory via Path Finding in Discretized Phase Space. In: Becker J.D., Eisele I. (Eds.), WOPPLOT86: Parallel Processing: Logic, Organization and Technology. Lecture Notes in Computer Science 253:29-39, Springer (Heidelberg).

[12] Ritter H., Martinetz T., Schulten K. (1989) Topology-Conserving Maps for Learning Visuo-Motor-Coordination. Neural Networks 2:159-168.

List of General References

Aarts, E.H.L., Korst, J.H.M., Simulated Annealing and Boltzman Machines (J. Wiley, Chichester, 1989)

Aleksander, I. (ed.), Neural Computing Architectures (North Oxford Academic Publ., London, 1989)

Amit, D.J., Moldeling Brain Function Cambridge University Press, Cambridge, 1989)

Anderson, J.A., Rosenfeld, E. (eds.), Neurocomputing: A Collection of Classic Papers (MIT Press, Cambridge, 1987)

Arbib, M.A., The Metaphorical Brain (J. Wiley, New York, 1989)

Baron, R.J., The Cerebral Computer - An Introduction to the Computational Structure of the Human Brain (L. Erbaum, Hillsdale N.J., 1987)

Cotterill, R.M.J. (ed.), Models of Brain Function (Cambridge University Press)

DARPA Study on Neural Networks (ASCEA International Press, 1988)

Dowling, J., The Retina, an Approachable Part of the Brain (Harvard University Press, 1987)

Durbin, R., Miall, C., Mitchison, G. (eds.), The Computing Neuron (Addison-Wesley, Working UK, 1989)

Eckmiller, R., v.d. Malsburg, C., (eds.), Neural Computers (Springer, Heidelberg, 1988, reprinted 1989)

Eckmiller, R., Hartmann, G., Hauske, G. (eds.), Parallel Processing in Neural Systems and Computers (Elsevier, Amsterdam, 1990)

Grossberg, S., The Adaptive Brain, Vol. 1+2 (Elsevier, New York, 1987)

Grossberg, S., Kuperstein, M., Neural Dynamics of Adaptive Sensory Motor Control (Pergamon Press, New York, 1989)

Haken, H. (ed.), Neural and Synergetic Computers (Springer, Heidelberg, 1988)

Hubel, D.H., Eye, Brain, and Vision (Scientific Americal Library), New York, 1988

Ito, M., The Cerebellum and Neural Control (Raven Press, New York, 1984)

Ito, M., (ed.), Neural Programming (Karger, Basel, 1989)

Klar, H., Ramacher, U. (eds.), Microelectronics for Artificial Neural Nets (VDI-Verlag, Düsseldorf, 1989)

Kohonen, T., Content-Adressable Memories, (Springer, Berlin, Heidelberg, 1987 2nd Edition)

Kohonen, T., Self-Organization and Associative Memory, (Springer, Berlin, Heidelberg, 1984, 1988 2nd Edition, 1989 3rd Edition)

Mead, C.A., Analog VLSI and Neural Systems (Addison-Wesley, Reading Mass., 1989)

Minsky, M.L., Papert, S.A., Perceptrons, an Introduction to Computational Geometry (MIT Press, Cambridge, 1988, expanded edition)

Pao, Y.H., Adaptive Pattern Recognition and Neural Networks (Addison-Wesley, Reading Mass., 1989)

Pfeifer, R., Schreter, Z., Fogelman F., Steels, L. (eds.), Connectionism in Perspective (Elsevier, Zürich, 1989)

Proc. Int. Joint Conf. Neural Networks (IJCNN), Washington, June 1989, (IEEE, Piscataway N.J., 1989)

Proc. Int. Joint Conf. Neural Networks (IJCNN 90, Washington) Washington, January 1990, (IEEE, Piscataway N.J., 1990)

Proc. Int. Joint Conf. Neural Networks (IJCNN 90, San Diego), San Diego, June 1990, (IEEE, Piscataway N.J., 1990)

Rakic, P., Singer, W. (eds.), Neurobiology of NeoCortex (J. Wiley, New York , 1988)

Rosenblatt, F., Principles of Neurodynamics, (Spartan Books, New York, 1962)

Rumelhart, D.E., McClelland, J.L. (eds.), Parallel Distributed Processing, Vol. 1-2 (MIT Press, Cambridge, 1986)

v. Seelen, W., Shaw, G., Leinhos, U.M. (eds.), Organization of Neural Networks, (VCH Verlagsges., Weinheim, 1988)

Touretzky, D.S. (ed.), Advances in Neural Information Processing Systems Vol. 2 (Morgan Kaufmann, San Mateo, 1990)

Widrow, B., Stearns, S.D., Adaptive Signal Processing (Prentice-Hall, Englewood Cliffs N.J., 1985)

Zornetzer, S.F., Davis, J.L., Lau, C. (eds.), An Introduction to Neural and Electronic Networks (Academic Press, Orlando, 1990)

REFERENCES FROM ALL CONTRIBUTIONS

Abbruzzese, F. and Lauria, F.E., An assembler for a McCulloch and Pitts network, IEEE 1st Int. Conf. on Neural Network, San Diego, Vol.IV, (1987) pp.601–608.

Abu–Mostafa, Y.S., The Vapnik–Chervonenkis dimension: Infomation versus complexity in learning, Neural Computation 1, (1989) pp.312–317.

Ackley, D.H., Hinton, G.H., and Sejnowski, T.J., A learning algorithm for Boltzmann machines, Cognitive Science 9, (1985) pp.147–169.

Agre, P.E. and Chapman, D., Pengi: An implementation of a theory of activity, Proc. AAAI, (1987) pp.268–272.

Akers, L.A., Walker, M., Grondin, R., and Ferry, D., A synthetic neural integrated circuit, Proc. IEEE 1989 Custom Integ. Circuits Conf., San Diego, (1989) pp.12.6.1–4.

Albert, A., Regression and the Moore–Penrose Pseudo–Inverse, (Academic Press, New York, 1972).

Albus, K., Exp. Brain Res. 24, (1975) pp.159–179 and 181–202.

Aleksander, I. and Morton, H.B., An Introduction to Neural Computing, Ch.10 and Ch.5, (Chapman and Hall, 1990).

Aleksander, I. and Morton, H.B., An overview of weightless neural systems, Proc. IJCNN90, Vol.II, (Washington, 1990) pp.499–502.

Aleksander, I., Ideal neurons for neural computers, in: R. Eckmiller, G. Hartmann, and G. Hauske (eds.), Parallel Processing in Neural Systems and Computers, (Elsevier, North Holland, Amsterdam, 1990) pp.225–228.

Almeida, L.B., Backpropagation in non–feedforward networks, in: I. Aleksander (ed.), Neural Computing Architectures, (MIT Press, 1989) pp.74–91.

Aloimonos, J., Bandopadhay, A., and Weiss, I., Active vision, Int. J. Computer Vision 4, (1988) pp.333–356.

Amaral, D.G. and Price, J.L., Amygdalo–cortical projections in the monkey (Macaca fascicularis), J. Comp. Neurol. 230, (1984) pp.465–496.

Amaral, D.G., Amygdalohippocampal and amygdalocortical projections in the primate brain, in: R. Schwarz and Y. Ben–Ari (eds.), Excitatory Amino Acids and Epilepsy, (Plenum Press, New York, 1986) pp.3–17.

Amaral, D.G., Memory: Anatomical organization of candidate brain regions, in: Handbook of Neurophysiology, Section 1, The Nervous System, Vol.V, (Am. Physiol. Soc., Washington, 1987) pp.211–294.

Amit, D.J., Gutfreund, H., and Sompolinsky, H., Information storage in neural networks with low levels of activity, Physical Review A 35, (1987) pp.2239–2303.

Anastasio, T.J. and Robinson, D.A., Distributed parallel processing in the vestibulo–oculomotor system, Neural Computations 1, (1989) pp.230–241.

Anderson, R.A., Essick, G.K., and Siegel, R.M., The encoding of spatial location by posterior parietal neuron, Science 230, (1985) pp.456–458.

Angle, C.M., Genghis, a six legged autonomous walking robot, (MIT S.B. Thesis in Electrical Engineering and Computer Science, 1989).

Anninonos, P.A., Beek, B., Csermely, T.J., Harth, E., and Pertile, G., Dynamics of neural structures, J. Theoret. Biol. 26, (1970) pp.121–148.

Arbib, M.A., The Metaphorical Brain 1, (John Wiley & Sons, New York, 1989).

Ashby, W.R., Design for a Brain, (John Wiley & Sons, New York, 1952/1960).

Atkeson, C.G., Learning arm kinematics and dynamics, Ann. Rev. Neurosci. 12, (1989) pp.157–183.

Bailey, J. and Hammerstrom, D., Why VLSI implementations of associative VLCNs require connection multiplexing, Proc. Int. Conf. on Neural Networks, (1988).

Baker, J. and Wickland, C., Kinematic properties of the vestibulocollic reflex, in: Peterson and Richmond (eds.), Control of Head Movement, (Oxford University Press, New York, 1988).

Baker, J., Goldberg, G., Hermann, G., and Peterson, B., Optimal response planes and canal convergence in secondary neurons in vestibular nuclei of alert cats, Brain Res. 294, (1984) pp.133–137.

Baker, J., Goldberg, J., and Peterson, B., Spatial and temporal response properties of the vestibulocollic reflex in decerebrate cats, J. Neurophysiol. 54, (1985) pp.735–756.

Baker, J., Wickland, C., and Peterson, B., Dependence of cat vestibulo–ocular reflex direction adaptation on animal orientation during adaptation and rotation in darkness, Brain Res. 408, (1987) pp.339–343.

Baker, J.F., Perlmutter S.I., Peterson, B.W., Rude, S.A., and Robinson, F.R., Simultaneous opposing adaptive changes in cat vestibulo–ocular reflex direction for two body orientations, Exp. Brain Res. 69, (1988) pp.220–224.

Ballard, D.H., Eye movement and spatial cognition, Technical Report TR–218, (Computer Science Dep., Univ. of Rochester, 1987).

Ballard, D.H. and Ozcandarli, A., Eye fixation and early vision, kinetic depth, Proc. 2nd IEEE Int. Conf. on Computer Vision, (1988).

Barhen, J., Gulati, S., and Zak, M., Neural learning of constrained nonlinear transformations, IEEE Computer 22, (1989) pp.67–76.

Barlow, H.B., Single units and sensation: A neuron doctrine for perceptual psychology?, Perception 1, (1972) pp.371–394.

Barrow, H., Learning receptive fields, Proc. IEEE 1st Int. Conf on Neural Networks, Vol.IV, (San Diego, 1987) pp.115–121.

Barto, A.G. and Sutton, R.S., Landmark learning, an illustration of associative search, Biol. Cybern. 42, (1981) pp.1–8.

Barto, A.G., Sutton, R.S., and Anderson, C.W., Neuronlike elements that can solve difficult learning control problems, IEEE Trans. on Systems, Man, and Cybernetics, SMC–13, (1983) pp.835–846.

Basar, E., EEG–Brain Dynamics, (Elsevier, North Holland, Amsterdam, 1980).

Batschelet, E., Circular Statistic in Biology, (Academic Press, London, 1981).

Baum, E. and Haussler, D., What size net gives valid generalization?, Neural Computation 1, (1989) pp.151–160.

Baylis, G.C., Rolls, E.T., and Leonard, C.M., Functional subdivisions of temporal lobe neocortex, J. of Neuroscience 7, (1987) pp.330–342.

Baylis, G.C., Rolls, E.T., and Leonard, C.M., Selectivity between faces in the responses of a population of neurons in the cortex in the superior temporal sulcus of the monkey, Brain Res. 342, (1985) pp.91–102.

Becker, S. and le Cun, Y., Improving the convergence of back–propagation learning with second order methods, Proc. Connec. Models Summer School, (Carnegie–Mellon Univ., 1988).

Beerhold, J.R., Jansen, M., and Eckmiller, R., Pulse–processing neural net hardware with selectable topology and adaptive weights and delays, Proc. IJCNN, Vol.II, (San Diego, 1990) pp.567–574.

Berkinblit, M.B., Feldman, A.G., and Fukson, O.I., Adaptability of innate motor patterns and motor control mechanisms, Behavioral and Brain Sciences 9, (1986) pp.585–638.

Berthoz, A. and Melvill–Jones, G., Adaptive mechanisms in gaze control, Reviews in Oculomotor Research, (Elsevier, North Holland, Amsterdam, 1985).

Biedermann, I., Recognition–by–components: A theory of human image understanding, Psychol. Rev. 94, (1987) pp.115–147.

Biguer, B., Prablanc, C., and Jeannerod, M., The contribution of coordinated eye and head movements in hand pointing accuracy, Exp. Brain Res. 55, (1984) pp.462–469.

Bijl, P. and Koenderink, J.J., Visibility of blobs with a Gaussian luminance profile, Vision Res. 29, (1989) pp.447–456.

Bilbro, G., Mann, R., Miller III, T., Snyder, W., Van den Bout, D.E., and White, M., Mean field annealing and neural networks, in: Advances in Neural Information Processing Systems, (Morgan–Kaufmann, San Mateo, 1989) pp.91–98.

Bienenstock, E. and Malsburg v.d., C., A neural Network for invariant pattern recognition, Europhysics Letters 4, (1987) pp.121–126.

Bizzi, E., Accornero, N., Chapple, W., and Hogan, N., Posture control and trajectory fomation during arm movements, J. Neurosci. 4, (1984) pp.2738–2744.

Bizzi, E., Polit, A., and Morasso, P., Mechanisms underlying achievement of final head position, J. Neurophysiol. 39, (1976) pp.435–444.

Blazis, D.E., Desmond, J.E., Moore, J.W., and Berthier, N.E., Simulation of the classically conditioned nictitating membrane response by a neuron–like adaptive element, a real–time variant of the Sutton–Barto model, Proc. 8th Ann. Conf. of the Cogn. Sci. Soc., (Erlbaum, Hillsdale, 1986) pp.176–186.

Bock, O. and Eckmiller, R., Goal–directed arm movements in absence of visual guidance: Evidence for amplitude rather than position control, Exp. Brain Res. 62, (1986) pp.451–458.

Bock, O., A neural network predicting posterior parietal cortex function in the control of goal–directed arm movements, Neural Networks 2, (1989) pp.351–358.

Bock, P. and Becker, G., A design tool for modeling large networks of simple parallel processors, Proc. 19th Ann. Pittsburgh Conf. on Modeling and Simulation, (1988).

Bock, P., A massively parallel architecture for collective learning systems, J. of the Latin Am. Soc. on Artificial Intelligence, (1988).

Bock, P., A perspective on artifical intelligence, learning to learn, Ann. of Operations Res. 16, (1988).

Bourlard, H. and Morgan, N., A continuous speech recognition system embedding MLP into HMM, Proc. Neural Inf. Processing Systems Conf., (Denver, 1989).

Bourlard, H. and Wellekens, C.J., Links between Markov models and multilayer perceptrons, in: Touretzky, D. and Kaufmann M. (eds.), Advances in Neural Information Processing 1, (1988) pp.502–510.

Bourlard, H. and Wellekens, C.J., Speech pattern discrimination and multilayer perceptrons, Computer, Speech and Language 3, (1989) pp.1–19.

Braitenberg, V., Charting the visual cortex, in: A. Peters and E.G. Jones (eds.), Cerebral Cortex 3, (Plenum Press, New York, London, 1985) pp.379–414.

Brooks, R.A., A robot that walks: Emergent behavior from a carefully evolved network, Neural Computation 1, (1989) pp.253–262.

Brooks, R.A., A robust layered control system for a mobile robot, IEEE J. of Robotics and Automation, RA–2, (1986) pp.14–23.

Brown, C.M. (ed.), Ballard, D.H., Becker, T.G., Gans, R.F., Martin, N.G., Olson, T.J., Potter, R.D., Rimey, R.D., Tilley, D.G., and Whitehead, S.D., The Rochester Robot, TR–257, Comp. Sci. Dept., U. Rochester, (1988)

Brown, C.M., Gaze controls with interactions and delays, to appear, IEEE Trans. on Systems, Man, and Cybernetics 20, (1990).

Brown, C.M., Prediction and cooperation in gaze control, to appear in: Biol. Cybern., (1990).

Buhmann, J., Lange, J., and Malsburg v.d., C., Distortion invariant object recognition by matching hierarchically labeled graphs, Proc. IJCNN Int. Conf. on Neural Networks, Vol.I, (Washington, 1989) pp.155–159.

Bullock, B. and Grossberg, S., Neural dynamics of planned arm movements: Emergent invariants and speed–accuracy properties during trajectory formation, in: S. Grossberg (ed.), Neural Networks and Natural Intelligence, (MIT Press, Cambridge, 1988) pp.553–622.

Bullock, D. and Grossberg, S., Adaptive neural networks for control of movement trajectories invariant under speed and force rescaling, Human Movement to appear in: Science 9, (1990).

Bullock, D. and Grossberg, S., VITE and FLETE: Neural modules for trajectory formation and postural control, in: W.A. Hershberger (ed.), Volitional Action, (Elsevier, Amsterdam, 1989) pp.253–297.

Burnod, Y., An adaptative neural network: The Cerebral Cortex, (Masson, Paris, 1988).

Caianiello, E.R. and Capocelli, R.M., On form and language: The Procuste's algorithms for feature extraction, Kybernetik 8, (1971) pp.223.

Caianiello, E.R. and Capocelli, R.M., Structural analysis of hierarchical systems, Proc. 3rd Joint Conf. Pattern Recognition, (1976).

Caianiello, E.R. and Crocchiolo, Programma procuste per l'analisi linguaggi naturali, Calcolo 2, (1965) pp.83.

Caianiello, E.R., On the analysis of natural languages, Odessa, Proc. of the 3rd All Union SSR Congress on Cybern., (1965).

Caianiello, E.R., Outline of a theory of thought processes and thinking machines, J. of Theor. Biol. 2, (1961) pp.204–235.

Caianiello, E.R., Some remarks on organization and structure, Biol. Cybern. 26, (1977) pp.151.

Caianiello, P., Neural models, structure and learning, Proc. 1st Italian Workshop on Parallel Architecture and Neural Networks, (Word Scientific, Singapore, 1988).

Caianiello, P., Learning by data compression in neural nets, Proc. 2nd Italian Workshop on Parallel Architecture and Neural Networks, (Word Scientific, Singapore, 1989).

Caminiti, R., Johnson, P.B., and Urbano, A., Making arm movements within different parts of space; dynamic aspects in the primate motor cortex, J. of Neuroscience, (1990) in press.

Canny, J.F., Finding edges and lines in images, MIT AI Lab, TR–720, (1983).

Cantoni, V. and Levialdi, S. (eds.), Pyramidal Systems for Computer Vision, (Springer, Berlin, 1986).

Carpenter, G. and Grossberg, S., ART 3 hierarchical search, chemical trans–mitters in self–organizing pattern recognition architectures, Proc. IJCNN, Vol.II, (Washington, 1990) pp.30–33.

Carpenter, G.A. and Grossberg, S., Neural dynamics of category learning and recognition: Attention, memory consolidation, and amnesia, in: J. Davis, R. Newburgh, and E. Wegmann (eds.), Brain Structure, Learning, and Memory, AAAS Symp. Series, (1987).

Chan, L.W. and Fallside, F., An adaptive training algorithm for back propagation networks, Computer Speech and Language 2, (1987) pp.205–218.

Chater, N., Learning to respond to structure in time, UC, (London, 1989).

Cheney, P.D. and Fetz, E.E., Functional classes of primate corticomotoneuronal cells and their relation to active force, J. Neurophysiol. 44, (1980) pp.773–791.

Cheney, P.D., Mewes, K., and Fetz, E.E., Encoding of motor parameters by corticomotoneuronal (CM) and rubromotoneuronal (RM) cells identified by spike–triggered averaging in the awake monkey, Behav. Brain Res. 28, (1988) pp.181–191.

Chiang, A. et al., A programmable CCD signal processor, Digest of Tech. Papers of the Int. Solid State Circuits Conf. 33, (San Francisco, 1990) p.146.

Churchland, P., Neurophilosophy, towards a unified Understanding of the Mind–Brain, (Bradford Books, MIT Press, Boston, 1985).

Coggins, J.M. and Jain, A.K., A spatial filtering approach to texture analysis, Pattern Recognition Letters 3, (1985) pp.195–203.

Coggins, J.M., Fay, F.S., and Fogarty, K.E., Development and application of a three–dimensional artificial visual system, Computer Methods and Programs in Biomedicine 22, (1986) pp.69–77.

Cohen, B., Vestibular and oculomotor physiology, Ann. N.Y. Acad. Sci. 347, (1981) p.892.

Cohen, M. and Grossberg, S., Absolute stability of global pattern formation and parallel memory storage by competitive neural networks, IEEE Trans. Systems, Man, and Cybern., SMC–13, (1983) pp.815–826.

Cole, R., Muthusamy, Y, Atlas, L., Leen, T., and Rudnick, M., Speaker–independent vowel recognition: Comparison of backpropagation and trained classification trees, in: Proc. IEEE Hawaii Int. Conf. on System Sciences, (1990).

Collins, T.J., Cerebral cortical parallel processing using a metric tensor, Proc. Int. Neural Network Soc. 2nd Ann. Meeting 85, (1988).

Connell, J.H., A colony architecture for an artificial creature, MIT AI Lab, TR–1152, (1989).

Cowey, A., Cortical maps and visual perception, Quart. J. Exp. Psychol. 31, (1979) pp.1–17.

Cutting, J.E., Motion parallax and visual flow: How to determine direction of locomotion, 4th Meeting, Int. Soc. for Ecological Psychology, (Hartford, 1982).

Daan, S. and Berde, C., Two coupled oscillators: Simulations of the circardian pacemaker in mammalian activity rhythms, J. Theor. Biol. 70, pp.297–313.

Daugman, J., in: J.G. Taylor and C.L.T. Mannion (eds.), New Developments in Neural Computing, (Adam Hilger, 1989) pp.233–250.

Daunicht, W. and Pellionisz, A., Spatial arrangement of the vestibular and the oculomotor system in the rat, Brain Res. 435, (1987) pp.48–56.

David, C. and Zucker, S.W., Potentials, valleys, and dynamic global coverings, TR–CIM–89–1, McGill Research Center for Intelligent Machines, (Montreal, 1989).

Debenham, R.M. and Garth, S.C.J., Investigations into the effect of numerical resolution on the performance of back propagation, Neural Networks from Models to Applications, (IDSET, Paris, 1988) pp.752–755.

Denker, J.S., Gardner, W.R., Graf, H.P., Henderson, D., Howard, R.E., Hubbard, W., Jackel, L.D., Baird, H.S., and Guyon, I., Neural network recognizer for handwritten zip code digits, in: D.S. Touretzky (ed.), Advances in Neural Information Processing Systems 1, (Morgan Kaufmann, San Mateo, 1989) pp.323–331.

Desimone, R. and Gross, C.G., Visual areas in the temporal lobe of the macaque, Brain Res. 178, (1979) pp.363–380.

Desimone, R., Schein, S., Moran, J., and Ungerleider, L., Contour, colour, and shape analysis beyond the striate cortex, Vision Res. 25, (1985) pp.441–452.

Dobbins, A., Zucker, S.W., and Cynader, M.S., Endstopping and curvature, Vision Research 29, (1989) pp.1371–1387.

Dobbins, A., Zucker, S.W., and Cynader, M.S., Endstopping in the visual cortex as a substrate for calculating curvature, Nature 329, (1987) pp.438–441.

Doman, D., Bock, O., and Eckmiller, R., Interaction of visual and non–visual signals in the initiation of smooth pursuit eye movements in primates, Behav. Brain Res. 32, (1989) pp.95–99.

Dowling, J., The Retina, an Approachable Part of the Brain, (Harvard Univ. Press, Cambridge, 1987).

Duncan, R., A survey of parallel computer architectures, IEEE Computer 23, (1990) pp.5–17.

Duranton, M. and Sirat, J.A., Learning on VLSI, a general–purpose digital neurochip, Proc. IJCNN, Vol.II, (Washington, 1989) pp.613.

Eccles, J.C., The cerebral neocortex: A theory of its operation, in: E.G. Jones and A. Peters (eds.), Cerebral Cortex 2, Functional Properties of Cortical Cells, (Plenum Press, New York, 1984) pp.1–36.

Eckmiller, R. and Malsburg v.d., C., Neural Computers, (Springer, Heidelberg, 1988, 1989).

Eckmiller, R., Beckmann, J., Werntges, H., and Lades, M., Neural kinematics net for a redundant robot arm, Proc. IJCNN, Vol.II, (1989) pp.333–339.

Eckmiller, R., Concerning the emerging role of geometry in neuroinformatics, in: R. Eckmiller, G. Hartmann, and G. Hauske (eds.), Parallel Processing in Neural Systems and Computers, (Elsevier, North Holland, Amsterdam, 1990) pp.5–8.

Eckmiller, R., Internal representation of space in neural networks of primates and other sensorimotor mapping machines, Proc. IJCNN, Vol.I, (Washington, 1990) pp.165–168.

Eckmiller, R., Neural nets for sensory and motor trajectories, IEEE Control Systems Magazine 9, (1989) pp.53–60.

Eckmiller, R., Neural networks for generation of eye and arm movement trajectories, in: M. Ito (ed.), Neural Programming, (Karger, Basel, 1989) pp.173–187.

Eckmiller, R., The design of intelligent robots as a federation of geometrical machines, in: S. Zornetzer, J. Davis, and C. Lau (eds.), An Introduction to Neural and Electronic Networks, (Academic Press, Orlando, 1990) pp.109–128.

Elman, J.L., Finding structure in time, CLR Tech. Report 8801, (UC San Diego, 1988).

Erkelens, C.J. and Collewijn, H., Eye movements and stereopsis during dichoptic viewing of moving random–dot stereograms, Vision Res. 25, (1985) pp.1689–1700.

Fahlman, S., Faster–learning variations on back–propagation: An empirical study, Proc. Connec. Models Summer School, (Carnegie–Mellon Univ., 1988).

Feldman, A.G., Functional tuning of the nervous system with control of movement of maintenance of a steady posture, Biophysics 11, (1966) pp.565–578.

Feldman, A.G., Once more on the equilibrium–point hypothesis (λ–model) for motor control, J. of Motor Behav. 18, (1986) pp.17–54.

Fernandez, C. and Goldberg, J.M., Physiology of peripheral neurons innervating otolith organs of the squirrel monkey, I. Response to static tilts and to long duration centrifugal force, J. Neurophysiol. 39, (1976) pp.970–984.

Ferster, D. and Koch, C., TINS–10, (1987) pp.487–492.

Fetz, E.E., Cheney, P.D., Mewes, K., and Palmer, S., Control of forelimb muscle activity by populations of corticomotoneuronal and rubromoto–neuronal cells, in: J.A.H. Allum and M. Hulliger (eds.), Peripheral Control of Posture and Locomotion, Progress in Brain Research 80, (1990) pp.437–449.

Fetz, E.E., Shupe, L.E., and Murthy, V.N., Neural networks controlling wrist movements, Proc. IJCNN, (San Diego, 1990) in press.

Flash, T. and Hogan, N., The coordination of arm movements: An experimentally confirmed mathematical model, J. Neurosci. 5, (1985) pp.1688–1703.

Flynn A.M., Brooks, R.A., and Tavrow, L.S., Twilight zones and cornerstones: A gnat robot double feature, (MIT AI Memo 1126, 1989).

Foldiak, P., Adaptive network for optimal linear feature extraction, Proc. IJCNN, Vol.I, (Washington, 1989) pp.401–405.

Freeman, R., User–programmable gate arrays, IEEE Spectrum, (1988) pp.32–35.

Freeman, W., Simulation of chaotic EEG patterns with a dynamic model of the olfactory system, Biol. Cybern., (1987).

French, A.S. and Stein, R.B., A flexible neural analog using integrated circuits, IEEE Trans. Biomed. Eng. 17, (1970) pp.248–253.

Fukushima, K. and Miyake, S., Neocognitron, a new algorithm for pattern recognition tolerant of deformations and shifts in position, Pattern Recognition 15, (1982) pp.455–469.

Fukushima, K. and Wake, N., Handwritten alphanumeric character recognition by the neocognitron, to appear in: Neural Networks, (1990).

Fukushima, K., Miyake, S., Ito, T., and Kouno, T., Handwritten numeral recognition by the algorithm of the neocognitron – an experimental system using a microcomputer, Trans. Inf. Processing Society of Japan 28, (1987) pp.627–635.

Fukushima, K., Neocognitron, a hierarchical neural network capable of visual pattern recognition, Neural Networks 1, (1988) pp.119–130.

Fukushima, K., Neocognitron, a self–organizing neural network model for a mechanism of pattern recognition unaffected by shift in position, Biol. Cybern. 36, (1980) pp.193–202.

Fukushima, K., Neural network model for selective attention in visual pattern recognition and associative recall, Applied Optics 26, (1987) pp.4985–4992.

Gaál, G., Non–orthogonal hormonal coordinate axes calculated from correlation matrices according to tensor network theory, Neurosci. 22, Suppl. 146, (1987).

Gaines, B., Uncertainty as a foundation of computational power in neural networks, Proc. IEEE 1st Int. Conf. on Neural Networks, Vol.III, (San Diego, 1987) pp.51–57.

Gardner, E. The space of interactions in neural network models, J. of Physics A, (1988) pp.257–270.

Gardner, E. and Derrida, B., Optimal storage properties of neural network models, J. of Physics A, (1988) pp.271–284.

Garth, S.C.J., A dedicated computer for simulation of large systems of neural networks, in: R. Eckmiller and C. v.c. Malsburg (eds.), Neural Computers, (Springer, Heidelberg, 1988, 1989) pp.435–444.

Gelperin, A., Hopfield, J.J., and Tank, D.W., The logic of Limax learning, in: A. Selverston (ed.), Model Neural Networks and Behavior, (Plenum Press, New York, 1985) pp.237–261.

Georgopoulos, A.P., Coding of the direction of reaching by neural populations, Proc. IJCNN, Vol.I, (Washington, 1990) p.169.

Georgopoulos, A.P., Neural integration of movement: Role of motor cortex in reaching, Faseb Journal 2, (1988) pp.2849–2857.

Georgopoulos, A.P., On reaching, Ann. Rev. Neurosci. 9, (1986) pp.147–170.

Georgopoulos, A.P., Schwarz, A.B., Kettner, R.E., Neuronal population coding of a movement direction, Science 233, (1986) pp.1416–1419.

Gersho, A., On the structure of vector quantizers, IEEE Trans. Inform. Theory 28, (1982) pp.157–166.

Gertner, I. and Tolimieri, R., A group theoretic approach to image representation, to appear in: J. Visual Communication and Image Representation, (1990).

Gielen, C.C.A.M. and Van Zuylen E.J., Coordination of arm muscles during flexion and supination: Application of the tensor analysis approach, Neurosci. 17, (1986) pp.527–539.

Ginosar, R. and Telishevski, R., Intelligent scan image processors, Techn. Report, Dept. of Electrical Engineering, Technion, Haifa, (1988).

Ginosar, R., Zeevi, Y.Y., and Hilsenrath, O.A., Adaptive sensitivity/intelligent scan imaging sensor chips, Proc. SPIE Vis. Comm. Image Proc., (Cambridge, MA, 1988).

Gluck, M.A. and Thompson, R.F., Modeling the neural substrates of associative learning and memory: A computational approach, Psychol. Rev. 94, (1987) pp.176–191.

Goerke, N., Schöne, M., Kreimeier, B., and Eckmiller, R., A network with pulse processing neurons for generation of arbitrary temporal sequences, Proc. IJCNN, Vol.III, (San Diego, 1990) pp.315–320.

Görke, W., Kazmierczak, H., and Wagner, S.W., Anwendungen der Lernmatrix, in: H. Billing (ed.), Lernende Automaten, (R. Oldenbourg, München, 1961).

Goldberg, J.M. and Fernandez, C., Responses of peripheral neurons to angular and linear accelerations in the squirrel monkey, Acta Otolaryngol. 80, (1975) pp.101–110.

Golubitsky, M. and Schaeffer, D., Singularities and Groups in Bifurcation Theory 1, (Springer, Berlin, 1984).

Graf, H.P., A reconfigurable CMOS neural network, Digest of Tech. Papers of the Int. Solid State Circuits Conf. 33, (San Francisco, 1990) p.144.

Granger, R., Ambros–Ingerson, J., Staubli, U., and Lynch, G., Memorial operation of multiple, interacting simulated brain structures, in: M. Gluck and D. Rumelhart (eds.), Neuroscience and Connectionist Models, (Erlbaum Associates, 1989).

Granger, R., Whitson, J.W., and Lynch, G., Asymmetry in cortical networks enhances hierarchical clustering, Biol. Cybern., (1989).

Gray, C.M., König, P., Engel, A.K., and Singer, W., Oscillatory responses in cat visual cortex exhibit inter–columnar synchronization which reflects global stimulus properties, Nature 338, (1989) pp.334–337.

Gross, C.G., Inferotemporal cortex and vision, Progr. Physiol. Psychol. 5, (1973) pp.77–123.

Grossberg, S. and Carpenter, G., A massively parallel architecture for a self–organizing neural pattern recognition machine, Computer Vision, Graphics, and Image Processing 37, (1987) pp.54–115.

Grossberg, S. and Carpenter, G., ART 2: Self–organization of stable category recognition codes for analog input patterns, Applied Optics 26, (1987) pp.4919–4936.

Grossberg, S. and Kuperstein, M., Neural Dynamics of Adaptive Sensory Motor Control, (Pergamon Press, New York, 1989) expanded edition.

Grossberg, S., Adaptive pattern classification and universal recoding, Vol.II: Feedback expectation, olfaction, and illusions, Biol. Cybern. 23, (1976) pp.187–202.

Grossberg, S., Contour enhancement, short–term memory, and constancies in reverberating neural networks, Studies in Applied Mathematics 52, (1973) pp.217–257.

Grossberg, S., Pavlovian pattern learning by nonlinear neural networks, Proc. Nat. Acad. of Sci. USA 68, (1971) pp.828–831.

Grossberg, S., Studies of Mind and Brain, (Reidel, Boston, 1982).

Grossberg, S., The Adaptive Brain, Vol.1+2, (North–Holland, New York, 1987).

Hakala, J., Steiner, R., and Eckmiller, R., Quasi–local solution for inverse kinematics of a redundant robot arm, Proc. IJCNN, Vol.III, (San Diego, 1990) pp.321–326.

Harris, J. et al., Resistive fuses, analog hardware for detecting discontinuities in early vision, in: C. Mead and M. Ismail (eds.), Analog VLSI Implementation of Neural Systems, (Kluwer Academic Publ., 1989) pp.27–56.

Harth, E., Csermely, T.H., Beek, B., and Lindsay, R.D., Brain Functions and Neural Dynamics, J. Theoret. Biol. 26, (1970) pp.93–120.

Hasler, P. and Akers, L.A., VLSI neural circuits and systems, Proc. 9th Ann. Int. Phoenix Conf. on Computers and Communications, (1990).

Hasselmo, M.E., Rolls, E.T., and Baylis, G.C., The role of expression and identity in the face–selective responses of neurons in the temporal visual cortex of the monkey, Behav. Brain Res. 32, (1989) pp.203–218.

Hasselmo, M.E., Rolls, E.T., Baylis, G.C., and Nalwa, V., Object–centered encoding by face–selective neurons in the cortex in the superior temporal sulcus of the monkey, Exp. Brain Res. 75, (1989) pp.417–429.

Hatze, H., Myocybernetic control models of skeletal muscle, characteristics and applications, University of South Africa, Pretoria, (1981).

Hebb, D.O., The Organization of the Behavior, a Neurophsychological Theory, (John Wiley & Sons, New York, 1949).

Hecht–Nielsen, R., Theory of the backpropagation neural network, Proc. IJCNN, Vol.I, (Washington, 1989) pp.593–611.

Hecht–Nielsen,R., TRW Inc. Internal Technical Report, (1987).

Heinke, D., Giannakopoulos, F., and Best, J., The thalamo–cortical feedback–system: a nonlinear network model for binocular interaction, in: R. Eckmiller, G. Hartmann, and G. Hauske (eds.), Parallel Processing in Neural Systems and Computers, (Elsevier, North Holland, Amsterdam, 1990) pp.113–116.

Held, R. and Bauer, J.A., Development of sensorially–guided reaching in infant monkeys, Brain Research 71, (1974) pp.265–271.

Henn, W. and Cohen, B., Proc. Symp. of Barany Soc., Representation of 3–dimensional space in the vestibular, oculomotor and visual systems, (Bologna, 1988).

Henneman, E., The size–principle: A deterministic output emerges from a set of probabilistic connections, J. of Exp. Biol. 115, (1985) pp.105–112.

Hinton, G.E., Sejnowski, T.J., and Ackley, D.H., Boltzmann machines: Constraint satisfaction networks that learn, Tech. Report CMU–CS–84–119, Pittsburgh, Carnegie–Mellon University, Computer Science Department, (1984).

Hönerloh, H.J. and Kraft, H., Technische Verwirklichung der Lernmatrix, in: H. Billing (ed.), Lernende Automaten, (R. Oldenbourg, München, 1961).

Hogan, N., An organizing principle for a class of voluntary movements, J. Neuroscience 4, (1984) pp.2745–2754.

Holler, M., Tam, S., Castro, H., and Benson, R., An electrically trainable artificial neural network (ETANN) with 10,240 floating gate synapses, in: Proc. IJCNN, Vol.II, (Washington, 1989) pp.191.

Hopfield, J.J. and Tank, D.W., Computing with neural circuits: A model, Science 233, (1986) pp.625–633.

Hopfield, J.J. and Tank, D.W., Neural computation of decisions in optimization problems, Biol. Cybern. 52, (1985) pp.141–152.

Hopfield, J.J., Neural networks and physical systems with emergent collective computational abilities, Proc. Nat. Acad. Sci. USA 79, (1982) pp.2554–2558.

Hopfield, J.J., Neurons with graded response have collective computational properties like those of two state neurons, Proc. Nat. Acad. Sci. USA 81, (1984) pp.3088–3092.

Horner, H., Neural networks with low levels of activity, Ising vs. McCulloch–Pitts neurons, Z. Phys. B., (1988) pp.1–10.

Horswill, I.D. and Brooks, R.A., Situated vision in a dynamic world: Chasing objects, AAAI–88, (St Paul, MN, 1988) pp.796–800.

Houk, J.C. and Gibson, A.R., Sensorimotor processing through the cerebellum, in: J.S. King (ed.), New Concepts in Cerebellar Neurobiology, (Alan Liss Inc., 1987) pp.387–416.

Hounsgaard, J., Hultborn, H., and Kiehn, O., Transmitter–controlled properties of α–motoneurones causing long–lasting motor discharge to brief excitatory inputs, Prog. in Brain Res. 64, (1986) pp.31–50.

Hubel, D.H. and Wiesel,T.N., Receptive fields of single neurons in the cat's striate cortex, J. Physiol. 148, (1959) pp.574–591.

Hubel, D.H., Eye, Brain, and Vision, Scientific American Library, (New York, 1988).

Hummel, R. and Zucker, S.W., On the foundations of relaxation labelling processes, IEEE Trans. PAMI–5, (1983) pp.267–287.

Humphrey, D.R. and Reed, D.J., Separate cortical systems for control of joint movement and joint stiffness: Reciprocal activation and coactivation of antagonist muscles, in: J.E. Desmedt (ed.), Motor Control Mechanisms in Health and Disease, (Raven Press, New York, 1983) pp.347–372.

Hwang, Y.K., Robot path planning using potential field representation, Thesis, Univ. of Illinois at Urbana–Champaign, (1988).

Ito, M., The Cerebellum and Neural Control, (Raven Press, New York, 1984).

Ito, T., Fukushima, K., and Miyake, S., Realization of a neural network model neocognitron on a hypercube parallel computer, to appear in: Int. J. of High Speed Computing, (1990).

Iwamida, H., Katagiri, S., McDermott, E., and Tohkura, Y., A hybrid speech recognition system using HMMs with and LVQ–trained codebook, ATR Tech. Report TR–A–0061, (ATR Auditory and Visual Perception Research Laboratories, Japan, 1989).

Jacobs, R., Increased rates of convergence through learning rate adaptation, Neural Networks 1, (1988).

Jelinek, F., Continuous speech recognition by statistical methods, Proc. IEEE 64, (1976) pp.532–555.

Johnson, K., Daniell, C., and Burman, J., Feature extraction in the Neocognitron, Proc. IEEE, Vol.II, (1988) pp.117–127.

Jones, J.P. and Palmer, L.A., An evaluation of the two–dimensional Gabor filter model of simple receptive fields in cat striate cortex, J. Neurophysiol. 58, (1987) pp.1233–1258.

Jones, J.P. and Palmer, L.A., The two–dimensional spatial structure of simple receptive fields in cat striate cortex, J. Neurophysiol. 58, (1987) pp.1187–1211.

Jordan, M.I., Supervised learning and systems with excess degrees of freedom, COINS 88–27, Techn. Rep. MIT, (1988) pp.1–41.

Jordan, M.L., Serial order: A parallel distributed processing approach, UCSD, Tech. Report 8604, (1986).

Juang, B.H. and Rabiner, L.R., Mixture autoregressive hidden Markov models for speech signals, IEEE Trans. ASSP–33, (1985) pp.1404–1412.

Julesz, B., Toward an axiomatic theory of preattentive vision, in: G. Edelman, M. Cowan, and E. Gall (eds.), Dynamic Aspects of Neocortical Function, (John Wiley & Son, New York, 1984).

Kahan, S., Pavlidis, T., and Baird, H.S., On the recognition of printed characters of any font or size, IEEE Trans. PAMI–9, (1987) pp.274–288.

Kangas, J., Kohonen, T., and Laaksonen, J., Variants of self–organizing maps, IEEE Trans. on Neural Networks 1, (1990) pp.93–99.

Kangas, J., Kohonen, T., Laaksonen, J., Simula, O., and Ventä, O., Variants of self–organizing maps, Proc. IJCNN, Vol.II, (Washington, 1989) pp.517–522.

Kano, M., Kawato, M., and Suzuki, R., Acquisition of inverse–kinematics and inverse–dynamics model of redundant arm by feedback error learning, Jpn IEICE Tech. Report MBE88–171, (1989) pp.91–96, in Japanese.

Kass, M., Witkin, A., and Terzopoulos, D., SNAKES, active contour models, Int. J. Computer Vision 1, (1988) pp.321–332.

Katayama, M. and Kawato, M., Learning control of a redundant controlled–object by feedback error learning, Jpn IEICE Tech. Report MBE89–76, (1989) pp.83–90, in Japanese.

Kato, H. et al., A parallel neurocomputer architecture towards billion connection updates per second, Proc. IJCNN, Vol.II, (Washington DC, 1990) pp.47–50.

Kawato, M., Furukawa, K., and Suzuki, R., A hierarchical neural–network model for control and learning of voluntary movement, Biol. Cybern. 57, (1987) pp.169–185.

Kawato, M., Uno, Y., Isobe, M., and Suzuki, R., Hierarchical neural network model for voluntary movement with application to robotics, IEEE Control Systems Magazine 8, (1988) pp.547–561.

Kesten, H., Accelerated stochastic approximation, Ann. of Mathematical Statistics 29, (1957) pp.41–59.

Khatib, O., Real time obstacle avoidance for manipulators and mobile robots, Int. J. Robotics Res. 5, (1986) pp.90–98.

Klar, H. and Ramacher, U. (eds.), Microelectronics for Artificial Neural Nets, (VDI–Verlag, Düsseldorf, 1989).

Klopf, A.H. and Morgan, J.S., The role of time in natural intelligence: Implications of classical and instrumental conditioning for neuronal and neural network modeling, in: M. Gabriel and J. Moore (eds.), Learning and Computational Neuroscience, (MIT Press, Cambridge, MA, 1990) in press.

Klopf, A.H., A drive–reinforcement model of single neuron function: An alternative to the Hebbian neuronal model, in: J.S. Denker (ed.), Neural Networks for Computing, (American Inst. of Physics, New York, 1986) pp.265–270.

Klopf, A.H., A neuronal model of classical conditioning, Psychobiology 16, (1988) pp.85–125.

Klopf, A.H., Brain function and adaptive systems – a heterostatic theory, Report 133 (AFCRL–72–0164), L.G. Hanscom Field, Bedford: Air Force Cambridge Research Laboratories, (1972), DTIC Report AD 742259.

Klopf, A.H., Drive–reinforcement learning, a real–time learning mechanism for unsupervised learning, Proc. IEEE 1st Int. Conf. on Neural Networks, (San Diego, 1987) pp.21–24.

Klopf, A.H., The hedonistic neuron: A theory of memory, learning, and intelligence, Hemisphere, (Washington, 1982).

Koch, J.C., Poggio, T., and Torre, V., Trends in Neurosciences 7, (1986) pp.204–211.

Koenderink, J.J. and Richards, W., Two–dimensional curvature operators, J. Opt. Soc. Am. A5, (1988) pp.1136–1141.

Koenderink, J.J. and Van Doorn, A.J., Representation of local geometry in the visual system, Biol. Cybern. 55, (1987) pp.367–375.

Koenderink, J.J., Operational significance of receptive field assemblies, Biol. Cybern. 58, (1988) pp.163–171.

Koenderink, J.J., The structure of images, Biol. Cybern. 50, (1984) pp.363–370.

Kohonen, T., An introduction to neural computing, Neural Networks 1, (1988) pp.3–16.

Kohonen, T., Barna, G., and Chrisley, R., Statistical pattern recognition with neural networks: Benchmarking studies, Proc. IEEE Int. Conf. on Neural Networks, Vol.I, (San Diego, 1988) pp.61–68.

Kohonen, T., Learning vector quantization for pattern recognition, Report TKK–F–A601, Helsinki University of Technology, Dept. of Tech. Physics, Lab. of Computer and Infomation Science, (1986).

Kohonen, T., Learning vector quantization, Neural Networks 1, Suppl. 1, (1988) p.303.

Kohonen, T., Mäkisara, K., and Saramäki, T., Phonotopic maps – insightful representation of phonological features for speech recognition, Proc. 7th Int. Conf. on Pattern Recognition, (Montreal, 1984) pp.182–185.

Kohonen, T., Self–Organization and Associative Memory, (Springer, Heidelberg, Berlin, 1984, 1988 2nd edition, 1989 3rd edition).

Kohonen, T., Self–organized formation of topologically correct feature maps, Biol. Cybern. 43, (1982) pp.56–69.

Kohonen, T., The 'neural' phonetic typewriter, Computer 21, (1988) pp.11–22.

Kosko, B., Differential Hebbian learning, in: J.S. Denker (ed.), Neural Networks for Computing, (American Inst. of Physics, New York, 1986) pp.277–282.

Kraft, T., Artificial neural systems – technology of today, Proc. 'Neural Computing – the Marketplace' IBC Technical Services Ltd., (London, 1990).

Kravitz, E.A., Hormonal control of behavior: Amines and the biasing of behavioral output in lobsters, Science 241, (1988) pp.1775–1781.

Kronauer, R.E. and Zeevi, Y.Y., Reorganization and diversification of signals in vision, IEEE Trans. SMC–15, (1985) pp.91–101.

Kuffler, S.W., Neurons in the retina: Organization, inhibition and excitation problems, Cold Spring Harbor Symp. on Quant. Biol. 17, (1952) pp.281–292.

Kung, S.Y. and Hwang, J.N., Parallel architectures for artificial neural nets, IEEE Int. Conf. on Neural Networks, Vol.II, (San Diego, 1988).

Kuperstein, M., An adaptive neural model for mapping invariant target position, Behav. Neurosci. 102, (1988) pp.148–162.

Kuperstein, M., Neural network model for adaptive hand–eye coordination for single postures, Science 239, (1988) pp.1308–1311.

Lakshmivarahan, S., Learning algorithms theory and applications, (Springer, Heidelberg, New York, 1981).

Lange, T.E. and Dyer, M.G., High–level inferencing in a connectionist network, Connection Science 1, (1989) pp.181–216.

Lauria, F.E., A connectionist approach to knowledge acquisition, Cybern. and Syst. 19, (1988) pp.35–88.

Lauria, F.E., A cybernetic approach to the Hebb rule implementation in a McCulloch and Pitts network, in: R. Trappl (ed.), Cybern. and Syst., (World Scientific, Singapore, 1990) in print.

Lauria, F.E., A general purpose neural network as a new computing paradigm, in: E.R. Caianiello (ed.), 2nd Italien Workshop on Parallel Architectures and Neural Networks, (World Scientific, Singapore, 1990) in print.

Lauria, F.E., An universal, loops free, digital neural network, in: E.R. Caianiello (ed.), 1st Italien Workshop on Parallel Architectures and Neural Networks, (World Scientific, Singapore, 1989) pp.274–308.

Lauria, F.E., Learning as the high level language for a neural network, in: R. Trappl (ed.), Cybern. and Syst., (Kluwer Acad. Pub., Dordrecht, 1988) pp.383–390.

Lauria, F.E., Learning implementation on a deterministic general purpose network, Neural Networks 1, (1988) p.548.

Lauria, F.E., On a learning neural network, in: L.M. Ricciardi (ed.), Biomathematics and Related Computational Problems, (Kluwer Acad. Pub., Dordrecht, 1988) pp.483–496.

Le Cun, Y., Boser, B., Denker, J.S., Henderon, D., Howard, R.E., Hubbard, W., and Jackel, L.D., Handwritten digit recognition with a backpropagation network, in: D.S. Touretzky (ed.), Advances in Neural Information Processing Systems 2, (Morgan Kaufmann, San Mateo, 1990).

Le Cun, Y., Boser, B., Denker, J.S., Henderson, D., Howard, R.E., Hubbard, W., and Jackel, L.D., Back–propagation applied to handwritten zipcode recognition, to appear in: Neural Computation 4, (1990).

Le Cun, Y., Denker, J.S., and Solla, S.A., Optimal brain damage, to appear in: D.S. Touretzky (ed.), Advances in Neural Information Processing Systems 2, (Morgan Kaufman, San Mateo, CA, 1990).

Le Cun, Y., Generalization and network design strategies, in: R. Pfeifer, Z. Schreter, F. Fogelman–Soulié, and L. Steels (eds.), Connectionism in Perspective, (Elsevier, North Holland, Amsterdam, New York, 1989) pp.143–155.

Le Cun, Y., Learning in an asymmetric–threshold network, in: E. Bienenstock, F. Fogelmann–Souli, and G. Weisbuch (eds.), Disordered Systems and Biological Organization, (Springer, Berlin, 1986).

Le Cun, Y., Une procedure d'apprentissage pour reseau a seuil asymetrique (A learning procedure for an asymmetric threshold network), Proc. Cognitiva, (1985) pp.559–604.

Leen, T., Rudnick, M., and Hammerstrom, D., Hebbian feature discovery improves classifier efficiency, Proc. IJCNN, Vol.??, (Washington, 1990) pp.???–???.

Lemon, R., The output map of the primate motor cortex, TINS–11, (1988) pp.501–506.

Leonard, C.M., Rolls, E.T., Wilson, F.A.W., and Baylis, G.C., Neurons in the amygdala of the monkey with responses selective for faces, Behav. Brain Res. 15, (1985) pp.159–176.

Levin, E., Speech recognition using hidden control neural network architecture, Proc. IEEE Int. Conf. on ASSP, (New Mexico, 1990).

Li, D. and Wee, W., A new Neocognitron structure modified by ART and backpropagation, Proc. IJCNN, Vol.I, (Washington, 1990) pp.420–423.

Libet, B., Wright, E.W., Feinstein, B., and Pearl, D.K., Subjective referral of the timing for a conscious sensory experience: A functional role for the somatosensory specific projection system in man, Brain 102, (1979) pp.193–224.

Linsker, R., Self–organization in a perceptual network, IEEE Computer 21, (1988) pp.105–117.

Lippmann, R.P. and Gold, B., Neural classifiers useful for speech recognition, Proc. 1st IJCNN, Vol.IV, (San Diego, 1987) p.417.

Lippmann, R.P., An introduction to computing with neural nets, IEEE ASSP Magazine 3, (1987) pp.4–22.

Ljung, L., Analysis of recursive stochastic algorithms, IEEE Trans. Automatic Control 22, (1977) pp.551–575.

Llinás, R., Neurobiology of cerebellar evolution and development, Am. Med. Assoc. Chicago, (1969).

Lyon, R.F. and Mead, C., An analog electronic cochlea, IEEE Trans. on Acoustics, Speech and Signal Processing 36, (1988).

Mackie, S., Implementation of neural network models in silicon, in: R. Eckmiller and C. v.d. Malsburg (eds.), Neural Computers, (Springer, Heidelberg, 1987, 1988, 1989) pp.467–477.

MacLane, S. and Birkhoff, G., Algebra, (Macmillan, New York, 1967).

Maes, P., The dynamics of action selection, IJCAI–89, (Detroit, 1989) pp.991–997.

Maher, M., DeWeerth, S., Mahawold, M., and Mead, C., Implementing neural architectures using analog VLSI circuits, IEEE Trans. on Circuits and Systems 36, (1989) pp.643–652.

Makhoul, J., Roucos, S., and Gish, H., Vector quantization in speech coding, Proc. IEEE 73, (1985) pp.1551–1588.

Makhoul, J., Schwartz, R. and El Jaroudi, A., Classification, capabilities of two–layer neural networks, Proc. ICASSP–89, (Glasgow, Scotland, 1989) pp.635–638.

Mallat, S., A theory for multiresolution signal decomposition: The wavelet representation, IEEE Trans. PAMI–11, (1989) pp.674–693.

Mallot, H.A. and Giefing, G.–J., Retinal sampling grids and space–variant image compression, in: R. Eckmiller, G. Hartmann, and G. Hauske (eds.), Parallel Processing in Neural Systems and Computers, (Elsevier, Amsterdam, 1990) pp. 125–128.

Mallot, H.A., Schulten, E., and Storjohann, K., Neural network strategies for robot navigation, in: L. Personnaz and G. Dreyfus (eds.), Neural Networks: From Models to Application, (IDSET, Paris, 1989) pp.560–569.

Mallot, H.A., v. Seelen, W., and Giannakopoulos, F., Neural mapping and space–variant image processing, Neural Networks, (1990) in press.

Malsburg v.d., C. and Bienenstock, E., Statistical coding and short–term synaptic plasticity: A scheme for knowledge representation in the brain, in: E. Bienenstock, F. Fogelman, and G. Weis (eds.), Disordered Systems and Biological Organization, (Springer, Berlin, Heidelberg, 1986) pp.247–272.

Malsburg v.d., C. and Bienenstock, E., A neural network for the retrieval of superimposed connection patterns, Europhysics Letters 3, (1987) pp.1243–1249.

Malsburg v.d., C. and Singer, W., Principles of cortical network organization, in: P. Rakic and W. Singer (eds.), Neurobiology of Neocortex, (Wiley, 1988) pp.69–99.

Malsburg v.d., C., Self–organization of orientation sensitive cells in the striate cortex, Kybernetik 14, (1973) pp.85–100.

Malsburg v.d., C., How are nervous structures organized?, in: E. Başar, H. Flohr, H. Haken, and A.J. Mandell (eds.), Synergetics of the Brain, (Springer, Heidelberg, 1983) pp.238–249.

Malsburg v.d., C., Nervous structures with dynamical links, Ber. Bunsenges. Phys. Chem. 89, (1985) pp.703–710.

Malsburg v.d., C., Am I thinking assemblies ?, in: G. Palm and A. Aertsen (eds.), Brain Theory, (1984), (Springer, Berlin, Heidelberg, 1986).

Malsburg v.d., C., Goal and architecture of neural computers, in: R. Eckmiller and C. v.d. Malsburg (eds.), Neural Computers, (Springer, Berlin, 1988) pp.23–28.

Malsburg v.d., C., Pattern recognition by labeled graph matching, Neural Networks 1, (1988) pp.141–148.

Malsburg v.d., C., A neural architecture for the representation of sciences, in: J.L. McGaugh, N.M. Weinberger, and G. Lynch (eds.), Brain Organization and Memory: Cells, Systems and Circuits, (Oxford Univ. Press, New York, 1990).

Marr, D., A computational investigation into the human representation and processing of visual information, in: Vision, (W.H. Freeman, San Francisco, 1982).

Martin, K.A.C., Neuronal circuits in cat striate cortex, in: E.G. Jones and A. Peters (eds.), The Cerebral Cortex 2, Functional properties of cortical cells, Ch.9, (Plenum Press, New York, 1984) pp.241–285.

Martinetz, T., Ritter, H., and Schulten, K., Three–dimensional neural net for learning visuomotor coordination of a robot arm, IEEE Trans. on Neural Networks 1, (1990) pp.131–138.

Martinetz, T., Ritter, H., and Schulten, K., Learning of visuomotor coordination of a robot arm with redundant degrees of freedom, in: R. Eckmiller, G. Hartmann, and G. Hauske (eds.), Parallel Processing in Neural Systems and Computers, (Elsevier, Amsterdam, 1990) pp.431–434.

Massone, L. and Bizzi, E., A neural network model for limb trajectory formation, Biol. Cybern. 61, (1989) pp.417–425.

Massone, L., and Bizzi, E., On the role of input representations in sensorimotor mapping, Proc. IJCNN, Vol.I, (Washington, 1990) pp.173–176.

Mataric, M.J., Environment learning using a distributed representation, Proc. IEEE Int. Conf. Robotics and Automation, (Cincinnati, 1990).

Maunsell, J. and Newsome, W., Visual processing in monkey extrastriate cortex, Ann. Rev. Neuroscience 10, (1987) pp.363–401.

Max, J., Quantizing for minimum distortion, IRE Trans. Inform. Theory 6, (1960) pp.7–12.

May, N. and Hammerstrom, D., Fltsim detailed description and operation, Tech. Report CS/E–88–021, (Oregon Graduate Inst., 1988).

McCulloch, W.S. and Pitts, W., A logical calculus of the ideas immanent in nervous activity, Bull. Math. Biophys. 5, (1943) pp.115–133.

McDermott, E. and Katagiri, S., Shift–invariant, multi–category phoneme recognition using Kohonen's LVQ2, Proc. Int. Conf. Acoust., Speech, Signal Processing, (Glasgow, 1989) pp.81–84.

Mead, C.A., Analog VLSI and Neural Systems, (Addison–Wesley, Reading Mass., 1989).

Mead, C.A. et al., VLSI–architectures for implementation of neural networks, in: J. Denker (ed.), Neural Networks for Computing, (AIP, New York, 1986).

Mel, B.W., Building and using mental models in a sensory–motor domain: A connectionist Approach, Proc. of 5th Int. Conf. on Machine Learning, Ann Arbor, (Morgan Kaufmann, San Mateo, 1988) pp.207–213.

Minsky, M.L. and Papert, S.A., Perceptrons, an Introduction to Computational Geometry, (MIT Press, Cambridge, MA, 1988) expanded edition.

Mishkin, M., A memory system in the monkey, Phil. Trans. Roy. Soc. London, Ser.B 298, (1982) pp.85–95.

Moran, J. and Desimone, R., Selective attention gates visual processing in the extrastriate cortex, Science 229, (1985) pp.782–784.

Morasso, P., Mussa Ivaldi, F.A., Vercelli, G., and Zaccaria, R., in: Pfeiffer, Schreter, Fogelman–Soulié, and Steels (eds.), Connectionism in Perspective, (Elsevier, North Holland, Amsterdam, 1989) pp.413–420.

Morgan, J.S., Patterson, E.C., and Klopf, A.H., A network of two drive–reinforcement neurons that learns a solution to a real–time dynamic control problem, Neural Networks 1, Suppl., (1988) pp.???

Mountcasle, V.B., An organizing principle for cerebral function: The unit module and the distributed system, in: F.O. Schmitt (ed.), The Mindful Brain, (MIT Press, Cambridge, MA, 1978) pp.7–50.

Mozer, M.C., A focused back–propagation algorithm for temporal pattern recognition, Toronto U., Tech. Report CRG–TR–88–3, (1988).

Murveit, H. and Brodersen, R.W., An integrated–circuit–based speech recognition system, IEEE Trans. on ASSP–34, (1986) pp.1465–1472.

Mussa Ivaldi, F.A., Morasso, P., and Zaccaria, R., Kinematic networks – a distributed model for representing and regularizing motor redundancy, Biol. Cybern. 60, (1988) pp.1–16.

Nadal, J.–P. and Toulouse, G., Information storage in sparsely–coded memory nets, Networks, to appear Computation in Neural Systems, (1990).

Nadas, A., Nahamoo, D., and Picheny, M.A., On a model–robust training method for speech recognition, IEEE Trans. on ASSP–35, (1988) pp.1432–1436.

Nakayama, K., The iconic bottleneck and the tenuous link between early visual processing and perceptron, in: C. Blakemore (ed.), Vision: Coding and Efficiency, (Cambridge Univ. Press, 1988).

Narendra, K.S. (ed.), Special issue on learning automata, J. of Cybern. and Info. Sci. 1, (1977) pp.2–4.

Nelson, J.J. and Frost, B.J., Intracortical facilitation among co–oriented, co–axially aligned simple cells in cat striate cortex, Exp. Brain Res. 61, (1985) pp.54–61.

Ney, H., The use of one–stage dynamic programming algorithm for connected word recognition, IEEE Trans. on ASSP–32, (1984) pp.263–272.

Niles, L., Silverman, H., Tajchman, G., and Bush, M., How limited training data can allow a neural network classifier to outperform an 'optimal' statistical classifier, Proc. IEEE Int. Conf. on AAAP 1, (Glasgow, Scotland, 1989) pp.17–20.

Noton, D. and Stark, L., Scanpaths in eye movements during pattern perception, Science 171, (1971) pp.308–311.

Oja, E., A simplified neuron model as a principal component analyzer, J. Math. Biol. 15, (1982) pp.267–273.

Oja, E., Neural networks, principal components, and subspaces, Int. J. of Neural Systems 1, (1989) pp.61–68.

Olshausen, B.A., A survey of visual preprocessing and shape representation techniques, RIACS Techn. Report 88.35, Res. Inst. for Advanced Computer Science, NASA Ames Research Center, (1988).

Olson, T.J. and Potter, R.D., Real–time vergence control, TR 264, Comp. Sci. Dept. U. Rochester, (1988).

Orban, G.A., Neuronal operations in the visual cortex, in: Studies of Brain Function, (Springer, Berlin, 1984).

Ott, D. and Eckmiller, R., Dynamic adaption of the blind pointing characteristic to stepwise lateral tilts of body, head, –and trunk, Behav. Brain Res. 30, (1988) pp.99–110.

Ott, L., An Introduction to Statistical Methods and Data Analysis, (Duxbury Press, 1984).

Palm, G., Local synaptic rules with maximal information storage capacity, in: H. Haken (ed.), Neural and Synergetic Computers, (Springer, Heidelberg, 1988) pp.100–110.

Palm, G., On associative memory, Biol. Cybern. 36, (1980) pp.19–31.

Palm, G., On the asymptotic information storage capacity of neural networks, in: R. Eckmiller and C. v.d. Malsburg (eds.), Neural Computers, (Springer, Heidelberg, 1988, 1989) pp.271–280.

Palmer, S.S. and Fetz, E.E., Discharge properties of primate forearm motor units during isometric muscle activity, J. of Neurophysiology 54, (1985) pp.1178–1193.

Pao, Y.H., Adaptive Pattern Recognition and Neural Networks, (Addison–Wesley, Reading Mass., 1989).

Parent, P. and Zucker, S.W., Trace inference, curvature consistency, and curve detection, IEEE Trans. on PAMI–11, (1989) pp.823–839.

Parker, D.B., Learning logic, (Invention Report 581–64, File 1, Stanford Univ., Office of Techn. Licensing, CA, 1982).

Parker, D.B., Learning–logic, (Tech. Report 47, MIT, Center for Computational Research in Economics and Management Science, MA, 1985).

Parker, D.B., Optimal algorithms for adaptive networks, second order back propagation, second order direct propagation, and second order Hebbian learing, Proc. IEEE First Int. Conf. on Neural Networks, Vol.II, (San Diego, 1987) pp.593–600.

Partridge, L.D. and Benton, L.A., Muscle, the motor, in: Handbook of Physiology: The Nervous System, Vol.II, Bethesda, Amer. Physiol. Soc., (1981) pp.43–106.

Pavlov, I.P., Conditioned Reflexes, (Oxford University Press, 1927; Dover Edition, 1960).

Peeling, S.M. and Moore, R.K., Isolated digit recognition experiments using the multi–layer perceptron, Speech Communicaton 7, (1988) pp.403–409.

Pellionisz, A. and Llinás, R., Brain modeling by tensor network theory and computer simulation, the cerebellum, distributed processor for predictive coordination, Neurosci. 4, (1979) pp.323–348.

Pellionisz, A. and Llinás, R., Tensorial approach to the geometry of brain function, cerebellar coordiation via metric tensor, Neurosci. 5, (1980) pp.1125–1136.

Pellionisz, A. and Llinás, R., Tensor network theory of the metaorganization of functional geometries in the CNS, Neurosci. 16., (1985) pp.245–274.

Pellionisz, A., Coordination: A vector–matrix description of transformations of overcomplete CNS coordinates and a tensorial solution using the Moore–Penrose generalized inverse, J. Theoret. Biol. 110, (1984) pp.353–375.

Pellionisz, A., Tensor geometry: A language of brain & neurocomputers, generalized coordinates in neuroscience & robotics, in: R. Eckmiller and C. v.d. Malsburg (eds.), Neural Computers, (Springer, Heidelberg, 1988, 1989) pp.381–391.

Penz, P. and Wiggins, R., Digital signal processor accelerators for neural network simulations, in: J.S. Denker (ed.), Neural Networks for Computing, (Amer. Inst. Physics, New York, 1986) pp.345–355.

Perrett, D.I., Rolls, E.T., and Caan, W., Visual neurons responsive to faces in the monkey temporal cortex, Exp. Brain Res. 47, (1982) pp.329–342.

Peters, A. and Jones, E.G., The cerebral cortex, Cellular Components of the Cerebral Cortex 1, (Plenum Press, New York, 1984).

Peterson, B.W., Modeling of spatial transformations in vestibular reflex systems, Proc. IJCNN, Vol.I, (Washington, 1990) pp.152–156.

Peterson, B.W., Pellionisz, A.J., Baker, J.A., and Keshner, E.A., Functional morphology and neural control of neck muscles in mammals, Am. Zoology 29, (1989) pp.139–149.

Pineda, F.J., Generalization of backpropagation to recurrent and higher order neural networks, in: D.Z. Anderson (ed.), Neural Information Processing Systems, (Am. Inst. Phys., New York, 1988) pp.602–611.

Polit, A. and Bizzi, E., Characteristics of motor programs underlying arm movements in monkeys, J. Neurophysiology 42, (1979) pp.183–190.

Pollen, D.A., Gaska, J.P., and Jacobson, L.D., Physiological constraints on models of visual cortical function, in: R. Cotterill (ed.), Models of Brain Function, (Cambridge Univ. Press, Cambridge, 1989) pp.115–135.

Pompeiano, O., Recurrent inhibition, in: R.A. Davidoff (ed.), Handbook of the Spinal Cord, Vol.2+3, Anatomy and Physiology, (Marcel Dekker, New York, 1984).

Porat, M. and Zeevi, Y.Y., The generalized Gabor scheme of image representation in vision, IEEE Trans. on PAMI–10, (1988) pp.452–468.

Powers, W.T., Behavior, the Control of Perception, (Aldine, New York, 1973).

Pylyshyn, Z.W. and Storm, R., Tracking multiple independent targets: Evidence for parallel tracking mechanism, Spatial Vision 3, (1988) pp.179–197.

Rajapakse, J., Jakubowicz, O., and Acharya, R., A real time ART 1 based vision system for distortion invariant recognition and autoassociation, Proc. IJCNN, Vol.II, (Washington, 1990) pp.298–301.

Ramacher, U. and Beichter, J., Architecture of a systolic neuro–emulator, Proc. IJCNN, Vol.II, (Washigton, 1990) pp.59–63.

Raviv, D. and Herman, M., Towards an understanding of camera fixation, Techn. Report, Robot Systems Division, Nat. Inst. of Standards and Technology, (1989).

Renshaw, B., Central effects of centripetal impulses in axons of spinal ventral roots, J. of Neurophys. 9, (1946) pp.191–204.

Rimey, R.D. and Brown, C.M., Selective attention as sequential behavior, modeling eye movements with an augmented hidden Markov model, TR–327, Comp. Sci. Dept., (Rochester, 1990).

Ritter, H. and Schulten, K., Planning a dynamic trajectory via path finding in discretized phase space, in: J.D. Becker and I. Eisele (eds.), WOPPLOT86: Parallel Processing: Logic, Organization and Technology, Lecture Notes in Computer Science 253, (Springer, Heidelberg, 1986) pp.29–39.

Ritter, H., Martinetz, T., and Schulten, K., Topology–conserving maps for learning visuo–motor–coordination, Neural Networks 2, (1989) pp.159–168.

Robinson, D.A., The coordinates of neurons in the vestibuloocular reflex, Adaptive Mechanisms in Gaze Control Facts and Theories, (1985) pp.297–311.

Robinson, D.A., The use of control systems analysis in the neurophysiology of eye movements, Ann. Rev. Neurosci. 4, (1981) pp.463–503.

Robinson, D.A., The use of matrices in analyzing the three–dimensional behavior of the vestibulo–ocular reflex, Biol. Cybern. 46, (1982) pp.53–66.

Rolls, E.T., Neurons in the cortex of the temporal lobe and in the amygdala of the monkey with responses selective for faces, Human Neurobiol. 3, (1984) pp.209–222.

Rolls, E.T., Baylis, G.C., and Leonard, C.M., Role of low and high spatial frequencies in the face–selective responses of neurons in the cortex in the superior temporal sulcus, Vision Res. 25, (1985) pp.1021–1035.

Rolls, E.T. and Baylis, G.C., Size and contrast have only small effects on the responses to faces of neurons in the cortex of the superior temporal sulcus of the monkey, Exp. Brain Res. 65, (1986) pp.38–48.

Rolls, E.T., Baylis, G.C., and Hasselmo, M.E., The responses of neurons in the cortex in the superior temporal sulcus of the monkey to band–pass spatial frequency filtered faces, Vision Res. 27, (1987) pp.311–326.

Rolls, E.T., Baylis, G.C., Hasselmo, M.E., and Nalwa, V., The effect of learning on the face–selective responses of neurons in the cortex in the superior temporal sulcus of the monkey, Exp. Brain Res. 76, (1989) pp.153–164.

Rolls, E.T., The representation and storage of information in neuronal networks in the primate cerebral cortex and hippocampus, in: R. Durbin, C. Miall, and G. Mitchison (eds.), The Computing Neuron, Ch.8, (Addison–Wesley, Wokingham, England, 1989) pp.125–159.

Rolls, E.T., Functions of the primate hippocampus in spatial processing and memory, in: D.S. Olton and R.P. Kesner (eds.), Neurobiology of Comparative Cognition, Ch.12, (Erlbaum, Hillsdale, 1990) pp.339–362.

Rosenblatt, F., Principles of Neurodynamics, (Spartan Books, New York, 1962).

Rosenblatt, F., The perceptron: A probalistic model for information storage and organization in the brain, Psychological Review 65, (1958) pp.386–408.

Ross, M.D., Morphological evidence for parallel processing of information in rat macula, Acta Otolaryngol. 106, (1988) pp.213–218.

Rossignol, S., Lund, J.P., and Drew, T., The role of sensory inputs in regulating patterns of rhythmical movements in higher vertebrates, in: A. Cohen, S. Rossignol, and S. Grillner (eds.), Neural Control of Rhythmic Movements in Vertebrates, (John Wiley & Sons, New York, 1988) pp.201–283.

Rubner, J. and Schulten, K., Development of feature detectors by self–organization, a network model, Biol. Cybern., (1990) in press.

Rückert, U. and Goser, K., VLSI design of associative networks, Int. Workshop on VLSI for Artificial Intelligence, (Uni. Oxford, 1988).

Rumelhart, D.E. and McClelland, J.L. (eds.), Parallel Distributed Processing, Explorations in the Microctructure of Cognition, Vol.I+II, Ch.5+8, (MIT Press, Cambridge, 1986).

Rumelhart, D.E., Hinton, G.E., and Williams, R.J., Learning internal representations by error propagation, in: D.E. Rumelhart and J.L. McClelland (eds.), Parallel Distributed Processing, Explorations in the Microstructure of Cognition 1, (MIT Press, Cambridge, 1986) pp.318–364.

Sagi, D. and Julesz, B., Where and what in vision, Science 228, (1985) p.1217.

Sanger, T., An optimality principle for unsupervised learning, in: D.S. Touretzky (ed.), Advances in Neural Information Processing Systems, (Morgan–Kaufmann, San Mateo, 1989) pp.11–19.

Schank, R.C. and Abelson, R.P., Scripts, plans, goals and understanding, (Erlbaum, Hillsdale, N.J., 1977).

Schild, D., Biophys. J. 54, (1988) p.100.

Schmitt, F. and Worden, F. (eds.), The Neurosciences: Fourth Study Program, (MIT Press, Cambridge, 1979).

Schor, R.H., Miller, A.D., Timerick, S.J.B., and Tomko, D.L., Responses to head tilt in cat central vestibular neurons, Vol.II, Frequency dependence of neural response vectors, J. Neurophysiol. 53, (1985) pp.1444–1452.

Schäfli, L., Gesammelte mathematische Abhandlungen, Vol.1, (Birkhäuser, Basel, 1950).

Schürmann, B., Stability and adaptation in artificial neural systems, Phys. Rev. A40, (1989) p.2681.

Sejnowski, T.J. and Rosenberg, C.R., NETtalk, a parallel network that learns to read aloud, Johns Hopkins University EE & CS Techn. Report, JHU/EECS–86/01, (1986).

Seltzer, B. and Pandya, D.N., Afferent cortical connections and architectonics of the superior temporal sulcus and surrounding cortex in the rhesus monkey, Brain Res. 149, (1978) pp.1–24.

Sharkey, N.E., A PDP learning approach to natural language understanding, in: Aleksander, I. (ed.), Neural Computing Architectures, (MIT Press, Boston, 1989) pp.92–116.

Shepherd, G.M., The Synaptic Organization of the Brain, (Oxford University Press, New York, 1979).

Simpson, P.K., A review of artificial neural systems, Part I & II, CRC Critical Review in Artificial Intelligence, (1988).

Smith, D.V. and Travers, J.B., A metric for the breadth of tuning of gustatory neurons, Chemical Senses 4, (1979) pp.215–229.

Soechting, J.F., Lacquaniti, F., and Terzuolo, C.A., Coordination of arm movements in three–dimensional space, sensorimotor mapping during drawing movement, Neuroscience 17, (1986) pp.295–311.

Sorek, N. and Zeevi, Y.Y., On–line visual data compression along a one–dimensional scan, Proc. SPIE 1001, (1988) pp.764–770.

Squire, L., Mechanisms of memory, Science 232, (1986) pp.1612–1619.

Squire, L.R. and Zola–Morgan, S., Memory, brain systems and behavior, TINS–11, (1988) pp.170–175.

Steinbuch, K., Die Lernmatrix, Kybernetik 1, (1961) pp.36–45.

Steinbuch, K. and Frank, H., Nichtdigitale Lernmatrizen als Perzeptoren, Kybernetik 1, (1961), pp.117–124.

Stratford, K., Mason, A., Larkman, A., Major, G., and Jack, J., The modelling of pyramidal neurones in the visual cortex, in: Durbin, Miall, and Mitcheson (eds.), The Computing Neuron, (Addison–Wesley, 1989) pp.296–321.

Sutton, R.S. and Barto, A.G., A temporal–difference model of classical conditioning, Proc. 9th Ann. Conf. of the Cogn. Sci. Soc., (Erlbaum, Hillsdale, 1987) pp.355–378.

Sutton, R.S. and Barto, A.G., Toward a modern theory of adaptive networks: Expectation and prediction, Psychol. Rev. 88, (1981) pp.135–170.

Sutton, R.S., Two problems with backpropagation and other steepest–descent learning procedures for networks, Proc. 8th Ann. Conf. of the Cogn. Sci. Soc., (1986) pp.823–831.

Tanaka, S.C., Tseng, H.F., and Wang, W.L., A 512 x 512 random access photodiode array for industrial applications, Proc. Electronic Imaging, (Boston, 1989) pp.868–873.

Taylor, J.G., A model of early vertebrate visual processing, in: R. Cotterill, Models of Brain Function, (Cambridge University Press, 1989) pp.231–253.

Taylor, J.G., Temporal patterns and leaky integrator neurons, Proc. ICANN, (Paris, 1990).

Tesauro, G., Simple neural models of classical conditioning, Biol. Cybern. 55, (1986) pp.187–200.

Thakoor, A.P. and Moopenn, A., Electronic neural network with optically modulated variable strength, resistive a–SI:H interconnects for analog computation, MRS Spring Meeting, paper E 7.5, (Reno, Nevada, 1988).

Treisman, A., Preattentive processing in vision, Comp. Vision, Graphics and Image Proc. 31, (1985) pp.156–177.

Tsividis, Y.P. and Anastassiou, D., Switched–capacitor neural networks, Electronic Letters 23, (1987).

Tsotsos, J., A complexity level analysis of vision, in: Proc. IJCCV, (London, 1987).

Tsukahara, N. and Kawato, M., Dynamic and plastic properties of the brain stem neuronal networks as the possible neuronal basis of learning and memory, in: S. Amari and M.A. Arbib (eds.), Lecture Notes in Biomathematics 45, Competition and Cooperation in Neural Nets, (Springer, Berlin, Heidelberg, New York, 1982) pp.430–441.

Tubiana, R., The Hand, Vol.I, (W.B. Saunders Co., Philadephia, 1981).

Turner, B.H., The cortical sequence and terminal distribution of sensory related afferents to the amygdaloid complex of the rat and monkey, in: Y. Ben–Ari (ed.), The Amygdaloid Complex, (Elsevier, Amsterdam, 1981) pp.51–62.

Van den Bout, D.E. and Miller III, T.K., A digital architecture employing stochasticism for the simulation of Hopfield neural nets, IEEE Trans. on Circuits and Systems 36, (1989) pp.732–738.

Van den Bout, D.E. and Miller III, T.K., Graph partitioning using annealed neural networks, IEEE Trans. on Neural Networks 1(2), (1990).

Van den Bout, D.E. and Miller III, T.K., Improving the performance of the Hopfield–Tank neural network through normalization and annealing, Biol. Cybern. 62, (1989) pp.129–139.

Van den Bout, D.E. and Miller III, T.K., TInMANN: The integer Markovian artificial neural network, Proc. IJCNN, Vol.II, (Washington, 1989) pp.205–211.

Van Hoesen, G.W., The differential distribution, diversity and sprouting of cortical projections to the amygdala in the rhesus monkey, in: Y. Ben–Ari (ed.), The Amygdaloid Complex, (Elsevier, Amsterdam, 1981) pp.79–90.

Van Hoesen, G.W., The parahippocampal gyrus, new observations regarding its cortical connections in the monkey, TINS–5, (1982) pp.345–350.

Vidal, P.P., Graf, W., and Berthoz, A., The orientation of the cervical vertebral column in unrestrained awake animals, I., Resting position, Exp. Brain Res. 61, (1986) pp.549–559.

Viola, P., Neurally inspired plasticity in oculomotor processes, in: D.S. Touretzky (ed.), Advances in Neural Information Processing Systems 2, (Morgan Kaufmann, San Mateo, 1989).

Waibel, A., Hanazawa, T., Hinton, G., Shikano, K., and Lang, K., Phoneme recognition using time–delay neural networks, Proc. IEEE Int. Conf. on ASSP, (New York, 1988).

Watrous, R.L. and Shastri, L., Learning phonetic features using connectionsist networks: An experiment in speech recognition, Proc. IEEE First Int. Conf. Neural Networks, (San Diego, 1987).

Watrous, R.L., Learning algorithms for connectionist networks, applied gradient methods of nonlinear optimization, Proc. IEEE First Int. Conf. on Neural Networks, Vol.II, (San Diego, 1987) pp.619–627.

Wehmeier, U., Dong, D., Koch, C., and Van Essen, D., Modeling the visual system, in: C. Koch and I. Segev (eds.), Methods in Neuronal Modeling, (MIT Press, Cambridge) pp.335–359.

Wellekens, C.J., Explicit time correlation in hidden Markov models for speech recognition, Proc. IEEE Int. Conf. on ASSP, (Tokyo, Japan, 1987).

Whitehead, S.D. and Ballard, D.H., A role for anticipation in reactive systems that learn, Proc. 6th Int. Workshop on Machine Learning, (Cornell U., Ithaca, NY, 1989).

Whitehead, S.D., The Rochester robot, TR 257, Computer Science Dept., U. Rochester, (1988).

Widrow, B. and Hoff, M.E. Jr., Adaptive switching circuits, IRE WESTON Conv. Record, Part 4, (1960) pp.96–104.

Widrow, B. and Stearns, S.D., Adaptive Signal Processing, (Prentice–Hall Inc., Englewood Cliffs, N.J., 1985).

Widrow, B., Adaptive inverse control, in: Adaptive Systems in Control and Signal Processing, (Int. Federation of Automatic Control, 1986).

Widrow, B., Generalization and information storage in networks of ADALINE neurons, in: M.C. Yovits, G.T. Jacobi, and G.D. Goldstein (eds.), Self–organizing Systems–1962, (Spartan Books, Washington, 1962) pp.435–461.

Wiener, N., Cybernetics, (MIT Press, Cambridge, MA 1948/1961).

Wike, W. and Van den Bout, D.E., STONN, a stochastic neural network chip, Proc. 6th MIT Conf. on Adv. Res. in VLSI, (1990).

Williams, R.J. and Zipser, D., A learning algorithm for continually running fully recurrent neural networks, Neural Computation 1, (1989) pp.270–280.

Willshaw, D., Longuet–Higgins, H.C., and Buneman, P., A simple network capable of inductive gneralization, Proc. R. Soc. London B. 182, (1972) pp.233–247.

Wilson, D.M., Insect walking, Ann. Rev. of Entymology 11, reprinted in: C.R. Gallistel (ed.), The Organization of Action: A New Synthesis, (Lawrence Erlbaum, Hillsdale, NJ, 1980).

Winograd, T., Understanding Natural Language, (Academic Press, New York, 1972).

Works, G., The creation of Delta: A new concept in ANS processing, Proc. IEEE Int. Conf. on Neural Networks, Vol.II, (1988) pp.159–164.

Yarbus, A.L., Eye Movements and Vision, (Plenum Press, New York, 1967).

Yeshurun, Y. and Schwartz, E.L., Cepstral filtering on a columnar image architecture, a fast algorithm for binocular stereo segmentation, IEEE Trans. PAMI–11, (1989) pp.759–767.

Young, R.A., The gaussian derivative theory of spatial vision: Analysis of cortical cell receptive field line–weighting profiles, General Motors Res. Tech. Rep. GMR–4920, (1985).

Yuille, A.L., Kammen, D.M., and Cohen, D.S., Quadrature and the development of orientation selective cortical cells by Hebb rules, Biol. Cybern. 61, (1989) pp.183–194.

Zador, P.L., Asymptotic quantization error of continuous signals and the quantization dimension, IEEE Trans. Inform. Theory 28, (1982) pp.139–142.

Zak, M. and Barhen, J., Neural networks with creative dynamics, Math. Comp. Model, (1990) in press.

Zak, M., Non–lipschitzian dynamics for neural net modelling, Appl. Math. Letters 2, (1989) pp.69–74.

Zak, M., Terminal attractors in neural networks, Neural Networks 2, (1989) pp.259–274.

Zeevi, Y.Y. and Ginosar, R., Neural computers in vision, in: R. Eckmiller and C. v.d. Malsburg (eds.), Neural Computers, (Springer, Heidelberg, 1988, 1989) pp.169–178.

Zeevi, Y.Y. and Hilsenrath, O.A., Random scan system, U.S. Pat. 4,858,014, (1989).

Zeevi, Y.Y., Peterfreund, N., and Shlomot, E., Pyramidal image representation in nonuniform systems, Proc. SPIE 1001, (1988) pp.563–570.

Zielke, Th., Storjohann, K.II, Mallot, A., and Seelen v., W., Adapting computer vision systems to the visual environment: Topographic mapping, in: O. Faugeras (ed.), Proc. 1st European Conf. on Computer Vision INRIA, (1990).

Zipser, D. and Andersen, R.A., A back propagation programmed network that simulates response properties of a subset of posterior parietal neurons, Nature 311, (1988) pp.679–684.

Zucker, S.W. and Iverson, L., Computational networks in early vision: From orientation selection to optical flow, in: R. Eckmiller and C. v.d. Malsburg (eds.), Neural Computers, (Springer, Heidelberg, 1988, 1989) pp.179–188.

Zucker, S.W., David, C., Dobbins, A., and Iverson, L., The organization of curve detection: Coarse tangent fields and fine spline coverings, Proc. 2nd Int. Conf. on Computer Vision, (Tarpon Springs, Fla, 1988).

Zucker, S.W., Dobbins, A., and Iverson, L., Two stages of curve detection suggest two styles of visual computation, Neural Computation 1, (1989) pp.68–81.

List of Contributors

Name / Affiliation	Address	Page
Akers, L.A. (USA) Arizona State University Center for Solid State	Tempe, AZ 85287-6206 (602) 965-3808 AKERS@ASU.CSNET	161
Aleksander, I. (UK) Imperial College of Science Exhibition Road	London SW7 2BT (1) 589-5111 I.ALEKSANDER@VAXA.CC.IMPERIAL.AC.UK	97
Almeida, L.G. (P) University of Lisboa Inst. Eng. Comp. Systems, INESC	P-1000 Lisboa Codex (1) 544607 LBA@INESC.MCVAX.UUCP	151
Angeniol, B. (F) Thomson CSF-DSE 1 rue des Mathurins, BP 10	F-92223 Bagneux Cedex (1) 4084-4239	167
Ballard, D.H. (USA) University of Rochester Dept. of Computer Science	Rochester, NY 14627 (716) 275-3772 DANA@CS.ROCHESTER.EDU	229
Barhen, J. (USA) Caltech Jet Propulsion Labortory	Pasadena, CA 91109 (818) 354-9218 BAHREN@JPL-VLSI.ARPA	103
Bock, P. (FRG) FAW-Ulm Helmholtzstraße 16	D-7900 Ulm (731) 501-610	237
Boser, B. (USA) AT&T Bell Lab. Cranfords Corner Road	Holmdel, NJ 07733 (201) 949-7733	193
Bourlard, H. (B) Philips Research Lab. of Brüssels Av. van Becelaere 2, Box 8	B-1170 Brussels (2) 674 22 74 BOURLARD@PRLB.PHILIPS.BE	247
Brooks, R.A. (USA) MIT 545 Technology Square	Cambridge, MA 02139 (617) 253-5223 BROOKS@WHEATIES.AI.MIT.EDU	341
Büttner, W. (FRG) Siemens AG, ZFE F 2 INF 2 Otto-Hahn-Ring 6	D-8000 München 83 (89) 636-46310 BUETTNER ZTIVAX.SIEMENS.COM	255
Bullock, D. (USA) Boston University Cogn. & Neural Systems Program	Boston, MA 02215 (617) 353-9486 DANB@BUCASB.BU.EDU	349
Burnod, Y. (F) Inst. des Neurosciences 9, quai St. Bernard	F-75 015 Paris	33

Caianiello, E.R. (I) Universita di Salerno Dipartimento di Fisica Teorica	I-84100 Salerno (89) 82 21 11	3
Caminiti, R. (I) Universita La Sapienza Instituto di Fisiologia	I-00185 Roma (6) 49910967 NEURAL@IRMUNISA.BITNET	33
Christensen, S.S. (DK) Technical University of Denmark Dept. of Biophysics, Bld. 307	DK-2800 Lyngby (42) 88 24 88	113
Cotterill, R.M.J. (DK) Technical University of Denmark Dept. of Biophysics, Bld. 307	DK-2800 Lyngby (42) 88 24 88 FYMCOT@NEUYM1.BITNET	113
Denker, J.S. (USA) AT&T Bell Lab. Cranfords Corner Road	Holmdel, NJ 07733 (201) 949-7733	193
De Pinto, P. (I) Inst. Ricerca Sistemi Informatici	I-80125 Napoli	121
Dobbins, A. (Canada) Mc Gill University Res. Center for Int. Machines	Montreal, P.Q.	331
Eckmiller, R. (FRG) H.-Heine Universität Düsseldorf Universitätsstraße 1	D-4000 Düsseldorf 1 (211) 311-4540 ECKMILLE@DDØRUD81.BITNET	357
Fetz, E.E. (USA) University of Washington Dept. of Phys. & Biophysics SJ-40	Seattle, WA 98915 (206) 543-4839 FETZ@UWALOCKE.BITNET	43
Fukushima, K. (JAPAN) Osaka University 1-1, Machikaneyama, Toyonaka	Osaka 560 (81) 6-844-1151	263
Garth, S.C.J. (UK) Myriad Solutions LTD. St. John's Innovation Center	Cambridge, CB2 1PZ (44) 223-332743 DP@UK.AC.CAM.ENG.IBM	177
Geiger, H. (FRG) Fa. Kratzer Automatisierung Maxfeldhof 6	D-8044 Unterschleissheim (89) 310-2037	271
Ginosar, R. (Israel) Technion Israel Inst. Technol. Dept. of Electrical Engineering	Haifa 32000 (4) 293111	323
Graf, H.P. (USA) AT&T Bell Lab. Cranfords Corner Road	Holmdel, NJ 07733 (201) 949-7733	193

Contributor	Address	Page
Granguillaume, PH. (F) Inst. des Neurosciences 9, quai St. Bernard	F-75 015 Paris	33
Grossberg, S. (USA) Boston University Cogn. & Neural Systems Program	Boston, MA 02215 (617) 353-9486	349
Guyon, I. (USA) AT&T Bell Lab. Cranfords Corner Road	Holmdel, NJ 07733 (201) 949-7733	193
Haghighi, S. (USA) Arizona State University Center for Solid State	Tempe, AZ 85287-6206 (602) 965-3808	161
Hammerstrom, D. (USA) Adaptive Solutions Inc. 1400 N.W. Compton Drive, Suite 3	Beaverton, OR 97006 (503) 609-1234	185
Hartmann, G. (FRG) Universität Paderborn Electrical Engineering Dept.	D-4790 Paderborn (5258) 60-2206 HARTMANN@PBINFO.UUCP	279
Hecht-Nielsen, R. (USA) Hecht-Nielsen Neurocomputer, Inc. 5501 Oberlin Drive	San Diego, CA 92121 (619) 546-8877 HNIELSEN@A.ISI.EDU	129
Iverson, L. (Canada) McGill University Dept. of Electrical Engineering	Montreal, P.Q. (514) 398-7134	331
Jackel, L.D. (USA) AT & T Bell Lab Crawfords Corner Rd.	Holmdel, NJ 07733 (201) 949-7773	193
Johnson, K. (USA) Rockwell International Science 1049 Camino Dos Rios	Thousand Oaks, CA 93106 (805) 373-4487 KBJ@RICS.COM	287
Johnson, P. (I) Universita La Sapienza Instituto di Fisiologia	I-00185 Roma (6) 49910967	33
Kawato, M. (JAPAN) ATR, Soraku-gun Sanpeidani, Inuidani, Seika-cho	Kyoto 619-02 (7749) 5-1452 KDDLAB!ATR.HR.ATR.JUNET!KAWATO@UUNET.UU.NET	365
Klopf, A.H. (USA) Wright Res. and Devel. Center Wright Patterson Air Force Base	Wright-Patterson AFB, OH 5433-6523 (513) 255-7649	201
Koch, C. (USA) Caltech Division of Biology 216-76	Pasadena, CA 91125 (818) 356-6855 KOCH@CALTECH.BITNET	87

Kocinski, C.J. (FRG) FAW-Ulm Helmholzstr. 16	D-7900 Ulm	237
Koenderink, J.J. (NL) Rijksuniversiteit Utrecht Princetonplein 5	NL-3508 TA Utrecht (30) 532808/3985 KOENDERINK@HUTRUU51.BITNET	295
Kohonen, T. (Finland) Helsinki University of Technology Lab. of Comp. & Inform. Science	SF-02150 Espoo (0) 451-3268 TEUVO@HUTMC.HUT.FI	137
Lauria, F.E. (I) Universita di Napoli Dip. di Scienze Fisiche	I-80125 Napoli (81) 7253-411 LAURIA%VAXNA.INFNET@CERNVAX.BITNET	121
Le Cun, Y. (USA) AT&T Bell Lab. Cranfords Corner Road	Holmdel, NJ 07733 (201) 949-7733	193
Leen, T. (USA) Oregon Graduate Inst. Dept. of Com. Sci. and Engineering	Beaverton, OR 97006-1999	185
Mallot, H.A. (FRG) Universität Bochum Dept. Theoret. Biology	D-4630 Bochum 1 (234) 700-7974	79
Malsburg, v.d. C. (FRG) Universität Bochum Dept. of Neuroinformatics	D-4630 Bochum 1 (234) 700-1	303
Means, E. (USA) Oregon Graduate Inst. Dept. of Com. Sci. and Engineering	Beaverton, OR 97006-1999	185
Miller III, T.K. (USA) North Carolina State University Dept. Electr. and Comp. Engineering	Raleigh, NC 27650 (919) 737-2336	219
Morasso, P. (I) University of Genoa Dept. of Computer Science	I-16145 Genoa (10) 3532749 PIERO.MORASSO@DIST.UNIGE.IT	51
Morgan, J.S. (USA) Wright Res. and Devel. Center Wright Patterson Air Force Base	Wright-Patterson AFB, OH 5433-6523 (513) 255-7649	201
Morton, H. (UK) Brunel University Dept. of Human Sciences	Uxbridge	97
Niebur, E. (USA) Caltech Division of Biology 216-76	Pasadena, CA 91125 (818) 356-6855	87

Name / Address	Location / Contact	Page
Nielsen, C. (DK) Technical University of Denmark Dept. of Biophysics, Bld. 307	DK-2800 Lyngby (42) 88 24 88	113
Nguyen, D. (USA) Stanford University Dept. of Elect. Engineering	Stanford, CA 94305-4055 (415) 723-4949	11
Opitz, R. (FRG) IBP Pietzsche GmbH Hertzstraße 32-34	D-7505 Ettlingen (7243) 709-134	373
Otto, I. (F) Inst. des Neurosciences 9, quai St. Bernard	F-75 015 Paris	33
Palm, G. (FRG) H.-Heine Universität Düsseldorf Inst. for Brain Research	D-4000 Düsseldorf 1 (211) 311-2789 PALM@DDØRUD81.BITNET	145
Pellionisz, A.J. (USA) New York University Dept. Physiology and Biophysics	New York, NY 10016 (212) 340-5422	61
Peterson, B.W. (USA) Northwestern University 550 First Ave	Chicago, IL 60611 (312) 908-6216 PETERSON@NUACC.BITNET	61
Ramacher, U. (FRG) Siemens AG Corporate Research & Development	D-8000 München 83 (89) 636-41296 RAMACHER%ZTRZVL@ZTIVAX.UUCP	209
Rao, A. (USA) Arizona State University Center for Solid State	Tempe, AZ 85287-6206 (602) 965-3808	161
Ritter, H. (USA) Univ. Illinois at Urbana-Champaign Beckman Institute	Urbana, IL 61801 (217) 244-1613 11074@NCSAVMSA.BITNET	381
Rolls, E.T. (UK) University of Oxford Dept. of Exp. Psychology	Oxford, OX1 3UD (865) 271-348 EROLLS@VAX.OXFORD.AC.UK	69
Rovner, R. (FRG) FAW-Ulm Helmholtzstr. 16	D-7900 Ulm	237
Seelen, v. W. (FRG) Universität Bochum Dept. Theoret. Biology	D-4630 Bochum 1 (234) 700-7965	79
Sette, M. (I) Inst. Ricerca Sistemi Informatici	I-80125 Napoli	121

Shupe, L.E. (USA) Seattle, WA 98915 43
University of Washington (206) 543-4839
Dept. of Phys. & Biophysics SJ-40

Silva, F.M. (P) P-1000 Lisboa Codex 151
University of Lisboa (1) 544607
Inst. Eng. Comp. Systems, INESC

Snyder, W.E. (USA) Raleigh, NC 27650 219
North Carolina University (919) 737-2336
Dept. Electr. and Comp. Engineering WES@ECELET.NCSU.EDU

Steinbuch, K. (FRG) D-7505 Ettlingen 21
TH Karlsruhe (7243) 12686
Adalbert-Stifter-Straße 4

Taylor, J.G. (UK) London WC2R 2LS 313
King's College London (1) 836-5454
Department of Mathematics UDAH057@UK.AC.KCL.CC.ASH

Tomko, D.L. (USA) Moffet Field, CA 94035 61
NASA Ames Research Center (415) 694-5723
Vestibular Research Faculity

Toomarian, N. (USA) Pasadena, CA 91109 103
Caltech
Jet Propulsion Lab.

Treleaven, P. (UK) London, WC1E 6BT 167
Univ. College London (1) 380-7288
Dept. of Comp. Sci., Gower Street TRELEAVEN@CS.UCL.AC.UK

Van den Bout, D.E. (USA) Raleigh, Nc 27650 219
North Carolina University (919) 737-2336
Dept. Electr. and Comp. Engineering

Van Doorn, A.J. (NL) NL-3508 TA Utrecht 295
Rijksuniversiteit Utrecht (30) 532808/3985
Princetonplein 5

Viola, P.A. (USA) Cambridge, MA 02139 341
MIT (617) 253-5223
545 Technology Square

Wake, N. (Japan) Osaka 560 263
Osaka University (81) 6-844-1151
1-1, Machikaneyama, Toyonaka

Widrow, B. (USA) Stanford, CA 94305-4055 11
Stanford University (415) 723-4949
Dept. of Elect. Engineering WIDROW@ISL.STANFORD.EDU

Wörgötter, F. (BRD) D-4630 Bochum 87
Ruhr. Univ. Bochum (234) 700-3849
Inst. für Neurophysiologie

Zak, M. (USA) Caltech Jet Propulsion Lab.	Pasadena, CA 91109	103
Zeevi, Y.Y. (Israel) Technion Israel Inst. Technol. Dept. of Electrical Engineering	Haifa 32000 (4) 293111 ZEEVI%ENDOR@HUSC6.BITNET	323
Zucker, S.T. (Canada) McGill University Dept. of Electrical Engineering	Montreal, P.Q. (514) 398-7134 ZUCKER@LARRY.MCRCIM.MCGILL.EDU	331

AUTHOR INDEX

SUBJECT INDEX